SYBEX
READY
REFERENCE
SERIES

# dBASE III PLUS™ PROGRAMMER'S REFERENCE GUIDE

**Alan Simpson**

SAN FRANCISCO · PARIS · DÜSSELDORF · LONDON

SYBEX Ready Reference Series
Editor in Chief: Rudolph S. Langer
Series Editor: Barbara Gordon
Editor: Bonnie Gruen

Book and cover design by Thomas Ingalls + Associates

Screenprinting in this book was produced with Xenofont from Xenosoft, Berkeley, CA.



Hardcover: Library of Congress Card Number: 87-61336
ISBN 0-89588-382-1
Papercover: Library of Congress Card Number: 87-62212
ISBN 0-89588-508-5
Manufactured in the United States of America
Printed by Haddon Craftsmen

10 9 8 7 6 5

To Susan and the Egg

# *TABLE OF CONTENTS*

## PART 5: The Programming Environment



## PART 6: Beyond the Programming Environment



## PART 7: Commonly Used Algorithms

# *LIST OF TABLES*

# PREFACE

This book was designed to meet the needs of dBASE programmers on two fronts. First, as a reference work, the book provides the reader with access to all the commands and functions available in the dBASE language, as well as specific programming techniques used in many dBASE applications. Second, the book provides discussions of program design and development, database design, and other more theoretical topics that go beyond the nuts and bolts of what the individual commands and functions do. When you need background information, such as how a particular command or function can be used in an application, or how to create a routine or program to perform a specific task, you can find that information in the discussion sections of the chapters. The organization of the book and the extensive indexes are designed to make access to all of this information as quick and easy as possible.

Most chapters in this book begin with a discussion of the subject of that chapter and end with more structured reference entries for each dBASE command covered in the chapter. When you need background on the techniques used to meet a particular programming goal, you should read the discussion section of the chapter. For quick reference to a particular command or function, you can skip the discussion section and move directly to the reference section.

Unlike many reference books, this book is not organized in a simple encyclopedic or alphabetical order. Instead, it is divided into chapters that represent specific components of applications, such as reports, custom screens, data entry, and so forth, making it easier to find all the information on a given topic. For example, when you want to develop the report formats for your application, you can find that topic treated in depth in Chapter 9, "Printing Formatted Reports." If there is related information in another chapter, you will be informed of this within the chapter as well as in the chapter summary.

## WHY PROGRAM IN dBASE III PLUS?

Programming in dBASE allows you to develop custom systems that anybody can use, even people with virtually no computer experience. You can design your system so that a user need enter only a single command at the DOS prompt. From that point on, your custom system can allow the user to perform tasks of any complexity simply by selecting items from custom menus that you have designed.

The types of custom systems that you can develop with dBASE include the following, among others:

- Inventory management
- Sales order processing
- Accounts payable/receivable
- General ledger
- Time and billing
- Project/job accounting
- Scheduling
- Data analysis

There are several reasons for the professional programmer to consider switching from another language to dBASE:

- dBASE III PLUS has become the industry standard programming language for developing business applications software on microcomputers.
- dBASE offers advanced file-handling techniques, which are necessary in most business settings.
- dBASE has many powerful built-in commands that greatly reduce the time required to develop custom applications.

For both the beginning programmer and the old pro, dBASE is perhaps the easiest and most powerful tool available for getting a project from the idea stage to a final, polished product.

## Who Should Use This Book

This book is designed for people who want to use dBASE III PLUS as a programming language to develop custom business applications. The book assumes that you already know the basics of using dBASE III PLUS at the Assistant level, or that you have some familiarity with basic programming concepts with some language other than dBASE III PLUS.

Those readers who have some dBASE experience but only limited programming experience should possess the following basic dBASE III PLUS skills before using this book:

- The ability to create database files using the dBASE CREATE command or the Create a Database File option from the Assistant menu.
- The ability to add new records to a database, change and delete database records, and display those records on the screen or printer.

- A minimal ability to display only records that meet some search criterion, such as individuals in a mailing list database who live in California.
- Some familiarity with dBASE full-screen commands and pull-down menus, such as those on the dBASE Assistant, MODIFY REPORT, and MODIFY LABEL screens.

A reader with neither dBASE nor any programming experience would be better off reading an introductory book, such as my own *Understanding dBASE III PLUS* (SYBEX, 1986), before attempting to use this reference book.

## STRUCTURE OF THE BOOK

This book is divided into major sections, as listed below:

***Part 1:*** Provides an overview of dBASE III PLUS as a programming language, as well as discussions of software design and development and database designs used in custom business applications. These chapters provide valuable information for planning a custom dBASE III PLUS application.

***Part 2:*** Discusses the basics of creating, running, and debugging command files (programs). Readers with little or no programming experience will gain a solid background in dBASE programming from these chapters. Topics in this part include general program construction, memory variables, procedures, debugging, and others.

***Part 3:*** Covers the commands and programming techniques you need to develop sophisticated data-entry screens and formatted reports.

***Part 4:*** Discusses commands and techniques for managing a database with custom programs, including adding, editing, sorting, searching, and calculating data. This section also discusses techniques used for managing multiple related database files.

***Part 5:*** Discusses the programming environment and commands and functions used to handle that environment. It covers commands and techniques that allow you to change parameters such as screen color, file directory paths, dBASE's response to error conditions, and so forth. These techniques let you refine the interaction between your application and the user.

***Part 6:*** Covers topics that are related to dBASE programming and are of particular interest to dBASE programmers, such as networking, dBASE compilers, and assembly language subroutines.

***Part 7:*** Contains a library of prewritten solutions to common programming problems, allowing you to extend dBASE III PLUS beyond its off-the-shelf capabilities.

## ACKNOWLEDGMENTS

This book was an ambitious project from the start and would have never been completed without the skills and talents of many people. Though only one author's name appears on the cover, this book is actually the creation of many people. Much credit (and my heartfelt thanks) are owed to the following people:

To everyone at SYBEX who guided and supported me through this project, including Rudolph Langer and Barbara Gordon, who came up with the original idea and provided me with the design and goals of the book; Bonnie Gruen, who edited the entire manuscript; Joel Kroman and Greg Hooten, who provided all technical editing as well as many useful additional techniques; John Kadyk, word processing supervisor; Jeff Giese, design coordinator; Cheryl Vega, typesetter; Aidan Wylde, proofreading supervisor; Amparo Del Rio, production artist, and Anne Leach, indexer.

To Mitchell E. Timin, PhD, of Timin Engineering Inc., who wrote the assembly language subroutines and accompanying text in Chapter 22.

To Sally Campbell, who wrote most of the material on program design in Chapter 2.

To Mick Keily, who wrote Chapters 17 and 18 in this book.

To Bill and Cynthia Gladstone, of Waterside Productions Inc., my literary agents.

And to my wife Susan, who once again supported me through a long and demanding project.

# *OVERVIEW OF dBASE PROGRAMMING*

Part 1 provides a background in general program design and development techniques. The techniques discussed in this section are relevant to all applications that you might consider developing with dBASE III PLUS. This part is designed for dBASE users with little or no programming experience and for programmers with minimal knowledge of dBASE.

Chapter 1 outlines the capabilities and limitations of dBASE III PLUS as a programming language. This information is geared toward programmers with experience in languages other than dBASE, though some of the information will also be useful to readers with previous dBASE experience.

Chapter 2 discusses software design and development. It presents a series of steps for bringing your custom application from the idea stage to a working software system. The tips and techniques appearing in this chapter will be particularly useful to dBASE users with minimal programming experience, because they provide a structured framework within which to build your application.

Chapter 3 discusses how to design a database and store data in database files to make both storing and accessing data as efficient as possible. This chapter also demonstrates basic commands and techniques for managing and relating data stored on separate database files.

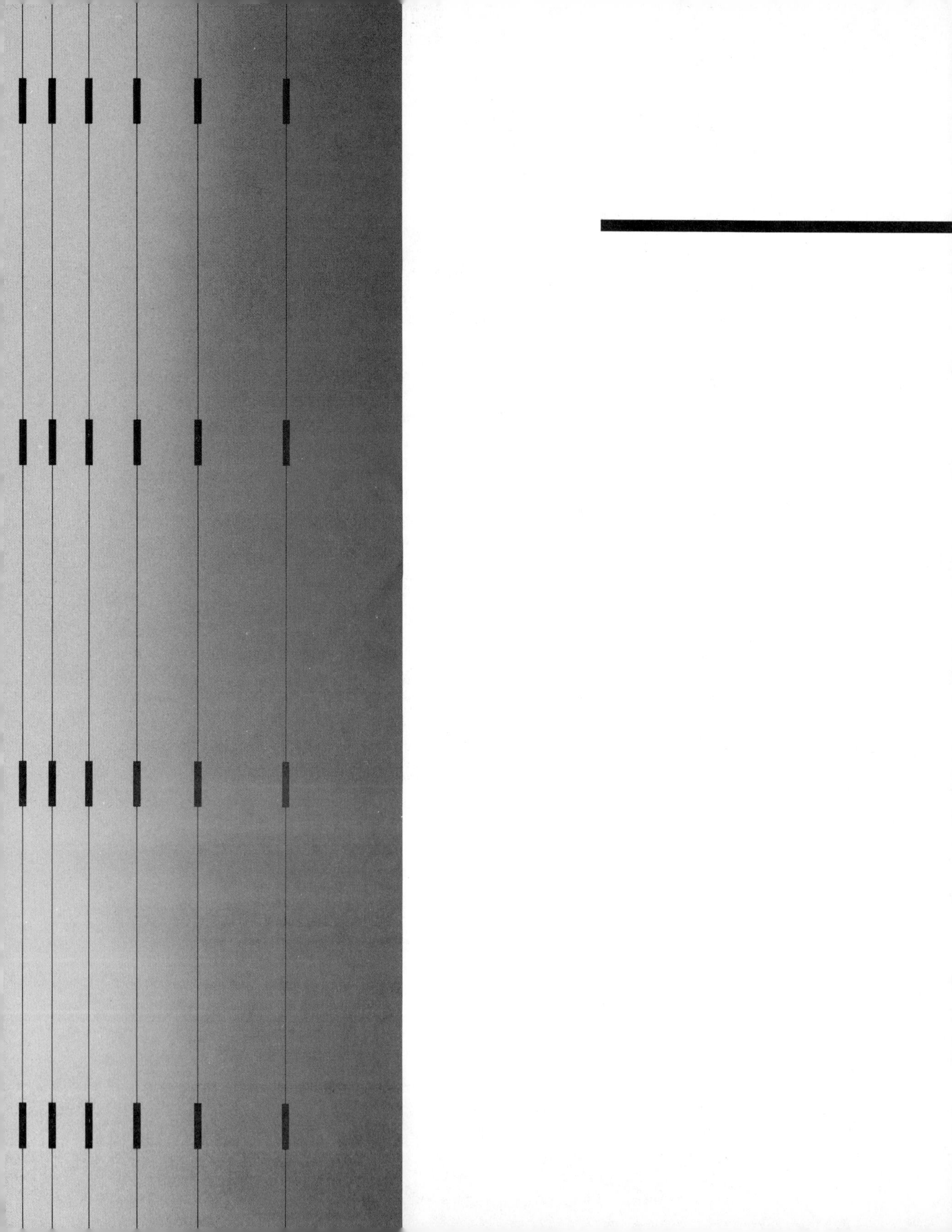

# OVERVIEW OF THE dBASE LANGUAGE

# Overview of the dBASE Language

This chapter provides an overview of dBASE III PLUS as a programming language. For the experienced dBASE user, much of this material will be review. For the experienced programmer with little or no background in dBASE III PLUS, this chapter will provide a general overview of the capabilities and limitations of dBASE III PLUS as a programming language.

The chapter begins with some of the basics of configuring DOS for running dBASE and getting dBASE up and running. Then it discusses the various modes of operation within dBASE, and from there it focuses on the more technical details of dBASE, particularly those that are of interest to the programmer. The chapter concludes with two tables listing and briefly describing all the dBASE commands and functions, grouping them by the type of task they perform.

## Configuring DOS for dBASE

While dBASE allows a maximum of 15 files to be open simultaneously, DOS does not provide enough file handles for this in its default state. To remedy this situation, you need to alter or create the file named Config.sys on your boot-up disk. (On a floppy disk system, this would be the disk you use to boot up your computer. On a hard disk system, this would be the root directory.)

To see the contents of the Config.sys file, use the DOS TYPE command. Log onto the disk from which you usually boot your computer and at the DOS A> or C> prompt, enter the command **TYPE Config.sys** and press Return. If there is no Config.sys file, you'll need to create one. If there is one, it should specify at least 20 files and 15 buffers, as follows:

```
FILES = 20
BUFFERS = 15
```

You can use any word processor or text editor (including the dBASE MODIFY COMMAND editor discussed in Chapter 4, "Command Files") to alter or create the Config.sys file. Just be sure that you store the resulting file on the disk or directory you use to boot the system.

If there is no Config.sys file at all on your boot-up disk, you can quickly create it with the COPY command. At the DOS prompt, type the command **COPY CON Config.sys** and press Return. Type the lines

**FILES = 20**
**BUFFERS = 15**

pressing Return once after each line. Next press F6 (or Ctrl-Z, whichever displays ^Z on the screen) and Return. When the DOS A> or C> prompt reappears, you're done. To verify that you've created the file, enter the **TYPE Config.sys** command once again at the A> or C> prompt. You should see the FILES and BUFFERS commands in the file exactly as you typed them. The Config.sys file settings will take effect *after* you reboot your computer and on all future boot-ups.

Be forewarned that dBASE III PLUS will run even without the proper settings in the Config.sys file. However, if the FILES setting in the Config.sys file is less than 20, you will get the "Too many files are open" error before you reach the dBASE maximum of 15 open files.

## INSTALLING dBASE III PLUS

Different versions of dBASE require different installation procedures. For example, the copy-protected version 1.0 of dBASE III PLUS uses a different installation procedure than the non-copy-protected version 1.1. Furthermore, networks require still other installation procedures.

I recommend that you refer to the dBASE user's manual for information on installing your particular version of dBASE. That way, you'll be sure to get the information that's best for your computer and your needs. You can also refer to Appendix B, "Installing dBASE III PLUS," for general installation techniques. In addition, Chapter 20, "Networking and Security," discusses how to install dBASE III PLUS on a network.

## STARTING dBASE

After installing dBASE on your computer, you can get it up and running with a single command. However, instructions for starting dBASE will vary somewhat, depending on whether your computer has a hard disk.

### Starting from a Hard Disk

Assuming you've already installed dBASE III PLUS on your computer and your computer is already booted up (the C> prompt is showing), you first need to log onto the appropriate directory using the DOS CD\ command. Then enter the command **dBASE** at the DOS prompt. You'll see a copyright notice and instructions to press Return to continue. After pressing Return, you'll see the dBASE Assistant menu.

### Starting from Floppy Disks

If you are using a computer with floppy disks and no hard disk, first boot up in the usual fashion (using your DOS disk or a copy of it). Be sure that the floppy disk that you boot up from has the appropriate Config.sys file on it, as discussed above.

After the A> prompt appears on your screen, place the dBASE System Disk #1 in drive A and type the command **dBASE**. Press Return. You'll see a copyright notice. Press Return to continue. You'll see a message telling you to place dBASE System Disk #2 in drive A. Remove the disk currently in drive A, put in System Disk #2, and press Return. You'll see the dBASE Assistant menu when dBASE is fully loaded and ready to run.

## dBASE Operating Modes

Because dBASE III PLUS is designed to reach a wide range of users, it offers three basic modes of user interaction: the assist mode, the interactive (or dot prompt) mode, and the programming language.

### The Assist Mode

When run in its off-the-shelf configuration, dBASE always begins by displaying the Assistant menu at the top of the screen. The Assistant menu allows the user to select major categories of commands (using the arrow keys and the Return key) and then build commands from the pull-down menus that appear beneath each menu item as it is highlighted. The assist mode is of little or no value to the programmer.

### The Interactive Dot Prompt Mode

As a dBASE programmer, you will most often begin your work at the dBASE dot prompt level. To leave the assist mode and work interactively with dBASE at the dot prompt, press the Esc key at any time while the menu is showing.

If you would like to remove the status bar from the bottom of the screen to make more room, you can enter the command **SET STATUS OFF** next to the dot prompt, and press Return.

The dot prompt is the dBASE "ready-to-accept-commands" signal. At this point you can enter any valid dBASE command, and dBASE will attempt to interpret and execute the command immediately.

To bypass the assist mode and go straight into the interactive mode when dBASE is first loaded into memory, you can remove the lines

```
COMMAND = ASSIST
STATUS = ON
```

from the Config.db file on the same disk (or directory) as dBASE. You can use any text editor or the dBASE MODIFY COMMAND editor (discussed in Chapter 4, "Command Files") to remove these commands.

The interactive dot prompt mode is valuable for programming: it lets you test procedures that you want to use in a program, develop screen and report formats, and perform other tasks that help in the overall development of custom applications.

To bring the status bar and Assistant menu back onto the screen, enter the commands below at the dot prompt:

```
SET STATUS ON
ASSIST
```

### dBASE as a Programming Language

Beyond the dBASE assist and dot prompt modes is the dBASE III PLUS programming language. This third aspect of dBASE, the programming language, is what this book is all about. Whereas the assist and dot prompt modes allow you to interact with dBASE in a "one-command-at-a-time" manner, the dBASE language lets you create fully customized software systems to suit particular applications.

## PROGRAMMING IN dBASE

The remainder of this chapter provides a general overview of the dBASE programming language. If you are not already a programmer or well versed in dBASE, some of this information might seem a bit abstract. However, do keep in mind that all of the topics summarized in this chapter are discussed in detail throughout the book. Table 1.1 lists the technical specifications and limitations of dBASE III PLUS that you will have to keep in mind while programming.

### Data Types

When you store information in databases or memory variables, the data must be one of four data types: character, numeric, date, or logical. In addition,

| |
|---|
| **DATABASE FILE LIMITATIONS**<br>• 1 billion records per file maximum<br>• 2 billion bytes per file maximum<br>• 128 fields or 4,000 bytes maximum record size (additional 512K in memo fields)<br>• Maximum length of field names: 10 characters |
| **DATA LIMITATIONS**<br>• Character data: 0–254 characters<br>• Numeric data: 19 bytes maximum length<br>• Date data: always requires 8 bytes<br>• Logical data: always requires 1 byte in database, 2 bytes in memory<br>• Memo fields: 5,000 bytes or the capacity of external word processor |
| **FILES OPEN SIMULTANEOUSLY**<br>• All types: 15 files total, including database, index, command, procedure, format, and other files<br>• Database files: 10 maximum; database with memo fields counts as two open files<br>• Index files: 7 per open database file<br>• Format files: 1 per open database file |
| **MEMORY VARIABLES**<br>• 256 maximum memory variables active in RAM, or 6,000 bytes (modifiable through Config.db) |
| **COMMAND FILES**<br>• 254 characters maximum command line length<br>• 5,000 characters maximum command file length if created and edited with built-in MODIFY COMMAND editor; otherwise, limited only by word processor used |
| **NUMERIC ACCURACY**<br>• Computational accuracy: 15.9 digits<br>• Accuracy for nonzero comparisons: 13 digits<br>• Largest number: $10^{308}$<br>• Smallest positive number: $10^{-307}$ |

**TABLE 1.1:** dBASE Technical Specifications

database files can store data in memo fields. The various data types are summarized below:

- The character data type is used to store nonnumeric types of information, such as names and addresses. The maximum length of a character string is 254 characters.
- The numeric data type can store numbers up to 19 digits long (including the plus or minus sign and decimal point). Numeric accuracy is to 15.9 digits, excluding the decimal point, which means that the 15 most significant digits in the number will be reliable. When comparing nonzero numbers (with operators such as $<$, $>$), numeric accuracy is to 13 digits. Although dBASE cannot display numbers with more than 19 digits, you can store and manipulate much larger numbers in variables. The largest allowable number in dBASE III PLUS is $10^{308}$. The smallest positive number is $10^{-307}$.
- The date data type stores dates in MM/DD/YY format (the format can be modified). In most cases, dates are checked automatically for validity without programmer intervention. Date arithmetic is also supported. The date data type consumes 8 bytes of disk space.
- The logical data type stores one of two conditions, true (.T.) or false (.F.). Though always stored as .T. or .F., the true condition can be entered as .T., .t., .Y., or .y.. The false condition can be entered as .F., .f., .N., or .n.. dBASE automatically converts any valid entry to the .T. or .F. equivalent. Each logical data type entry takes up one byte of disk space.
- Memo fields are stored in files outside of the actual dBASE database file. Memo fields cannot be stored in variables in main memory (RAM). The maximum length of a memo field is 4,000 characters, or whatever limit is imposed by an external word processor.

## dBASE Databases

Database files store data that most dBASE commands operate upon. The data in database files is organized into records and fields. Theoretically, a database can have a maximum of one billion records or two billion bytes, whichever occurs first. However, the practical limitation of the size of a dBASE database on today's microcomputers is probably under 100,000 records when the size and speed of disk drives is taken into consideration.

Each database field has to have a name that can be a maximum of 10 characters in length, with no spaces. The only punctuation allowed in a field name is the underscore (_) character. Each record in a database file can contain a maximum of 128 fields or 4,000 bytes, whichever comes first. (Including memo fields, the maximum number of bytes in a record is 512K.)

To create a database structure, start at the dBASE dot prompt and enter the **CREATE** command followed by a valid DOS file name for the database file (i.e., eight or fewer letters, no spaces or punctuation). The screen will prompt you for the field name, data type, width, and decimal. When you are done, press **Ctrl-W** or **Ctrl-End** to save the database structure.

The sample dBASE database structure shown in Figure 1.1 shows the name, data type, width, and decimal places (for numbers) for each field in the database structure. The C:Sample.dbf portion of the display shows that the name of the database is Sample.dbf, and it is stored on drive C. The total width of each record is 144 characters in this example, which is the sum of the widths plus one. dBASE stores an "invisible" field on each record for marking records for deletion.

Following is a brief summary of the basic commands used to create, open, view, and modify the structure of dBASE databases:

| | |
|---|---|
| CREATE | Allows you to name and define the structure of a database. |
| USE | Opens an existing database for all dBASE operations. |
| DISPLAY STRUCTURE | Displays the structure of the database in use. |
| MODIFY STRUCTURE | Lets you modify the structure of an existing database, even if it already contains data. |

dBASE III PLUS allows a maximum of 10 simultaneously open database files. Keep in mind that an open database that contains memo fields counts as

```
Structure for database: C:Sample.dbf

Field  Field Name  Type       Width    Dec
    1  LName       Character     15
    2  FName       Character     15
    3  Company     Character     20
    4  Address     Character     20
    5  City        Character     15
    6  State       Character      2
    7  Zip         Character     10
    8  Phone       Character     13
    9  Extension   Character      4
   10  Date_Hired  Date           8
   11  Salary      Numeric       10      2
   12  Active      Logical        1
   13  Comments    Memo          10

** Total **                     144
```

**FIGURE 1.1:** Sample dBASE database structure, created with the dBASE CREATE command. Field names, in the second column, can be up to 10 characters long. Data types, in the third column, can be character, date, numeric, logical, or memo. The maximum widths vary with the data types. The decimal setting (Dec) is used only with the numeric data type.

two files. The number of open database files should not be confused with the 15 *total* files (of all types) that dBASE allows to be open simultaneously.

## Memory Variables

All databases are stored on disk. In addition, data can be stored in RAM in *memory variables*. Memory variables are used as a sort of scratchpad to store values temporarily during the current session with dBASE. For a complete discussion of memory variables, see Chapter 6, "Memory Variables."

Memory variable names follow the same rules as field names: a maximum of 10 characters, no spaces, and no punctuation except the underscore character (_). The same data types used in fields are allowed in memory variables, except for the memo data type. Memo fields are allowed only in database files.

## dBASE Operators

An operator is a symbol that performs an arithmetic or other operation or is used for logical comparisons. For example, the + operator means add. Operators are used in many situations in dBASE. For example, the command

```
? 2 + 3
```

means "display the results of 2 plus 3." Relational operators, such as < (less than), can be used to find information that compares to some value. For example, the command

**LIST FOR Salary < 10000**

would display all records in which the Salary field contains a number less than 10,000.

Many practical examples of the use of operators for manipulating character strings, numbers, and dates are provided throughout this book, particularly in Chapter 15, "Managing Data, Records, and Files." The three types of dBASE operators (mathematical, relational, and logical) are summarized below and in Tables 1.2 through 1.4:

- Mathematical operators generally perform basic arithmetic on numeric values, though the + and – operators can be used with character strings, as listed in Table 1.2.

- Relational operators compare two values and result in one of two possible outcomes: true (.T.) or false (.F.). Relational operators can be used to compare numeric, character, or date data types. However, both sides of the equation must be of the same data type. For example, you cannot compare character data to numeric data, or date data to character data.

| OPERATOR | FUNCTION |
|---|---|
| + | Adds two numbers or concatenates two character strings. For example, **3 + 5** produces 8. **"Hello " + "there"** produces "Hello there". |
| – | Subtracts two numbers or concatenates two character strings without any trailing blank spaces. For example, **10 – 6** produces 4. **"Hello " – "there"** produces "Hellothere". |
| * | Multiplies two numbers. For example, **20*2** produces 40. |
| / | Divides two numbers. For example, **40/2** produces 20. |
| ^ or ** | Exponentiation. For example, **3 ^ 3** produces 27, and **27**(1/3)** produces 3. |
| ( ) | Used for grouping. For example, **2*3+4** evaluates to 10, because multiplication takes precedence over addition. However, the expression **2*(3+4)** results in 14, because the addition inside the parentheses takes precedence over (occurs before) the multiplication. |

**TABLE 1.2:** The Mathematical Operators

(However, there are many functions, discussed in Chapter 17 "dBASE Functions," that can convert data types so that you can still perform logical comparisons among different data types.) The relational operators are listed in Table 1.3.

- Logical operators produce a true or false result after comparing two or more expressions that use the mathematical or relational operators discussed above. The logical operators are listed in Table 1.4.

## Operator Precedence

When dBASE calculates expressions, it follows the standard order of precedence (as opposed to a strict left-to-right order). For example, the expression **3 + 4*2** evaluates to 11 (because the multiplication occurs first). The expression **(3 + 4)*2** evaluates to 14, because the parentheses take precedence. The order of precedence for mathematical operators is listed below:

1. Unary + (positive) and – (negative) signs
2. Exponentiation
3. Multiplication and division
4. Addition and subtraction

| OPERATOR | FUNCTION |
|---|---|
| < | Less than. For example, **1 < 10** is true, **"A" < "B"** is true, and **12/31/86 < 01/01/87** is true. |
| > | Greater than. For example, **1 > 10** is false, **"A" > "B"** is false, and **12/31/86 > 01/01/87** is false. |
| = | Equal. For example, **1 = 1** is true, **"Smith" = "Jones"** is false, and **12/01/86 = 12/01/87** is false. |
| <> or # | Not equal. For example, **1 <> 10** is true, while **1 <> 1** is false. The command **LIST FOR City # "San Diego"** lists all records in a database file where the field named City does not contain "San Diego". |
| < = | Less than or equal to. For example, 9 < = 10 is true. **"Adams" < = "Bowers"** is also true, because "Adams" is alphabetically less than "Bowers". The date expression **01/01/87 < = 12/31/86** is false, and the expression **10 < = 10** is true. |
| > = | Greater than or equal to. For example, **10 > = 9** is true, **"Bowers" > = "Adams"** is true, **12/31/86 > = 01/01/87** is false, and **10 > = 10** is true. |
| $ | Character for comparing whether one character string is embedded in another. For example, **"dog" $ "Hot dog and a Coke"** is true, because the characters "dog" appear within the character string "Hot dog and a Coke". (See the UPPER and LOWER functions in Chapter 17 for techniques in handling upper- and lowercase distinctions.) |

**TABLE 1.3:** The Relational Operators

The order of precedence for logical operators is as follows:

1. .NOT.
2. .AND.
3. .OR.

Relational operators and operators that work on character strings follow no order of precedence. They are performed from left to right.

When an expression includes many different kinds of expressions, the order of precedence is mathematical, relational, then logical. All operations at the same level of precedence are performed from left to right.

While the rules of operator precedence might seem complex, they are actually designed to make the syntax of expressions intuitively obvious. For example, the command

```
LIST FOR X + Y < 10 .OR. X + Y > 20
```

| OPERATOR | FUNCTION |
|---|---|
| .AND. | States that two things must be true. For example, **LIST FOR LName = "Smith" .AND. State = "NY"** displays all Smiths in the state of New York. |
| .OR. | States that one or two things must be true. For example, **LIST FOR Past_Due >= 90 .OR. Notice2** displays all records with a number greater than or equal to 90 in the PastDue field, in addition to all records with .T. in the logical field named Notice2. |
| .NOT. | States that one thing must not be true (works with a single expression). For example, **LIST FOR .NOT. "Apple" $ Address** displays all records except those with the word Apple in the field named Address. |
| ( ) | Parentheses used for grouping logical expressions. For example, **LIST FOR LName = "Smith" .AND. (State = "NY" .OR. State = "NJ")** displays all Smiths in the states of New York and New Jersey. |

**TABLE 1.4:** The Logical Operators

will locate all records wherein the sum of X and Y is less than 10 or greater than 20. When in doubt about how dBASE will interpret an expression, you can specify precedence with parentheses, as below:

**LName = "Miller" .AND. (State = "CA" .OR. State = "NY")**

The parentheses process the .OR. expression before the .AND. expression. Hence, the parentheses ensure that only Millers in the states of NY or CA will be accessed. On the other hand, if you wanted to access all the Millers in the state of California, and everyone (regardless of last name) in the state of New York, you could move the parentheses, as below:

**(LName = "Miller" .AND. State = "CA") .OR. State = "NY"**

## dBASE Files

A summary of the types of files that dBASE creates and manipulates, along with their default file names, is shown in Table 1.5. Generally speaking, you assign the initial file name (eight characters with no spaces and only the underscore character allowed) whenever you enter the CREATE or MODIFY command used to create the file. dBASE automatically adds the file-name extension. It also assumes the extension when trying to locate a file.

| FILE-NAME EXTENSION | TYPE OF FILE |
|---|---|
| .cat | Catalog files, used to store the names of files used in a single application, created by SET CATALOG TO command |
| .db | File for configuring dBASE at startup; always uses the full name Config.db |
| .dbf | Database files created with the CREATE command |
| .dbt | Database text files used to store memo fields |
| .fmt | Format files used to display custom data entry and editing screens, created by the CREATE/MODIFY SCREEN command |
| .frm | Report format files used to display formatted reports, created by the CREATE/MODIFY REPORT command |
| .lbl | Mailing-label format files created by the CREATE/MODIFY LABEL command |
| .mem | Memory variables stored on disk with a SAVE command |
| .ndx | Index files used to maintain sort orders, expedite searches, and link related database files; created by the INDEX ON command |
| .prg | Command (program) files created with the CREATE/MODIFY COMMAND editor or an external word processor |
| .qry | Query files created with the CREATE/MODIFY QUERY command |
| .scr | Intermediate files between the MODIFY SCREEN editor and the finished format (.fmt) file |
| .txt | Text files created by the SET ALTERNATE command |
| .vue | View files created by the CREATE/MODIFY VIEW command |

**TABLE 1.5:** Types of dBASE Files

## THE dBASE CONFIGURATION FILE

When first started from DOS, dBASE automatically checks the current directory for a special file named Config.db and executes any commands within that file. You can use the Config.db file to control the status of numerous parameters in dBASE, including screen color, function key commands, external editors used, memory and buffer size allocations, and command files processed automatically. For more information on the Config.db file and a complete listing of commands used in Config.db, see Appendix C, "Configuring dBASE III PLUS."

## CATEGORICAL SUMMARY OF dBASE COMMANDS AND FUNCTIONS

Table 1.6 summarizes all dBASE commands and groups them according to the basic operations they perform. Even if you are already familiar with dBASE, you should browse through this list, because you might find a new command or two that you weren't already familiar with. The commands that are of particular interest to the programmer are discussed in detail throughout the book. For additional information on a specific command, consult the command index inside the front cover of this book for page references.

Table 1.7 provides a brief summary of all dBASE functions. They are grouped by the type of data they operate on and the type of task they perform. For more details on dBASE functions, see Chapter 17, "dBASE Functions."

| | COMMAND | DESCRIPTION |
|---|---|---|
| **User-Assistance Commands** | ASSIST | Switches from the interactive dot prompt mode to the menu-driven assist mode. |
| | DIR | Displays the names of database (.dbf) files on the currently logged drive and directory. |
| | DISPLAY | Displays the data from records in a database (.dbf) file. |
| | DISPLAY MEMORY | Displays the names, data types, and contents of all currently active memory variables. |
| | DISPLAY STATUS | Displays information about the database (.dbf) files currently in use and other dBASE environmental parameters. |
| | DISPLAY STRUCTURE | Displays the structure of the database file currently in use. |
| | HELP | Provides on-line assistance for specific dBASE commands and other information. |

**TABLE 1.6:** dBASE Commands

| | COMMAND | DESCRIPTION |
|---|---|---|
| **Commands to Create Files** | COPY | Copies the database in use to another file. |
| | COPY FILE | Makes a copy of any file. |
| | CREATE | Creates a new database (.DBF) file. |
| | CREATE LABEL | Creates a format (.lbl) file for printing mailing labels. |
| | CREATE QUERY | Creates a query (.qry) file for filtering out records from a database that do not match a specified search criterion. |
| | CREATE REPORT | Creates a report format (.frm) file that defines the format and heading for a printed report. |
| | CREATE SCREEN | Creates a format (.fmt) file for entering and editing records on a database through a custom screen. |
| | CREATE VIEW | Creates a view (.vue) file for setting up a relationship between related files with at least one identical field. |
| | EXPORT | Creates a PFS file from a dBASE database file. |
| | IMPORT | Creates a database file from a PFS file. |
| | INDEX | Creates an index (.NDX) file from the database file in use, for maintaining sort orders, maximizing the speed of searches, and defining relationships among multiple databases. |
| | JOIN | Combines the fields of two related databases into a new database. |
| | MODIFY COMMAND | Creates a command (.prg) file (a program). |
| | MODIFY STRUCTURE | Allows changes to an existing database (.dbf) file. |

**TABLE 1.6:** dBASE Commands (continued)

| | COMMAND | DESCRIPTION |
|---|---|---|
| **Commands to Create Files (continued)** | SAVE | Saves memory variables to a memory (.mem) file on disk. |
| | SET ALTERNATE | Opens a text file that captures all activity on the screen. |
| | SET CATALOG | Creates a catalog (.cat) file of all the files used in a particular application. |
| | TOTAL | Creates a summary of an existing file containing totals of specified numeric fields. |
| **Commands to Add New Data** | APPEND | Adds new records to the bottom of the database file in use. |
| | APPEND BLANK | Adds a new, blank record to the bottom of a database file. |
| | BROWSE | Allows full-screen, spreadsheet-like editing and entering of data to the database file in use. |
| | INSERT | Inserts new data into a database at a specified record position. |
| **Commands to Reorganize Existing Data** | INDEX | Creates an index (.ndx) file from the database file in use, for maintaining sort orders, maximizing the speed of searches, and defining relationships among multiple databases. |
| | SORT | Creates a new, sorted database (.dbf) file from the database file currently in use. |
| **Commands to Change Existing Data** | BROWSE | Allows full-screen, spreadsheet-like editing and entering of data to the database file in use. |
| | CHANGE | Allows editing of all fields in a single database record. |
| | DELETE | Marks records in a database for eventual deletion. |
| | EDIT | Same as the CHANGE command. |

**TABLE 1.6:** dBASE Commands (continued)

| | COMMAND | DESCRIPTION |
|---|---|---|
| **Commands to Change Existing Data (continued)** | PACK | Permanently removes records from a database that have been marked for deletion with the DELETE, CHANGE, EDIT, or BROWSE commands. |
| | READ | Allows modification or entering of data in database files or memory variables in conjunction with the GET command and custom screen format (.fmt) files. |
| | RECALL | Reclaims records that have been marked for deletion. |
| | REPLACE | Replaces the data in a database field with a new value. |
| **Commands to Display Data** | @...SAY | Specifies a row and column position on the screen or printer and displays data at that position. |
| | @...TO | Draws a line or box. |
| | ? | Prints information starting on a new line. |
| | ?? | Prints information at the current cursor or printer position. |
| | DISPLAY | Displays the contents of a database record. |
| | LABEL | Prints mailing labels in the format specified by the CREATE LABEL command. |
| | LIST | Displays database records. |
| | REPORT | Prints a report with the format specified by the CREATE REPORT command. |
| **Commands to Locate a Particular Record** | CONTINUE | Finds the next record matching the search criterion (used in conjunction with the LOCATE command). |
| | FIND | Locates a value in an index file. |

**TABLE 1.6:** dBASE Commands (continued)

| | COMMAND | DESCRIPTION |
|---|---|---|
| **Commands to Locate a Particular Record (continued)** | GO | Moves the record pointer to a specific record according to its position (record number). |
| | LOCATE | Positions the record pointer to the first record in the database that matches a search criterion. |
| | SEEK | Locates a value in an index file. |
| | SKIP | Moves the record pointer forward or backward relative to its current position. |
| **Commands to Calculate Data** | AVERAGE | Calculates and displays the average of a numeric field in a database. |
| | COUNT | Counts how many records in a database meet a specified criterion. |
| | SUM | Calculates and displays the sum of a numeric field in a database. |
| | UPDATE | Changes the values of fields in a database based on the fields in a separate related database. |
| **Commands to Manipulate Database Files** | APPEND FROM | Adds records from one database file to the bottom of another database file. Can also be used to import data from foreign files into database files. |
| | CLOSE | Closes files. |
| | COPY | Copies the currently open database to another database or to a foreign file format. |
| | ERASE | Permanently erases a file from the directory. |
| | MODIFY STRUCTURE | Changes the structure of the database in use. |
| | REINDEX | Rebuilds all currently active index files. |

**TABLE 1.6:** dBASE Commands (continued)

| | COMMAND | DESCRIPTION |
|---|---|---|
| **Commands to Manipulate Database Files (continued)** | RENAME | Changes the name of any file. |
| | SELECT | Allows up to ten database files to be open simultaneously; also allows switching from one to the next. |
| | USE | Opens an existing database file for future operations. |
| **Commands to Modify Nondatabase Files** | MODIFY COMMAND | The dBASE word processor for editing command (.prg) files. |
| | MODIFY LABEL | Modifies a mailing label (.lbl) format. |
| | MODIFY QUERY | Modifies a filter query (.qry) file. |
| | MODIFY REPORT | Changes an existing report (.frm) format. |
| | MODIFY SCREEN | Changes an existing screen (.fmt) format file. |
| | MODIFY VIEW | Alters an existing view (.vue) file. |
| **Commands to Control Peripherals** | CLEAR | Clears the screen. |
| | EJECT | Ejects the page in the printer. |
| | SET COLOR | Determines the colors used on screen displays. |
| **Commands to Manipulate Memory Variables** | ACCEPT | Stores user input in a character memory variable. |
| | CLEAR ALL | Initializes dBASE III PLUS to its default startup mode. |
| | CLEAR MEMORY | Erases all current memory variables. |
| | DISPLAY MEMORY | Displays all current memory variables. |
| | INPUT | Waits for user entry and stores input in a numeric memory variable. |
| | READ | Allows data to be entered via the @...SAY...GET commands. |

**TABLE 1.6:** dBASE Commands (continued)

| | COMMAND | DESCRIPTION |
|---|---|---|
| **Commands to Manipulate Memory Variables (continued)** | RELEASE | Erases memory variables. |
| | RESTORE | Brings memory variables that have been stored on disk in a .mem file back into memory. |
| | SAVE | Saves memory variables in a memory (.mem) file on disk. |
| | STORE | Creates a memory variable and assigns a value to it. |
| | WAIT | Waits for the user to press a single key and optionally stores that keypress in a character memory variable. |
| **Programming Commands** | * | Specifies a programmer comment when used as the first character in a line. |
| | && | Specifies a programmer comment to the right of a command line in a program. |
| | CANCEL | Terminates command file processing and returns control to the dot prompt. |
| | CASE | Begins an option within a DO CASE clause. |
| | DO | Runs a command file or procedure. |
| | DO CASE | Begins a block of several mutually exclusive routines. |
| | DO WHILE | Begins a loop in a command file. |
| | ELSE | Used within an IF clause as the alternate path when the IF expression is false. |
| | ENDCASE | Marks the bottom of a DO CASE clause. |
| | ENDDO | Marks the bottom of a DO WHILE loop. |
| | ENDIF | Marks the bottom of an IF clause. |
| | ENDTEXT | Marks the bottom of a TEXT block. |

**TABLE 1.6:** dBASE Commands (continued)

| | COMMAND | DESCRIPTION |
|---|---|---|
| **Programming Commands (continued)** | EXIT | Passes control to outside a DO WHILE loop. |
| | IF | Makes a decision based on a single expression. |
| | LOOP | Passes control to the top of a DO WHILE loop. |
| | NOTE | Marks a programmer comment in a command file (same as *). |
| | ON ERROR | Executes a specified command when an error occurs. |
| | ON ESCAPE | Executes a specified command when the Esc key is pressed (SET ESCAPE ON parameter must be set). |
| | ON KEY | Executes a specified command when the user presses any key. |
| | OTHERWISE | Used as an alternative path in a DO CASE clause when no CASE statements evaluate to true. |
| | PARAMETERS | Specifies internal names for values passed to a procedure. |
| | PRIVATE | Specifies that a memory variable is local to a given command file or procedure. |
| | PROCEDURE | Assigns a name to a procedure within a procedure file. |
| | PUBLIC | Makes a memory variable global to all levels of command files and procedures. |
| | QUIT | Terminates command file processing, closes all open files, and exits dBASE III PLUS. |
| | RETURN | Passes control back to a calling command file or procedure and resumes processing at the next line. |
| | TEXT | Begins a block of text in the command file to be displayed on the screen or printer. |

**TABLE 1.6:** dBASE Commands (continued)

| | COMMAND | DESCRIPTION |
|---|---|---|
| **Commands to Interface with External Programs** | CALL | Runs an assembly language (binary) subroutine that has already been loaded into memory. |
| | LOAD | Copies an assembly language subroutine into memory. |
| | RUN | Runs an external DOS program and automatically returns control to the dot prompt. |
| | ! | Same as RUN. |
| **Debugging Commands** | DISPLAY HISTORY | Displays commands stored in the history file (the SET DOHISTORY ON parameter must be set to record command file lines). |
| | LIST HISTORY | Same as DISPLAY HISTORY, but does not pause after each screen-ful of information. |
| | RESUME | Resumes command file processing after temporary suspension. |
| | SET DEBUG | Sends the results of the SET ECHO command to the printer rather than the screen. |
| | SET DOHISTORY | Determines whether lines from command files are recorded in the history file. |
| | SET ECHO | Displays command lines from command files on the screen before executing them. |
| | SET HISTORY | Specifies the number of lines to be recorded in the history file. |
| | SET STEP | Pauses execution after every line in a command file. |
| | SUSPEND | Temporarily suspends processing of a command file and returns control to the dot prompt. |

**TABLE 1.6:** dBASE Commands (continued)

| | COMMAND | DESCRIPTION |
|---|---|---|
| **Commands to Control the Environment** | SET ALTERNATE | Determines whether ensuing text is stored on a disk file. |
| | SET ALTERNATE TO | Sets up a disk file for capturing text that appears on the screen. |
| | SET BELL | Determines whether the bell sounds during data entry and editing. |
| | SET CARRY | Determines whether data from the previous record are carried over to the next record during data entry. |
| | SET CATALOG | Determines whether new files are added to an active catalog. |
| | SET CATALOG TO | Creates, opens, or closes a catalog file. |
| | SET CENTURY | Determines whether the century appears in dates. |
| | SET COLOR | Automatically set at startup depending on whether a monochrome or color monitor is in use. |
| | SET COLOR TO | Determines colors (or shading) for the screen. |
| | SET CONFIRM | Determines whether a carriage return is required after filling in a data-entry field. |
| | SET CONSOLE | Turns the screen on or off. |
| | SET DATE | Sets a format for displaying dates. |
| | SET DEBUG | Sends the output from the SET ECHO command to the printer. |
| | SET DECIMALS | Determines the number of decimal places displayed in the results of mathematical calculations. |
| | SET DEFAULT | Specifies the disk drive used to store and retrieve files. |
| | SET DELETED | When ON, records that are marked for deletion are not displayed. |

**TABLE 1.6:** dBASE Commands (continued)

| | COMMAND | DESCRIPTION |
|---|---|---|
| **Commands to Control the Environment (continued)** | SET DELIMITERS | Determines whether delimiters appear around fields on screen displays. |
| | SET DELIMITERS TO | Specifies the characters to use as delimiters around fields on screen displays. |
| | SET DEVICE | Determines whether output from @...SAY commands is directed to screen or printer. |
| | SET DOHISTORY | When ON, command file lines are recorded in the history file. Otherwise, only commands entered at the dot prompt are recorded in the history file. |
| | SET ECHO | Determines whether lines from command files are displayed on the screen before execution. |
| | SET ESCAPE | Determines whether pressing the Esc key interrupts command file processing. |
| | SET EXACT | Determines whether exact matches are required in character string searches. |
| | SET FIELDS | Activates or deactivates the most recent SET FIELDS command. |
| | SET FIELDS TO | Determines which fields from a database or multiple related databases are to be displayed and edited. |
| | SET FILTER | Hides database records that do not match a specified search criterion. |
| | SET FIXED | Determines whether a fixed number of decimal places will be displayed (used in conjunction with SET DECIMALS). |
| | SET FORMAT | Determines the format (.fmt) file to be used with APPEND, EDIT, and READ commands; also closes a format file. |

**TABLE 1.6:** dBASE Commands (continued)

| | COMMAND | DESCRIPTION |
|---|---|---|
| **Commands to Control the Environment (continued)** | SET FUNCTION | Assigns tasks to function keys. |
| | SET HEADING | Determines whether field names appear at the top of the output from LIST and DISPLAY commands. |
| | SET HELP | Determines whether the "Do you want some help?" message appears on the screen after an error occurs. |
| | SET HISTORY | Determines whether commands are recorded in the history file. |
| | SET HISTORY TO | Determines the number of lines to be recorded in the history file. |
| | SET INDEX | Opens index files for the database currently in use. |
| | SET INTENSITY | Determines whether enhanced display with reverse video is used for full-screen operations. |
| | SET MARGIN | Adjusts the left margin setting on the printer. |
| | SET MEMOWIDTH | Determines the display width of memo fields. |
| | SET MENUS | Determines whether help menus above full-screen operation are displayed automatically. |
| | SET MESSAGE | Displays a message centered at the bottom of the screen (if SET STATUS is ON). |
| | SET ODOMETER | Determines the frequency of updating on the odometer displayed with COPY and other commands (when SET TALK is ON). |
| | SET ORDER | Determines which of several open index files will be the controlling index file. |
| | SET PATH | Specifies a path of directories to search for files. |
| | SET PRINT | Directs screen output to the printer. |
| | SET PRINTER | Directs printing to a specified device. |

**TABLE 1.6:** dBASE Commands (continued)

| | COMMAND | DESCRIPTION |
|---|---|---|
| **Commands to Control the Environment (continued)** | SET PROCEDURE | Opens a procedure file. |
| | SET RELATION | Defines a common field and relationship between two open database files. |
| | SET SAFETY | Determines whether the prompt "<File name> already exists, overwrite it? (Y/N)" appears on the screen when a file is about to overwritten. |
| | SET SCOREBOARD | Determines whether dBASE messages appear on the status bar (or row zero on the screen if SET STATUS is OFF). |
| | SET STATUS | Determines whether the status bar appears on the screen. |
| | SET STEP | Determines whether dBASE pauses before processing each line in a command file. |
| | SET TALK | Determines whether the results of commands and calculations are displayed on the screen. |
| | SET TITLE | Determines whether the SET CATALOG command prompts for file names as new files are added to the catalog. |
| | SET TYPEAHEAD | Specifies the number of keystrokes stored in the typeahead buffer. |
| | SET UNIQUE | Determines whether only unique records are included in an INDEX ON command. |
| | SET VIEW | Opens multiple database files and sets up their relationships based on a previous CREATE VIEW or MODIFY VIEW command. |

**TABLE 1.6:** dBASE Commands (continued)

| | COMMAND | DESCRIPTION |
|---|---|---|
| **Networking Commands** | DISPLAY USERS | Displays the names of all currently logged dBASE network users. |
| | LIST STATUS | Displays information about the current status of dBASE III PLUS on the network. |
| | LOGOUT | Logs a user out of the network, allowing a new user to log on. |
| | RETRY | Returns to a calling program and executes the same line. |
| | SET ENCRYPTION | Determines whether protected files are encrypted when copied. |
| | SET EXCLUSIVE | Sets a file open attribute to either exclusive or shared mode. |
| | SET PRINTER | Selects a printer on the network. |
| | UNLOCK | Removes record and file locks. |
| | USE EXCLUSIVE | Opens a database for use in exclusive (single-user) mode. |

**TABLE 1.6:** dBASE Commands (continued)

| | FUNCTION | DESCRIPTION |
|---|---|---|
| **Date Functions** | CDOW( ) | Returns the day of the week as a character string (e.g., Monday). |
| | CMONTH( ) | Returns the month as a character string (e.g., April). |
| | DATE( ) | Returns the current system date. |
| | DAY( ) | Returns the day of the month as a number. |
| | DOW( ) | Returns the day of the week as a number. |
| | MONTH( ) | Returns the month as a number (1–12). |
| | TIME( ) | Returns the current system time. |
| | YEAR( ) | Returns the year of a date. |

**TABLE 1.7:** dBASE Functions

| | FUNCTION | DESCRIPTION |
|---|---|---|
| **Character Manipulation Functions** | & | Macro substitution. |
| | AT( ) | Returns the position of a substring within a string. |
| | LEFT( ) | Returns the substring counting from the leftmost characters. |
| | LEN( ) | Returns the length of a character string. |
| | LOWER( ) | Returns the lowercase equivalent of a string. |
| | LTRIM( ) | Trims leading blanks. |
| | REPLICATE( ) | Repeats a character string a specific number of times. |
| | RIGHT( ) | Returns the substring from the rightmost characters. |
| | RTRIM( ) | Removes trailing blanks. |
| | SPACE( ) | Generates blank spaces. |
| | STUFF( ) | Replaces or inserts a substring into a character string. |
| | SUBSTR( ) | Returns a substring from a larger character string. |
| | TRANSFORM( ) | Displays data in a predefined format. |
| | TRIM( ) | Removes trailing blanks. |
| | UPPER( ) | Returns the uppercase equivalent of a string. |
| **Mathematical Functions** | ABS( ) | Returns the absolute (positive) value. |
| | EXP( ) | Returns the exponential (value of $e^x$). |
| | INT( ) | Returns the truncated integer equivalent. |
| | LOG( ) | Returns the natural logarithm. |
| | MAX( ) | Returns the largest of the numbers compared. |
| | MIN( ) | Returns the smallest of the numbers compared. |

**TABLE 1.7:** dBASE Functions (continued)

| | FUNCTION | DESCRIPTION |
|---|---|---|
| **Mathematical Functions (continued)** | MOD( ) | Returns the modulus of two numbers. |
| | ROUND( ) | Rounds a number to the specified decimal place. |
| | SQRT( ) | Returns the square root. |
| **Data Type Conversion Functions** | ASC( ) | Converts character data to numeric ASCII code. |
| | CHR( ) | Converts numeric data to ASCII characters. |
| | CTOD( ) | Converts character data to the date data type. |
| | DTOC( ) | Converts date data to the character data type. |
| | STR( ) | Converts numeric data to the character data type. |
| | VAL( ) | Converts character data to the numeric data type. |
| **Testing Functions** | BOF( ) | Tests for the beginning of database file. |
| | COL( ) | Indicates the current column position of the cursor. |
| | DELETED( ) | Indicates whether a record is marked for deletion. |
| | DISKSPACE( ) | Returns the available space on disk. |
| | EOF( ) | Tests for the end of database file. |
| | ERROR( ) | Returns the number generated by an ON ERROR command. |
| | FILE( ) | Tests whether a file exists. |
| | FOUND( ) | Indicates whether a database search was successful. |
| | IIF( ) | Immediate if, embedded inside command lines or report columns. |
| | ISALPHA( ) | Indicates whether the first character in a string is part of the alphabet. |
| | ISCOLOR( ) | Indicates whether a color monitor is in use. |

**TABLE 1.7:** dBASE Functions (continued)

| | FUNCTION | DESCRIPTION |
|---|---|---|
| **Testing Functions (continued)** | ISLOWER( ) | Indicates whether the first character in a string is lowercase. |
| | ISUPPER( ) | Indicates whether the first character in a string is uppercase. |
| | LUPDATE( ) | Returns the last update of a database file in date format. |
| | MESSAGE( ) | Generates an error message during ON ERROR. |
| | PCOL( ) | Returns the current printer column position. |
| | PROW( ) | Returns the current printer row position. |
| | RECCOUNT( ) | Returns the number of records in the current database file. |
| | RECNO( ) | Returns the number of the current record. |
| | RECSIZE( ) | Returns the size of a selected record in a database file. |
| | ROW( ) | Returns the row number of the current cursor position on the screen. |
| | TYPE( ) | Returns a C, N, L, M, or U character depending on data type. |
| **Data Entry Functions** | INKEY( ) | Returns an integer representing the key pressed as a program is running. |
| | READKEY( ) | Returns an integer representing the key pressed to exit a full-screen editing session. |
| **Identification Functions** | DBF( ) | Returns the name of the database file currently in use. |
| | FIELD( ) | Returns the name of the chosen field in the current database file. |
| | FKLABEL( ) | Returns the name of a function key. |
| | FKMAX( ) | Returns the number of programmable function keys on the keyboard. |

**TABLE 1.7:** dBASE Functions (continued)

| | FUNCTION | DESCRIPTION |
|---|---|---|
| **Identification Functions (continued)** | GETENV( ) | Returns data on the operating system environment. |
| | NDX( ) | Returns the names of any open index files. |
| | OS( ) | Returns the name of the operating system in use. |
| | VERSION( ) | Returns the version of dBASE III PLUS in use. |
| **Networking Functions** | ACCESS( ) | Indicates the level of access for the last logged-in user. |
| | ERROR( ) | Traps and recovers from networking errors. |
| | FLOCK( ) | Tries to lock a database file. |
| | LOCK( ) | Tries to lock a database record. |
| | MESSAGE( ) | Traps the message generated by a networking error. |
| | RLOCK( ) | Same as LOCK. |

**TABLE 1.7:** dBASE Functions (continued)

## SUMMARY

This chapter overviewed dBASE III PLUS as a programming language. The next chapter focuses on the other side of the coin that the programmer needs to deal with: the application.

*For a discussion of techniques used to design and develop custom software systems:*

- Chapter 2, "Software Design and Development"

*For an in-depth discussion of database design with dBASE III PLUS:*

- Chapter 3, "Database Design"

*For specific information on creating dBASE III PLUS command files (or programs), and using the MODIFY COMMAND editor:*

- Chapter 4, "Command Files"

*For a complete discussion of memory variables:*

- Chapter 6: "Memory Variables"

*For more information on dBASE functions and how to use them to convert data types:*

- Chapter 17: "dBASE Functions"

*For general information on installing dBASE on a network:*

- Chapter 20: "Networking and Security"

*For a listing of the commands used in the Config.db file:*

- Appendix C: "Configuring dBASE III PLUS"

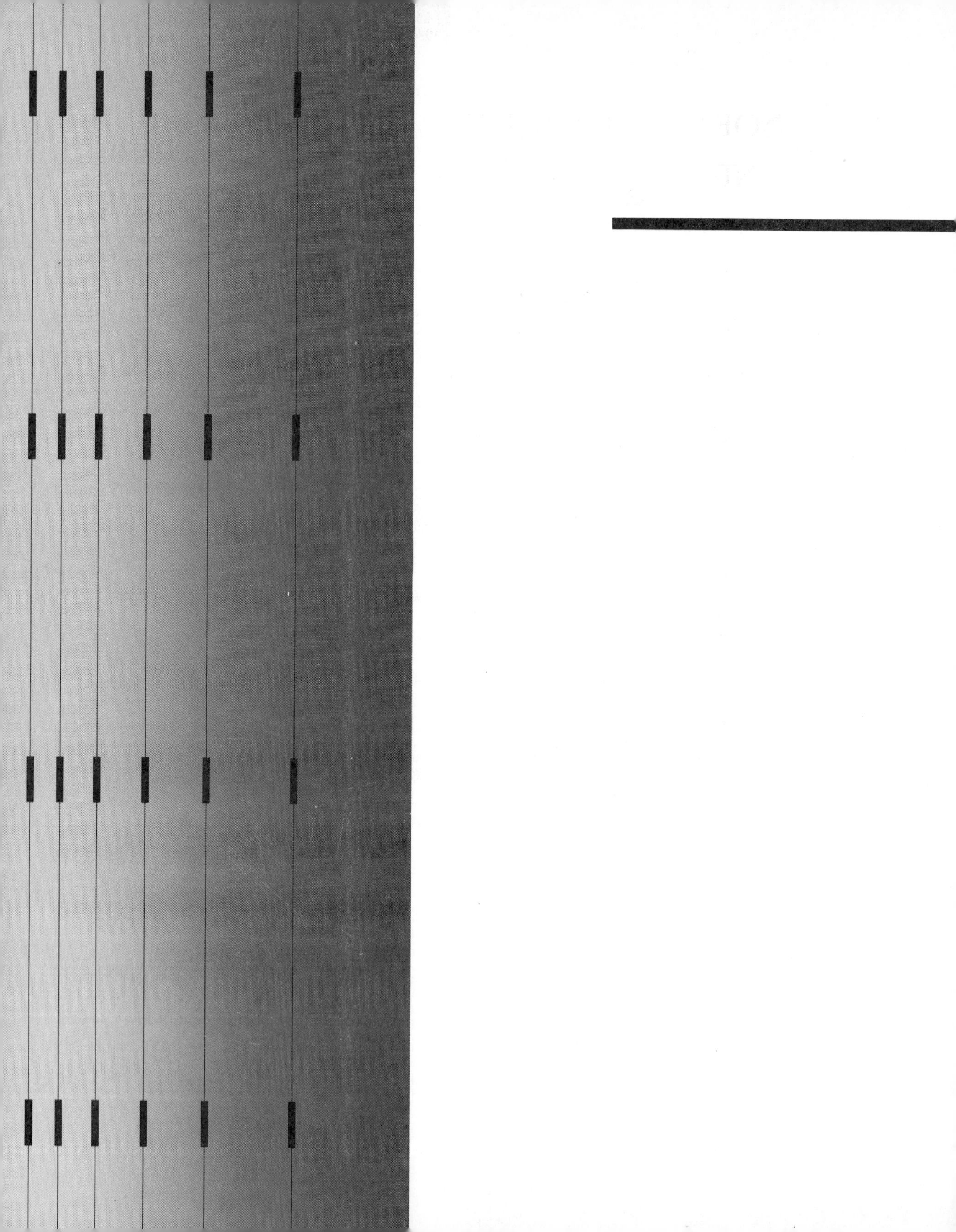

# SOFTWARE DESIGN AND DEVELOPMENT

# SOFTWARE DESIGN AND DEVELOPMENT

Developing a custom application with dBASE III PLUS is a creative process, though certainly not a haphazard one. Carrying a large, sophisticated project from the idea stage to the finished product requires more than just dBASE commands and functions. Custom applications require planning and structure to prevent great ideas from turning into hapless catastrophes.

This chapter looks at the design tools and techniques of the software development cycle and how they can help the dBASE programmer build large, sophisticated software systems. You will learn the various phases of the development cycle in the order in which they take place:

1. Problem definition
2. Database design
3. Modular program design
4. Coding
5. Testing, debugging, and enhancing

## PHASE 1: PROBLEM DEFINITION

The first step of the problem definition phase is to develop clear and unambiguous goals about your project. Usually, the goals for a software project begin with a general statement such as

> Create a payroll management system for a small business.

That problem definition gives you a direction in which to move, but there is much more to consider before you sit down at the keyboard.

To start with, you'll want some clues as to the size of the database and the frequency with which payroll is paid. Assuming that the business under consideration has no more than 100 employees and pays its employees weekly, the first refinement to the problem definition might be as follows:

> Generate a weekly payroll system for a business with a maximum of 100 employees.

The next step in the refinement process is to start pinning down the input to and output from the system being developed.

## Specifying the Input and Output

As soon as you have a vague idea of what the overall function of the custom system will be, you'll want to get down to the specifics of what, exactly, the program is going to produce (the output), and what data are available to produce that information (the input). Later you'll also need to determine what calculations are required to develop the finished output from the raw input.

If you are automating an existing manual system, this job can be fairly easy. You just collect copies of all the reports currently being generated manually; those define your program's output. (Invariably, somebody will want something different on the computer's output, but you can just pencil in any changes along these lines on the existing forms.) To determine the input, collect whatever forms are used to supply information to the people currently producing the reports manually. These will determine your input (unless, again, changes in the automated system require additional information).

If you are not automating an existing manual system, your job will be different. First of all, you'll need a subject-matter expert (in this example, this would be the person who is in control of payroll at this business) to sit down with you and explain what he or she needs. Ideally, this person will be able to sketch out examples of forms for data input and reports for data output.

In other cases, you, the programmer, are also the subject-matter expert, particularly when developing programs for your own personal use or to mass produce for marketing on a wide scale. This being the case, it is still to your benefit to jot down forms representing information going into the computer and reports coming out. Let's get back to our payroll example and see how this will help matters.

### Focusing on Output

At this point you must narrow down exactly what this custom software system is going to produce. Again, if available, the documents from an existing manual system can help answer this question. If you are developing an entirely new system, however, you may have to sketch out sample reports from scratch.

Getting back to the payroll example, assume that the program will need to generate the following information:

- Paychecks
- Paystubs showing
  - current, quarterly, and year-to-date gross pay
  - current, quarterly, and year-to-date net pay
  - current, quarterly, and year-to-date federal, FICA, and state withholding taxes
- Management reports including
  - total wages paid this period

        total taxes withheld per employee
        total vacation hours paid this period
        total overtime wages paid this period
        payroll account check register
    W-2 forms
    W-4 forms

If you can get copies of the above reports (from either the existing manual system or a sketch), do so. They will certainly come in handy when designing the database structure and report formats.

With the outputs of the custom system defined, you can also refine the original problem definition, as below:

> Generate a weekly payroll system for a business with a maximum of 100 employees. Each week, the system produces a paycheck and a pay stub detailing gross and net pay, federal and state withholding amounts, and FICA tax. The system also produces a summary of all payroll activity, W-2 forms, and W-4 forms.

Now that you know what the system needs to produce, you need to make sure that enough data will be available to produce those reports. Of course, the computer needs only raw (uncalculated) data; it can perform any necessary calculations on those data.

## Focusing on Input

Next you need to take inventory of what information is going to be available for data entry. You also need to make sure that there is enough raw data being entered to produce the desired reports (output). In this hypothetical payroll model, the following items of information might be readily available:

| | |
|---|---|
| Employee records | Including employee number, name, address, social security number, hourly pay/salary status, regular hourly pay rate, overtime pay rate, salary, number of federal and state exemptions, date hired |
| Time cards | Including pay-period dates, employee name, social security number, total hours worked, regular hours, overtime hours, sick leave hours, vacation hours |
| Tax tables | Including tables for calculating federal and state withholding taxes, contribution amount for FICA, other taxes |

Given the current application, the inputs appear to be sufficient to produce the outputs. If they were not, it would be the responsibility of the programmer to determine what additional information needs to be added and how and where that information should be entered (with every payroll period, each time a new employee is added, and so forth).

Now you can refine your original problem definition as below:

> Generate a weekly payroll system for a business with a maximum of 100 employees. Each week, the system produces a paycheck and a pay stub detailing gross and net pay, federal and state withholding amounts, and FICA tax. The system also produces a summary of all payroll activity, W-2 forms, and W-4 forms.
>
> Data for the payroll system will come from employee records, time cards, and existing tax tables.

If you can get copies of the forms used for input, do so. They will be valuable references during the database design and coding phases of the project. Furthermore, instructions or booklets on how to perform the calculations (i.e., how to calculate federal and state withholding) will most certainly come in handy during the coding and testing phases of the software development cycle.

Now that the input and output are defined, it's a good idea to start thinking about *exceptions*—situations that will not go through the normal flow of things. Preparing for exceptions early in the process will help you avoid having to go back and modify a lot of existing programs to handle that occasional nuisance that creeps into the data.

## Preparing for Exceptions

The sooner you begin thinking (and asking) about possible exceptions to the general flow of information in your system, the less often these situations will come back and haunt you after you've already written a lot of software.

A frequent problem that arises in payroll systems is employee termination in the middle of a pay period. The employee may be due vacation and sick pay and perhaps additional severance pay. Exceptions such as this should be added to your problem definition, as below:

> Generate a weekly payroll system for a business with a maximum of 100 employees. Each week, the system produces a paycheck and a pay stub detailing gross and net pay, federal and state withholding amounts, and FICA tax. The system also produces a summary of all payroll activity, W-2 forms, and W-4 forms.

Data for the payroll system will come from employee records, time cards, and existing tax tables.

Employees who were terminated during the payroll period will receive checks that include vacation and sick leave back pay.

Following these same basic steps, you can continue to develop and refine the problem definition. Your end goal will be a collection of documents that you and any other programmers on the same project can refer to throughout the software development process. Again, written copies of any data-entry forms and reports (data output) will be very helpful. A well-written description or outline of the overall system will also provide a solid foundation to build upon.

## Phase 2: Database Design

Once you've clearly defined your overall goals on paper, you can begin designing the databases for your application. You'll want to decide what information needs to be stored on databases. In general, you'll want databases to store the following:

- Any raw data needed for immediate processing
- Any raw data required for general long-term processing
- Any raw data necessary for performing calculations
- Any accumulated totals, such as quarter-to-date and year-to-date

I've emphasized raw data above to point out that the results of any calculations usually need not be entered into the keyboard or stored on any databases. Let's look at some examples.

Raw data required for immediate processing of the paychecks might be the employee number and hours worked. Raw data for general (long-term) processing might include the employee's name, address, pay rate, hire date, and so forth. Data used to aid in calculations might include tables of federal and state tax cutoffs.

While entering data to process the payroll, the system could allow the operator to key in only the employee number and hours worked. Given that information, the system could produce the following data:

1. It could calculate the employee's gross pay by locating the appropriate employee on the database and multiplying the hours worked by the hourly rate.
2. It could calculate and subtract the withholding tax by looking up cutoffs in the tax table databases and subtracting the appropriate withholding.

3. It could accumulate quarter-to-date and year-to-date totals by first seeing whether the value needs to be reset to zero (depending on the current date) and then adding the current tax withholding and gross pay to the accumulated totals.

There is more to database design, however, than simply storing data on a few files of information. Some applications will require many separate database files. Of these files, some may be entirely independent, while others are related to one another in a one-to-many or many-to-many relationship. These more complicated aspects of database design are discussed in Chapter 3, "Database Design."

## Database Planning

While you are identifying the types of data needed for the system, it is helpful to plan how these data may be grouped in your database (.dbf) files. As discussed in Chapter 3, "Database Design," there are several reasons and techniques for dividing data into separate database files. In this example of the payroll system, you could group the data into the following files:

| | |
|---|---|
| Employee master file | Including the employee number, name, address, social security number, hourly pay/salary status, regular hourly pay rate, overtime pay rate, salary, number of federal and state exemptions, hire date, termination date |
| Employee pay file | Including year-to-date totals for gross pay, federal and state tax withheld, FICA withheld, sick leave taken, vacation taken |
| Time card detail file | Including pay period date, employee number, name, hours worked, regular hours, overtime hours, sick leave hours, vacation hours |
| Paycheck file | Including the pay period date, employee number, employee name and address, current and year-to-date gross pay, federal and state withholding, FICA withholding, sick leave hours, and vacation hours |
| Company payroll file | Including quarter-to-date totals for gross wages, federal and state withholdings, FICA withholdings, FICA employer contribution |
| Tax table files | Including tables indicating federal tax withholding, state tax withholding, maximum contribution amount for FICA |

The employee data were put into two database files because the employee master information will probably not be changed during the weekly payroll cycle. Also, by separating the data, the programs can keep the user from changing data used to calculate the paychecks.

## Database Sizing

Now that you know what the database files should contain, you can begin to estimate the amount of file space the custom system will require. The first step in calculating the amount of space you will need is to multiply the maximum number of records by the size of each record. (dBASE always adds one byte to each record for storing the "marked for deletion" symbol.) You could size the 100-record (100 employees) employee master file as follows:

| | |
|---|---|
| Employee number | 4 digits |
| Employee name | 30 characters |
| Employee address | 40 characters |
| Social security number | 11 characters |
| Hourly/salary status | 1 character |
| Regular hourly pay rate | 5 digits |
| Overtime percentage rate | 4 digits |
| Federal exemptions | 3 characters (e.g., M02) |
| State exemptions | 3 characters |
| Date hired | 8 characters |
| Date terminated | 8 characters |
| dBASE "deleted" field | 1 character |
| Total bytes | 118 bytes × 100 records = 11,800 |

In addition, the database header record uses about 64 bytes, plus 32 bytes per field. In the above example, there are 11 fields (excluding the "deleted symbol" field), so we need to add 416 bytes (32 × 11 + 64) to the overall file size, leaving a total of 12,216 bytes for the entire file with 100 employees.

A rough estimate of the sizes of other files in this sample application is listed below:

- Employee pay file: 100 records × 38 digits for an estimated size of 3,800 bytes
- Time card detail file: 100 records × 59 digits for 5,900 bytes
- Paycheck file: 100 records × 162 bytes = 16,200 bytes
- Company payroll file: 1 record × 80 bytes = 80 bytes

- Tax table files: 1 file per table, each table size is the number of rows multiplied by the size of each row. For example, a typical state tax table contains 560 rows, with 18 digits and 4 spaces separating the dollar amounts, for a size of 11,700 bytes.

Something to keep in mind when you're calculating file sizes is whether the maximum number of records will be enough for the company in, say, three to five years. If not, you need to adjust the file size to account for terminated employees in addition to the maximum of 100 active employees, as well as for growth of the company.

The complete custom system for any given application will consist of far more than the database files (created with the dBASE CREATE command) and programs. There will probably be some combination of index, format, report, label, and other types of files in the system. These you can develop at the dot prompt immediately after creating your database files. (Techniques for creating index, format, report, and label files are discussed in Chapters 8, 9, and 12.) You may want to test all of these related files before you even begin programming, to help further refine the database structures as well as the input and output requirements.

## Phase 3: Modular Program Design

After developing a satisfactory database design for your application, you can begin thinking about the design of the actual software. Our original problem definition for the payroll system defines what we need the system to do and what we have to work with. But it does not give us too many clues as to how to start the actual programming. Trying to tackle the entire system at once can be a bit overwhelming. Instead, think about the tasks that the system needs to perform and make a list, as below:

1. Set up a new employee's master record.
2. Change an employee's record.
3. Terminate an employee.
4. Enter time card information.
5. Calculate and print the payroll.
6. Print reports.
7. Print W-2 forms.

You can think of this list as a table of contents. In fact, a similar list might appear on the system's initial screen or main menu. Each item on the list can be thought of as a module in the system. You might wish to view this modularity by using a structure chart like the one in Figure 2.1.

Some of these modules can be broken down into still smaller tasks. For example, Figure 2.2 shows the "Change Employee" module further refined into specific tasks.

You can continue breaking down the logical tasks as much as necessary in order to feel comfortable that each task will be reasonably small, easy to code, and easy to debug. For example, calculating the payroll represents a lot of processing, particularly if you consider all the controls you should incorporate in your design. If you break down this module into submodules, you could design the program as in Figure 2.3.

The routines for these submodules could be contained in separate programs, or they could be combined in one larger program. In either case, by breaking down the modules into smaller logical units you can concentrate on the code that needs to be written for each process. Once you've drawn the design for your program, you are prepared to begin your coding.

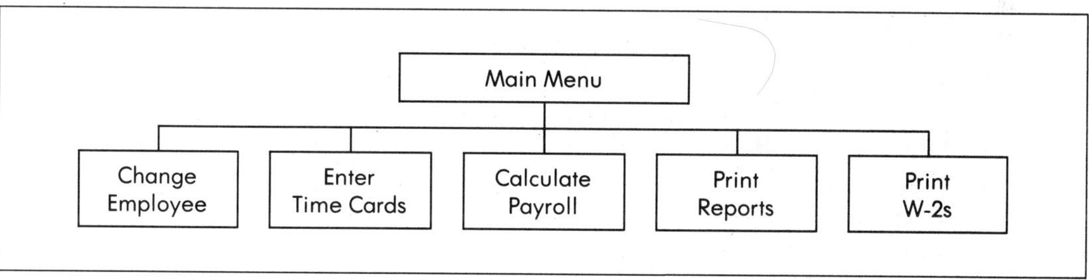


**FIGURE 2.1:** A modularized view of the major tasks to be performed in a payroll application. Breaking down the overall goal of the project into modules creates smaller, more manageable tasks. Each individual task can be broken down into still smaller tasks, as in Figure 2.2.

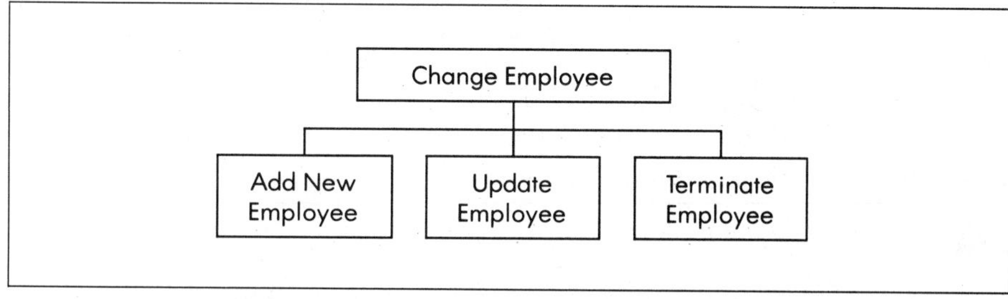


**FIGURE 2.2:** The "Change Employee" module of the payroll application further broken down into still smaller modules. Each smaller module might represent an individual program within the overall application system. Each program can be broken down further into individual routines.

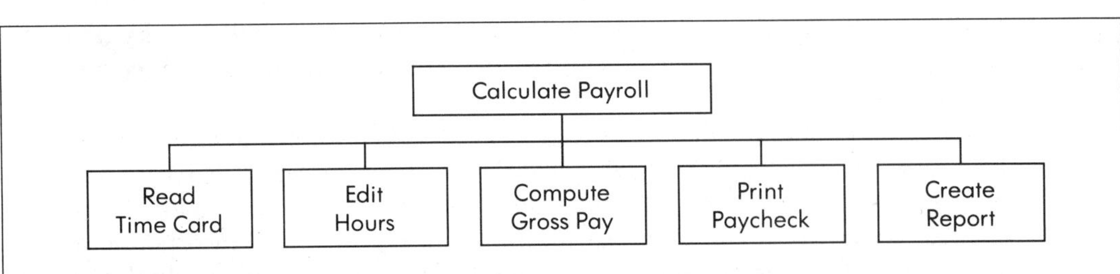


**FIGURE 2.3:** The "Calculate Payroll" module of the payroll application broken down into smaller tasks. Each of these smaller tasks could represent a routine in a single program. Or they could be broken down into even smaller individual tasks.

# PHASE 4: CODING TECHNIQUES

With a good design to work from, the programmer can begin writing the actual programs for the application. This phase is often called the *coding* phase. The best place to start coding is at the top, which in most systems is the main menu, as in the payroll system design. The main menu program is the easiest; starting there allows you to build your system from the general to the most detailed logic, which is how most people think.

## Structured Programming

Modularized program design provides you with the framework for what is called *structured programming.* You can use structured programming techniques to make your programs *self-documenting* (easy for anyone to read and work with). There is nothing mysterious about structured programming; it is simply a series of guidelines designed to make your programs easier to write, easier to debug, and easier to modify or enhance in the future.

You will need to learn the guidelines of structured programming when you are actually creating a program. Chapter 4, "Command Files," discusses this topic in more detail, along with other aspects of creating programs.

## Edit and Validation Checks

When you code your program, you should anticipate that the users of the system will make mistakes in entering the data. Your programs should contain logic that protects the database files from these mistakes. The two basic types of program error checks are edits for reasonableness and validation of values.

Edit checks are tests the program performs to ensure that the data entered is reasonable. For example, an edit of the base rate of pay may reject an hourly pay rate over $40.00. This edit check will not, however, be able to detect whether the amount entered is necessarily the right amount.

A validation test checks for the correctness of the data entered. Typically, this requires looking up the data in the database files and notifying the user if the value doesn't match. For example, one of the first validation tests that should be made in the Enter Time Card module would be for the employee number. If the number entered is not a valid employee number, the entry card should be rejected by the system.

In designing edit and validation checks, you should keep in mind the "garbage-in-garbage-out" principle. The more accidental "garbage" your system allows to sneak into the database files, the more garbage your system will be spewing out. Try to write your programs so that they catch as many errors as possible *before* they reach the database files. Chapter 19, "Event Processing and Error Trapping," discusses many techniques for validating data entry and trapping errors.

# Phase 5: Testing, Debugging, and Enhancing

Even when your design is great and your coding techniques are superlative, your program is not complete. In fact, it will probably never be complete, because you or your users will continue to think of things it should be doing. Also, as the system is used, problems with it will likely arise. Below are some ways that you can reduce the amount of time you'll need to spend maintaining the system.

## Testing the System

The goal of testing your programs is to identify, isolate, and correct as many bugs as possible. All programs have bugs, the most insidious of which appear only with unique combinations of data or events. A custom application needs to be tested thoroughly before entrusting critical data and calculations to it.

The most obvious form of testing is what's called positive testing, where you demonstrate that the program does what it's supposed to do when the data being used are accurate. In the payroll example a positive test would be to enter an employee and his time-card data (ensuring visually that all the data are correct) and generate his paycheck.

Conversely, negative testing involves deliberately trying to enter and process data that are not accurate. For example, if you enter an invalid employee number into the system, will the system accept it? Will it print a check for this nonexistent employee? During negative testing, you want to anticipate the potential errors made during data entry and editing to see how well your application handles them.

Complete testing can require an inordinate amount of time, especially if the system is complex. Your testing task will be much easier if you concentrate on specific tasks in the program, as you did when you set up your modularized program design. In this case, however, you'll need to concentrate on all possible paths through your program logic.

Testing of the modules can be conducted either *top-down* or *bottom-up,* whichever you prefer. In top-down testing, you begin by testing only the main menu module, to ensure that it calls the right submodule and that it rejects numbers that are not listed in the menu. Once that module is free of bugs, you could test the add-new-employee process, then the change-employee process, and so forth.

Bottom-up testing, on the other hand, starts with the most detailed or specific module and adds the more general modules over it until the entire system has been tested. The advantage of bottom-up testing is that the detailed processing is repeatedly tested and therefore should be well exercised.

It's a good idea to develop a testing strategy that you can use both during the original program development and after you've made modifications to the programs. By writing this strategy or plan down and using it on test database files, you'll know that the new code hasn't corrupted the logic of the original program.

## Debugging the Code

Detecting a bug is only the beginning. If the problem cannot be repeated, it's likely that you won't be able to locate the logic flaw in the code. Therefore, it's imperative that you work slowly and methodically, force the error to recur, and document exactly what it is that causes the bug to appear. This will help you isolate the problem in the code.

But isolating a bug is only half the solution. It's very important that the coding changes you make to resolve the bug do not adversely affect the rest of the program. Take time to think through the fix you propose. Also, modify your testing strategy to ensure that the problem cannot be repeated, the code works as planned, and the other, already tested logic paths are still okay. Specific dBASE techniques for debugging are discussed in detail in Chapter 7, "Debugging Commands and Techniques."

## Enhancing the System

Usually, at just about the time you're finished coding the system, someone will ask you to make a small change to it. Be forewarned! A "small" change in one part of a custom system may have a very large (and unpleasant) effect on some other part of the system. Before being too generous with the small changes you are willing to place in an application, remember that constant design changes to the system tend to reduce its reliability, even before the system is up and running.

When you do make enhancements to the system, make them in new modules if at all possible. By isolating the new logic, your testing and debugging tasks will be greatly reduced and the integrity of the system will be maintained. If, however, you must make modifications to existing code, do so very carefully and be certain to test thoroughly all areas that could be affected.

Any program changes made after the system is being used should be documented. Set aside space at the beginning of the module where a diary of changes can be described in paragraphs. You may want to include a special code or character at the beginning of these lines so that they can be pulled out automatically and summarized by a program.

Each paragraph should correlate to a design change, be dated, indicate who has made the change, and provide a brief description of the change, as in the example in Figure 2.4. Then, before you make a change to an existing module, review the diary to see if something like this has already been done, been eliminated, or the like.

If the diary of a module becomes quite long and the program itself is becoming unwieldy, it may be time to implement an enhancement by redesigning the module and perhaps separating the logic into smaller modules.

```
**************************************** PrinRep.PRG

*---------- Reports menu for the payroll application.

*====================================================
*                                                  *
*  The //symbol marks diary of changes.            *
*                                                  *
* // 02/01/87: Employee summary report added: Alan *
* // 03/01/87: Color capability added: Susan       *
*====================================================

*--- Begin actual program...
SET TALK OFF
IF ISCOLOR()
   SET COLOR TO GR+/B,W+/BR,R
ENDIF
CLEAR

*--- Rest of program follows...
```

**FIGURE 2.4:** Diary of changes listed near the top of a program. Each change includes the date, the person's name who made the change, and a brief description of the change. Notice that above the diary comments also display the name of the program and its general function. This is also useful information in programs.

## SUMMARY

This chapter discussed the general principles and techniques involved in designing and developing custom dBASE III PLUS applications. The individual commands and techniques that accompany each phase in the development cycle are discussed throughout the book.

*For more information on database design:*

- Chapter 3, "Database Design"

*For more information on creating command files and structured programming:*

- Chapter 4, "Command Files"

*For more information on debugging techniques and commands:*

- Chapter 7, "Debugging Commands and Techniques"

*For additional information on error trapping:*

- Chapter 19, "Event Processing and Error Trapping"

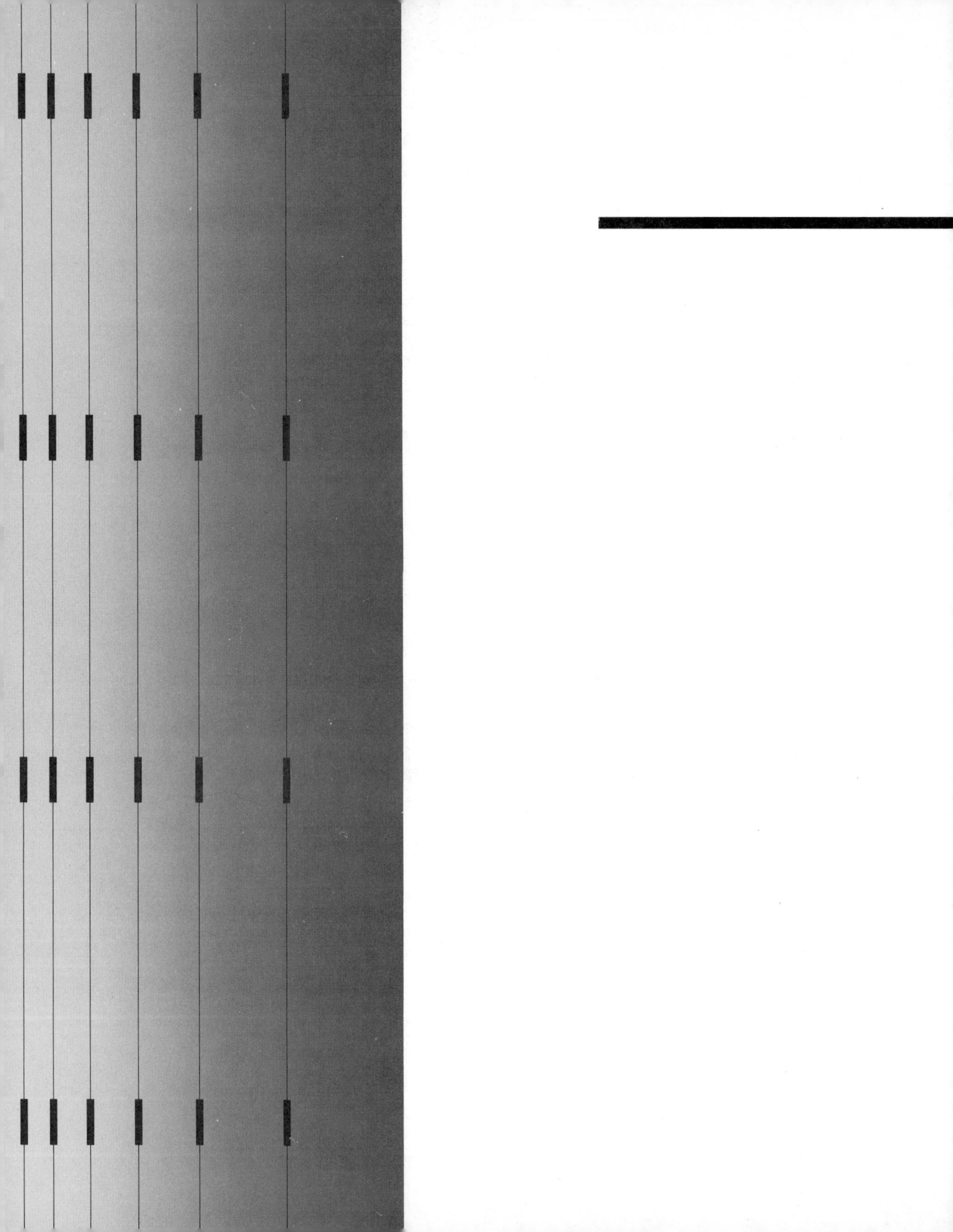

CHAPTER 3

# DATABASE DESIGN

# DATABASE DESIGN

Deciding what to store in a database is one of the first steps in creating any custom application. Many applications, such as those that manage a mailing list or customer list, require only a single database file and maybe an index file or two. Larger business applications typically require more complex designs, using several related database files. The task of determining how to divide data into separate, related files is called *database design.*

This chapter looks at some commonly used database designs along with practical examples. It discusses basic database design theory as well as the dBASE commands used for defining relationships among database files. Following these discussions is more detailed information on the commands necessary for defining relationships and managing multiple related database files.

## THE ONE-TO-ONE DATABASE DESIGN

The *one-to-one* relationship is the simplest and perhaps most common database design. A simple mailing list might have a one-to-one design, as shown in the database structure in Figure 3.1. The term *one-to-one* means that for every name on the database, there is *one* company affiliation, *one* address, *one* city, *one* state, and so forth.

```
Structure for database: C:Mail.dbf

Field  Field Name  Type        Width    Dec

    1  Mr_Mrs      Character       4
    2  FName       Character      15
    3  MI          Character       2
    4  LName       Character      15
    5  Company     Character      25
    6  Address     Character      25
    7  City        Character      20
    8  State       Character       5
    9  Zip         Character      10
   10  Country     Character      12
   11  Phone       Character      13
   12  Phone_Ext   Character       4
```

**FIGURE 3.1:** A sample mailing-list database, illustrating a one-to-one database design. For every name on the database, there is one company affiliation, one address, one city, and so forth.

# The One-to-Many Database Design

The *one-to-many* design is used in situations where many (usually an unknown number) items of data are associated with another data item. For example, in an accounts receivable system, each individual customer might charge several items during the course of the month. In other words, there could be *many* charge transactions placed by *one* customer.

If you attempt to design the database for an accounts receivable system using a single database file, you'll quickly see the problems inherent in the design. If the file has a single record for each charge transaction, where would you store the customer's name, address, city, state, zip code, and so forth? If you store this information with each charge transaction, there will be a great deal of redundant data.

For example, even though there are only three unique customers (Smith, Miller, and Jones) in the charges transactions listed in Figure 3.2, the database file uses a lot of disk space because of all the redundant data in the name and address fields. A data-entry operator will waste a lot of time typing the name and address of each customer repeatedly; and if one of the customers moves, it is not easy to change his address.

One solution is to store one record for each customer and have several fields for charges. But such a design limits the number of transactions a particular customer can be assigned to the number of fields created in the database structure. It also makes it virtually impossible to answer questions such as, How many charge transactions this month involved part number A-123?

## Using a Key Field to Relate Databases

To resolve the problems inherent in trying to store accounts receivable data on a single database file, the data can be stored on two database files. Then a single *common field* or *key field* can be used to relate the two database files.

```
Jones      Fred      345 Grape St.   Encinitas     6457.42
Smith      Albert    345 C St.       San Diego        5.10
Smith      Albert    345 C St.       San Diego     1000.00
Adams      Martha    P.O. Box 1107   Alameda         76.50
Smith      Albert    345 C St.       San Diego     4567.89
Adams      Martha    P.O. Box 1107   Alameda         99.00
Adams      Martha    P.O. Box 1107   Alameda        123.45
Adams      Martha    P.O. Box 1107   Alameda       3245.69
Jones      Fred      345 Grape St.   Encinitas      333.33
Smith      Albert    345 C St.       San Diego      596.43
Jones      Fred      345 Grape St.   Encinitas      764.32
```

**FIGURE 3.2:** In this poor example of an accounts-receivable database, customers' names and addresses are listed with each charge transaction (rightmost column). Even though there are records for 11 transactions, there are only 3 customers listed, so 8 records include redundant names and addresses.

For example, Figure 3.3 shows the structures of two database files named Customer and Charges. The Customer database contains a single record for each customer in the hypothetical accounts receivable system. Each customer is assigned a unique customer number in the field named CustNo. The Charges database stores each individual charge transaction on a single record. The CustNo field in the Charges database identifies which customer on the Customer database the transaction belongs to.

Note that the common field in the two databases, CustNo, has been given the exact same name, data type, width, and decimals in both file structures. This is essential to the success of relational database design.

Figure 3.4 shows sample listings of the two database files. It is easy to see which charges belong to which customers, as the arrows linking customer number 1001 to his charges indicate.

Note that dividing the information into two separate data files minimizes the redundant data. Each customer and his address (and other related information) fills a single record on the Customer database. Each transaction for each

```
Structure for database: Customer.dbf

Field  Field name  Type       Width  Dec   Description

    1  CustNo      Numeric        4        Customer number
    2  LName       Character     15        Last name
    3  FName       Character     10        First name
    4  Address     Character     25        Address
    5  City        Character     20        City
    6  State       Character      2        State
    7  Zip         Character     10        Zip code
    8  Phone       Character     13        Phone number
    9  Last_Updat  Date           8        Last updated
   10  Start_Bal   Numeric        8   2    Staring balance
   11  Chg_Curr    Numeric        8   2    Current charges
   12  Pay_Curr    Numeric        8   2    Current payments
   13  Bal_30      Numeric        8   2    Balance last month
   14  Bal_60      Numeric        8   2    Balance 2 months ago
   15  Bal_90      Numeric        8   2    Balance 3 months ago
   16  Bal_90Plus  Numeric        8   2    Balance over 3 months
   17  Terms       Character     20        Credit terms

   ==============================================================

Structure for database: Charges.dbf

Field  Field Name  Type       Width  Dec  Description

    1  CustNo      Numeric        4       Customer number
    2  Part_No     Character      5       Part number
    3  Qty         Numeric        4       Quantity purchased
    4  Unit_Price  Numeric        9   2   Unit price
    5  Date        Date           8       Date of purchase
```

**FIGURE 3.3:** Structures of the Customer and Charges databases. Each record on the Customer database contains information about a single customer. For each customer, there may be several transactions listed in the Charges database. The common CustNo field tells which transaction belongs with which customer.

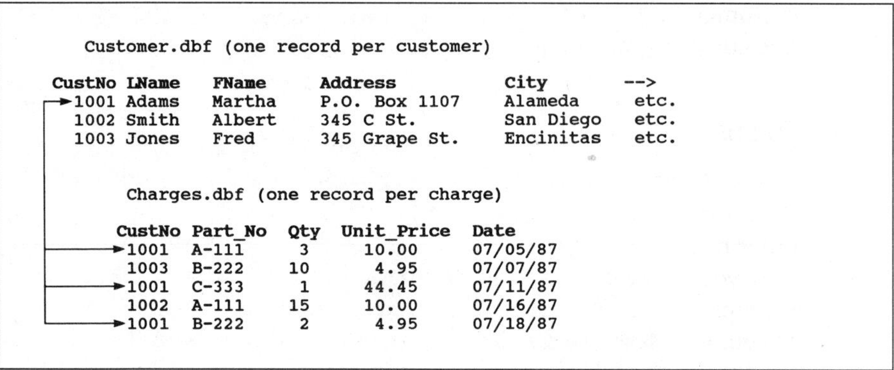

Customer.dbf (one record per customer)

| CustNo | LName | FName | Address | City | --> |
|---|---|---|---|---|---|
| 1001 | Adams | Martha | P.O. Box 1107 | Alameda | etc. |
| 1002 | Smith | Albert | 345 C St. | San Diego | etc. |
| 1003 | Jones | Fred | 345 Grape St. | Encinitas | etc. |

Charges.dbf (one record per charge)

| CustNo | Part_No | Qty | Unit_Price | Date |
|---|---|---|---|---|
| 1001 | A-111 | 3 | 10.00 | 07/05/87 |
| 1003 | B-222 | 10 | 4.95 | 07/07/87 |
| 1001 | C-333 | 1 | 44.45 | 07/11/87 |
| 1002 | A-111 | 15 | 10.00 | 07/16/87 |
| 1001 | B-222 | 2 | 4.95 | 07/18/87 |

**FIGURE 3.4:** Sample data from the Customer and Charges databases. The arrows show how the customer number links charge transactions to customers. This figure shows a typical one-to-many relationship.

customer requires one record on the Charges database. Only the customer number is repeated on both databases, and there is no limit to the number of transactions that can be assigned to each customer.

## Guidelines for Creating a Key Field

The key field or common field that relates the two databases is an important one, and there are a few guidelines that you should follow when designing your own databases and key fields.

### Make Key Fields Unique

If there is a one-to-many relationship involved, the key field on the "one" side of the relationship must be unique to each record. Otherwise, there will be no way of matching a given record with the appropriate record on the "many" side of the relationship. For example, suppose the last name field (LName) rather than CustNo was the common field between the Customer and Charges databases above. Furthermore, suppose there are ten customers with the last name Smith on the Customer database. If one of the charges in the Charges database is charged to Smith, you have no way of knowing which Smith it refers to. You could refine the relationship a bit by trying to link the two databases by both last and first name, but if you have two customers with the same first and last name your problem will not be solved.

The customer number is the best way to set up the common field between the Customer and Charges database, because it is easy to ensure that each customer has a unique customer number. That way, when a record on the Charges database refers to customer number 1005, there can be no ambiguity about which customer on the Customer database gets the bill (assuming, of course, that only one customer has the number 1005).

### Make Key Fields Meaningless

A second guideline in creating key fields is to make them meaningless. A random four-digit number (from 1001 to 9999) is a good choice, because it has no other meaning in the database.

If you decide to place encoded information into the customer number (for example, by assigning numbers such as SDC5112, where SD stands for San Diego, C5 stands for credit rating of 5, and 112 is the customer number), you might have some difficulty in ensuring that each customer has a unique number. Furthermore, if the encoded information changes (the customer moves away from San Diego or his credit rating changes), you'll have to change his customer number. As soon as you change the customer number on the Customer database, you have to make sure both that the new number is not already in use and that the same change is made to all the related database files.

To avoid this problem, put any meaningful information into a field of its own, and make the customer number a plain, arbitrarily assigned number.

### Make Key Fields Numeric

The third guideline is to use a numeric value for the key field. (This may not be feasible if you are using some pre-existing numbering scheme, such as inventory part numbers or social security numbers.) That way, you can easily create a program that automatically assigns the next unique number to each new record. Such a program is discussed in Chapter 10, "Adding New Data."

Some relatively safe nonarbitrary key fields might include social security numbers or a manufacturer's part numbers. Social security numbers are unique to every individual, but you'll want to use these only if you can be sure that you can get a social security number from everyone on your database. Using manufacturer's or vendor's part numbers as a key field in your own database is safe only if you are sure that it will not be the same as a number used by a different manufacturer or vendor.

Remember, it is up to you, the programmer, to make sure that the key fields in the "one" side of your one-to-many related files are unique. A mistake in this area could lead to serious problems.

## The Master-File/Transaction-File Structure

One of the most common applications of the one-to-many design is the master-file/transaction-file relationship. In this design, the master file keeps track of current, ongoing balances, while the transaction file records individual transactions that affect those balances. The master file tells us the status of things at the moment, while the transaction files maintain a history, or audit trail, of the events that produced those current balances.

A retail store inventory database provides a good example. The master database stores one record for each item that is kept in stock and the quantity currently in stock. Two other databases are used to keep track of individual sales transactions and individual purchases (items received into the stockroom or warehouse).

Through a process called *updating*, dBASE can subtract the quantities of items sold from the appropriate in-stock quantity on the master database. The quantities of items received into the stockroom can be added to the appropriate in-stock quantities. The net result is that the master database reflects the true quantity of each item in stock, while the databases recording individual sales and purchase transactions still retain their useful information.

The accounts receivable system can be structured with a master-file/transaction-file relationship as well. The master file records the customer number, name, address, and current balance for each credit customer. Charges and payments are stored in separate databases.

Through updating, the current charges can be added to each customer's balance, and his payments can be subtracted from his balance. So current information is readily available (current balances), and historical information (the individual charges and payments that produced the balances) is maintained.

There are a couple of ways to perform updates, either in a batch (all together at the end of the day, week, or month), or instantaneously as the transaction occurs. These *updating algorithms* are discussed and demonstrated in Chapter 16, "Managing Multiple Database Files."

## THE MANY-TO-MANY DATABASE DESIGN

The many-to-many relationship occurs in situations such as scheduling or exploded inventories. For example, when scheduling students for classes, there will be *many* students in each of *many* classes, and *many* classes each with *many* students. In an exploded inventory, a manufacturer might produce *many* products from *many* components. Likewise, each of *many* components might be used in *many* products. Let's discuss each example independently.

### A Scheduling Database

The class scheduling problem mentioned above is the classic example of the many-to-many relationship. To avoid redundancies in storing data, the information is split into several files. The Courses database contains information about each course or each section of each course. Each course has a unique number assigned to it, which is the key field that links specific students to specific courses. The structure and sample data for the Courses database are shown in Figure 3.5. (This database is simplified, because each course might really be offered in several different sections or time slots.)

The Students database contains one record for each student in the school. To help individually identify students, each student is assigned a unique student number. The structure and sample data for the students database are shown in Figure 3.6.

```
Structure for database: Courses

Field  Field Name  Type       Width    Dec

    1  CourseID    Character      5
    2  CourseName  Character     10
    3  Room_No     Character      5
    4  Teacher     Character     20
================================================================

CourseID  CourseName  Room_No  Teacher
 A-111     English     J-222    Watson
 B-222     Spanish     E-345    Holmes
 C-333     Greek       G-445    Moriarty
```

**FIGURE 3.5:** Structure and sample contents of the Courses database file used in the example of a many-to-many relationship. To simplify the example, only three records are included. The CourseID field uniquely identifies each course and is also used to link students to courses, via the linking file named SCLink.dbf.

```
Structure for database: Students

Field  Field Name  Type       Width    Dec

    1  StudentID   Numeric        5
    2  LastName    Character     10
    3  FirstName   Character     10
    4  Address     Character     20
    5  City        Character     20
    6  State       Character      2
    7  Zip         Character      5
    8  Phone       Character     13
================================================================

StudentID  LastName  FirstName  Address    -->
 10001      Adams     Angela     123 A St.  etc.
 10002      Baker     Bobbi      345 B st.  etc.
 10003      Carlson   Carla      345 C St.  etc.
```

**FIGURE 3.6:** Structure and sample contents of the Students database file used in the example of a many-to-many relationship. The StudentID field uniquely identifies each student and is also used to link students to courses, via the linking file named SCLink.dbf.

To link the *many* students to their appropriate *many* courses, a third database contains one record for each student enrolled in each class. For this example, the linking database is called SCLink and has the structure and sample data shown in Figure 3.7. From the contents of the SCLink database, you can clearly see that student number 10001 is enrolled in courses B-222 and C-333. Student number 10002 is enrolled in courses A-111, B-222, and C-333.

If you were to sort the SCLink database by course number rather than student number, you could see at a glance which students were enrolled in which courses (particularly if you also reversed the order of the fields, as in Figure 3.8).

In this example, there are two key fields on the linking database: CourseID, which links the file to course information, and StudentID, which links the file to

```
Structure for database: SClink

Field  Field Name  Type        Width    Dec

    1  StudentID   Numeric         5
    2  CourseID    Character       5
=================================================================

StudentID  CourseID
 10001       B-222
 10001       C-333

 10002       A-111
 10002       B-222
 10002       C-333

 10003       A-111
 10003       C-333
```

**FIGURE 3.7:** Structure and sample contents of the SCLink database file used in the example of a many-to-many relationship. The file contains only two fields, StudentID and CourseID. These fields link individual students in the Students database to courses in the Courses database. The blank lines between the sample records help show more clearly which students are enrolled in which courses, but they are not actually in the database file.

```
CourseID  StudentID
 A-111      10002
 A-111      10003

 B-222      10001
 B-222      10002

 C-333      10001
 C-333      10002
 C-333      10003
```

**FIGURE 3.8:** Sample contents of the SCLink database file, sorted and grouped into course number order. This display shows the enrollments in each class. In this simple example, only two students are enrolled in the courses numbered A-111 and B-222. Course number C-333 has three students enrolled.

student information. In some situations, the linking database will contain more than two key fields, as the next section demonstrates.

## An Exploded Inventory Database

Another example of a many-to-many relationship among databases is the *exploded inventory* model. One database, named Products, stores one record for each product the company produces. The structure and sample data for the Products file are shown in Figure 3.9. (The [Other fields] can be any other relevant information, such as quantity in stock, selling price, and so forth.)

A second database, named Componen, contains one record for each component that the manufacturer purchases to create its products. Each component has a unique component number, stored in the field named Comp_No. The structure and sample data for the Componen database are shown in Figure 3.10. (Again, [Other fields] refers to any other relevant information, such as purchase price, date of last shipment received, quantity on order, expected date of next shipment, vendor, and so forth.)

There is a many-to-many relationship between the Products and Componen database files, because each product uses *many* components, and each component is used in *many* products. A *linking* database, named Linker in this example, sets up the link between these two databases. It describes which products use which components.

Because some products use more than one of a particular component, the Linker database includes the number of each component that each product uses. This information is stored in the Qty_Used field of the Linker database. The

```
Structure for database: Products

Field Name          Type        Width   Dec  Description

Prod_No             Character     5          Product number
Prod_Name           Character    25          Product name

[other fields]
=================================================================
Record#  Prod_No   Prod_Name                        Other fields...
      1  A-123     Personal Computer 1000
      2  B-123     Personal Computer 2000
      3  C-123     Business Computer 3000
```

**FIGURE 3.9:** Structure and sample contents for the Products database used in the "exploded inventory" example. The sample database file uses only the product number (Prod_No) and product name (Prod_Name) fields to simplify the example. The Prod_No field uniquely identifies each product that the company manufactures and also links products to components, using the Linker database file as an intermediary.

structure and sample contents of the Linker database for this example are shown in Figure 3.11.

Note that product number A-123 uses one component number TT-1234 and two component numbers ZZ-1234. You can see the relationships among the

```
Structure for database: Componen

Field Name  Type        Width    Dec   Description

Comp_No     Character       7          Component number
Comp_Name   Character      21          Component name
In_Stock    Numeric         3      0   Qty. in stock

[Other fields]
==================================================================
Record#  Comp_No  Comp_Name                In_Stock  Other Fields...
      1  TT-1234  80286 microprocessor          500
      2  UU-1234  Color monitor                 500
      3  VV-1234  Monochrome monitor            500
      4  WW-1234  Hard disk                     500
      5  YY-1234  Floppy controller             500
      6  ZZ-1234  Floppy disk drive             500
```

**FIGURE 3.10:** Structure and sample contents for the Componen database used in the exploded inventory example. In most real-world applications, this database might include other information that is relevant to each component, such as vendor information. The Comp_No field on this database uniquely identifies each component and is used as the link to the products database, via the Linker database.

```
Structure for database: C:Linker

Field Name  Type        Width    Dec  Description

Prod_No     Character       5         Product number
Comp_No     Character       7         Component number
Qty_Used    Numeric         3         Quantity used
==================================================================
Record#  Prod_No Comp_No Qty_Used
      1  A-123   TT-1234      1
      2  A-123   VV-1234      1
      3  A-123   YY-1234      2
      4  A-123   ZZ-1234      2
      5  B-123   TT-1234      1
      6  B-123   UU-1234      1
      7  B-123   YY-1234      2
      8  B-123   ZZ-1234      2
      9  C-123   TT-1234      1
     10  C-123   UU-1234      1
     11  C-123   WW-1234      1
     12  C-123   YY-1234      1
     13  C-123   ZZ-1234      1
```

**FIGURE 3.11:** Structure and sample contents of the Linker database file. Prod_No is the link to the products database, and Comp_No is the link to the Componen database. The Qty_Used field describes how many of each component each product requires. For example, the sample data show that product number A-123 requires two of component number YY-1234.

Products, Linker, and Componen databases in Figure 3.12, which uses arrows to show which components make up product number B-123.

With a bit of programming, you can use these three files to answer questions such as, If I plan to manufacture 75 personal computers and 50 business computers, how many of each component will I need? Or, Given that I've manufactured 22 personal computers and 17 business computers today, how many of each component is left in stock? (Techniques for answering such questions are discussed in Chapter 16, "Managing Multiple Database Files.")

With a little imagination, the many-to-many design can handle quite a few diverse applications that might seem extraordinarily complicated at first glance. For example, consider the problem of managing a database from the manufacturer's side of the application, where the customers assign their own part numbers to products that they order. The customers want to be able to order parts using their own part numbers rather than the manufacturer's part numbers.

To solve this problem, you could set up a database of customers and assign each customer a unique customer number. Then you could link the customer database to the products database through a linking file that contains the customer number, the part number the customer wants to use, and the part number the manufacturer uses. Now the customers can order parts using their own part numbers, because the linking file can automatically translate the customer's part number into the part number used internally.

## NORMALIZING A DATABASE

The practice of storing data in separate files to minimize redundancy and simplify basic database file management is called *normalization*. The process of

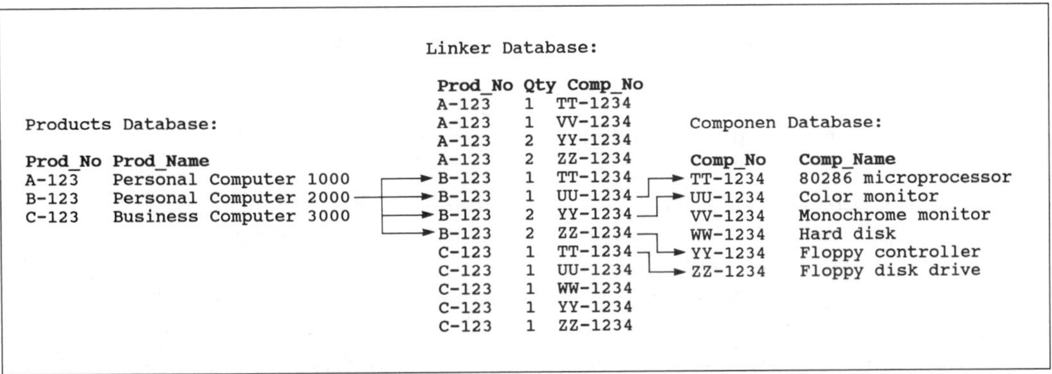


**FIGURE 3.12:** Relationships among the Products, Linker, and Componen databases. The arrows show how you can determine which components and how many of each component are used to manufacture a single product. This structure represents the many-to-many relationship among databases.

normalizing a database involves three rules:

1. Remove all redundant data.
2. Remove all partial dependencies.
3. Remove all transitive dependencies.

Each step in the process is called one of the *normal forms.*

## Remove Redundant Data

The first step in normalizing a database file is to remove repeating data from the single database file and place it in a separate database file, using a key field to link the redundant information. When you've removed the redundant data from a single database by placing it into two separate related databases, the database files are said to be in the *first normal form* of database design.

The sample accounts receivable design discussed earlier in this chapter and illustrated in Figures 3.3 and 3.4 demonstrates a database in the first normal form, because the redundant customer names and addresses were removed from the Charges databases and placed on a separate Customer database.

## Remove All Partial Dependencies

Partial dependencies might occur in a database file that contains more than one key field. In that situation, any information that is not dependent on all key fields should be removed into a separate database file.

For example, the Linker database in the exploded inventory example contained two key fields: Prod_No, which acted as the link to the Products database, and Comp_No, which was the link to the Componen database. This database also included the Qty_Used field, which is directly dependent on *both* the product number and component number (because it describes how many of each component each product requires).

Any other information stored on this database would have been dependent on only one of the key fields (either Prod_No or Comp_No). For example, the product name would have been directly relevant only to the Prod_No field. To avoid any such partial dependencies, all information that is specific to individual products is stored on the separate Products database, and all information that is specific to individual components is stored in the Componen database. When only the data that are directly relevant to all of the key fields in a database record remain in that database, the database has reached the *second normal form.*

## Remove Transitive Dependencies

The third step in normalizing a database design is to remove the *transitive dependencies:* those fields that are occasionally (though not always) dependent on some other nonkey field in the same record. For example, in the Componen database, where information about components purchased by the manufacturer is listed, you might want to place the name and address of the vendor who supplies the component. However, if this were the only component purchased from that vendor and you later stopped using that component and deleted the record, you would lose the vendor's name and address. Hence, the dependence between the particular component and the vendor was a temporary, or transitive, one.

To avoid this situation, you could store a vendor code in the Componen database and use that to relate each component to a vendor in a separate file of vendors' names and addresses named Vendors. That way, your list of vendors would remain intact, regardless of the components you were using at a particular moment.

To use a bookkeeping example, you wouldn't want the chart of accounts to be dependent on (or derived from) the individual transactions that transpired within a given month, because some accounts might not be used in that particular month.

When all the transitive dependencies have been removed from the records, the database is said to be in the *third normal form.*

## The Fully Normalized Database Design

Like most theories, perhaps this discussion tends to make abstract what is actually intuitively obvious. When you take away all the fancy terminology, a *fully normalized* database is one that is easy to manage because the data are grouped into database files of similar information. For example, in an inventory system, the data are simply divided into product information, component information, vendor information, and information that defines which components go into which products. If you think about it for a moment, it makes perfect sense to store information in such a manner.

Furthermore, if you look at most manual systems that are used to store and manage information, you'll often find that the information is already structured in the third normal form. So don't let a lot of theory confuse you. Strive to reduce the redundancies in your database files and make particular bodies of information independent and easy to work with, and you'll find that your databases will naturally fall into the desired third normal form.

## DEFINING DATABASE RELATIONSHIPS

Let's take a look at the commands commonly used to relate database files and manage multiple databases. As a programmer, you'll probably want to experiment with these commands at the interactive (dot prompt) level before writing any programs. Such experiments will help refine your overall database design.

This discussion covers only the basic dBASE built-in commands. More complex algorithms for managing multiple databases appear in examples throughout the book, particularly in Chapter 16, "Managing Multiple Database Files."

As mentioned earlier in this chapter, two database files must have a common field (a field with the same name, data type, and width) in order to be related. It is this common field (also called a key field) that is used in conjunction with the dBASE SET RELATION command to define a relationship. Once you have set up this relationship, you will be able to display data from two related databases simultaneously.

### Setting Up Index Files

First you need to create an index file of the common field for the database on the "one" side of the relationship (because the SET RELATION command actually uses the index file of the related database). In many cases, you'll be using index files on both sides of the relationship, so at this point you may want to set up an index file of the common field for the "many" side too.

To illustrate this using the Customer and Charges databases discussed earlier in this chapter, create index files for the CustNo fields in both the Customer and Charges databases, by entering the following commands:

```
USE Customer
INDEX ON CustNo TO Customer
USE Charges
INDEX ON CustNo TO Charges
```

### Linking Files with SELECT and SET RELATION

Now to link the two files, use a combination of the SELECT and SET RELATION commands as follows:

```
SELECT A
USE <"many" side with optional index file>
SELECT B
USE <"one" side with index file>
SELECT A
SET RELATION TO <common field> INTO <"one" side>
```

where <"many" side> is the name of the file on the "many" side of the one-to-many relationship, <"one" side> is the name of the file on the "one" side of the relationship, and <common field> is the name of the field that the two files have in common.

In the example of the Customer and Charges databases, Charges has *many* transactions for every *one* customer in the Customer database. The common field is CustNo. Hence, to set up the relationship, you would enter these commands:

**SELECT A**
**USE Charges**
**SELECT B**
**USE Customer INDEX Customer**
**SELECT A**
**SET RELATION TO CustNo INTO Customer**

In the series of commands above, the SELECT commands allow multiple database files to be opened simultaneously. In this example, the Charges database was opened in work area A. The Customer database was opened in work area B. The second SELECT A command defines Charges as the *selected* or *current* database. That means that any dBASE command that uses a database file (such as APPEND, EDIT, LIST, DISPLAY, etc.) will operate on the Charges database.

The SET RELATION command sets up a relationship between the currently selected database (Charges) and the Customer database, based on the common CustNo field. From this point on, any movement through the Charges database (with a LIST, GOTO, LOCATE, or any other command) will cause dBASE to always "point" to the record in the Customer database that has the same customer number as the record in the Charges database. The next section demonstrates techniques for using that relationship.

## Displaying Data in One-to-Many Relationships

Now that your databases are linked and Charges is the selected database, you can use all the usual dBASE commands to display records from the Charges database (LIST, REPORT, DISPLAY, etc.). To display data from the Customer database, you need only use the symbol **B->** or the *alias* **Customer->.** (The arrow consists of a hyphen followed by a greater-than sign.) The B-> symbol followed by a field name refers to a field from the SELECT B work area. If you don't want to use a letter such as B->, you can use an alias—either the name of the database file or a name you create with the ALIAS command. In the example above, Customer-> is equivalent to B-> because Customer is the name of the database in the second work area.

To view data from the Charges database only, you could just enter the command **LIST OFF**, which would display the data below:

| | | | | |
|---|---|---|---|---|
| 1001 | A-111 | 3 | 10.00 | 07/05/87 |
| 1003 | B-222 | 10 | 4.95 | 07/07/87 |
| 1001 | C-333 | 1 | 44.45 | 07/11/87 |
| 1002 | A-111 | 15 | 10.00 | 07/16/87 |
| 1001 | B-222 | 2 | 4.95 | 07/18/87 |

To view the customer name along with some information from the Charges database, use the command line below:

**LIST CustNo, B->FName, B->LName, Part_No**

Optionally, you could use the command

**LIST CustNo, Customer->FName, Customer->LName, Part_No**

The result is a display containing the customer number and part number fields from the Charges database and the appropriate customer names from the Customer database, as below:

| | | | |
|---|---|---|---|
| 1001 | Martha | Adams | A-111 |
| 1003 | Fred | Jones | B-222 |
| 1001 | Martha | Adams | C-333 |
| 1002 | Albert | Smith | A-111 |
| 1001 | Martha | Adams | B-222 |

To display the customer number, product number, customer last name, and address from the two related files you could enter the command

**DISPLAY ALL CustNo, Part_No, B->LName, B->Address**

The LIST and DISPLAY commands are used only as examples. Because these two databases are linked, you can treat them as a single database and use just about any dBASE command, including REPORT, REPLACE, @, and ? (though not APPEND or INSERT).

Note that the order in which you open the database files is not important. What is important is that the SET RELATION command points from the "many" side of the relationship to the indexed field in the file of the "one" side. For example, you can open the Customer database and its index file in work area A and the Charges database in work area B. Again, you would set the relationship from the currently active Charges database into the Customer database, as below:

**SELECT A**

```
USE Customer INDEX Customer
SELECT B
USE Charges INDEX Charges
SET RELATION TO CustNo INTO Customer
```

In this case, the LIST command will still display records from the Charges database (because B is the currently selected database). To "borrow" data from the Customer database, you need to use the A-> or Customer-> alias. For example, the command

```
LIST CustNo, A->FName, A->LName, Part_No
```

will list the CustNo and Part_No fields from the currently selected Charges database and the FName and LName fields from the Customer database in work area A.

Take a look at what happens when you set a relationship from the "one" side of the relationship into the "many" side. Consider the following commands:

```
SELECT A
USE Customer INDEX Customer
SELECT B
USE Charges INDEX Charges
SELECT A
SET RELATION TO CustNo INTO Charges
```

Here you have the relationship from the Customer ("one" side) database pointing into the Charges ("many" side) database. Entering a LIST command shows all the records on the Customer database, a portion of which are shown below:

```
1001    Adams    Martha    P.O. Box 1107
1002    Smith    Albert    345 C St.
1003    Jones    Fred      345 Grape St.
```

You can "borrow" data from the Charges database using the usual B-> alias:

```
LIST CustNo,LName,FName,B->Part_No,B->Qty
```

But because there is only one record on Customer to several records on Charges, only the data from the first matching record in Charges will be displayed, as shown below:

```
1001    Adams    Martha    A-111     3
1002    Smith    Albert    A-111    15
1003    Jones    Fred      B-222    10
```

While the relationship performs correctly, the information is of little value, because you can see only a small fraction of the data stored in Charges.

If you now select the Charges database with the **SELECT B** command and then type **LIST**, you see all the records from Charges, as shown below:

```
1001    A-111     3    10.00    07/05/87
1003    B-222    10     4.95    07/07/87
1001    C-333     1    44.45    07/11/87
1002    A-111    15    10.00    07/16/87
1001    B-222     2     4.95    07/18/87
```

If you attempt to "borrow" data from the Customer database, you're in for a bit of a surprise, as shown in the results of the LIST command below:

**LIST CustNo,A->FName,A->LName,Part_No**

```
1001                A-111
1001                C-333
1001                B-222
1002                A-111
1003                B-222
```

Even though you specified data from the Customer database using the A-> alias, you got only blanks. That's because the relationship is pointing from Customer into Charges. Therefore, while you can still select and list data from either database, you can "borrow" data only from Charges to Customer, not vice versa.

## Relating Three or More Files

You can link three or more files, as long as you remember to use only one SET RELATION command per work area. For example, look at the commands below:

```
SELECT A
USE Orders
SELECT B
USE Master INDEX Master
SELECT C
USE Vendors INDEX Vend_Code
* ---- Set relationship from Orders into Master (A into B).
SELECT A
SET RELATION TO PartNo INTO Master
* ---- Set relationship from Master into Vendors (B into C).
```

**SELECT B**
**SET RELATION TO Vend_Code INTO Vendors**

The Master database has a field named PartNo that relates it to Orders. The command **INDEX ON PartNo to MASTER** creates the Master.ndx index file. The Master database also contains a field named Vend_Code, which is a small code representing the name of the vendor that manufactures or sells the product. Vend_Code relates each product to the vendor's name and address in the Vendors database. The Vendors index file in use with the Vendors database contains the Vend_Code field.

The first SET RELATION command sets up a relation from the Orders database (in work area A) into the Master database. (There are many orders for every product in Master.) The second SET RELATION command sets up a relationship from Master (work area B) into Vendors (there are many products from each vendor in Vendors). Each relation is set from its own work area, and each one points from the "many" side of the relationship into the "one" side.

If you were to enter a command such as

**LIST PartNo,B->Part_Name,B->Vend_Code,C->Vend_Name**

you would see the part number for each order on Orders, the name of the part "borrowed" from Master, the vendor code for that item (also borrowed from Master), and the name of the appropriate vendor (from Vendors).

Incidentally, this technique for opening three related database files has its limitations in the many-to-many design discussed in the scheduling and exploded inventory examples above. More sophisticated programming techniques to overcome these limitations are discussed in Chapter 16, "Managing Multiple Database Files."

## COMMANDS FOR MANAGING MULTIPLE DATABASES

The remainder of this chapter discusses the individual commands that define relationships among databases. This section focuses on the technical aspects of these commands rather than the design issues involved.

More advanced techniques for managing related database files are discussed in Chapter 16, "Managing Multiple Database Files." In addition, Chapter 10, "Adding New Data," includes some material on multiple databases.

### The USE Command

The USE command opens an existing database file, can activate any existing index files, and can assign an alias name for use as a pointer when multiple database files are in use.

## SYNTAX

**USE <file name> [INDEX <index files>] [ALIAS <alias name>]**

where <file name> is the name of an existing database file. The optional INDEX <index files> command can include up to seven index files that have been created previously with the INDEX ON command. The optional ALIAS <alias name> command can provide a name that can be used as a pointer when using multiple databases simultaneously.

If you've intentionally assigned a file-name extension other than .dbf to a database, you must specify the extension in the USE command, as in **USE Customer.dat**.

## USAGE

The USE command alone (with no file name listed) closes the database in the currently selected work area. Therefore, the following command closes whatever database was originally opened in the SELECT 2 work area:

```
SELECT 2
USE
```

If the database opened by the USE command contains a memo field, the .dbt file containing the memo field is opened automatically by the USE command. If the .dbt file has been erased or corrupted, the following error message will appear:

**.DBT file cannot be opened**

See Chapter 23, "Foreign and Damaged Files," for tips on managing memo fields and problems with memo fields.

### USE WITH VARIABLES

If the name of the database you want to open is stored in a memory variable, the variable name must be treated as a macro. For example, the commands below store the file name MyFile in a variable named SomeFile. The USE command attempts to open MyFile (rather than SomeFile) because of the macro substitution (&):

```
SomeFile = "MyFile"
USE &SomeFile
```

## USE WITH THE INDEX COMMAND

Any index files that are listed to the right of the INDEX portion of the USE command are automatically updated whenever any command adds, changes, deletes, or packs data. By default, the first listed index file is the controlling (or *master*) index file, which determines the sort order for displays and the field(s) that can be located with the FIND and SEEK commands. (The SET ORDER command, however, can specify any index file in the list as the controlling index file.)

If no index files are specified in the USE command, the record pointer points automatically to the first record in the database when the database is opened. If one or more index files are listed in the INDEX portion of the command, the pointer will be pointing to the first (top) record in the controlling (first-listed) index file.

## USE WITH THE ALIAS COMMAND

The optional ALIAS command specifies a name to be used with a work area pointer when multiple database files are in use simultaneously. In the example below, the file named Customer is opened with the alias Lookup. The LIST command uses this alias to display the LName and FName fields from the Customer database:

```
SELECT A
USE Charges
SELECT B
USE Customer INDEX Customer ALIAS Lookup
SELECT A
SET RELATION TO CustNo INTO Lookup
LIST CustNo,Lookup->FName,Lookup->LName,Part_No
```

Note also that the alias is used directly in the SET RELATION command. The alias can be used as the name of the file or the work area. For example, the command **SELECT Lookup** is equivalent to the command **SELECT B** in the example above.

## USE WITH CATALOGS

If a data catalog has been created and opened, the command **USE ?** displays the names of all database files in the catalog, along with any index files that were created while the catalog was in effect. **USE <file name>** will also add a new file name to an open catalog if the file name was not already defined for the catalog. Generally speaking, however, catalogs are used in the assist mode or during command level (dot prompt) work and are of little concern to the programmer.

#### EXAMPLES

The command below opens a database named Members and two index files named Names.ndx and Zips.ndx:

**USE Members INDEX Names,Zips**

In the example above, Names is the *controlling index* or *master index* and will determine both the sort order in which records are displayed and the field(s) that can be accessed with the SEEK and FIND commands. However, both the Names and Zips index files will be updated whenever any data is added to, changed, or deleted from the database.

#### TIPS

To see which database, index files, and aliases are in use at any given moment, use the DISPLAY STATUS command. To close all open databases, use the CLOSE DATABASES command. To close all active index files, use the CLOSE INDEXES command.

Once you've created an index file for a database using the INDEX ON command, you should remember to include that index file in the USE command if you plan on changing data on the database. Any index files that are not included to the right of the INDEX command in the USE command line will not be updated, and hence will be corrupted. Once corrupted, an index file needs to be regenerated with either the INDEX ON or the REINDEX command.

#### SEE ALSO

SELECT
INDEX
CLOSE
SET INDEX
SET ORDER

## The SELECT Command

The SELECT command is used both to assign databases to work areas and to move from one work area to another. By assigning databases to separate work areas, the SELECT command makes it possible to open up to ten database files simultaneously. You can define the ten work areas as either 1 through 10 or A through J. You can also assign aliases to work areas through the USE command; see the section "USE with the ALIAS Command" in this chapter for more information.

Use the SELECT command when you have clearly established the relationships between database files. The full potential of the SELECT command is best realized when used in conjunction with other commands such as SET RELATION.

## SYNTAX

**SELECT <work area / alias >**

where <work area> is a letter A through J or a number 1 through 10 and <alias> is the name of the database or an alias defined in the ALIAS portion of a USE command.

## USAGE

Once you have defined work areas with the SELECT and USE commands, you can select a new work area without affecting the current record position of the pointer in the unselected work area. This is best explained with a couple of examples.

If you issue the commands

```
USE Charges
GOTO 15
```

the record pointer will be pointing to record 15 in the Charges database. If you then issue the commands

```
USE Customer
GOTO 10
```

the Charges database is closed, and the record pointer points to the tenth record in the Customer database. If you then issue the command

```
USE Charges
```

the record pointer is once again pointing to the first record in Charges, and the Customer database is closed.

On the other hand, if you issue the commands

```
SELECT 1
USE Charges
SELECT 2
USE Customer
SELECT 1
GOTO 15
```

the record pointer points to record 15 in the Charges database. If you then type

```
SELECT 2
GOTO 10
```

the record pointer points to record 10 in the Customer database. But the Charges database is still open, and its record pointer is still pointing to record 15. Hence, if you issue the command

```
SELECT 1
```

the record pointer is still pointing to record 15 in Charges (and is also pointing to record 10 in Customer).

Generally, any command that changes the contents of a field (APPEND, EDIT, BROWSE, READ, and so forth) works only on the currently active database (the one specified by the most recent SELECT command). However, you can *display* fields from any database by using a pointer. For example, the command

```
LIST Prod_No, B->ProdName, C->Vendor
```

displays the Prod_No field from the currently selected database, the ProdName field from the database in work area B, and the Vendor field from the database in work area C. You can use aliases in lieu of the B-> and C-> symbols, as discussed in the preceding section on the USE command.

## Opening Too Many Files

In some cases, dBASE will not allow the full ten database files to be open. For example, if a catalog is in use, it occupies the tenth file position; hence only nine other files can be opened with the SELECT and USE commands. Furthermore, if the Config.sys file does not specify FILES = 20 and BUFFERS = 15, the "Too many files are open" error will occur before ten files are open. Command files and other open files may also reduce the maximum of ten open database files.

## SELECT with Variables

If you wish to use a memory variable to determine the work area to activate, you must treat the variable name as a macro. For example, the two commands below select work area B:

```
WorkArea = "B"
SELECT &WorkArea
```

#### EXAMPLES

In the example below, the Master database and Master index file are assigned to work area A. The Charges database and the Charges and ChrgDate index files are assigned to work area B:

```
SELECT A
USE Master INDEX Master
SELECT B
USE Charges INDEX Charges, ChrgDate
```

At this point, the Charges database and its index files are currently active. To make the Master database and Master index files active (so that commands such as LIST, APPEND, and EDIT access the Master database and its index file), you can enter the command

```
SELECT A
```

#### TIPS

Be careful to use the SELECT command rather than the USE command to switch among multiple open database files. Remember that USE opens a file in the current work area and closes whatever file was already open in that work area.

From a practical standpoint, the SELECT command is best understood in relation to other commands and concepts. Therefore, I encourage you to take the time to read this entire chapter to gain a full understanding of the use of SELECT in programming. Examples throughout the book demonstrate additional programming techniques for managing multiple database files.

#### SEE ALSO

USE
SET RELATION
SET VIEW
CREATE/MODIFY VIEW
SET FIELDS

## The SET RELATION Command

The SET RELATION command defines a relationship between two databases that are open simultaneously. The databases must have a field or group of fields in common.

## SYNTAX

**SET RELATION TO <common field or RECNO( )> INTO <file name>**

where <common field> is the key field that both files share and is indexed on the linked file. In lieu of a common field, you can use RECNO( ), which sets a one-to-one relationship between multiple database files and is generally used to bypass the 128-field-per-record limitation. The <file name> parameter can be the name of the file being linked, the work area for that file, or an alias specified in the USE command.

## USAGE

SET RELATION links the currently active database (as defined by the SELECT command) to another open database. The active database should be the "many" side in a one-to-many relationship. The field name next to the TO portion of the command is a common field that is identical in name, data type, and width on both databases, but may also be any combination of common fields in both databases. The index expression in the linked file must match the expression to the right of the TO portion of the SET RELATION command.

For example, if you wished to link a database named Payments to a database named Register, based on account number and check number, the index expression in the "one" side of the relationship would need to include both fields, as shown below. (In the example, the Check_No field is the numeric data type, and Acct_No is the character data type.)

```
USE Register
INDEX ON STR(Check_No,4) + Acct_No TO RegIndex
```

The SET RELATION expression would need to match this index expression exactly, as shown in the series of commands below:

```
SELECT A
USE Payments
SELECT B
USE Register INDEX RegIndex
SELECT A
SET RELATION TO STR(Check_No,4) + Acct_No INTO Register
```

Remember, the SET RELATION command "looks into" the index file for matches, not the actual database file. Therefore, the field expression in the SET RELATION command must always exactly match the index file expression.

Once a relation is set, any movement through the currently selected database file causes dBASE to move the record pointer to the corresponding record in the linked file. The actual positioning takes place via an index file; hence the linked file must be indexed on the common field. If no value in the linked file matches the value in the active database, the record pointer in the linked file is set to EOF( ).

Note that only one relationship can be set from one work area into another work area. Hence, the second SET RELATION command below cancels the first one, because both are set from the work area A:

```
SELECT A
USE Charges
SELECT B
USE Payments
SELECT C
USE Customer INDEX CustNo
SET RELATION TO CustNo INTO Charges
* -- The following command cancels the previous relation,
* -- because both are set from work area C.
SET RELATION TO CustNo INTO Payments
```

However, you can set up relationships from *several* work areas into a *single* work area. For example, the commands below are valid and allow you to use the C-> alias from either the SELECT A or SELECT B work areas:

```
SELECT A
USE Charges
SELECT B
USE Payments
SELECT C
USE Customer INDEX CustNo
* -- The following are valid relations,
* -- because they both point into work area C.
SELECT A
SET RELATION TO CustNo INTO Customer
SELECT B
SET RELATION TO CustNo INTO Customer
```

The command SET RELATION TO without any following parameters closes the relationship in the currently selected work area.

dBASE III PLUS allows up to seven relationships to be active at any given time. Hence, if at least eight database files are open simultaneously (SELECT A through SELECT H), seven SET RELATION commands can be issued, each one set from its own work area (A through H).

With the CREATE VIEW and MODIFY VIEW commands, you can set up relationships with a full-screen assisted approach and store the commands defining the relationship in a view (.vue) file. The command **SET VIEW TO <file name>** can then restore the relationship at any time. These commands, however, do not actually offer the programmer any more than SET RELATION does. They simply present a means for the nonprogrammer to define relationships among files.

## Using RECNO( ) as the SET RELATION Expression

If you use RECNO( ) as the SET RELATION expression, the open files will be linked based on matching record numbers. This technique allows you to bypass the 128 field-per-record limit. For example, suppose you need a database with 250 fields for a particular application. You could create two database files, one named MyData and another named MyData2.

The commands below would open both database files and set up a relationship based on matching record numbers (notice that index files are not required when RECNO( ) is used):

```
SELECT A
USE MyData
SELECT B
USE MyData2
SELECT A
SET RELATION TO RECNO( ) INTO MyData2
```

From this point on, any command that moves the record pointer to a particular record in the MyData database will also move the record pointer to the same record in the MyData2 database. However, all commands that add or change data, including APPEND, EDIT, DELETE, and PACK, must work with each file independently. For example, to add new records, you would need a routine similar to the one below to ensure that both databases received a new record:

```
SELECT A
APPEND BLANK
READ
SELECT B
APPEND BLANK
READ
```

When deleting and packing records, it is imperative that both database files be treated equally. If you delete and pack any records on one database but not the other, the two databases will have an unequal number of records, and the SET RELATION command will no longer accurately link records in the packed database to records in the unpacked database.

## EXAMPLES

The file named Products contains the part number (PartNo), part name (PartName), and selling price (Sel_Price) for each product sold in a store. Products was indexed on the PartNo field using the command **INDEX ON Part_No TO Products**.

The Orders database contains a record for each order. Each record includes the part number (PartNo) and the quantity ordered (Qty). However, the part name and selling price are not stored on Orders.

To see a list of all orders from Orders, with the part name and extended price (quantity × selling price), first set a relationship from Orders into the Products.dbf and Products.ndx files, as below:

```
SELECT A
USE Orders
SELECT B
USE Products INDEX Products
SELECT A
SET RELATION TO PartNo INTO Products
```

To view the orders with part names and extended prices, enter the command

```
LIST PartNo,B->PartName,(Qty * B->Sel_Price)
```

## TIPS

Chapter 9, "Printing Formatted Reports," gives tips for printing reports from two or three related database files. Chapter 10, "Adding New Data," discusses techniques for validating data on related files.

## SEE ALSO

SELECT
USE
INDEX
CREATE/MODIFY VIEW
SET FIELDS

## SUMMARY

This chapter presented numerous commonly used database designs, as well as techniques for designing databases. In addition, it covered several dBASE commands that can be used at the dot prompt or in command files to define relationships among database files. For more advanced information on managing multiple databases, see the references listed below.

*For information on printing reports from multiple related database files:*

- Chapter 9, "Printing Formatted Reports"

*For information on entering and validating data on multiple files:*

- Chapter 10, "Adding New Data"

*For information on entering and verifying data on related databases and performing updates on database files related in a master-file/transaction-file relationship:*

- Chapter 16, "Managing Multiple Database Files"

# PART 2

## *dBASE AS A PROGRAMMING LANGUAGE*

Making the transition from dBASE user to dBASE programmer requires an understanding of the commands and techniques that are unique to programming in dBASE III PLUS. Part 2 focuses on these dBASE III PLUS commands and techniques, including creating command files (dBASE programs) and using procedures and procedure files, memory variables, and debugging techniques.

Chapter 4 discusses all the basics of creating and running dBASE command files. This chapter also discusses the general programming constructs, such as looping and decision making, that make up most programs.

Chapter 5 discusses procedure files and parameter passing: two advanced programming techniques that can help you develop quick and efficient applications. With these techniques, you can build custom libraries of commonly used routines that speed up and simplify the overall application development process.

Chapter 6 discusses memory variables, which are vital to all custom dBASE applications. Memory variables allow you to store data temporarily to aid in performing calculations, storing users' answers to questions, controlling decision-making processes in programs, and more.

Chapter 7 discusses dBASE debugging commands and techniques. Debugging is the fine art of removing the "bugs" (errors) from programs. No application is complete until all the bugs are removed. The techniques in this chapter will help you locate and fix the bugs in an application quickly and efficiently.

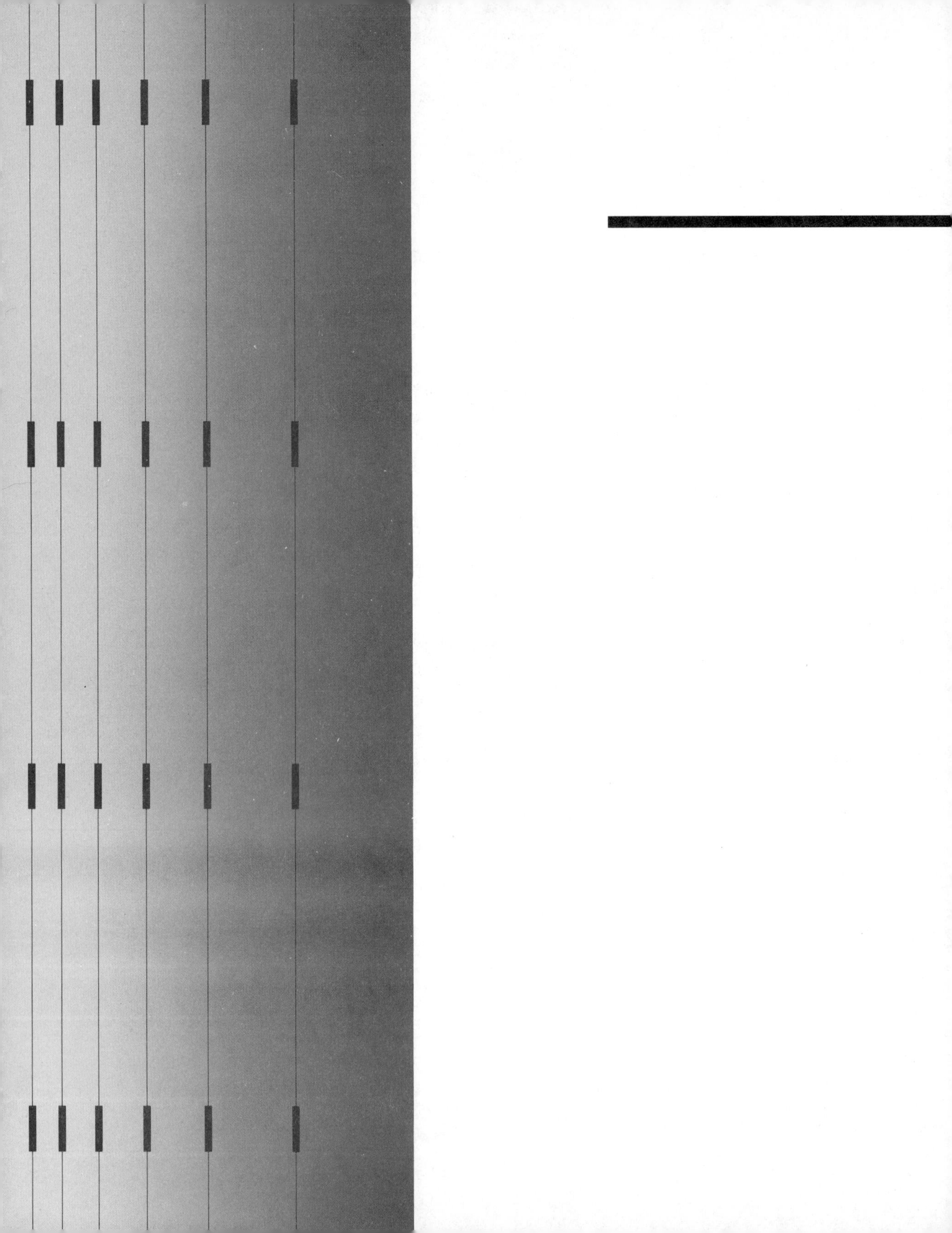

# Command Files

# COMMAND FILES

This chapter begins by covering the basic techniques for creating command files. (Because all command files are actually computer programs, the terms *command file* and *program* are used interchangeably.) It then goes on to discuss the dBASE commands that control a program's flow. To help you create neater and more efficient programs, a section explaining the techniques of structured programming is included.

The reference section of the chapter provides in-depth technical discussions of the dBASE commands used to create and comment programs, and to control a program's flow. The commands are organized according to the programming construct they support, such as user-interface, looping, decision making, and branching.

## CREATING COMMAND FILES

The first part of this chapter explains how to write, run, and modify a command file. It covers how to use the dBASE built-in text editor as well as external word processors to write dBASE programs.

### Writing Command Files Using MODIFY COMMAND

dBASE III PLUS has a built-in text editor for writing command files. To use the text editor, type **MODIFY COMMAND** and the name of the file you want to create or edit. (If you're using a floppy-disk system, you might want to use the command **SET DEFAULT TO B** before creating the command file. This ensures that the command file you create is stored on the disk in drive B.)

For example, at the dot prompt type **MODIFY COMMAND Test** and press the Return key. You'll see the message **Edit: Test.prg** at the top of the screen, along with a menu of cursor-control, editing, and file-manipulation commands, as shown in Figure 4.1. Beneath this menu is a blank area for composing your command file. (The ^ symbol in the menu means "hold down the Ctrl key while typing the next letter(s).") You can create more space for your program by pressing F1 to get rid of the menu. Pressing F1 again will bring it back. The control keys that you can use while creating your command file are summarized in Table 4.1.

```
Edit: C:Test.prg

CURSOR:  <-- -->  |          UP    DOWN |    DELETE    | Insert Mode:      Ins
 Char:      ←  →  | Line:     ↑     ↓   | Char:    Del | Insert line:     ^N
 Word:  Home End  | Page: PgUp   PgDn   | Word:     ^T | Save: ^W  Abort:Esc
 Line:     ^← ^→  | Find:    ^KF        | Line:     ^Y | Read file:       ^KR
 Reformat: ^KB    | Refind: ^KL         |              | Write file:      ^KW

_
```

**FIGURE 4.1:** The dBASE text editor help menu. The ^ symbol means "hold down the Ctrl key while typing the next letter(s)." To toggle this help menu on and off, press the F1 key.

| | KEY | ALTERNATIVE | FUNCTION |
|---|---|---|---|
| **Cursor-Movement Commands** | ↑ | Ctrl-E | Moves cursor up one line |
| | ↓ | Ctrl-X | Moves cursor down one line |
| | ← | Ctrl-D | Moves cursor left one character |
| | → | Ctrl-S | Moves cursor right one character |
| | Home | Ctrl-A | Moves cursor left one word |
| | End | Ctrl-F | Moves cursor right one word |
| | Ctrl-← | Ctrl-Z | Moves cursor to beginning of line |
| | Ctrl-→ | Ctrl-B | Moves cursor to end of line |
| | PgUp | Ctrl-R | Scrolls screen up a page (18 lines) |
| | PgDn | Ctrl-C | Scrolls screen down a page (18 lines) |

**TABLE 4.1:** Keyboard Control Commands for MODIFY COMMAND

| | KEY | ALTERNATIVE | FUNCTION |
|---|---|---|---|
| **Insert Commands** | Return | Ctrl-M | Ends line and begins new line; also inserts a new line if the Insert mode is on |
| | Ins | Ctrl-V | Toggles Insert mode on and off |
| | | Ctrl-N | Inserts a blank line at cursor position |
| **Delete Commands** | ← | Rub | Deletes the character to the left of the cursor |
| | Del | Ctrl-G | Deletes the character over the cursor |
| | | Ctrl-T | Deletes the word to the right of the cursor |
| | | Ctrl-Y | Deletes the entire line over the cursor |
| **File-Manipulation Commands** | Ctrl-End | Ctrl-W | Saves command file with all changes |
| | Esc | Ctrl-Q | Returns to dot prompt without saving current changes to command file |
| | Ctrl-KB | | Reformats text in a paragraph (used with memo fields rather than command files) |
| | Ctrl-KF | | Locates the first occurrence of any word(s) you specify |
| | Ctrl-KL | | Locates the next occurrence of word(s) specified in Ctrl-KF |
| | Ctrl-KR | | Reads an external command file stored on disk into the current command file starting at the cursor position |
| | Ctrl-KW | | Saves a copy of the current command file with a new name |
| **Help Screen Toggle** | F1 | Ctrl-\ | Toggles help menu on and off |

**TABLE 4.1:** Keyboard Control Commands for MODIFY COMMAND (continued)

To illustrate how command files are created, run, and modified, you can type the commands

**CLEAR**
**? "Hi! I'm a test program."**

into the Test file. If you see any errors, use the arrow keys on your keyboard to move the cursor around and then type your changes.

When you've correctly typed both lines of the command file and pressed Return so that your cursor is on a new line, type Ctrl-End or Ctrl-W. dBASE saves the command file and returns control to the dot prompt. dBASE also adds the extension .prg (program) to the file name, so the name of the file you've stored on disk will be Test.prg.

## Running Command Files

Once you've created and saved a command file, the DO command will run the program. In this example, type the command **DO Test** next to the dBASE dot prompt and press the Return key. dBASE should clear the screen (the CLEAR command) and then display the message **Hi! I'm a test program.** on the screen (the ? command means print or display). After both commands in the command file have been executed, dBASE once again returns control to the dot prompt.

## Modifying Existing Command Files

If you want to change something in your program, you can use MODIFY COMMAND again to make the changes. For this example, type **MODIFY COMMAND Test** and press the Return key. dBASE will display the existing program on the screen, with the cursor under the first letter of the first line, as below:

**CLEAR**
**? "Hi! I'm a test program."**

Now change the word Hi to Hello by pressing ↓ once and then → four times to place the cursor under the letter i in Hi. Next press the Del key to delete the letter i. To insert the letters ello into the sentence, press the Ins key on your keyboard until you see the symbol Ins appear at the top of the screen. With the insert mode on, any new letters (or spaces) that you type will be inserted into existing text. Next just type the letters ello so that the line reads **? "Hello! I'm a test program."**

Note that if you accidentally press the Return key while insert mode is on, dBASE will cut your command line into two lines at the current cursor position.

For example, pressing Return after typing ello would tell dBASE to cut the line as follows:

```
? "Hello
! I'm a test program."
```

dBASE cannot read lines that are arbitrarily broken, so you have to "unbreak" the line. To do so, make sure that the cursor is at the very end of the top line, then press the Del key. The line will be reunited into a single line.

## Breaking Long Lines

You can intentionally break a very long command line into two or more lines by ending the top line(s) with a semicolon. When using a semicolon to break a line, try to do so at a natural space preceding a command. For example, the following long command line

```
@ 10,2 SAY "Enter your name please " GET LName PICTURE "@!"
```

could be broken into two lines with the semicolon command, as below:

```
@ 10,2 SAY "Enter your name please " ;
GET LName PICTURE "@!"
```

A single command line can be broken as many times as necessary. The command below is actually a single REPLACE command:

```
REPLACE ALL LName WITH UPPER(LName), ;
            FName WITH UPPER(FName), ;
            City WITH UPPER(City) FOR ;
            Date > = CTOD("01/01/87") .AND. ;
            Past_Due > = 90
```

However, even with semicolons to break a long line into smaller parts, the total number of characters in a single command cannot exceed 254 characters.

Whenever you press Return to end a line in the MODIFY COMMAND editor, a < symbol indicates a *hard carriage return* and separates individual command lines. dBASE also automatically word-wraps any lines that extend beyond 66 characters. These wrapped lines do *not* display the < symbol at the right edge of the screen. Furthermore, wrapped lines are treated as a single command line and do not require semicolons.

When you've finished editing your command file, type Ctrl-W or Ctrl-End to save it again. dBASE stores the modified command file under the same file name (Test.prg in this example). It also stores a backup copy of the unedited command file under the file name Test.bak.

### COMMAND FILE LENGTH

The dBASE text editor imposes a limit of 5,000 characters within a single command file. The only way around this limitation is to use another text editor or word processor, as discussed below.

## Using External Word Processors

You can use external word processors, such as WordStar or WordPerfect, to create and edit command files. However, you must make sure that you save a nondocument or ASCII format of the command file to disk. In WordStar, you accomplish this by selecting N (nondocument) rather than D (document mode) when creating or editing a file. With WordPerfect, you press Ctrl-F5 and select option 1.

Failure to save the command file in the proper format may cause your word processor to put special characters in the command file that are not immediately visible to you but are very visible to dBASE. These characters can cause your command file to "crash" for no apparent reason.

To see whether there are any special characters in a command file, use the DOS or dBASE TYPE command to view the file. Just use the syntax **TYPE <file name>**, where <file name> is the complete name of the file to view, as in the command **TYPE Test.prg**.

If the command file scrolls by too quickly, you can use the Ctrl-S key combination to start and stop scrolling. Any special embedded characters in the command file will probably appear as graphics symbols, or they may cause your computer to beep. Unfortunately, these special characters are not always easy to remove. You may need to go back into the command file and completely retype the lines with the special characters. If you have experience programming in BASIC or Pascal, you can probably write a program to remove all the special characters by subtracting 128 from all characters with ASCII values over 128.

When using external word processors, be sure to add the .prg extension to the command file name. dBASE will assume that the command file name has this extension and will search for that file in response to a DO command. (If you forget to add the .prg extension when you are creating the file, you can use the DOS or dBASE RENAME command to change the file name later.)

To save word processor files as programs or dBASE command files, see the reference manual that came with your word processor or text editor. You'll want to look for the commands that save files as either ASCII text files or DOS text files.

### CALLING EXTERNAL WORD PROCESSORS WITH RUN

One disadvantage to using external word processors can be the time required to quit dBASE, load up your word processor to create the file or make changes, then exit your word processor and reload dBASE from the DOS prompt. However, if you have 384K or more of RAM memory, you can use the RUN (or !) command at the dBASE dot prompt to run your external word processor. Once you exit the word processor, you'll be returned to the dBASE dot prompt automatically.

The RUN and abbreviated ! commands are identical. To load WordStar from the dBASE dot prompt, you can enter either **RUN WS** or **!WS**, assuming that WordStar is stored under the file name WS.COM and is available from the currently logged drive.

Note that the RUN or ! commands will search a path set by the DOS PATH command but not by the dBASE SET PATH command.

## USING CONFIG.DB TO CALL EXTERNAL WORD PROCESSORS

Rather than using RUN to call external word processors, you can modify the Config.db file so that MODIFY COMMAND will call the word processor. (Config.db is discussed in more detail in Appendix C "Installing dBASE III PLUS.") Like the RUN command, this technique requires 384K or more of memory. To make this modification, use the command **TEDIT = <word processor command>**, where <word processor command> is the command used to call up the word processor. For example, to call WordStar from dBASE, you would type **TEDIT = WS** in the Config.db file.

The use of TEDIT in the Config.db file causes dBASE to substitute the external word processor for the MODIFY COMMAND editor. So if you've placed the command TEDIT = WS in your Config.db file, the command **MODIFY COMMAND MyProg** will automatically create (or edit) a file named MyProg.prg using WordStar as the word processor. (Unfortunately, WordStar may be in document mode. You should reinstall WordStar to start in nondocument mode if you wish to use the TEDIT method.)

When you are finished creating or editing the command file, exit your word processor in the usual manner. You'll be returned to the dot prompt.

## USING RAM-RESIDENT EDITORS

You can also use a RAM-resident editor, such as Sidekick's Notepad, as an external editor. RAM-resident editors have a few advantages over other alternatives. For one, they pop onto and off of the screen almost instantly and are therefore faster than most other editors. Another advantage is that they do not have large RAM memory requirements. Finally, they usually save their text in the plain ASCII format required by dBASE, so you need not be concerned about word processing codes creeping into your command files.

# PROGRAMMING CONSTRUCTS

In its simplest form, a command file is simply a collection of commands that might otherwise be typed individually at the dot prompt. dBASE reads and interprets the commands in the same order that you are reading this page: from left to right and from top to bottom.

In most applications, however, you need command files that are more than simple collections of commands: you need command files that can pause and get information from the user, make decisions based on new information, and perform certain tasks repeatedly and automatically. There are several general *programming constructs*—elements that make up an effective program—that allow you to build these capabilities into a command file.

This section covers the programming constructs in a general sense, discussing the situations in which they are used. The specific commands used for these programming constructs are discussed in more technical detail in the reference section of this chapter.

## Programmer Comments

Command files can include *programmer comments,* which, unlike commands and functions, do nothing at all. Instead, comments serve as notes to themselves and other programmers. These notes come in handy when you need to go back and modify a program that you have not worked with for a long time, or when you need to work with a command file that somebody else created.

In a command file, any line beginning with an asterisk (*) or the command NOTE is a programmer comment that dBASE will ignore. The example below shows two programmer comments added to the simple Test command file:

```
************************* Test.prg.
* ------- First sample command file.

CLEAR
? "Hello! I'm a test program."
```

Notice that each comment begins with an asterisk. Additional asterisks and hyphens in the example above simply make the comment stand out. You'll also note a blank line between the comments and the first command (CLEAR). Blank lines are permissible anywhere in a command file.

Another technique for placing comments in command files is to precede the comment with two ampersands (&&). Comments beginning in this way are placed to the right of a dBASE command. For example, in the command below, dBASE displays all the FName and LName fields from the database currently in use and ignores the && and comment to the right:

**LIST FName, LName      && Show customers' names**

The comment simply presents an English interpretation of what the LIST command is doing.

## Interacting with the User

Often a program needs to ask for information and then wait for an answer from the user. For example, a program that prints an inventory report might first ask the user whether the report should be displayed on the screen or sent to the printer. Then it would display the report according to the user's answer. The ACCEPT, INPUT, WAIT, and READ commands all present a question to the user, wait for a response, and store that answer to a field or memory variable.

### Using the ACCEPT Command

The ACCEPT command presents a question to the user, waits for a response (followed by a press on the Return key), and stores that response to a character-type memory variable. For example, the command

**ACCEPT "Send report to printer? (Y/N) " TO YN**

displays the message **Send report to printer? (Y/N)** on the screen and waits for an answer of any length. When the user presses Return, the answer is stored in a character memory variable named YN. Because the ACCEPT command always stores information as character data, it should not be used when the program needs to ask about numeric data.

### Using the INPUT Command

The INPUT command also displays a prompt on the screen and waits for the user's response (and a Return), but the type of data entered determines the type of variable created. For example, the command

**INPUT "Enter your age " TO Age**

presents the prompt **Enter your age** and stores the user's answer to a numeric memory variable named Age. If data are to be stored as character data, INPUT requires that the response be enclosed in quotation marks.

Be careful not to use the INPUT command to get date information from the user. The command

**INPUT "Enter today's date" TO Date**

accepts information in date format (MM/DD/YY), but it actually stores the entered date as a quotient. For example, 03/31/85 would be stored as the quotient of 3 divided by 31 divided by 85.

## Using the WAIT Command

The WAIT command presents a prompt and waits for a single keystroke (without a carriage return). If WAIT is used without a prompt or memory variable, dBASE presents the message

**Press any key to continue . . .**

and waits for any key to be pressed (the keystroke is not stored in this case). If a prompt and memory variable name are included in the command, the program displays a message and waits for a response. For example,

**WAIT "Send data to printer? (Y/N) " TO YN**

displays the message **Send data to printer? (Y/N)** and waits for a key to be pressed. In this case, the keystroke is stored in the memory variable YN.

The WAIT command always stores the user's keystroke as character data. If you want to use WAIT to ask for a number, you must use the VAL function to convert the character data to numeric data:

**WAIT "Enter your choice (1–5) " TO Choice**
**Choice = VAL(Choice)**

In this example, the WAIT command accepts a single character, and the VAL function converts it to numeric data.

## Using the READ Command

The READ command can be used to get field or memory-variable data. It is always used in conjunction with the @...SAY...GET commands. Unlike ACCEPT, INPUT, and WAIT, READ works only with field or memory variable names that already exist. For example, to use the READ command to get information for a menu choice and store that information in a memory variable named Choice, you must create the Choice memory variable before using the READ command:

**Choice = 0**
**@ 9,5 SAY "Enter choice " GET Choice**
**READ**

This sequence of commands first creates a numeric memory variable named Choice (Choice = 0) and then displays the prompt **Enter choice** on row 9, column 5 of the screen. Then the program waits for an answer to the prompt (GET Choice) and stores that answer to the variable Choice (READ).

The @...SAY...GET...READ commands are often used for entering and editing data on a database through custom screens. For detailed information on all aspects of the @...SAY...GET...READ commands, see Chapter 8, "Managing Screen Displays."

## Looping

One of the most frequently used command structures in dBASE programming is the DO WHILE loop. A loop tells dBASE to repeat a series of commands as long as some condition exists. The DO WHILE command marks the start of the loop, and the ENDDO command marks the end of the loop.

For example, the Count program in Figure 4.2 contains a loop that repeats 20 times. After the programmer comments, the CLEAR command clears the screen. The SET TALK OFF command keeps extraneous dBASE messages from appearing on the screen as the program is running. Then the STORE command creates a memory variable named X that contains the number 1 (an alternative form for this command is X = 1).

The next line begins the loop. **DO WHILE X < = 20** tells dBASE to start a loop that will repeat as long as X is either less than or equal to 20. The command **? X** simply prints the current value of the memory variable X. Then the command **X = X + 1** increments the current value of the memory variable X by one. The ENDDO command marks the end of the DO WHILE loop. Every DO WHILE command in a program must have an ENDDO command associated with it. The last line prints the message **All done** on the screen when the program

```
****************************** Count.prg
*-------------- Test the DO WHILE loop.

CLEAR
SET TALK OFF

STORE 1 TO X
DO WHILE X <= 20
   ? X
   X = X + 1
ENDDO

? "All done"
```

**FIGURE 4.2:** Sample program to test the DO WHILE loop. In this example, the loop repeats 20 times. Each time, the ? command displays the current value in the variable named X, and the X = X + 1 command increments X by one. When X reaches 21, the loop stops and the last command prints **All done** on the screen.

is done (X is greater than 20). As long as X is less than or equal to 20, all commands within the loop are executed repeatedly.

When this program is run, it produces the screen shown in Figure 4.3. If you were to change the program so that the loop repeated as long as X was less than or equal to 40, as in Figure 4.4, dBASE would count to 40 before displaying the **All done** message.

```
          1
          2
          3
          4
          5
          6
          7
          8
          9
         10
         11
         12
         13
         14
         15
         16
         17
         18
         19
         20
All done

. _
```

**FIGURE 4.3:** Results of the Count program shown in Figure 4.2. Each pass through the DO WHILE loop displays the current value of the variable named X, until X goes beyond the value of 20. At that point, the loop ends, and the **All done** message is displayed.

```
****************************** Count.prg
*-------------- Test the DO WHILE loop.

CLEAR
SET TALK OFF

STORE 1 TO X
DO WHILE X <= 40
   ? X
   X = X + 1
ENDDO

? "All done"
```

**FIGURE 4.4:** The modified Count program. In this example, the DO WHILE loop will repeat 40 times, displaying the numbers 1 through 40, before printing the **All done** message.

One of the most common uses for the DO WHILE command is to step through each record in a database and perform some action on every record. The command DO WHILE .NOT. EOF() is often used for this type of loop. In English, the command translates to "Do the following procedure as long as the last record in the database (EOF()) has not been encountered." This and other uses of the DO WHILE command are discussed later in this chapter and throughout the book.

## Decision Making

You can write a command file so that it can make decisions about what to do next based on current information. There are several techniques that you can use in command files to make decisions: they employ the IF clause, the IIF function, the CASE clause, and macro substitution.

### THE IF CLAUSE

If a command file needs to make a decision with only one or two alternative outcomes, the IF...ELSE...ENDIF commands can handle the job. The example program in Figure 4.5 demonstrates the use of an IF clause.

The command

**ACCEPT "Turn on printer? (Y/N) " TO YesNo**

presents the prompt **Turn on printer? (Y/N)** on the screen and waits for the user to type an answer and press the Return key. Whatever the user types is stored in

```
***************************************** IfTest.prg
*-------------- Test the IF...ELSE...ENDIF commands.
CLEAR
ACCEPT "Turn on printer? (Y/N) " TO YesNo

*------ Decide what to do based on answer (YesNo).
IF UPPER(YesNo)="Y"
   SET PRINT ON
   ? "You chose the printer"
   EJECT
   SET PRINT OFF
ELSE
   CLEAR
   ? "You chose the screen."
ENDIF
```

**FIGURE 4.5:** The IfTest program. In this example, the program asks whether the user wants the printer turned on. If the user enters Y (or y), the program sets the printer on and displays the message **You chose the printer.** Otherwise, the program clears the screen and displays the message **You chose the screen.**

a memory variable named YesNo. The next line, **IF UPPER(YesNo) = "Y"**, checks whether the uppercase equivalent of the user's answer is a capital Y (so it won't matter whether the user enters Y or y). If it is, dBASE performs all the lines between the IF and ELSE statements. If the user's answer is not Y or y, dBASE skips the lines between the IF and ELSE statements and processes all lines between the ELSE and ENDIF statements instead. In either case, the program returns to the dot prompt when done.

The last line in the command file, ENDIF, marks the end of the commands to be included within the IF clause. Every IF statement in a command file must have an ENDIF associated with it, but the ELSE statement is optional. For example, if you simply want the program to turn on the printer when the user answers Yes to a prompt, you can use an IF...ENDIF clause without the ELSE, as in Figure 4.6. If the user decides to use the printer in this case, the output from the LIST command is displayed on the printer. Otherwise, the output is displayed on the screen.

## THE IIF FUNCTION

An abbreviated form of the IF command is the IIF function (immediate IF), which can be used in a command line or even in a column definition in a report format or label format. The syntax for IIF is

**IIF(this is true, do this, otherwise do this)**

For example, the IIF command below prints the words **Less Than** if a memory variable named X is less than 10. Otherwise, the command line prints the words **Greater Than**:

**? IIF(X<10,"Less Than","Greater Than")**

```
***************************************** IfTest.prg
*-------------- Test the IF...ELSE...ENDIF commands.
CLEAR
ACCEPT "Turn on printer? (Y/N) " TO YesNo

*------ Decide what to do based upon answer (YesNo).
IF UPPER(YesNo)="Y"
   SET PRINT ON
ENDIF

LIST LName, FName, Address
SET PRINT OFF
```

**FIGURE 4.6:** A program with IF...ENDIF but no ELSE. This program asks whether the user wants the printer turned on. If the user answers with a Y or y, the output from the LIST command is displayed on the printer. Otherwise, the output is displayed on the screen.

The IF command clause below performs exactly the same task:

**IF X < 10**
**? "Less Than"**
**ELSE**
**? "Greater Than"**
**ENDIF**

Notice that with the IIF function the ? (print) command begins the line, and the IIF function determines how to finish the command line. The IF command requires two separate ? commands to achieve the same goal.

Generally speaking, the IIF function is used where one condition leads to a single "either/or" result. The IF...THEN...ELSE commands can perform any number of steps based on the result of a condition. The IIF function is discussed in more detail in Chapter 17, "dBASE Functions."

## The CASE Clause

A DO CASE...ENDCASE clause tells a program what to do based on any one of several mutually exclusive possibilities. A simple example is shown in Figure 4.7.

```
*************************************** CaseTest.prg
*-------------- Test the DO CASE...ENDCASE Commands.
CLEAR
INPUT "Enter a number from 1 to 4 " TO X

DO CASE

   CASE X = 1
        ? "You entered one."

   CASE X = 2
        ? "You entered two."

   CASE X = 3
        ? "You entered three."

   CASE X = 4
        ? "You entered four."

   OTHERWISE
        ? "I said from one to four!"

ENDCASE
```

**FIGURE 4.7:** The CaseTest command file. The INPUT command waits for a number between one and four. If the user enters a number within that range, a CASE statement shows a message with the number in English (e.g., **You entered one.**). If the user does not enter a number between one and four, the OTHERWISE command displays the message **I said from one to four!**

The INPUT command presents the message

**Enter a number from 1 to 4**

on the screen and waits for the user to enter a response and press the Return key. The user's response is stored to a numeric memory variable named X. The next line, **DO CASE**, marks the beginning of the conditional clause. Beneath this, the lines **CASE X = 1** and **? "You entered one."** tell dBASE that if the user's answer is a 1 (X = 1), it should print the message **You entered one.**

The next CASE statement, **CASE X = 2**, prints the message **You entered two.** if a 2 is typed in, and so forth for **CASE X = 3** and **CASE X = 4**. The optional OTHERWISE command is used to cover all other possibilities. For example, if you run this command file and type in the number 37 in response to the prompt, the program displays the message **I said from one to four!** Unlike the optional OTHERWISE command, the ENDCASE command *must* be used to mark the end of a DO CASE clause in a program.

The DO CASE command is commonly found in menu programs, where the program displays a list of options to the user, waits for a response, and decides what to do next based on the user's menu choice. For an example of this, see the section "A Typical Menu Program" later in this chapter.

## MACRO SUBSTITUTION

Yet another technique for making decisions while a program is executing is *macro substitution.* With this technique, a portion of a command is stored in a character memory variable and then substituted into the command using the ampersand (&) symbol.

For example, the REPORT FORM command uses the TO PRINT option to display a report on the printer rather than on the screen. You would use the command

**REPORT FORM AnyRept**

to display a report on the screen and the command

**REPORT FORM AnyRept TO PRINT**

to display the report on the printer.

A program could decide whether to include the TO PRINT part of command using macro substitution, as below:

```
PMacro = " "
ACCEPT "Send report to printer? (Y/N) " TO PrintIt
IF UPPER(PrintIt) = "Y"
    PMacro = "TO PRINT"
```

```
ENDIF
REPORT FORM AnyRept &PMacro
```

In this example, the variable PMacro is initially a blank. If the user answers **Y** in response to the prompt **Send report to printer? (Y/N)**, the variable PMacro becomes "TO PRINT", and the last command becomes

```
REPORT FORM AnyRept TO PRINT
```

If the user does not answer Y to the prompt about the printer, PMacro remains a blank and dBASE substitutes a blank for PMacro. So the last command becomes

```
REPORT FORM AnyRept
```

Macro substitution is a very powerful programming technique; it is discussed in more detail in Chapter 6, "Memory Variables."

## Branching

In dBASE, *branching* usually refers to the technique of calling one command file from another with the DO command. The called program automatically passes control back to the calling program when either a RETURN command is issued or there are no more commands to process in that file.

The called programs (*subroutines*) can be either separate command files or procedures stored in memory. Procedures and procedure files are discussed in detail in Chapter 5, "Procedures and Parameters."

The section that follows presents a menu program that illustrates the branching technique.

## A Typical Menu Program

The menu program developed in this section is typical because it does the following three things:

1. It presents a number of options and allows the user to select an option.
2. It performs some task based on the user's selection.
3. It automatically redisplays the menu when that task is done (unless the user selects an option to exit the application).

The program demonstrates the use of programmer comments, looping, branching, and decision making (and also serves as an example of structured programming, which is discussed in the next section). The entire program, named MainMenu.prg, is shown in Figure 4.8.

The first two lines of the program, beginning with the * character, are programmer comments. For convenience to the programmer, these display the program name and its basic function. Some programmers also like to add the programmer's name, the date of the last change to the program, a copyright notice (if relevant), and perhaps additional information to the top of a program.

Looking at the logic of the program, you can see that the variable MChoice is first initialized to zero. Then a DO WHILE loop is set up to continually redisplay the menu as long as the user does not choose to exit the program (WHILE MChoice # 5).

```
**************************************** MainMenu.prg
*--------------------------- A typical menu program.
SET TALK OFF
MChoice = 0

DO WHILE MChoice # 5

   CLEAR
   TEXT
             Accounts Payable Main Menu

             1. Add new transactions

             2. Edit transactions

             3. Print reports

             4. Post transactions

             5. Exit

   ENDTEXT
   @ 12,10 SAY "Enter choice (1-5) " ;
     GET MChoice PICTURE "9" RANGE 1,5
   READ

   DO CASE

      CASE MChoice = 1
           DO APAdd

      CASE MChoice = 2
           DO APEdit

      CASE MChoice = 3
           DO APPrint

      CASE MChoice = 4
           DO APPost

   ENDCASE

ENDDO
*----- End of program.
```

**FIGURE 4.8:** A typical menu program. The DO WHILE loop redisplays the menu until the user opts to exit by selecting option 5. The GET and READ commands wait for the user's entry. If the user selects a number between 1 and 4, the CASE statements in the DO CASE clause branch to the appropriate program.

Within the loop, dBASE clears the screen and displays the menu of options. (dBASE will display any text that appears between the TEXT and ENDTEXT commands on the screen or even the printer.) Beneath the ENDTEXT command, the @...SAY...GET...READ commands ask the user to select an option and then store the selection in the variable named MChoice.

If the user selects a number in the range of one to four, the DO CASE clause passes control to another program (via the various DO commands beneath each CASE command). When the program called by the DO command completes its task, it returns control to the main menu program. Once control is returned to the main menu program, the rest of the CASE statements are ignored, and the ENDDO command causes control to loop back to the top of the DO WHILE loop, thereby redisplaying the menu on the screen.

If the user selects option 5, none of the CASE statements is true, so no external task is performed. Furthermore, the ENDDO command notes that MChoice *is* equal to 5, so it does not repeat the DO WHILE MChoice # 5 loop. Therefore, control falls out of the ENDDO loop, the program terminates, and the dot prompt is redisplayed. (Placing the command QUIT beneath the ENDDO command would cause dBASE to quit and control to be passed all the way back to the DOS prompt.)

Note that if the user selects option 1, control is passed to a program named APAdd (actually APAdd.prg, because dBASE always assumes the .prg extension). Let's assume that the APAdd.prg program looks like the one in Figure 4.9.

The APAdd command file clears the screen, sets up a custom screen named APScreen, and allows the user to add as many new records to the database as he or she wishes. When done adding records, the user just presses the Return key without adding a record, and control passes back to the first line beneath the DO APAdd command in MainMenu.prg.

## STRUCTURED PROGRAMMING

Structured programs are *self-documenting,* that is, easy for you and other programmers to read and therefore easy to debug or modify in the future. Naturally, programs are easier to read if they follow some basic structural techniques. The

```
***************************************** APAdd.prg
CLEAR
SET FORMAT TO APScreen
APPEND
RETURN
```

**FIGURE 4.9:** The APAdd command file, called by the main menu program. This program allows the user to add new records to the database file. When the user is done, it passes control back to the calling program (MainMenu.prg) with the RETURN command.

following rules of thumb can help make your dBASE III PLUS command files easier to read and work with:

1. Use highly visible programmer comments that make it easy to locate the portions of the program that perform specific tasks.
2. Indent program lines within loops and decision-making routines, so you can see the beginning and ending points of these routines.
3. Try to select commands and variable names that are descriptive rather than cryptic.

These rules can best be demonstrated by comparing a program that doesn't use structured-programming techniques to one that does. Both programs perform exactly the same job: they present a main menu for a hypothetical library-management system, ask the user for a choice from the menu, and then perform the task that the user requests. Figure 4.10 presents a main menu program that does not follow the structured programming rules of thumb.

First of all, while there are some programmer comments in the program (lines preceded by a single asterisk), they are not highly visible. You need to skim through many lines of dBASE code to find the comment that reads * **EXIT**.

```
USE LIBRARY
DO WHILE .T.
CLEAR
@ 1,20 SAY "Library Management System"
@ 3,25 SAY "1. Add New Records"
@ 4,25 SAY "2. Print Reports"
@ 5,25 SAY "3. Edit Data"
@ 6,25 SAY "4. Exit"
STORE 0 TO CHOICE
@ 8,20 SAY "Enter choice (1-6) " GET CHOICE
READ
* BRANCH ACCORDINGLY
IF CHOICE=1
APPEND
ELSE
IF CHOICE=2
REPORT FORM LIBRARY
ELSE
IF CHOICE=3
DO LIBEDIT
ELSE
* EXIT
IF CHOICE=4
RETURN
ENDIF
ENDIF
ENDIF
ENDIF
ENDDO
```

**FIGURE 4.10:** An unstructured menu program. The lack of basic structured programming principles in this program make it difficult to read and understand. Figure 4.11 shows this same program written with the structured programming guidelines in mind.

Second, there are no indentations in the program, making it difficult to figure out what is going on; the list of seemingly disconnected ENDIF commands near the bottom of the file is particularly daunting. If for some reason this program didn't work, it would not be easy to figure out why.

Third, there are some commands that are not very descriptive or even logical in a programming sense. For example, the fourth line reads **DO WHILE .T.** In the dBASE language, .T. means true. In fact, .T. is a value in the logical data type and is always true. Therefore, this line suggests that the loop will run forever. However, if you examine the lines below, you'll find that the loop will not actually run forever. When the user selects option 4 from the menu, dBASE executes a RETURN command, bypassing the loop and returning to the dot prompt.

At the bottom of the command file is the ENDDO command. There are no comments associated with it. If this were a larger program with many DO WHILE commands, it would be difficult to determine which DO WHILE this ENDDO belongs to. The same is true for the many ENDIF commands.

The program in Figure 4.11 performs exactly the same task as the previous program, but it is written using the rules for structured programming.

```
****************************************** Library.prg.
***************************** Library system main menu.
USE Library
Choice = 0

DO WHILE Choice # 4
   CLEAR
   @ 1,20 SAY "Library Management System"
   @ 3,25 SAY "1. Add New Records"
   @ 4,25 SAY "2. Print Reports"
   @ 5,25 SAY "3. Edit Data"
   @ 6,25 SAY "4. Exit"
   @ 8,20 SAY "Enter choice (1-6) " GET Choice
   READ

   ************ Perform according to user's request.
   DO CASE

      CASE Choice = 1
           APPEND

      CASE Choice = 2
           REPORT FORM Library

      CASE Choice = 3
           DO LibEdit

   ENDCASE

ENDDO (while Choice # 4)

*************************** When Choice = 4, exit.
RETURN
```

**FIGURE 4.11:** A structured main menu program. The programmer comments, indentations on clause commands, and more descriptive command lines make the program easier to read.

This structured command file is much easier to read than the preceding one. To begin with, all of the programmer's comments are visible at a glance. Furthermore, they're written in plain English syntax and upper- and lowercase. Highly visible, descriptive comments make it much easier to spot a specific routine in a mass of program lines, and therefore make the program much easier to debug or modify later. Also, there is a heading at the top of the program that gives the name of the program and a brief description of what it does.

All the lines within the DO WHILE...ENDDO loop are indented three spaces. It is easy to find the beginning and ending points of the loop simply by running your finger down the margin from the DO WHILE command until you encounter an ENDDO in the same column.

This program also uses the DO CASE...ENDCASE commands to decide which task to perform, based on the user's request. This eliminates those confusing ENDIFs in the first program, making the program easier to read. The commands within the DO CASE...ENDCASE lines are also evenly indented, which makes the entire DO CASE...ENDCASE clause stand out.

Finally, some of the commands chosen are more descriptive than the commands in the first program. The command **DO WHILE Choice # 4** immediately informs us that this loop is not going to repeat itself forever. It is going to stop when the memory variable Choice equals 4. So you won't need to dig around in the program to find the mysterious end to a seemingly infinite loop. In addition, the ENDDO command at the bottom of the program has a comment after it (while Choice # 4). This simple comment pinpoints which DO WHILE command is associated with this ENDDO (many programs have more than one such loop) and makes the program easier to read and work with at a later date. In the dBASE programming language, anything that you type to the right of an ENDDO, ENDIF, or ENDCASE command is assumed to be a programmer's comment. You can do yourself a big favor by including these reminders about which particular DO WHILE, IF, or DO CASE each ENDDO, ENDIF, or ENDCASE command belongs to.

In spite of your hard work in designing and structuring your programs, you may still find bugs in them when you first try to run them. The art of quickly finding and removing bugs from programs is called *debugging,* and this topic is discussed in detail in Chapter 7, "Debugging Commands and Techniques."

## Commands for Creating and Commenting Programs

As discussed earlier in this chapter, MODIFY COMMAND allows you to create and edit command files. As an alternative, however, you can use any external word processor or text editor to create and modify command files.

One of the first "commands" you will place in your programs will be comments to yourself and other programmers. In addition to covering the MODIFY

COMMAND command, this section discusses in more detail the three commands you can use to place programmer comments in command files.

## The MODIFY COMMAND Command

The MODIFY COMMAND command calls up the dBASE text editor for creating or modifying command files. dBASE automatically adds the extension .prg to command files created with the MODIFY COMMAND text editor. The command MODIFY FILE is similar to MODIFY COMMAND, except that it does not assume the .prg extension when creating or searching for a file.

### SYNTAX

**MODIFY COMMAND <file name>**

where <file name> is a valid DOS file name (up to eight characters, no spaces or punctuation).

### USAGE

Use MODIFY COMMAND to create and edit command files. When you enter the command, dBASE searches for the file specified. If the file is found, it is brought to the screen for editing. If the file is not found, dBASE creates it.

Unless specified, the current drive and directory are assumed. You can specify drive and directory designators at the beginning of the file name using the usual DOS sequence. For example, the command

**MODIFY COMMAND C:\DB\PRGFILES\MyProg**

creates or edits a command file named MyProg on the PRGFILES subdirectory under the DB directory on drive C.

When saving edited command files, dBASE stores a copy of the previous (unedited) version of the command file using the same file name but with the extension .bak.

For a complete list of the control-key commands used within the dBASE text editor, see Table 4.1 earlier in this chapter.

#### File Length Limit

The MODIFY COMMAND editor cannot hold more than 5,000 characters. When the 5,000-character limit is exceeded, a warning message appears at the top of the screen. If you were typing new material when the 5,000-character warning appeared, you could save all the text prior to the 5,000th character by typing Ctrl-W or Ctrl-End as usual. If you inadvertently load a command file into MODIFY COMMAND, not realizing it is already over 5,000 characters long, do not save the command file! Saving the command file at this point would cut off all characters beyond 5,000. Instead, abandon the command file with the Esc key or the Ctrl-Q combination.

### Hard and Soft Carriage Returns

The dBASE text editor automatically word-wraps command lines at the 66th character. When you press Return after typing in a line, dBASE ends the line with a *hard carriage return.* This hard carriage return shows up as a < symbol at the extreme right edge of the screen. Lines that dBASE wraps automatically are broken by *soft carriage returns,* which do not show any symbol at the right edge of the screen.

Lines that are broken by soft carriage returns are treated as single command lines when the program is running. Any lines broken by hard carriage returns are considered two separate commands. If a single command line is broken with a hard carriage return, a semicolon character must end the top line. When you use the semicolon to break lines, be sure to place at least one space between words. For example, the command below will not work, because there is no space between FOR and City:

```
LIST CustNo, LName, FName, Company FOR;
City = "San Diego"
```

However, either of these two versions will work because of the inserted space:

```
LIST CustNo, LName, FName, Company FOR ;
City = "San Diego"
```

or

```
LIST CustNo, LName, FName, Company FOR;
 City = "San Diego"
```

### Printing Command Files

To print a hard copy of a file created with the MODIFY COMMAND editor, exit the editor so that the dot prompt reappears. Then use the TYPE command with the TO PRINT option to print the file. For example, if you use the command **MODIFY COMMAND MyProg** to create and edit a file, the commands

```
TYPE MyProg.prg TO PRINT
EJECT
```

will print a copy of the program on the printer.

## The NOTE, *, and && Commands

The NOTE, *, and && commands serve exactly the same purpose in a command file: they define a line as a programmer comment to be ignored by the dBASE interpreter.

### SYNTAX

**NOTE <any text>**
*** <any text>**
**<dBASE command> && <any text>**

where <any text> is any information you wish to place in a program as a note to yourself or other programmers, and <dBASE command> is any dBASE command and accompanying parameters that precede the && command.

### USAGE

NOTE and * define an entire line, beginning in the leftmost column of a command file, as a comment. The && command marks in-line comments to the right of an existing command.

### EXAMPLE

In the example below, only the command ExtPrice = Qty * U_Price is actually processed by dBASE:

```
NOTE: ExtPrice is the extended price of the transaction.
        * Qty is the Quantity, U_Price is unit price.
ExtPrice = Qty * U_Price        && Calculate extended price
```

### TIPS

Use programmer comments liberally in your programs to aid in debugging and later modifications.

## USER-INTERFACE COMMANDS

The ACCEPT, INPUT, WAIT, and READ commands halt program execution and allow the user to input data. The program can then respond to these user inputs or store the information from these inputs in memory variables for later use. (Memory variables are discussed in detail in Chapter 6 "Memory Variables.") The ACCEPT, INPUT, and WAIT commands are discussed in the following sections; the @...SAY...GET...READ commands are discussed in Chapter 8, "Managing Screen Displays."

The INKEY() and READKEY() functions also accept user input from the screen, but they are used only for special cases. They are discussed in Chapter 17, "dBASE Functions." In addition, the ON command responds to user inputs without disrupting the flow of a program; again, it is used only for special situations. See Chapter 19, "Event Processing and Error Trapping," for details on the ON command.

## The ACCEPT Command

The ACCEPT command presents a prompt on the screen and waits for the user to respond by typing some text and pressing the Return key. Whatever the user types is stored in a memory variable.

### SYNTAX

**ACCEPT [<prompt>] TO <memory variable>**

where <prompt> is optional and <memory variable> is the name of the character memory variable that will store the user's entry.

### USAGE

Use ACCEPT to present a prompt to the user and wait for a response. (Although technically the prompt is optional, it is generally included.) The user's response is stored in a memory variable of the character data type. The data stored in the memory variable can be from 1 to 254 characters in length.

If the user presses the Return key without typing any characters, the stored memory variable has an ASCII value of zero and a length of zero. For example, if the user presses Return in response to the command

**ACCEPT "Enter your name " TO Name**

ASC(Name) will be zero, and LEN(Name) will also be zero. The statement IF LEN(Name) = 0 will evaluate to true (.T.) in this case.

#### PROGRAMMING THE PROMPT

The optional prompt can be surrounded by quotation marks, apostrophes, or brackets. The examples below are equivalent:

**ACCEPT "Enter your name " TO Name**

```
ACCEPT 'Enter your name ' TO Name
ACCEPT [Enter your name ] TO Name
```

To embed an apostrophe or other character in the prompt, just use different characters for the outside delimiters:

```
ACCEPT "What's your name " TO Name
```

The prompt itself can be stored in a memory variable. In the example below, the variable Prompt is assigned a character string. That character string is then used in the ACCEPT command as the prompt to display on the screen:

```
Prompt = "What is your name? "
ACCEPT Prompt TO Name
```

A macro can be placed anywhere in the prompt. For example, the first command line below creates a bent arrow similar to the Return key symbol on IBM keyboards and stores the symbol in a variable named Ret. To show the bent-arrow symbol inside of the prompt, use macro substitution with the variable name, as in the second line below:

```
Ret = CHR(17) + CHR(196) + CHR(217)
ACCEPT "Enter your name, then press &Ret " TO Name
```

## Handling the User's Entry

The character data that the user types in response to the ACCEPT prompt can be treated as any other character string memory variable. For example, in the routine below, the ACCEPT command asks for the name of a database file to open and stores the answer in a memory variable named FileName. Then the routine adds the extension .dbf to the contents of the FileName variable. Next, an IF clause checks whether the requested file exists. If it does, the USE command opens the appropriate data file. Otherwise, the ELSE portion of the IF clause displays a message indicating that no database file with the requested file name exists:

```
* - - - - - - - - - - Ask for name of file to open.
ACCEPT "Enter name of file to use " TO FileName

* - - - - - - - - - Add .dbf extension to file name.
FileName = FileName + ".dbf"

* If file exists open it, else display a message.
IF FILE(FileName)
      USE &FileName
```

```
ELSE
     ? "Can't find file named",FileName
ENDIF
```

## EXAMPLE

The command line

**ACCEPT "Enter your name " TO Name**

displays the prompt **Enter your name** on the screen and waits for the user to type in some text and press Return. Whatever the user types before pressing the Return key is stored in the variable Name as a character string.

## TIPS

Any data entered via the ACCEPT command can be used for macro substitution.

ACCEPT will work with character strings of any length up to 254 characters. To restrict the size of the memory variable character string, use the @...READ command combination instead.

To convert the character data entered via the ACCEPT command to numeric or date data, use the VAL or CTOD functions.

To detect whether the user pressed Return without entering any text in response to the ACCEPT command prompt, check for either a length greater than zero, an ASCII value greater than zero, or a null string (""). In the example below, the IF clause returns control to a main menu when the user presses Return without entering any text or numbers. (The expressions within the IF clause are redundant and are used only to display the three options. In your own programs, you can use any one of these expressions to test for an empty character string.)

```
ACCEPT "Enter your choice " TO Answer
* If user pressed only Return, branch to main menu.
IF LEN(Answer) = 0 .OR. ASC(Answer) = 0 .OR. Answer = ""
     RETURN TO MASTER
ENDIF
```

## SEE ALSO

@...READ
INPUT
WAIT

# The INPUT Command

The INPUT command presents a message on the screen and waits for the user to enter some data and press the Return key. The data entered via the INPUT command is assumed to be numeric unless it is enclosed in quotation marks.

### SYNTAX

**INPUT [<prompt>] TO <memory variable>**

where <prompt> is an optional character string enclosed in double or single quotation marks or brackets and <memory variable> is any valid memory variable name.

### USAGE

INPUT is usually used to request numeric data from the user. The optional prompt can be enclosed in double quotation marks, apostrophes, or brackets. Hence, each of the three commands below is identical:

```
INPUT "Enter your age " TO Age
INPUT 'Enter your age ' TO Age
INPUT [Enter your age ] TO Age
```

To embed an apostrophe or other character in the prompt, use different characters for the outside delimiters, as in the example below:

```
ACCEPT "What's your age " TO Age
```

The prompt can be stored in a memory variable. In the example below, the variable named InPrompt is assigned a character string. The INPUT command then displays the contents of the InPrompt memory variable as the prompt on the screen:

```
InPrompt = "What is your name? "
ACCEPT InPrompt TO Name
```

A macro can be substituted directly into the prompt. For example, the first command line below creates a bent arrow similar to the Return key symbol on IBM keyboards and stores the symbol in a variable named Ret. To show the bent-arrow symbol inside the prompt, use macro substitution with the variable name, as in the second line below:

```
Ret = CHR(17) + CHR(196) + CHR(217)
INPUT "Enter your age, then press &Ret " TO Age
```

To enter nonnumeric data in response to the INPUT command, a user must enclose the entry in quotation marks. For example, consider the prompt below:

**INPUT "Enter your name " TO Name**

The user must type "Smith", including the quotation marks, or dBASE will display the error message "Variable not found" and redisplay the prompt. For this reason, the ACCEPT and @...READ commands are better than the INPUT command for accepting nonnumeric data from the screen.

If the user presses Return in response to the prompt INPUT displays without first entering some data, dBASE will reject the entry and redisplay the prompt until the user types in a value.

## EXAMPLE

The command below displays the prompt **What's 5 + 5?** and waits for the user to enter an answer:

**INPUT "What's 5 + 5? " TO Answer**

The answer is stored in a numeric variable named Answer.

## TIPS

To limit the user's entry to a range of numbers via the INPUT command, initialize the variable in the TO portion of the command to some number outside the desired range, then place the INPUT command inside a DO WHILE loop that repeats as long as the number is out of range. In the example below, the INPUT command accepts only numbers in the range of 1 to 5.

```
* - - - - - - -- Initialize numeric variable Choice.
Choice = 0
* - - - - - - - - - -- Restrict Choice to range 1-5.
DO WHILE Choice < 1 .OR. Choice > 5
     INPUT "Enter choice (1-5) : " TO Choice
ENDDO
```

A slightly more sophisticated version of the above routine sounds a beep and displays an error message when an out-of-range number is entered, as shown below:

```
* - - - - - - -- Initialize numeric variable Choice.
Choice = 0
* - - - - - - - - - -- Restrict Choice to range 1-5.
DO WHILE Choice < 1 .OR. Choice > 5
     @ 9,0
```

```
        INPUT "Enter choice (1-5) : " TO Choice
        IF Choice < 1 .OR. Choice > 5
            @ 23,1 SAY CHR(7) + "Acceptable range is 1 to 5!"
        ENDIF
    ENDDO
    CLEAR
```

The @...READ commands provide yet greater control over the size, decimal portion, and appearance of the number entered by the user.

### SEE ALSO

@...READ
ACCEPT
WAIT

## The WAIT Command

The WAIT command suspends processing of a program and waits for the user to press any key. It accepts only a single keystroke and does not require the Return key to be pressed.

### SYNTAX

**WAIT [<prompt>] TO [<memory variable>]**

where both the <prompt> and <memory variable> are optional.

### USAGE

When the WAIT command is used alone in a command file, it presents the message **Press any key to continue** on the screen and delays processing until the user presses any key. The user's keypress is not stored in any field or variable.

If the programmer specifies a prompt, either enclosed in double or single quotation marks or in brackets, the WAIT command displays that prompt in lieu of the default prompt. For example, each of the WAIT commands below displays the message **Press any key to return to menu...**:

```
WAIT "Press any key to return to menu..."
WAIT 'Press any key to return to menu...'
WAIT [Press any key to return to menu...]
```

If you want the WAIT command to pause without presenting any message at all, use a blank as the prompt, as below:

```
WAIT " "
```

If you specify a variable name to store the keystroke in, the keystroke is stored in that memory variable as a character string (regardless of whether the user typed in a letter or number). If the user presses a nonprinting character such as the Return key, the variable is stored as a single ASCII character zero with a length of zero (i.e., ""). For example, the WAIT command below displays the prompt shown in quotation marks and waits for the user to press any key:

```
WAIT "Press a key to return to menu " TO AnyKey
```

Whatever character or number the user presses is stored in the variable named AnyKey as a character string. If the user presses a nonprinting key (such as Return or PgDn), the AnyKey variable contains a null string that has a length of zero and an ASCII value of zero (AnyKey = "", LEN(AnyKey) = 0, and ASC(AnyKey) = 0).

## EXAMPLES

This routine asks the user whether he or she wishes to continue with some task. If the user presses the letter N, the IF clause returns control to the calling program:

```
WAIT "Do you wish to continue? (Y/N) " TO YesNo
IF UPPER(YesNo) = "N"
    RETURN
ENDIF
```

## TIPS

To restrict the user's entry to a particular group of letters (for example, the letters A through F, and X), initialize the variable used in the TO portion of the command to a blank, and place the WAIT command in a DO WHILE loop that repeats as long as letters outside of the desired group are entered. In the example below, the WAIT prompt will reappear until the user enters one of the letters A, B, C, D, E, F, or X:

```
Choice = " "
DO WHILE .NOT. UPPER(Choice) $ "ABCDEFX"
    WAIT "Enter your choice (A-F or X) " TO Choice
ENDDO
```

A more sophisticated version of the above routine displays an error message until the user enters one of the appropriate letters:

```
Choice = " "
DO WHILE .NOT. UPPER(Choice) $ "ABCDEFX"
```

```
        @ 9,0
        WAIT "Enter your choice (A-F or X) " TO Choice
        IF .NOT. UPPER(Choice) $ "ABCDEFX"
            @ 23,1 SAY CHR(7) + "Must be in the range A-F or X"
        ENDIF
    ENDDO
    CLEAR
```

To detect whether the user pressed Return or another nonprinting key, check the length or ASCII value of the keypress. In the example below, the WAIT command stores the user's keypress in a variable named KeyPress. If the user presses a nonprinting key, the program returns control to the main menu program. This example redundantly demonstrates all three techniques for detecting the empty character string; you need use only one of the methods shown in the IF condition:

```
* - Create Return key symbol for WAIT prompt.
Ret = CHR(17) + CHR(196) + CHR(217)
* - Pause for user to press any key.
WAIT "Enter your choice, 1-5 or &Ret to exit: " TO Choice

* - If nonprinting key pressed, return to main menu.
IF LEN(Choice) = 0 .OR. ASC(Choice) = 0 .OR. Choice = ""
    RETURN TO MASTER
ENDIF
```

### SEE ALSO

ACCEPT
INPUT
@...READ
INKEY()
ON KEY
READKEY()

## The Looping Commands

dBASE offers a single command structure for setting up loops in a program: the DO WHILE...ENDDO commands with the associated EXIT and LOOP commands.

## The DO WHILE...ENDDO Commands

The DO WHILE...ENDDO commands are used to construct repetitive (*iterative*) loops in a program. As long as the condition that repeats the loop is true, all commands between the DO WHILE and ENDDO commands are executed repeatedly. When the looping condition becomes false, processing continues at the first command beneath ENDDO.

### SYNTAX

```
DO WHILE <condition>
    <commands...>
    [LOOP]
    [EXIT]
    <commands...>
ENDDO
```

where <condition> is a logical statement that determines the condition under which the loop should continue repeating. The <commands...> are any commands to be repeated within the loop. The LOOP and EXIT commands are optional and are used to exit the loop before all the commands within the loop are executed. The ENDDO command is required; it marks the end of the commands to be repeated within the loop.

### USAGE

The DO WHILE loop is one of the most frequently used structures in dBASE programming. A loop tells dBASE to repeat a series of commands as long as a certain condition exists. The DO WHILE command marks the start of the loop, and the ENDDO command marks the end of the loop. For an example of a simple loop illustrating the DO WHILE...ENDDO commands, see the section "Looping" earlier in this chapter.

If the DO WHILE condition is not true upon entering the loop, the loop will not be processed at all. For example, in the routine below, the variable Mem_LName is initialized as 25 blank spaces. The DO WHILE loop immediately beneath states that the loop is to be repeated only as long as Mem_LName is not a blank:

```
Mem_LName = SPACE(25)

DO WHILE Mem_LName # " "
    @ 2,10 SAY "Enter name to look for " GET Mem_LName
    READ
```

```
        <more commands...>
    ENDDO
```

Because Mem_LName is a blank before the loop begins, dBASE ignores all commands between the DO WHILE and ENDDO commands. To execute a loop that is set up to terminate when a character field is blank, you must assign a dummy value to the variable above the loop and then reset the variable to a blank value inside the loop, as below:

```
Mem_LName = "X"          && Temporary dummy value

DO WHILE Mem_LName # " "
    Mem_LName = SPACE(20)
    @ 2,10 SAY "Enter name to look for " GET Mem_LName
    READ
    <more commands...>
ENDDO
```

In the above example, the commands beneath the READ command will be processed no matter what the user types in as the value for Mem_LName. In some situations, you might want dBASE to skip over the commands beneath the READ command if the user does not enter a value for Mem_LName (that is, if the user just presses Return without typing in a value). To do so, use the LOOP command within an IF clause to pass control back to the DO WHILE command so that the looping condition can be reevaluated. The routine below shows an example:

```
Mem_LName = "X"          && Temporary dummy value

DO WHILE Mem_LName # " "
    Mem_LName = SPACE(20)
    @ 2,10 SAY "Enter name to look for " GET Mem_LName
    READ

    *- If user presses only Return, pass control to DO WHILE.
    IF Mem_LName = " "
        LOOP
    ENDIF

    <more commands...>
ENDDO
```

As an alternative to the structure above, you could have the IF clause pass control to the first command outside of the DO WHILE loop (the first command beneath the ENDDO command). To do so, use the EXIT command in place of the LOOP command, as below:

```
Mem_LName = "X"          && Temporary dummy value

DO WHILE Mem_LName # " "
     Mem_LName = SPACE(20)
     @ 2,10 SAY "Enter name to look for " GET Mem_LName
     READ

     *- If user presses only Return, get out of loop.
     IF Mem_LName = " "
          EXIT
     ENDIF

     <more commands...>
ENDDO
```

### EXAMPLES

In this section, four different uses of the DO WHILE loop are demonstrated. Numerous other examples appear throughout the book.

#### LOOPING THROUGH RECORDS

One of the most common programming constructs is the DO WHILE .NOT. EOF() loop, which repeats until the record pointer is beyond the last record in the currently open database. In the example below, the routine positions the record pointer at the first record in the currently open database (GO TOP). The loop condition repeats all commands between the DO WHILE and ENDDO commands until the record pointer is past the last record in the database:

```
GO TOP
DO WHILE .NOT. EOF()
     ? PartNo, PartName
     ? Qty,U_Price,(Qty*U_Price)
     SKIP
ENDDO
```

Within the DO WHILE loop, the ? command displays the fields PartNo, PartName, Qty, and U_Price from a single record, as well as the extended price (Qty * U_Price). The SKIP command moves the pointer to the next record in the database.

If the SKIP command were excluded, the DO WHILE loop above would simply redisplay the first record from the database forever. The SKIP command moves the record pointer to the next record in the database, ensuring that dBASE eventually reaches the end of the database file (EOF()), which in turn terminates the loop.

### LOOPING TO VALIDATE DATA

In the routine below, the user must enter the letter A, B, C, D, or X. Otherwise, the error message appears on the screen and the READ command requests the user to reenter a value for the Choice variable:

```
* - - - - - - - -- Get a value for Choice.
Choice = " "
@ 20,25 SAY "Enter choice (A-D or X) " ;
     GET Choice PICTURE "!"

* - - - - - - - -- Insist on A-D or X.
DO WHILE .NOT. Choice $ "ABCDX"
     READ
     * -- Print error message if not acceptable.
     IF .NOT. Choice $ "ABCDX"
          @ 23,1 SAY CHR(7) + "Please try that again!"
     ENDIF
ENDDO
CLEAR
```

Notice that the Choice variable is initialized as a single blank. The user is then prompted to type in a new value for Choice. (The PICTURE "!" command converts the single character the user enters to uppercase.)

The READ command is placed inside the DO WHILE loop (which will repeat as long as Choice is not an A, B, C, D, or X). If the user's entry is not A, B, C, D, or X, the IF clause causes the computer to beep (CHR(7)) and display the error message **Please try that again!**, then the DO WHILE loop repeats, and the READ command again waits for the user's entry.

If the user does enter an A, B, C, D, or X, both the IF and DO WHILE conditions are false, so no error message is displayed and the loop does not repeat. Instead, processing continues at the CLEAR command beneath the ENDDO command. For more on error trapping and validation techniques, see Chapter 19, "Event Processing and Error Trapping."

### LOOPS IN MENUS

Another common application of the DO WHILE loop is to redisplay a menu until the user selects an option to exit the menu. Figure 4.8 earlier in this chapter demonstrates such a menu program.

### THE DO WHILE LOOP AS A TIMER

You can also use the DO WHILE loop to act as a timer or pause. You'll need to extract the seconds from the current system time, convert that string to a number, and add the number of seconds that you want to pause to this value. Store this number in a memory variable. Then create an empty DO WHILE loop that repeats until the number of seconds in the current time catches up with the number of seconds stored in the memory variable.

In the example below, the loop pauses for ten seconds:

```
CLEAR
? "Timing......"

* - - Set up finish time (10 seconds from now).
Done = VAL(RIGHT(TIME( ),2)) + 10
Done = (IIF(Done<60, Done, Done -60))

* - - Loop until seconds = Done.
DO WHILE VAL(RIGHT(TIME( ),2)) # Done
     @ 1,70 SAY TIME( )
ENDDO

? "Time is up!"
```

In the example above, a running clock is displayed on row 1, column 70 of the screen. If you do not want this clock displayed, remove the command inside the DO WHILE...ENDDO loop.

### NESTED LOOPS

When placing loops inside of loops, be sure that each DO WHILE loop has an ENDDO associated with it. Also, keep in mind that a LOOP or EXIT command operates only on the loop at its own nesting level. An example of a command file with nested loops appears in Figure 4.12. The output from this program is shown in Figure 4.13.

Notice the structure of the nested loops in this program. In English (or pseudocode), the structure appears as follows:

```
Set starting value for outer loop
DO WHILE command for outer loop
     <commands...>

     Set starting value for inner loop
```

```
****************************************** Nested.prg.
*--------------------------- Demonstrate nested loops.
SET TALK OFF
CLEAR
*--------- Set beginning value for outer loop.
OutLoop = 1
DO WHILE OutLoop <= 5
   ? "Outer loop = ",OutLoop
   ?
   ?
   *----- Set beginning value for inner loop.
   InLoop = 1
   DO WHILE InLoop <= 40
      ?? TRANSFORM(InLoop,"##")
      *------- Increment inner loop counter.
      InLoop = InLoop + 1
   ENDDO (InLoop)
   *--------- Increment outer loop counter.
   OutLoop = OutLoop + 1
ENDDO (OutLoop)
?
? "All done"
```

**FIGURE 4.12:** Sample program with nested loops. Indentations and comments next to the ENDDO commands help make the nesting more visible. In this example, the outer loop repeats 5 times, and the inner loop repeats 40 times within each outer loop.

```
Outer loop =          1

 1 2 3 4 5 6 7 8 910111213141516171819202122232425262728293031323334353637383940

Outer loop =          2

 1 2 3 4 5 6 7 8 910111213141516171819202122232425262728293031323334353637383940

Outer loop =          3

 1 2 3 4 5 6 7 8 910111213141516171819202122232425262728293031323334353637383940

Outer loop =          4

 1 2 3 4 5 6 7 8 910111213141516171819202122232425262728293031323334353637383940

Outer loop =          5

 1 2 3 4 5 6 7 8 910111213141516171819202122232425262728293031323334353637383940


All done

. _
```

**FIGURE 4.13:** Output from the nested loop program shown in Figure 4.12. The outer loop repeated 5 times. Within each outer loop, the inner loop displayed the numbers 1 through 40 across the screen.

```
    DO WHILE command for inner loop
        <commands...>
        Increment counter for inner loop
    ENDDO for inner loop

    Increment counter for outer loop
ENDDO for outer loop
```

All nested loops must have a similar structure. Chapter 7, "Debugging Commands and Techniques," discusses debugging techniques that will help you avoid and find improperly nested loops. For examples of programs using nested loops to calculate subtotals in printed reports, see Chapter 9, "Printing Formatted Reports."

## TIPS

You can use macro substitution anywhere within the body of a DO WHILE loop. However, you must be careful when using a macro in the condition of the DO WHILE command. A macro is acceptable in the WHILE condition as long as the name of the field or variable in the macro does not change within the DO WHILE loop. That's because dBASE will perform the macro substitution only once before beginning the loop.

In the following example, notice that the variable named LoopCond is defined above the loop and is then used as a macro in the DO WHILE condition. Within the loop, no commands alter the contents of the LoopCond variable, so the &LoopCond macro in the condition of the DO WHILE command is acceptable:

```
USE Sample INDEX Names
LoopCond = 'LName = "Smith"'

FIND Smith
DO WHILE &LoopCond
    ? TRIM(FName),LName
    ? Address
    ? TRIM(City) + ", " + State,Zip
    SKIP
ENDDO (LoopCond)
```

If you place a RETURN command within a DO WHILE loop, the loop may still affect processing, even though control returned to the calling program. To avoid this, place the RETURN command beneath the ENDDO command. If necessary, you can use the EXIT or LOOP command from within the loop to exit the loop.

#### SEE ALSO

LOOP
EXIT

## The LOOP Command

LOOP passes control within a DO WHILE loop back to the top of the loop. The looping condition is reevaluated before repeating the loop.

#### SYNTAX

**LOOP**

#### USAGE

LOOP is an optional command used to pass control back to the current DO WHILE command. It prevents a series of commands within a loop from being processed unnecessarily. It can be used only inside an IF...ENDIF or DO CASE...ENDCASE clause.

#### EXAMPLE

In the sample routine shown in Figure 4.14, the READ command waits for the user to enter a person's last name and stores that entry in a variable named Search. If the user enters a name, the SEEK command attempts to find the name and the IF clause that follows responds accordingly. However, if the user presses Return without typing a last name to search for, the LOOP command passes control back to the top of the DO WHILE loop, ignoring the SEEK command and IF clause altogether (and terminating the **DO WHILE Search # " "** loop in this example as well).

#### SEE ALSO

EXIT
IF...ENDIF
DO CASE...ENDCASE
DO WHILE...ENDDO

```
*--- Sample program to demonstrate the LOOP command.
USE AnyFile INDEX LastName

Search = "X"
DO WHILE Search # " "
   Search = SPACE(20)
   @ 5,5 SAY "Enter last name to search for ";
   GET Search
   READ

   *---- If no name entered, skip lower commands.
   IF Search = " "
      LOOP
   ENDIF (Search = " ")

   *--- Attempt to find entered name.
   SEEK UPPER(Search)

   *--- If found, edit it.
   IF FOUND()
      EDIT RECNO()
   *--- If not found, display message.
   ELSE
      @ 23,1 SAY "No such person on file!"
   ENDIF (found)

ENDDO (while Search # " ")

RETURN
```

**FIGURE 4.14:** LOOP command in a DO WHILE loop. The program allows the user to repeatedly enter a last name to search for on the database. When the user leaves this name blank, the LOOP command passes control back to the **DO WHILE Search #** " " command, which in turn terminates the loop (and the program, in this example).

# The EXIT Command

The EXIT command passes control to the first line beneath the ENDDO command in a DO WHILE loop and terminates the loop regardless of the DO WHILE condition.

### SYNTAX

**EXIT**

### USAGE

EXIT forces termination of a DO WHILE loop, regardless of the condition stated in the DO WHILE command. Whereas the LOOP command passes control back to the top of the loop, the EXIT command passes control to the first command below the ENDDO command.

## EXAMPLE

Figure 4.15 shows a routine that displays the message **Press Space Bar to stop printer** on the screen and then prints records from the currently open database using a **DO WHILE .NOT. EOF( )** loop. If the user presses the space bar while the program is running, however, the **IF INKEY( ) = 32** command senses this, and the enclosed EXIT command passes control to the SET PRINT OFF command beneath ENDDO.

## TIPS

In most cases, you can build the condition to exit a loop into the DO WHILE command, thereby creating tighter, more structured command files. For example, in Figure 4.15 the IF clause (and EXIT command) can be eliminated altogether by placing the INKEY( ) function in the DO WHILE condition, as shown below:

```
DO WHILE .NOT. EOF( ) .AND. INKEY( ) # 32
    ? Name, Company, Address
    SKIP
ENDDO (not EOF( ))
```

The only difference between the loop above and the one shown in Figure 4.15 is that this one does not react to the space bar keypress until after the SKIP command moves to the next record. In Figure 4.15, the **IF INKEY( ) = 32** command will pass control out of the loop before the SKIP command is processed.

```
*-- Sample program to demonstrate EXIT command.
SET TALK OFF
CLEAR
@ 5,5 SAY "Press Space Bar to stop printer"
SET PRINT ON
SET CONSOLE OFF

DO WHILE .NOT. EOF()
   ? Name, Company, Address
   *--- If space bar pressed, exit the loop.
   IF INKEY() = 32
      EXIT
   ENDIF
   SKIP
ENDDO (not EOF())

*----- Set printer off and screen on.
SET PRINT OFF
EJECT
SET CONSOLE ON
```

**FIGURE 4.15:** A program demonstrating the EXIT command. In this sample program, the **DO WHILE .NOT. EOF( )** loop prints the Name, Company, and Address fields for each record in the database until the end of the file or until the user presses the space bar [INKEY( ) = 32]. If the user does press the space bar, the EXIT command passes control outside of the DO WHILE loop, thereby ending the program.

## Commands Used for Making Decisions

The IF...ELSE...ENDIF and DO CASE...CASE...OTHERWISE...ENDCASE command structures allow a program to make decisions about what step to perform next, based on current information.

## The IF...ELSE...ENDIF Commands

The IF...ELSE...ENDIF clause allows a program to make decisions while it is running. The IF command means the same thing that it does in English: IF *this is the case* THEN *do this* ELSE *do that instead*.

### SYNTAX

**IF <condition>**
    **<commands...>**
**[ELSE]**
    **<commands...>**
**ENDIF**

where <condition> is a valid dBASE logical expression, ELSE is an optional branch to alternative commands, and ENDIF is the command required to close the IF clause. (If you forget to include the ENDIF command, dBASE will not give you any error message. Instead, your program will just behave in a strange and unpredictable manner.)

### USAGE

When dBASE encounters an IF command in a command file, it evaluates the condition as either true or false. What happens next depends on how the IF clause is structured. See the examples below for a demonstration of how to set up IF clauses.

Any text to the right of the ENDIF command is ignored, so you can place programmer comments to the right of an ENDIF command without the leading && characters. (Do leave at least one space between ENDIF and the comment, however.)

### EXAMPLES

In the sample routine below, the ACCEPT command asks whether the user wants to send output to the printer. If the user types in the letter Y, the IF clause sets the printer on. Otherwise, the IF clause does not set the printer on. Either way, processing continues at the CLEAR command beneath the ENDIF command:

```
* - - - - - - - - - - - - - - - - - Ask about printer.
ACCEPT "Send results to printer? (Y/N) " TO YesNo

* -- If user enters Y or y, set the printer on.
IF UPPER(YesNo) = "Y"
     SET PRINT ON
ENDIF (yesno)

CLEAR
```

Note that in the example above, the text (yesno) to the right of the ENDIF command is a programmer comment.

In the following example, the IF clause includes an ELSE command. In this sample routine, the IF condition determines whether the date in a field named Due_Date is more than 90 days past. If the date is not more than 90 days past, the routine prints the message **Thank you**. If the due date is more than 90 days past, the routine prints the message **Please pay immediately!**

```
IF DATE() - Due_Date < = 90
     ? "Thank you"
ELSE
     ? "Please pay immediately!"
ENDIF (due date past 90 days)
```

Again, the text to the right of the ENDIF command is simply a programmer comment.

## Nested IF Clauses

IF clauses can be nested one inside the other as long as each IF command has an ENDIF command associated with it. Nesting IF clauses within one another has a very different effect than stacking IF clauses above one another.

For example, suppose you know the following to be true:

```
LName = "Smith"
State = "CA"
```

In the routine below, the command **? LName,State** prints **Smith** and **CA**, because both IF clauses are true:

```
IF LName = "Smith"
     IF State = "CA"
```

```
            ? LName,State
        ENDIF (state)
    ENDIF (lname)
```

In the next routine, the command **? LName,State** is never encountered, because the outermost IF command evaluates to false. Because the outermost IF clause is evaluated as false, *all* commands between the outermost IF and the outermost ENDIF are completely ignored by dBASE:

```
IF LName = "Jones"
    IF State = "CA"
        ? LName, State
    ENDIF (state)
ENDIF (lname)
```

The effect of nesting one IF clause inside the other is the same as using .AND. in a single IF clause. That is, nesting the IF for the state inside the IF for the last name is the same as using the construction

```
IF LName = "Smith" .AND. State = "CA"
    ? LName, State
ENDIF (LName and State)
```

Another way to view nested IF clauses is in English, as below:

```
IF <this conditions exists>
    <then do these commands...>
    IF <furthermore, this condition also exists>
        <then do these commands as well...>
    ENDIF (inner IF)
ENDIF (outer if )
```

## Stacked IF Clauses

If you *stack* IF clauses rather than nest them, you end up with something more of an "or" relationship between conditions. Suppose dBASE is currently pointing to a database record with the name "Smith" in the LName field and "CA" in the State field. The stacked IF clauses below will print **Smith CA** on the screen, because it is true that LName is Smith and State is CA.

```
IF LName = "Smith"
    ? LName
ENDIF

IF State = "CA"
```

```
    ?? State
ENDIF
```

Now consider this modification of the upper IF clause:

```
IF LName = "Jones"
    ? LName
ENDIF

IF State = "CA"
    ?? State
ENDIF
```

The command **?? State** prints **CA**, but the **? LName** command is never executed, because LName in this example is Smith, not Jones. The important point here is that the two IF clauses are completely independent, because they are stacked one atop the other. In the nested IF clauses above, the innermost IF clause was partially dependent on the outer IF clause surrounding it.

### Macro Substitution

Macro substitution can be used anywhere in an IF command. For example, in the commands

```
Condition = 'State = "CA"'
IF &Condition
```

the IF command becomes

```
IF State = "CA"
```

before being processed. You can also use variables, as in the example below. Note that the ACCEPT command stores the user's entry in a variable named Answer. Then the IF clause checks whether a field (or variable) named State is equal to the user's entry:

```
ACCEPT "Enter a state to list " TO Answer
IF State = Answer
```

## TIPS

An abbreviated form of the IF command is the IIF (immediate IF) function, which can be used in a command line or even in a column definition in a report format or label format. Chapters 8, "Managing Screen Displays," 9, "Printing Formatted Reports," and 17 "dBASE Functions," discuss the IIF function.

### SEE ALSO

DO CASE
IIF
&(macro substitution)

## The DO CASE...ENDCASE Commands

The DO CASE...CASE...OTHERWISE...ENDCASE construct selects a single course of action from a set of alternatives. It differs from the IF...ENDIF clause in that you can list many mutually exclusive options between the DO CASE and ENDCASE commands.

### SYNTAX

```
DO CASE
    CASE <condition>
        <commands...>
    [CASE <condition>
        <commands...>]
    [OTHERWISE
        <commands...>]
ENDCASE
```

where any number of CASE commands can be listed between DO CASE and ENDCASE. The OTHERWISE command is optional. A single ENDCASE command is required at the end of every DO CASE clause.

### USAGE

The DO CASE clause is used when only one option out of several alternatives is to be selected. As soon as a single CASE statement evaluates to true, dBASE performs all commands between that CASE statement and the next one. From that point on, all other CASE statements are ignored (whether they evaluate to true or not), and processing begins at the first command below the ENDCASE command.

If none of the CASE statements in a DO CASE clause evaluates to true, the commands listed beneath the optional OTHERWISE command are executed. If there is no OTHERWISE command and none of the CASE statements evaluates to true, all commands between DO CASE and ENDCASE are ignored.

Like the DO WHILE...ENDDO and IF...ENDIF constructs, DO CASE clauses can be nested inside one another as long as each clause begins with the DO CASE command and ends with an ENDCASE command.

The DO CASE clause differs from a series of stacked IF clauses, because the alternatives in a DO CASE clause are always mutually exclusive. For example, the variable X below is given a value of 5. Then two stacked IF clauses make decisions about the value of X:

```
X = 5

IF X < 10
    ? "X is less than ten"
ENDIF

IF X = 5
    ? "X is equal to five"
ENDIF
```

The output from the small routine above is

```
X is less than ten
X is equal to five
```

On the surface, the routine below appears to be almost identical (in logic) to the routine above:

```
X = 5

DO CASE

    CASE X < 10
        ? "X is less than ten"

    CASE X = 5
        ? "X is equal to five"

ENDCASE
```

However, the output from this routine is simply **X is less than ten**. Although it is true that X is equal to five, the second CASE statement is never evaluated. In a DO CASE clause, only the first alternative that evaluates to true is processed; all remaining commands and CASE statements up to the ENDCASE command are ignored completely. In other words, the alternatives in the DO CASE clause are mutually exclusive.

## EXAMPLES

The DO CASE clause is usually used to tell dBASE to take an action based on a user's menu selection. Figure 4.8 earlier in this chapter shows an example of a

DO CASE clause used within a sample menu program. Figure 4.7 shows a simple DO CASE clause in a command file.

### TIPS

Use the DO CASE clause in place of nested IF statements where possible, because it is much easier to construct and modify. Do not confuse the stacked appearance of the DO CASE clause with the logic of stacked IF statements. Stacked IF statements are independent, while CASE statements are mutually exclusive.

### SEE ALSO

IF...ELSE...ENDIF

# The Branching Commands

The DO and RETURN commands allow a program to pass control to another program and return control back to the calling program. These commands can also be used in conjunction with the SET PROCEDURE, PROCEDURE, and PARAMETERS commands to pass control to a procedure, as discussed in Chapter 5, "Procedures and Parameters." In addition, these commands can be used in conjunction with the ON command to respond to program errors, as discussed in Chapter 19, "Event Processing and Error Trapping."

## The DO Command

The DO command tells dBASE to perform all of the commands stored in a command file or procedure. It can be entered directly at the dot prompt or used within a command file to call another command file.

### SYNTAX

**DO <program name> [WITH <parameters>]**

where <program name> is the name of a command file with the assumed extension .prg, or a procedure within a procedure file. See Chapter 5 "Procedures and Parameters," for a discussion of procedure files and the optional WITH portion of the command.

## USAGE

The DO command executes all of the commands in a command file or procedure. It cannot call a file that is already open (that is, you cannot call a command file or procedure file recursively in dBASE III PLUS).

If the DO command is entered at the dot prompt, the dot prompt reappears when the command file or procedure is done running. If DO is used as a command in a command file, control returns to the first line beneath the calling DO command when the called program is finished running or when a RETURN command passes control back to the calling program.

Programmers should note that every DO command opens a file, which counts as an open file within the limit of 15 total open files. Therefore, it is quite possible to hit the "Too many files are open" error message through a series of DO commands, even though only a few database and index files are actually open. (Database, index, format, report, and other active files all count as open files.)

When a DO command is entered, dBASE will search only the current disk and directory for the appropriate file. To specify another disk drive, you can use the dBASE SET DEFAULT command, or you can specify the disk drive in the file name. In the example below, dBASE will run the command file named Test.prg on the disk in drive B:

**DO B:Test**

The current directory is assumed, unless another is specified in the file name or with the SET PATH command. In the example below, dBASE runs a program named Test.prg on the directory named PrgFiles on drive C:

**DO C:\PrgFiles\Test**

## EXAMPLES

The command **DO MyProg** first searches for a procedure named MyProg in the currently open procedure file. If no such procedure exists, or if there is no open procedure file, the command searches for a command file named MyProg.prg on disk. If neither a procedure or command file with the correct name can be found, dBASE returns the error message **File does not exist**.

## TIPS

Be sure to read about procedures in Chapter 5, "Procedures and Parameters," to gain complete mastery over the DO command. See Chapter 7, "Debugging Commands and Techniques," for debugging techniques. Also, refer to the various ON commands in Chapter 19, "Event Processing and Error Trapping," to see how the DO command can respond to errors that occur while a program is running.

### SEE ALSO

RETURN
SET PROCEDURE
PROCEDURE
PARAMETERS
ON

## The RETURN Command

The RETURN command passes control back to the line beneath the DO command that called the program. If a command file was called directly from the dot prompt, the RETURN command simply passes control back to the dot prompt. When RETURN is used to terminate a command file, it closes the called command file and subtracts one file from the number of files currently open.

The command RETURN TO MASTER passes control from a called program all the way back to the highest-level program in an application (usually the main menu program). It also closes all open files along the way.

### SYNTAX

**RETURN [TO MASTER]**

where the [TO MASTER] portion of the command is optional.

### USAGE

RETURN is generally used as the last command in a program (or procedure) to pass control back to the calling program, but it can be placed anywhere within a command file. However, you should avoid placing RETURN commands within DO WHILE loops. Forcing a program to return control to a calling program within a DO WHILE loop leaves the looping condition active. Hence, the old loop might still have some effect on the currently running program. In the example below, the RETURN command passes control back to the calling program from within a DO WHILE loop, demonstrating a situation to avoid:

```
DO WHILE .T.
    <commands...>
    IF Choice = "X"
        RETURN
    ENDIF
ENDDO
```

By structuring the loop properly, you not only tighten the routine, but you also ensure that the RETURN command is issued after the loop has run its course. All you have to do is move the IF condition to the DO WHILE condition and drop the RETURN command to beneath the loop, as below:

```
DO WHILE Choice # "X"
    <commands...>
ENDDO
RETURN
```

When there is no elegant way to have control fall naturally out of a loop onto the RETURN command, you can still place the RETURN command outside of the loop and use the EXIT command to force termination of the loop.

## SUMMARY

This chapter discussed all of the basic commands for creating command files and controlling the flow through a command file. For more information related to these topics, consult the following guide.

*For a discussion of general software design and development techniques:*

- Chapter 2, "Software Design and Development"

*For a discussion of procedures and procedure files:*

- Chapter 5, "Procedures and Parameters"

*For more information on memory variables:*

- Chapter 6, "Memory Variables"

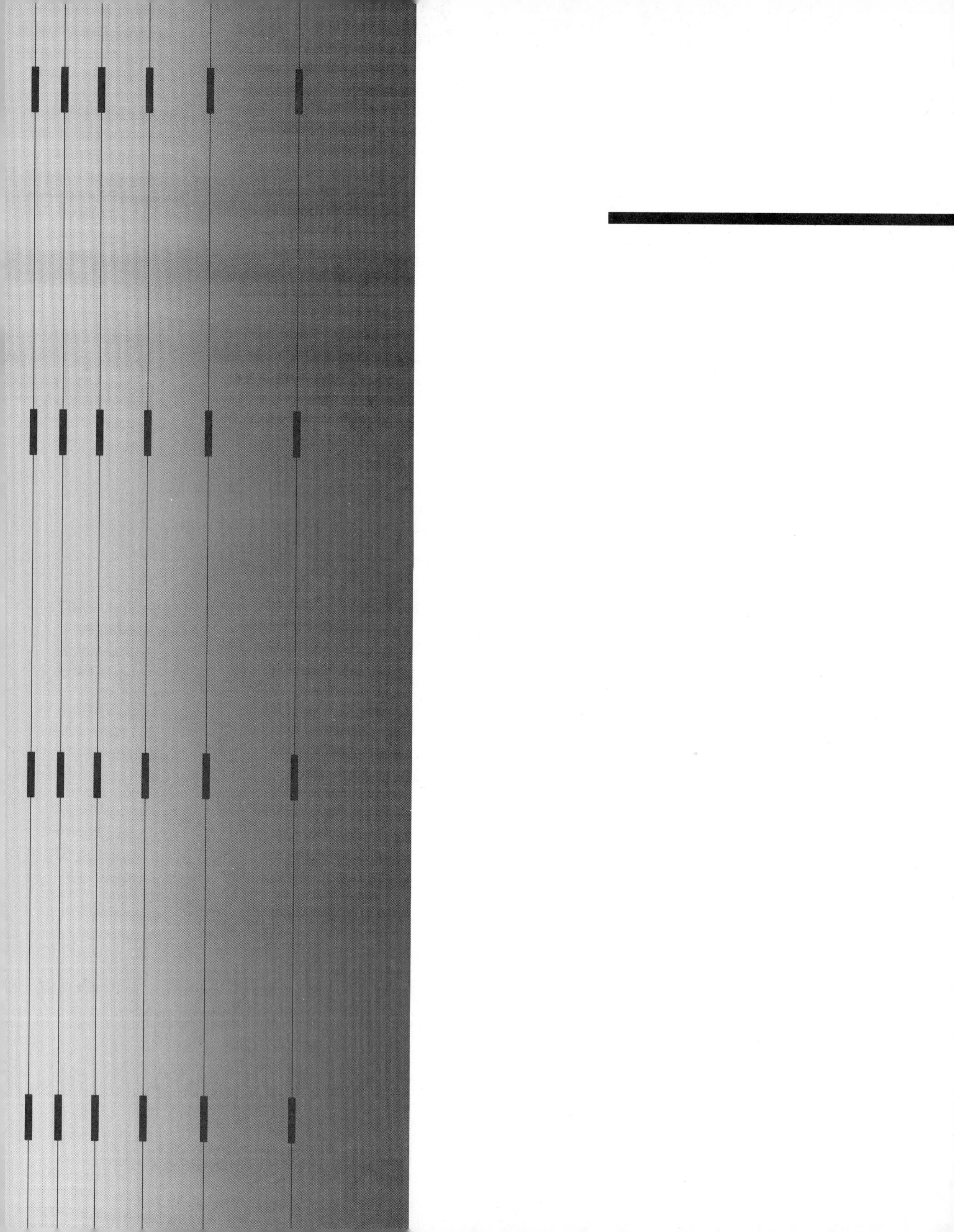

CHAPTER 5

# PROCEDURES AND PARAMETERS

# Procedures and Parameters

This chapter discusses a special type of command file known as a *procedure file*. A procedure file is a single command file that contains small, very specialized programs that are stored in RAM. With the use of *parameter passing* (sending information to and from the procedures), you can develop many custom routines that are easily adapted to many different applications. Over time, you can build up a library of flexible custom routines that will speed the development of your custom applications.

## Working with Procedure Files

Procedure files should contain routines that can be used in many places within an application and even across several applications. Though the procedure itself might require several lines of code, you can easily use it over and over in different programs because it can be accessed with a single command line. The following sections explain how to write, modify, and use these specialized programs.

### Creating Procedure Files

You create a procedure file in the same way that you create a command file: you simply use the MODIFY COMMAND editor or an external word processor. Give your file any name you like, along with the .prg extension. Within the procedure file, each procedure must begin with the PROCEDURE command followed by the name of the procedure. Each procedure must end with the RETURN command, which returns control to the dot prompt or calling program.

If you want to pass parameters to and from a procedure, you must use the PARAMETERS command, which lists the names of the parameters being passed. The PARAMETERS command must be the second command in the procedure, immediately beneath the PROCEDURE command.

Figure 5.1 shows a procedure that calculates the area of any rectangle by multiplying the length by the width. This example command file is named TestProc.prg and can be created with the command **MODIFY COMMAND TestProc**.

```
********************************** TestProc.prg
*---------------------- Sample procedure file.
PROCEDURE CalcArea
PARAMETERS Length,Width,Area
  Area = Length * Width
RETURN
```

**FIGURE 5.1:** The CalcArea procedure in the TestProc procedure file. Like all procedures, this one begins with the PROCEDURE command and ends with the RETURN command. The optional PARAMETERS command is included immediately beneath the PROCEDURE command.

Notice that the name of the procedure is CalcArea and that three parameters are assigned: Length, Width, and Area. The variable Area is calculated by multiplying the length by the width (Area = Length * Width). The procedure ends with the RETURN command.

## Opening Procedure Files

A procedure file needs to be opened before any of the procedures in it can be run. To do so, you must use the SET PROCEDURE command along with the name of the file. For this example, you would enter the command **SET PROCEDURE TO TestProc** at the dot prompt. From this point on, the procedure in the TestProc file is stored in RAM and can be quickly accessed from the dot prompt or any command file.

## Using Procedures and Passing Parameters

To use a procedure, issue the DO command with the name of the procedure. To pass data to and from a procedure, you use the DO command to specify the procedure you want to run and the WITH command to specify the parameters you want to pass. Separate each parameter in the WITH portion of the command by a comma.

When several parameters are used in a procedure, both the sending DO...WITH command and the receiving PARAMETERS command must have exactly the same number of parameters listed. The CalcArea procedure in the previous section specified three variables in its PARAMETERS statement: Length, Width, and Area. Therefore, three parameters need to be sent to the CalcArea procedure.

There are several ways to pass information to and from the procedure. First, of course, the procedure file must be opened with the SET PROCEDURE command. Then variables can be passed from existing memory variables, as in the steps below:

**. X = 5**

```
. Y = 10
. Z = 0
. DO CalcArea WITH X,Y,Z
```

If you now print the value of Z, you get the results of the calculation, as below:

```
. ? Z
        50
```

The variables being passed can have the same name as the variables listed in the PARAMETERS statement, as in the example below (remember that CalcArea includes the parameters Length, Width, and Area):

```
. Length = 20
. Width = 25
. Area = 0
. DO CalcArea WITH Length,Width,Area
. ? Area
        500
```

If you attempt to pass variables that do not exist, dBASE generates an error message, as below:

```
. Do CalcArea with J,K,L
Variable not found
                ?
Do Area with J,K,L
```

You can also pass constants to the procedure. However, any data sent back from the procedure to the dot prompt or calling program must be created first. In this example, the procedure calculates and returns the area in a variable named Area, so you first need to create the memory variable Area and then pass both the numbers and the Area variable, as below:

```
. Area = 0
. DO CalcArea WITH 30,20,Area
```

To see the results, print the current value of the Area variable:

```
. ? Area
        600
```

Calculations can be sent to the procedure too, as shown below:

```
. Area = 0
. DO CalcArea WITH (27 ^ (1/3)), (5*5), Area
```

Print the results again, as below:

```
. ? Area
        75.00
```

Most importantly, you must *always* send the same number of parameters as there are in the PARAMETERS statement. In the example below, only two variables were sent, so dBASE responded with an error message, wondering where the third parameter was:

```
. L = 100
. W = 277
. DO CalcArea WITH L,W

Syntax error
                                        ?
PARAMETERS Length, Width, Area
```

If you forget to specify any parameters, as in the command **DO CalcArea**, you'll get the cryptic error message shown below:

```
*** Unrecognized command verb.
                        ?
PARAMETERS Length, Width, Area
Called from - C:genprocs.prg
Cancel, Ignore, or Suspend? (C, I, or S) Cancel
```

Press C to terminate the command file and try again; this time remember to specify the appropriate number of parameters with the WITH command.

## Modifying Procedure Files

New procedures can be added easily to a procedure file with the MODIFY COMMAND editor. Before you can change a procedure file, however, you must close it. If you forget to close a procedure file before editing it, dBASE will display the message "File is already open". To close the procedure file, enter the command **CLOSE PROCEDURE** from the dot prompt. Now type **MODIFY COMMAND TestProc** to open the TestProc file. Add the Center procedure to the bottom of the TestProc procedure file (below the RETURN command), so the procedure file looks like Figure 5.2.

The Center procedure uses two parameters: Title (a title to be centered on the screen or printer), and RM (the right margin used to calculate the center). It operates by creating a variable named Pad, which is used to pad the title with leading blanks so that it will be centered. The procedure calculates the width of the Pad variable by dividing the right margin by two (RM/2) and subtracting half the width of the title (LEN(TRIM(Title)/2)) to create a string of spaces.

```
*********************************** TestProc.prg
*---------------------- Sample procedure file.
PROCEDURE CalcArea
PARAMETERS Length,Width,Area
  Area = Length * Width
RETURN

*------------- Center procedure centers any string.
PROCEDURE Center
PARAMETERS Title,RM
  Pad = SPACE((RM/2)-(LEN(Title)/2))
  CTitle = Pad + TRIM(Title)
RETURN
```

**FIGURE 5.2:** TestProc procedure file with new Center procedure. The Center procedure pads a title with enough blank spaces to center it on the screen or printer.

Then the spaces stored in Pad, as well as the original title, are stored in a variable named CTitle.

Once you've entered the new procedure, save the command file with the usual Ctrl-W or Ctrl-End. To use the procedure file again, you must reenter the command **SET PROCEDURE TO TestProc** to open it.

## Passing Public Memory Variables

When a variable is created in a particular procedure, it is *local* to that procedure and will be erased automatically when the RETURN command is executed. To avoid this situation and to allow a memory variable to be passed back to the calling program, you can declare the variable as *public*.

To experiment with local and public memory variables using the Center procedure shown in Figure 5.2, first enter the command **SET TALK OFF** so that dBASE does not display any extraneous messages. Then type

**DO Center WITH "Sample Title",80**

This command tells dBASE to do the Center procedure, using the title **Sample Title** and a right margin of 80. When the dot prompt reappears, enter the command **? CTitle** to view the centered title. You'll notice that you get an error message, indicating that there is no variable named CTitle. Because CTitle is a local variable, it was erased when the RETURN command was issued from the procedure. To keep the CTitle variable from being erased, you need to make it public. To do so, type **PUBLIC CTitle**. Now the CTitle variable will always be available. Once again, enter the command

**DO Center WITH "Sample Title",80**

When the dot prompt reappears, enter the command **? Ctitle** to see the title centered on the screen.

When you make a memory variable public, you make it readily accessible throughout all levels of a system of programs. The procedure files in the following chapters (particularly Chapter 24 "Algorithms to Extend dBASE") use public memory variables as a means of making the procedures more accessible, thereby making it easier to integrate these procedures into custom software systems.

## Procedure File Limitations

There are a few limitations to keep in mind when creating and working with procedure files. First, a single procedure file can contain a maximum of 32 procedures. Procedure names can contain a maximum of eight characters, no spaces or punctuation allowed, and must begin with a letter (A–Z).

Only one procedure file can be open at any given time. If a procedure file is already open when you issue a SET PROCEDURE command, the currently open procedure file will be closed before the new one is opened. To see whether a procedure file is currently open at any given time, enter the command **DISPLAY STATUS** at the dot prompt. If a procedure file is open, its name will be displayed along with the other information displayed by this command.

The MODIFY COMMAND editor can handle a maximum of about 5,000 characters in any command file or procedure file. Therefore, very large procedure files are best created with external word processors or text editors such as WordStar or WordPerfect.

## Moving Procedures among Files

As your collection of procedures grows, you may find that different applications can use different procedures. You'll want to be able to "mix-and-match" your procedures into various procedure files. The best way to do so is to treat individual procedures as blocks of text and move them from file to file.

For example, suppose you have a procedure file named Inventry.prg that contains several procedures used in a custom inventory system you've developed. One of the procedures, named NumCheck, would be useful in your new accounts receivable system. How do you move the NumCheck procedure from the Inventry procedure file into your new AR procedure file? Here is a suggested technique.

First, create a temporary copy of the Inventry procedure file to work with. For this example, name the file Temp.txt by typing **MODIFY COMMAND Temp.txt**.

Next, read in a copy of the Inventry procedure file by typing **Ctrl-KR** and entering **Inventry.prg** as the name of the file to read in. When the copy of Inventry is on the screen, use the usual Ctrl-Y command to delete lines from the file, leaving only the procedure(s) you wish to copy to the other procedure file. When only the procedures to be copied remain in the Temp file, save the file using Ctrl-W or Ctrl-End.

Next, bring the receiving procedure file (AR in this example) into the editor by typing **MODIFY COMMAND AR**. When the procedure file is on the screen, position the cursor at the place where you want the outside procedures to appear. This can be at the top of the file or between two existing procedures. Next, type **Ctrl-KR** and specify the name of the temporary file (Temp.txt in this example). The outside procedures will be inserted into the current procedure file, starting at the cursor position. To save your work, type the usual Ctrl-W or Ctrl-End commands.

Don't forget the limits of 5,000 characters (with MODIFY COMMAND) and 32 procedures when juggling procedures around. Remember, you can get around the 5,000 character limit by using an external word processor. Furthermore, most word processors have more sophisticated capabilities for moving blocks of text from one file to the next, which makes it much easier to move procedures from file to file.

# COMMANDS USED WITH PROCEDURES

The remainder of this chapter discusses the commands used with procedure files in more technical detail.

## The PROCEDURE Command

The PROCEDURE command marks the beginning of a procedure and assigns a name to the procedure within a procedure file.

### SYNTAX

**PROCEDURE <procedure name>**

where <procedure name> is no more than eight characters long.

### USAGE

Each individual procedure within a procedure file must begin with the PROCEDURE command followed by the name of the procedure. The procedure name must begin with a letter and contain no more than eight characters. Numbers and underscores can be used within the procedure name.

Every procedure in a procedure file must end with a RETURN command, which passes control back to the calling command file or procedure. One procedure can call another within the same procedure file.

When dBASE encounters the PROCEDURE command within a command file that was not loaded with the SET PROCEDURE command, it ignores the command and instead performs a RETURN immediately.

### EXAMPLE

Figure 5.3 shows a procedure file containing two procedures, one named Center and the other named ErrMsg. The name of the procedure file in this example is GenProcs.prg. To open the procedure file and display the error message **No such person on file!** using the ErrMsg procedure, you would enter the following commands:

**SET PROCEDURE TO GenProcs**
**DO ErrMsg WITH "No such person on file!"**

### TIPS

Once a procedure file is opened and a DO command is issued, dBASE scans the names of all procedures. If no such procedure is found, dBASE checks the disk for a command file with the procedure name and the .prg extension. Therefore, if you attempt to call a procedure that is not in the currently open procedure file (or if there is no open procedure file), dBASE will display the error message

**File does not exist**

```
*************************************** GenProcs.prg
*------- Sample procedure file with two procedures.

*-------------- Center procedure centers any string.
PROCEDURE Center
PARAMETERS Title,RM
   Pad = SPACE((RM/2)-(LEN(Title)/2))
   ? Pad + TRIM(Title)
RETURN

*-- ErrMsg procedure beeps, displays error
*-- message, waits for a keypress.
PROCEDURE ErrMsg
PARAMETERS Msg
   @ 22,1 SAY Msg
   ? CHR(7)
   WAIT
   @ 22,1 CLEAR
RETURN
```

**FIGURE 5.3:** Sample procedure file with two procedures. Each procedure begins with the PROCEDURE command and ends with the RETURN command.

### SEE ALSO

SET PROCEDURE
PARAMETERS
DO...WITH
RETURN

## The PARAMETERS Command

The PARAMETERS command assigns variable names to data passed to a procedure. These variable names are local to the procedure (that is, they are known only to the procedure) and are not automatically passed back to the calling program. These local variable names receive their values from those listed in the WITH portion of the DO. . .WITH command.

### SYNTAX

**PARAMETERS <parameter list>**

where <parameter list> is a list of up to seven variable names, each separated by a comma.

### USAGE

The PARAMETERS command must be the first executable command beneath the PROCEDURE command in a procedure (which means only programmer comments can be placed between the PROCEDURE and PARAMETERS commands). The PARAMETERS command assigns local variable names to the data passed to the procedure in a DO...WITH command. The number of parameters passed to a procedure must be the same in the DO...WITH and PARAMETERS commands.

If the variable name in the PARAMETERS statement is the same as a variable name that has already been created in the calling program, the original variable is used and its contents may be altered by the procedure. If the variable name used in the PARAMETERS command is unique and has not already been created, the variable is erased before control is returned to the calling program.

The information passed to a PARAMETERS command through a DO . . . WITH command can be literal data, data stored in variables, or calculated data.

Usually, field names and database names passed as parameters need to be treated as macros within the called procedure. For example, in the DO...WITH command below, ARecs is the name of a database file, and Over90 is the name of a field in that database file:

**DO SumField WITH "ARecs","Over90"**

In the small procedure below, the parameter DBName receives the database name (ARecs), and FldName receives the field name (Over90). Then, using macro substitution, the procedure substitutes the names into the USE and SUM commands:

```
PROCEDURE SumField
PARAMETERS DBName,FldName
    USE &DBName
    SUM &FldName TO GrandTot
RETURN
```

Though usually used with procedures, the PARAMETERS command can also be used in a command file, as long as it is the first executable line in the command file. The command file can be run and parameters passed using the usual DO...WITH command syntax. The only difference is that the command file will take longer to load and execute than a procedure would, because the command file is stored on disk, and the procedure is stored in RAM.

## EXAMPLES

The procedure in Figure 5.4 calculates the monthly payment on a loan using data passed as parameters named Principal, Interest, and Term (where Interest is the annual percentage rate and Term is the number of years). The Pmt parameter is used to store the results of the calculation.

After entering the SET PROCEDURE command to open the procedure file, you can calculate the monthly payment on any mortgage. In the example below, the Pmt = 0 command initializes the variable for storing the calculated payment.

```
*---- Payment procedure calculates
*---- monthly payment on a mortgage.
PROCEDURE Payment
PARAMETERS Principal,Interest,Term,Pmt
  *-- Convert APR to monthly rate.
  Interest = (Interest/12)/100
  *-- Convert years to months.
  Term = (Term*12)
  Pmt = Principal*Interest/(1-1/(1+Interest)^Term)
RETURN
```

**FIGURE 5.4:** Sample procedure that calculates payment on a loan. This procedure accepts four parameters named Principal, Interest, Term, and Pmt. It calculates and returns the payment on the loan in a variable named Pmt.

The DO...WITH command calls the Payment procedure, using a loan with a principal of $200,000.00, an annual interest rate of 12.5%, and a term of 25 years. The ? Pmt command then displays the results of the calculation.

```
Pmt = 0
DO Payment WITH 200000,12.5,25,Pmt
? Pmt
        2180.71
```

#### TIPS

Instead of passing an "empty" variable to a procedure to bring back a value, you can use public memory variables. See the tutorial at the beginning of this chapter and Chapter 6, "Memory Variables," for more information.

#### SEE ALSO

PROCEDURE
SET PROCEDURE
DO...WITH

## The SET PROCEDURE Command

The SET PROCEDURE command loads a procedure file from disk into RAM. Once loaded, all of the procedures within the file are accessible with the DO command.

#### SYNTAX

**SET PROCEDURE TO <file name>**

where <file name> is the name of the procedure file. The .prg file-name extension is assumed unless another is specified.

#### USAGE

One of the biggest advantages of procedure files is speed. A DO command can locate and execute a procedure in RAM far more quickly than it can locate, load, and execute a command file stored on disk.

The SET PROCEDURE command opens a procedure file and makes all procedures within that file accessible. If the SET PROCEDURE command is issued and another procedure file is already open, that procedure file is closed before the new one is opened. Only one procedure file can be open at a time.

A procedure file can have a maximum of 32 procedures within it. Each of these procedures must begin with the PROCEDURE command and the procedure name and end with a RETURN command.

### EXAMPLE

The command **SET PROCEDURE TO GenProcs** searches the disk for a file named GenProcs.prg. If found, the command closes any currently open procedure file, then loads the GenProcs.prg procedure file into RAM.

### TIPS

Programmers should keep in mind that the actual process of loading a procedure file into RAM with the SET PROCEDURE command is relatively slow; only the DO command that calls a procedure is fast. Therefore, when developing a custom application, you'll probably want to issue a single SET PROCEDURE command near the beginning of the main menu program (outside of the loop that displays the main menu). That way, the slower process takes place only once when the user first runs the application.

While you can use the SET PROCEDURE command anywhere within any command file, you should never place it within a procedure file. In dBASE III PLUS version 1.0, using the command SET PROCEDURE within a procedure file can cause the computer to hang up (which means you will need to reboot). In version 1.1, a SET PROCEDURE command within a procedure file causes a "File is already open" error but does not hang up the computer.

The DISPLAY STATUS command displays the name of any currently open procedure file.

### SEE ALSO

PROCEDURE
RETURN
PARAMETERS
DO...WITH

## The CLOSE PROCEDURE Command

The CLOSE PROCEDURE command closes any currently open procedure file.

### SYNTAX

**CLOSE PROCEDURE**

### USAGE

CLOSE PROCEDURE clears an open procedure file from RAM. (It does not affect the permanent disk copy of the procedure file.)

### EXAMPLE

If you attempt to edit an open procedure file with the MODIFY COMMAND editor, you'll get the error message "File is already open". To close the procedure, enter **CLOSE PROCEDURE** and try the MODIFY COMMAND editor again.

### TIPS

The DISPLAY STATUS command displays the name of any currently open procedure file.

### SEE ALSO

CLOSE
CLEAR
SET PROCEDURE

## The DO...WITH Command

The DO...WITH command runs a command file or procedure and passes parameters to it. The PARAMETERS command in the called command file or procedure receives the passed values.

### SYNTAX

**DO <file name> WITH <parameter list>**

where <file name> is the name of the command file or procedure to run and <parameter list> is a list of up to seven parameters, separated by commas, to be passed.

### USAGE

The DO command executes a command file or a procedure. When the command is issued, dBASE checks whether a procedure file has been opened with the SET PROCEDURE command. If it has, dBASE checks whether a procedure with the given file name exists in the procedure file. If it does, dBASE executes that procedure. If no procedure file is open or no procedure with the given file name exists, dBASE checks the directory for a command file with the specified file name and .prg extension. If the command file exists, dBASE executes it. If neither the procedure nor the command file are available, dBASE returns the "File does not exist" error.

The same rules of disk drives and directories that apply to the DO command apply to the DO...WITH command, as discussed in Chapter 15, "Managing Data, Records, and Files."

The WITH portion of the command passes parameters to the PARAMETERS statement in the procedure or command file being executed. The number of items in the PARAMETERS command must match the number of items in the WITH portion of the DO...WITH command. Also, the order of items in the DO...WITH command must match the order of items in the PARAMETERS command. Data in the WITH portion of the command can be literal, variable, or calculated.

## EXAMPLES

In this sample PARAMETERS command, the variable Amount is a numeric data type, Name is a character data type, and Date is a date data type:

```
PARAMETERS Amount, Name, Date
```

In the example below, all three items of information are passed literally. Note that the character data type is enclosed in quotation marks, while the numeric and date data types are not:

```
DO Sample WITH 123.45, "Joe Smith", DATE()
```

In the next example, all three items are passed as variables. Both the LName and Exp_Date fields are assumed to be fields on the currently open database:

```
Salary = 25000
LastName = LName
Date = Exp_Date
DO Sample WITH Salary, LastName, Date
```

The following example shows all data calculated in the WITH portion of the command. This example assumes that LName and FName are fields on the currently open database:

```
DO Sample WITH Hrs*Rate,TRIM(FName) + " " + LName,;
   DATE() - 30
```

If part of a passed parameter is to be enclosed in quotation marks, use a combination of single and double quotation marks to pass the information. In the example below, the PARAMETERS command expects two items of data: a field name (FldName) and a condition (Condition).

```
PROCEDURE Stats
PARAMETERS FldName,Condition
     SET TALK ON
     SUM &FldName FOR &Condition
     AVERAGE &FldName FOR &Condition
     SET TALK OFF
RETURN
```

To add and average the Qty field using only California residents (State = "CA"), you could pass the parameters as below:

```
DO Stats WITH "Qty",'State = "CA"'
```

Note that within the Stats procedure, the passed values are treated as macros. That's because they are actually a part of the command lines SUM and AVERAGE.

## TIPS

Using the DO . . . WITH method of passing information to procedures helps reduce the size and increase the speed of your code by eliminating the need to create and pass a lot of memory variables.

For example, without parameter passing, you might need to perform the following steps to pass four items of information to to a hypothetical command file or procedure named TintBox:

```
Left = 1
Top = 19
Bottom = 23
Right = 79
DO TintBox
```

However, if TintBox were a procedure with a PARAMETERS statement to accept the data, you could perform the same task with a single command, eliminating four unnecessary steps from the process:

```
DO TintBox WITH 1,19,23,79
```

## SEE ALSO

PARAMETERS
DO

SET PROCEDURE
PROCEDURE
PUBLIC

## SUMMARY

This chapter discussed procedures and parameter passing. The techniques covered here will help you to develop general-purpose routines that you can access from different places within a given application. Also, if your procedures are general enough, you'll probably be able to use them in many different applications.

*For more information on public memory variables:*

- Chapter 6, "Memory Variables"

*For examples of powerful, general-purpose procedures that might come in handy in your own work:*

- Chapter 24, "Algorithms to Extend dBASE"

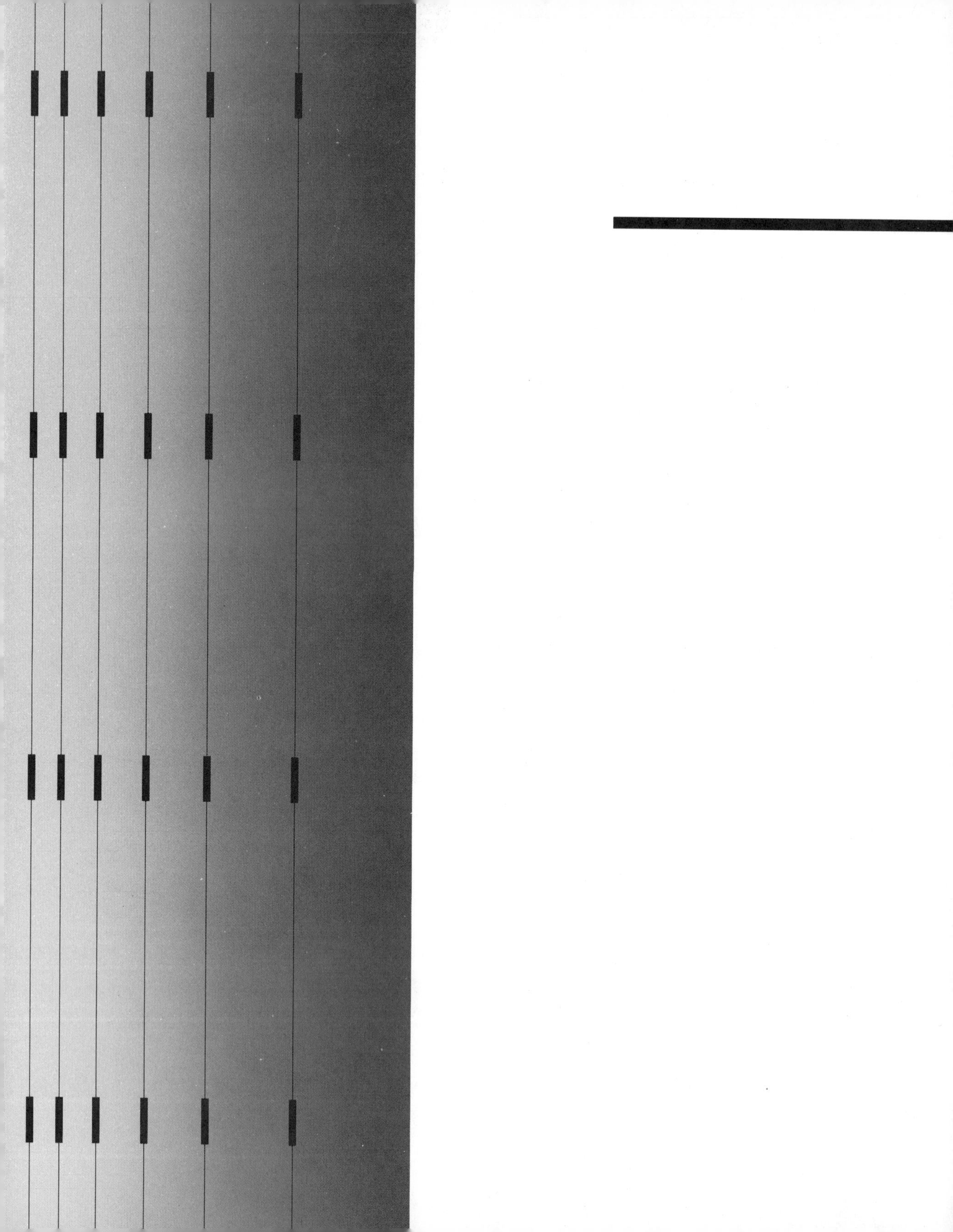

CHAPTER 6

# MEMORY VARIABLES

# Memory Variables

Data stored in a database file are stored on disk. With dBASE III PLUS, you can also store information in the computer's main memory (also called random-access memory or RAM for short). Data stored in RAM are called *memory variables* (or *memvars*). Unlike database data, data stored in memory variables are usually erased as soon as you exit dBASE.

Generally, memory variables are used to store *scratchpad* data, values used temporarily to aid in a calculation or process. This chapter covers the many common uses of memory variables in dBASE programming, as well as the commands that provide for these techniques.

## Creating Memory Variables

There are two ways to create memory variables: you can use either the STORE command or the = (assign) operator. For example, both lines below create a variable named Choice and store the number zero in that variable:

**STORE 0 TO Choice**
**Choice = 0**

### Naming Variables

Memory variable names can be up to ten characters long, must begin with a letter, and can contain numbers and the underscore character. You should be careful not to use the names of dBASE functions or commands as memory variable names, as these might cause problems and confusion. Keep in mind that any dBASE command can be abbreviated to four letters, so you do not want to use even the first few letters of a command.

For example, because you can use the command OTHERWISE within a DO CASE clause, creating a memory variable named Other could cause problems. dBASE would probably accept the command **Other = 123.45** unless it were inside a DO CASE clause. If this command were in a DO CASE clause, dBASE would assume that Other was an abbreviation for OTHERWISE and treat the command and the lines beneath it accordingly. It would not generate an error message, but it would cause the program to behave very strangely.

Incidentally, you should also avoid using commands as field names. For example, if you were to assign the field name Next to a field in the database and then enter the command **LIST Next**, dBASE would consider it an error, because NEXT is a command used with the LIST command, and it requires a number (e.g., LIST NEXT 5 means "display the next 5 records").

## Assigning Data Types

The data types assigned to memory variables can be the same as those assigned to fields, except that there is no memory variable equivalent to the memo field. The data types are discussed in Chapter 1, "Overview of the dBASE Language." They are summarized in Table 6.1.

dBASE assigns data types automatically based on either a reasonable guess or the command used to create the memory variable. Chapter 4, "Command Files" discussed several user-interface commands that create memory variables. These are listed in Table 6.2, along with the data type of the memory variable they create. (The INPUT command can actually store character data, but it is usually used to store numbers.) Other commands, such as COUNT, SUM, and AVERAGE can be used to create numeric variables that are calculated from database data. See Chapter 14, "Calculating Numbers," for information on these commands.

| DATA TYPE | DESCRIPTION |
|---|---|
| Character | Nonnumeric data such as names and addresses |
| Numeric | Numeric values |
| Date | Dates stored in MM/DD/YY format |
| Logical | A value that is either true (.T.) or false (.F.) |

**TABLE 6.1:** The dBASE Data Types

| COMMAND | DATA TYPE OF VARIABLE |
|---|---|
| ACCEPT | Character |
| INPUT | Numeric |
| WAIT | Character |
| READ | Same as existing entry |

**TABLE 6.2:** User-Interface Commands that Create Memory Variables

If you use the STORE command or = operator to create a variable, the data type is assumed from the context. For example, the command **STORE "Smith" TO LName** creates a memory variable named LName of the character data type, containing the name Smith. The command **BotLine = −1234.56** creates a numeric variable named BotLine, with the value −1234.56. The command **Maybe = .T.** creates a logical data type variable named Maybe, which contains true (.T.). The values .t., .Y., and .y. can be entered in place of .T., but dBASE always converts the entry to .T. Similarly, .f., .N., and .n. are all synonymous with .F. and are converted automatically to .F.. Therefore, the expression **YesOrNo = .y.** creates a logical memory variable that contains .T..

The following commands create a date data type:

```
Yesterday = DATE( ) - 1
Today = CTOD("12/31/87")
```

In the first example, Yesterday is the date data type simply because DATE( ) always equals the current date, and its data type is date. In the second example, the data type is date because the CTOD (character-to-date) function converts the character string "12/31/87" to the date data type.

Note that the date data type is a little trickier than the others. If you attempt to create a memory variable of the date data type using the command **Today = 12/01/87**, you'll get a numeric data type with the value 0.14 (the quotient of 12 divided by 1 divided by 87). If you attempt to create the data type by typing **Today = "12/31/87"**, the variable Today will be the character data type because of the quotation marks. Therefore, to create a memory variable of the date data type you must assign existing date data type values to a memory variable, as follows:

```
NinetyAgo = DATE( ) - 90
DeadLine = CTOD("12/01/87")
Date_Hired = Hire_Date
```

In the last example, Hire_Date is assumed to be a date field on the currently open database.

## MANIPULATING DATA TYPES IN VARIABLES

You can convert and mix the data types in memory variables just as you can with database fields. The dBASE functions that convert data types are summarized below:

| | |
|---|---|
| CTOD( ) | Converts character data to date data |
| DTOC( ) | Converts date data to character data |

| | |
|---|---|
| STR( ) | Converts numeric data to character data |
| VAL( ) | Converts character data to numeric data |

In most cases when you want to combine data types, you'll want to convert all of the data to the character type. For example, if you had the memory variables

**Name = "Harry Jones"**
**Age = 33**
**BirthDate = CTOD("06/11/54")**

you could combine them into this single character variable:

**Line = Name + " – Age: " + STR(Age,2) + " DOB: " + ;**
**DTOC(BirthDate)**

The command above creates a single memory variable named Line, which contains

**Harry Jones – Age: 33 DOB: 6/11/54**

Chapter 15, "Managing Data, Records, and Files," demonstrates more techniques for combining data types, and Chapter 17, "dBASE Functions," discusses dBASE functions in depth. Note that the functions discussed in Chapter 17 act on memory variables in the same ways that they act on database fields.

## Using Literals, Variables, and Fields

To avoid confusing variables, literals, and database fields, there are a few rules of thumb to keep in mind. First of all, character literals are always enclosed in quotation marks; literal numbers always begin with a numeric digit, plus or minus sign, or decimal point; and logical literals are always surrounded by periods. Examples of the various literals are shown in Table 6.3. If you look at the examples, you'll see that none could possibly be mistaken for a field or variable name, because a field or variable name must begin with a letter.

| CHARACTER LITERALS | NUMERIC LITERALS | LOGICAL LITERALS |
|---|---|---|
| "123 A St." | –123.45 | .T. |
| "Joe Smith" | .00001 | .Y. |
| "East Bend, IN" | +334456 | .F. |
| 'Say "Hi Ho!" ' | 1234.56 | .N. |

**TABLE 6.3:** Examples of Character, Numeric, and Logical Literals

If a currently active database field has the same name as a currently active memory variable, the field name takes precedence. For example, suppose the currently active database has a field named LName, and that field contains the name "Smith". If you enter the command **LName = "Jones"**, you've just created a memory variable called LName that contains "Jones". (Doing so has no effect on the database field.) However, if you enter the command **? LName**, you'll see Smith, because the field takes precedence over the memory variable.

A quick and easy way around this is to use the M-> alias to specify the memory variable over the field value. For example, the command **? M->LName** will display Jones, because M-> specifies the contents of the memory variable named LName.

### Memory Variable Limitations

At any given time, dBASE allows a maximum of 256 active memory variables, or up to 6,000 bytes (6K) worth. However, you can change the 6K limit to any value between 1K and 31K using the MVARSIZE option in the Config.db file, as discussed in Appendix C, "Configuring dBASE III PLUS."

## Managing Memory Variables

There are five commands that you can use to manage memory variables: DISPLAY MEMORY, RELEASE, CLEAR, SAVE, and RESTORE. The DISPLAY MEMORY command displays the names, data types, and contents of all existing memory variables. The RELEASE command erases memory variables. You can use RELEASE with a specific name (e.g., RELEASE BotLine), with ALL, or with skeletal names. The CLEAR ALL and CLEAR MEMORY commands erase all active memory variables.

The SAVE command saves all active files to a disk file for future use. The RESTORE command retrieves memory variables from disk back into RAM memory. These commands are all discussed in detail in the reference section at the end of this chapter with the exception of the CLEAR command, which is discussed in Chapter 15, "Managing Data, Records, and Files.".

## Macro Substitution

You can use any memory variable of the character data type in a command line by using the macro substitution (&) symbol. For example, suppose you create a memory variable named MyMacro by typing **MyMacro = "AnyText"**. dBASE always checks a command line for macros and substitutes the contents of the macro prior to executing the command. Therefore, if you type **USE**

**&MyMacro**, dBASE will first substitute "AnyText" for &MyMacro and then attempt to open the database file named AnyText.

The command

**REPORT FORM &MyMacro TO PRINT**

will be converted to

**REPORT FORM AnyText TO PRINT**

prior to execution, so the command will print the AnyText.frm report format. The command

**COPY TO &MyMacro DELIMITED WITH BLANK**

will copy records to a delimited ASCII file named AnyText.txt. In the command

**LIST &MyMacro TO PRINT**

the substitution produces

**LIST AnyText TO PRINT**

prior to execution, so the command lists the field named AnyText.

## Including Quotation Marks in Macros

If you want your macro to contain quotation marks, use a combination of single and double quotation marks. For example, note that the command below stores the text enclosed in single quotation marks in a character memory variable named Condition:

**Condition = 'LName = "Smith" .AND. Qty > 100'**

If you were then to enter the command

**LIST FOR &Condition**

dBASE would substitute the Condition variable as shown below:

**LIST FOR LName = "Smith" .AND. Qty > 100**

The command would result in the display of all records with Smith in the LName field and values greater than 100 in the Qty field.

## Placing Macros in Literals

dBASE will even scan literal data and place macros into the literals. For example, the command below combines three graphics characters to produce a bent-arrow symbol similar to that on the Return key on the IBM keyboard:

**BentArrow = CHR(17) + CHR(196) + CHR(217)**

In the command below, the bent arrow will appear at the end of the prompt displayed by the ACCEPT command:

**ACCEPT "Enter your name, then press &BentArrow :" TO Name**

And the screen will display

**Enter your name, then press ↵ :**

## Linking Macros

Two macros can be linked contiguously (with no space in the middle) and still work correctly, as in the following example:

```
Drive = "B:"
FileName = "Contest"
USE &Drive&FileName
```

These commands cause dBASE to open the Contest database on drive B (the macro substitution produces USE B:Contest).

Linking a macro to a literal is a different matter. Look at the commands below, which attempt to open a database named Contest on drive B:

```
Drive = "B:"
USE &DriveContest
```

dBASE cannot find a memory variable named DriveContest, so the command fails. You cannot place a space between the literal and macro, because the substitution would produce USE B: Contest, and dBASE syntax does not allow this space. In a situation such as this, however, you can place a period between the macro and the literal, as below:

```
Drive = "B:"
USE &Drive.Contest
```

dBASE will properly translate this command to **USE B:Contest** before executing it.

# USING PSEUDO ARRAYS

Programmers who are accustomed to programming languages that use arrays (subscripted variables) are usually surprised to find that dBASE offers no equivalent capability. (However, an index file can perform the sorting and searching capabilities of an array.)

If you need a small array of data, you can append subscripts to variable names and access the elements of the array by using macros as the subscripts. The process isn't as quick as it is in a language that supports true arrays, but the basic technique is similar.

For example, the commands below create a small array of 12 month names, Month1 through Month12:

```
Month1 = "January"
Month2 = "February"
Month3 = "March"
Month4 = "April"
Month5 = "May"
Month6 = "June"
Month7 = "July"
Month8 = "August"
Month9 = "September"
Month10 = "October"
Month11 = "November"
Month12 = "December"
```

To convert a number such as 6 to its related month (Month6), you convert the number to a character string (making sure to trim off any leading blanks) and attach the character-string equivalent of the number to the variable name.

For example, the command **MonthNumb = 6** stores the number 6 in a variable named MonthNumb. Then the following command stores the character equivalent of MonthNumb, with leading blanks trimmed off, in a variable named Sub:

```
Sub = LTRIM(STR(MonthNumb))
```

Now if you enter the command

```
? Month&Sub
```

dBASE first performs the macro substitution, converting the command to

```
? Month6
```

Then it executes the command, which displays June, the contents of the Month6 variable.

The routine below demonstrates a loop that can print all 12 months. To do so, it appends the string equivalent of the current loop number to the Month variable name, thereby printing the appropriate month:

```
Counter = 1
DO WHILE Counter < = 12
     Sub = LTRIM(STR(Counter))
```

```
        ? Month&Sub
        Counter = Counter + 1
    ENDDO
```

One of the biggest advantages of the dBASE pseudo arrays is that they allow you to pass an unknown number of parameters to a procedure. You create the array in the calling program, pass the number of elements in the array to the procedure, and let the procedure process each element in the array. The Bar Graph and Lite-Bar Menu routines in Chapter 24, "Algorithms to Extend dBASE," show how this is done.

# PUBLIC, PRIVATE, AND HIDDEN VARIABLES

As a programmer, you need to have a thorough understanding of the three states of memory variables: *public, private,* and *hidden.* First, however, you must understand the terms *lower-level* and *higher-level* programs.

## Lower-Level versus Higher-Level Programs

Any command file or procedure that calls another command file or procedure with a DO command is the higher-level program. The called program, which returns control to the calling program at some point, is the lower-level program.

In the hierarchical diagram shown in Figure 6.1, the program MainMenu.prg is the higher-level program because it calls AddNames.prg with a DO command. After AddNames.prg is called and performs its job, it returns control to the higher-level program, MainMenu.prg, using the RETURN command. These levels are important, because they affect the way memory variables are created and used in command files.

## Private Memory Variables

By default, all dBASE III PLUS variables are private. This means that they are accessible only to the command files that created them and any programs that are at a lower level. A RETURN command erases all variables that were created in the current program. Memory variables that were created in the highest-level program are erased as soon as control is returned to the dot prompt.

In Figure 6.1, any memory variables created in the MainMenu command file are accessible to both MainMenu and AddNew. These variables will not be erased until control is returned to the dot prompt.

However, any memory variables created in AddNew are, by default, private to AddNew and any other lower-level programs or procedures that AddNew might call. As soon as AddNew returns control to MainMenu, the private variables that were created in AddNew are automatically erased.

## Public Memory Variables

Public memory variables are available to programs and procedures at all levels, as well as at the dot prompt. Variables created at the dot prompt are public by default. To create public variables within a command file, you must use the PUBLIC command. The placement of the PUBLIC command in the command file is also important. It must come *before* the variable is assigned a value. To declare the variable named Choice as PUBLIC and to assign it a value of 10, the command **PUBLIC Choice** must occur at some time before the command **Choice = 10** occurs in a command file (or group of command files). Typically, all variables that are to be public in a given application are declared at the top of the highest-level program in the application (usually the main menu program).

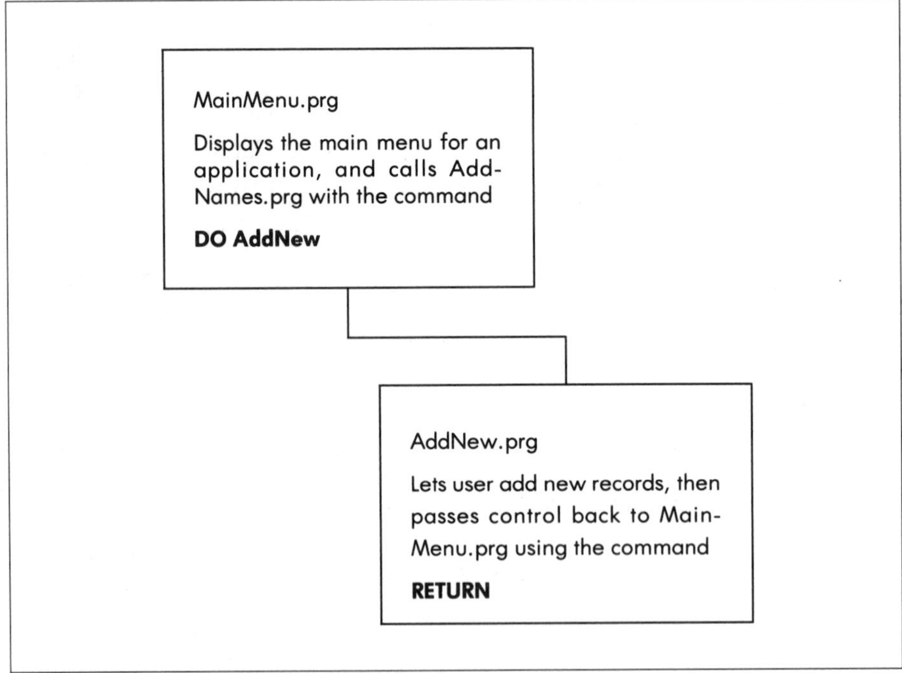


**FIGURE 6.1:** Higher- and lower-level command files. MainMenu.prg calls AddNew.prg with a DO command. Variables created in MainMenu.prg are available to AddNew.prg, because MainMenu.prg is the higher-level program. Variables created in AddNew.prg, on the other hand, are not available to MainMenu.prg, because they are automatically erased when AddNew.prg returns control to MainMenu.prg.

Once a memory variable is declared public, only the RELEASE, CLEAR MEMORY, CLEAR ALL, or QUIT commands will erase the memory variable.

## Hidden Variables

Hidden memory variables are those that have the same names as variables in lower-level programs but are temporarily set aside or hidden while the lower-level programs are running. For example, if a program or procedure issues the command **PRIVATE Counter**, any existing memory variable named Counter in higher-level programs becomes temporarily hidden from any changes made by the current program. When the current program returns control to a higher-level program, the original Counter variable comes out of hiding.

To illustrate, suppose MainMenu.prg (in Figure 6.1) creates a variable named Choice and assigns it a value of 10. Then the lower-level program AddNew.prg declares a private variable named Choice (using the command PRIVATE Choice) and assigns it a value of 1. The Choice variable that was created in MainMenu will be temporarily hidden, while AddNew and any other lower-level programs use the new variable named Choice, with its value of 1. When AddNew returns control to MainMenu, the private Choice variable disappears, and the original Choice variable "comes out of hiding," retaining its original value of 10.

The purpose in all of this is to allow you to create general-purpose programs and procedures that will not affect variable names used in a particular application. For example, in the procedure in Figure 6.2, the variable Counter is used to control a simple DO WHILE loop.

```
*---------- Pause for a few seconds.
PROCEDURE Pause
   *-- Don't disrupt outside Counter variable.
   PRIVATE Counter
   Counter = 1
   *-- Count to 500 to take up time.
   DO WHILE Counter < 500
      Counter = Counter + 1
   ENDDO (counter)
   *-- Counter in calling program will now
   *-- retain its original value, because the Counter
   *-- variable in this procedure is private
   *-- (local) to this procedure.
RETURN
```

**FIGURE 6.2:** Procedure with a private variable. In this example, the command **PRIVATE Counter** creates a unique variable named Counter to be used only in this procedure. When the RETURN command passes control back to the calling routine, the private Counter variable will be erased, and any other variable named Counter will retain its original value.

In this case, any program can call the Pause routine to interrupt processing for a few seconds. When Pause passes control back to the calling program, any variable previously named Counter will have its original value, because Counter was declared private within the Pause procedure. If, on the other hand, Counter had not been declared private in the Pause procedure, the Counter variable would have a value of 500 in the calling program when control was passed back to it, because the DO WHILE loop uses the counter variable to count to 500. This could disrupt the processing of other commands in the calling program that use a variable named Counter.

So the real value of public and private variables is that they allow you to mix-and-match general-purpose procedures within a specific application without having to worry about conflicting variable names.

In some cases, you *will* want the variables created in a lower-level procedure to affect variables at a higher level. Chapter 5, "Procedures and Parameters," discusses how you can use public variables to pass values calculated within procedures back to the calling program.

## Viewing Variables for Debugging

When an error occurs in a program, you are given the options presented below:

**Cancel, Ignore, or Suspend? (C, I, or S)**

If you select the Cancel option by typing C, you'll be returned to the dot prompt. If you then enter the command DISPLAY MEMORY to view the memory variables, you'll find that they've been erased (because canceling a command file has the same automatic memory-erasure effect as a RETURN or CANCEL command).

If you wish to check your memory variables when an error occurs, select the Suspend option (by typing S) rather than the Cancel option. Doing so will return you to the dot prompt without erasing any memory variables. Then enter the DISPLAY MEMORY command to check your memory variables.

Before you make any changes to your command file, enter the command **RESUME** to resume processing, press Esc, and select Cancel to get back to the dot prompt. *Then* use the MODIFY COMMAND editor to change your command file. For more details on this and other debugging techniques, see Chapter 7, "Debugging Commands and Techniques."

## Commands to Create and Manage Memory Variables

This section covers the commands used to create and manage memory variables. Memory variables are used widely in all dBASE programming, so it is to the programmer's advantage to gain a complete understanding of the commands used with memory variables, as well as the more subtle concepts of private and public memory variables and macro substitution. For more information on memory variable data types, see Chapter 15, "Managing Data, Records, and Files."

## The STORE Command

The STORE command, like the assignment operator ( = ), places a value into a memory variable.

### SYNTAX

**STORE <expression> TO <variable name>**

where <expression> is a literal, a variable name, an expression, or a field name, and <variable> is the name of the variable, or several variables, that will store the value.

### USAGE

STORE can be used to create a new variable and place a value in it or to place a new value into an existing memory variable. An alternative to the STORE command is the assignment operator ( = ), with the following syntax:

**<variable name> = <expression>**

A maximum of 256 memory variables can be active at any one time. Unless otherwise modified in the Config.db file, the amount of space allotted for memory variables is 6,000 bytes.

The STORE command and the assignment operator always place their values into a memory variable, even if there is a field on the open database with the same name. On the other hand, commands that display or use memory variables will give a field precedence over a memory variable when the field and memory variable have the same name. When a field and memory variable have the same name, you can use the M-> alias to specify the memory variable. For example, the command **? M->LastName** displays the data stored in the memory variable named LastName, even if there is a field on the currently open database named LastName.

When assigning values to variables, numbers can be added to themselves, and character strings can be concatenated to themselves, as some of the examples below will demonstrate.

## EXAMPLES

The command

**STORE 123.45 TO Amount**

stores the value 123.45 to a memory variable named Amount, with the numeric data type. The command

**Amount = 123.45**

performs exactly the same task as STORE 123.45 TO Amount.

With the STORE command, you can place a value into many variables:

**STORE 0 TO Top, Bottom, Left, Right**

This command creates four memory variables named Top, Bottom, Left, and Right, and assigns each the numeric value of zero. The assignment operator ( = ) technique does not allow you to assign a value to multiple memory variables.

The command below increments the current value of the variable named Counter by 1:

**STORE Counter + 1 TO Counter**

The command below increments the numeric quantity stored in the memory variable named Ext_Price by six percent:

**STORE Ext_Price * 1.06 TO Ext_Price**

The next command places a blank space and the name "Joe" at the end of a character string named Greeting:

**STORE Greeting + " " + "Joe" TO Greeting**

The command below converts the contents of a memory variable named Search to uppercase:

**Search = UPPER(Search)**

## TIPS

Remember that STORE and the assignment operator always operate on memory variables, not database fields. A similar command for database fields is REPLACE.

Don't use dBASE commands as variable names, particularly when using the assignment operator. For example, the command

**Else = 123.45**

is likely to cause problems, because dBASE will interpret the variable name as the ELSE command, ignoring the rest of the line.

### SEE ALSO

PUBLIC
PRIVATE
DISPLAY MEMORY
RELEASE
SAVE
RESTORE

## The DISPLAY MEMORY Command

The DISPLAY MEMORY command shows the names, data types, sizes, contents, and other information concerning currently active memory variables.

### SYNTAX

**DISPLAY MEMORY [TO PRINT]**

where the optional TO PRINT command echoes the output to the printer.

### USAGE

If the DISPLAY MEMORY command is used after a command file has terminated, only public memory variables will be displayed. However, if it is used while a command file is suspended, all variables that are active at that moment are displayed. (See Chapter 7, "Debugging Commands and Techniques," for a discussion of suspending a command file.)

The status of each variable is displayed as public (pub), private (priv), or hidden (hidden). The data type of each variable is also displayed as either numeric (N), character (C), logical (L), or date (D).

Each number is displayed in two formats: as it is represented internally in memory and as you see it on the screen. For example, the number 123.456 might be stored internally as 123.45600000.

Very large numbers are displayed in scientific notation but stored internally as rounded numbers. For example, the command

**jj = 9999999999999999**

stores a large number in a variable named jj. The DISPLAY MEMORY command displays the contents of the jj variable as follows:

**JJ pub N .1000000000E + 17 (10000000000000000.0)**

The DISPLAY MEMORY command pauses for a keypress after each screenful of information. If you don't want the display to pause, use the LIST MEMORY command instead of DISPLAY MEMORY.

Both the DISPLAY MEMORY and LIST MEMORY commands allow the TO PRINT option to send the display to the printer. To store a copy of the memory variable display on a disk file, use the SET ALTERNATE command with the DISPLAY or LIST MEMORY command.

## EXAMPLE

Figure 6.3 shows the output from a DISPLAY MEMORY command executed after suspending the processing of a procedure. Note that the variable named Company is a public (pub) variable, of the character (C) data type, containing the text "ABC Corporation". Presumably, this variable was created at the dot prompt.

All other variables are private (priv). The Amount variable is numeric (N), with a value of 123. The Maybe variable is logical (L) with a value of .T. The

```
. DISPLAY MEMORY
COMPANY      pub   C  "ABC Corporation"
AMOUNT       priv  N          123  (        123.00000000)           C:test.prg
MAYBE        priv  L  .T.                                           C:test.prg
TODAY        priv  D  03/23/87                                      C:test.prg
X            priv  (hidden)  C  "Original"                          C:test.prg
X            priv  C  "Now"                                     C:GenProcs.prg
    6 variables defined,        52 bytes used
  250 variables available,    5948 bytes available

. _
```

**FIGURE 6.3:** Sample output from the DISPLAY MEMORY command. Variable names are listed in the left column. The status, data type, contents, and program in which the variable was created is also listed for each variable. The bottom of the screen describes both used and available memory variable space.

Today variable is the date (D) data type with the value 03/23/87. Each of these three variables was created in the command file named Test.prg on drive C.

There are two variables named X currently in use, both of which are of the character (C) data type. The one created in Test.prg is currently hidden. It contains the word Original. The second memory variable named X was created in a file named GenProcs.prg and contains the word Now. This variable named X is not hidden, so its value is the one currently being used in processing.

The display also shows that six memory variables are in use, occupying 52 bytes of memory. There is still room for 250 variables, or a maximum of 5948 bytes.

### TIPS

When debugging command files, you can press Esc and select Suspend, or even put the SUSPEND command directly in your command file, to get back to the dot prompt without losing memory variables. Then the DISPLAY MEMORY or LIST MEMORY commands will display the accurate status of memory variables at the moment.

### SEE ALSO

STORE
PUBLIC
PRIVATE

## The PUBLIC Command

The PUBLIC command defines a variable as accessible and modifiable to all levels of command files within a system. Public memory variables are not automatically erased when the command file that created them ends.

### SYNTAX

**PUBLIC <variable names>**

where <variable names> is a list of variable names separated by commas.

### USAGE

You must issue the PUBLIC command earlier in the program than the STORE command or the = assignment operator that creates the variables. When first declared public, memory variables are defined as the logical data type with the .F. value. Any later assignments to that variable will change the data type accordingly.

Any public variable can be temporarily hidden using the PRIVATE command. This allows you to create procedures that use memory variable names of their own which do not interfere with or modify any public memory variables already assigned that name.

### EXAMPLE

To declare several variables as public simultaneously, list the variable names separated by commas, as below:

**PUBLIC Qty, Unit_Price, Tax, Ext_Price**

### TIPS

To avoid any potential problems when trying to declare existing variables as public, programmers should make an effort to declare all public variables early in an application, perhaps above the main menu, which the user sees first.

For techniques on using public variables to pass values from procedures to the calling program, see Chapter 5, "Procedures and Parameters."

### SEE ALSO

PRIVATE
STORE
DISPLAY MEMORY
SUSPEND
DO...WITH

## The PRIVATE Command

The PRIVATE command temporarily hides the current value of a public memory variable, so that a lower-level command file or procedure can use the variable name.

### SYNTAX

**PRIVATE <variable list> [ALL[LIKE/EXCEPT <skeleton>]]**

where <variable list> is a list of variable names, each separated by a comma. The optional ALL command declares all variables as private. The optional LIKE and EXCEPT commands can be used with a *skeleton* to define a group of variable names using the * and ? wild-card characters.

## USAGE

The main reason for using the PRIVATE command is to create general-purpose procedures and programs that use local variable names which do not interfere with existing public or higher-level variables with the same names. Once a variable is declared private, the value in the public or higher-level variable retains its value but is hidden. Any new operations take place only on the private variable.

When the program or procedure that created the private variable ends, the public or higher-level memory value retains its original value, unaffected by changes to the private variable with the same name.

If you were to think of the PRIVATE command as a verb rather than a declaration, perhaps the correct equivalent would be HIDE. For example, the command **PRIVATE Counter,X,Company** hides the current values of the variables Counter, X, and Company while the currently running procedure or program uses these variable names for its own purposes. When the current program or procedure returns control to the calling program, Counter, X, and Company will regain their original values.

When creating skeletons for use with the optional LIKE and EXCEPT components, * stands for any combination of characters, and ? stands for any single character. Hence, Sm?th would match any five-letter name beginning with Sm and ending with th, such as Smith, Smyth, Smeth, Smuth, etc. The skeleton A*t matches any name beginning with the letter A and ending with the letter T, such as Amount, Art, and At.

## EXAMPLES

The command **PRIVATE ALL** declares all public variables currently in use as private (hidden) from variable names being created at the current program level and lower.

The command **PRIVATE ALL LIKE C*** hides all memory variables that begin with the letter C. The command **PRIVATE ALL EXCEPT Day?** hides all variables except those beginning with the letters Day and ending with an additional single character.

For an example of the PRIVATE command used in a procedure, see Figure 6.2.

## TIPS

If you plan to develop a library of general-purpose procedures, you might want to declare any frequently used variable names private, such as Counter. That way, the Counter variable in the procedure will not interfere with another variable named Counter in any of the applications in which that procedure is used.

#### SEE ALSO

PUBLIC
STORE
RELEASE

## The RELEASE Command

The RELEASE command erases memory variables and reclaims the space occupied by the variable(s). RELEASE is also used to remove assembly language subroutines from memory (as discussed in Chapter 22, "Assembly Language Subroutines").

#### SYNTAX

**RELEASE <variable list> [ALL[LIKE/EXCEPT <skeleton>]] ;**
**[MODULE <subroutine name>]**

where <variable list> is the name of the variable to release or a list of variable names separated by commas. The ALL, LIKE, and EXCEPT components are optional. The <skeleton> allows you to define variables using the * and ? wildcard characters. The <subroutine name> is the name of an assembly language subroutine to be released from memory using the optional RELEASE MODULE combination.

#### USAGE

The RELEASE command removes memory variables from memory to make room for new ones. Note that when entered at the dot prompt, the RELEASE ALL command releases all memory variables. When used in a command file, however, the RELEASE ALL command erases only those variables created by the current program or procedure. On the other hand, the CLEAR MEMORY command releases all public and private memory variables created at all program levels.

#### EXAMPLES

The command

**RELEASE Choice, X, MyVar**

erases the memory variables Choice, X, and MyVar and frees up the memory used by them. The command

**RELEASE ALL LIKE Month***

releases all memory variables beginning with the letters Month. The command

**RELEASE ALL EXCEPT ???C***

erases all memory variables except those that have C as the fourth letter.

### TIPS

To temporarily erase memory variables and make room for new ones, you can first save all current memory variables and then release (or clear) them. To bring back the original memory variables, use the RESTORE command.

For information on expanding the amount of memory variable space, see Appendix C, "Configuring dBASE III PLUS."

### SEE ALSO

CLEAR
STORE
PRIVATE

## The SAVE Command

The SAVE command places a copy of active memory variables on a disk file.

### SYNTAX

**SAVE TO <file name> [ALL LIKE/EXCEPT <skeleton> ]**

where <file name> is the name of the file to store the variables on and <skeleton> is an ambiguous variable name used with the ALL LIKE or ALL EXCEPT options to specify a group of memory variables to be stored.

### USAGE

The SAVE command can store all or some of the currently active memory variables on a disk file. The disk file will have the name you supply followed by the extension .mem. Saving memory variables has no effect on data stored in database files.

File names must be valid DOS file names (eight letters maximum length, no spaces, and no punctuation except the underscore). Unless otherwise specified, the file will be created on the currently logged disk drive and directory.

If you do not use the ALL LIKE or ALL EXCEPT options, all currently active memory variables are stored on the file. The ALL LIKE and ALL EXCEPT options allow you to specify skeletal file names with the ? and * wild-card characters, where the ? symbol represents a single character and * represents any group of characters.

Saving a copy of an active memory variable does not erase it from memory. To erase saved variables from memory, use the RELEASE or CLEAR MEMORY command. To retrieve saved variables from disk back into memory, use the RESTORE command.

### EXAMPLES

The command

**SAVE TO MemVars**

stores a copy of all active memory variables on a disk file named MemVars.mem. The command

**SAVE ALL LIKE New* TO SetUp**

stores all memory variables starting with the letters New in a disk file named SetUp.mem. The command

**SAVE ALL EXCEPT ??Temp TO MVars**

saves all current memory variables in a file named MVars.mem, except those that begin with any two characters and end with the four characters Temp.

### TIPS

Memory variable files are useful if you are creating applications that you want to be hardware independent; that is, the applications will be used by many different clients on many different computer systems.

### SEE ALSO

RESTORE
RELEASE
CLEAR MEMORY

## The RESTORE Command

RESTORE loads memory variables from disk into memory.

### SYNTAX

**RESTORE FROM <file name> [ADDITIVE]**

where <file name> is the name of the memory (.mem) file to retrieve the variables from. The ADDITIVE component is optional.

## USAGE

Any memory variables that were stored on disk with a SAVE command can be retrieved into memory using the RESTORE command. If you don't specify the ADDITIVE option, all memory variables currently in memory are erased before the new variables are retrieved. If the ADDITIVE option is used, retrieved variables are combined with existing variables. If both a retrieved and existing variable have the same name, the retrieved variable overwrites the existing variable.

Restored variables are always private to the level at which they were restored. For example, suppose Prog1.prg calls Prog2.prg with a DO command. Prog2.prg, in turn, uses the command RESTORE FROM MemVars ADDITIVE to bring in memory variables from MemVars.mem. These new variables are available to Prog2.prg and all lower-level programs and procedures. However, when Prog2.prg passes control back to Prog1.prg, the restored variables will be erased automatically (just as though they'd been created in Prog2.prg).

To treat restored variables as public to an entire system, you can either restore them at the highest-level program in an application or declare them public before they are restored.

RESTORE searches the currently logged disk drive and directory for the specified file, unless a drive and/or directory are included. For example, the command RESTORE FROM D:\MemFiles\MyVars restores memory variables from the file named MyVars.mem on the directory named MemFiles on drive D. The RESTORE command will also search the path specified in a dBASE SET PATH command.

## EXAMPLES

The command

**RESTORE FROM SetUp**

deletes all variables currently in memory and reads in memory variables stored on the file named SetUp.mem. The command

**RESTORE FROM SetUp ADDITIVE**

reads in memory variables from the file named SetUp.mem without first deleting existing memory variables.

### TIPS

If you receive the error message **Out of memory variable slots** while using a RESTORE FROM...ADDITIVE command, you've gone over the 256-variables limit. Try using SAVE and RELEASE to make room for the incoming variables.

The error message **Out of memory variable memory** means you've gone over the 6,000-byte limit while trying to restore saved variables. Again, you can use the SAVE and RELEASE commands to make more room, or you can extend the amount of memory available for variables through the Config.db file.

Chapter 18, "Setting Parameters," shows techniques for using memory files to provide users with options for customizing an application.

### SEE ALSO

SAVE
STORE
RELEASE

## SUMMARY

This chapter covered dBASE III PLUS memory variables. Memory variables are always used extensively in custom applications, so you'll see them used in many examples throughout this book.

*For information on creating variables with the SUM, AVERAGE, and COUNT commands, as well as on using memory variables to perform quick interactive calculations:*

- Chapter 14, "Calculating Numbers"

*For general information on manipulating data types:*

- Chapter 15, "Managing Data and Records"

*For more information on functions to manage and manipulate memory variables as fields:*

- Chapter 17, "dBASE Functions"

*For tips on using memory variables to create portable, hardware-independent systems:*

- Chapter 18, "Setting Parameters"

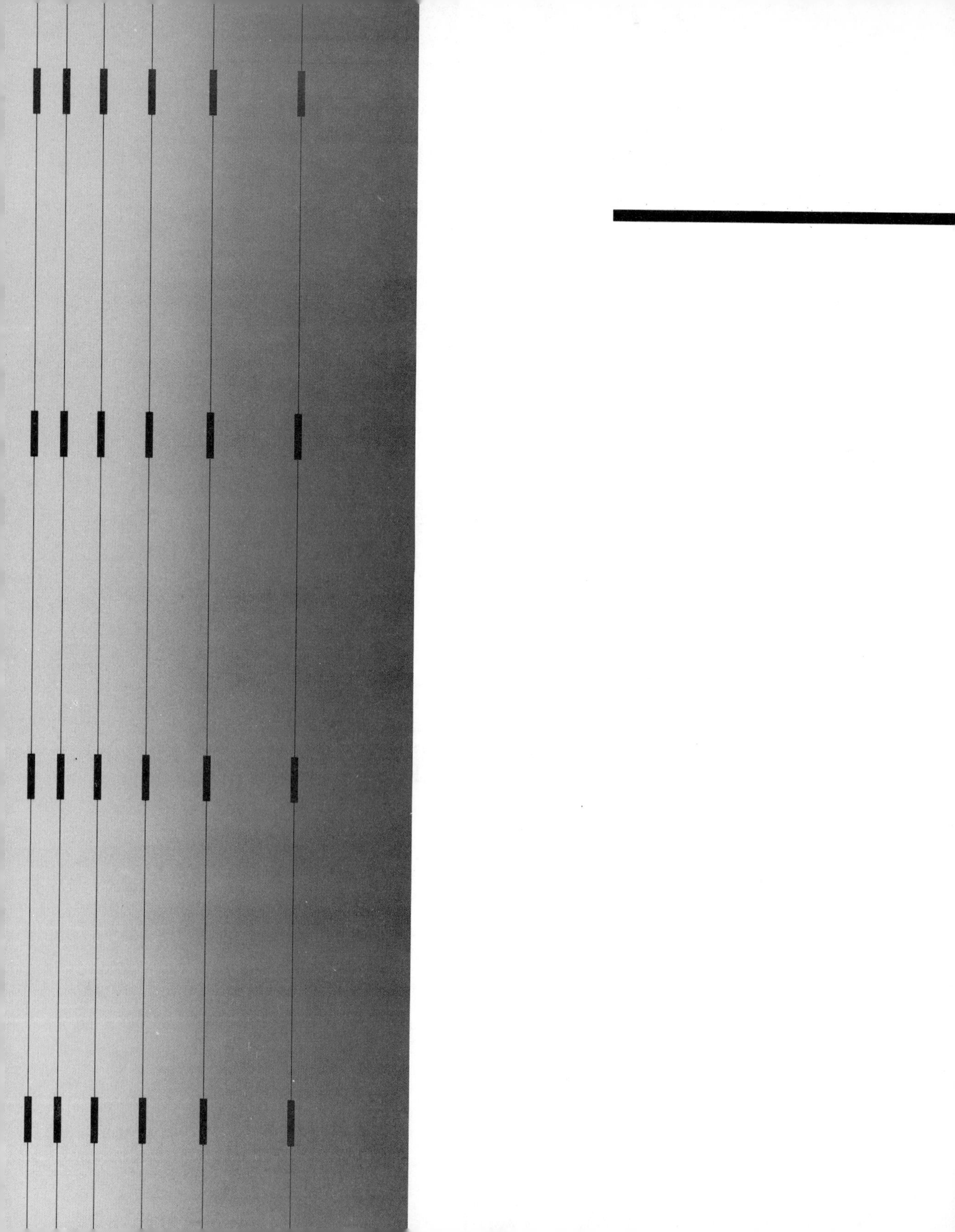

CHAPTER 7

# DEBUGGING COMMANDS AND TECHNIQUES

# DEBUGGING COMMANDS AND TECHNIQUES

No matter how carefully a programmer designs and plans an application, the programs are sure to have a few bugs (errors) in them. Program bugs come in all varieties: from obvious ones that cause dBASE to crash on the spot to more subtle ones that may not be immediately apparent. This chapter covers general debugging techniques and the dBASE III PLUS commands that can help you debug programs.

## TYPES OF PROGRAMMING ERRORS

Virtually all programs have bugs in them initially; some are easy to detect and fix, and others may require many tedious hours to isolate and correct. You can classify the various types of bugs that creep into programs as follows:

| | |
|---|---|
| Syntax errors | Errors caused by misspellings, omissions, or syntax-rule violations |
| Limitation errors | Errors caused by going beyond a dBASE boundary, such as the maximum number of files open |
| Structural errors | Errors caused by improper construction of IF, DO WHILE, DO CASE, or TEXT clauses in programs, or by other improperly sequenced commands |
| Logical errors | Errors caused when the programmer thinks one thing but inadvertently tells the program to do something else |

The sections below describe each of these types of errors and suggest steps and techniques you can use to locate and fix the error as quickly as possible.

## Syntax Errors

Syntactical errors are usually pretty obvious in a program, because dBASE immediately halts program execution and displays an error message. The example below demonstrates how the screen might look when dBASE encounters a syntactical error in a program:

```
*** Unrecognized command verb.
        ?
LITS CustNo,LName,FName
Called from - RepProg.prg
Called from - MainMenu.prg
Cancel, Ignore, or Suspend? (C, I, or S)
```

The error message ***** Unrecognized command verb** is displayed at the top. The question mark indicates the approximate position where dBASE gave up trying to interpret the line. The next line is the command line that contains the unrecognizable command. The series of **Called from** messages beneath the command line display the command files that generated the error. The topmost command file, RepProg.prg, is the file that actually contains the error. (RepProg.prg was called by MainMenu.prg.)

The bottom line of the display presents the options Cancel, Ignore, or Suspend. To select an option, type the letter C, I, or S. These options are summarized below:

| | |
|---|---|
| Cancel | Terminates program execution, erases all private memory variables (those created within this program), and returns to the dot prompt. The program can be edited immediately with MODIFY COMMAND or another editor. |
| Ignore | Ignores the line with the error in it and continues processing the program at the next line. |
| Suspend | Leaves the command file open and all memory variables intact and returns to the dot prompt. DISPLAY, LIST, and all other commands display the accurate status of the program environment when the error occurred. The command file cannot be edited immediately, however, because it is still open. To resume processing, enter the RESUME command. To cancel processing and edit the command file immediately, enter the CANCEL command. |

### Misspelled Commands and Fields

Syntax errors, like the one in the example above, are very common. In this case, the error is pretty obvious; the LIST command is spelled wrong. Here you would probably just select Cancel to return to the dot prompt or Ignore to continue with the rest of the program. If the error were not quite so obvious, you could select Cancel to return to the dot prompt and then enter the command HELP LIST for some information on the LIST command.

A second common error is that of misspelled field or variable names, as in the example below:

**Variable not found.**
**?**
**LIST CustNo,LastName,FirstName**
**Called from - C:Test.prg**
**Cancel, Ignore, or Suspend? (C, I, or S)**

In this case, it might be best to suspend operation and return to the dot prompt. Then use DISPLAY STRUCTURE to double-check on the spelling of field names or DISPLAY MEMORY to check on the spelling of memory variable names (DISPLAY MEMORY is discussed in Chapter 6, "Memory Variables."). For example, in the DISPLAY STRUCTURE output in Figure 7.1, you can see that LastName and FirstName are not valid field names (LName and FName are). At this point, you can cancel program execution and use an editor to fix the error in the program.

Sometimes the **Variable not found** error might mean that the wrong database is in use or the wrong one has been selected with the SELECT command. The DISPLAY STATUS command will show you the names of all open database files, as well as the currently selected database file.

```
Structure for database: C:Customer.dbf
Number of data records:       999
Date of last update    : 03/09/87
Field  Field Name  Type         Width     Dec
    1  CUSTNO      Numeric          4
    2  LNAME       Character       15
    3  FNAME       Character       10
    4  ADDRESS     Character       25
    5  CITY        Character       20
    6  STATE       Character        2
    7  ZIP         Character       10
    8  PHONE       Character       13
    9  LAST_UPDAT  Date             8
   10  START_BAL   Numeric          8       2
```

**FIGURE 7.1:** Structure of a sample database file as displayed by the DISPLAY STRUCTURE command. The display includes the database name, the number of records, the date of the most recent change, and the field name, data type, width, and decimal places of each field.

## DATA-TYPE MISMATCHES

A third common syntactical error is caused by data-type mismatches. For example, in the command below, dBASE is complaining about the CustNo field name being an argument to the TRIM function:

```
Invalid function argument
                          ?
LIST TRIM(CustNo),LName,FName
Called from - C:Bugs.prg
Cancel, Ignore, or Suspend? (C, I, or S)
```

(dBASE might also display the message **Data type mismatch** when there is a problem with mixed data types.)

Again, in a case like this you may want to suspend operation and check the data type of CustNo using DISPLAY STRUCTURE (or DISPLAY MEMORY if a memory variable is being questioned). Also, use the HELP TRIM command or another resource to check on the data type expected by the TRIM command. In this example, CustNo is numeric, and TRIM expects character data. You need to cancel the command file and fix the error with an editor.

## UNBALANCED PARENTHESES

Another common error is the use of unbalanced parentheses, as in the example below:

```
Unbalanced parenthesis.
                          ?
? SQRT((A ^ 2) + B ^ 2))
Called from - C:Bugs.prg
Cancel, Ignore, or Suspend? (C, I, or S)
```

In a case such as this, you might as well just select Cancel and then edit the command file immediately. A handy technique for counting parentheses is to start at 0, add 1 for every open parenthesis, and subtract 1 for every closed parenthesis. You should end up back at 0. In the example below you end up with −1, indicating that there is an extra closed parenthesis (or missing open parenthesis):

```
? SQRT( (A ^ 2) + B ^ 2) )
0      1 2   1        0 -1
```

You'll need to correct the line so that there are an equal number of open and closed parentheses.

### General Syntax Debugging Procedures

These are just a few examples of syntax-related errors that might occur in a program. Appendix A, "Error Messages," contains a list of all the possible error messages you might receive, along with a description of each. In general, when a syntax-related bug causes dBASE to crash and displays the Cancel, Ignore, and Suspend options, you should follow these steps to correct the problem:

1. Make sure you know what the error message means. If not, look it up in Appendix A, "Error Messages," or the dBASE manual.
2. If the problem is not obvious, select Suspend and use the DISPLAY STATUS, DISPLAY STRUCTURE, DISPLAY MEMORY, and other commands to determine what was going on when the error occurred. Be especially watchful of data types.
3. If necessary, use the online HELP feature of dBASE or printed reference material for additional information about the command or function causing the error.
4. If you suspended operation, be sure to cancel processing with the CANCEL command before editing the command file (otherwise, you'll just get the additional error message **File is already open!**).

## Limitation Errors

Limitation errors are those that cause dBASE to crash because some command attempted to go beyond dBASE's limitations. Perhaps the most common example is the infamous **Too many files are open** error, which can become a problem in larger applications. This error can be caused by two things:

1. An improper or missing Config.sys file on the boot-up disk (or the root directory on a hard disk)
2. More than 15 files open at once

The first is easy to fix; just place the proper Config.sys file on the appropriate disk, as discussed in Chapter 1, "Overview of the dBASE Language." If the Config.sys file is the correct one and the error still occurs, you'll need to find a way to have fewer files open. Remember, each active database, index, procedure, and command file counts as an open file. Each time a command file calls another with a DO command, another open file is added to the list.

There are only two ways around this problem. One is to use the DISPLAY STATUS command to see what files are open, and if possible, use CLOSE commands in the command files to close any unnecessary files. A second solution is to try to reduce the number of command files called by placing a few in a procedure file. Even though a procedure file can contain up to 32 procedures, they are all accessible with a single SET PROCEDURE command, which opens only a single file.

As with syntax errors, when you receive an error message that is caused by going beyond a dBASE limitation, be sure to look up the error message and any related information to gain a full understanding of what went wrong. In some cases, there will be a way around the limitation (for example, the Config.db file allows you to alter limitations for memory variable memory, PICTURE commands, RANGE commands, and GET commands). In other cases, you'll just need to find some other way to work around the limitation.

## Structural Errors

Structural errors are not always easy to find, because dBASE may not generate an error message. Instead, the program will continue to run, but it will behave unexpectedly. For example, a DO WHILE loop may attempt to run forever until you press the Esc key to terminate execution. Or the statements inside or outside an IF clause will be executed when they should not be. These errors are commonly caused by missing or improperly nested clause commands.

If your program is properly indented, it should not be too difficult to spot any missing clause commands or improperly nested clauses. But to be doubly sure, you can use the dBASE command

**TYPE <file name.prg> TO PRINT**

(or any word processor) to make a hard copy of your program. Then, using a pen or pencil, draw arrows to connect each DO WHILE, IF, DO CASE, and TEXT command with its appropriate ENDDO, ENDIF, ENDCASE, and ENDTEXT command, as shown in Figure 7.2. Each clause command should have one, and only one, closing command. Furthermore, they should all be nested within one another.

Any crossed-over clauses, as in Figure 7.3, must be corrected. You can nest any clauses *within* any other clauses, but each clause must have its starting and ending points completely inside of the clause surrounding it.

Figure 7.4 shows a diagrammatic sketch of properly nested clause commands. Note that there is no rule stating that only certain types of clauses can be embedded within other clauses. The rule is that if one clause command begins inside of another clause, it must also end inside that same clause.

Structural errors are often difficult to find, and perhaps the best approach is to use a hard copy of the program and draw arrows as suggested above. However, in Chapter 24, "Algorithms to Extend dBASE," you will find a debugging aid that can help you find structural errors in a program.

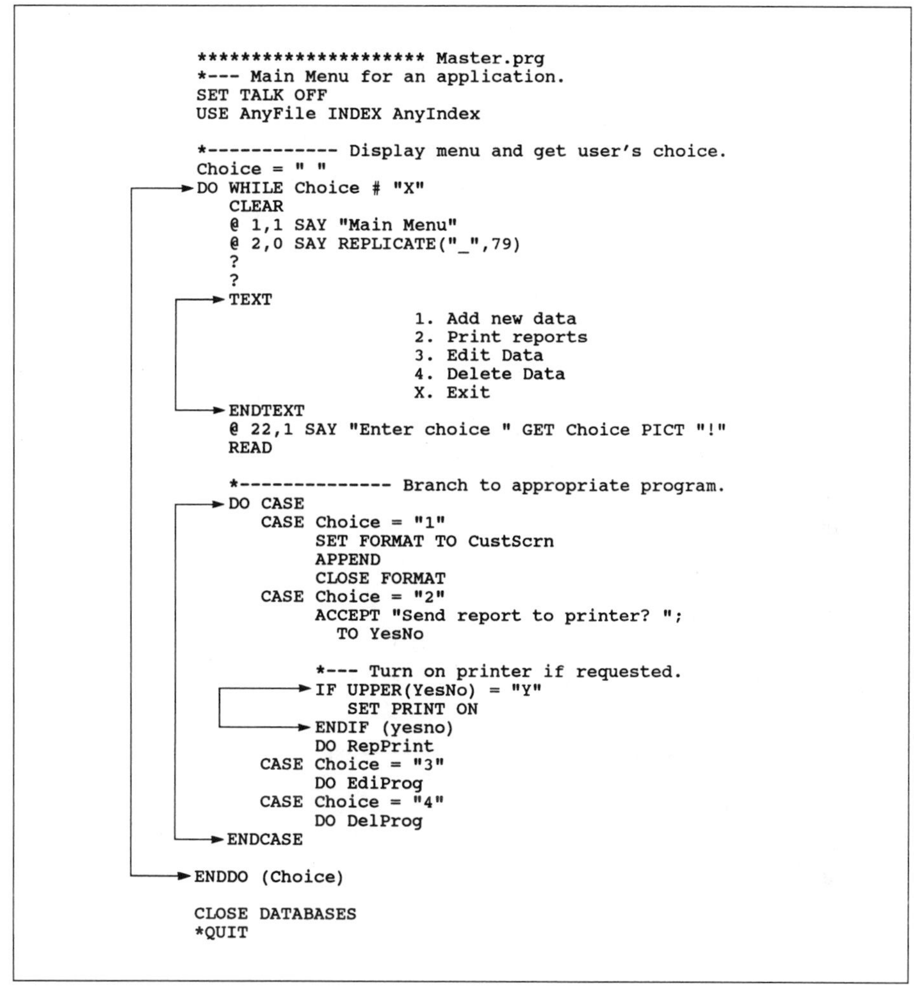

```
********************* Master.prg
*--- Main Menu for an application.
SET TALK OFF
USE AnyFile INDEX AnyIndex

*------------ Display menu and get user's choice.
Choice = " "
DO WHILE Choice # "X"
   CLEAR
   @ 1,1 SAY "Main Menu"
   @ 2,0 SAY REPLICATE("_",79)
   ?
   ?
   TEXT
                    1. Add new data
                    2. Print reports
                    3. Edit Data
                    4. Delete Data
                    X. Exit
   ENDTEXT
   @ 22,1 SAY "Enter choice " GET Choice PICT "!"
   READ

   *-------------- Branch to appropriate program.
   DO CASE
      CASE Choice = "1"
           SET FORMAT TO CustScrn
           APPEND
           CLOSE FORMAT
      CASE Choice = "2"
           ACCEPT "Send report to printer? ";
             TO YesNo

           *--- Turn on printer if requested.
           IF UPPER(YesNo) = "Y"
              SET PRINT ON
           ENDIF (yesno)
           DO RepPrint
      CASE Choice = "3"
           DO EdiProg
      CASE Choice = "4"
           DO DelProg
   ENDCASE

ENDDO (Choice)

CLOSE DATABASES
*QUIT
```

**FIGURE 7.2:** Sample program with arrows that connect clause commands. Because there are no missing clause commands and no crossing over of clauses, the clauses in this program are correctly structured and nested.

## Logical Errors

Of all the errors in a program, logical errors are the most difficult to find. With logical errors, the program may seem to run just fine, but it just does not do what you want it to do. In this case, everything in the program is "legal," but what it's doing is just not what you had in mind.

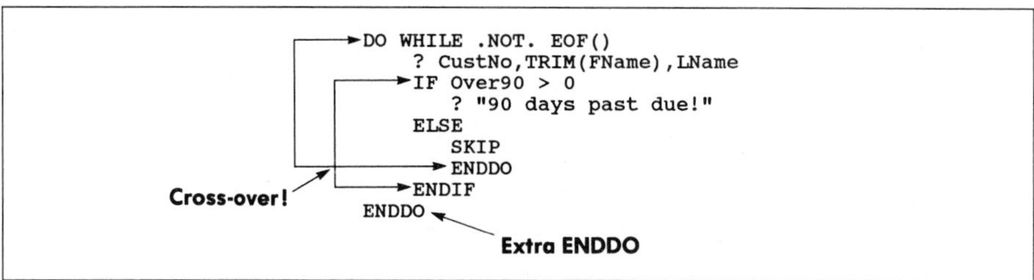


**FIGURE 7.3:** This routine has a couple of problems. First, there are two ENDDO commands and only a single DO WHILE command. Second, the IF clause is not fully nested within the DO WHILE loop clause.

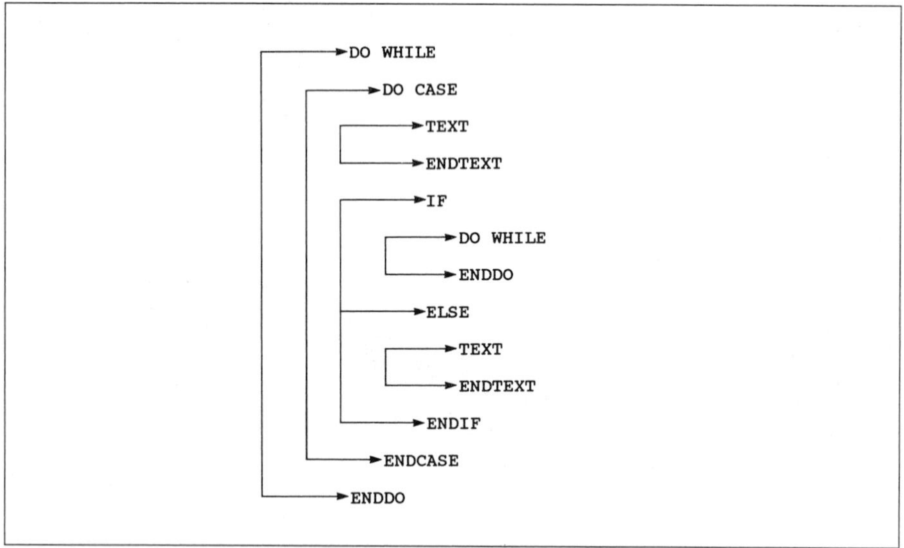


**FIGURE 7.4:** Diagram of properly nested clause commands. Note that each clause is fully nested within the clause that surrounds it, and none of the connecting lines overlaps any others.

Many logical errors are errors of carelessness. For example, the error in the routine in Figure 7.5 is not immediately apparent, but the DO WHILE loop in this program will never do anything.

The reason the DO WHILE loop will never do anything is that part of the looping condition is WHILE .NOT. EOF( ). The COUNT command above the DO WHILE command will *always* leave the record pointer pointing at EOF( ), so the DO WHILE condition will never be true. (Many other commands, such as LIST, DISPLAY ALL, SUM, AVERAGE, REPLACE, REPORT FORM, and LABEL FORM, might also leave the record pointer at EOF( ).) To fix this,

```
*--- Count how many records are
*--- marked for deletion.
COUNT FOR DELETED() TO HowMany

*---- Double-check before packing.
DO WHILE .NOT. EOF() .AND. HowMany > 0
   IF DELETED()
      DISPLAY
      WAIT "Pack this record? (Y/N) " TO YesNo
      IF UPPER(YesNo) # "Y"
         RECALL
      ENDIF (yesno)
    ENDIF (deleted)
    SKIP
ENDDO (eof)
```

**FIGURE 7.5:** Subtle logical error in a program caused by beginning a DO WHILE .NOT. EOF() loop directly beneath a COUNT command. The DO WHILE loop will never do anything because the COUNT command leaves the record pointer at the EOF() position.

the program needs a GO TOP command between the COUNT and DO WHILE commands.

## Correcting Logical Errors

Your best bet in attacking these tough, subtle logical errors is to use the various debugging commands covered in the reference section of this chapter. The SET ECHO, SET STEP, and SET DEBUG commands are especially useful for watching the flow of logic, one line at a time, so you can see exactly what is going on.

It helps to have a hard copy of the program nearby while you are watching for logical errors on the screen, so that you can mark the exact locations where things seem to start going astray. Doing so helps you *isolate* the problem to a specific part of the program.

Once you've isolated the general area, you can place testing commands directly into the program to analyze the problem more deeply. You might want to place SUSPEND, DISPLAY STATUS, DISPLAY STRUCTURE, or DISPLAY MEMORY commands directly in the program at the problem areas to see what is going on in the program at that moment.

You can place any temporary command in a command file to help find an error. For example, a handy technique to find the error shown in Figure 7.5 would be to view the values of EOF( ) and HowMany just above the DO WHILE loop by inserting the following command:

```
COUNT FOR DELETED( ) TO HowMany
? EOF( ),HowMany        && Just checking here...
DO WHILE .NOT. EOF( ) .AND. HowMany > 0
```

Next time you ran the program, you would see that EOF( ) is true (.T.) before the DO WHILE command, so you would know why the loop was never processed.

In general, the best techniques for fixing the hard-to-find logical errors in a program can be summarized as follows:

1. Make a hard copy of the program. (Check for structural errors.)
2. Try to isolate the problem to a small area of code. (SET ECHO, SET STEP, SET DEBUG, and other commands can help with this step.)
3. Once isolated, if more information is needed, embed temporary commands directly in the program to provide additional feedback as the program is running.
4. Modify the command file and test it again. If the error persists, keep trying to isolate, test, and modify until all works well.

Unfortunately, not even this sort of persistence will solve all problems. For example, if there appears to be data missing from a report, you might spend a great deal of time trying to work with the report format (.frm) file or the code to print the report, when in actuality there is a problem with a much earlier SET RELATION command. The DISPLAY STATUS command can be a good reminder of *all* the factors affecting a routine at any given time. Be sure to consider all the possibilities before spending a great deal of time in one isolated area.

## Commands Used for Debugging

This section covers the specific dBASE commands that can help you debug a program. Keep in mind, however, that the best debugging tool you have is your own knowledge and understanding of every dBASE command, function, and error message.

### The SET ECHO Command

The SET ECHO command displays each line in a command file as it is being processed.

#### SYNTAX

**SET ECHO ON/OFF**

where ON turns on the echoing and OFF turns it off.

### USAGE

This command allows a programmer to view each line in a command file while it is being processed. To see the entire program echoed, just type SET ECHO ON at the dot prompt before running the program. If you have already isolated the error, you can place the SET ECHO command directly in the command file so that echoing begins and ends in the vicinity of the error.

### EXAMPLE

In the program below, a DO WHILE loop is causing problems in a command file. In order to view the processing, you can surround the routine with SET ECHO commands:

```
SET ECHO ON
DO WHILE .NOT. EOF( )
      ? LName, FName
ENDDO (eof)
SET ECHO OFF
```

### TIPS

SET ECHO displays its output pretty quickly. Unless the program or segment you want to view with SET ECHO is very short, you may want to use the SET STEP and SET DEBUG commands to slow it down.

### SEE ALSO

SET TALK
SET STEP
SET DEBUG
SET DOHISTORY

## The SET STEP Command

SET STEP pauses program execution after each line is processed, allowing the programmer to view processing one line at a time.

### SYNTAX

**SET STEP ON/OFF**

where ON starts the stepping process and OFF disables it and returns to normal processing.

## USAGE

When STEP is on, each line in a program is individually processed, its results (if any) are displayed, and the screen displays this message before processing the next line:

**Press SPACE to step, S to suspend, or Esc to cancel...**

Pressing the space bar simply moves processing to the next line in the command file. Pressing the Esc key completely terminates processing, closes the command file, erases all private memory variables, and returns to the dot prompt.

Typing S to suspend returns control to the dot prompt without closing the command file or erasing any memory variables. The programmer can use the DISPLAY MEMORY, DISPLAY STRUCTURE, DISPLAY STATUS, and other commands at that point to analyze the environment. To resume processing, enter the RESUME command. To stop processing and edit the command file, enter the CANCEL command.

When ECHO is on, the SET STEP command displays each command line before processing it, displaying the results, and presenting the stepping options.

Like all commands, SET STEP can be placed anywhere inside a command file. Therefore, if you've isolated a problem to a particular place in a program, you can surround the area with SET STEP ON and SET STEP OFF commands to pause program execution in that area only.

## EXAMPLES

To view each line in a command file as it is processing and step through each line as well, enter the commands

**SET ECHO ON**
**SET STEP ON**

directly at the dot prompt.

## TIPS

SET STEP offers not only a technique for pausing execution but also a technique for suspending program execution at a specific location. If you select Suspend from the SET STEP options, remember to type C for Cancel before editing the command file. (If you suspend a procedure file, you'll need to close it with CLOSE PROCEDURE.) If you don't want to close the file, however, you can use the RESUME command to continue processing.

### SEE ALSO

SET ECHO
SET DEBUG
SUSPEND
RESUME

## The SET DEBUG Command

SET DEBUG sends the output from a SET ECHO command to the printer rather than the screen.

### SYNTAX

**SET DEBUG ON/OFF**

where ON sends echoed output to the printer and OFF sends it to the screen.

### USAGE

Use the SET DEBUG ON command to view the normal screen activity of a program while generating a printed copy of the output produced by the SET ECHO command. (If SET ECHO is not on, SET DEBUG does nothing.) As with SET ECHO and SET STEP, the SET DEBUG command can be placed anywhere within a command file so that you get a printout of only part of the file.

The programmer can use the printed output from SET ECHO and SET DEBUG to follow each line in the program as dBASE processed it. Doing so provides an exact picture of how dBASE executed the command file and should help isolate logical errors that might otherwise be very difficult to find.

### EXAMPLE

The routine in Figure 7.6 is surrounded by SET ECHO and SET DEBUG commands. After running the program, the printout displays

```
COUNT FOR DELETED( ) TO DelRecs
DO WHILE DelRecs > 0 .AND. .NOT. EOF( )
SET DEBUG OFF
```

indicating that none of the commands within the DO WHILE loop was processed, and therefore the WHILE condition was false before the loop was ever performed.

```
SET ECHO ON
SET DEBUG ON
COUNT FOR DELETED() TO DelRecs
DO WHILE DelRecs > 0 .AND. .NOT. EOF()
   IF DELETED()
      ? "Deleted - ",RECNO(),CustNo,LName,FName
   ENDIF
   SKIP
ENDDO
SET DEBUG OFF
SET ECHO OFF
EJECT
```

**FIGURE 7.6:** A sample routine surrounded by SET ECHO and SET DEBUG commands to aid in the debugging process. As the routine executes, the command lines are displayed on the printer, showing that none of the commands within the DO WHILE loop was processed.

### TIPS

SET DEBUG is very useful for digging out hard-to-find logical errors. You might want to combine it with a LIST STATUS TO PRINT command to get a printed view of the program environment as well.

### SEE ALSO

SET ECHO
SET DOHISTORY
SET ALTERNATE
SET TALK
LIST STATUS

## The SUSPEND Command

The SUSPEND command suspends execution of a command file without closing the file or erasing any memory variables.

### SYNTAX

**SUSPEND**

### USAGE

The SUSPEND command forces a program to go into suspension at a specific place (presumably a location where you've isolated an error). When dBASE encounters a SUSPEND command, it displays the message **Do suspended** and the dot prompt reappears. At this point, all commands including DISPLAY

MEMORY, DISPLAY STRUCTURE, DISPLAY STATUS, DISPLAY HISTORY, and ? will display information about the program environment at that exact point in the program.

To edit a suspended command file, you must first close the file with the CANCEL command. If you suspend a procedure file, you must close it with the CLOSE PROCEDURE command prior to editing. To resume processing without editing, enter the command RESUME.

If you create any memory variables at the dot prompt while a command file is suspended, those memory variables will be private to the suspended command file.

### EXAMPLE

After isolating a program bug near a particular routine, the programmer places a SUSPEND command in a good position for checking parameters near that routine, as shown below:

```
SEEK Search
SUSPEND
LIST WHILE .NOT. EOF( )
```

When the program runs, it is suspended immediately after executing the SEEK command. At this point, the programmer can enter any useful DISPLAY commands, or commands such as ? FOUND( ) or ? EOF( ) to see if the item was found or the end of the file was encountered.

After determining the cause of the problem, the programmer can then cancel processing and edit the command file (also removing the now unnecessary SUSPEND command).

### TIPS

Remember that you can use the ? command as well as the DISPLAY commands to get specific information while a program is suspended. Some examples include ? EOF( ), ? BOF( ), ? DISKSPACE( ), ? ERROR( ), ? TYPE(variable), ? FOUND( ), and ? RECNO( ). See Chapter 17, "dBASE Functions," for discussions of these dBASE functions.

### SEE ALSO

RESUME
CANCEL
LIST HISTORY
DISPLAY MEMORY
DISPLAY STATUS
DISPLAY STRUCTURE

## The RESUME Command

The RESUME command continues processing a suspended command file.

### SYNTAX

**RESUME**

### USAGE

Use the RESUME command to restart execution of a suspended command file at the first line beneath the one that caused the error or the first line beneath the SUSPEND command.

### EXAMPLE

If you want to continue running a program after suspending it and experimenting with some commands at the dot prompt, type **RESUME** at the dot prompt.

### TIPS

If your experimentation at the dot prompt during suspension has left the screen cluttered, you can use the CLEAR command to clear the screen before entering the RESUME command.

### SEE ALSO

SUSPEND

## The CANCEL Command

CANCEL terminates execution and closes all command files.

### SYNTAX

**CANCEL**

### USAGE

The most common use of the CANCEL command is to close a suspended command file so that it can be edited. (CANCEL does not, however, close open procedure files; the CLOSE PROCEDURE command does that.) It can be used directly in a command file to terminate all program execution, close all program files, and return control to the dot prompt. Doing so also erases all private memory variables.

### TIPS

You can edit a suspended command file or procedure file without first closing it by using an external word processor with the RUN command. However, doing so changes only the copy on disk, not the suspended command file or procedure file in memory. Because you will usually want to rerun the file once you've edited it, always cancel a suspended command file or close a procedure before editing it with any text editor.

### SEE ALSO

SUSPEND
RESUME
CLOSE PROCEDURE

## The DISPLAY STATUS Command

This command displays the current status of dBASE parameters, pausing with each full screen.

### SYNTAX

**DISPLAY STATUS [TO PRINT]**

where TO PRINT optionally echoes the display to the printer.

### USAGE

The DISPLAY STATUS command shows the following information about each currently open database file:

- Database name
- Active index files
- Index file keys
- SELECT area
- Alias name
- Relations set
- Open memo file names

If no databases are open, none of the above are displayed.

DISPLAY STATUS also shows the status of the following parameters:

- ALTERNATE file in use (if any)
- SET PATH command
- Default disk drive
- Print destination
- SET MARGIN setting
- Currently selected work area (from SELECT)
- ON ERROR destination
- Current settings for most SET commands
- Function key assignments

The LIST STATUS command is equivalent to DISPLAY STATUS, except that it does not pause for a filled screen, which is why it is preferred when the TO PRINT option is used.

### EXAMPLE

Figure 7.7 shows a sample display from the DISPLAY or LIST STATUS command. In the example, two database files are open, ABCTemp.dbf in SELECT area 1 and ABCProd.dbf in SELECT area 2. ABCTemp.dbf is related to ABCProd.dbf on a field named Product. The alias for ABCTemp.dbf is "Manyside", and the alias for ABCProd.dbf is "OneSide". ABCTemp.dbf is the currently selected database.

The ABCProd database has a single active index file named ABCProd.ndx, using the Product field as the key.

The SET ALTERNATE command in use specifies a file named TaxRept.txt. The path set with the SET PATH command is C:\DBFiles. Drive C is the default disk drive, and LPT1: is the printer port. The current left margin setting for the printer is zero (modifiable with the SET MARGIN command). The currently selected work area is 1. The most recent ON ERROR command specifies DO ErrProc as the action to take when an error occurs.

The status of the various SET commands that use ON/OFF switches (as well as the SET DEVICE command) are displayed, as are the current settings for the function keys. (Function keys can be customized using the SET FUNCTION command.)

### TIPS

The DISPLAY or LIST STATUS command will give you general information about environmental parameters. For more specifics about individual fields

```
Currently Selected Database:
Select area:  1, Database in Use: C:ABCTemp.dbf   Alias: ManySide
    Related into: ABCProd
    Relation: Product

Select area:  2, Database in Use: C:ABCProd.dbf   Alias: OneSide
    Master index file:  C:ABCProd.ndx  Key: product

Alternate file: C:TaxRept.txt
File search path: C:\DBFILES
Default disk drive: C:
Print destination:  LPT1:
Margin =      0
Current work area =    1
On Error:       DO ErrProc

ALTERNATE  - ON   DELETED    - OFF  FIXED      - OFF  SAFETY     - OFF
BELL       - ON   DELIMITERS - OFF  HEADING    - ON   SCOREBOARD - ON
CARRY      - OFF  DEVICE     - SCRN HELP       - OFF  STATUS     - OFF
CATALOG    - OFF  DOHISTORY  - OFF  HISTORY    - ON   STEP       - OFF
CENTURY    - OFF  ECHO       - OFF  INTENSITY  - ON   TALK       - OFF
CONFIRM    - OFF  ESCAPE     - ON   MENU       - ON   TITLE      - ON
CONSOLE    - ON   EXACT      - OFF  PRINT      - OFF  UNIQUE     - OFF
DEBUG      - OFF  FIELDS     - OFF

Programmable function keys:
F2  - assist;
F3  - list;
F4  - dir;
F5  - display structure;
F6  - display status;
F7  - display memory;
F8  - display;
F9  - append;
F10 - edit;
```

**FIGURE 7.7:** Sample output from the DISPLAY STATUS command showing information about all open database files, the status of most SET commands, and commands assigned to the programmable function keys.

and memory variables, use the DISPLAY STRUCTURE and DISPLAY MEMORY commands. To put a copy of the output of the DISPLAY STATUS command on a disk file (for program documentation), use the SET ALTERNATE command.

### SEE ALSO

DISPLAY MEMORY
DISPLAY STRUCTURE
SUSPEND

## The DISPLAY STRUCTURE Command

DISPLAY STRUCTURE displays the structure of the currently open database file.

### SYNTAX

**DISPLAY STRUCTURE [TO PRINT]**

where TO PRINT optionally echoes the display to the printer.

### USAGE

The DISPLAY STRUCTURE command displays the name, disk drive, location, number of records, date of last change, and total number of bytes per record for the database, as well as the name, data type, width, and decimal places for each field. The total number of bytes per record includes the extra byte used to store the deletion marker.

If SET FIELD is on, a triangle symbol appears to the left of the currently accessible fields. The LIST STRUCTURE command presents the same display but does not pause between full screens.

### EXAMPLES

Figure 7.1 earlier in the chapter shows the results of the DISPLAY STRUCTURE command when used to display the structure of a database file name Customer.

### TIPS

To store a copy of the structure in a text file, use the SET ALTERNATE command.

### SEE ALSO

DISPLAY STATUS
COPY

## The SET DOHISTORY Command

SET DOHISTORY records commands from the command file being processed in a history file, in the same manner that interactive commands are stored in a history file.

### SYNTAX

**SET DOHISTORY ON/OFF**

where ON records command file commands in the history file and OFF terminates the recording.

## USAGE

dBASE records all interactive commands in a history file that can be reviewed with the LIST HISTORY command or with the ↑ and ↓ keys. If SET DOHISTORY is ON, commands from command files are recorded in the history file as well. In a sense, SET DOHISTORY is similar to SET DEBUG, except that commands are echoed into a file rather than to the printer.

The default number of commands recorded in the history file is 20. However, the SET HISTORY command allows you to set this value to any number within a range of 0 to 16,000.

The DISPLAY HISTORY and LIST HISTORY commands display all commands in the history file on the screen. The optional TO PRINT parameter displays them on the printer.

## EXAMPLE

To record 500 command lines from a command file in the history file, enter the commands

**SET HISTORY TO 500**
**SET DOHISTORY ON**

at the dot prompt before running the command file.

When the command file is finished running, enter the commands below to terminate the recording of program commands and to review the commands as they were processed:

**SET DOHISTORY OFF**
**DISPLAY HISTORY**

## TIPS

When SET DOHISTORY is on, a program runs very slowly. Be sure to turn SET DOHISTORY off when you no longer need to record commands. The SET DEBUG command is usually better to use, because it sends the echoed output directly to the printer.

Be sure to read about the SET HISTORY command in Chapter 16, "Managing Multiple Database Files," if you plan to record many command lines in a history file. With large history settings you must take into consideration the interaction between memory variable space and the RUN command.

**SEE ALSO**

SET HISTORY
DISPLAY HISTORY
LIST HISTORY
SUSPEND
RESUME
SET DEBUG

## SUMMARY

This chapter presented a basic tutorial on debugging and included discussions of each debugging tool dBASE offers.

*For tips on designing systems to minimize the likelihood of bugs:*

- Chapter 2, "Software Design and Development"

*For information on displaying memory variables:*

- Chapter 6, "Memory Variables"

*For more information on avoiding data-type mismatch errors:*

- Chapter 15, "Managing Data, Records, and Files"

*For more information on dBASE functions:*

- Chapter 17, "dBASE Functions"

*For more information on SET commands:*

- Chapter 18, "Setting Parameters"

*For more information on trapping errors as they occur:*

- Chapter 19, "Event Processing and Error Trapping"

*For a debugging aid that can help find structural errors:*

- Chapter 24, "Algorithms to Extend dBASE"

*For help with specific error messages:*

- Appendix A, "Error Messages"

# PART 3

# *SCREEN DISPLAYS AND REPORTS*

Custom screens and reports are the means by which your application communicates with its users: the custom screens allow the user to enter data, and the reports display the data and perhaps results of calculations that the application produces. Even the casual dBASE user is probably familiar with the basics of custom screens and reports. However, the chapters in this part go beyond the basics to provide you with the necessary techniques for attaining complete control of screen displays and formatted reports.

Chapter 8 discusses custom screens, format files, and the dBASE III PLUS screen painter. In addition, the chapter covers more advanced topics, such as custom graphics characters, which you can use to enhance your screen displays.

Chapter 9 discusses techniques for displaying data on printed reports. In addition to discussing the built-in dBASE report generator, this chapter presents programming techniques that allow you to develop formatted reports beyond the capabilities of the report generator, including techniques for calculating and displaying an unlimited number of subtotals in a report.

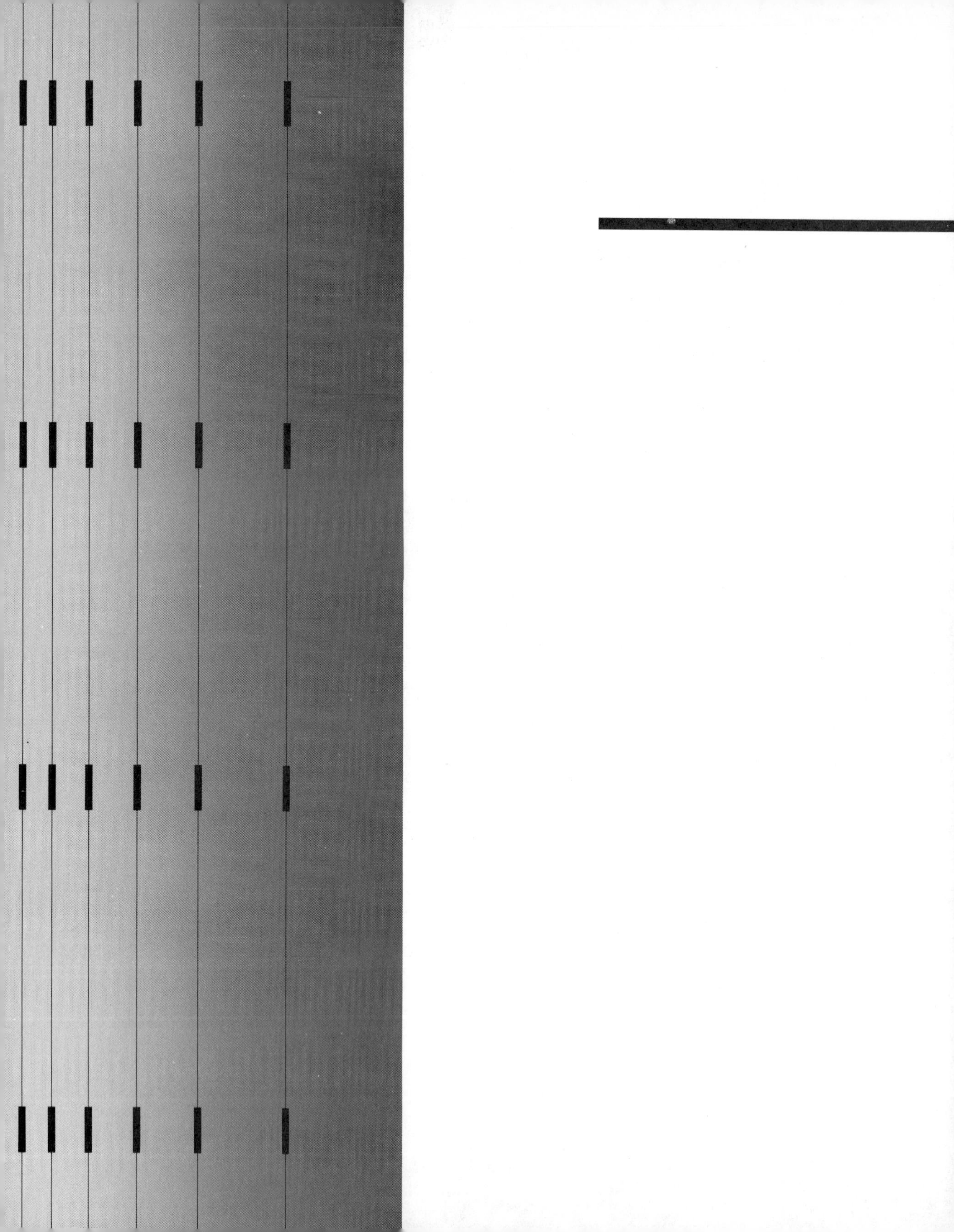

CHAPTER 8

# Managing Screen Displays

# Managing Screen Displays

When you issue the dBASE APPEND or EDIT command without a custom screen (or *form*) in use, dBASE will draw a very basic form for entering and editing data. This basic form, as you are probably aware, only lists field names down the left side of the screen, with a prompt to the right of each field name.

For custom applications, such simplified screens are rarely sufficient: you'll want to create forms that are visually appealing, easy to use, and efficient for entering and editing data. These custom forms usually include prompts that are more descriptive than the field names alone. They also employ a variety of enhancement techniques, including color, boxes, graphics characters, data checking, and validation.

This chapter discusses custom forms and the commands that create and use them, particularly the built-in dBASE screen painter. It also discusses techniques for enhancing custom forms, such as graphics characters, intensity, and color. The reference section of the chapter covers the basic commands used to create custom forms.

## Creating a Form with the Screen Painter

dBASE III PLUS provides a tool called the *screen painter,* which allows you to "paint" a custom form on your monitor. To access the screen painter, type

**MODIFY SCREEN <file name>**

at the dot prompt, where <file name> is a valid DOS file name with no extension (that is, eight letters with no spaces or punctuation). dBASE will add the extension .scr to the screen file and the extension .fmt to the format file that the screen painter generates. The format file that the screen painter eventually generates is the one you will use with your application programs and is discussed in the section "Using Format Files."

Note that the screen painter is only a handy tool for creating custom forms. A programmer can also create a format file directly with the MODIFY COMMAND editor or any word processor. However, it is much easier to "draw" a custom form with the screen painter than it is to guess how the format file will look based on the @...SAY...GET commands you type into a format file.

Once loaded, the screen painter displays a menu of options at the top of the screen, a status bar at the bottom of the screen, and a blank area on which you can compose your custom form. The two lines at the bottom of the screen provide help and instructions as you work. Figure 8.1 shows how the screen painter looks when it is first brought up.

Each of the menu options at the top of the screen has a pull-down menu associated with it. To pull down the other menus across the top of the screen, press the ← and → keys. To highlight options within a pull-down menu, use the ↑ and ↓ keys. To select an option in a pull-down menu, move the highlight to that option and press the Return key.

## Selecting the Database for the Form

The first step in creating a custom form is to select the database file for the form. (The database should already exist.) To do so, highlight the Select Database File option on the Set Up menu and press Return. dBASE will display a list of your database (.dbf) file names. Move the highlight to the name of the database file that

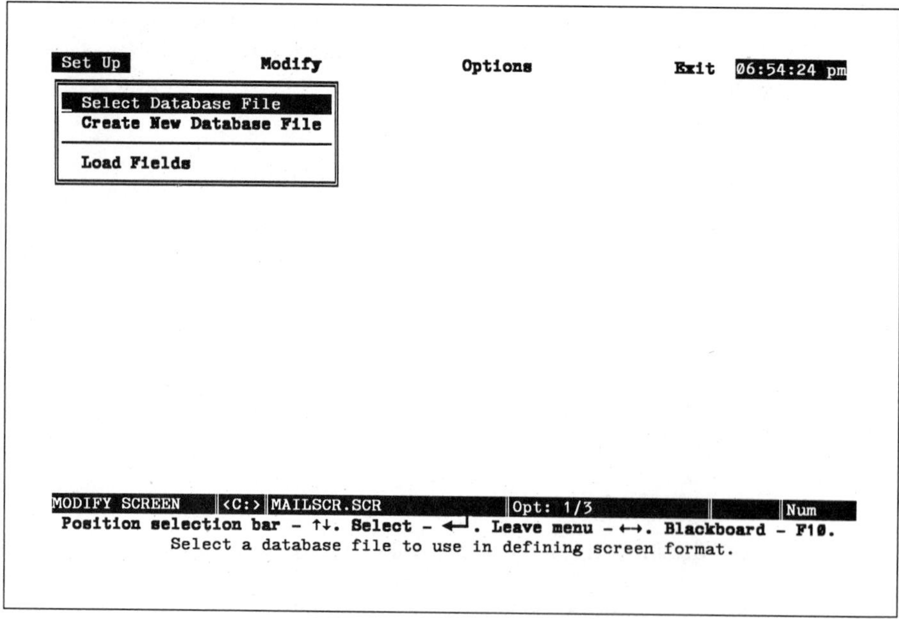


**FIGURE 8.1:** The screen painter before loading any fields onto the form. The bottom two lines provide help and instructions as you design a custom form. The main menu appears at the top of the screen, and the Set Up menu is currently displayed. The status bar near the bottom of the screen displays the name of the screen file being edited (MailScr in this example). It will also display the row and column position of the cursor when you begin placing fields on the screen.

the form will serve, and press Return. The menu of database file names will disappear, and the highlight bar will return to the first pull-down menu.

You can also select the appropriate database file with the USE command before entering the screen painter. The commands below preselect Mail.dbf as the database to paint a form for and assign the name MailScr to the custom form:

**USE Mail**
**MODIFY SCREEN MailScr**

## Loading Fields for the Form

Selecting the fields that you want displayed on the form is the second step in creating a new form. To do so, select the Load Fields option from the Set Up menu. This brings up a list of fields on the currently selected database.

You can use the ↑ and ↓ keys to highlight field names and the Return key to select them to display on the form. A triangle symbol will appear next to each field that you select for display. (To *unselect* a selected field, highlight it and press Return again.) You need not include all field names on your form.

After selecting the fields you want to include on your form, press the ← or → key to leave the field names submenu. The field names you selected will appear on the screen, with highlights showing the size and default templates for each field immediately to the right of each field name. Figure 8.2 shows an example using a hypothetical Mail.dbf database.

## The Screen Painter Blackboard

The portion of the screen that the fields are on is called the *screen painter blackboard.* The blackboard is where you compose your form. It is important to keep the following points in mind when using the blackboard:

- The lower-right corner always displays the current position of the cursor on the screen. Each page or screenful of a form should begin at row 1 or lower (not row 0) and should not extend beyond row 24.
- To use the menus at the top of the screen at any time, press F10. To return to the blackboard, press F10 again.

Table 8.1 lists the keys that you can use to write, erase, and move items on the blackboard.

### Inserting Lines, Text, and Fields

To insert text into a form (such as prompts for fields, a screen title, or instructions), first make sure that the cursor is *not* in a field highlight. Then turn on the

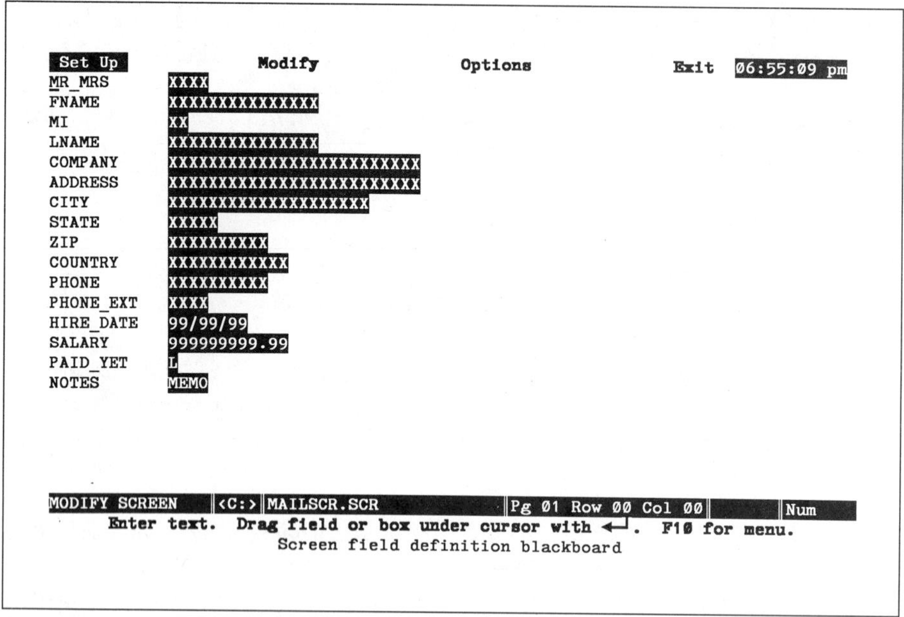


**FIGURE 8.2:** Fields from a database file named Mail.dbf have been loaded onto the screen painter. In the default templates, Xs accept any character, 9s accept only numbers, Ls accept only logical data, and MEMO represents a memo field.

insert mode by pressing the Ins key. You will notice that Ins appears in the status bar at the bottom of the screen.

Once the insert mode is on, pressing the Return key inserts a new line at the current cursor position. (Typing Ctrl-N at any time, regardless of the insert mode, inserts a blank line at the cursor position.)

While the insert mode is on, any letters that you type will be inserted at the current cursor position, and all characters to the right of the cursor will move to the right. To type over existing text (rather than insert the text), turn the insert mode off before typing.

To insert new fields onto the form, first move the cursor to where you want the new field to appear. Then press F10 to bring back the menu, and highlight the Set Up option at the top of the screen. From the Set Up menu, select Load Fields. Highlight the field you wish to add, then press Return to select it. Press the ← or → key to leave the submenu and F10 to return to the blackboard. The newly selected field and its highlight will appear at the cursor position.

| KEY | ALTERNATE | EFFECT |
|---|---|---|
| F10 | | Switches between menu and blackboard |
| ← | | Moves cursor left one character |
| → | | Moves cursor right one character |
| ↑ | | Moves cursor up one line |
| ↓ | | Moves cursor down one line |
| Ins | Ctrl-V | If cursor is not in a field highlight, turns the insert mode on and off; otherwise, extends the length of the field highlight |
| Ctrl-N | | Inserts a blank line at the cursor position |
| End | Ctrl-F | Moves cursor to beginning of next word |
| Home | Ctrl-A | Moves cursor to beginning of current or previous word |
| Return | Ctrl-M | If insert mode is on, inserts a new line; otherwise, just moves down a line (also used for moving field highlights and boxes) |
| Del | Ctrl-G | Deletes character over cursor, or decreases the size of a field highlight if the cursor is inside a field highlight |
| Backspace | | Deletes character to left of cursor |
| Ctrl-T | | Deletes word to right of cursor |
| Ctrl-Y | | Deletes an entire line |
| Ctrl-U | | Deletes a field highlight or box at the current cursor position |
| PgDn | Ctrl-C | Scrolls down 18 lines on screen |
| PgUp | Ctrl-R | Scrolls up 18 lines on screen |

**TABLE 8.1:** Control Keys Used on the Screen Painter Blackboard

## Deleting Lines, Text, and Fields

To delete an entire line from a form, put the cursor on that line and type Ctrl-Y. To delete only the text (such as a field name), place the cursor to the left of the text to be deleted. Then press Del, Ctrl-G, or the Backspace key to delete individual characters, or Ctrl-T to delete entire words. To erase text without repositioning anything on the line, turn the insert mode off and press the space bar repeatedly over the existing text.

To delete a field from the form, move the cursor inside the field highlight and type Ctrl-U. dBASE will ask whether you want to delete the field from the database as well. You probably will not want to, because doing so permanently deletes all the data in that field. Enter N to delete the field from the form but not the associated database.

### MOVING FIELD HIGHLIGHTS

To move a field highlight, first place the cursor inside the highlight you wish to move. Then press the Return key. The navigation line at the bottom of the screen will give you some basic instructions on moving the field, as well as the name, data type, and size of the field. Use the arrow keys to move the cursor to the new position for the field, then press Return to complete the move. (If you change your mind before pressing Return, you can press Esc to cancel the move.)

### CHANGING FIELD WIDTHS

To change the size of a highlight on the form, first place the cursor inside the field highlight. To lengthen the highlight, press the Ins key until the highlight is the desired length. To decrease the highlight width, press the Del key until the field is the desired width.

You can also change the width of a field by using the Modify option from the top menu. However, doing so changes the width of the field on the database as well as on the form. In general, this is not good practice because it can result in the loss of data. Use the Ins and Del keys to alter field widths on the form. To alter database field sizes, use the MODIFY STRUCTURE command outside of the screen painter.

### ADDING BOXES AND LINES TO FORMS

You can add single- and double-bar boxes and lines to custom forms by pressing F10 and highlighting the Options pull-down menu. Highlight either the Double-bar or Single-bar option and press Return. The navigation line at the bottom of the screen will give you instructions for drawing the box. Basically, you just need to position the cursor where you want a corner of the box to appear, then press Return. Use the arrow keys to position the cursor to the opposite corner, then press Return again. The box will appear on the form.

You can use the same technique for drawing lines on the form. Select the Single- or Double-bar option, move the cursor to the start of the line, and press Return. Then move the cursor to the end of the line and press Return once again. Figure 8.3 shows a sample form with double-bar boxes drawn around the form title and bottom menu and some single-bar lines within the bottom menu.

To delete a box that has already been drawn, move the cursor to any place on the box and type Ctrl-U. The entire box or line will disappear. To expand or shrink a box, move the cursor to a corner of the box and press Return. Then use the arrow keys to resize the box, and press Return.

## Changing Entry Characteristics

The Modify option from the main screen painter menu offers several options for altering the characteristics of fields on the form. Before using this option, move the cursor to a specific field highlight on the form. Then press F10 and → to display the Modify pull-down menu. The menu will display the current characteristics for that field, as shown in Figure 8.4.

On the top half of the menu, the Source, Content, Type, Width, and Decimal options define the database, field name, data type, and size of the field currently highlighted on the blackboard. Any changes made here will affect the actual

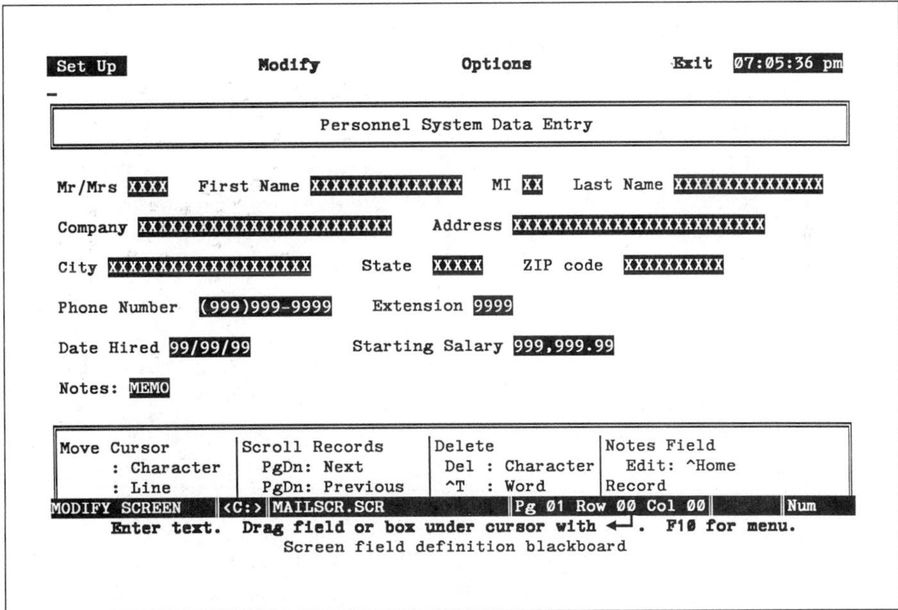


**FIGURE 8.3:** A fancier custom form on the screen painter blackboard. Fields have been rearranged, and abbreviated field names have been replaced by more descriptive titles. A title, help menu (partially obscured), boxes, and lines have been added to present a more appealing display.

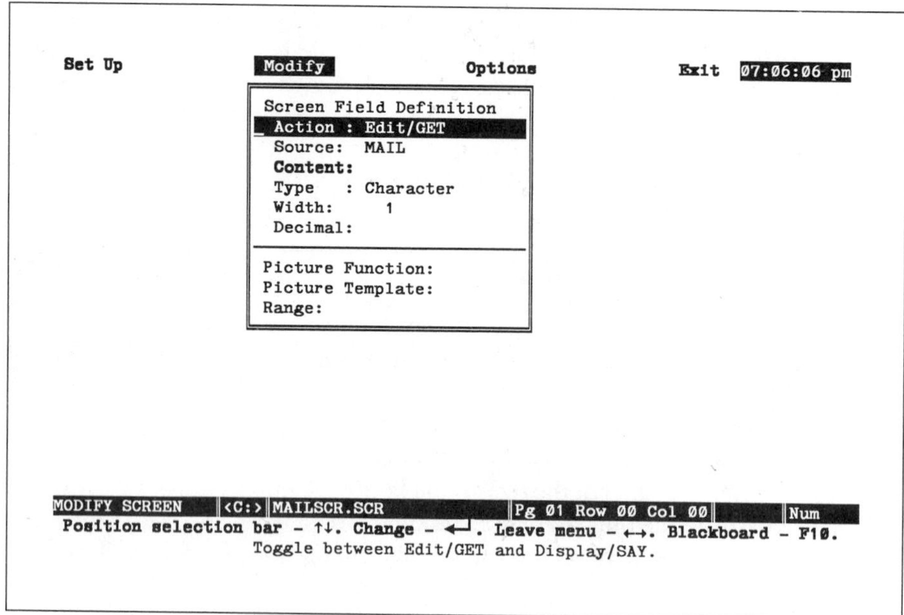


**FIGURE 8.4:** The Modify pull-down menu on the screen painter. In most cases, you will want to stay away from the Source, Content, Type, Width, and Decimal options, because these affect the database structure directly. The Action option converts fields from "editable" to "display-only," and the Picture and Range options add templates and data-verification capabilities to the form.

database structure, so you should avoid these options. (Use MODIFY STRUCTURE to alter a database structure; use the screen painter only to paint forms.)

In some situations, you'll want to display a field but not allow it to be edited (as with a customer number or part number that should not be changed). The Action option on the Modify menu determines whether a field can be edited. If this option reads Edit/GET, the field can be edited on the custom form. If the option reads Display/SAY, the field will be displayed but cannot be edited. Highlighting the option and pressing Return toggles it between the Display and Edit modes. The Picture Function, Picture Template, and Range options add data transformation, templates, and verification to your custom form.

***The Picture Function Option*** When you select Picture Function, you will see some of the options listed in Table 8.2 (only the options relevant to the data type of the currently selected field will be displayed). For a more complete discussion and examples of picture functions, see the discussion of the @...SAY...GET command and Table 8.5 in the reference section later in this chapter.

| OPTION | EFFECT |
|---|---|
| ! | Converts all alphabetic characters placed in the field to uppercase |
| A | Allows only letters (A–Z and a–z) to be entered into the field; any previously entered nonalphabetic characters are hidden if displayed by a SAY command |
| R | Used in combination with a template to ensure that data are always *displayed* within a predefined template but *stored* on disk without the extra template characters; e.g., phone number is *displayed* as (123)555-1919 but compactly *stored* on disk as 1235551919 |
| D | Displays date in American mm/dd/yy format |
| E | Displays date in European dd/mm/yy format |
| S | Allows horizontal scrolling on a wide character field |
| B | Left-justifies a number |
| Z | Displays a blank instead of a zero value |

**TABLE 8.2:** Picture Function Options Available from the Screen Painter

To select a picture function, type in the appropriate letter (or letters) in the box presented at the bottom of the screen and press Return. You can combine two or more picture functions. For example, typing in the function **BZ** would display all numbers left-justified within the highlight. It would display a blank instead of the number zero if the field contained the number zero.

The picture function that you specify here will automatically be incorporated into the format file that the screen painter generates. For example, if you specify the picture function **BZ** for the Salary field, the generated format file will contain a command such as the one below:

**@ 10,15 SAY "Salary" GET Salary FUNCTION "BZ"**

(*Note:* Programmers who create their own format files might be more familiar with the syntax PICTURE "@BZ" than FUNCTION "BZ". The two are equivalent, except that if you use PICTURE to define a function, the function must begin with the @ character.)

***The Picture Template Option*** The Picture Template option allows you to specify a character-for-character template for a field (rather than an overall template for the field). This can be used in conjunction with a previously defined picture function. Your options for defining a picture template are summarized in Table 8.3.

A common example of a picture template would be **(999)999-9999** for phone numbers. With this template the user can type only numeric characters (because of the "9" template), and dBASE automatically puts in the parentheses and

| OPTION | EFFECT |
|---|---|
| A | Allows only letters (upper- and lowercase) to be entered into the field; no numeric characters |
| X | Allows any character, including letters, numbers, and punctuation, to be entered into the field |
| # | Allows only numbers, spaces, plus ( + ), and minus ( − ) signs to be entered into the field |
| ! | Converts any letter entered into the field to uppercase |
| N | Allows both alphabetical letters and numeric digits |
| 9 | Allows only numeric digits to be entered into the field |
| . | Specifies the exact position of decimal point in a number |
| , | Displays commas in "thousands" places if number is large enough |
| L | Allows only logical data to be entered into the field (upper- or lowercase T, F, Y, or N) |
| Y | Allows a Y or N |
| other | Inserts any other character automatically into the user's entry (unless the R function is used) |

**TABLE 8.3:** Picture Template Options Available from the Screen Painter

hyphen. Therefore, if the user types in **6195551212**, dBASE automatically converts the entry to **(619)555-1212**.

As with the picture functions, you can type your template directly into the box provided on the screen painter blackboard. Press Return after entering the template. The template is automatically incorporated into the format file that the screen painter eventually generates. For example, if you were to specify the template

**(999)999-9999**

for the Phone field, the generated format file would contain a command like the one below:

```
@ 2,5 SAY "Phone number";
GET Phone PICTURE "(999)999-9999"
```

Examples of additional picture templates are summarized in Table 8.7 in the reference section of this chapter, in the discussion of the @...SAY...GET... PICTURE commands.

***The Range Option*** The Range option from the Modify menu lets you define a range of acceptable values for a numeric or date field. (Range is not a valid selection if the field currently highlighted on the blackboard is not of the date or numeric data type.) When you select the Range option from the Modify menu, the screen presents two options:

**Lower Limit:**
**Upper Limit:**

First highlight Lower Limit, to specify the smallest number or earliest date that can be entered into the field, then press Return to enter a value. Then highlight Upper Limit, to specify the highest number or latest date that can be entered into the field, and press Return to enter a value. Press the ← or → key to leave the submenu when you are done.

The range options that you select are automatically incorporated into the format file that the screen painter creates. For example, if you specified a range of 10000 to 99000 for the Salary field, the generated format file would contain a command such as

**@ 10,15 SAY "Salary" GET Salary RANGE 10000, 99000**

#### SAVING A TEXT-FILE IMAGE OF THE FORM

To save a text-file image of the form that can be displayed on the printer (which can be useful when developing documentation), select the Generate a Text File Image option from the top of the Options menu. The generated file will have the same name as the screen file, but with the extension .txt. This file can be printed or incorporated into any text file, using a standard word processor. You can also use the dBASE **TYPE <file name> TO PRINT** command to print the text file.

### Saving the Form

When you've finished designing your form, press F10 to Select the top menus, and move the highlight to the Exit menu. Select the Save option to save your work (or Abandon if you want to abandon changes made during the most recent session). Selecting Save saves the screen painter file (with the extension .scr), the format file that has been created automatically (with the extension .fmt), and the text-image file if you requested one (with the extension .txt).

## EDITING FORMS WITH MODIFY SCREEN

To edit an existing form with MODIFY SCREEN, first select the associated database at the dot prompt with the USE command. Then enter the MODIFY

SCREEN command with the name of the screen file to edit. When the blackboard appears, press F10 to bring the form onto the screen. (If the form does not appear, try selecting the Select a Database File option first, then select the appropriate database, and then try F10 again.)

When the form appears on the blackboard, you can use the usual keys and menu items to make changes, then select Exit and Save to save the changes.

## USING FORMAT FILES

The format file that the screen painter creates is like any other command file or program, except that it contains only @...SAY...GET...PICTURE...RANGE and perhaps READ commands. For example, Figure 8.5 shows the format file generated from the screen in Figure 8.3.

```
@  2, 27  SAY "Personnel System Data Entry"
@  5,  1  SAY "Mr/Mrs"
@  5,  8  GET  MAIL->MR_MRS
@  5, 15  SAY "First Name"
@  5, 26  GET  MAIL->FNAME  PICTURE "XXXXXXXXXXXXXXX"
@  5, 44  SAY "MI"
@  5, 47  GET  MAIL->MI
@  5, 52  SAY "Last Name"
@  5, 62  GET  MAIL->LNAME
@  7,  1  SAY "Company"
@  7,  9  GET  MAIL->COMPANY
@  7, 38  SAY "Address"
@  7, 46  GET  MAIL->ADDRESS
@  9,  1  SAY "City"
@  9,  6  GET  MAIL->CITY
@  9, 31  SAY "State"
@  9, 38  GET  MAIL->STATE
@  9, 47  SAY "ZIP code"
@  9, 57  GET  MAIL->ZIP
@ 11,  1  SAY "Phone Number"
@ 11, 15  GET  MAIL->PHONE  PICTURE "(999)999-9999"
@ 11, 32  SAY "Extension"
@ 11, 42  GET  MAIL->PHONE_EXT  PICTURE "9999"
@ 13,  1  SAY "Date Hired"
@ 13, 12  GET  MAIL->HIRE_DATE
@ 13, 30  SAY "Starting Salary"
@ 13, 46  GET  MAIL->SALARY  PICTURE "999,999.99"
@ 15,  1  SAY "Notes:"
@ 15,  8  GET  MAIL->NOTES
@ 18,  1  SAY "Move Cursor       Scroll Records      Delete          Notes Field"
@ 19,  6  SAY ": Character     PgDn: Next         Del : Character   Edit: ^Home"
@ 20,  6  SAY ": Line          PgDn: Previous     ^T  : Word      Record"
@ 21,  2  SAY "End : Word right Insert Mode        ^Y  : Field       ^End: Save changes"
@ 22,  2  SAY "Home: Word left      Ins: On/off     ^U  : Record      Esc: Abandon changes"
@ 17,  0  TO 23, 79     DOUBLE
@  1,  0  TO  3, 79     DOUBLE
@ 18, 18  TO 22, 18
@ 18, 37  TO 22, 37
@ 18, 54  TO 22, 54
```

**FIGURE 8.5:** Format file generated by the screen painter. The format file contains only @...SAY...GET... PICTURE...RANGE and perhaps READ commands. The format file always has the .fmt extension on its file name.

To activate a format file, first select the associated database (and any index files, if relevant), and then use the SET FORMAT command. For example, given a database named Mail and a form named MailScr, the following commands will open the format file:

**USE Mail**
**SET FORMAT TO MailScr**

Any ensuing APPEND, EDIT, READ, INSERT, or CHANGE command will display the custom MailScr form rather than the basic dBASE editing form. To return to the database and remove the form from use, issue the CLOSE FORMAT command. Be forewarned that even READ commands that are not meant to access the custom form will continue to do so if the format file is inadvertently left open.

For specific instructions on adding new data through custom forms, see Chapter 10, "Adding New Data." More specific techniques for editing data through custom forms are discussed in Chapter 11, "Editing and Deleting Records."

## MULTIPLE-PAGE CUSTOM FORMS

If your database contains many fields and you want to create a custom form for it, you will probably have to separate the form into *pages* (screenfuls). For example, Figure 8.6 shows a portion of a sample database named Taxes with many fields. Obviously, all of the fields shown will not fit on one screen. To handle this situation, you can use the MODIFY SCREEN command to create a custom form. Using the same control keys that you use to create a single-page form, you can design the first page of the form as in Figure 8.7.

Once the first page is defined, you can press PgDn to move to the next page. Now it becomes tricky, because you can't rely on your eye to tell you where the next page begins. You have to use both Ctrl-N (to insert blank lines) and Ctrl-Y (to delete blank lines) to place the cursor at the top of the screen. The status bar tells you that you are at the top of page 2 by displaying

**Pg 02 Row 01 Col 01**

At the top of page 2, design the next page of the form. Figure 8.8 shows a second page for the Taxes form. The cursor has been repositioned to the upper-left corner of the screen, so the status bar shows the starting position of the text on the screen.

Notice that the client number, last name, and first name are repeated on the second page of the form. These are for informational purposes only and need not be reentered by the operator. To place these fields on the second page and make them uneditable, first type a prompt for the field anywhere on the screen. Then

```
Structure for database: Taxes.dbf

Field  Field Name  Type        Width    Dec
    1  CLIENT_NO   Character       4
    2  LNAME       Character      15
    3  FNAME       Character      15
    4  MI          Character       1
    5  ADDRESS     Character      20
    6  CITY        Character      20
    7  STATE       Character       2
    8  ZIP         Character      10
    9  PHONE       Character       8
   10  SSN         Character      12
   11  SPOUSESSN   Character      12
   12  OCCUPATION  Character      20
   13  SPOUSEOCC   Character      20
   14  ELECTION    Character       1
   15  SPOUSEELEC  Character       1
   16  SINGLE      Character       1
   17  MARJOINT    Character       1
   18  MARSEPARAT  Character       1
   19  SPOUSENAME  Character      20
   20  HEAD        Character       1
   21  CHILDNAME   Character      20
   22  WIDOW       Character       1
   23  SPDEATHYR   Numeric         2
   24  SELF        Character       1
   25  OVER65      Character       1
   26  BLIND       Character       1
   27  SPOUSE      Character       1
   28  SPOVER65    Character       1
   29  SPBLIND     Character       1
   30  BOX6AB      Numeric         2
   31  BOX6C       Numeric         2
   32  CHILDNMS    Character      40
   33  OTHERDEP1   Character      20
   34  RELATE1     Character      15
   35  MONTHS1     Numeric         3
   36  INCOME1     Character       1
   37  HALF1       Character       1
   38  OTHERDEP2   Character      20
   39  RELATE2     Character      15
   40  MONTHS2     Numeric         3
   41  INCOME2     Character       1
   42  HALF2       Character       1
   43  OTHERBOX1   Numeric         2
   44  WAGES       Numeric        10        2
   45  INTEREST    Numeric        10        2
```

**FIGURE 8.6:** Partial structure of the large sample database named Taxes. Obviously, several pages of data-entry fields will be required to enter and edit each record on this database.

place the cursor where you want the field highlight to start, as below:

**Client: _**

Call up the menu by pressing F10 and select Content under the Modify menu. dBASE will show you a list of existing fields. Highlight the field that you want to place at the cursor position and press Return to select it.

To make sure that the field is for display only, move the highlight to the Action option and press Return to change it from Edit/GET to Display/SAY. Press F10 to return to the blackboard and continue designing the form. Field highlights for Display/SAY fields are not displayed in reverse video.

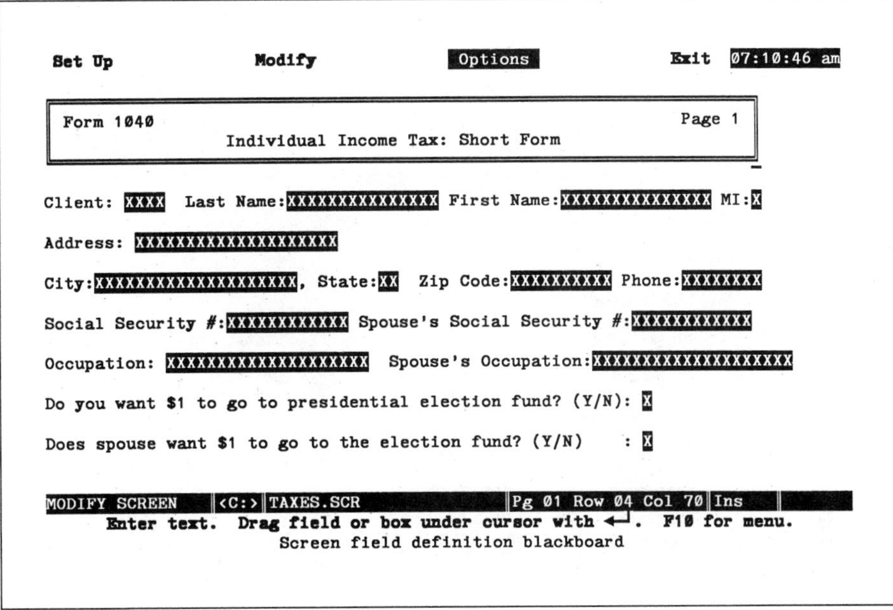


**FIGURE 8.7:** First page of a custom Taxes form on the screen painter blackboard. Only a few of the fields will fit on this page. Remaining fields for each record are on other pages. The PgUp and PgDn keys allow the user to scroll through multiple-page forms.

You can create as many as 32 pages for a single data-entry form, repeating whatever information you like on each page. When you finish creating the entire form, save your work by highlighting the Exit option and selecting Save.

## Using a Multiple-Page Form

Once you've saved your multiple-page form, you can treat it as you would any custom form. At the dot prompt, use the SET FORMAT TO command, along with the name of the file (e.g., **SET FORMAT TO Taxes**). The APPEND, EDIT, INSERT, CHANGE, and READ commands will use the custom form as usual. The only difference in control-key commands is that PgUp and PgDn will scroll from page to page before they scroll from record to record.

If you look at the contents of the format (.fmt) file, you'll see that the screen painter has simply inserted a READ command between each page. Should you ever decide to develop your own multiple-page format files without the aid of the screen painter, just remember to place a READ command between each screenful of data-entry fields.

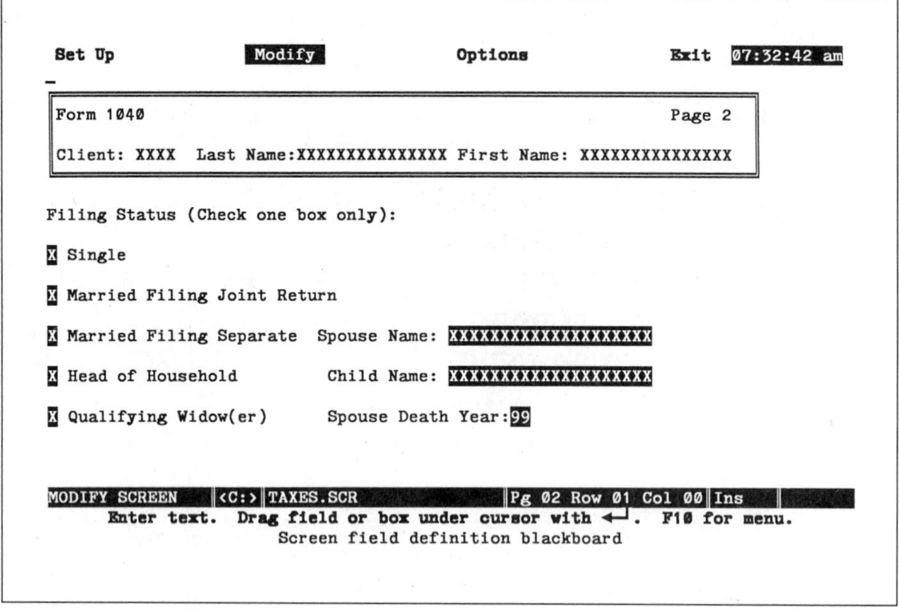


**FIGURE 8.8:** Second page of the Taxes form designed on the screen painter blackboard. Up to 32 more such pages can be placed in a single custom form. The client number and name from the first page are displayed on all pages in the form as a reminder to the user.

## A Problem with Boxes on Multiple-Page Forms

An early release of dBASE III PLUS had a slight problem with boxes on multiple-page forms—all the boxes appeared together on the last page of the form. If this problem occurs when you create multiple-page forms, there is a remedy.

At the dot prompt, enter the MODIFY COMMAND command with the name of the format file (the file name you assigned to the form, followed by the extension .fmt). When you see the format file, press PgDn until you get to the

**@ <r>,<c> TO <r>,<c>**

commands (where <r> and <c> are row and column numbers) at the bottom of the form, as below:

```
@ 1, 0 TO 4, 70 DOUBLE
@ 2, 0 TO 6, 70 DOUBLE
```

These @...TO... commands draw the boxes on the forms. You need to put these on each page rather than clumped together at the end of the format file. You can tell where the pages begin and end by looking for the READ commands that mark the end of one page and the beginning of the next.

If you use an external word processor, such as WordStar in the nondocument mode, you can block move the @...TO... commands to their appropriate locations for each page (e.g., the first @...TO... command belongs above the first READ command, the second @..TO... command belongs above the second READ command, and so forth). If you use MODIFY COMMAND, you'll have to type the @...SAY...DOUBLE command at the new position and erase it from its original position. You may have to experiment a bit to get all the pages exactly how you want them.

## Adding Graphics Characters to Forms

You can add other graphics characters in addition to boxes and lines to your custom forms to make the display fancier or more descriptive. For example, if you look near the lower-left corner of the form shown in Figure 8.9, you'll see that it uses several arrow-key symbols. These arrow-key symbols were added directly to the format (.fmt) file after all work with the screen painter was complete (the screen painter was used to create everything in the form except the arrows).

The dBASE III PLUS CHR( ) function can display any graphics symbol available to the screen or printer. Some of the symbols most commonly used in data-entry forms are listed in Table 8.4.

To add these characters to your format files, use MODIFY COMMAND or another editor to edit the format (.fmt) file directly. (Be sure to specify the .fmt extension no matter which editor you use.) Concatenate the CHR( ) function to existing literals with the plus ( + ) operator. (You may need to experiment with the column setting in the @ command as well.)

As an example, the form shown in Figure 8.9 was originally drawn with only blank spaces where the arrows were to be placed. The screen painter generated

| CHR FUNCTION | SYMBOL DISPLAYED |
|---|---|
| CHR(24) | ↑ |
| CHR(25) | ↓ |
| CHR(26) | → |
| CHR(27) | ← |
| CHR(17) + CHR(196) + CHR(217) | ↵ |
| CHR(249) | • |
| CHR(219) | ■ |

**TABLE 8.4:** Graphics Characters Used in Data-Entry Forms

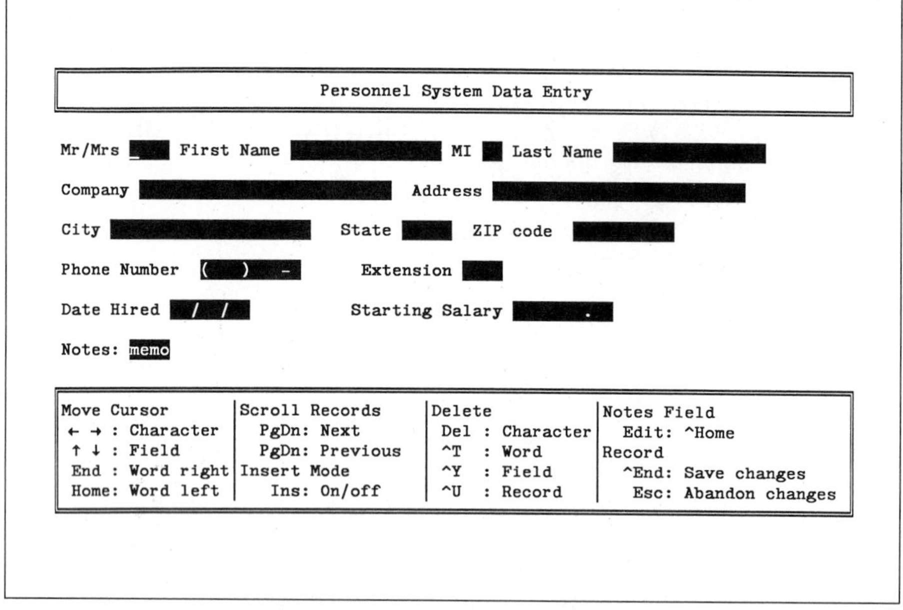

Personnel System Data Entry

Mr/Mrs First Name MI Last Name

Company Address

City State ZIP code

Phone Number ( ) - Extension

Date Hired / / Starting Salary .

Notes: memo

| Move Cursor | Scroll Records | Delete | Notes Field |
|---|---|---|---|
| ← → : Character | PgDn: Next | Del : Character | Edit: ^Home |
| ↑ ↓ : Field | PgDn: Previous | ^T : Word | Record |
| End : Word right | Insert Mode | ^Y : Field | ^End: Save changes |
| Home: Word left | Ins: On/off | ^U : Record | Esc: Abandon changes |

**FIGURE 8.9:** A custom form that includes graphics characters. The arrows near the lower-left corner of this custom form were placed directly into the format file with the MODIFY COMMAND editor and the dBASE CHR() function.

the lines where the arrows belong as below:

> **@ 19, 6 SAY ": Character..."**
> **@ 20, 6 SAY ": Line..."**

To add the graphics characters to the left of each line with a space between the characters and the text, the column position in the @ command needed to be shifted four columns to the left to make room. Then the appropriate CHR( ) functions with + signs were filled in, as below:

> **@ 19, 2 SAY CHR(27) + " " + CHR(26) + ": Character..."**
> **@ 20, 2 SAY CHR(24) + " " + CHR(25) + ": Line..."**

You can place any graphics character at any position in a custom form as long as you remember to place the CHR( ) function directly in the format file. You should add these characters as the very last step in developing your form: if you use the screen painter to make any additional changes to the form, the newly generated format file will overwrite the changes you made to the original file.

To see a complete set of graphics characters on the screen, type in and run the command file named ASCII.prg shown in Figure 8.10. Figure 8.11 shows the result.

```
*************************************** ASCII.prg
*--------------------- Display ASCII characters.
SET TALK OFF
CLEAR
Row = 1
Counter = 0
*--- Set up loop for 256 characters.
DO WHILE Counter < 256
   Col = 0
   *--- Set up loop for individual rows.
   DO WHILE Col <= 72 .AND. Counter < 256
      @ Row,Col SAY STR(Counter,3)+" "+CHR(Counter)
      Col = Col + 6
      Counter = Counter + 1
   ENDDO (col and counter)
   Row = Row + 1
ENDDO (counter <= 256)
RETURN
```

**FIGURE 8.10:** A simple command file that displays all of the ASCII codes and characters on the screen.

```
  0     1 ☺   2 ☻   3 ♥   4 ♦   5 ♣   6 ♠   7 •   8 ◘   9 ○  10 ◙  11 ♂  12 ♀
 13 ♪  14 ♫  15 ☼  16 ►  17 ◄  18 ↕  19 ‼  20 ¶  21 §  22 ▬  23 ↨  24 ↑  25 ↓
 26 →  27 ←  28 ∟  29 ↔  30 ▲  31 ▼  32    33 !  34 "  35 #  36 $  37 %  38 &
 39 '  40 (  41 )  42 *  43 +  44 ,  45 -  46 .  47 /  48 0  49 1  50 2  51 3
 52 4  53 5  54 6  55 7  56 8  57 9  58 :  59 ;  60 <  61 =  62 >  63 ?  64 @
 65 A  66 B  67 C  68 D  69 E  70 F  71 G  72 H  73 I  74 J  75 K  76 L  77 M
 78 N  79 O  80 P  81 Q  82 R  83 S  84 T  85 U  86 V  87 W  88 X  89 Y  90 Z
 91 [  92 \  93 ]  94 ^  95 _  96 `  97 a  98 b  99 c 100 d 101 e 102 f 103 g
104 h 105 i 106 j 107 k 108 l 109 m 110 n 111 o 112 p 113 q 114 r 115 s 116 t
117 u 118 v 119 w 120 x 121 y 122 z 123 { 124 ¦ 125 } 126 ~ 127   128 Ç 129 ü
130 é 131 â 132 ä 133 à 134 å 135 ç 136 ê 137 ë 138 è 139 ï 140 î 141 ì 142 Ä
143 Å 144 É 145 æ 146 Æ 147 ô 148 ö 149 ò 150 û 151 ù 152 ÿ 153 Ö 154 Ü 155 ¢
156 £ 157 ¥ 158 ₧ 159 ƒ 160 á 161 í 162 ó 163 ú 164 ñ 165 Ñ 166 ª 167 º 168 ¿
169 ⌐ 170 ¬ 171 ½ 172 ¼ 173 ¡ 174 « 175 » 176 ░ 177 ▒ 178 ▓ 179 │ 180 ┤ 181 ╡
182 ╢ 183 ╖ 184 ╕ 185 ╣ 186 ║ 187 ╗ 188 ╝ 189 ╜ 190 ╛ 191 ┐ 192 └ 193 ┴ 194 ┬
195 ├ 196 ─ 197 ┼ 198 ╞ 199 ╟ 200 ╚ 201 ╔ 202 ╩ 203 ╦ 204 ╠ 205 ═ 206 ╬ 207 ╧
208 ╨ 209 ╤ 210 ╥ 211 ╙ 212 ╘ 213 ╒ 214 ╓ 215 ╫ 216 ╪ 217 ┘ 218 ┌ 219 █ 220 ▄
221 ▌ 222 ▐ 223 ▀ 224 α 225 ß 226 Γ 227 π 228 Σ 229 σ 230 µ 231 τ 232 Φ 233 Θ
234 Ω 235 δ 236 ∞ 237 ø 238 ∈ 239 ∩ 240 ≡ 241 ± 242 ≥ 243 ≤ 244 ⌠ 245 ⌡ 246 ÷
247 ≈ 248 ° 249 • 250 · 251 √ 252 ⁿ 253 ² 254 ■ 255

. _
```

**FIGURE 8.11:** ASCII codes as displayed by the ASCII.prg command file shown in Figure 8.10. The number for each character is to the left of each character. Hence, CHR(13) shows a musical note, and CHR(25) shows a down arrow.

To display any graphics character, use the number to the left of the character with the CHR function. For example, the number 25 appears to the left of the ↓ character, indicating that CHR(25) displays the down arrow.

To view your printer's ASCII character set (which will likely be different from the screen's), enter the command

**SET DEVICE TO PRINT**

before running the ASCII program. (Be forewarned that some of the codes may cause your printer to do strange things!) After the program is done, enter the command

**SET DEVICE TO SCREEN**

to return to normal processing. If necessary, enter the command EJECT to empty the print buffer and return to the complete display.

## USING INTENSITY, DELIMITERS, AND COLOR

You can use other commands to alter the appearance of custom forms. These commands, however, are used in your command file and not directly in a format file.

Normally, the field highlights displayed with the GET commands are displayed in reverse video (because the SET INTENSITY command is on). You can use the command SET INTENSITY OFF to remove the reverse video from the custom form.

To display delimiters around GET fields, use the SET DELIMITERS command. Normally, SET DELIMITERS is off, so fields are displayed without delimiters. If SET DELIMITERS is on, each GET field will be surrounded by colons (:). The SET DELIMITERS TO command lets you specify a character other than the colon. For example, the command **SET DELIMITERS TO "[ ]"** places square brackets around the GET highlights.

Figure 8.12 shows a custom form with intensity off and the delimiters set to the square bracket characters. The series of commands that produced the modified screen are listed below. Notice that the SET INTENSITY and SET DELIMITERS commands are executed before the SET FORMAT command:

**USE Mail**
**SET INTENSITY OFF**
**SET DELIMITERS TO "[ ]"**
**SET DELIMITERS ON**
**SET FORMAT TO Mail2**
**APPEND**

In addition to the SET INTENSITY and SET DELIMITERS commands, the SET COLOR command allows you to define colors on a color monitor and other display attributes on a monochrome monitor. You can also control intensity and blinking with the SET COLOR command. This and all other SET commands are discussed in more detail in Chapter 18, "Setting Parameters."

```
                     Personnel System Data Entry

Mr/Mrs [_   ] First Name [               MI [  Last Name [                    ]

Company [                            Address [                         ]

City [                     ]   State  [     ]  ZIP code  [          ]

Phone Number  [(   )   -     ]  Extension [    ]

Date Hired [  /  /  ]        Starting Salary [        .  ]

Notes: [memo]

Move Cursor       |Scroll Records     |Delete            |Notes Field
 ← →: Character   | PgDn: Next        |Del  : Character  | Edit: ^Home
 ↑ ↓: Line        | PgDn: Previous    |^T   : Word       |ecord
 End : Word right |Insert Mode        | ^Y   : Field     |  ^End: Save changes
 Home: Word left  |    Ins: On/off    | ^U   : Record    |   Esc: Abandon changes
```

**FIGURE 8.12:** Custom form displayed after the commands SET INTENSITY OFF (to cancel reverse-video highlights), SET DELIMITERS TO "[ ]", and SET DELIMITERS ON to display square brackets around GET highlights.

# BEYOND FORMAT FILES

There are far more techniques for controlling the screen activity than those presented in this chapter. Chapter 10, "Adding New Data," explains how to develop programs that simultaneously validate data entered onto the form, perform calculations and display their results on the form, move data from one file to another or from one record to another, and so forth. These capabilities are not possible through format files.

Nevertheless, a good basic background in the screen painter, format files, and the SET FORMAT command are valuable tools for the programmer. For many tasks where data entry and editing are quite straightforward, the screen painter and format files will be sufficient.

# COMMANDS USED WITH CUSTOM FORMS

The remainder of this chapter discusses the commands used specifically for displaying, entering, and editing data on the screen.

# The MODIFY SCREEN Command

The MODIFY SCREEN command activates the menu-driven screen painter for drawing custom data-entry forms.

### SYNTAX

**MODIFY SCREEN <file name>**

where <file name> is the first eight letters of the original screen (.scr) file and also the name of the generated format (.fmt) file. The command CREATE SCREEN is equivalent to the command MODIFY SCREEN.

### USAGE

MODIFY SCREEN brings up the dBASE screen painter, which allows you to develop a custom form for any database (.dbf) file in an interactive, what-you-see-is-what-you-get fashion. When you save your work, dBASE automatically creates a format (.fmt) file that can be used with the SET FORMAT command to define a custom form for use with the APPEND, EDIT, CHANGE, INSERT, and READ commands.

The keys used for navigating the screen painter blackboard (the area in which you compose your custom form) are listed in Table 8.1 at the beginning of this chapter. The menu options that appear at the top of the screen and in the pull-down menus are also discussed at the beginning of this chapter.

The screen painter always opens a file with the name provided in the MODIFY SCREEN command and the extension .scr. This file is required for future modifications to the custom form. If this file is erased, there is no way to convert the .fmt file back into a form usable by the MODIFY SCREEN command.

Note that any changes made directly to the .fmt file will not affect the .scr file. Furthermore, any changes made to the custom form through the MODIFY SCREEN command will overwrite any previous changes made directly to the format (.fmt) file. (The screen painter always completely overwrites the existing .fmt file.)

The screen painter can create forms for multiple files linked together in a view (.vue) file. Before issuing the MODIFY SCREEN command, make sure that the .vue file has already been created and that the SET FIELDS TO command was used to define fields for the view. Then use the SET VIEW TO command to open the view file and the SET FIELDS ON command to activate the previous SET FIELDS TO command. From this point on, the screen painter will treat the view file as a single database file. However, the options in the Modify menu that would normally alter the database structure will have no effect on databases in the view file.

## EXAMPLES

The commands

```
USE Customer
MODIFY SCREEN CustScrn
```

open a database file named Customer.dbf and allow you to create a format file named CustScrn.fmt. The screen painter will also create its own working file named CustScrn.scr.

The commands below open a view file named ThreeFil.vue, which presumably has already been established using the CREATE VIEW or MODIFY VIEW command:

```
SET VIEW TO ThreeFil
SET FIELDS ON
MODIFY SCREEN ThreeFil
```

The SET FIELDS ON command specifies fields previously defined in the SET FIELDS TO command. Then the MODIFY SCREEN command allows the programmer to create a custom form named ThreeFil.vue to serve the entire view file. When creating a form for a view file in this manner, there is no need to select the Select Database File option from the screen painter top menu.

## TIPS

Even if a format file is not sufficient for your application, you can still use the MODIFY SCREEN command to generate all the @...SAY...GET commands for the basic user interface. Then read the generated .fmt file into a command file, or rename the .fmt file to a file with the .prg extension using the DOS or dBASE RENAME command. From that point on, you can use the DO command rather than the SET FORMAT command to activate the @...SAY...GET commands.

## SEE ALSO

SET FORMAT
CLOSE FORMAT
READ
@...SAY...GET...PICTURE...RANGE
APPEND
EDIT
INSERT
CHANGE

# The @...SAY...GET...PICTURE...RANGE Commands

These commands position the cursor to a location on the screen, display a prompt, and allow data entry into a field or memory variable. The optional PICTURE statement provides data verification, transformation, and/or a template. The RANGE statement limits numeric or date entries to a particular range of values.

## SYNTAX

**@ <row>,<col> [SAY <message>] [GET <variable>] ;**
**[PICTURE <template>] [RANGE <value>,<value>] ;**
**[CLEAR] [TO]**

where <row> is the row number and <col> is the column number for the screen or printer. The optional <message> can be a literal, variable, field, or combination of elements concatenated with the + sign. The <variable> can be a database field or memory variable. The <template> must consist of valid picture functions and template characters. The <value> parameters are dates or numbers. The optional CLEAR is used to clear a portion of the screen, and the optional TO is used to draw lines or boxes.

## USAGE

Each component of the @ command is discussed independently below.

### @ <row>,<col>

The first component of the command, @, positions the cursor (or printer head) to the row and column position specified by <row> and <col>. Both <row> and <col> can be a number, variable, field, expression, or function that evaluates to a number.

On the standard 24 × 80 monitor, the row value must be between 0 and 23. The column value must be between 0 and 79. Keep in mind, however, that row 0 is generally reserved for *scoreboard displays* (like the Ins and NumLock key settings), and line 22 generally displays the status bar. If you wish to use rows 0 and/or 22 for your own application, the SET SCOREBOARD OFF and SET STATUS OFF commands will free these rows for your use.

The functions ROW( ) and COL( ) return the current position of the cursor on the screen. These can be used for relative addressing, as in the example below, where the instructions place the cursor two rows down and five columns to the left of the cursor's current position:

**@ ROW( ) + 2, COL( ) – 5**

ROW( ) + 2 and COL( ) – 5 must evaluate to valid row and column numbers.

If the command @ <row>,<col> is used with nothing else following it, all the characters to the right of <col> on the specified <row> are erased from the screen.

When the command SET DEVICE TO PRINT is issued, the output from @...SAY commands is routed to the printer. (The GET portion of the command is never displayed on the printer.) When sending text to the printer, the maximum <row> and <column> coordinates are each 255.

A problem to watch out for when sending @...SAY output to the printer is decreasing row numbers. For example, in the commands below dBASE will print each line on a separate page:

```
@ 2,1 SAY "Page 1"
@ 1,40 SAY "Summary Report"
```

That's because the printer cannot move backwards from row 2 to row 1. To ensure that these end up on the same page, always place the smaller row number above the larger row number when sending @...SAY output to the printer. (As an alternative, use the ? command when printing reports instead of @.)

The PROW( ) and PCOL( ) functions are the printer equivalents of the screen's ROW( ) and COL( ) functions and can be used in the same manner for calculating relative row and addresses. (However, you cannot decrease the row or column position when sending text to the printer.)

## SAY

The optional SAY portion of the command displays any text or the contents of any database field or memory variable (though not memo fields). The PICTURE template can be used with the SAY command to format the displayed text. If the SAY command is to display literal text, it must be enclosed in quotation marks, as below:

```
@ 2,40 SAY "This is printed literally"
```

Only the plus sign ( + ) concatenator is allowed in SAY commands to join literals and variables. For example, the Up memory variable in the following example contains the character string for displaying an up arrow. The @ command below it displays the up arrow in midsentence:

```
Up = CHR(24)
@ 20,1 SAY "Press" + Up + "to make corrections."
```

Optionally, a macro can be embedded directly in the SAY command, as below:

```
Up = CHR(24)
@ 20,1 SAY "Press &Up to make corrections."
```

If the data to be concatenated is not the character data type, it must be converted to the character data type. For example, given that Amount in the following example is numeric data and Date is the date data type, the STR and DTOC functions are required to convert the data to character strings, as below:

```
@ 2,1 SAY "You won" + LTRIM(STR(Amount,9,2)) + "dollars,"
@ 3,1 SAY "on this day," + DTOC(Date) + ". Lucky you!"
```

SAY can display information from the currently open database as well as related databases. For example, if a database named Charges is currently selected in work area 1, a database named Customer is open in work area 2, and the SELECT 1 command is in effect, the following command displays the FName, LName, and Address fields from the Customer database:

```
@ 5,50 SAY TRIM(B->FName) + " " + B->LName
@ 6,50 SAY B->Address
```

Of course, you can use the full alias in place of the B->, (e.g., @ 6,50 SAY Customer->Address).

## GET

The optional GET component of the command displays the contents of an existing field or memory variable in a template that matches the size and data type of the field or variable. When a READ, APPEND, EDIT, INSERT, or CHANGE command is issued, the user can change the contents of the field or variable displayed in the GET command.

Note that unlike the SAY command, the GET command can be used to read data into a memo field. However, this works only when the GET command appears in a format file that is opened with the SET FORMAT command.

Unlike the STORE command (and assignment operator), GET cannot create a new variable from scratch. If the field or variable that GET is attempting to display does not exist in memory or the currently selected database, the error message

```
Variable not found
```

will appear on the screen. If you use GET to read in a variable, you must predefine the data type and size.

For example, the commands below create a character memory variable named FullName consisting of 30 spaces. The GET command beneath displays a 30-character template for the user to fill in a value for FullName:

```
FullName = SPACE(30)
@ 2,15 SAY "Enter your name" GET FullName
READ
```

In the example below, the Choice variable is initialized as the number zero, then the GET command requests a value for it (the PICTURE component displays the zero as a blank space and limits the user's entry to a single digit):

```
Choice = 0
@ 10,2 SAY "Select a number" ;
    GET Choice PICTURE "@Z 9"
READ
```

With a view (.vue) file in effect, the GET command can read in values for the nonselected database during editing. For example, the following commands are legal:

```
@ 10,2 GET Charge->Amount
@ 12,2 GET Customer->Name
```

However, trying to get data for two separate databases simultaneously can be very tricky and should be avoided. Chapters 10, "Adding New Data," and 16, "Managing Multiple Database Files," discuss managing multiple databases in more detail.

Unlike the ACCEPT command, any data entered into a memory variable through a GET command retains its original size. For example, if in response to the commands

```
AnyName = SPACE(15)
ACCEPT "Enter name" TO AnyName
```

the user enters Albert, the AnyName variable simply contains Albert.

However, if in response to the commands

```
AnyName = SPACE(15)
@ 2,2 SAY "Enter name" GET AnyName
READ
```

the user enters Albert, the variable AnyName actually contains Albert plus nine spaces, because GET retains the original length of 15 characters. This subtle difference can cause confusion in applications programs, particularly in memory variables used with the SEEK command. See Chapter 12, "Sorting and Indexing," for more information on using the GET and SEEK commands for data searching.

## PICTURE

The optional picture template performs three functions:

- It translates data from one format to another.
- It weeds out invalid entries.
- It adds template characters to data.

Picture templates must be enclosed in quotation marks unless they are previously defined in a memory variable. For example, the command

**@ 2,10 GET Phone PICTURE "(999)999-9999"**

is equivalent to the following two commands:

**PicTemp = "(999)999-9999"**
**@ 2,10 GET Phone PICTURE PicTemp**

A PICTURE clause can contain a picture function, a picture template, or both. If both are used, they must be separated by a space. For example, the clause "**@Z 999**" contains the picture function @Z and the picture template 999. Picture functions affect the entire SAY display or GET entry. The picture functions are summarized in Table 8.5. Note that the table includes a list of the acceptable data types for each picture function.

The @S and @R picture functions are more abstract than the others and therefore merit some additional discussion. @S is generally used to set up a partial highlight for a long character field. For example, suppose you have a character field named Notes that is 254 characters long. However, you only want to dedicate one row of your form to this field. If you use the command

**@ <row>,<col> SAY "Notes:" GET Notes PICTURE "@S70"**

the display highlight for the Notes field will be only 70 characters long. However, the user will be able to scroll all 254 characters through this 70-character window using either the arrow keys or the Ctrl-A and Ctrl-F keys. Also, if the user types beyond the 70th character, the character string will automatically scroll to the left.

The @R function is much easier to use than it is to explain. It is used primarily to save storage space. For example, suppose you create a character field named Phone on your database and you assign a length of 10 characters to it. If you use the command

**@ X,Y GET Phone PICTURE "@R (999)999-9999"**

to enter data into the field, the template will be displayed as below:

```
:(   )   -    :
```

| FUNCTION | DATA TYPES | EFFECT IN SAY | EFFECT IN GET |
|---|---|---|---|
| @( | N | Displays negative number in parentheses | None |
| @B | N | Left-justifies a number | Left-justifies a number in display |
| @C | N | Displays CR (credit) after positive number | None |
| @X | N | Displays DB (debit) after negative number | None |
| @Z | N | Displays a zero as a blank space | Displays a zero as a blank space |
| @D | C,N,D | Displays date in American MM/DD/YY format | Displays date in MM/DD/YY format, though date is stored on file in SET DATE format |
| @E | C,N,D | Displays date in European DD/MM/YY format | Displays date in DD/MM/YY format, though date is stored on file in SET DATE format |
| @A | C | None | Permits only alphabetic characters to be entered |
| @! | C | Displays all letters in uppercase | Converts all letters to uppercase |
| @R | C | Inserts template characters into displayed data | Displays template characters in highlight, but does not store them on the file |
| @S<n> | C | Displays the left <n> characters of the data | Creates a highlight that is <n> spaces wide; if data are longer than <n> spaces wide, user can scroll with arrow keys |

**TABLE 8.5:** Picture Functions Used with the PICTURE Clause

After the user types in the phone number, however, only the actual numbers will be stored, not the parentheses or hyphen. To view the data later with parentheses and hyphen, you'll need to use the syntax

**@ X,Y SAY Phone PICTURE "@R (999)999-9999"**

or

**LIST TRANSFORM(Phone, "@R (999)999-9999")**

The alternative to using the @R function is to assign a large enough field width to the field to accommodate the template characters. For example, if you were to assign a width of 13 to the Phone field, you could use the phone number template without the @R function, as below:

**@ X,Y GET Phone PICTURE "(999)999–9999"**

This time the screen will display the parentheses and hyphen and also *store* them on the file. While this takes up a little extra disk space, it prevents you from having to add templates to display data.

Picture templates apply to all of the characters in the data displayed by SAY and GET. The picture template characters are summarized in Table 8.6.

Table 8.7 shows several examples of the effects of picture functions and templates on various types of data. Note that when two or more picture functions are combined, they are preceded by a single @ sign (e.g., @CX). When a picture function and picture template are combined, they are separated by a single space and enclosed in a single pair of quotation marks (e.g., "@CX $999,999.99").

## RANGE

The optional RANGE component of the @ command specifies an acceptable range of numbers or dates for an entry. The lowest acceptable value is listed first, followed by a comma and then the highest acceptable value. If the user enters any value outside the acceptable range, dBASE beeps and displays an error message, along with the lowest and highest acceptable values, near the top of the screen. To try again, the user must press the space bar.

In the example below, Amount is assumed to be a field or variable of the numeric data type. The acceptable range of values is 1,000 to 99,000:

**@ X,Y GET Amount PICTURE "99999.99" RANGE 1000,99000**

In the example below, Today is assumed to be a field or variable of the date data type. Note that the CTOD function is used to convert the range of acceptable dates from the character to the date data type:

**@ 10,10 GET Today RANGE CTOD("01/01/87"),;**
**CTOD("12/31/87")**

| TEMPLATE CHARACTER | DATA TYPES | EFFECT IN SAY | EFFECT IN GET |
|---|---|---|---|
| A | C | None | Accepts only an alphabetic character |
| X | C | None | Accepts any character |
| ! | C | Displays the letter in uppercase | Converts the letter to uppercase |
| L | L,C | None | Accepts only upper- or lowercase T, F, Y, or N |
| Y | L,C | Converts .T. to Y and .F. to N | Accepts only Y or N and converts lowercase to uppercase |
| 9 | C,N,N | None | Accepts only a number |
| # | C,N | None | Accepts a number, space, decimal, plus, or minus sign |
| $ | N | Displays leading $ in front of number if space permits | Fills highlight with leading dollar signs |
| * | N | Displays asterisk in place of leading zeros | Displays asterisk in place of leading zeros |
| , | N | Displays comma if digits are present on both sides | Displays comma if digits are present on both sides |
| Other | | Any other characters are added as template characters | Any other characters are added as template characters |

**TABLE 8.6:** Picture Template Characters Used with the PICTURE Clause

The values specified in the RANGE command can be variables, field values, or the results of calculations. For example, in the commands below, LowDate and HighDate are predefined date values that limit the entry to the year 1987:

```
LowDate = CTOD("01/01/87")
HighDate = CTOD("12/31/87")
Today = DATE()
@ 10,10 GET Today RANGE LowDate,HighDate
```

In the commands below, LowVal and HighVal are numbers stored in database fields or memory variables. Each is multiplied by 1,000 to determine the highest

| PICTURE CLAUSE | OUTPUT |
|---|---|
| "Hello" PICTURE "@!" | HELLO |
| "jones" PICTURE "!XXXXXXXXX" | Jones |
| 1234.56 PICTURE "@CX" | 1234.56 CR |
| −987.65 PICTURE "@CX" | 987.65 DB |
| 1234.56 PICTURE "@B 999,999,999.9" | 1,234.5 |
| −987.65 PICTURE "@B(" | (987.65) |
| DATE() PICTURE "@E" | 03/04/87 |
| "Long text here" PICTURE "@S2" | Lo |
| .T. PICTURE "Y" | Y |
| 1234.56 PICTURE "@CX $9,999.99" | $1,234.56 CR |
| −9876.54 PICTURE "@( $99,999.99" | ($$9,876.54) |
| 1235551212 PICTURE "(999)999-9999" | (123)555–1212 |
| 0 PICTURE "@Z" | |
| 123 PICTURE "*9,999.99" | ***123.00 |

**TABLE 8.7:** Displays from Various Picture Templates

and lowest acceptable values:

**@ 10,10 GET Amount RANGE LowVal*1000,HighVal*1000**

## CLEAR

The optional CLEAR command is used only with @ <row>,<col> to clear the screen from the specified coordinates down. For example, the command

**@ 20,0 CLEAR**

clears all rows from number 20 down on the screen.

(The @ <row>,<col> coordinates with no other commands clear the current line from the <col> position to the right. For example, the command **@ 20,5** clears columns 5 through 79 on row 20.)

## TO

The optional TO component is used only for drawing boxes. For example, the command

**@ 1,2 TO 5,79**

draws a single-bar box on the screen, starting at row 1, column 2 and ending at row 5, column 79.

The addition of the word DOUBLE draws a double-bar box, as in the example below:

**@ 1,2 TO 5,79 DOUBLE**

The CLEAR command can also be used within the @...TO commands. For example, the command

**@ 1,2 CLEAR TO 5,79**

erases the box drawn at coordinates 1,2 to 5,79, as well as the contents of the box.

## EXAMPLES

For a hands-on demonstration of the @...SAY...GET commands in action, try keying in the command file named DemoGet.prg, shown in Figure 8.13. Then run the command file with the usual DO command.

After running the entire DemoGet program, your screen will look like Figure 8.14. Notice the boxes drawn (and cleared in the middle) with the @...TO commands and the effects of the various picture templates and functions on the data stored in memory variables.

## TIPS

The screen painter called up with MODIFY SCREEN provides the quickest way to put together a series of @...SAY....GET....PICTURE commands, whether for use in a format file or command file.

If a picture template is used with a number containing a decimal point, be sure to place the decimal point within the template.

Picture templates with character strings less than two characters long do not always work properly.

You can set the number of simultaneously active PICTURE, RANGE, and GET commands through the BUCKET and GETS commands within the Config.db file, as discussed in Appendix C, "Configuring dBASE III PLUS."

## SEE ALSO

MODIFY SCREEN
SET FORMAT
CLEAR GETS
READ
?
TEXT...ENDTEXT

APPEND
EDIT
CHANGE
INSERT
SET DELIMITERS
SET INTENSITY
SET COLOR
SET DEVICE

```
************************************* DemoGet.prg.
*----------- Demonstrate various @ command lines.
*----------- Set up color, if available.
CLEAR              && Clear the screen.
SET TALK OFF

*--------- Set up a few memory variables.
SSN = "123456789"
PosNumb = 12345.67
NegNumb = -98765.432
Logical = .T.
Today = DATE()
Right = CHR(26)
Left = CHR(27)
Text1 = "Press &Right to scroll this line."

*-------- Demonstrate @S picture function.
@ 1,1 TO 3,79 DOUBLE
@ 2,5 SAY "Sample screen with @...SAY...GET commands"
@ 5,5 GET Text1 PICTURE "@S17"
@ 19,1 TO 23,79 DOUBLE
@ 20,5 SAY "Test &Right and &Left arrow keys"
@ 21,5 SAY "Then press Return."
READ

*-------- Demonstrate Y picture template.
@ 7,5 SAY "Yes or No? " GET Logical PICTURE "Y"
@ 20,2 CLEAR TO 22,78
@ 20,5 SAY "The next field will accept only"
@ 21,5 SAY "A Y or an N.  Try it"
READ

*--------- Demonstrate miscellaneous templates.
@ 9,5 SAY SSN PICTURE "@R 999-99-9999"
@ 11,5 SAY PosNumb PICTURE "@( $99,999.99"
@ 13,5 SAY NegNumb PICTURE "@X $99,999"
@ 15,5 SAY "European date today is: "
@ 15,29 SAY Today PICTURE "@E"

*--------- Rearrange boxes.
@ 20,2 CLEAR TO 22,78
@ 20,10 TO 22,68
@ 21,11 SAY REPLICATE(CHR(176),57)
@ 21,35 SAY "All done!"
```

**FIGURE 8.13:** The DemoGet program demonstrates several aspects of the @...SAY commands. For a demonstration, key it in with MODIFY COMMAND and use the DO command to run it. Press the → key a few times to watch the scrolling of the @S function. Refer back to the original program to see the effects of other pictures and commands.

## The SET FORMAT Command

The SET FORMAT command opens a format (.fmt) file for use with APPEND, EDIT, READ, INSERT, and CHANGE commands.

### SYNTAX

**SET FORMAT TO <file name>**

where <file name> is the name of an existing format file created with either the screen painter or any text editor.

### USAGE

SET FORMAT opens an existing format file, reading only the @...SAY ...GET...PICTURE...RANGE and READ commands within the file. It ignores any other commands within the format file.

Once a format file is opened, all ensuing APPEND, EDIT, READ, CHANGE, and INSERT commands use the format specified in the format file

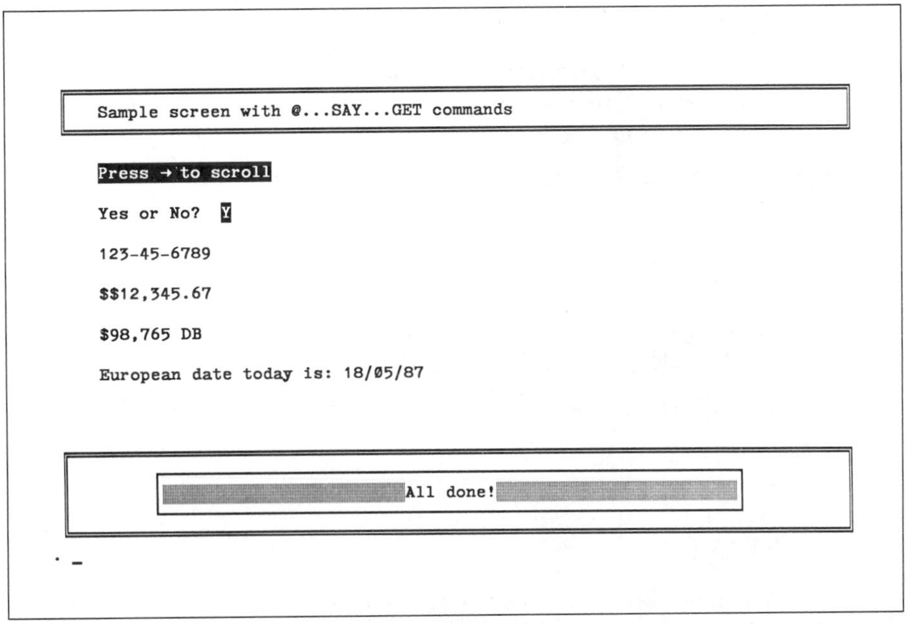

```
Sample screen with @...SAY...GET commands

Press → to scroll

Yes or No? Y

123-45-6789

$$12,345.67

$98,765 DB

European date today is: 18/05/87

All done!
```

**FIGURE 8.14:** The screen display after the DemoGet command file has been run. The box at the bottom of the screen is cleared twice and at the end of the program displays **All Done!**

rather than the simpler default screens these commands usually generate. Once opened, a format file stays in effect until either a CLOSE FORMAT or different SET FORMAT command is issued.

If the format file consists of several pages (screens), the PgUp and PgDn keys scroll through pages before they scroll through records on the database. Note that each page in a format file must be separated by a READ command. Furthermore, multiple-page forms work only with the SET FORMAT command and cannot be used with the DO command.

### EXAMPLE

Assuming that you've already created a format file named MailScrn.fmt (using the MODIFY SCREEN command or a text editor), the following commands open the Mail database and the MailScrn format file and use the format file to add new records to the Mail database:

```
USE Mail
SET FORMAT TO MailScr
APPEND
```

### TIPS

Use the SET FORMAT command for data entry and editing that require minimal verification and calculation. For more powerful data-entry and editing techniques, use @...SAY...GET commands directly in command files, as discussed in Chapters 10, "Adding New Data," and 11, "Editing and Deleting Records."

### SEE ALSO

MODIFY SCREEN
@...SAY...GET
READ
APPEND
EDIT
INSERT
CHANGE
SET DEVICE

## The READ Command

The READ command activates the GET commands displayed on the screen so that the user can enter or edit data.

## SYNTAX

**READ [SAVE]**

where [SAVE] is optional.

## USAGE

READ is used to enter or edit memory variables or fields on a single database record. Often, the READ command is used in conjunction with the APPEND BLANK command to append a single record to a database file. READ can be used either with an open format file or in a command file containing GET commands. READ is also used to separate individual pages within a format file.

The READ command allows the user to move the cursor about freely to make changes to the data displayed on the screen. The cursor-control keys used with other full-screen operations (such as MODIFY COMMAND, EDIT, and APPEND) also operate when the READ command is issued and active GET commands are on the screen.

Only the GET commands displayed on the screen since the last CLEAR, CLEAR GETS, CLEAR ALL, or READ command are activated by READ. After the user cycles through all the GET commands on the screen, they are all cleared from further access.

Unlike READ, the READ SAVE command does not automatically clear the GET commands that were just cycled through. Therefore, if you use READ SAVE instead of READ to edit a database record, the next READ SAVE or READ command will access the same fields.

The ACCEPT, INPUT, and WAIT commands also accept data typed in by the user. These commands, however, store data only in memory variables and do not provide full-screen editing capabilities.

Note that there is a limit to the number of GET commands per READ command. The default limit is 128 GET commands per READ, though this value can be changed to any value from 35 to 1023 through the Config.db GETS setting. The CLEAR GETS command will also free up GET space between READ SAVE commands.

## EXAMPLES

The commands below add a blank record to the currently open database file, open a format file named AScreen.fmt, and allow the user to enter new values into the blank record through the format file:

**APPEND BLANK**
**SET FORMAT TO AScreen**

**READ**
**CLOSE FORMAT**

The small sample command file in Figure 8.15 creates a few memory variables and displays them on the screen with some prompts. The READ SAVE command allows you to enter or change values, then the READ command allows you to do so again. The DISPLAY MEMORY command displays the results of the data entry.

## TIPS

READ is the only dBASE command that allows a user to edit memory variables through a command file. See Chapter 10, "Adding New Data," for tips on using READ to enter data into a database file. See Chapter 11, "Editing and Deleting Records," for information on using READ to edit database data.

## SEE ALSO

@...SAY...GET
CLEAR GETS
APPEND
EDIT
INSERT
CHANGE
SET FORMAT
MODIFY SCREEN

```
********** Test the READ SAVE and READ commands.
*----- Create memory variables.
Name = SPACE(20)
Date = DATE()
Time = TIME()
Amount = 0

CLEAR
*---- Display prompts and "gets".
@ 2,1 SAY "Name " GET Name
@ 4,1 SAY "Date " GET Date
@ 6,1 SAY "Time " GET Time
@ 8,1 SAY "Amount " GET Amount PICTURE "999.99"
*---- Read once, then again.
READ SAVE
READ
*---- Show results.
DISPLAY MEMORY
```

**FIGURE 8.15:** Sample program to demonstrate the READ and READ SAVE commands. The READ SAVE command allows data to be entered into the variables or changed. The second READ command is able to access the same GET commands, because the previous READ SAVE command did not clear the GET statements.

# The CLEAR GETS Command

CLEAR GETS releases GET commands from future access with the READ command and initializes the number of used GET commands to zero.

### SYNTAX

**CLEAR GETS**

### USAGE

This command prevents any previously issued GET commands from being accessed by the next READ command. The number of active GET commands is limited by the amount of memory and the GETS setting in the Config.db file. (The default value is 128.) To avoid running out of memory for GET commands, you can issue the CLEAR GETS command where convenient in your programs.

Any data displayed on the screen by a GET command will be displayed in reverse video and the enhanced-display colors specified in the SET COLOR command. In some applications, you might want to display all the fields from a record in reverse video but allow the user to change only some of the fields. In such a situation, issue the @...GET commands for the fields that you do not want the user to edit first, then issue a CLEAR GETS command. Next, issue the @...GET commands for the fields you do want the user to edit, and then issue the READ command.

### EXAMPLE

Assume that all of the GET commands in Figure 8.16 are sending data straight to a database file (no memory variables). All of the fields will be displayed on the screen in reverse video (as shown in Figure 8.17), but the operator can change only the Cust_Name and Cust_Add fields.

### TIPS

Remember that CLEAR GETS only releases GET commands displayed on the screen from READ access, it does not release memory variables.

### SEE ALSO

READ
@...SAY...GET
CLEAR

```
******************************* ClearGet.prg
*-- Command file demonstrates a practical
*-- use for the CLEAR GETS command.

CLEAR
@  1,  0  TO  3, 50
@ 11,  0  TO 17, 50    DOUBLE

*------ Set up "uneditable" fields.
@  2,  1  SAY "Customer Number"
@  2, 17  GET  CustNo
@  5,  1  SAY "*** Only Name and Address below may be edited ***"
@ 12,  5  SAY "Starting Balance"
@ 12, 22  GET  Start_Bal
@ 14,  6  SAY "Current Charges"
@ 14, 22  GET  Curr_Bal  PICTURE "999999999.99"
@ 16,  6  SAY "Current Payment"
@ 16, 22  GET  Curr_Pay
CLEAR GETS               && Release from read access.

*------ Now set up "editable" fields.
@  7,  1  SAY "Customer Name"
@  7, 18  GET  Cust_Name
@  9,  1  SAY "Customer Address"
@  9, 18  GET  Cust_Add
READ                 && Read values for editable fields.
```

**FIGURE 8.16:** This routine displays all fields in reverse video on the screen. The CLEAR GETS command deactivates all but the Cust_Name and Cust_Add fields before the READ command is issued, so the user can edit only the Cust_Name and Cust_Add fields. Figure 8.17 shows how the screen looks after running this program.

```
Customer Number 1001

*** Only Name and Address below may be edited ***

Customer Name     Joe Smith

Customer Address  123 A St.

    Starting Balance      1000.00

     Current Charges       500.00

     Current Payment       500.00
```

**FIGURE 8.17:** The screen produced by the routine in Figure 8.16. Even though many fields on the database are displayed in reverse video, the user can alter only the Cust_Name and Cust_Add fields because of the CLEAR GETS embedded in the program displayed in Figure 8.16.

## SUMMARY

This chapter discussed many aspects of custom forms and screens for applications. Refer to the following chapters if you want some specific techniques for entering and editing data through custom forms.

*For information on using the @...SAY commands to print formatted reports:*

- Chapter 9, "Printing Formatted Reports"

*For an in-depth discussion of adding new records to a database file:*

- Chapter 10, "Adding New Data"

*For more on editing records in a database:*

- Chapter 11, "Editing and Deleting Records"

*For tips on developing custom forms that serve multiple related database files:*

- Chapter 16, "Managing Multiple Database Files"

*For more information on the SET COLOR, SET DELIMITER, and SET INTENSITY commands:*

- Chapter 18, "Setting Parameters"

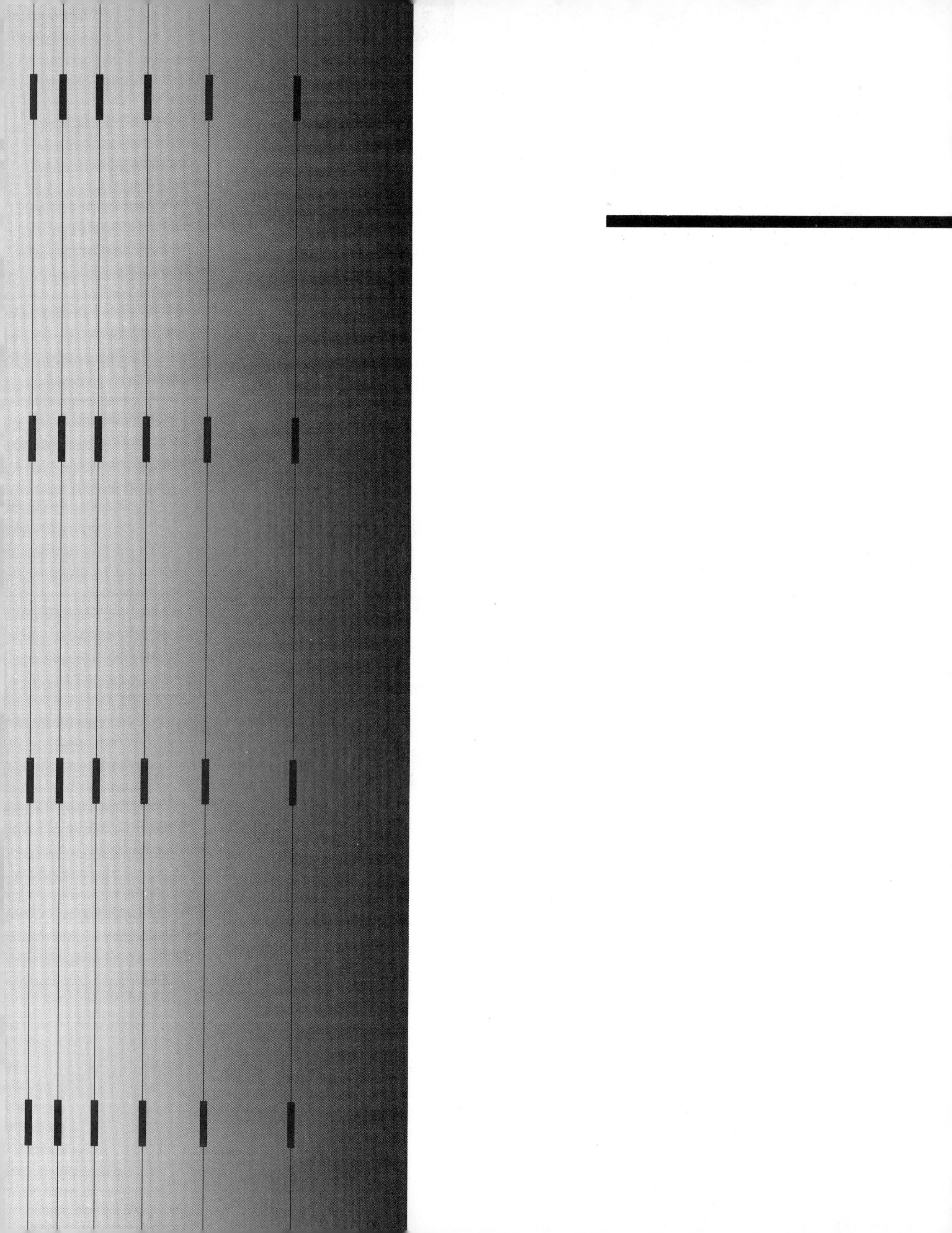

CHAPTER 9

# PRINTING FORMATTED REPORTS

# PRINTING FORMATTED REPORTS

This chapter covers the basic commands and techniques for displaying data in formatted reports. The first part of the chapter discusses the built-in report and label generators. Then techniques for displaying reports with command files are discussed. The reference part of the chapter discusses all the menu options available on the report generator screen and the individual report-printing commands.

## USING THE REPORT GENERATOR

The dBASE report generator, accessed through the CREATE REPORT or MODIFY REPORT command, is the simplest way of developing a format for a report.

Before you enter the report generator, you must open all database files to be used in the report. If you want to include data from two or more databases, you must open all the database files and establish the relationships with the SET RELATION (or SET VIEW) command.

To illustrate the features of the report generator, I will use the Sales and Master sample databases, whose structures are shown in Figures 9.1 and 9.2, respectively. The Sales database contains information on individual sales transactions, while the Master database contains information on individual products. The Master database has been indexed on the PartNo field for rapid access to parts, creating the file PartNos.ndx. To presort the Sales data into part number and

```
Structure for database: Sales.dbf

Field  Field Name  Type       Width     Dec
    1  PARTNO      Character      5
    2  INVOICE_NO  Numeric        5
    3  CLERK       Character      5
    4  CUSTOMER    Character     20
    5  QTY         Numeric        4
    6  DATE_SOLD   Date           8
** Total **                      48
```

**FIGURE 9.1:** Structure of a sample Sales database. In the sample generated report this database holds individual sales transactions and is the "many" side of the one-to-many relationship. This will also be the currently selected database when designing and printing the Sales report.

salesperson order, the following command creates the index file named Sales.ndx, which will be used in developing and printing the sample Sales report:

**INDEX ON UPPER(PartNo + Clerk) TO Sales**

To print a report of records from the Sales database, "borrowing" some information from the Master database, you must open both databases and set up the relationship (pointing from the "many" side into the "one" side) with the following commands:

**SELECT A**
**USE Sales Index Sales**
**SELECT B**
**USE Master INDEX PartNos**
**SELECT A**
**SET RELATION TO PartNo INTO Master**

Note that Sales.dbf is the currently selected database. The report generator will only "see" fields from Sales.dbf, but you can still "borrow" data from Master.dbf.

## Designing a Report

Once you have opened your database files and have established the relationships between multiple files, you can enter the MODIFY REPORT (or the equivalent CREATE REPORT) command, followed by a valid DOS file name for the report format file, directly at the dot prompt. For this example, to name the report Sales.frm, enter the command

**MODIFY REPORT Sales**

```
Structure for database: Master.dbf

Field  Field Name  Type       Width    Dec
    1  PARTNO      Character      5
    2  PARTNAME    Character     20
    3  IN_STOCK    Numeric        4
    4  UNIT_PRICE  Numeric        9      2
    5  TAXABLE     Logical        1
    6  REORDER     Numeric        4
    7  ON_ORDER    Numeric        4
    8  BACKORDER   Numeric        4
    9  REC_DATE    Date           8
   10  LOCATION    Character      4
   11  VEND_CODE   Character      4
** Total **                      68
```

**FIGURE 9.2:** Structure for the Master database. This database holds information about individual products. In the Sales report, this file is on the "one" side of the one-to-many relationship and is in work area B. The sample Sales report generated in this chapter "borrows" the PartName, Unit_Price, and Taxable fields from this database by using the B-> alias.

dBASE automatically adds the .frm extension to the file name.

The report generator appears on the screen as in Figure 9.3. You can move to the various menus along the top of the screen with the ← and → keys. The ↑ and ↓ keys move the highlight within the pull-down menus. Pressing Return selects the currently highlighted menu item. To remove the help information boxed in the lower part of the screen, you can press F1 (pressing F1 again will bring it back).

## The Options Menu

The first pull-down menu, Options, presents options for the page layout. The suggested values on the menu are adequate for most printers, though you may want to experiment with the settings for some reports. To create a report heading, leave the highlight on the Page title option and press Return. You'll see a box that allows you to enter up to four lines of text for a title (which is centered automatically when the report is printed). After typing in the title, type Ctrl-End to return to the Options menu.

If you are using a laser printer, you may want to change the Page eject after printing option from No to Yes by moving the highlight to that option and

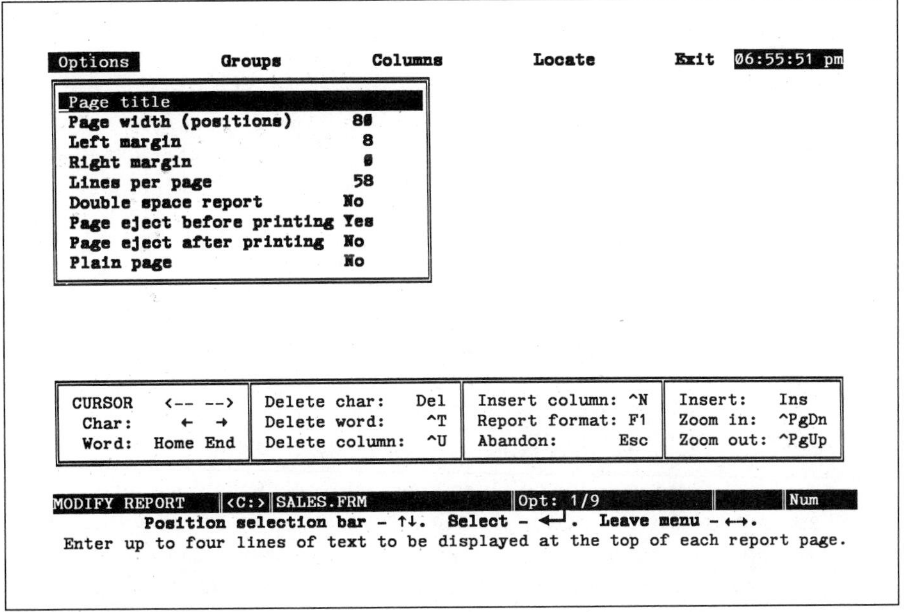


**FIGURE 9.3:** The report generator screen for designing formatted reports. The ← and → keys pull down the menus across the top of the screen. The ↑ and ↓ keys move the highlight within the pull-down menus. Pressing Return selects the currently highlighted menu item. The help information in the box at the bottom of the screen can be toggled on and off with the F1 key.

pressing Return. Doing so will ensure that the page is ejected from the printer after the report is printed, even if the last page is not entirely filled.

## THE GROUPS MENU

The second menu, Groups, lets you group data on the report into subtotals and subsubtotals. The data file must be indexed (or sorted) on the fields that determine the groups. In this example, the Sales database was indexed on the PartNo and Clerk fields, so these can be used for grouping records.

The first option on the Groups menu is Group on expression. This represents the first level of grouping (and subtotals) and must be the first-listed field in the index file expression. In this example, you would type **PartNo** as the grouping field.

The second option, Group heading, lets you enter text for a heading that will appear above each subtotal group on the printed report. Typically, you'll want to place an English version of the database field name, such as **Part Number** for the PartNo field.

The Summary report only option determines whether all of the data from the database file are shown, or only the subtotals and subsubtotals. To show the actual data, leave this setting as No.

The Page eject after group option determines whether each subtotal group begins on a new page. To print groups without page ejects, leave this setting at No.

The Sub-group on expression option allows you to determine a second level of subtotals or grouping. This field must be the second listed field in the INDEX (or previous SORT) command. In the example above, Clerk was defined as the secondary index field. So to subgroup on the Clerk field, you would enter the expression **UPPER(Clerk)** (the UPPER function prevents any incorrect grouping based on upper- and lowercase discrepancies).

You can place a heading on the subgroups by filling in the Sub-group heading option. In this example, you might enter **Salesperson** as the description of the Clerk field name. Figure 9.4 shows how the Groups menu might look after filling in data for the sample Sales report.

## PLACING COLUMNS ON THE REPORT

The Columns menu options allow you to place field values into columns on the report. On this menu, you select each option by moving the highlight to the option and pressing Return. Then enter your value and press Return again.

To create a report column, first highlight the Contents option and press Return. You can then type the field name directly or press F10 to see a list of field names. If you press F10 to see the field names and then press Return while the PartNo field is highlighted, PartNo will be selected as the field for the first column.

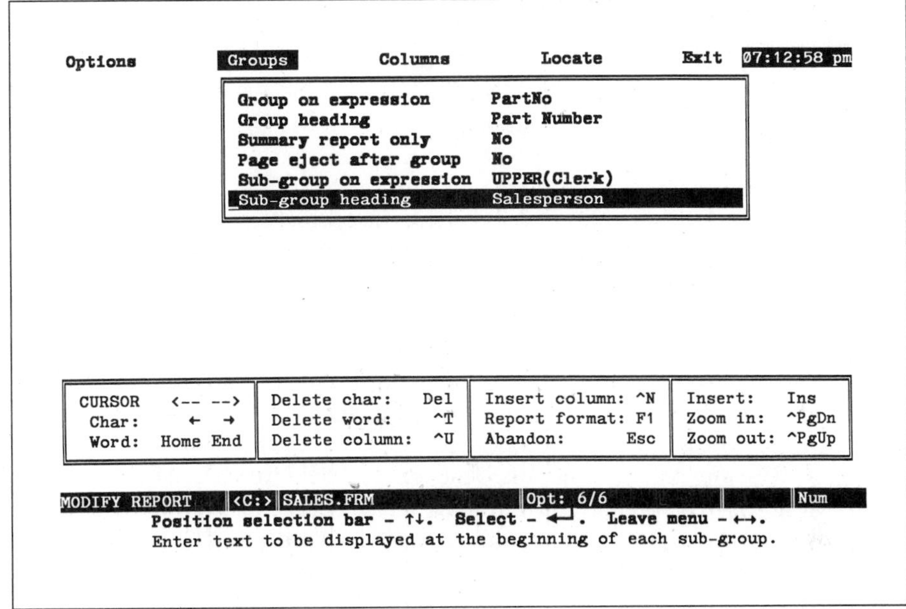


**FIGURE 9.4:** The Groups menu completed for the sample Sales report. Because the database was indexed on the expression PartNo + Clerk, these two fields can be used as the group and subgroup expressions. The printed report will display subtotals for each part number and for each Salesperson within each part number group.

Next, move the highlight to the Heading option and press Return. Again, a small box appears for you to fill in a heading. In this case, enter the two-line heading

**Part**
**Number**

Then press Ctrl-End to return to the pull-down menu. dBASE automatically fills in the Width portion of the menu, as shown in Figure 9.5. Notice also that the semicolon (;) shows where the column heading is broken into two lines. Near the bottom of the screen, the Report Format box shows the column heading and XXXXX beneath the column heading, to show you how the columns are laid out so far. Each X represents a single character that will be printed on the actual report.

To move to the next column on the report, press PgDn.

## DISPLAYING A FIELD FROM ANOTHER DATABASE

To place a field from another database onto your report, for example, the PartName field from the Master database, select the Contents option and type **B–>PartName** as the field to display. Pressing F10 does not work in this case, because it shows only fields from the currently selected database (unless a view file has been created and opened with the SET VIEW and SET FIELDS commands). Press Return after entering the correct field name.

Then select the Heading option and enter the heading **Part Name**. Type Ctrl-End when you are done.

You can continue placing fields in your report by selecting Contents and typing the field names directly (or using F10 to select the fields). The example report has the Clerk and Qty fields in the next two columns. Because both of these fields are stored on the currently selected Sales database, there is no need to use an alias arrow.

The fifth column contains Unit_Price, a field from the Master database file, so it needs to be preceded with the B–> alias in the Contents box of the pull-down menu. You can enter whatever heading you like. (In addition, you should change the last item in the box, Total this column, from Yes to No, because there is no need to total the unit price.)

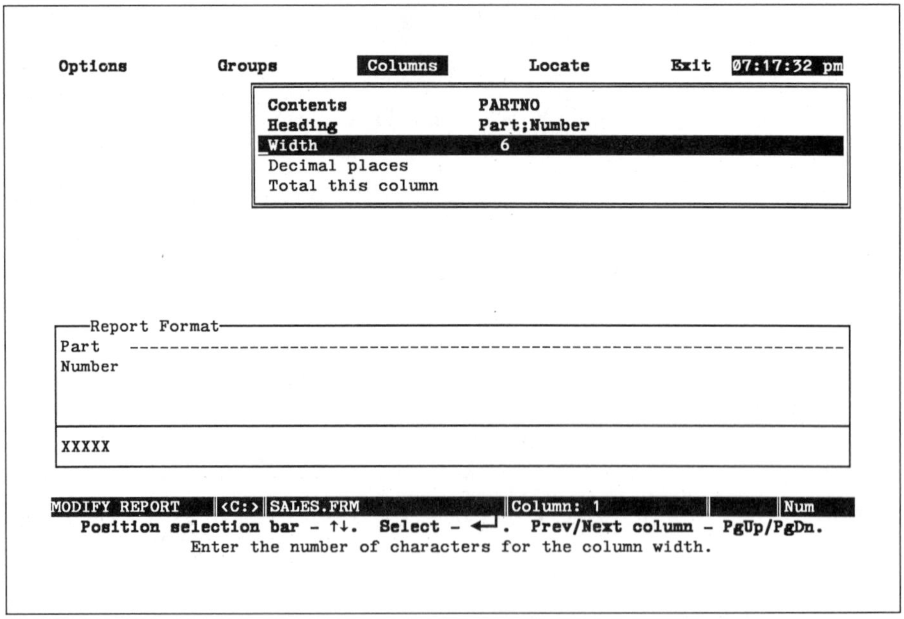

```
Options        Groups        Columns        Locate        Exit  07:17:32 pm

                      Contents                  PARTNO
                      Heading                   Part;Number
                      Width                       6
                      Decimal places
                      Total this column

Report Format
Part    -------------------------------------------------------------
Number

XXXXX

MODIFY REPORT  |<C:>|SALES.FRM          |Column: 1          |    |Num
   Position selection bar - ↑↓.  Select - ↵.  Prev/Next column - PgUp/PgDn.
              Enter the number of characters for the column width.
```

**FIGURE 9.5:** First column defined on the report generator screen. The semicolon indicates where the column heading is broken onto two lines. The lower portion of the screen shows the space occupied by the field as a series of Xs.

Figure 9.6 shows how the example screen might look after adding the B->PartName, Clerk, Qty, and B->Unit_Price fields to the report format.

## Using IIF in Report Columns

You can have a report column make a decision about what to display based on current data by using the IIF function. For example, suppose you want to display the logical field Taxable in the next column, but you want to display the value as Y or N rather than .T. or .F. In the Contents box under the Columns menu, enter the expression **IFF(B->Taxable,"Y","N")**, which, in English, translates to "If the Taxable field is .T., display the letter Y, otherwise display the letter N." Once again the B-> alias is required in this example, because the Taxable field is stored on the database in work area B.

Suppose you want to display the extended price in the next column. This is simply the quantity times the unit price if the item is not taxable, or the quantity times the unit price plus the tax if the unit is taxable. The following commands define the contents of the extended price column, given that the sales tax rate is 6 percent:

```
IIF(B->Taxable,(Qty*B->Unit_Price)*1.06,;
  (Qty*B->Unit_Price))
```

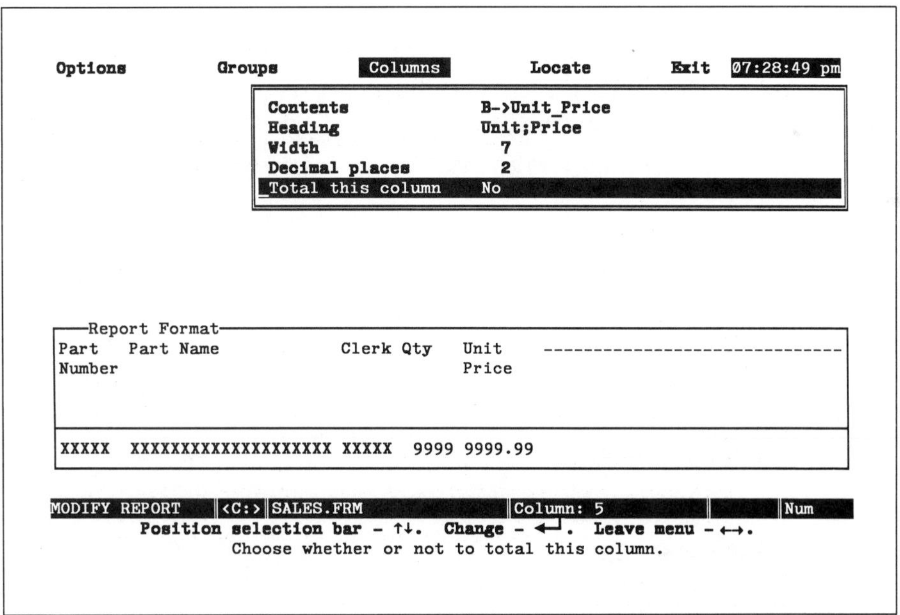


**FIGURE 9.6:** More columns defined on the Sales report format. The PartName and Unit_Price fields require B-> aliases because they are taken from the Master database in work area B. At the bottom of the screen, the 9s indicate the space taken by numeric fields.

(The expression is broken in half only to fit in the book. In the report generator, it must be entered as a single line without the semicolon.) In English this expression translates to "If the item is taxable, display the quantity times the unit price with 6 percent sales tax added, otherwise just display the quantity times the unit price."

## Using TRANSFORM to Format Data

You can use the TRANSFORM function to specify a format for the data displayed in a report column in the same way that you can use PICTURE to format the display in an @ command. Unfortunately, however, if you use TRANSFORM to format a numeric field, you cannot total that column in the report. Furthermore, TRANSFORM does not support the logical picture templates L or Y, nor the date functions D or E, as the PICTURE command does. (You can use IIF to convert logical data to Y or N, as discussed above, and you can use the SET DATE command to format the date data.)

Let's look at how TRANSFORM could be used with the Unit_Price column, which does not need to be totaled. Suppose you wanted to display the data in the format 1,234.56. Using the PgUp and PgDn keys, scroll to the Unit_Price column in the pull-down menu and change the Contents entry from the current **B->Unit_Price** to the following expression:

**TRANSFORM(B->Unit_Price,"9,999.99")**

If you wanted to display a leading dollar sign, you could place it as a literal in front of the TRANSFORM function, as below:

**"$" + TRANSFORM(B->Unit_Price,"9,999.99")**

The dollar sign would then be left justified on all numbers, as follows:

```
$1,234.56
$  123.56
$    9.99
```

Or you could use the "$" picture template in the TRANSFORM function, as below:

**TRANSFORM(B->Unit_Price,"$9,999.99")**

In this case, the dollar sign will fill the leading blank spaces, as follows:

```
$1,234.56
$$$123.56
$$$$$9.99
```

To combine a TRANSFORM function with an IIF function, you simply place it in front. In this particular example, you would not want to transform the Extended Price column, because it will be totaled in the report. But for the sake of example, we will use it to combine TRANSFORM with the IIF function.

To display the extended price with the single leading dollar sign and punctuated with commas, you could define the column contents as follows:

```
"$" + TRANSFORM(IIF(B->Taxable, ;
                    (Qty*B->Unit_Price)*1.06, ;
                    (Qty*B->Unit_Price)),"99,999.99")
```

(Note that the expression is broken only to fit onto the page; it must be typed in as a single line without the semicolons.)

## Editing Long Strings of Text

When entering or editing a long expression in the report generator, you can use Ctrl-PgDn and Ctrl-PgUp to "zoom" into and out of the expression. The "zoomed" expression appears just above the status bar near the bottom of the screen, in a longer 80-column prompt.

## Eliminating Rounding Errors

It is not unusual to see rounding errors in reports, particularly where dollars and cents are concerned. For example, if you were to run the sample Sales report without correcting for rounding errors, the subtotal for the first printed group might come out like the example in Figure 9.7. If you add up the pennies in the right column of the display, you'll see that they total .39, not .40 as the report displays.

To correct this error, you can round all of the extended price calculations to two decimal places using the ROUND function. Type the following expression

```
** Part Number A-111
* Salesperson Adam
A-111  Baseball      Adam      5   14.95  Y       79.23
A-111  Baseball      Adam      1   14.95  Y       15.85
A-111  Baseball      Adam      2   14.95  Y       31.69
A-111  Baseball      Adam      4   14.95  Y       63.39
A-111  Baseball      Adam      5   14.95  Y       79.23
* Subsubtotal *                                --------
                                                 269.40
```

**FIGURE 9.7:** A small section of a report with totals in the right column. Due to rounding errors, the rightmost column of numbers does not add up properly.

at the Contents option (as a single expression, leaving out the semicolon):

**ROUND(IIF(B->Taxable,(Qty*B->Unit_Price)*1.06,;**
**(Qty*B->Unit_Price)),2)**

Adding the ROUND function to the extended price calculation produces the output shown in Figure 9.8. As you can see, the extended prices are rounded upward in a couple of rows, and the pennies total up correctly.

After adding the ROUND function to the Contents option of the report column, be sure to double-check (and correct if necessary) the Width and Decimal settings for the column. Adding the ROUND function often changes these.

## STACKING INFORMATION IN REPORT COLUMNS

The report generator is designed primarily to print a single field in each column of the report. However, you can stack several fields in a single column by carefully wrapping them around within the column.

For example, suppose you wanted to stack four fields in a single report column, as below:

**Smith, Sandy**
**ABC Company**
**12/31/87**

Furthermore, suppose these fields had the following names, data types, and widths:

| | | |
|---|---|---|
| LName | Character | 20 |
| FName | Character | 15 |
| Company | Character | 40 |
| Date | Date | 8 |

First, you need to decide on a width for the column. The easiest way to do this is to select the widest field as the width of the column (40 in this example).

```
** Part Number A-111
* Salesperson Adam
A-111  Baseball       Adam     5   14.95  Y        79.24
A-111  Baseball       Adam     1   14.95  Y        15.85
A-111  Baseball       Adam     2   14.95  Y        31.69
A-111  Baseball       Adam     4   14.95  Y        63.39
A-111  Baseball       Adam     5   14.95  Y        79.24
* Subsubtotal *                                 --------
                                                  269.41
```

**FIGURE 9.8:** The same section of the report shown in Figure 9.7 after the ROUND() function was used within the report column definition. Using ROUND() eliminates the error that occurred in Figure 9.7.

Next, you want to concatenate all of the fields into a single character string. Furthermore, each segment that occupies a single row must have a width of exactly 40 characters. In this example, the Contents of this report column would be

**TRIM(LName) + ", " + FName + SPACE(23 – LEN(TRIM(LName))) ;**
**+ Company + DToc(Hire_Date)**

(Once again, the long expression is divided into two columns only to fit on the book page. In practice, it must be entered as a single expression without the semicolon.)

If you study the expression, you'll see that each column does total 40 characters. Given that LName is 20 characters long and FName is 30 characters long, the expression

**TRIM(LName) + ", " + FName + SPACE(23 – LEN(TRIM(LName))) ;**

fills in exactly 40 characters, because the comma, blank space, and FName fields occupy exactly 17 characters (leaving 23 characters for the last name). The last name is printed on this line, with blanks trimmed (so we do not know how many characters it occupied). However, the SPACE function adds enough spaces to round out the column to 40 characters by printing the remaining 23 spaces minus however many spaces the trimmed last name occupied (i.e., SPACE (23 –LEN(TRIM(LName)))).

The Company field already occupied 40 characters, so nothing needed to be added to that. The Date field is the last one in the column, so it does not need to be padded. However, it does need to be converted to the character data type with the DTOC function, because it is concatenated to a character string. (Similarly, a number would need to be converted using the STR function.)

To separate individual records when items are stacked in columns, change the Double space report option on the report generator Options menu to Yes. If you need to stack columns in a report to print labels of some sort, use the MODIFY LABEL and LABEL FORM commands rather than the report generator, as discussed in the section "Using the Label Generator" later in this chapter.

## Saving the Report Format

Once you are satisfied with the appearance of your report format, move the highlight to the Exit menu and select Save. (To abandon the format, select Abandon instead.) The report format will be saved with the file name you originally provided plus the .frm extension.

## Printing a Report

After you have created and saved the report format, use the REPORT FORM command to print the report. REPORT FORM assumes that the appropriate database file is open. If multiple related databases were used to create the report format, all the files must be open and related in the same manner as they were when the report was created. Using the Sales report example discussed earlier, the routine in Figure 9.9 would open the database files, set the relationship, and print the report.

A copy of the formatted Sales report is shown in Figure 9.10 with some sample data. To display the report on the printer rather than the screen, use the command **REPORT FORM Sales TO PRINT**.

The REPORT FORM command supports all of the sorting and searching features of dBASE III PLUS, including WHILE and FOR. If the currently selected database is indexed, records in the report are displayed in the index order. There are also options to control the heading, printer, page ejects, memo fields, and other elements. See the discussion of the REPORT FORM command in the reference section of this chapter for more information.

### Letting the User Select Screen or Printer

When you use the REPORT FORM and LABEL FORM commands in command files, you can include a user prompt, an IF clause, and a macro to allow the user to decide whether to send the report to the screen or the printer. (The LABEL FORM command is discussed in the section "Printing Mailing Labels" later in this chapter.)

For example, in the routine in Figure 9.11, the variable named PMacro is initialized as a blank. If the user answers Yes to the prompt about sending the report

```
*-------- Open both database files.
SELECT A
USE Sales
SELECT B
USE Master INDEX PartNos

*-------- Set relation from Sales into Master.
SELECT A
SET RELATION TO PartNo INTO Master

*-------- Print the Sales.frm report.
REPORT FORM Sales
```

**FIGURE 9.9:** A small routine that opens the Sales and Master database files and establishes a relationship from the Sales file into the Master file. The REPORT command then prints the report using data from both files.

to the printer, the PMacro variable receives the words "TO PRINT" rather than the blank space.

Before executing the REPORT FORM command, dBASE first substitutes the appropriate text for the macro. If the user opted to send the report to the printer, the words TO PRINT are tacked onto the command, and output is channeled to the printer. If the user did not opt for the printer, only a blank space is added to the REPORT FORM command, and output is channeled to the screen.

```
Page No.     1
04/08/87
                                  Sample Report

Part    Part Name    Clerk  Qty    Unit Tax   Extended Date
Number                            Price          Price


** Part Number A-111

* Salesperson Adam
A-111   Baseball     Adam     5   14.95 Y        79.24 02/28/87
A-111   Baseball     Adam     1   14.95 Y        15.85 02/28/87
A-111   Baseball     Adam     2   14.95 Y        31.69 02/28/87
A-111   Baseball     Adam     4   14.95 Y        63.39 02/28/87
A-111   Baseball     Adam     5   14.95 Y        79.24 02/28/87
* Subsubtotal *
                                                269.41

* Salesperson Susan
A-111   Baseball     Susan    1   14.95 Y        15.85 02/28/87
A-111   Baseball     Susan    4   14.95 Y        63.39 02/28/87
* Subsubtotal *
                                                 79.24
** Subtotal **
                                                348.65

** Part Number B-222

* Salesperson Adam
B-222   Tomatoes     Adam    10   19.95 N       199.50 02/28/87
B-222   Tomatoes     Adam     1   19.95 N        19.95 02/28/87
* Subsubtotal *
                                                219.45

* Salesperson Susan
B-222   Tomatoes     Susan    1   19.95 N        19.95 02/28/87
B-222   Tomatoes     Susan    1   19.95 N        19.95 02/28/87
* Subsubtotal *
                                                 39.90
** Subtotal **
                                                259.35
*** Total ***
                                                539.19
```

**FIGURE 9.10:** Sample report printed by the report generator. Each line is based on a record in the Sales database, but the Part Name, Unit Price, and Taxable fields are "borrowed" from the Master inventory database. The extended price is calculated by multiplying quantity times the unit price and adding 6 percent sales tax if the item is taxable.

```
*------------- Ask about sending report to printer.
PMacro = " "
YesNo = .F.
@ 10,2 SAY "Send report to printer? (Y/N) " ;
  GET YesNo PICTURE "Y"
READ
*------------- If printer requested, set up PMacro.
IF YesNo
   PMacro = "TO PRINT"
ENDIF
*------------- Display the report on screen or printer.
REPORT FORM Sales &PMacro
```

**FIGURE 9.11:** A routine that asks the user whether the report should be sent to the printer. If the user selects Yes, the variable named PMacro receives the character string TO PRINT, which is in turn substituted into the REPORT FORM command.

# USING THE LABEL GENERATOR

To print mailing labels, you can use the dBASE III PLUS label generator. Like the report generator, you must first open the database from which the labels will be printed. Then enter the MODIFY LABEL command with a valid DOS file name, as in the example below:

**USE Mail**
**MODIFY LABEL ThreeUp**

These commands prepare the label generator to create a label format file named ThreeUp.lbl for the Mail database.

## Designing Mailing Labels

When the label generator first appears, it provides options for formatting the labels, as shown in Figure 9.12. You can either scroll through various predefined label sizes (by pressing the Return key while the top item is highlighted) or individually select items in the lower portion of the menu and enter new values.

To design the label format, press → to highlight the Contents option at the top of the screen. You can place field names or expressions in any of the columns. When placing multiple field names on a single line, a comma displays fields separated by a space and the plus sign displays fields with no spaces. Figure 9.13 shows a sample label format defined on the screen. After designing a label format, highlight the Exit option at the top menu and select Save.

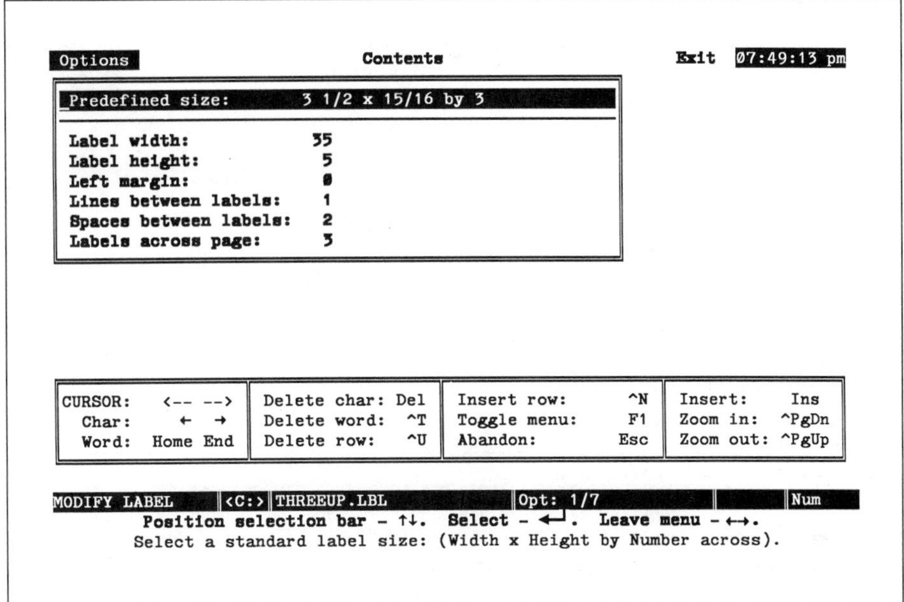


**FIGURE 9.12:** The first menu in the label generator lets you select mailing-label size and the number of labels to print across each page. You can cycle through predefined sizes by pressing Return while the top menu item is highlighted, or you can select individual items in the lower menu by moving the highlight with the arrow keys and pressing Return.

## Printing Mailing Labels

After you've defined and saved the format for mailing labels, use the LABEL FORM command to print the labels. As with the REPORT FORM command, the database file must be opened before the LABEL FORM command is issued. In the commands below, the Mail database is opened and labels are printed from the ThreeUp.lbl format:

**USE Mail**
**LABEL FORM ThreeUp TO PRINT**

See the discussions of the MODIFY LABEL and LABEL FORM commands in the reference section of this chapter for more details on creating and printing mailing labels.

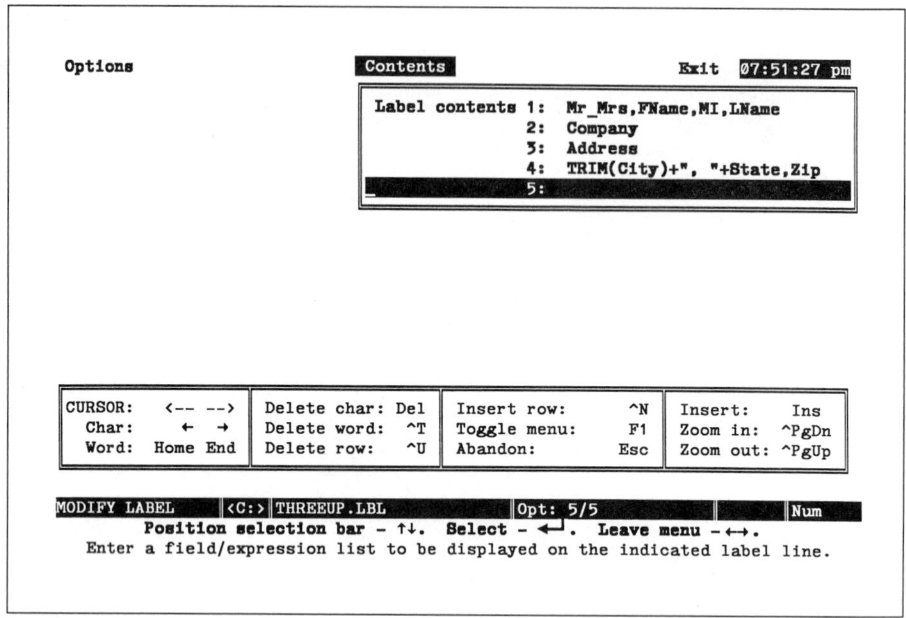


**FIGURE 9.13:** A sample label format defined on the screen. The database fields Mr_Mrs, FName, MI, and LName will be displayed on the top line of each mailing label (separated by a single space). On the third line, the city, state, and zip code will be displayed in the format **San Diego, CA 92122.**

# USING PROGRAMS TO PRINT REPORTS

In many programming situations, the report and label generators simply do not have the power or flexibility to display data in the format you require. With a few basic programming techniques, you can set up programs to display reports in any format you wish.

Figure 9.14 shows the structure of a sample database named Donate. Figure 9.15 shows a sample report printed from this database. The report was printed by the program named Donate.prg shown in Figure 9.16. In the sections that follow, we'll look at individual components of the Donate command file.

## The Main Program Loop

The main body of the donation summary report is printed by the DO WHILE .NOT. EOF() loop near the middle of the program. (The record pointer is at the first record before this loop begins because of the USE command near the top of the program.)

```
Structure for database: Donate.dbf

Field  Field Name  Type       Width    Dec
    1  MR_MRS      Character      4
    2  FNAME       Character     15
    3  MI          Character      2
    4  LNAME       Character     20
    5  COMPANY     Character     40
    6  ADDRESS     Character     25
    7  CITY        Character     20
    8  STATE       Character      5
    9  ZIP         Character     10
   10  PHONE       Character     10
   11  JOIN_DATE   Date           8
   12  PLEDGED     Numeric       12      2
   13  DONATED     Numeric       12      2
** Total **                     184
```

**FIGURE 9.14:** Structure of the hypothetical Donate database file, used in conjunction with the Donate.prg command file to demonstrate printing a report from a command file.

```
04/08/87                 Donations Summary               Page    1


Magilicutty, Miss Zeppo Z.

     1086 Crest Dr.                           Phone: (619)555-4306
     Albany, NY     12121                     Date joined:  03/18/87

     Amount pledged:    800.00                Donated to date:    100.00


Mendez, Dr. Thalia G.
     Petticoat Junction
     P.O. Box 1234                            Phone: (123)555-2222
     La Jolla, CA     92038                   Date joined:  03/28/87

     Amount pledged:  1,000.00                Donated to date:    500.00


Stravinsky, Mr. Igor
     Green Acres
     345 Willow Grove Ave                     Phone: (213)555-0909
     Philadelphia, PA     24345               Date joined:  03/23/87

     Amount pledged: 25,000.00                Donated to date:  1,200.00


Watson, Mr. Joe A.
     ABC Corporation
     123 Fifth Ave.                           Phone: (123)555-1111
     San Diego, CA     92122                  Date joined:  04/02/87

     Amount pledged:  5,000.00                Donated to date:  2,500.00
```

**FIGURE 9.15:** Sample report printed by the Donate.prg command file using data from the Donate database.

```
**************************************** Donate.prg
*------- Print report from the Donate.dbf database.

*------- Set parameters and variables.
SET TALK OFF
SET MARGIN TO 4
LineCount = 1
PageCount = 1
PageLength = 55
Title = "Donations Summary"

*------- Open database and index file.
USE Donate INDEX Names

*------- Ask about printer.
CLEAR
ToPrinter = .F.
@ 10,10 SAY "Send report to printer (Y/N)? ";
  GET ToPrinter PICTURE "Y"
READ

IF ToPrinter
   SET PRINT ON
ENDIF (toprinter)

*------ Print report title.
? DATE(),SPACE(20),Title
?? SPACE(20)+"Page "+STR(PageCount,3)
?
?
LineCount = 3

*------- Start main loop through database file.
DO WHILE .NOT. EOF()
   ? TRIM(LName)+", "+TRIM(Mr_Mrs),TRIM(FName),MI
   ? SPACE(5)+Company
   ? SPACE(5)+Address+SPACE(10)+"Phone: "
   ?? TRANSFORM(Phone, "@R (999)999-9999")
     FullCSZ = Trim(City)+", "+State+"  "+Zip
   ? SPACE(5)+FullCSZ+SPACE(35-LEN(FullCSZ))
   ?? "Date joined: ",Join_Date
   ?
   ? "     Amount pledged:",TRANSFORM(Pledged,"99,999.99")
   ?? SPACE(10)
   ?? "Donated to date:",TRANSFORM(Donated,"99,999.99")
   ?
   ?
   LineCount = LineCount + 8
   *----- See if time for a page break yet.
   IF LineCount >= PageLength .AND. ToPrinter
      EJECT
      PageCount = PageCount + 1
      ? DATE(),SPACE(20),Title
      ?? SPACE(20)+"Page "+STR(PageCount,3)
      ?
      ?
      LineCount = 3
   ENDIF  (lincount)
   SKIP
ENDDO (eof)

*---- If report printed, eject before finishing.
IF ToPrinter
   SET PRINT OFF
   EJECT
ENDIF (to printer)

*---- All done.
RETURN
```

**FIGURE 9.16:** The Donate program that printed the report shown in Figure 9.15. The main body of the report is printed by the DO WHILE .NOT. EOF() loop near the middle of the program. Other modules set the necessary parameters and variables, open the database and index file, determine whether to set the report to the printer or the screen, print the report title, and eject the paper if the report is printed.

Within the loop, the ? and ?? commands display text on the screen (or printer if the SET PRINT parameter is ON). Note that ? always prints text starting on a new line, while ?? always begins printing at the current cursor (or printer-head) position.

There are a number of SPACE functions within the ? commands that print blank spaces to align columns. In many cases, the number of blank spaces to print is calculated, as in the line

**? SPACE(5) + FullCSZ + SPACE(35 – LEN(FullCSZ))**

which prints five blank spaces and the FullCSZ memory variable, and then moves the cursor or print head to the 40th column. (First **SPACE(5)** prints 5 spaces, then **FullCSZ** prints an unknown number of characters, then the next part of the command, **SPACE(35 – LEN(FullCSZ))** prints enough additional spaces to get to the 40th column.)

A couple of TRANSFORM functions are used, such as TRANSFORM(Phone, @R "(999)999-9999"), which inserts parentheses and a hyphen into the phone number. The TRANSFORM(Pledged,"99,999.99") expression displays the Pledged field with a comma in the thousands place.

The information for a single record occupies eight lines on the report. The command

**LineCount = LineCount + 8**

keeps track of the number of lines printed in the memory variable named LineCount.

Near the bottom of the loop are the SKIP and ENDDO commands, which move the record pointer to the next database record and continue processing the DO WHILE loop until the end of the file (EOF( )) has been reached.

## PRINTING WITH ? VERSUS @

As an alternative to using the ? and ?? commands to print information within the DO WHILE loop, you can use @, SAY, and PICTURE commands. To do so, however, you must also remember to use the command SET DEVICE TO PRINT in place of SET PRINT ON and SET DEVICE TO SCREEN in place of SET PRINT OFF.

The advantage to using @...SAY commands in place of ? commands is that the @ command makes it easier to place data directly into a column. Also, the PICTURE clause is more flexible with logical and date data than the TRANSFORM function. However, these differences are easily overcome with IIF and SET DATE functions.

The real advantage of using ? and ?? commands to print formatted reports is that the SET ALTERNATE command can be used to store a copy of the output on disk. This means that you can use a word processor or print spooler to print a copy of the report later, which in turn means that there is no need to sit around and wait for each report to be printed. (Print spoolers are discussed later in this chapter.)

Another, albeit smaller, advantage to using ? and ?? commands to print reports from within a command file is that you need not be concerned with the exact row position of the cursor or print head at any given time.

## Headings and Pagination

If you use a program to print a report, the program will need to take care of formatting the report, which includes providing page headings, page numbers, and page breaks. The Donate.prg command file shown in Figure 9.16 has all the necessary routines to handle headings and paginations.

Several variables in Donate.prg are used to keep track of information. LineCount keeps track of the number of lines printed, PageCount keeps track of the page number, PageLength stores the maximum number of lines to print on each page, and Title stores the report title. These variable are all initialized near the top of the Donate.prg command file, in the following lines:

```
LineCount = 1
PageCount = 1
PageLength = 55
Title = "Donations Summary"
```

The routine in Donate.prg (Figure 9.16) that begins with the comment line

```
* - - - - -Ask about printer.
```

creates a logical variable named ToPrinter and uses it to ask the user whether the report should be sent to the printer. As you can see in Donate.prg, if the user answers Y or y to the prompt, the SET PRINT ON command is executed.

The routine below prints the page title (including the date and page number) and a couple of blank lines and sets the LineCount variable to 3 (because three lines have just been printed):

```
* - - - Print report title.
? DATE( ),SPACE(20),Title
?? SPACE(20) + "Page  " + STR(PageCount,3)
?
?
LineCount = 3
```

The routine for handling pagination appears inside the DO WHILE loop that prints each record on the database. After each record is printed with a series of ? commands, the line

```
LineCount = LineCount + 8
```

increments the line counter by eight (because each record occupies eight lines on the report, if you count blank lines). The next routine in Figure 9.16, which begins with the comment line

```
* - - - See if time for a page break yet.
```

checks whether the printer is on and whether the number of lines printed exceeds that specified in the PageLength variable (set to 55 in this example). If so, the routine ejects the page in the printer, increments the page counter variable by 1, prints the report heading, page number, and a couple of blank lines, and resets the line counter to 3.

After the report has been printed, the last routine in the program ejects the last page from the printer and turns off the printer (assuming the report was indeed sent to the printer).

## Screen Pauses

If you would like your custom report to pause for the user to press a key between each screenful of information, you can add a routine such as the one below. Note that the routine checks whether the ToPrinter variable is false (indicating that the printer was not selected), and the number of lines printed is about 22 (you may need to experiment with this routine in different programs, trying different values in place of 22):

```
IF .NOT. ToPrinter .AND. LineCount > = 22
    WAIT
    LineCount = 0
ENDIF (not toprinter)
```

In the Donate.prg command file, this routine would be placed in the routine to break pages, below the ENDIF command and above the SKIP command. (In Donate.prg, you may want to try a value of 16 in place of 22, so that complete records would be displayed.)

## Pause for Paper Change

If you do not have a tractor feed on your printer, or you want to print reports on letterhead, you may need to feed sheets of paper one at a time into your printer. If a command file prints your report, it's easy have your program pause for paper change between pages.

All you need to do is have the screen display a message to change pages and wait for the user to press a key after the EJECT command is issued. If you are using SET PRINT ON to print the report, use an @...SAY command to display the prompt. If you are using SET DEVICE to print the report, use a ? command to display the prompt. Both techniques prevent the prompt from being sent to the printer.

In the sample Donate.prg command file (in Figure 9.16), which uses SET PRINT ON and ? to print data, the modification to the pagination routine (shown in Figure 9.17) would pause between pages for paper change.

## A Keypress to Stop the Printer

Another handy feature to build into a report-printing program is a keypress that stops the printer. You can use any key you wish, but this example uses the End key. When the user begins printing the report, the screen displays the prompt **Press the End key to abort print job...** and starts printing the report. If the user does not press End, the entire report is printed. If the user does press End, the program stops printing, as though the DO WHILE .NOT. EOF( ) condition were true. (The actual printing stops when the printer buffer is empty.)

To add this capability to a program, the console should be set off with the SET CONSOLE OFF command when the report is being printed, so that the message stays on the screen. If you were to modify the Donate.prg command file to include this feature, you would alter the IF ToPrinter clause as shown below:

```
IF ToPrinter
    CLEAR
    ? "Press any key to abort print job..."
    SET CONSOLE OFF
    SET PRINT ON
ENDIF (toprinter)
```

```
IF LineCount >= PageLength .AND. ToPrinter
   EJECT

   *--------- Routine for paper change.
   @ 10,10 SAY "Insert new page, then press any key..."
   WAIT " "
   @ 10,10 CLEAR

   *--------- End of page-pause routine.
   PageCount = PageCount + 1
   ? DATE(),SPACE(20),Title
   ?? SPACE(20)+"Page "+STR(PageCount,3)
   ?
   ?
   LineCount = 3
ENDIF  (linecount)
```

**FIGURE 9.17:** A routine that pauses for a page change after ejecting a page. The @ command displays instructions to insert a new page, and the WAIT command waits for the user to press any key before continuing.

Then, to ensure that the program stops printing records when the End key is pressed, the DO WHILE .NOT. EOF( ) loop includes a second condition, as shown below:

**DO WHILE .NOT. EOF( ) .AND. INKEY( ) # 6**

The .AND. INKEY( ) # 6 causes the DO WHILE loop to end when the user presses the End key. (You can use keys other than End if you prefer. See the discussion of INKEY( ) in Chapter 17, "dBASE Functions," for more details.)

One important point to remember in such a program, however, is that the console must be set back on as soon as the report is printed. To accomplish this, place the SET CONSOLE ON command immediately below the ENDDO that marks the bottom of the DO WHILE .NOT. EOF( ) .AND. INKEY( ) < > 6 loop, as shown below:

```
    SKIP
ENDDO (eof )
SET CONSOLE ON
```

## Using Printer Control Codes

Most printers use codes for special attributes such as underlining, boldface, compressed and expanded print, and other features. Unfortunately, different printers use different codes, so the only way to learn the codes for your particular printer is to read the printer manual.

If you can determine the ASCII decimal values for printer control codes, you can embed them directly in report or label columns, as well as in programs. For example, suppose your printer uses ASCII 15 to start underlining and ASCII 16 to stop underlining. If you want to underline a particular field in a REPORT FORM or LABEL FORM report, you could enter the Contents of that column with these codes surrounding the field name(s):

**CHR(15) + TRIM(FName) + " " + LName + CHR(16)**

Let's look at another example. Suppose your printer uses Esc-C to start compressed print and Esc-N to stop compressed print. You want to print an entire report in compressed print to squeeze 120 columns across an 80-column page. First, your REPORT FORM format needs to have the right margin set to some larger value, such as 132. To set this, you need to change the Page width (positions) option in the report generator Options menu.

When you get back to the dot prompt, the commands

```
SET PRINT ON
? CHR(27) + "C"
SET PRINT OFF
```

will send the Esc-C sequence to your printer to start compressed print. (The Esc key is *always* expressed as CHR(27)). Next, the command

**REPORT FORM <file name> TO PRINT**

will display your report in compressed print. When the report is done, the commands

```
SET PRINT ON
? CHR(27) + "N"
SET PRINT OFF
```

will return the printer to normal print mode. (Again, Esc-C and Esc-N are only examples; your printer will likely require different codes.)

If you use a command file, such as Donate.prg above, to print your report, you can place the printer codes within the program. As usual, use the ? command with CHR and the appropriate ASCII decimal value. For example, suppose your printer uses Esc-E to begin emphasized print, Esc-C to begin compressed print, and Esc-N for normal print. You could use the routine below to print the heading in emphasized print:

```
* - - - Print report title.
? CHR(27) + "E"
?? DATE(),SPACE(20),Title
?? SPACE(20) + "Page " + STR(PageCount,3)
?? CHR(27) + "N"
?
```

(You might have to reduce the number of spaces specified inside the SPACE functions to get everything aligned properly.)

To print the body of the report in compressed print, place the command

```
? CHR(27) + "C"
```

above the DO WHILE .NOT. EOF() loop, and the command

```
? CHR(27) + "N"
```

below the ENDDO command for that loop.

To underline a particular field in the report, surround the field name with the appropriate codes as in the example below, which uses the hypothetical codes CHR(1) and CHR(2) to start and stop underlining:

```
?? CHR(1),"Date joined:", Join_Date,CHR(2)
```

In this example a comma is used between Join_Date and CHR(2), because Join_Date is the date data type and cannot be concatenated directly to CHR(2), which is the character data type.

# Using Print Spoolers

In most dBASE applications, when the user opts to print a report, the keyboard and monitor are tied up until the report is completely printed. On systems with large database files and slow printers, this can be a long time.

To avoid the long wait and free up the computer while the printer does its job, you can send copies of your reports to disk files, then have dBASE automatically run a print spooler to print the report. As the report is being printed, you are free to interact with dBASE or your application as usual.

## Sending Reports to Disk Files

Before you can use a print spooler, your application needs to be able to send reports to a disk file. If the report is being printed via REPORT FORM or LABEL FORM, you can just add TO FILE to the command line in place of the TO PRINT command.

If a command file is printing the report, the SET ALTERNATE command will channel all ? and ?? commands to a disk file. (There is no way to channel @ commands to a disk file, which is a good reason to use @ commands only in screen formats.)

Within the program that prints the report, place the following commands above any commands that print the report title:

```
SET SAFETY OFF
SET ALTERNATE TO Spool.txt
SET ALTERNATE ON
```

Doing so will ensure that all remaining text is stored on a file named Spool.txt.

Beneath the ENDDO that marks the bottom of the main DO WHILE .NOT. EOF( ) loop in the program that prints the report, place the command

```
CLOSE ALTERNATE
```

to safely close the completed Spool.txt disk file.

Once the disk file is created, you can use the dBASE RUN command to run a print spooler. (*Note:* RUN requires at least 380K RAM.)

## Accessing the Print Spooler

dBASE III PLUS does not come with a built-in print spooler, but DOS does. The DOS print spooler is stored on one of the DOS disks under the file name Print.com. To use it, copy it on the same disk (or the same drive and directory if you have a hard disk) that your applications programs are stored on.

Within the program that prints reports, you can use the command

**RUN PRINT <file name>**

where <file name> is the entire name of the file to be printed.

If you are using floppy disks and all of the files are stored on the disk in drive B, you can use the command **RUN B:PRINT B:Spool.txt** to access the print spooler on drive B.

To demonstrate the use of the print spooler, the commands below write a report named Sales.frm to a file named Sales.txt and mailing labels from the ThreeCol.lbl format to a file named ThreeCol.txt. Then the two RUN PRINT commands use the DOS print spooler to print the reports "in the background" while dBASE continues to run normally:

```
SET SAFETY OFF
REPORT FORM Sales TO FILE Sales.txt
LABEL FORM Threecol TO FILE Threecol.txt
RUN PRINT Sales.txt
RUN PRINT ThreeCol.txt
```

There will be some wait while the disk files are created, but generally not nearly as long as the printer requires.

## Working with Print.com

The first time you run Print.com, it will display a prompt such as

**Name of list device [PRN]:**

if it is not already initialized to a print device. To prevent Print.com from asking this, place the command

**PRINT /D:PRN**

somewhere near the top of your application program, where it will be executed only once. (If your printer is not hooked to the PRN port, substitute the appropriate port in place of PRN. Your options are LPT1, LPT2, LPT3, COM1, COM2, AUX, etc., as described in the DOS manual.)

The default maximum number of files that can be queued for printing in the Print.com queue is 10. This can be expanded to 32 with the /Q option using the DOS command **PRINT /Q:32** or the equivalent **RUN PRINT /Q:32** from within dBASE. Like the /D option, this command should be executed only once at the beginning of your application.

The /T option terminates all print jobs in the print queue. The /C option terminates a particular print job. From dBASE, the command **RUN PRINT /T** terminates all print jobs, and the command **RUN PRINT Sales.txt /C** cancels only the printing of Sales.txt.

Be forewarned that certain aspects of Print.com might vary from one version of DOS to the next. Take the time to read up on Print.com in your DOS manual. Also, remember that Print.com is part of a copyrighted software product, so you cannot freely distribute it with any software products that you plan to mass-produce.

## UNLIMITED SUBTOTALS IN REPORTS

The dBASE III PLUS report generator allows you to print reports with two levels of subtotals: subtotals and subsubtotals. With some programming, however, you can bypass the report generator and develop your own reports with just about any number of subtotals or levels of grouping that you want. While there is no quick-and-easy procedure that you can develop to handle this job, there are some basic, straightforward programming techniques that you can use to develop reports with multiple levels of subtotals.

This section explains how to build a program with three levels of subtotals, starting with a program with only one level. By building the program in this manner, you should be able to see how each level of subtotaling uses basically the same logic or *algorithm.*

Figure 9.18 shows the database used with the sample programs developed in this section. The database contains the fields PartNo, PartName, Clerk (which contains the salesperson's initials), Qty, UnitPrice, and Date. To show the potential for subtotaling, the file is sorted by part number, by salesperson within each part number, and by date for each salesperson.

```
PartNo PartName        Clerk      Qty UnitPrice  Date
A-111  Floppy Drive    ABC         10    150.00  01/01/87
A-111  Floppy Drive    ABC         11    150.00  01/01/87
A-111  Floppy Drive    ABC          9    150.00  01/02/87
A-111  Floppy Drive    ABC         11    150.00  01/02/87
A-111  Floppy Drive    ZEM         11    150.00  01/01/87
A-111  Floppy Drive    ZEM         12    150.00  01/01/87
A-111  Floppy Drive    ZEM          5    150.00  01/01/87
A-111  Floppy Drive    ZEM          5    150.00  01/02/87
A-111  Floppy Drive    ZEM          7    150.00  01/02/87
B-222  Hard Disk       ABC          4   1495.00  01/01/87
B-222  Hard Disk       ABC          5   1495.00  01/01/87
B-222  Hard Disk       ABC          4   1495.00  01/02/87
B-222  Hard Disk       ABC          6   1495.00  01/02/87
B-222  Hard Disk       ABC         14   1495.00  01/02/87
B-222  Hard Disk       ZEM          2   1495.00  01/01/87
B-222  Hard Disk       ZEM          4   1495.00  01/01/87
B-222  Hard Disk       ZEM          2   1495.00  01/02/87
B-222  Hard Disk       ZEM         10   1495.00  01/02/87
```

**FIGURE 9.18:** Contents of the SubTots database. This sample database is used by the SubTot1, SubTot2, and SubTot3 command files in this chapter to display one-, two-, and three-level subtotaled reports.

To print subtotals, the file must first be indexed (or sorted) on the field being used to define subtotal groups. Therefore, if you are printing a report with subtotals based on the part number, the database must be indexed or sorted on the part number field.

Next, for each subtotal group you need a DO WHILE loop that has the basic structure shown in pseudocode below:

```
Store subtotal group identifier in a memory variable
Initialize subtotal accumulator to zero
Print subtotal heading (if any)
Start loop to repeat while still in subtotal group
    Print record from database
    Increment subtotal by current record amount
    Skip to next record in database
End loop when this subtotal group ends
Print subtotal
```

Each subtotal group will be represented by a loop, like the one above, in a command file. Furthermore, each of the subtotal loops must be nested inside a single DO WHILE .NOT. EOF( ) that ensures that all records from the database will be printed.

## One-Level Subtotals

The sample program in Figure 9.19 prints a single level of subtotals based on the PartNo field. Of course, the dBASE report generator can do the same thing that this program can do, because this program displays only one level of subtotals. However, this program is only the first step in demonstrating how to develop programs that can print many levels of subtotals. The output from this program is shown in Figure 9.20.

Because PartNo is the field that defines subtotal groups, the database must be indexed on the PartNo field. The first command in the command file opens the SubTots database with the SubTots index file (previously created with the command INDEX ON PartNo TO SubTots). Then the GO TOP command ensures that the record pointer is at the top of the database.

The program then initializes a variable named GrandTot, which accumulates the grand total of all records displayed in the report. Then the outermost DO WHILE loop begins. It uses the condition WHILE .NOT. EOF( ) to ensure that all records in the database are printed.

Before actually printing any records, however, another DO WHILE loop is needed to control the subtotal group. As shown in the pseudocode version discussed previously, this loop stores the part number of the current record in the database in a memory variable (named ThisPart in this example). The variable

```
***************************************** SubTot1.prg
*---- Displays subtotals based upon the PartNo field.

*-- File must be indexed on the PartNo field.
USE SubTots INDEX SubTots
GO TOP
CLEAR

*-- GrandTot variable accumulates grand total.
GrandTot = 0

*----------- Outermost loop does entire file.
DO WHILE .NOT. EOF()

   *--------- Loop to print first subtotal.
   *--------- Initialize subtotal field and value.
   ThisPart = PartNo
   PartTot = 0
   *---------Subtotal heading (optional).
   ? "---Part Number "+ThisPart+" : "+PartName
   ?

   DO WHILE PartNo = ThisPart .AND. .NOT. EOF()
      *---- Print a record from the database.
      ? PartNo," ",Clerk," ",Date,Qty,UnitPrice
      ?? TRANSFORM(Qty*UnitPrice,"999,999.99")
      *---- Increment grandtotal and subtotals.
      GrandTot = GrandTot + (Qty * UnitPrice)
      PartTot = PartTot + (Qty * UnitPrice)
      SKIP
   ENDDO (part number subtotal)

   *----- Print subtotal.
   ? SPACE(37),"---------"
   ? "Part &ThisPart total:",SPACE(19)
   ?? TRANSFORM(PartTot,"999,999.99")
   ?
   ?
ENDDO (entire file)
*--- Print grand total.
? SPACE(36),"----------"
? "Grand Total:",SPACE(24)
?? TRANSFORM(GrandTot,"999,999.99")
RETURN
```

**FIGURE 9.19:** The SubTot1.prg command file displays data from the sample SubTots database file with a single level of subtotals. The output from this program is shown in Figure 9.20.

to accumulate the subtotal, named PartTot in this example, is intialized as zero:

**ThisPart = PartNo**
**PartTot = 0**

At this point, you can display a heading for the subtotal group, though it is not absolutely necessary to do so. This routine prints a heading for the subtotal group, which consists of the part number, part name, and some text:

**? " --Part Number " + ThisPart + " : " + PartName**
**?**

Now the inner DO WHILE loop to control the part number subtotal begins.

```
---Part Number A-111 : Floppy Drive

A-111   ABC   01/01/87   10      150.00  1,500.00
A-111   ABC   01/01/87   11      150.00  1,650.00
A-111   ABC   01/02/87    9      150.00  1,350.00
A-111   ABC   01/02/87   11      150.00  1,650.00
A-111   ZEM   01/01/87   11      150.00  1,650.00
A-111   ZEM   01/01/87   12      150.00  1,800.00
A-111   ZEM   01/01/87    5      150.00    750.00
A-111   ZEM   01/02/87    5      150.00    750.00
A-111   ZEM   01/02/87    7      150.00  1,050.00
                                        ---------
Part A-111 total:                       12,150.00

---Part Number B-222 : Hard Disk

B-222   ABC   01/01/87    4     1495.00  5,980.00
B-222   ABC   01/01/87    5     1495.00  7,475.00
B-222   ABC   01/02/87    4     1495.00  5,980.00
B-222   ABC   01/02/87    6     1495.00  8,970.00
B-222   ABC   01/02/87   14     1495.00 20,930.00
B-222   ZEM   01/01/87    2     1495.00  2,990.00
B-222   ZEM   01/01/87    4     1495.00  5,980.00
B-222   ZEM   01/02/87    2     1495.00  2,990.00
B-222   ZEM   01/02/87   10     1495.00 14,950.00
                                        ---------
Part B-222 total:                       76,245.00


                                       ----------
Grand Total:                            88,395.00
```

**FIGURE 9.20:** Report printed by the SubTot1.prg program. The subtotal field is PartNo. The database is indexed on the PartNo field.

Notice that the loop repeats as long as the current record has the same part number that began this group (PartNo = ThisPart) and that the loop also repeats the condition of the previous loop (.NOT. EOF( )). The most common mistake that people make when developing programs that print subtotals is forgetting this rule: *each nested loop in a subtotaling program must repeat the conditions stated in all previous loops.* In this example, that rule has not been forgotten:

```
DO WHILE PartNo = ThisPart .AND. .NOT. EOF( )
```

Within this loop, the program prints a record from the database (a row in the report) and then increments the grand total and subtotal values by the amount being totaled and subtotaled (total sale, or quantity, times the unit price in this example):

```
? PartNo," ",Clerk," ",Date,Qty,UnitPrice
?? TRANSFORM(Qty*UnitPrice,"999,999.99")
*-- Increment grandtotal and subtotals.
GrandTot = GrandTot + (Qty * UnitPrice)
PartTot = PartTot + (Qty * UnitPrice)
```

With the job of printing the record and incrementing the total and subtotal done, the program can skip to the next record in the database with the SKIP command.

The process of printing a record and incrementing the total and subtotal will continue until a new part number is encountered in the database (because of the condition WHILE PartNo = ThisPart stated in the inner DO WHILE loop).

When the innermost loop is done, all the records for the current part number have been printed and accumulated in the total and subtotal variables. Therefore, the program can now print something beneath the subtotal group. In this example, it prints an underline beneath the totals in the right column of the report, some text, and the subtotal for the current part number (stored in the PartTot variable):

```
? SPACE(37),"---------"
? "Part &ThisPart total:",SPACE(19)
?? TRANSFORM(PartTot,"999,999.99")
?
?
```

The report is not done, however, because only a single part number group has been printed. The closing ENDDO loop keeps printing records because the outermost loop has the condition WHILE .NOT. EOF( ). The outermost ENDDO command causes processing to resume at the lines within the outermost DO WHILE loop that reset the ThisPart variable to the new current part number and the PartTot accumulating variable to zero. Hence, the innermost loop will print the next subtotal group and subtotal amount. This process continues until all the records in the database have been printed, at which time the outermost DO WHILE .NOT. EOF( ) loop terminates and the program prints the grand total:

```
? SPACE(36),"----------"
? "Grand Total:",SPACE(24)
?? TRANSFORM(GrandTot,"999,999.99")
```

To include page numbers and headings in this report, refer to the section "Headings and Pagination" earlier in this chapter.

## Two-Level Subtotals

To add a second level of subtotaling to the report SubTot1.prg is printing, you need to nest another DO WHILE loop inside the innermost loop. This new loop will look very much like the loop for subtotaling part numbers and will use the same technique discussed in the pseudocode version of the algorithm earlier.

The new subtotal group will be based on the salesperson's initials (stored in the Clerk field). So the report will display subtotals by part number, and within each part number it will display a subtotal by salesperson. In view of this, the database must be sorted by part number and by salesperson within each part number. Hence, the SubTots index file now needs to be created with the command

```
INDEX ON PartNo + Clerk TO SubTots
```

Figure 9.21 shows the SubTot2.prg program, which has the new loop for subtotaling on the Clerk field nested within the original SubTot1.prg command file.

Only the following lines have been added to the original SubTot1.prg command file to create the SubTot2.prg command file. First, nested within the loop to subtotal part numbers are the commands to store the salesperson's initials from the current record in a variable named ThisPerson. Second, a command creates a variable named PersonTot, which will be used to accumulate the salesperson's subtotal. PersonTot is initialized as zero:

```
ThisPerson = Clerk
PersonTot = 0
```

Next the DO WHILE loop to print and accumulate a subtotal for a single salesperson begins. As before, the loop states its own condition (Clerk = ThisPerson) to isolate the current salesperson, and also repeats the conditions of all previous loops (PartNo = ThisPart .AND. .NOT. EOF( )), as shown below:

```
DO WHILE Clerk = ThisPerson .AND. ;
     PartNo = ThisPart .AND. .NOT. EOF( )
```

The innermost loop then performs the task of printing a record from the database and accumulating all subtotals and totals. To accumulate the subtotal for each salesperson, SubTot2.prg has the new line

```
PersonTot = PersonTot + (Qty * UnitPrice)
```

When all the records representing the current salesperson have been printed, the loop ends and the program prints some text and the subtotal for the current salesperson:

```
ENDDO (salesperson subtotal)
? SPACE(37),"---------"
? " Salesperson &ThisPerson Part &ThisPart subtotal:"
?? TRANSFORM(PersonTot,"999,999.99")
?
```

Everything else in the program is exactly as it was in the original SubTot1 program.

Figure 9.22 shows the report printed by the SubTot2.prg command file. Notice that subtotals for each part number still appear on the report, but there are also subtotals for each salesperson within each part number.

```
****************************************** SubTot2.prg
*- This program adds a DO WHILE loop to calculate
*- and display subtotals based upon the Clerk field.

*-- File must be indexed on the PartNo + Clerk fields.
USE SubTots INDEX SubTots
GO TOP
CLEAR
*-- GrandTot variable accumulates grand total.
GrandTot = 0
*----------- Outermost loop does entire file.
DO WHILE .NOT. EOF()
   *--------- Loop to print first subtotal.
   *--------- Initialize subtotal field and value.
   ThisPart = PartNo
   PartTot = 0
   *---------Subtotal heading (optional).
   ? "---Part Number "+ThisPart+" : "+PartName
   ?
   DO WHILE PartNo = ThisPart .AND. .NOT. EOF()

      *-- Next loop handles subtotals for salesperson.
      ThisPerson = Clerk
      PersonTot = 0
      DO WHILE Clerk = ThisPerson .AND. ;
         PartNo = ThisPart .AND. .NOT. EOF()
         *---- Print a record from the database.
         ? PartNo," ",Clerk," ",Date,Qty,UnitPrice
         ?? TRANSFORM(Qty*UnitPrice,"999,999.99")
         *---- Increment grandtotal and subtotals.
         GrandTot = GrandTot + (Qty * UnitPrice)
         PartTot = PartTot + (Qty * UnitPrice)
         PersonTot = PersonTot + (Qty * UnitPrice)
         SKIP
      ENDDO (salesperson subtotal)
      ? SPACE(37),"---------"
      ? " Salesperson &ThisPerson Part &ThisPart subtotal:"
      ?? TRANSFORM(PersonTot,"999,999.99")
      ?

   ENDDO (part number subtotal)
   *----- Print subtotal.
   ? SPACE(37),"---------"
   ? "Part &ThisPart total:",SPACE(19)
   ?? TRANSFORM(PartTot,"999,999.99")
   ?
   ?
ENDDO (entire file)
*--- Print grand total.
? SPACE(36),"----------"
? "Grand Total:",SPACE(24)
?? TRANSFORM(GrandTot,"999,999.99")
RETURN
```

**FIGURE 9.21:** The SubTot2.prg command file displays data from the SubTots database subtotaled on both the PartNo and Clerk fields. The report produced by this program is shown in Figure 9.22.

## Three-Level Subtotals

In this example, the date field is the third subtotal field, so that subtotals will be displayed by part number, by salesperson within each part number, and by date for each salesperson.

```
---Part Number A-111 : Floppy Drive

A-111   ABC   01/01/87   10    150.00  1,500.00
A-111   ABC   01/01/87   11    150.00  1,650.00
A-111   ABC   01/02/87    9    150.00  1,350.00
A-111   ABC   01/02/87   11    150.00  1,650.00
                                       ---------
 Salesperson ABC Part A-111 subtotal:  6,150.00

A-111   ZEM   01/01/87   11    150.00  1,650.00
A-111   ZEM   01/01/87   12    150.00  1,800.00
A-111   ZEM   01/01/87    5    150.00    750.00
A-111   ZEM   01/02/87    5    150.00    750.00
A-111   ZEM   01/02/87    7    150.00  1,050.00
                                       ---------
 Salesperson ZEM Part A-111 subtotal:  6,000.00

                                       ---------
Part A-111 total:                     12,150.00

---Part Number B-222 : Hard Disk

B-222   ABC   01/01/87    4   1495.00  5,980.00
B-222   ABC   01/01/87    5   1495.00  7,475.00
B-222   ABC   01/02/87    4   1495.00  5,980.00
B-222   ABC   01/02/87    6   1495.00  8,970.00
B-222   ABC   01/02/87   14   1495.00 20,930.00
                                      ---------
 Salesperson ABC Part B-222 subtotal: 49,335.00

B-222   ZEM   01/01/87    2   1495.00  2,990.00
B-222   ZEM   01/01/87    4   1495.00  5,980.00
B-222   ZEM   01/02/87    2   1495.00  2,990.00
B-222   ZEM   01/02/87   10   1495.00 14,950.00
                                      ---------
 Salesperson ZEM Part B-222 subtotal: 26,910.00

                                      ---------
Part B-222 total:                     76,245.00

                                     ----------
Grand Total:                          88,395.00
```

**FIGURE 9.22:** Report printed by SubTot2.prg. Data are subtotaled by the PartNo field and by SalesPerson within each part number. The database needs to be indexed on the expression PartNo + Clerk to display this report.

Because there are three levels of subtotals, there now must be three sort levels: PartNo, Clerk, and Date. So the command to create the SubTots index file must be

**INDEX ON PartNo + Clerk + DTOC(Date) TO SubTots**

(The DTOC function is necessary to combine the date data type used for the date field with the character data types of PartNo and Clerk.)

Notice that the order of the fields in the INDEX statement matches the levels of grouping in the report: from outermost level to innermost level. The sort order *must* match the grouping order in the report.

Figure 9.23 shows the SubTot3.prg command file, which contains the new inner loop to subtotal by date. Notice that all other parts of the program are identical to the SubTot2.prg command file.

```
****************************************** SubTot3.prg
*-- This program adds a DO WHILE loop to calculate
*-- and display subtotals based upon the Date field.

*-- File must be indexed on the
*-- PartNo, Clerk, and Date fields.
USE SubTots INDEX SubTots
GO TOP
CLEAR
*-- GrandTot variable accumulates grand total.
GrandTot = 0
*----------- Outermost loop does entire file.
DO WHILE .NOT. EOF()
   *--------- Loop to print first subtotal.
   *--------- Initialize subtotal field and value.
   ThisPart = PartNo
   PartTot = 0
   *---------Subtotal heading (optional).
   ? "---Part Number "+ThisPart+" : "+PartName
   ?
   DO WHILE PartNo = ThisPart .AND. .NOT. EOF()
      *-- Next loop handles subtotals for salesperson.
      ThisPerson = Clerk
      PersonTot = 0
      DO WHILE Clerk = ThisPerson .AND. ;
         PartNo = ThisPart .AND. .NOT. EOF()

         *-- Next loop handles subtotals for date.
         ThisDate = Date
         DateTot = 0
         DO WHILE Date = ThisDate .AND. ;
                  Clerk = ThisPerson .AND. ;
                  PartNo = ThisPart .AND..NOT. EOF()
            *---- Print a record from the database.
            ? PartNo," ",Clerk," ",Date,Qty,UnitPrice
            ?? TRANSFORM(Qty*UnitPrice,"999,999.99")
            *---- Increment grandtotal and subtotals.
            GrandTot = GrandTot + (Qty * UnitPrice)
            PartTot = PartTot + (Qty * UnitPrice)
            PersonTot = PersonTot + (Qty * UnitPrice)
            DateTot = DateTot + (Qty * UnitPrice)
            SKIP
         ENDDO (date subtotal)
         ? SPACE(37),"---------"
         ? SPACE(7),ThisPart,ThisPerson,ThisDate
         ?? " subtotal:",TRANSFORM(DateTot,"999,999.99")
         ?

      ENDDO (salesperson subtotal)
      ? SPACE(37),"---------"
      ? " Salesperson &ThisPerson Part &ThisPart subtotal:"
      ?? TRANSFORM(PersonTot,"999,999.99")
      ?
    ENDDO (part number subtotal)
    *----- Print subtotal.
    ? SPACE(37),"---------"
    ? "Part &ThisPart total:",SPACE(19)
    ?? TRANSFORM(PartTot,"999,999.99")
    ?
    ?
ENDDO (entire file)
*--- Print grand total.
? SPACE(36),"----------"
? "Grand Total:",SPACE(24)
?? TRANSFORM(GrandTot,"999,999.99")
RETURN
```

**FIGURE 9.23:** The SubTot3.Prg command file prints data from the SubTots database subtotaled on the PartNo, Clerk, and Date fields. The report displayed by this program is shown in Figure 9.24.

Once again, the new inner loop follows the same basic principles discussed throughout this section. The first new lines in the program are nested inside the previous innermost loop. Those lines store the current value of Date in a variable named ThisDate and initialize a variable, named DateTot in this example, to accumulate the Date subtotal:

```
ThisDate = Date
DateTot = 0
```

The DO WHILE loop for the Date subtotal uses the expression WHILE Date = ThisDate, and also repeats the conditions stated in all of the previous DO WHILE loops:

```
DO WHILE Date = ThisDate .AND. ;
             SalesMan = ThisPerson .AND. ;
             PartNo = ThisPart .AND..NOT. EOF( )
```

The commands to print a line and increment the total and subtotals are now within this new innermost DO WHILE loop. SubTot3.prg needs the additional command to increment the Date subtotal, as shown below:

```
DateTot = DateTot + (Qty * UnitPrice)
```

To mark the bottom of the new innermost DO WHILE loop, the program needs an ENDDO command, as well as commands to print the date subtotal (stored on the DateTot variable):

```
ENDDO (date subtotal)
? SPACE(37),"---------"
? SPACE(7),ThisPart,ThisPerson,ThisDate
?? " subtotal:",TRANSFORM(DateTot,"999,999.99")
?
```

The report printed by the SubTot3.prg command file is shown in Figure 9.24. The subtotal line for each date uses some abbreviated text to identify the total at a glance. For example, the line on the report that reads

```
A-111 ABC 01/01/87 subtotal:        3,150.00
```

indicates that the subtotal of $3,150.00 is for part number A-111, for salesperson ABC, on January 1, 1987.

You can now follow the techniques presented here to add more levels of subtotals or to develop your own subtotaling programs. The only limitation you need to be concerned with is the 256-character length limit dBASE imposes on command lines. At a certain point, the DO WHILE conditions for an inner loop might exceed that length, because each loop needs to repeat the conditions of the previous line. You can conserve space in the DO WHILE command lines by

```
---Part Number A-111 : Floppy Drive

A-111   ABC   01/01/87   10    150.00  1,500.00
A-111   ABC   01/01/87   11    150.00  1,650.00
                                       ---------
        A-111 ABC 01/01/87 subtotal:   3,150.00

A-111   ABC   01/02/87    9    150.00  1,350.00
A-111   ABC   01/02/87   11    150.00  1,650.00
                                       ---------
        A-111 ABC 01/02/87 subtotal:   3,000.00

                                       ---------
 Salesperson ABC Part A-111 subtotal:  6,150.00

A-111   ZEM   01/01/87   11    150.00  1,650.00
A-111   ZEM   01/01/87   12    150.00  1,800.00
A-111   ZEM   01/01/87    5    150.00    750.00
                                       ---------
        A-111 ZEM 01/01/87 subtotal:   4,200.00

A-111   ZEM   01/02/87    5    150.00    750.00
A-111   ZEM   01/02/87    7    150.00  1,050.00
                                       ---------
        A-111 ZEM 01/02/87 subtotal:   1,800.00

                                       ---------
 Salesperson ZEM Part A-111 subtotal:  6,000.00

                                       ---------
Part A-111 total:                     12,150.00

---Part Number B-222 : Hard Disk

B-222   ABC   01/01/87    4   1495.00  5,980.00
B-222   ABC   01/01/87    5   1495.00  7,475.00
                                       ---------
        B-222 ABC 01/01/87 subtotal:  13,455.00

B-222   ABC   01/02/87    4   1495.00  5,980.00
B-222   ABC   01/02/87    6   1495.00  8,970.00
B-222   ABC   01/02/87   14   1495.00 20,930.00
                                       ---------
        B-222 ABC 01/02/87 subtotal:  35,880.00

                                       ---------
 Salesperson ABC Part B-222 subtotal: 49,335.00

B-222   ZEM   01/01/87    2   1495.00  2,990.00
B-222   ZEM   01/01/87    4   1495.00  5,980.00
                                       ---------
        B-222 ZEM 01/01/87 subtotal:   8,970.00

B-222   ZEM   01/02/87    2   1495.00  2,990.00
B-222   ZEM   01/02/87   10   1495.00 14,950.00
                                       ---------
        B-222 ZEM 01/02/87 subtotal:  17,940.00

                                       ---------
 Salesperson ZEM Part B-222 subtotal: 26,910.00

                                       ---------
Part B-222 total:                     76,245.00

                                      ----------
Grand Total:                          88,395.00
```

**FIGURE 9.24:** Report printed by the SubTot3.prg program. The data are subtotaled on the PartNo field, on the Clerk field within each part number, and by Date within each salesperson. The database must first be sorted or indexed with the expression PartNo + Clerk + DTOC(Date) (assuming PartNo is a character field).

using brief variable names (e.g., L1, L2, and so forth), instead of the long variable names used in these examples.

Just remember that the database must be in properly sorted order for the subtotaling programs to work. I've seen people waste hours trying to figure out what was wrong with their subtotaling programs, only to discover that the program was fine—it was the index order that was wrong.

# COMMANDS FOR PRINTING REPORTS

The remainder of this chapter discusses individual commands used to display data on formatted reports. These include the MODIFY REPORT and MODIFY LABEL commands, for designing report and label formats, and the REPORT FORM and LABEL FORM commands, for printing the reports and labels. Also, the ?, ??, EJECT, and TEXT...ENDTEXT commands are discussed, which are of particular interest to the programmer who wants to develop custom programs to print reports.

## The MODIFY REPORT Command

MODIFY REPORT calls up the dBASE III PLUS report generator for designing report formats. The CREATE REPORT command is equivalent to MODIFY REPORT.

### SYNTAX

**MODIFY REPORT <file name>**

or

**CREATE REPORT <file name>**

where <file name> is any valid DOS file name. dBASE automatically adds the extension .frm to the report format file name if none is specified in this command.

### USAGE

MODIFY REPORT activates a full-screen, menu-driven report generator which lets you format reports that can be printed with the REPORT FORM command. The highlight can be moved to any menu option by pressing the arrow keys. Pressing Return while an option is highlighted selects that option.

The menus at the top of the screen are Options, Groups, Columns, Locate, and Exit. The options from each of these menus are discussed in the sections below.

## THE OPTIONS MENU

The Options menu provides options for formatting the margins, headings, and other aesthetic aspects of the report. Each option is summarized below.

***Title*** The Title option allows you to enter up to four lines of text as a report heading. After entering a heading, press Ctrl-End to return to the menu.

***Page Width*** The Page width option determines the number of characters to be printed across a page. The default value is 80 but you can change it to any value from 1 to 500. Note that the actual width of the printed report will be the total page width, minus the sum of the left and right margins, as set in the two options below.

***Left Margin*** The Left margin setting determines the number of blank spaces between the left edge of the paper and the first printed column.

***Right Margin*** The Right margin setting determines the number of columns between the right edge of the page and the character in the rightmost column.

***Number of Lines per Page*** The Number of lines per page option determines the number of lines that will be printed on a page before the paper is ejected and a new page is started. Any value between 1 and 500 is acceptable.

***Double Space Report*** The Double space report option places a blank line between each printed record if set to Yes. Otherwise, the report is single-spaced.

***Page Eject before Printing*** If the Page eject before printing option is Yes, REPORT FORM ejects the page currently in the printer before printing the report. If this option is set to No, the report starts printing at the current printer-head position. (This can also be controlled by the NOEJECT option in the REPORT FORM command.)

***Page Eject after Printing*** If the Page eject after printing option is set to Yes, the last page is ejected from the printer after the report is printed. If it is set to No, the printer head stays at the current page position after the report is printed. On laser printers, this option should be set to Yes. If you want to combine several smaller reports on a single page, set this option to No.

***Plain Page*** If the Plain page option is set to No, the report heading, page number, and date are printed on every page of the report. If it is set to Yes, the report heading is printed *only* on the first page of the report, and the page number and date are completely suppressed. (This can also be controlled with the PLAIN option in the REPORT FORM command.)

### THE GROUPS MENU

This menu allows you to group items of information in a report; it is typically used to print subtotals. It is important to remember that the database must be sorted or indexed on the subtotaled field. The features offered on this menu are entirely optional.

***Group on Expression*** The Group on expression option lets you group items in a report and optionally display subtotals for each group. For this setting to work correctly, the database must be indexed or sorted on the same expression. For example, if the grouping expression is PartNo, the database must be indexed or sorted on the PartNo field.

The grouping expression can consist of multiple keys, as in this example:

**PartNo + DTOC(Date) + STR(Amount,9,2)**

The database file must be sorted or indexed using exactly the same expression.

***Group Heading*** The Group heading option places a title at the top of each group on the report. The value that identifies the group will be displayed automatically at the top of each group. Any text that you enter here will be printed to the left of that value.

***Summary Report Only*** If the Summary report only option is No, the report displays all details (records) from the database. If it is changed to Yes, only subtotals and totals are displayed on the report. (This can also be controlled by the SUMMARY option in the REPORT FORM command.)

***Page Eject after Group*** If the Page eject after group option is Yes, each subtotal group will start on a new page. If it is left as No, each page can contain two or more subtotal groups.

***Sub-group on Expression*** The Sub-group on expression option lets you define a secondary level of grouping and subtotals. The database must be sorted (or indexed) on both the primary and secondary grouping expressions. For example, to print a report with subtotals by the Date Field and by the PartNo field within each date, Date is the primary grouping expression and PartNo the subgroup expression. The database must be sorted or indexed by the expression **DTOC(Date) + PartNo** or **DTOC(Date) + STR(PartNo,4,0)**, if PartNo is a numeric field.

***Sub-group Heading*** The Sub-group heading option allows you to define a heading for the subgroup, in the same manner that you create a heading for the primary group.

## THE COLUMNS MENU

The Columns menu lets you define the contents of each report column. A column can contain a field from the current database file or a related one. It can also contain an expression including calculations or any valid dBASE function.

***Contents*** The Contents option specifies what belongs in each column of the report. Pressing Return while the option is highlighted activates the item. Pressing F10 displays all fields from the currently selected database, which can be selected by highlighting and pressing Return. If an expression or field from a related database is to be entered, you must type it directly instead of selecting it from the F10 submenu.

To scroll up and down from one defined column to another, use the PgUp and PgDn keys. To delete the current column from the report format, type Ctrl-U. To insert a new column before the current column, type Ctrl-N.

***Heading*** To display a column heading at the top of each column, select the Heading option. You can enter up to four lines of text for each heading. Columns with headings of varying lines align on the top line, as shown in Figure 9.10 earlier in the chapter. After typing in your heading, press Ctrl-End to return to the Columns menu.

***Width*** The Width option determines the width of the column (though dBASE adds an additional space between each column). A suggested width is automatically calculated by the width of the field or the width of the heading, whichever is larger. You can change this setting by selecting the Width option and typing in a new value. If the column contains character data and the column width is narrower than the text to be printed, the text is automatically wrapped within the specified width. (This is also true for memo fields.)

***Decimal Places*** The Decimal places option specifies the number of decimals displayed for numeric values. The suggested size equals the size specified in the database file structure. If you set a lower size, the number will be rounded.

***Total this Column*** The Total this column option determines whether totals will be displayed for numeric columns. If it is set to Yes, the column is totaled at the bottom of every total and subtotal group. If it is set to no, the number is not totaled at all.

### THE LOCATE MENU

The Locate menu displays a list of all currently defined columns. To quickly bring one of these columns to the Columns menu, move the highlight to the column and press Return.

Any blank column that appears in this display should be removed. Blank columns cause the report to fail and display the error message **Syntax error in field expression**. To delete a blank column, move the highlight to it on the Locate menu. Select that column by pressing Return, then press Ctrl-U when the blank column appears on the Columns menu. Select Exit and Save to save the change.

### THE EXIT MENU

The Exit menu provides two means for leaving the report generator and returning to the dot prompt.

***Save*** The Save option saves the current report definition in a file with the extension .frm. Any previous report definition with the same name is completely overwritten.

***Abandon*** The Abandon option abandons the current report format. If an existing format was being modified, the current changes are abandoned and the original format remains intact.

## EXAMPLE

The commands

**USE OrdData**
**MODIFY REPORT Orders**

allow you to edit a report format file named Orders.frm, or create a new one if it does not already exist. The report format will use fields from the OrdData database. The discussion at the beginning of this chapter includes an example of creating a report using two related database files.

## TIPS

When a report uses many stacked fields, the LABEL FORM command or a custom command file is generally easier to use than MODIFY REPORT.

If you wish to create a report format that resembles an existing report format, you can copy the existing report format to another file name with the dBASE

COPY FILE command or the DOS COPY command. Then use MODIFY REPORT to edit the copied file.

When editing a column in an existing report format with MODIFY REPORT, keep an eye on the Width, Decimal, and Total settings. dBASE tends to change these automatically, even if you've previously defined them in earlier sessions.

#### SEE ALSO

REPORT FORM

## The REPORT FORM Command

REPORT FORM prints data using the format specified with the MODIFY REPORT or CREATE REPORT command. You can send the display to the screen, the printer, or an ASCII file.

#### SYNTAX

**REPORT FORM <file name> [<scope>][WHILE <condition>]**
**[FOR <condition>];[PLAIN] [HEADING <expression>]**
**[NOEJECT] [TO PRINT];**
**[TO FILE <text file name>] [SUMMARY]**

where <file name> is the name of the report (.frm) format file, <condition> is any valid search condition, <expression> is any valid character string expression, and <text file name> is the name of an ASCII text file.

#### USAGE

If two or more databases were used and related to create the report format, the databases must be open and related in the same manner to print the report. If the correct files are open but the wrong one is selected, the report will fail and the error message **Syntax error in field expression** will appear (other errors might also display this same message).

If the report displays groups or subtotals, the database must be sorted or indexed on the grouping fields for the report to be accurate.

The PLAIN option suppresses the display of the date and page number on all report pages and limits the heading display to the first page of the report.

The HEADING option specifies an additional title to be displayed on the same line as the page number on the report. If the heading is literal text, it should be enclosed in quotation marks, as below:

**REPORT FORM AnyFile HEADING "This is a literal heading"**

The heading can also be a variable or expression. In the example below, the variable RepHead is defined as text as well as a range of dates:

```
Start = CTOD("07/01/87")
End = CTOD("08/30/87")
RepHead = "The quarter " + DTOC(Start) + " to " + DTOC(End)
REPORT FORM AnyFile FOR Date >= Start .AND. Date <= End ;
HEADING RepHead TO PRINT
```

The NOEJECT option combined with the TO PRINT option causes the report to begin printing at the current page position in the printer rather than at the top of the next page.

The TO PRINT option sends output to the printer. The TO FILE option sends output to a file with the file name you specify. If you do not specify an extension for the output file name, the .txt extension is added automatically. The file output includes form-feed characters (Ctrl-L or CHR(12)) for automatic pagination. Hence, even a print spooler will properly paginate the text file.

The SUMMARY option suppresses the display of detail lines (individual records), displaying only the subtotals and totals specified in the report format.

## EXAMPLES

The commands

```
LookUp = "A-111"
SEEK LookUp
REPORT FORM AnyFile WHILE PartNo = LookUp;
        FOR Date = DATE( ) PLAIN NOEJECT TO PRINT
```

display all records with a part number equal to A-111 and a date equal to the current date on the printer without first ejecting the page and without page numbers or a report date.

See Figure 9.13 for an example routine that asks the user whether the report should be sent to the printer.

## TIPS

A strange anomaly occurs when the page width and left margin differ by exactly 256, causing dBASE to skip printing the page title. If your titles disappear on the printed report, check for this.

See the discussion of the WHILE and FOR commands in Chapter 13, "Searching a Database," for tips on maximizing the speed of the REPORT FORM command.

#### SEE ALSO

MODIFY REPORT

## The MODIFY LABEL Command

MODIFY LABEL provides an interactive, menu-driven technique for formatting mailing labels.

#### SYNTAX

**MODIFY LABEL <file name>**

or

**CREATE LABEL <file name>**

where <file name> is any valid DOS file name. If no extension is provided, dBASE adds the extension .lbl to the file name.

#### USAGE

The MODIFY LABEL command presents three pull-down menus for creating and editing mailing label formats. The menus are Options, Contents, and Exit. The arrow keys move the highlight to the various menu and submenu options, and the Return key selects the currently highlighted option. The F1 key toggles the help screen for manipulating the cursor on and off.

### THE OPTIONS MENU

The Options menu offers several predefined label sizes to choose from, as well as individual size specifications.

The Predefined size option lets you choose from the following predefined sizes by repeatedly pressing the Return key:

| Width | Height | Number of labels across |
|---|---|---|
| 3-1/2" | 15/16" | 1 |
| 3-1/2" | 15/16" | 2 |
| 3-1/2" | 15/16" | 3 |

4"      1-7/16"      1

3-2/10"      11/12"      3 (Cheshire labels)

Selecting one of the options above automatically adjusts all settings in the lower menu items.

The acceptable settings for the remaining menu items are shown in Table 9.1. Note, however, that the total width of all labels across the page cannot exceed 250 characters.

### THE CONTENTS MENU

Use the Contents menu to define what is to appear on each line of the mailing label. To enter something onto a line, move the highlight to that line and press Return. Then, to see a list of available field names, press F10. You can select a field from the submenu of field names by highlighting and pressing Return. Pressing ← or → returns you to the Contents menu.

Several fields can be combined on a single line. If a comma is used to join two fields, a space is inserted between those fields. If a plus sign is used to join two fields, no space is inserted. The LTRIM, RTRIM, and TRIM functions can be used to trim blank spaces. The TRANSFORM function can be used to format individual fields.

To delete a line from the label format, highlight the line and type Ctrl-U. To insert a new line above an existing line, highlight the line and type Ctrl-N. Ctrl-Y deletes all characters to the right of the cursor on the selected line.

### THE EXIT MENU

Select Exit when you've finished laying out your label format or when you wish to return to the dot prompt. The Save option saves all current changes to the mailing label format and stores them in the .lbl file. The Abandon option

| MENU OPTION | ACCEPTABLE RANGE |
| --- | --- |
| Label width | 1–120 characters |
| Label height | 1–16 characters |
| Left margin | 0–256 characters |
| Lines between labels | 0–16 lines |
| Spaces between labels | 0–120 characters |
| Labels across | 0–15 labels |

**TABLE 9.1:** Acceptable Ranges of Settings for Mailing Labels

abandons current changes and retains any settings in the previous .lbl file (if there is one.)

#### EXAMPLE

The command

**MODIFY LABEL ThreeCol**

allows you to create a mailing label format file named ThreeCol.lbl. The section "Designing Mailing Labels" and Figure 9.9 earlier in this chapter present a sample mailing label format.

#### TIPS

Blank lines in the label format, or lines that would otherwise print an empty field, are squeezed out of the label. To force a label format to print blank lines, place a nonprinting character, such as CHR(2), on the label line.

If you wish to create a label format that resembles an existing label format, you can copy the existing format to another file name using the dBASE COPY FILE command or the DOS COPY command. Then use MODIFY LABEL to edit the copied file.

#### SEE ALSO

LABEL FORM

## The LABEL FORM Command

LABEL FORM prints mailing labels in the format specified in a label file created by the MODIFY LABEL command.

#### SYNTAX

**LABEL FORM <file name> [SAMPLE] [<scope>]**
**[WHILE <condition>];[FOR <condition>] [TO PRINT]**
**[TO FILE <text file name>]**

where <file name> is the name of the associated label file, <condition> is any valid query expression, and <text file name> is the name of the disk file to store labels on.

#### USAGE

LABEL FORM prints mailing labels from the database currently in use, using the format specified in the label (.lbl) file created by the MODIFY LABEL command.

The optional WHILE and FOR commands specify records to be printed. The optional TO PRINT command sends the labels to the printer. If SAMPLE is used with TO PRINT, "dummy" labels are printed to help align the labels in the printer.

When dummy labels are printed, each one resembles the largest label to be printed but contains all Xs. SAMPLE will continue printing dummy labels and pausing to display the following prompt:

**Do you want more samples? (Y/N)**

To recheck the alignment, enter Y, to stop printing dummies and proceed with the actual labels, enter N.

The TO FILE option sends mailing labels to a disk file. The disk file is assigned the extension .txt unless another is provided in the command line.

#### EXAMPLES

The commands

**USE MailList**
**LABEL FORM ThreeUp SAMPLE TO PRINT**

display labels from the MailList database, using the format specified in the ThreeUp.lbl label file. Labels are sent to the printer, and the user is given the opportunity to print several dummy labels to help align the labels in the printer.

#### TIPS

See Chapter 13, "Searching a Datbase," for tips on maximizing the speed of the LABEL FORM command when you want to print labels for only certain records.

#### SEE ALSO

MODIFY LABEL

## The ? and ?? Commands

These commands display a field, memory variable, or the results of an expression. The ? command prints data on a new line, while ?? prints data at the current cursor position.

## SYNTAX

**? <expression>**

or

**?? <expression>**

where <expression> is any valid field name, existing memory variable, or expression.

## USAGE

Think of the ? command as meaning "What is..." or "Print the results of...". For example, the command

**? 5 * 6**

prints 30, the result of multiplying 5 by 6.

A single ? command always prints its data at the start of a new line. The ? command alone (with no expression) prints a blank line.

The ?? command prints its data at the current cursor position (or print-head position on the printer).

## EXAMPLES

**? EOF( )**

displays .T. if the currently active database is at the end of the file. The command

**? 27 ^ (1/3)**

displays the cube root of 27. The command

**? TRIM(City) + ", " + State + SPACE(5) + Zip**

prints the contents of the fields (or variables) City, State, and Zip in the following format:

**San Diego, CA      92122**

The commands

**? "Hello "**
**?? "there"**

display

**Hello there**

### TIPS

The TRANSFORM function can format character and numeric data displayed with ? and ?? similar to the way that PICTURE can format data displayed with @.

The SET PRINT ON command channels output from ? and ?? commands to the printer. The SET ALTERNATE command channels output from ? commands to a disk file. Because the output of ? and ?? commands can be stored in a disk file, these commands are usually preferred to @ commands for printing custom reports.

The ? command is also useful for quick debugging at the dot prompt while a command file is suspended, because it can print the current status of status functions. For example, **? EOF( )** displays the end-of-file status. **? DISKSPACE( )** displays the amount of available disk space on the default drive.

Try to avoid using ?? to display memo fields. An anomaly in dBASE III PLUS allows only the first memo field to be printed correctly with ??.

### SEE ALSO

@...SAY
TEXT...ENDTEXT

## The EJECT Command

EJECT causes the printer to eject the current page.

### SYNTAX

**EJECT**

### USAGE

The EJECT command is used primarily to force the printer to eject the last printed page, thereby ensuring that no text gets stuck in the printer buffer until the next report is printed.

To work properly, the paper must be properly aligned in the printer. To ensure proper paper alignment, move a page perforation to just above the printer head, *then* turn the printer on (or press the top-of-form button on the printer). Once the alignment is correct, do not hand crank the paper in the printer, because doing so will disrupt the alignment.

An EJECT command will cause an error if the printer is not currently connected and on line. Usually, turning on the printer will fix this, but, in some cases you may need to reboot the computer, potentially causing a loss of data.

### TIPS

Many laser printers will not print a page until the page is entirely filled or a form-feed character is sent. Therefore, be sure to follow all printed reports with an EJECT command when a laser printer is involved.

### SEE ALSO

SET PRINT ON

## The TEXT and ENDTEXT Commands

The TEXT and ENDTEXT commands can be used to mark off any block of text for display on the screen or printer.

### SYNTAX

**TEXT**
    **<text to be displayed>**
**ENDTEXT**

where <text to be displayed> is any amount of text to be displayed in the screen or printer.

### USAGE

To display a large body of text without using a series of @ or ? commands, enclose the text between the TEXT and ENDTEXT commands.

Note that dBASE ignores all text within the TEXT and ENDTEXT commands, including commands, functions, expressions, and macros. All text between TEXT and ENDTEXT commands is displayed *exactly* as it is written in the program.

If SET PRINT is on, all text between the TEXT and ENDTEXT commands is channeled to the printer. If a SET ALTERNATE file is active, all text is channeled to the text file. The SET DEVICE command has no effect on TEXT...ENDTEXT.

### EXAMPLE

The commands in Figure 9.25 present a menu of options to the user and wait for a selection.

```
TEXT
                         Main Menu
                1. Add new records
                2. Edit existing data
                3. Print reports
                4. Exit
ENDTEXT
Choice = 0
@ 20,2 SAY "Enter choice " GET Choice PICTURE "@Z 9"
READ
```

**FIGURE 9.25:** A routine that presents a menu of options to the user. The menu between the TEXT and ENDTEXT commands is displayed on the screen exactly as shown on the program. The routine beneath the ENDTEXT command asks the user to select a menu option and stores the user's selection in a variable named Choice.

### TIPS

Using TEXT...ENDTEXT in command files to display text reduces the clutter created by @ and ? commands and provides the easiest technique for formatting and printing text.

### SEE ALSO

? and ??
@...SAY

## SUMMARY

This chapter covered the various methods programmers can use to display data in formatted reports. It included discussions of both the built-in report and label generators, as well as general programming techniques that can extend your reporting capabilities beyond these generators.

*For more information on one-to-many relationships and the SET RELATION command:*

- Chapter 3, "Database Design"
- Chapter 16, "Managing Multiple Database Files"

*For more information on DO WHILE and other programming constructs:*

- Chapter 4, "Command Files"

*For tips on maximizing the speed of presorting data for printed reports:*

- Chapter 12, "Sorting and Indexing"

*For tips on maximizing searches for data to be displayed on printed reports:*

- Chapter 13, "Searching a Database"

*For a procedure that can print columnar reports alphabetized in telephone-directory format, as well as other procedures that might help you develop meaningful reports:*

- Chapter 24, "Algorithms to Extend dBASE"

# Part 4

# *Managing Information on the Database*

Part 4 discusses programming techniques for managing data on a database, including adding, editing, deleting, sorting, searching, and calculating data. Of course, even the casual dBASE user probably knows how to perform most of these tasks from the Assistant menu or the dBASE dot prompt. However, this part of the book focuses on programming techniques that allow you to manage database data with optimum efficiency.

Chapter 10 discusses techniques for entering data onto a database, including sophisticated techniques for error trapping, for displaying on-screen calculations, and even for allowing the user to carry data from one record to the next with the press of a key.

Chapter 11 covers techniques that allow the user to locate a record quickly, then edit or delete it. The programming techniques presented here provide a smooth interface between an application and an inexperienced user, and they also help prevent accidental changes and deletions of data.

Chapter 12 discusses sorting and indexing techniques, processing times required for various techniques for maintaining sort orders, and tips for creating complex sorts with combined ascending and descending orders.

Chapter 13 covers techniques used to search for a particular item of information or to search for groups of records that meet some criteria. Various techniques are compared in terms of the time required to complete a given task. You will see how the technique you use to search a database can greatly affect the overall speed at which an application runs.

Chapter 14 discusses techniques for calculating numbers in a database and for creating summary databases containing subtotals of certain fields.

Chapter 15 offers very general techniques for manipulating data at the field, record, and file levels. It discusses all aspects of manipulating and combining data types, as well as techniques for copying and combining data.

Chapter 16 discusses techniques for managing data on multiple related database files, including some very advanced techniques for managing data stored in many-to-many relationships. This chapter expands on the basic coverage of this topic provided in Chapter 3.

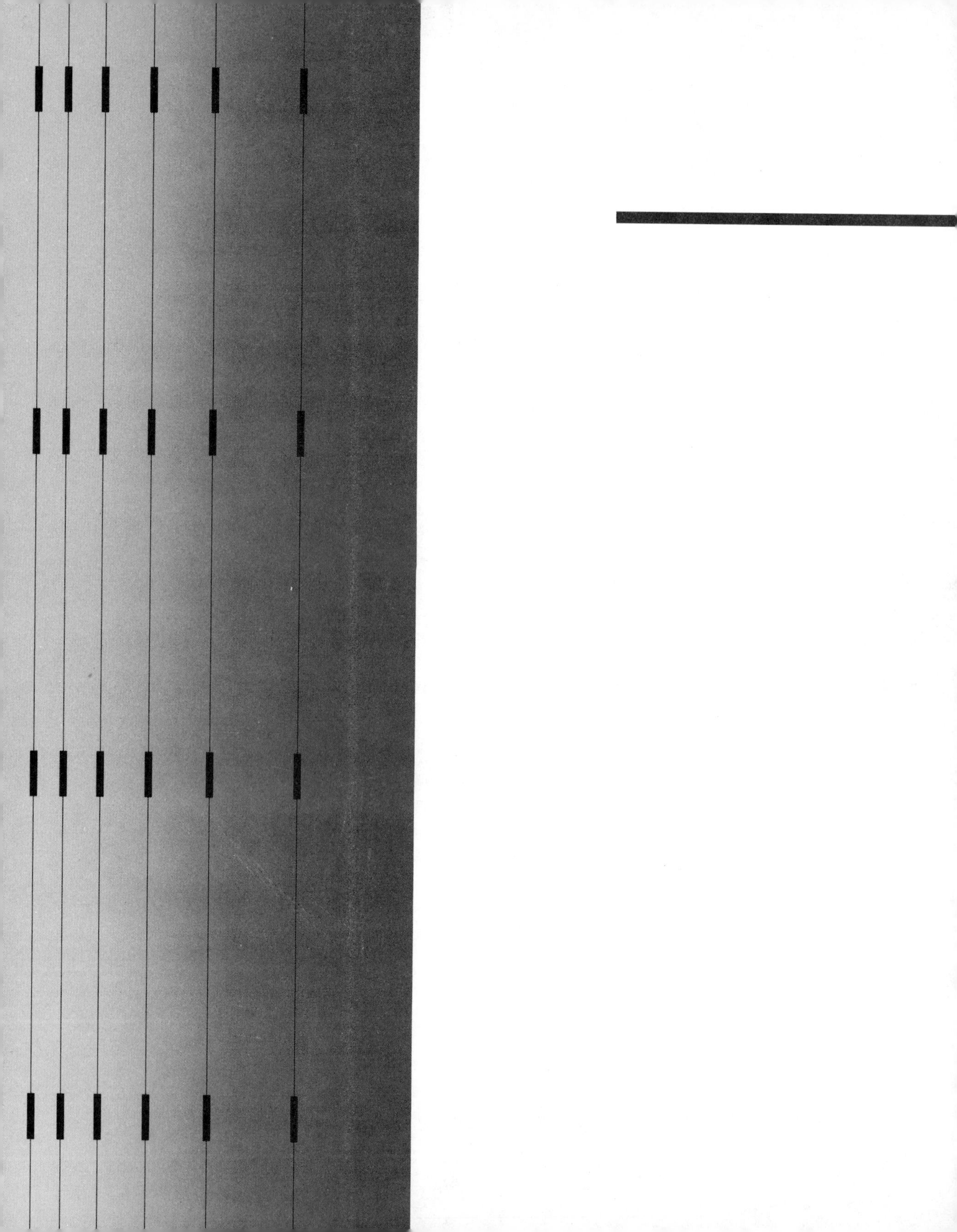

# ADDING NEW DATA

# Adding New Data

The casual dBASE user generally uses the simple APPEND command to add new records to a database file. The programmer can also use the APPEND command to allow users to enter data into a database file. With the addition of format files, the APPEND command can be used to enter data through a custom data-entry form.

However, the APPEND command can present a few potential problems for the programmer. First, it gives the user free reign when entering data, because it allows for only the minimal data-entry verification offered by the PICTURE and RANGE commands in @...SAY...GET commands. Second, it does not provide for on-screen calculations, which are so useful in applications that involve invoices and orders.

Therefore, in applications that require more power than the APPEND command offers, the READ command is generally preferred. Unlike APPEND, READ can be used to isolate and react to any individual entry that the user types on the screen.

This chapter discusses all of the techniques available for entering new records into a database, including APPEND, BROWSE, and READ. The primary focus, however, is on the more sophisticated data-entry techniques that the dBASE programmer is most likely to use in an application. The reference section of this chapter covers the APPEND and INSERT commands; the READ and BROWSE commands are covered in Chapter 8, "Managing Screen Displays," and Chapter 11, "Editing and Deleting Records," respectively.

## Adding Data with APPEND

The APPEND command provides the simplest technique for adding new records to a database. For example, the two lines below present a screen to enter new data and automatically update both the PartNo and OrdDate index files:

```
USE Orders INDEX PartNo,OrdDate
APPEND
```

Note that the APPEND command allows the user to enter as many records as he or she wishes. APPEND also allows a user to scroll back and forth through existing records using the PgUp and PgDn keys. When done entering records, the user can press either Return or PgDn when a blank record is on the screen.

To exit APPEND while a filled record is on the screen, the user can type Ctrl-W or Ctrl-End.

## Adding Data to Custom Screens

In place of the simple appending screen that dBASE generates automatically, the programmer can use a custom screen (as discussed in Chapter 8, "Managing Screen Displays"). To use the custom screen for appending, the programmer needs only four commands:

```
USE Orders INDEX PartNo,OrdDate
SET FORMAT TO CustScrn
APPEND
CLOSE FORMAT
```

## Carrying Data from One Record to the Next

If the data being entered into records are similar, you can use the SET CARRY ON command to automatically carry (or copy) data from the record just entered into the next new record. When SET CARRY is on, records are carried from one record to the next. When SET CARRY is off, the normal APPEND mode returns.

You can add these commands directly to your appending routine, as below:

```
USE Orders INDEX PartNo,OrdDate
SET CARRY ON
SET FORMAT TO CustScrn
APPEND
CLOSE FORMAT
SET CARRY OFF
```

The only drawback to the SET CARRY command is its "all-or-none" approach. Either all data are carried from one record to the next, or none. Later in this chapter you'll find techniques that give the user more control when carrying data from one record to the next.

# Adding Data with BROWSE

The BROWSE command allows you to enter data in a spreadsheetlike format. When you move the highlight beyond the bottom record, the screen will ask whether you want to add new data. Selecting Yes places the BROWSE screen into an appending mode. For details on the BROWSE command, see Chapter 11, "Editing and Deleting Records."

## ADDING DATA WITH READ

Using the READ command in your program rather than APPEND gives you more power over data-entry. Because the READ command reads data for only one record at a time, it gives a program time to perform calculations and verifications between records. Another good reason for using READ to enter records is that the dBASE compilers generally do not support the APPEND command.

There are several programming techniques you can use to develop fully customized data-entry routines for an application using the READ command. However, the READ command reads data into only one record at a time. Therefore, if you want your user to enter more than one record per session, your program will need a DO WHILE loop that repeats the READ command. Examples of the various techniques used with READ are discussed in the following sections.

These general techniques for using READ to enter new data can be expanded into larger programming techniques that allow you to provide default values for database fields, automatically calculate customer and invoice numbers, reject duplicate entries, and perform other sophisticated data-entry tasks. These more advanced techniques are discussed and demonstrated later in the chapter.

To demonstrate the basic data-entry techniques used with READ, this chapter uses the sample Orders database, which has the structure shown in Figure 10.1. In addition, the examples use the format file named OrdForm which contains the commands shown in Figure 10.2. Figure 10.3 shows how the OrdForm screen looks when displayed on the screen with the SET FORMAT TO command followed by a READ or APPEND command.

```
Structure for database: Orders.dbf

Field  Field Name  Type        Width    Dec
    1  PartNo      Character       5
    2  Invoice_No  Numeric         5
    3  Clerk       Character       5
    4  Customer    Character      20
    5  Qty         Numeric         4
    6  Price       Numeric         9      2
    7  Date_Sold   Date            8
** Total **                       57
```

**FIGURE 10.1:** Structure of the sample Orders database used in some programming examples in this chapter. The custom data-entry form defined in Figure 10.2 is used to set up the screen display.

## Using a Blank Record to Terminate Data Entry

If you want the user to be able to enter several records, the READ command needs to be enclosed in a DO WHILE loop that terminates on some condition. There are basically two ways to allow the user to exit from this loop: by leaving

```
*********************************** OrdForm.fmt
@  4,  0  SAY "Invoice No."
@  4, 12  GET  Invoice_No
@  4, 41  SAY "Salesperson Initials:"
@  4, 63  GET  Clerk
@  6,  0  SAY "Customer"
@  6, 12  GET  Customer
@  8,  5  SAY "Part Number      Quantity      Unit Price    Date Sold"
@ 10,  8  GET  Partno
@ 10, 24  GET  Qty
@ 10, 36  GET  Price
@ 10, 50  GET  Date_Sold
@  7,  0  TO  7, 67
@  2,  0  TO  2, 67     DOUBLE
@ 11,  0  TO 11, 66     DOUBLE
```

**FIGURE 10.2:** The OrdForm format file used in some programming examples in this chapter. It was created for the Orders database shown in Figure 10.1.

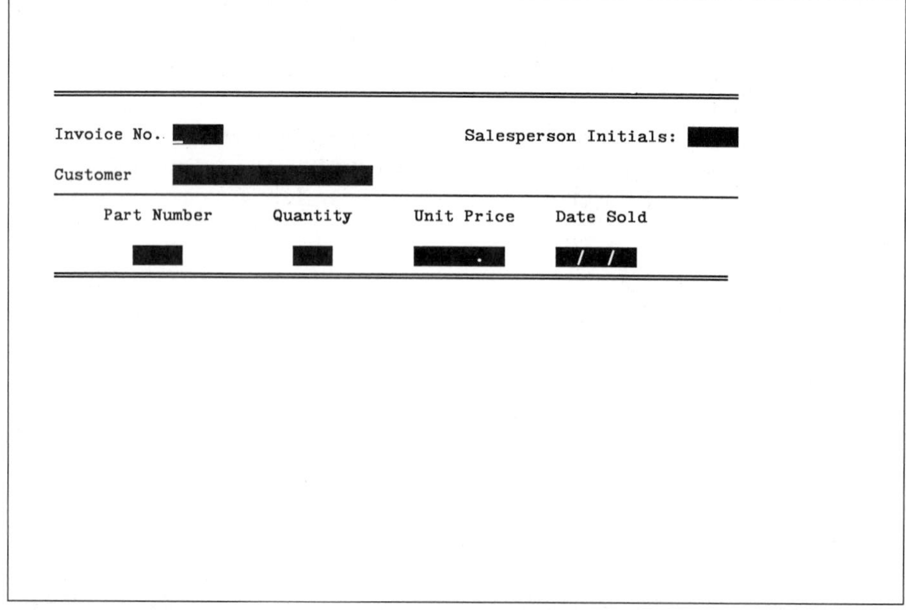


**FIGURE 10.3:** The OrdForm format file displayed on the screen with the SET FORMAT command followed by a READ or APPEND command. The database structure and format files for this screen are shown in Figures 10.1 and 10.2.

the record blank (as with the APPEND command) or by entering a specific value (such as X to exit).

If you want your users to be able to exit your appending routine by leaving the screen blank, you can set up your DO WHILE loop to continue as long as the first field on the screen is not blank (or zero in a numeric field). Using the Orders database and OrdForm format file as an example, the loop would be set up as in Figure 10.4.

This technique has the disadvantage of leaving a blank record on the database when the user exits (because the APPEND BLANK command is issued before the exit), which means that you must include a subsequent DELETE command to remove the blank record.

## Presenting Termination Options

As an alternative to exiting with a blank or zero value, you can place an extra field on the screen that accepts data into a memory variable. Then use that memory variable to control the DO WHILE loop.

The Entry2 program shown in Figure 10.5 uses a variable named Adding to control the loop. Additional commands have to be added to the OrdForm2 format file that allow the user to enter a value after filling in each screen. For this example, the following commands were added to the OrdForm format file:

**@ 22,1 SAY "Press " + CHR(24) + " to make corrections,"**
**@ 23,1 SAY "Return to continue, or X to exit";**

```
*********************************** Entry1.prg
*------ Open database, index, and format files.
USE Orders INDEX Orders, OrdDate
SET FORMAT TO OrdForm
Adding = .T.
DO WHILE Adding
   APPEND BLANK
   READ
   *---- If Invoice Number field left blank, exit.
   IF Invoice_No = 0
      Adding = .F.
   ENDIF
ENDDO
*-- To remove the extra blank record,
*-- use DELETE command as below.
DELETE
CLOSE FORMAT
RETURN
```

**FIGURE 10.4:** This program uses a DO WHILE loop and READ to allow the user to enter records into the Orders database. When the user saves a blank record, the Invoice_No field is zero. At that point, data-entry is terminated. This technique must include a DELETE Command to remove the resulting blank record.

These commands tell the user that he can press ↑ (CHR(24)) to make corrections to the current record, Return to add another record, or X to exit the appending routine. Figure 10.6 shows how the OrdForm screen looks with the brief instructions at the bottom of the form.

```
*********************************** Entry2.prg
*------ Open database, index, and format files.
USE Orders INDEX Orders, OrdDate
SET FORMAT TO OrdForm2

Adding = " "
DO WHILE Adding # "X"
   APPEND BLANK
   READ
ENDDO
CLOSE FORMAT
RETURN
```

**FIGURE 10.5:** The Entry2 program, which uses a DO WHILE loop to control data-entry with a READ command. In this example, the OrdForm format file has been altered to include a GET command that allows the user to enter a value into the Adding memory variable.

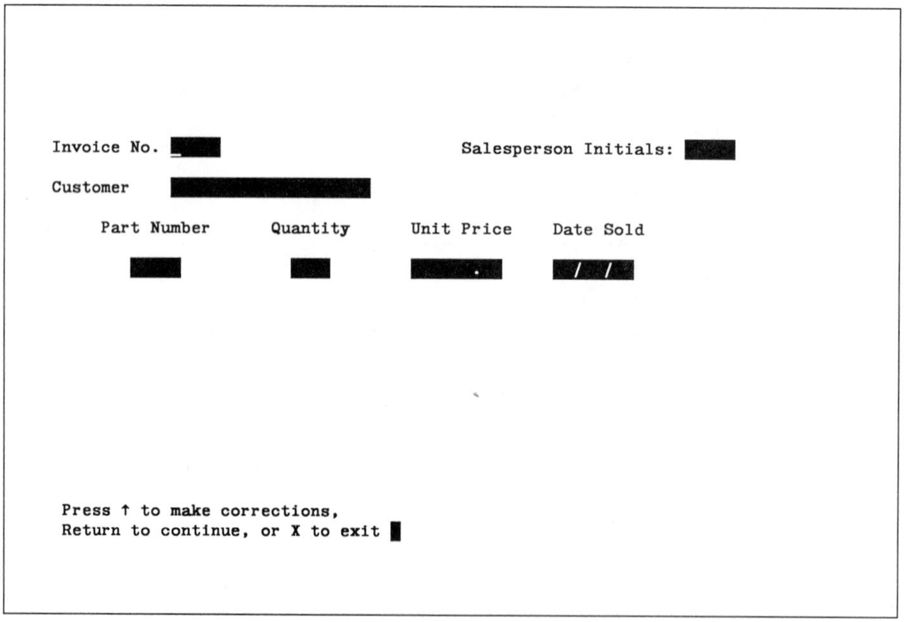

```
Invoice No. ████                         Salesperson Initials: ████

Customer    ████████████████

    Part Number     Quantity     Unit Price     Date Sold

      ████            ███        ████████.      █/ /█





 Press ↑ to make corrections,
 Return to continue, or X to exit █
```

**FIGURE 10.6:** The OrdForm2 form with additional prompts to give the user a choice at the bottom of each newly entered record. Data entered into the last prompt are stored in the Adding variable, which controls the loop for entering records.

The main advantage to this technique is that the user is given a chance to look over each new entry and make corrections, if necessary, before moving on. The disadvantage is that it is still possible for the user to enter a blank record onto the database by entering an X at the bottom prompt when the fields on the screen are empty.

## Using Memory Variables to Add Records

A third technique for using the READ command to append records is to store all the entered data in memory variables and then replace them in the database record. Figure 10.7 shows a program named Entry3.prg that uses this technique with the Orders database (shown in Figure 10.1).

This technique requires that the format file read data into the memory variables rather than directly into database fields. Therefore, the OrdForm format file has to be changed to include the memory variables.

```
*********************************** Entry3.prg
*------ Open database, index, and format files.
USE Orders INDEX Orders, OrdDate
SET FORMAT TO OrdForm3

Adding = " "
DO WHILE Adding # "X"
   *---- Initialize memory variables.
   MPartNo = SPACE(5)
   MInvoice = 0.00
   MClerk = SPACE(5)
   MCustomer = SPACE(20)
   MQty = 0
   MPrice = 0.00
   MDate = DATE()
   Adding = " "
   *---Read in values using OrdForm.fmt
   READ
   *------ If cancel not selected, and
   *------ invoice number > 0, append.
   IF Adding # "C" .AND. MInvoice > 0
      APPEND BLANK
      *--- Store memory variables on new record.
      REPLACE PartNo WITH MPartNo, ;
              Invoice_No WITH MInvoice, ;
              Clerk WITH MClerk, ;
              Customer WITH MCustomer
      REPLACE Qty WITH MQty, ;
              Price WITH MPrice, ;
              Date_Sold WITH MDate
   ENDIF (adding)
ENDDO
CLOSE FORMAT
RETURN
```

**FIGURE 10.7:** The Entry3 command file initializes memory variables as blanks, zeros, and the current date. Then the modified OrdForm format file reads data into the memory variables. If the user does not select C to Cancel and enters an invoice number greater than zero, the data are added to a new record on the database.

The new format file, shown in Figure 10.8, allows the user to enter data into memory variables that represent fields on a single database record. The format file also presents instructions telling the user to press the ↑ key to make corrections to the current data, Return to proceed to the next record, or C to cancel the current entry. The user's response to these instructions is stored in a memory variable named Adding.

In the Entry3 program shown in Figure 10.7, the IF...ENDIF clause copies the memory variables into the database fields only if the user did not select Cancel *and* the Invoice_No field is greater than zero. (The latter assumes that an invoice number of zero implies a blank record.)

The advantage of using memory variables to enter database data is that it gives you more control over the data entered into the database. In fact, most applications that require a great deal of data verification use this technique almost exclusively. The sample point-of-sale program presented a little later in this chapter uses this technique.

The disadvantage to this technique is that it takes more code (and more time) to get each record onto the database. On small databases, the extra time and code is small, but with large databases that have many fields, this method can slow things down a bit. Therefore, it is best to use this technique only in situations where the data entry requires much data verification or calculation.

## Using a Temporary Database for New Records

Another technique for entering records with the READ command is to store the newly entered records on a temporary database. When the user is done entering records, the program can automatically append the new records from the temporary database onto the "real" database.

```
********************************************** OrdForm3.fmt
@  4,  0  SAY "Invoice No."
@  4, 12  GET  MInvoice PICTURE "9999"
@  4, 41  SAY "Salesperson Initials:"
@  4, 63  GET  MClerk
@  6,  0  SAY "Customer"
@  6, 12  GET  MCustomer
@  8,  5  SAY "Part Number      Quantity      Unit Price     Date Sold"
@ 10,  8  GET  MPartNo
@ 10, 24  GET  MQty PICTURE "999"
@ 10, 36  GET  MPrice PICTURE "999999.99"
@ 10, 50  GET  MDate
@ 21,1 SAY "Press "+CHR(24)+" to make corrections,"
@ 22,1 SAY "Return to continue, C to Cancel,"
@ 23,1 SAY "or X to exit";
  GET Adding PICTURE "!"
```

**FIGURE 10.8:** The OrdForm3 format file to read data into memory variables rather than database fields. This format file is used with the Entry3.prg command file shown in Figure 10.7.

Figure 10.9 shows a program that uses a temporary database to add new records. The temporary database in this example is named OrdTemp. All new records are added to OrdTemp only, which is first purged of any old data with a ZAP command.

Near the bottom of the program, the **APPEND FROM OrdTemp FOR Invoice_No > 0** command line reads all records with invoice numbers greater than zero from the temporary database onto the OrdData database. (Records with invoice numbers of zero are excluded in this example because they are assumed to be blank.)

There are a couple of advantages to appending data to a temporary database rather than the actual database. For one, you can allow an intermediate step where the computer prints all the information on the temporary database, and an operator double-checks it and makes any corrections. After all the data have been corrected on the temporary database, they can be appended to the "real" database for further processing.

```
*********************************** Entry4.prg
*------ Open database, index, and format files.
USE OrdTemp
SET SAFETY OFF
ZAP
SET FORMAT TO OrdForm2

Adding = " "
DO WHILE Adding # "X"
   APPEND BLANK
   READ
ENDDO
CLOSE FORMAT

*--------- In some applications, you
*--------- might want to print newly
*--------- entered data here, for
*--------- verification.  Then, use
*--------- APPEND FROM later to transfer
*--------- corrected data to the real file.
CLEAR
? "Updating Orders database. Please wait..."
SET TALK ON

*----- Transfer records from OrdTemp to Orders.
USE Orders
APPEND FROM OrdTemp FOR Invoice_No > 0
*----- Update the index files.
SET INDEX TO Orders,OrdDate
REINDEX

SET TALK OFF
RETURN
```

**FIGURE 10.9:** A program that enters new records into a temporary database. In this example, OrdTemp.dbf holds newly entered records, which are later appended to Orders.dbf as a group. Any records with an invoice number of zero are considered to be blank in this application and are not copied from OrdTemp into Orders.

Using a temporary database is useful in a networking environment as well. If each operator can add data to his own temporary database, there are likely to be fewer of the problems inherent in many users trying to share a single database file.

The only disadvantage of using a temporary database to enter new records is the extra time required to add the new records to the actual database, along with the additional time required to rebuild index files. However, because this process is done all at once after the user has completed a data-entry session, the extra time required is generally not too inconvenient.

## PROVIDING DEFAULT VALUES

In some applications, data to be added to a record might be fairly predictable. For example, the date of a sale might be today's date, or the state might likely be the home state of the user. You can put default values onto data-entry screens as suggested responses. To accept the suggested response, the user need only press Return when the cursor is on the field. The user can, however, change the suggested value by typing a new one over the old one.

To add suggested responses directly to database fields, use REPLACE commands immediately after the APPEND BLANK command. For example, Figure 10.10 shows a data-entry command file with a REPLACE command that suggests the current date as the entry for the Date_Sold field.

If you want to place the default value into the record without allowing the user to change it, change the @...GET command in the format file to an @...SAY

```
*********************************** Entry5.prg
*------ Open database, index, and format files.
USE Orders INDEX Orders, OrdDate
SET FORMAT TO OrdForm2

Adding = " "
DO WHILE Adding # "X"
   APPEND BLANK
   *-- Suggest current date for Date_Sold field.
   REPLACE Date_Sold WITH DATE()
   READ
ENDDO
CLOSE FORMAT
RETURN
```

**FIGURE 10.10:** A data-entry program with the current date automatically placed into the Date_Sold field as a suggested entry. When entering data, the user can accept the suggested response by simply pressing Return when the cursor is on the field on the screen. Otherwise, the user can type a new value.

command. In this example, you would change the command in the OrdForm format file that reads

```
@ 10, 50 GET Orders->Date_Sold
```

to

```
@ 10, 50 SAY Orders->Date_Sold
```

If you do not want the user to even see the default value placed into the field, remove the associated @...GET line from the format file entirely.

If you are storing entered data in memory variables before they are entered onto the database file, you can store default values directly into memory variables before the READ command is issued. For example, in the program shown in Figure 10.7, the command

```
MDate = DATE( )
```

initializes the variable for storing the date as the current date.

## AUTOMATIC CALCULATION OF NEXT NUMBER

In many programs, each record entered must be assigned a unique number, such as an invoice number. If this number is increased by one for each record, you can easily use the next highest number as the default invoice number for each record.

First you must determine the highest invoice number. If the database is not indexed on the invoice number field, but you have always assigned numbers starting from the smallest and going up, the largest invoice number will be on the last database record. To get to the last record, open the database without an index file (with the USE command) and enter the GO BOTTOM command.

If the database is indexed on the field of interest (invoice number in this example), you can open the database with the invoice number index and use GO BOTTOM to find the largest invoice number.

Figure 10.11 shows a sample program that finds the largest invoice number at the bottom of the Orders database and stores it in a variable named MInvoice. MInvoice, in turn, is incremented by one and substituted into each new database record as the user adds new records.

To prevent the user from altering the calculated invoice number, change the GET Invoice_No command in the format file to a SAY command, as in the lines below (which are from the OrdForm format file in Figure 10.2):

```
@ 4, 0  SAY "Invoice No."
@ 4, 12  SAY  Invoice_No
```

```
*********************************** Entry6.prg

*------ Find the largest current invoice number.
USE Orders
GO BOTTOM
MInvoice = Invoice_No  && Assumes largest is last.

*----- Keep index files up to date.
SET INDEX TO Orders, OrdDate
SET FORMAT TO OrdForm5

Adding = " "
DO WHILE Adding # "X"
   APPEND BLANK
   MInvoice = MInvoice + 1
   REPLACE Invoice_No WITH MInvoice
   READ
ENDDO
CLOSE FORMAT
RETURN
```

**FIGURE 10.11:** In this sample program, the first routine positions the record pointer to the largest invoice number (presumably the last record) and stores that number in a memory variable named MInvoice. The variable is then used to automatically calculate a unique invoice number for each record. The REPLACE command puts this invoice number on each new record.

## REJECTING DUPLICATE ENTRIES

On some databases, the key field must be unique to every record, even if the field is not numeric or sequential. For example, in a master inventory database, each item typically has a unique part number, but this number might be assigned randomly and might contain nonnumeric characters. Nonetheless, an operator must enter a part number for a new item. If the part number is already in use, the program must reject the entry.

The database file named Master.dbf, which has a character field named PartNo, will illustrate this example. The database is indexed on the PartNo field using the command

**INDEX ON UPPER(PartNo) TO Master**

The command file shown in Figure 10.12 allows the user to enter records into the Master database file. The user first enters the part number. If that part number already exists, the screen displays the error message **Number already in use!** and allows the user to try again.

The Entry7.prg command file does not use a format file. Instead, the @...SAY...GET commands are listed right in the command file, mostly within the last CASE statement. Because format files will process only @...SAY... GET...READ...PICTURE...RANGE and READ commands, the SEEK, DO CASE, and other necessary commands would be ignored if they were stored in a

```
************************************* Entry7.prg
*---- Add new records to Master.dbf,
*---- but reject duplicate part numbers.
SET TALK OFF
CLEAR

*--- Open Master database and Master index file.
*--- Key for Master.ndx is UPPER(PartNo).
USE Master INDEX Master

Adding = .T.
DO WHILE Adding
   *------- Ask for new part number.
   MPartNo = SPACE(5)
   @ 10,5 SAY "Enter new part number "
   @ 12,5 SAY "or just press Return to exit ";
     GET MPartNo PICTURE "!!!!!"
   READ
   *------- See if that number is already in use.
   SEEK MPartNo

   DO CASE
      *---- No part number entered; exit.
      CASE MPartNo = " "
           Adding = .F.
           LOOP
      *----- Number already in use, beep and
      *----- Display error message.
      CASE FOUND()
           ? CHR(7)       && Beep
           @ 20, 5 SAY "Number already in use!"
           @ 21, 5 SAY "Press any key to try another"
           WAIT " "
      *----- Number not in use, proceed with transaction.
      CASE .NOT. FOUND()
           CLEAR
           APPEND BLANK
           REPLACE PartNo WITH MPartNo
           @ 3,5 SAY "Part number "+PartNo
           @ 5,5 SAY "Part Name " GET PartName
           @ 7,5 SAY "Unit Price " ;
                 GET Unit_Price PICTURE "9,999.99"
           *-- additional GET for each field in
           *-- Master.dbf can be listed here.
           READ
           CLEAR
   ENDCASE
ENDDO (while adding)
CLOSE DATABASES
RETURN
```

**FIGURE 10.12:** This program allows the user to add new records to the Master database, but it rejects any entry that duplicates a part number already in use. (Because PartNo is a key field on this database, it is imperative that each part number be unique.) This command file does not use a format file. Instead, @...GET commands are listed right in the program, within the last CASE clause.

format file. Therefore, all commands, including the @...SAY...GET commands, are together in the Entry7 program in this example. (In the interest of brevity, the sample program lists only a couple of fields, though you can include as many as necessary for a given application.)

The basic logic of the Entry7 program is as follows. The user enters a part number that is stored in a memory variable named MPartNo. The SEEK command checks the Master index file to see whether the part number already exists (the index file was created with the UPPER command, and the PICTURE clause converts MPartNo to uppercase, so there will not be a case conflict).

The DO CASE clauses test for the following three events:

1. If MPartNo is a blank, the user did not enter anything, so control is passed outside the DO WHILE loop and the program ends.
2. If the part number is found in the database, the program beeps and displays an error message. The loop repeats without changing any information on the database.
3. If the entered part number is not found, a blank record is added to the database, and this new part number is placed in the new record. Then a series of @...SAY...GET commands display this new part number and allow the user to fill in the rest of the information for the part.

## VIEWING AND EDITING DUPLICATES

In some applications, you might want to be able to catch duplicate entries before they occur. For example, in a mailing-list database, you might want the user to be able to type in a person's last and first name. If that person is already on the database, the appropriate record appears on the screen immediately. If that person is not already on the database, the new data can be entered immediately.

To demonstrate a technique for viewing a duplicate entry immediately, this section uses a database named Mail.dbf. The LName and FName fields, which store the last name and first name, have the structures shown below (there are, of course, other fields on this database, but only these are of concern at the moment):

| Field | Type | Width |
|---|---|---|
| LName | Character | 15 |
| FName | Character | 20 |

The database is indexed on these fields using the command INDEX ON UPPER(LName + FName) TO Names. The program for entering new data (and editing existing data) is shown in Figure 10.13. The program uses a simple format file named MailScr.fmt to display a custom screen.

The program allows the user to enter a last and first name. Then it uses a SEEK command to try to locate that name. (For more on seeking data in multiple fields, see Chapter 13, "Searching a Database.") If the name is found, a READ command allows the user to edit that record. If the name is not found, APPEND BLANK adds a new record, REPLACE substitutes in the last and first names, and READ allows the user to fill in the rest of the information through the format file.

```
************************************ Entry8.prg
*---- Add new records, but display record
*---- for editing if name already found.
SET TALK OFF
*--- Key for Mail.ndx is UPPER(LName+FName).
USE Mail INDEX Names
Adding = .T.
DO WHILE Adding
   *------- Ask for first and last name.
   *------- Note that the SPACE assignments here
   *------- here MUST exactly match field widths!
   CLEAR
   CLOSE FORMAT
   MLName = SPACE(20)
   MFName = SPACE(15)
   @ 10,5 SAY "Enter last name " GET MLName
   @ 12,5 SAY "Enter first name " GET MFName
   READ

   *------- Create lookup variable.
   Search = UPPER(MLName)

   *------- Only add MFName if not blank.
   IF MFName # " "
      Search = Search + UPPER(TRIM(MFName))
   ENDIF (mfname)

   *------ If nothing entered, leave program.
   IF Search = " "
      EXIT
   ENDIF (search)

   *------- See if that name already stored.
   SEEK Search
   SET FORMAT TO MailScr   && open format file.

   *-- If name found, edit it.
   IF FOUND()
      READ
   ENDIF (found)

   IF .NOT. FOUND()
      APPEND BLANK
      REPLACE LName WITH MLName
      REPLACE FName WITH MFName
      READ
   ENDIF (not found)

ENDDO (while adding)
CLOSE FORMAT   && close format file.
RETURN
```

**FIGURE 10.13:** A command file that allows a user to enter a name and then attempts to find that name on the database file. If the name is found, it is displayed immediately for editing. If the name is not found, a blank record is displayed so the user can fill in the rest of the information for the new record.

# PRESENTING AN OPTION TO COPY DATA TO A NEW RECORD

Earlier in the chapter, the SET CARRY command was discussed with its all-or-none treatment of repeating entered data. This section demonstrates a technique that allows the user to decide whether to carry data from one record to the next new record on a record-by-record basis.

The Orders database structure, shown in Figure 10.1, is used again for this example. Figure 10.14 shows the sample program that allows the user to carry data from one record to the next new record by simply typing the letter C.

Figure 10.15 shows the screen for entering data. Instructions are displayed at the bottom of the screen, and the record number is displayed at the top of the screen.

```
******************************************** Entry9.prg
*----------- Allows appending with optional "carry".
SET TALK OFF
SET SAFETY OFF

*----------- Use database without index files.
USE Orders

*--- Variables used in the Orders9 format file.
Ret = CHR(17)+CHR(196)+CHR(217)  && Return key
Up  = CHR(24)                    && Up arrow
Repeat = " "
SET FORMAT TO Orders9

*-------------- Add first blank record.
APPEND BLANK
REPLACE Date_Sold WITH DATE()

*-------------- Get data from user until done.
DO WHILE Repeat # "X"

   *----------- Read data from Orders9.fmt.
   Repeat = " "
   READ   && fill in Orders9.fmt screen.
   *---- If exit selected, done entering records.
   IF Repeat = "X"
      LOOP
   ENDIF (blank record)
   *-- If repeat requested, copy data to
   *-- the next new record.
   IF Repeat = "C"
      COPY TO Temp NEXT 1
      APPEND FROM Temp
      *--- Otherwise just add a new blank record.
      *--- and fill in the date.
   ELSE
      APPEND BLANK
      REPLACE Date_Sold WITH DATE()
   ENDIF

ENDDO (while not exiting)

*--- If any index files are used, update them all here.
CLEAR
? "Please wait a moment while I update the database..."
USE Orders INDEX Orders,OrdDate
REINDEX
CLOSE FORMAT
RETURN
```

**FIGURE 10.14:** The Entry9 command file allows the user to carry data from one record to the next blank record by typing the letter C at the bottom of the screen. Figure 10.15 shows the custom data-entry screen used with this program.

In Orders9.fmt, which produces the screen shown in Figure 10.15, the record number is displayed using the command

**@ 3, 0 SAY "Record number " + STR(RECNO( ),5)**

In addition, the commands below were added to Orders9.fmt to display instructions at the bottom of the screen:

```
@ 20, 2 SAY Up + " to correct:  " + Ret + " if done:"
@ 21, 2 SAY "C to carry data, or X to exit ";
           GET Repeat PICT "!"
```

The graphics symbols Up and Ret, as well as the Repeat variable, are created in the command file in Figure 10.14.

If you look at the general logic of the program in Figure 10.14, you can see that first the Orders database is opened without any index files. This speeds things along so that the copying of data from one record to the next is not slowed down by the automatic index updating.

Then the program sets up the graphics characters and Repeat variable used in the Orders9 format file and also opens that format file. The next commands add a blank record to the database and put the current date in it.

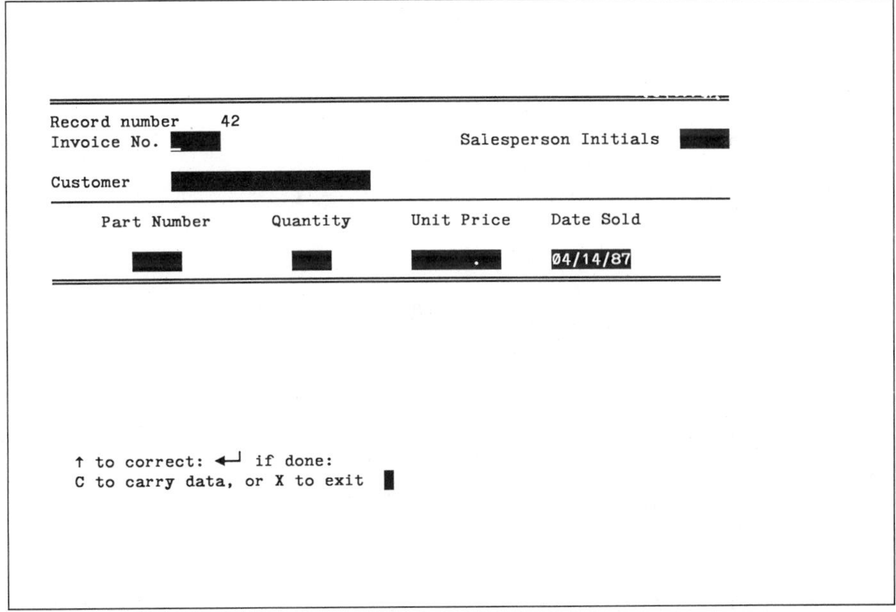


**FIGURE 10.15:** Screen used with optional data-carry technique presented in the Entry9.prg command file. Instructions appear at the bottom of the screen, and the record number appears at the top.

Then the DO WHILE command accepts new records until the user enters X into the Repeat variable to exit. Within the loop, the Repeat variable is initialized as a blank, and the Orders9 screen is displayed for the user to enter data into the new blank record:

```
DO WHILE Repeat # "X"
     Repeat = " "
     READ
```

If the user enters X at the bottom of the screen (to exit), the LOOP command passes control outside of the WHILE Repeat # "X" loop:

```
IF Repeat = "X"
     LOOP
ENDIF (blank record)
```

If the user entered C to carry the data from the current record to the next, the record is copied to a temporay database file named Temp and then appended back into the Orders database, thereby exactly duplicating the record just entered:

```
IF Repeat = "C"
     COPY TO Temp NEXT 1
     APPEND FROM Temp
```

If the user does not exit or request data carry, a blank record with the current date filled in is added to the Orders database:

```
     ELSE
          APPEND BLANK
          REPLACE Date_Sold WITH DATE( )
     ENDIF
ENDDO (while not exiting)
```

When the user exits the program, the commands below update the Orders and OrdDate index files and end the program:

```
CLEAR
? "Please wait a moment while I update the database..."
USE Orders INDEX Orders,OrdDate
REINDEX
CLOSE FORMAT
RETURN
```

## Partial Carrying of Data

In the program in Figure 10.14, the COPY command is used to carry all data from one record to the next. If you want to carry only a few fields, you can store those fields in memory variables, append a blank record onto the database, and then substitute those few fields into the new record. In the routine below, only the Clerk, Customer, and Date fields are carried over to the new record:

```
IF Repeat = "C"
     MClerk = Clerk
     MCust = Customer
     MDate = Date_Sold
     APPEND BLANK
     REPLACE Clerk WITH MClerk, ;
               Customer WITH MCust, ;
               Date_Sold WITH MDate
```

If you want to carry all but a few of the fields to the new record, you can first carry all the fields, then reset those you do not wish to carry. In the example below, the user never sees the PartNo, Qty, and Price fields carried to the new record, though all other fields are carried:

```
IF Repeat = "C"
     COPY TO Temp NEXT 1
     APPEND FROM Temp
     REPLACE Qty WITH 0, Price WITH 0, ;
               PartNo WITH "  "
```

## ADDING A SCROLLING FEATURE WITH READ

One nice feature of APPEND that READ does not offer is the ability to press PgUp and PgDn to scroll through records on the database. With a little programming, however, you can add this scrolling capability to any data-entry program. Doing so can provide the "best of both worlds" in a custom data-entry program—the ability to use the READ command and all of the features discussed previously in this chapter plus the convenience of scrolling offered by the APPEND command.

Figure 10.16 shows a sample program that allows the user to press the PgUp key to scroll back a record and PgDn to scroll forward a record. The database is opened without any index files so that the scrolling takes place in the natural order of the records.

The program uses the READKEY( ) function to determine the key pressed to exit the screen. This value is stored in the variable ExitKey. If the user presses PgUp and the record pointer is not already at the beginning of the file (BOF( )), the record pointer is skipped back 1. If the user presses PgDn and the record pointer is not already at the end of the file, the record pointer is skipped forward a record.

If the user just presses Return to add a new record, the last CASE clause adds a new blank record to the database, which is displayed on the screen on the next pass through the loop, ready to accept new data. (For more information on the numbers returned by the READKEY( ) function, see Chapter 17, "dBASE Functions.")

```
************************************ Entry10.prg
*------ Open database and format files.
USE Orders   && Leave off index files for scrolling.
SET FORMAT TO OrdFormS

Adding = " "
APPEND BLANK      && First blank record added.

DO WHILE Adding # "X"
   *---- Read in data via format file.
   READ
   ExitKey = READKEY()

   DO CASE
     *------------ PgUp key pressed.
     CASE (ExitKey = 6 .OR. ExitKey = 262) ;
          .AND. .NOT. BOF()
          SKIP -1
     *------------ PgDn key pressed.
     CASE (ExitKey = 7 .OR. ExitKey = 263) ;
          .AND. .NOT. EOF()
          SKIP
     *------------ Return pressed to leave record.
     CASE ExitKey = 15 .OR. ExitKey = 271;
          .AND. Adding # "X"
          APPEND BLANK

   ENDCASE

ENDDO (adding=x)

CLOSE FORMAT
*---------- Update the index files now.
CLEAR
? "Updating the index files..."
USE Orders INDEX Orders, OrdDate
REINDEX
CLEAR
RETURN
```

**FIGURE 10.16:** This program allows the user to press PgUp and PgDn to scroll through records while entering data. For more information on values returned by the READKEY command, see Chapter 17, "dBASE Functions."

The format file also provides appropriate instructions to the user for entering records and scrolling. Figure 10.17 shows the display produced by the OrdFormS format file.

## DATA ENTRY WITH MULTIPLE DATABASES

In applications that use multiple database files, you'll often want to develop sophisticated data-entry programs that use data from more than one file. For example, while adding records to a transaction file, you may want to verify an entry against data in a master file or display data from the master file. You might also want to transfer data from a separate file into the database you are currently adding records to, or use data from the foreign file to calculate some value.

This section presents a basic point-of-sale data-entry routine that adds transactions to the Orders database (shown in Figure 10.1) via a temporary database named OrdTemp. The program also uses the Master database (shown in Figure 10.2) to perform three functions:

1. Verify that the part number for the transaction is one that exists in the Master database.

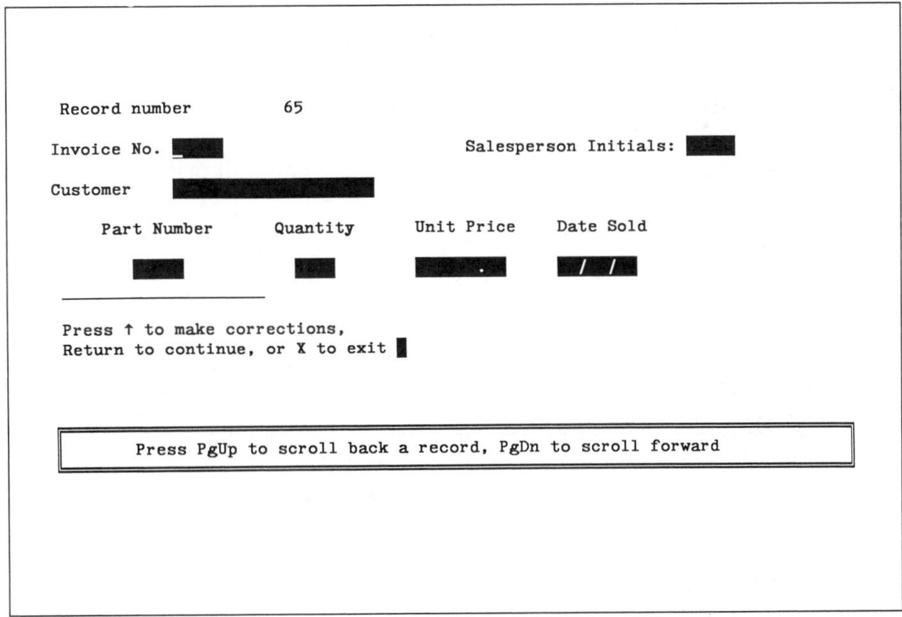


**FIGURE 10.17:** A custom data-entry screen including instructions for scrolling. This screen is produced by the OrdFormS format file.

2. Automatically display the part name, selling price, and taxable status for each transaction.
3. Use the selling price and taxable status from the Master database to calculate and display both individual transaction totals and a grand total for the invoice.

There is a master-file/transaction-file relationship between Master.dbf and Orders.dbf in this example, so it is important that individual transactions entered onto the Orders database contain valid part numbers from the Master database. Of course, there is also a one-to-many relationship here, where for every *one* product listed in the Master inventory, there might be *many* orders.

The user-interface for this program (which is called PosEntry.prg) is designed to resemble a typical paper invoice, where the invoice number, customer, and salesperson's name appear at the top of the invoice, and individual transactions are listed below. However, unlike the paper invoice, PosEntry provides feedback and performs calculations automatically.

## Point-of-Sale User Interface

When first run, PosEntry displays prompts for entering the customer and clerk names at the top of the screen. Once those are entered, it presents a prompt for entering the part number for the first transaction. If the user enters an invalid part number, the computer beeps and the screen displays the error message **No such part!!!** and waits for the user to reenter the part number. If the user enters a valid part number, the program displays the name of the part and the unit price, as shown in Figure 10.18.

After the program displays the part name and unit price for the transaction, it waits for the user to enter the quantity sold. The user actually has two choices. If the part name or unit price tip off the operator that he entered the wrong part number, he can just press Return rather than enter a quantity. Doing so cancels the individual transaction, and the cursor jumps back to the part number field, awaiting the new part number.

If the user enters a quantity, the program calculates the total for the transaction and moves to the next line for the next transaction, as shown in Figure 10.19.

The user can continue adding as many transactions for this customer as necessary. When done entering transactions, he just presses Return rather than enter a part number. The program displays the invoice total and asks whether the invoice should be printed, as shown in Figure 10.20. (The printed invoice looks very much like the screen display at this point.)

After the user decides whether to print the invoice, the screen asks the user if he or she wants to enter another invoice. If the answer is Y, the entire invoice process is repeated. If the answer is N, the program terminates.

```
04/14/87                              Invoice number:      1
Clerk  C.J. Jones                         Customer  Susita Marie

Part #  Name                              Qty   Price  Tax?      Total

A-111   Baseball                          _     14.95   Y
```

**FIGURE 10.18:** Data-entry screen displayed by PosEntry.prg. At this moment, the user has entered the customer and clerk names and the valid part number A-111. The program has automatically displayed the part name and unit price. The program is now waiting for the user to enter the quantity sold.

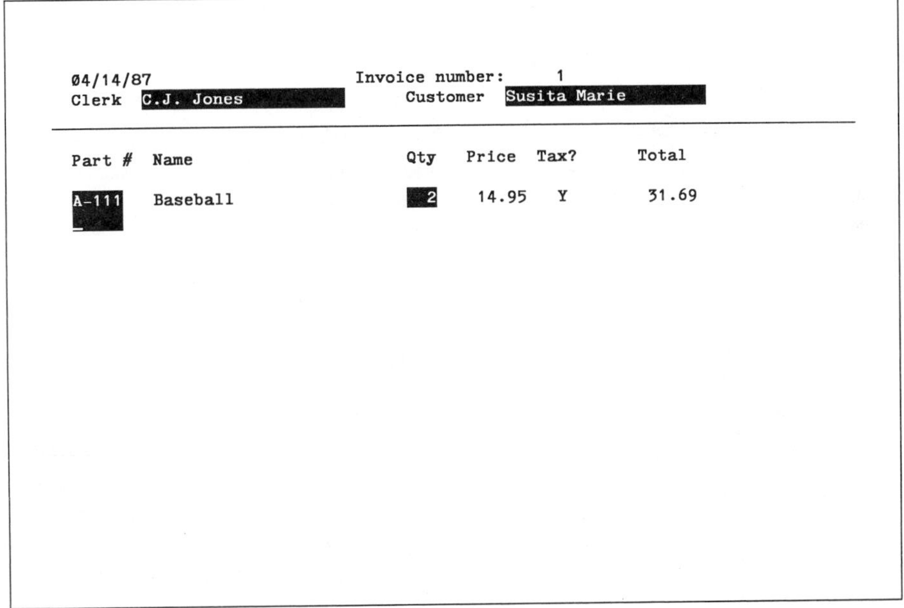


**FIGURE 10.19:** The user has entered a valid transaction, and the program has calculated and displayed the total for the transaction. Now the screen is waiting for the next transaction.

```
04/14/87                          Invoice number:    1
Clerk C.J. Jones                     Customer Susita Marie

Part #  Name                      Qty  Price  Tax?      Total

A-111   Baseball                    2   14.95   Y        31.69
B-222   Tomatoes                   10   19.95   N       199.50
C-333   Soccer Balls                1   12.00   Y        12.72
D-444   Baseball Gloves             1   35.00   Y        37.10

                                        Total:   $$$$281.01

Print invoice? (Y/N) Y
```

**FIGURE 10.20:** A complete invoice on the screen. Note that totals take into consideration whether the item is taxable (Y or N in the Tax column). At this point, the user can press Return to print the invoice or N to proceed to the next invoice.

Figure 10.21 shows the entire PosEntry command file. (The structures of the Orders and Master database files are shown in Figure 10.22.) The Master index file uses PartNo as the key field. The sections below, which discuss general programming techniques for entering data in an application with multiple database files, refer to the PosEntry program for clarification and to demonstrate the technique in an actual program.

## Initial Setup of a Multiple-Database Data-Entry Routine

If a custom data-entry program is to access data from more than one database file, all of the database files involved must be opened with the SELECT command. In addition, any external database that contains information you need to look up while entering new records should be indexed on the key field for the lookup. Furthermore, a SET RELATION command needs to be set from the database in which you are entering records into the database containing the information to be looked up or borrowed.

The SELECT and SET RELATION commands in the PosEntry program (Figure 10.21) show an example. In that program, new records are added to a

```
*********************************** PosEntry.prg
*  Point-of-sale data-entry program for Orders.
SET TALK OFF
SET HEADING OFF
SET BELL OFF

*---- Get last-used invoice number.
USE Orders
GO BOTT
MInvoice = Invoice_No
*------ Create an empty OrdTemp file.
SET SAFETY OFF
COPY STRUCTURE TO OrdTemp

*------- Open master and temporary files.
SELECT A
USE OrdTemp
SELECT B
USE Master INDEX Master
SELECT A
SET RELATION TO PartNo INTO Master

StartInv = 1    && First record for invoice.
PrintInv = .T.  && Print completed invoice?

*------- Set up loop for displaying invoice forms.
Again = .T.
DO WHILE Again

   *------- Display top of invoice on the screen.
   CLEAR
   MInvoice = MInvoice + 1
   STORE SPACE(20) TO MClerk, MCust
   MTotal = 0
   @ 1,2 SAY DATE()
   @ 1,30 SAY "Invoice number: " + STR(MInvoice,5)
   @ 2,2 SAY "Clerk " GET MClerk
   @ 2,35 SAY "Customer " GET MCust
   @ 3,0 SAY REPLICATE("_",80)
   ? "  Part #  Name",SPACE(20)
   ?? "Qty   Price  Tax?      Total"
   READ

   *------- Set up loop for each item on the invoice.
   Row = 7          && Screen row number.
   Adding = .T.

   DO WHILE Adding
      OK = .F.
      *- Loop to check validity of part number.
      DO WHILE .NOT. OK

         *------- Ask for part number.

         MPartNo = SPACE(5)
         @ Row,2 GET MPartNo PICTURE "@!"
         READ

         *------ Make sure part number exists.
         MPartNo = TRIM(MPartNo)
         SELECT B
         SEEK MPartNo
         *------- Decide next step based upon
         *------- existence of part number.
```

**FIGURE 10.21:** The PosEntry program demonstrates many techniques for entering records into a database, including techniques for validating, displaying, and calculating information based on data in a separate database.

```
DO CASE
   *---- No part number was entered.
   CASE LEN(MPartNo) = 0
      OK = .T.
      Adding = .F.

   *---- Part number does not exist.
   CASE .NOT. FOUND()
     @ Row,10 SAY "No such part!!!"
     OK = .F.

   *------- Part number does exist.
   CASE FOUND()
     *- Say part description,
     *- get quantity and price.
     MQty = 0
     MPrice = Unit_Price
     Tax=IIF(Taxable,1.06,1)
     @ Row,10 SAY PartName
     @ Row,35 GET MQty PICT "@Z 999"
     @ Row,40 SAY MPrice PICT "9999.99"
     @ Row,50 SAY Taxable PICT "Y"
     READ

     *------- If quantity is zero, loop.
     *------- Else, display line total.
     IF MQty = 0
        LOOP
     ELSE
        @ Row,55 SAY (MQty*MPrice)*Tax;
        PICT "99,999.99"
        MTotal = MTotal + (MQty*MPrice)*Tax
        OK = .T.
     ENDIF (mqty=0)

     *------- Add a blank record to
     *------- OrdTemp and fill it in.
     SELECT A
     APPEND BLANK
     REPLACE Date_Sold WITH DATE()
     REPLACE Clerk WITH MClerk
     REPLACE Invoice_No WITH MInvoice
     REPLACE Customer WITH MCust
     REPLACE PartNo WITH MPartNo
     REPLACE Qty WITH MQty
     REPLACE Price WITH MPrice

  ENDCASE

ENDDO (not valid)
Row = Row + 1      && Next screen row.

*----------- Scroll screen if near bottom.
IF Row >= 19
   @ 24,1
   ?
   Row = 19
ENDIF  (row>=19)
ENDDO (adding)

*------- Display grand total, and
*------- ask about printing invoice.
@ Row+2,45 SAY "Total: "
@ Row+2,54 SAY MTotal PICT "$99,999.99"

@ 23,2 SAY "Print invoice? (Y/N) ";
GET PrintInv PICT "Y"
```

**FIGURE 10.21:** The PosEntry program demonstrates many techniques for entering records into a database, including techniques for validating, displaying, and calculating information based on data in a separate database (continued).

```
READ

*------ Print invoice, readjust StartInv.
SELECT A
IF PrintInv
   SET PRINT ON
   ? "Date: ", DATE()
   ? "Invoice number: ",STR(MInvoice,5)
   ? "Customer: ",MCust,SPACE(20)
   ?? "Clerk: ",MClerk
   ? REPLICATE("_",80)
   ?
   GOTO StartInv
   LIST OFF PartNo,B->PartName,Qty,Price, ;
     IIF(B->Taxable,"Y","N"), ;
     TRANSFORM((Qty*Price)*Tax,"99,999.99") REST
   ?
   ?
   ? " Total: ",SPACE(36)
   ?? TRANSFORM(MTotal,"99,999.99")
   EJECT
   SET PRINT OFF
   StartInv = RECCOUNT()+1
   ENDIF (PrintInv)
   CLEAR
   @ 23,2 SAY "Do another transaction? (Y/N) ";
   GET Again PICT "Y"
   READ
ENDDO (again)

*------- Close databases and update Orders File.
CLOSE DATABASES
CLEAR
? "Updating transaction file, please wait..."
SET TALK ON
USE Orders
APPEND FROM OrdTemp
USE OrdTemp
ZAP
USE Orders INDEX Orders,OrdDate
REINDEX
SET TALK OFF
CLOSE DATABASES
RETURN
```

**FIGURE 10.21:** The PosEntry program demonstrates many techniques for entering records into a database, including techniques for validating, displaying, and calculating information based on data in a separate database (continued).

temporary database named OrdTemp. The Master file is opened (in work area B) with the Master index file (based on the PartNo field) so that information can be verified and borrowed as records are added to OrdTemp. The SET RELATION command points from the OrdTemp file into the Master file, as shown below:

**SELECT A**
**USE OrdTemp**
**SELECT B**
**USE Master INDEX Master**
**SELECT A**
**SET RELATION TO PartNo INTO Master**

```
Structure for database: Orders.dbf

Field  Field Name  Type       Width    Dec
    1  PartNo      Character      5
    2  Invoice_No  Numeric        5
    3  Clerk       Character      5
    4  Customer    Character     20
    5  Qty         Numeric        4
    6  Price       Numeric        9      2
    7  Date_Sold   Date           8

Structure for database: Master.dbf

Field  Field Name  Type       Width    Dec
    1  PartNo      Character      5
    2  PartName    Character     20
    3  In_Stock    Numeric        4
    4  Unit_Price  Numeric        9      2
    5  Taxable     Logical        1
    6  Reorder     Numeric        4
    7  On_Order    Numeric        4
    8  BackOrder   Numeric        4
    9  Rec_Date    Date           8
   10  Location    Character      4
   11  Vend_Code   Character      4
```

**FIGURE 10.22:** Structures of the Master and Orders database files used by the sample PosEntry command file shown in Figure 10.21. The Master database contains one record for each item in stock. New records are added to the Orders database by the PosEntry program, but information from the Master database is used to verify, display, and calculate data as the records are added.

The PosEntry program, however, does quite a bit more than simply open both database files. It includes a routine that automatically calculates invoice numbers and adds new transactions to a temporary database file, as discussed below.

The routine in PosEntry shown below moves the record pointer to the bottom of the Orders file to determine the largest existing invoice number. It stores this value in a variable named MInvoice:

```
USE Orders
GO BOTT
MInvoice = Invoice_No
```

This technique assumes that the data are entered sequentially, in which case the largest invoice number would always be at the bottom. If this were not the case, an index on the Invoice_No field would be required, to ensure that the GO BOTTOM command reaches the largest invoice number.

PosEntry uses a temporary database, named OrdTemp, to store new records. To ensure that OrdTemp is empty at the start of a session, the COPY STRUCTURE command is used to copy only the structure of the actual Orders database to the temporary database, as shown below:

```
SET SAFETY OFF
COPY STRUCTURE TO OrdTemp
```

Next, the StartInv variable is set to 1, because the first record for the first invoice to be entered will begin at record number 1 in the OrdTemp database. The variable PrintInv is used later to hold the user's answer to the question **Print invoice?**.

```
StartInv = 1
PrintInv = .T.
```

Next the main loop allows the user to continue adding invoices (*entire* invoices, not just individual transactions). The @...SAY...GET commands display the top portion of the invoice and wait for the user to enter the customer and clerk names:

```
Again = .T.
DO WHILE Again
    CLEAR
    MInvoice = MInvoice + 1
    STORE SPACE(20) TO MClerk, MCust
    MTotal = 0
    @ 1,2 SAY DATE( )
    @ 1,30 SAY "Invoice number: " + STR(MInvoice,5)
    @ 2,2 SAY "Clerk " GET MClerk
    @ 2,35 SAY "Customer " GET MCust
    @ 3,0 SAY REPLICATE("_",80)
    ? " Part # Name",SPACE(20)
    ?? "Qty      Price    Tax?         Total"
    READ
```

Then the program starts getting a little tricky. First, the variable Row stores the row number on the screen where the first transaction for this invoice will be entered, and the Adding variable is set to true. Then a loop is set up that repeats as long as the user adds transactions:

```
Row = 7
Adding = .T.
DO WHILE Adding
```

Within this loop, the memory variable MPartNo is prepared to accept the part number for the current transaction.

## Validating Entries against Another Database

In applications where the user is entering transactions into one database that relate to individual items in a separate master database, you'll want to ensure that the part number (or account number or customer number) the user enters is the same as one already existing on the master database. For example, if there were no part number Z-999 in the inventory, a record on the Orders database for part number Z-999 would create a good deal of confusion when it became time to fulfill the order.

The basic technique for verifying a number (or code) entered into a new record against a list of existing numbers (or codes) is fairly simple. You need to make the database that contains the list of valid numbers (or codes) the current database (using SELECT) and use a SEEK or FIND command to attempt to locate the entered value. If the SEEK or FIND command does not find a match, the value entered must be invalid and the program should reject the entry.

In an actual application program, you'll need to enclose the verification routine inside a loop that allows the user to reenter a number or code after inadvertently entering an invalid one. In the PosEntry program (Figure 10.21) this loop begins with the commands

```
OK = .F.
DO WHILE .NOT. OK
```

The program next displays the prompt for entering the part number for the transaction, as shown below:

```
MPartNo = SPACE(5)
@ Row,2 GET MPartNo PICTURE "@!"
READ
```

After the user enters the part number, the program checks the Master database to see whether the part number exists. It does so by making the Master database current (SELECT B) and looking for the part number in the Master index file, as shown below:

```
MPartNo = TRIM(MPartNo)
SELECT B
SEEK MPartNo
```

A DO CASE clause decides what to do next. If the user did not enter a part number, the **MPartNo = TRIM(MPartNo)** command above resulted in a character string with a length of zero. When this is the case, the program marks this as a valid entry (**OK = .T.**), but one that indicates that the user has finished adding transactions (**Adding = .F.**):

```
DO CASE
     CASE LEN(MPartNo) = 0
```

```
OK = .T.
Adding = .F.
```

If the user enters a part number that can't be found in the Master database, the next CASE statement displays an error message and sets the OK variable to false, as shown below:

```
CASE .NOT. FOUND( )
     @ Row,10 SAY "No such part!!!"
     OK = .F.
```

The DO WHILE .NOT. OK loop takes over from there to ask for a new part number. If the user did, indeed, enter a valid part number, the program proceeds with the transaction, using more data from the Master database.

## Using Data from a Separate Database

When entering data into one database and verifying it against data in another database, you'll often need to display data from the "outside" database as an aid to the user. For example, suppose the user enters a valid part number (such as A-111), but it turns out to be the incorrect part number (i.e., the user actually mistyped his intended entry of A-112). The program itself cannot detect this kind of an error. However, the program can display the part name for part number A-111, so that the user can quickly view the screen to ensure that the correct part number was entered. It is also useful to display price data from the foreign database. The PosEntry program (Figure 10.21) demonstrates a technique that displays data from the Master file on the screen while the user is entering orders. The commands appear in the routine that responds to the entry of a valid part number. The SELECT B command (above the DO CASE clause) has already selected the Master database file, and the SEEK command has already positioned the record pointer accordingly, so the PosEntry program can freely use data from the Master database. It does so in the CASE statement for a valid part number by assigning the unit price for the item to a memory variable named MPrice, determining the tax rate for the item, and displaying the part name field. In this example, the Tax variable is set to 1 if the item is not taxable and 1.06 (for 6 percent sales tax) if the item is taxable. Then the information is displayed directly on the screen in @...SAY and @...GET commands:

```
CASE FOUND( )
     *- Say part description,
     *- get quantity and price.
     MQty = 0
     MPrice = Unit_Price
     Tax = IIF(Taxable,1.06,1)
```

```
@ Row,10 SAY PartName
@ Row,35 GET MQty PICT "@Z 999"
@ Row,40 SAY MPrice PICT "9999.99"
@ Row,50 SAY Taxable PICT "Y"
READ
```

Later in the program, after the transaction is actually written to a record in OrdTemp, the commands

```
SELECT A
```

and

```
LIST OFF PartNo,B->PartName,Qty,Price, ;
        IIF(B->Taxable,"Y","N"), ;
        TRANSFORM((Qty*Price)*Tax,"99,999.99") REST
```

can use the B-> alias to display data from the Master database. The CASE FOUND( ) clause also asks the user to enter the quantity sold for the transaction and stores this value in the variable MQty. If the user does not enter a quantity for the transaction the program assumes the wrong (albeit valid) part number was entered, so a LOOP command repeats the DO WHILE .NOT. OK loop:

```
IF MQty = 0
   LOOP
```

This CASE statement, then, gives the user a chance to look at the screen to see the name of the part number he just typed in. If the name displayed is not what he was expecting, he can just press Return to enter a new part number.

## Performing On-Screen Calculations

In many application programs, you might want to use data from a separate database file to perform calculations for the database on which you are currently entering records. For example, if the user enters an order for 10 of part number A-111, it would be very helpful if the screen displayed the total amount of the sale (10 times the unit price, plus the tax if applicable). Since the unit price and tax status are likely to be stored on the separate master file, you will need to "borrow" this information from the master file to perform the calculation.

The PosEntry program (Figure 10.21) shows a technique to perform just this kind of calculation. As discussed above, the SELECT B and SEEK commands have already positioned the record pointer to the appropriate record in the Master database to match the part number on the order being entered. Furthermore, it has stored the unit price and tax rate in two memory variables named MPrice and Tax (using the commands **MPrice = Unit_Price** and

**Tax = IIF(Taxable,1.06,1)**. The user has already entered a quantity in the memory variable named MQty.

Next, the program calculates and displays the transaction total on the screen by multiplying the quantity by the unit price, multiplied by the Tax value. Then it increments the grand total for the entire invoice (in the variable MTotal) by this amount, as shown below. Because all data seem to be valid now, the OK variable is set to true:

```
        @ Row,55 SAY (MQty*MPrice)*Tax;
        PICT "99,999.99"
        MTotal = MTotal + (MQty*MPrice)*Tax
        OK = .T.
    ENDIF (mqty = 0)
```

The only reason the (MQty*MPrice)*Tax calculation can be reliably displayed on the screen at this point is that there are no more READ commands for this transaction in the program. The calculation has to be displayed after the final READ, because any further changes to the data would not recalculate the data. Another READ command for this transaction would simply put the cursor back onto the screen; it would ignore the commands necessary to perform the calculation.

However, because potential errors in both the part number and quantity fields have been eliminated, you can be certain that the entry is valid now, and therefore the program can reliably display the results of these entries.

## The Rest of PosEntry

While the rest of the PosEntry program shown in Figure 10.21 does not demonstrate techniques involving multiple database files per se, it does demonstrate some general programming techniques that can be applied to this particular application. These additional techniques are discussed below to describe the PosEntry program as a whole and to round out your understanding of this somewhat sophisticated data-entry program. First of all, the routine below reselects the OrdTemp database, appends a blank record to it, and places the data acquired up to this point into the new record:

```
SELECT A
APPEND BLANK
REPLACE Date_Sold WITH DATE( )
REPLACE Clerk WITH MClerk
REPLACE Invoice_No WITH MInvoice
REPLACE Customer WITH MCust
REPLACE PartNo WITH MPartNo
```

```
                REPLACE Qty WITH MQty
                REPLACE Price WITH MPrice
        ENDCASE
    ENDDO (not valid)
```

The routine below scrolls the screen up a line if the transactions for the invoice are nearing the bottom of the screen:

```
        Row = Row + 1
        IF Row > = 19
            @ 24,1
            ?
            Row = 19
        ENDIF (row> = 19)
    ENDDO (adding)
```

The next routine displays the grand total for the invoice (which has been accumulated in the memory variable MTotal) at the bottom of the screen and asks whether the user wants to print the invoice:

```
    @ Row + 2,45 SAY "Total: "
    @ Row + 2,54 SAY MTotal PICT "$99,999.99"
    @ 23,2 SAY "Print invoice? (Y/N) ";
    GET PrintInv PICT "Y"
    READ
```

If the user opts to print the invoice, the routine below does so. Note the use of the B-> alias to display data from the Master database that is not stored on the Orders database:

```
    SELECT A
    IF PrintInv
        SET PRINT ON
        ? "Date: ", DATE( )
        ? "Invoice number: ",STR(MInvoice,5)
        ? "Customer: ",MCust,SPACE(20)
        ?? "Clerk: ",MClerk
        ? REPLICATE("_",80)
        ?
        GOTO StartInv
        LIST OFF PartNo,B->PartName,Qty,Price, ;
            IIF(B->Taxable,"Y","N"), ;
            TRANSFORM((Qty*Price)*Tax,"99,999.99") REST
        ?
        ?
```

```
        ? " Total: ",SPACE(36)
        ?? TRANSFORM(MTotal,"99,999.99")
        EJECT
        SET PRINT OFF
        StartInv = RECCOUNT( ) + 1
    ENDIF (PrintInv)
    CLEAR
```

The routine below simply asks whether the user wishes to enter another invoice and repeats the outermost DO WHILE Again loop if the user answers yes:

```
        @ 23,2 SAY "Do another transaction? (Y/N) ";
        GET Again PICT "Y"
        READ
    ENDDO (again)
```

When the user is done entering invoices, the following routine uses an APPEND FROM command to copy records from the OrdTemp database onto the Orders database. This routine also deletes the appended records from OrdTemp using a ZAP command:

```
    CLOSE DATABASES
    CLEAR
    ? "Updating transaction file, please wait..."
    SET TALK ON
    USE Orders
    APPEND FROM OrdTemp
    USE OrdTemp
    ZAP
```

After the records from OrdTemp are appended to the Orders database, the index files for Orders are updated and the program terminates:

```
    USE Orders INDEX Orders,OrdDate
    REINDEX
    SET TALK OFF
    CLOSE DATABASES
    RETURN
```

## Commands Used to Append Data

The various versions of the APPEND command are discussed below. The @...SAY...GET and READ commands are discussed in detail in Chapter 8, "Managing Screen Displays," along with the SET FORMAT command and techniques for creating custom data-entry forms.

## The APPEND Command

APPEND allows new records to be added to the bottom of the database currently in use.

### SYNTAX

APPEND

### USAGE

The APPEND command initiates a full-screen data-entry mode for adding new records to a database. The command keys shown in Table 10.1 are used to control the screen and cursor.

If no format file is in use, APPEND generates a simple screen for entering records. If a format file is opened with the SET FORMAT command, the custom screen is used for data-entry.

APPEND can add data only to a single database file. If several database files are open and related, APPEND adds data only to the currently selected file.

Any currently active index files are automatically updated and resorted. Any inactive index files are not updated and will need to be rebuilt using the INDEX ON or REINDEX command.

The master index file, if any, will control the order in which PgUp and PgDn scroll through records. If there is no active index file, scrolling will take place in sequential record number order.

Some newly added records are stored in a buffer before being written to disk. The commands CLOSE DATABASES, CLOSE ALL, USE, or QUIT will transfer all new records from the buffer onto the database file.

### EXAMPLE

The commands below open the Mail database and MailScr format file and allow the user to add new records using the screen defined in the format file. The CLOSE FORMAT command sets the screen back to its default state.

```
USE Mail
SET FORMAT TO MailScr
APPEND
CLOSE FORMAT
```

| KEY | ALTERNATE | EFFECT |
|---|---|---|
| Return | | Finishes data entry in one field and moves cursor to next field |
| F1 | | Toggles help menu on and off (if no format file is in use) |
| Num Lock | | Toggles numbers/arrow keys on numeric keypad |
| → | Ctrl-D | Moves cursor right one character |
| ← | Ctrl-S | Moves cursor left one character |
| Home | Ctrl-A | Moves cursor to previous word, start of field, or previous field, depending on cursor's current position |
| End | Ctrl-F | Moves cursor to next word, end of field, or start of next field, depending on cursor's current position |
| PgUp | Ctrl-R | Scrolls to previous page or record, if any |
| PgDn | Ctrl-C | Scrolls to next page or record, if any; otherwise, exits EDIT mode |
| ↑ | Ctrl-E | Moves cursor to previous field |
| ↓ | Ctrl-X | Moves cursor to next field |
| Ins | Ctrl-V | Toggles insert mode on/off |
| Del | Ctrl-G | Deletes character at cursor |
| Backspace | | Moves cursor to left, erasing character |
| Ctrl-T | | Deletes word to right |
| Ctrl-Y | | Deletes all characters to right |
| Ctrl-U | | Marks record for deletion |
| Esc | Ctrl-Q | Aborts last entry and exits EDIT mode (if a memo field is being entered, aborts current entry and returns to EDIT screen) |
| Ctrl-End | Ctrl-W | Saves entry and exits EDIT mode |
| Ctrl-PgDn | Ctrl-Home | Edits a memo field |
| Ctrl-PgUp | Ctrl-End | Saves a memo field and returns to EDIT screen (when entering a memo field) |

**TABLE 10.1:** Command Keys Used with the APPEND Command

### TIPS

As a database and its index files grow larger, there will be an increased delay between newly added records. If the delay becomes too long, new records can be appended to a temporary file or to the actual database file without the index files. After editing, rebuild the index files with the INDEX ON or the faster REINDEX command.

For more control over entering records, use the READ command to add records individually, as discussed in the section "Adding Data with Read" earlier in this chapter.

See Chapter 8, "Managing Screen Displays," for an in-depth discussion of format files.

### SEE ALSO

APPEND BLANK
APPEND FROM
INSERT
SET FORMAT
BROWSE
READ
CLOSE FORMAT

## The APPEND BLANK Command

The APPEND BLANK command adds a blank record to the bottom of the database currently in use.

### SYNTAX

**APPEND BLANK**

### USAGE

APPEND BLANK adds a single blank record to a database that can be filled in using a READ command. If a format file is open, the READ command will use the screen defined in that file.

The newly added blank record is always the current record, until some action is taken to move the record pointer. Any active index files are immediately updated, just as with the APPEND command.

### EXAMPLE

In the commands below, the Mail database and MailScr format files are opened, a blank record is added to the database, and the READ command allows data to be entered into the new blank record.

```
USE Mail
SET FORMAT TO MailScr
APPEND BLANK
READ
CLOSE FORMAT
```

### TIPS

APPEND BLANK and READ can be used for advanced data-entry techniques, as discussed in the section "Using Memory Variables to Add Records" and demonstrated in Figure 10.21 earlier in this chapter. Also, the APPEND BLANK and READ commands are acceptable by most compilers, whereas APPEND is not.

### SEE ALSO

APPEND
APPEND FROM
INSERT
SET FORMAT
BROWSE
READ
CLOSE FORMAT

## The APPEND FROM Command

APPEND FROM appends database records from an external file into the currently selected database file.

### SYNTAX

**APPEND FROM <file name> [FOR <condition>] [TYPE<file type>]**

where <file name> is the name of the file to append records from, <condition> is any valid query condition, and <file type> defines the format of a foreign file.

## USAGE

The current disk drive and directory are assumed, unless otherwise specified. The extension .dbf is assumed in the file name being read, unless otherwise specified in the file name.

Only data with identical field names in both databases are appended into the currently active database. If the width for a field in the active database is smaller than the width in the database being read, the character data are truncated to fit the new width. Large numbers that do not fit are replaced with asterisks.

If SET DELETED is OFF, records that are marked for deletion are read into the current database but are *not* marked for deletion in the current database. However, if SET DELETED is ON, records marked for deletion are not read into the active database file at all.

The FOR expression works only with fields that exist in both database files.

The TYPE expression defines the structure of a non-dBASE data file. The foreign data file options are DELIMITED, SDF, DIF, SYLK, and WKS (discussed in Chapter 23, "Foreign and Damaged Files").

If the database from which you are reading records does not have a file-name extension, place a period at the end of the file name in the APPEND FROM command.

## EXAMPLE

The commands below append records from the OrdTemp.dbf database into the currently open Orders.dbf database. However, records that are marked for deletion in OrdTemp and records that have no entry in the PartNo field are *not* appended. (Both Orders and OrdTemp have a character field named PartNo.) After appending, all records are removed from the OrdTemp database with the ZAP command, so a future APPEND FROM command does not read these same records again.

```
USE Orders
SET DELETED ON
APPEND FROM OrdTemp FOR PartNo # "  "
*------- Empty the OrdTemp database.
USE OrdTemp
SET SAFETY OFF
ZAP
```

## TIPS

You can store newly entered records on a temporary database file and then use APPEND FROM to read these records into the "actual" database. This method is often preferred in networking environments or in situations where data needs to be verified after initial entry, before being processed in the "real" database.

### SEE ALSO

APPEND
IMPORT
COPY

## The INSERT Command

The INSERT command inserts a database record into a particular position on the database.

### SYNTAX

**INSERT [BLANK] [BEFORE]**

where [BLANK] and [BEFORE] are optional.

### USAGE

INSERT is identical to APPEND, except that it places the new record immediately after the current record, rather than at the bottom. For example, if the record pointer is at record 10 when INSERT is issued, the new record is entered as record 11, and all lower records move down a notch (i.e., the old record 11 becomes record 12, and so forth for all records).

INSERT allows data to be entered into only a single record, unless the inserted record is entered at the bottom of the file. In this case, INSERT allows multiple records to be added, just as APPEND does.

The optional BEFORE clause inserts the new record at the current pointer position. For example, if the pointer is at record 10, INSERT BEFORE places the new record at record 10 and moves record 10 and all others down a notch.

The INSERT BLANK command inserts a blank record into the database but does not enter full-screen mode for entering data. The SET CARRY and SET FORMAT commands work with INSERT in the same way as they do with APPEND. Command keys used in APPEND work similarly in INSERT. INSERT automatically updates all currently active index files.

### EXAMPLE

The commands below insert a record into the appropriate alphabetical position for the last name Miller (assuming that the Mail database is already sorted on the LName field, and LName contains last names). Data can then be entered through the MailScr format file:

```
USE Mail
SET FORMAT TO MailScr
LOCATE FOR LName > = "Miller"
INSERT BEFORE
CLOSE FORMAT
```

### TIPS

INSERT can be used to maintain a sort order in an unindexed file. However, the command tends to be slow and unreliable, so indexed files are by far the preferred method for maintaining sort orders.

In dBASE III PLUS version 1.0, INSERT caused the bottom record in the database file to disappear—a most unpleasant bug that should certainly be avoided by programmers.

### SEE ALSO

APPEND
APPEND BLANK
INDEX

## SUMMARY

This chapter discussed many commands and techniques for entering data into a database file. The PosEntry program, presented in the section "Data Entry with Multiple Databases," demonstrated a combination of techniques for developing a sophisticated, user-friendly data-entry process. This program is expanded even further in Chapter 16, "Managing Multiple Database Files," to provide instant updating to the master file, feedback about the current status of items in stock, and a back-ordering capability.

*For more information on master-file/transaction-file relationships:*

- Chapter 3, "Database Design"

*For more information on format files and the @ and READ commands:*

- Chapter 8, "Managing Screen Displays"

*For a more sophisticated point-of-sale data-entry program with instantaneous updating:*

- Chapter 16, "Managing Multiple Database Files"

*For more information on READKEY( ) and other dBASE functions:*

- Chapter 17, "dBASE Functions"

*For tips on using APPEND FROM to read data from foreign file formats into dBASE databases:*

- Chapter 23, "Foreign and Damaged Files"

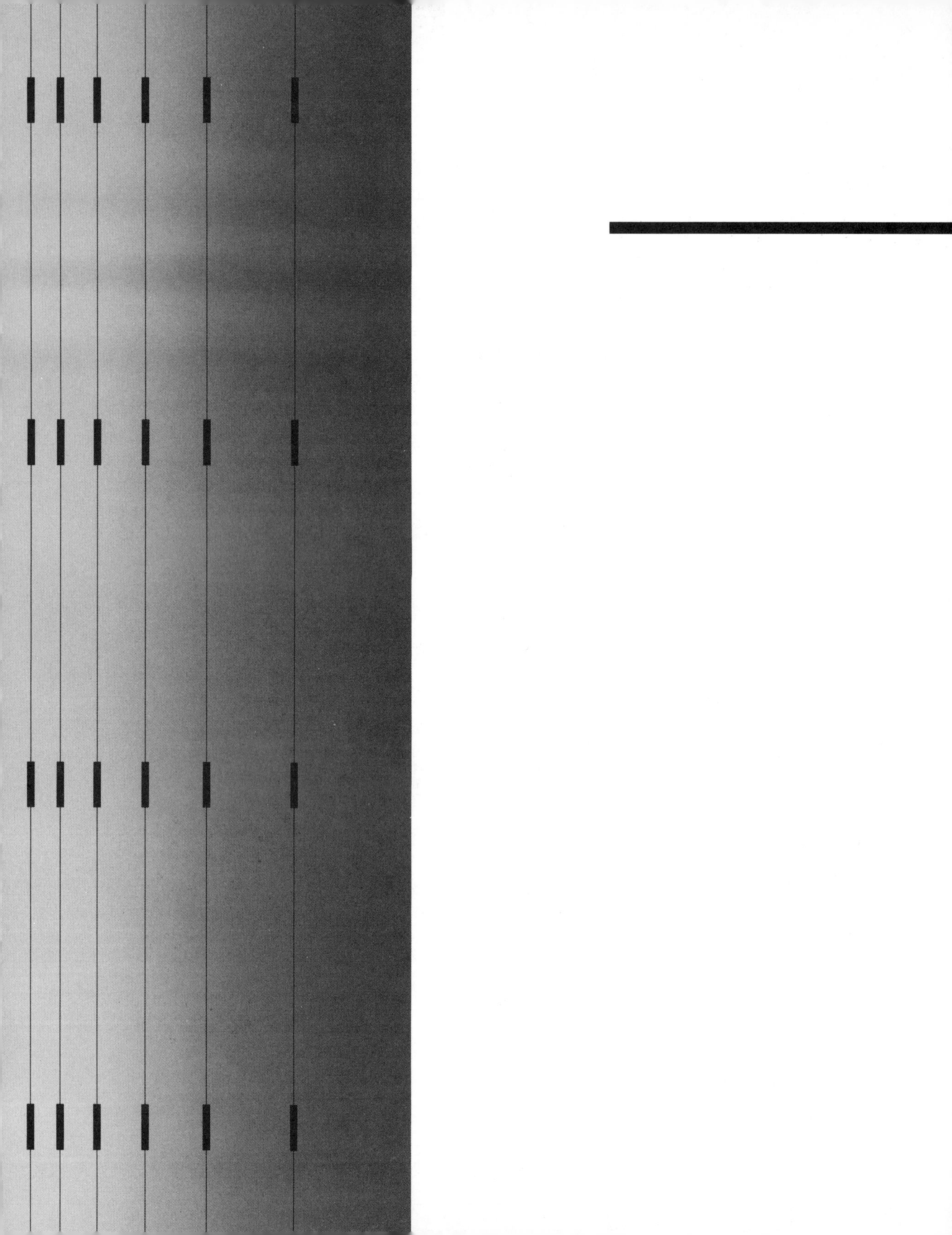

# EDITING AND DELETING RECORDS

# Editing and Deleting Records

For the average dBASE user, the full-screen EDIT, CHANGE, and BROWSE commands are usually adequate for changing and deleting records. However, the programmer usually needs more control over the user's edits. This chapter discusses the individual commands for editing and deleting records, as well as some techniques that help the programmer maintain control over edits and deletions.

## Editing Multiple Records

There are three dBASE commands that allow full-screen editing of dBASE records: EDIT, CHANGE, and BROWSE. These commands assume that the record pointer is positioned on the record to be edited (or in the general vicinity for BROWSE). They allow the user to scroll up and down through records, and they place no restrictions on edits other than those specified in PICTURE and RANGE commands within format files.

The CHANGE and EDIT commands are identical. (CHANGE is something of a vestigial appendage from dBASE II, where it originally acted as a sort of REPLACE command with a pause at each record.) For the sake of consistency, we'll discuss only the EDIT command in this chapter.

In many custom applications, neither the EDIT nor BROWSE command provides enough control over the user's changes in a record. Therefore, you'll probably want to use the READ command to perform some edits, as discussed later in the chapter.

## Editing with EDIT

The EDIT command works very much like the APPEND command. It creates a simple full-screen display of an individual record and allows the user to make changes. The user can also scroll up and down through records using the PgUp and PgDn keys. If a custom format file is opened with the SET FORMAT command, that form is used in place of the simple screen that EDIT would otherwise generate.

## Programming with EDIT

To allow the user to edit any group of records starting at a particular record, use the LOCATE, SEEK, or GOTO command to position the record pointer and then simply issue the EDIT command. Of course, if the user attempts to find a record that does not exist, your program should display some warning to this effect.

If several records have the value the user is searching for, you might want to also warn him or her of this situation. The sample program in Figure 11.1, named Edit1.prg, demonstrates all of these techniques. Keep in mind that the Names index was created with the command **INDEX ON UPPER (LName + FName) to Names**, and hence all the names in the index file are in uppercase.

Notice that the Edit1 program uses the SET FORMAT command to open a format file named MailSrc for use with the EDIT command. Furthermore, the format file is opened only for the duration of the edit, so it will not interfere with the READ command used to accept the name to search for. The routine below determines whether the name the user requested to edit exists on the database file and if so opens the custom screen, allows the edit, and then closes the custom screen:

```
*----- If found, edit...
IF FOUND()
     SET FORMAT TO MailScr
     EDIT
     CLOSE FORMAT
```

The Edit1 program allows the user to scroll freely up and down through records once a single record is brought to the screen. The DO WHILE loop in the Edit1 program allows the user to edit as many records as he or she wishes. When done entering records, the user simply presses Return rather than type in a name to look up, and the program ends.

### Limiting EDIT to Certain Records

You can use a FOR or WHILE command to limit editing to records that meet a search criterion. For example, to limit edits to individuals with the last name Miller, you could enter the command

```
EDIT FOR LName = "Miller"
```

If the database is indexed on the field used to locate the record to edit, you can use the faster WHILE approach to limit the edit to particular records. For example, the Edit1 program shown in Figure 11.1 uses the Mail database indexed on the LName and FName fields. The first SAY commands in the program ask for the last name of the individual whose record the user wants to edit

```
**************************** Edit1.prg
SET TALK OFF
USE Mail INDEX Names
*------------ Set up loop for editing.
More = .T.
DO WHILE More
    CLEAR
    Search = SPACE(20) && Same width as field.
    @ 10,5 SAY "Enter last name to edit"
    @ 12,5 SAY "or press <--' to exit " GET Search
    READ

    *------- Exit if nothing entered.
    IF Search = " "
        More = .F.
        LOOP
    ENDIF

    *------- Try to find the record.
    Search = UPPER(TRIM(Search))
    SEEK Search

    *------ See how many there are.
    COUNT WHILE UPPER(Lname) = Search TO HowMany

    *------ If more than one, tell user.
    IF HowMany > 1
       @ 20,1 SAY STR(HowMany,3)+" matches found"
       @ 22,1 SAY "Use PgDn, PgUp keys to scroll"
       ?
       WAIT "Press any key to edit..."
    ENDIF (howmany)
    SEEK Search   && Go back to first match.

    *------- If found, edit...
    IF FOUND()
        SET FORMAT TO MailScr
        EDIT
        CLOSE FORMAT
    ELSE
        *--- If not found, warn user.
        @ 22,0
        ? "Can't find: ",Search
        ?? CHR(7)
        WAIT
    ENDIF (found)
ENDDO (More)
RETURN
```

**FIGURE 11.1:** The Edit1 program allows the user to enter a last name. If several records have that name, the program tells the user this. If only one record has that name, the record can be edited immediately. If no records have the requested name, the user is warned and given the opportunity to try again.

and put the result in a variable called Search. Later in the program, the SEEK command moves the record pointer to the first record that matches the requested last name. To limit the forward and backward scrolling offered by the EDIT command to *only* those records with the requested last name (rather than all database records), change the EDIT command in the program to

**EDIT WHILE UPPER(LName) = Search**

In this situation, it is necessary to convert the last name in the database field to uppercase to match the Search variable, which was converted to uppercase earlier in the program (in the command **Search = UPPER(TRIM(Search))**.

### LIMITING EDIT TO CERTAIN FIELDS

There are a few techniques you can use to exclude whole fields from access in the EDIT command. If you are not using a custom screen, the SET FIELDS command allows you to select fields to display on the EDIT screen.

If you are using a custom screen, you need to exclude any fields from GET access within the format file. You can hide the field entirely by excluding it from the format file. Optionally, you can display the field but not let the user edit it by using a SAY command rather than a GET command in the format file.

## Editing with BROWSE

The BROWSE command displays records in a spreadsheet-like format for editing, as shown in Figure 11.2. It displays 17 records at a time, and as many

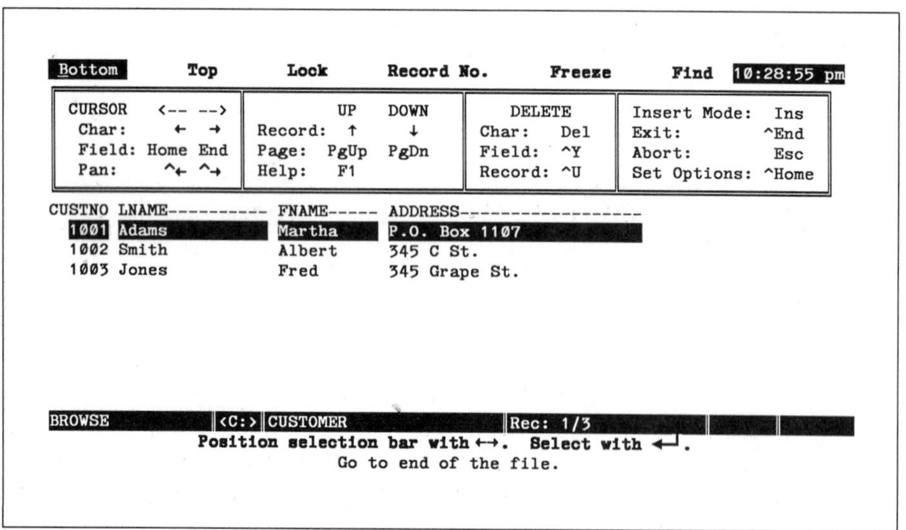


**FIGURE 11.2:** The BROWSE command displays records in a spreadsheet-like format, allowing users to edit individual records while viewing other records on the screen. BROWSE allows users full access to all records and fields in a database file. The programmer has no control over what the user places in fields. The user can freely scroll up and down through records and left and right through fields.

fields as will fit across the screen. The user can move the highlight up and down through records, as well as left and right through fields.

## Programming with BROWSE

For the programmer, the typical use of the BROWSE command is to ask the user for a record to edit, locate that record, and then go into the BROWSE mode with the record pointer in place. Of course, if the user attempts to edit a nonexistent record, the program should warn of this and give the user another try. Figure 11.3 shows a sample program named Edit2 that performs these tasks.

```
***************************** Edit2.prg
SET TALK OFF
USE Mail INDEX Names
*------------ Set up loop for editing.
More = .T.
DO WHILE More
    CLEAR
    Search = SPACE(20) && Same width as field.
    @ 10,5 SAY "Enter last name to edit"
    @ 12,5 SAY "or press <--' to Exit " GET Search
    READ

    *------- Exit if nothing entered.
    IF Search = " "
        More = .F.
        LOOP
    ENDIF

    *------- Try to find the record.
    Search = UPPER(TRIM(Search))
    SEEK Search

    *------- If found, edit...
    IF FOUND()
       BROWSE
    ELSE
        *--- If not found, warn user.
        @ 22,0
        ? "Can't find: ",Search
        ?? CHR(7)
        WAIT
    ENDIF (found)
ENDDO (More)
*---- Done editing.
RETURN
```

**FIGURE 11.3:** The Edit2 program asks the user for a last name to edit and attempts to find that name. If the user enters a name for which no match can be found, the program issues a warning. If a valid name is found, the program enters the BROWSE mode pointing at that record. The program continues asking for records to edit until the user leaves the prompt blank.

## USING READ TO EDIT A SINGLE RECORD

To allow the user to edit only one record at a time, you need to use the READ command instead of EDIT or BROWSE. This method gives you full control over what the user changes. Use the GOTO, LOCATE, or SEEK command to position the pointer to a particular record, and use a format file (or @...SAY-...GET commands) to present data on the screen. The READ command then allows the user to make changes to the record.

Generally, you'll want a routine to ask the user for the record to edit and then attempt to find that record with a SEEK or LOCATE command. If the record can be found, use SET FORMAT to display a custom screen, READ to edit the record, and CLOSE FORMAT to close the format file.

You should use this method only in situations where you are sure the user can pinpoint a record exactly, as in databases with a true key field. For example, the program in Figure 11.4 uses the Master database, which has a unique part number in every record.

The Master.fmt file defines the screen for editing records. It is a standard format file with @...SAY...GET commands. However, to prevent the user from changing the part number, the format file displays the part number with a SAY command, rather than GET, as follows:

```
@ 5, 13 SAY PartNo
```

## REJECTING DUPLICATES IN A KEY FIELD

When you allow a user to edit data on a master file that requires a unique identifier for each record in the key field, you'll want to be sure that the user does not change the existing identifier to one that already exists in the database file. For example, if a Master database file has a unique part number for every record and one of those part numbers is A-111, the user cannot be allowed to change the part number in another record to A-111.

Figure 11.5 shows a sample program that allows the user to edit a record on the sample Master database. The user is allowed to change the part number, but if the user changes the part number to one that already exists, the program displays an error message, and the user must reenter a new part number.

The following line in the Master2.fmt file uses the memory variable MPartNo to display and accept changes to the part number:

```
@ 5, 13 GET MPartNo PICTURE "@!"
```

The bulk of the error-checking for the duplicate part number is shown in the routine below. First, the variables named Original and MPartNo are assigned the same value as the part number being searched for. Then a DO WHILE

```
****************************** Edit3.prg
*--------------- Edit a single record.
SET TALK OFF
USE Master INDEX Master

*------------ Set up loop for editing.
More = .T.
DO WHILE More
    CLEAR
    Search = SPACE(5) && Same width as field.
    @ 10,5 SAY "Enter part number to edit"
    @ 12,5 SAY "or press <--' to Exit " GET Search
    READ

    *------- Exit if nothing entered.
    IF Search = " "
        More = .F.
        LOOP
    ENDIF

    *------- Try to find the record.
    Search = UPPER(TRIM(Search))
    SEEK Search

    *------- If found, edit...
    IF FOUND()
       SET FORMAT TO Master
       READ
       CLOSE FORMAT
    ELSE
        *--- If not found, warn user.
        @ 22,0
        ? "Can't find: ",Search
        ?? CHR(7)
        WAIT
    ENDIF (found)
ENDDO (More)
*---- Done editing.
RETURN
```

**FIGURE 11.4:** The Edit3 program asks the user for a part number. If no part number is entered, the program ends. If an invalid part number is entered, the program displays a warning. If a valid part number is entered, the user is allowed to edit that one record.

.NOT. OK loop will not let the user finish the edit until the part number in the current record is unique:

**OK = .F.**
**Original = Search**
**MPartNo = Search**
**SET FORMAT TO Master2**
**DO WHILE .NOT. OK**

The SEEK and READ commands then position the pointer to the appropriate record and allow the user to make changes. The GET command in the Master2.fmt format file allows only the MPartNo memory variable to be changed, not the actual PartNo field in the record (as discussed above).

```
*********************************** Edit4.prg
*-- Edit, disallowing duplicate part number.
SET TALK OFF
USE Master INDEX Master

*------------ Set up loop for editing.
More = .T.
DO WHILE More
   CLEAR
   CLOSE FORMAT
   Search = SPACE(5) && Same width as field.
   @ 10,5 SAY "Enter part number to edit"
   @ 12,5 SAY "or press <--' to Exit " GET Search
   READ

   *------- Exit if nothing entered.
   IF Search = " "
      More = .F.
      LOOP
   ENDIF

   *------- Try to find the record.
   Search = UPPER(TRIM(Search))
   SEEK Search
   *--- If not found, warn user.
   IF .NOT. FOUND()
      @ 22,0 SAY "Can't find: "+Search
      ?? CHR(7)
      WAIT
      LOOP
   ENDIF (found)

   *------- If found, edit...
   OK = .F.
   Original = Search  && Note original part number.
   MPartNo = Search   && Master2.fmt uses GET MPartNo.
   SET FORMAT TO Master2
   DO WHILE .NOT. OK
      *--- In this example, format file uses
      *--- GET MPartNo so user can change it.
      SEEK Original
      READ
      IF MPartNo # Original && If part number changed...
         SEEK MPartNo       && look for new number.
         IF FOUND()         && If taken, reject new number.
            @ 22,1 SAY "New part number taken!"
            @ 23,1 SAY "Original part number = "+Original
            WAIT "Press any key and reenter please."
         ELSE               && If not taken, accept it.
            SEEK Original
            REPLACE PartNo WITH MPartNo
            OK = .T.
         ENDIF (found)
      ELSE    && Part number not changed at all.
         OK =.T.
      ENDIF (Mpartno)
   ENDDO (ok)
ENDDO (More)
*---- Done editing.
RETURN
```

**FIGURE 11.5:** A program that allows the user to change any field on a record in the Master database. If, however, the user replaces the original part number with a part number that is already in use, the program displays an error message and rejects the new part number.

If the new part number does not match the original part number, the program looks for the new part number. If the number exists, the program displays an error message (and the OK variable remains false):

```
IF MPartNo # Original
    SEEK MPartNo
    IF FOUND()
        @ 22,1 SAY "New part number taken!"
        @ 23,1 SAY "Original part number = " + Original
        WAIT "Press any key and reenter please."
```

If, however, the new part number is indeed unique, the inner ELSE routine substitutes the new part number into the appropriate record. Because the change is acceptable, the OK variable is set to true. If the part number was not changed at all, the outer ELSE routine sets the OK variable to true and ends the DO WHILE loop.

## EDITING MULTIPLE DATABASES

When a database design involves multiple related databases, editing becomes slightly trickier, particularly if you want to display or use data from the nonselected database. You can "borrow" data for display purposes from the nonselected database during editing, but you should avoid making changes to that data.

While it is possible to make changes to the nonselected database with the SET VIEW command, the results can be unpredictable and particularly confusing to the user. Design your application so it is not necessary to edit the nonselected database.

If you use the -> alias, you can display data from the nonselected database while editing records. For example, suppose that a database named Customer contains the fields CustNo, LName, FName, and Address. The Charges database contains a single record for each charge transaction made by each customer. The CustNo field is the common field between the two files, and the relationship is set from the Charges database (the "many" side) into the Customer database (the "one" side) using the commands below:

```
SELECT A
USE Charges
SELECT B
USE Customer INDEX CustNo
SELECT A
SET RELATION TO CustNo INTO Customer
```

As long as Charges is the currently selected database, (i.e., SELECT A), a format file or any @...SAY command can contain a pointer into the Customer database, as below:

```
@ 5,5 SAY “Customer Number ” GET CustNo
@ 5,40 SAY “Name ” + TRIM(B->FName) + “ ” + B->LName
@ 6,4 SAY “Address ” + B->Address
@ 8,0 SAY “Invoice Number ” GET Invoice_No
```

The commands above will always display the name and address of the customer, whether the commands are in a command file or part of a format file used with EDIT. Note, however, that no GET commands are used with data from the B-> database. Again, you can display these data from the nonselected database, but it is to your advantage not to allow the user to change them. Your system should have a separate editing program for each database file.

## Editing Globally with REPLACE

You can edit a database globally using the REPLACE command. Normally, the user does not have direct access to this capability in an application, but the programmer may need to perform global operations on records in the database.

For example, suppose you have an accounts receivable system in which each customer's balance is stored in his or her record on the Customer database. The balance is calculated, in part, by adding the total charge transactions for the past month to each customer's current charges. You need to use some technique to ensure that once a transaction is *posted* to the customer's current totals, it is never posted again.

One way to do so would be to include a logical field named Posted on the Charges database and give it a value of false. After the posting takes place, you can change that value to true in all posted records. In the future, you post only records that still have false in the Posted field. The routine in Figure 11.6 presents an algorithm for accomplishing this kind of posting.

The first routine copies all nonposted transactions from the Charges database to a database named Temp. Then the SELECT commands open both the Charges and Temp databases. The UPDATE command adds all the transaction amounts from the Temp file to the current charge amount for each customer.

After the entire posting is complete, the last routine reopens the Charges database and marks all transactions as posted, so that this routine will never accidentally update the same transaction more than once.

This routine demonstrates a valuable use of the REPLACE command in applications that use the master-file/transaction-file relationship. For more on updating (posting) in general, see Chapter 16, "Managing Multiple Database Files."

```
*----- Copy nonposted transactions from Charges to Temp.
USE Charges INDEX ChargNo
COPY TO Temp FOR .NOT. Posted

*------------------------ Open both database files.
SELECT A
USE Customer INDEX CustNo
SELECT B
USE Temp

*------------------------ Perform the posting.
SELECT A
UPDATE ON CustNo FROM Temp REPLACE ;
   CurrChrg WITH CurrChrg + B->Amount

*------- Now mark all nonposted Charges as posted
CLOSE DATABASES
USE Charges
REPLACE ALL Posted WITH .T.
```

**FIGURE 11.6:** A small routine that updates a database named Customer from a database file named Charges. All records that have not been posted are copied to a database file named Temp. Then the UPDATE command performs the update. When updating is complete, the REPLACE ALL command at the bottom of the routine changes the Posted field to .T. in all records in the Charges database.

# DELETING RECORDS

There are many ways to delete records from a database in dBASE. While scrolling through records with the EDIT, CHANGE, APPEND, or BROWSE commands, the user can type Ctrl-U to mark a record for deletion.

Note that typing Ctrl-U does *not* work when editing a record with the READ command. However, a command such as

**@ <row>,<col> SAY DELETED( ) PICTURE "Y"**

will display whether a record is marked for deletion from within a format file. You can also use the DELETE command to mark a record for deletion from within a command file (or from the dot prompt).

There are two levels of deletion in dBASE. First, a record is marked for deletion. At this stage, the record can be hidden from view with the SET DELETED ON command. The record still exists in the database and can be undeleted with the RECALL command. All that really happens is that the hidden DELETED( ) field on the record is declared true, and the record appears with an asterisk to the left of it when displayed with the LIST or DISPLAY command.

At the second level of deletion, the database is *packed*. The PACK command permanently removes records that have been marked for deletion. The disk space used by these records is reclaimed, and records beneath the deleted ones move up a notch.

When providing deletion capabilities to the end user, you should accomplish the following:

1. Minimize the likelihood of a user accidentally deleting a record that should not be deleted.
2. Minimize the excessive time that the PACK command requires.

Figure 11.7 shows a sample program that handles both of these concerns. The program uses the Mail database and Names index file (created using UPPER(LName + FName)) as an example database.

## Pinpointing the Record to Delete

An application program must provide the user with a means of locating a particular record to delete, so the user must be given some means of entering data to identify the record to delete. Then the program should attempt to find that record and display it to the user for verification before deleting it.

If the value that the user enters to identify the record is matched in several records, the program should get further information from the user to pinpoint the exact record to delete. The program in Figure 11.7 demonstrates techniques for allowing a user to isolate an exact record to delete.

The program begins by asking the user for the last name of the individual to edit and storing that name in a variable named Search. If the user enters a name, the following lines attempt to find that name in the Names index file:

```
Search = UPPER(TRIM(Search))
SEEK Search
```

If the name cannot be found, the warning message **Can't Find** is displayed, and the user is asked to try again. If the name is found, the command

```
COUNT WHILE UPPER(LName) = Search TO HowMany
```

counts how many records on the database match the requested name. If more than one record contains the requested last name (IF HowMany > 1), the program displays the records, with the record number in the left column. Then the screen asks for the exact record (by record number) to delete.

As an extra precaution, the statement **IF Recno < = RECCOUNT() .AND. Recno > 0** determines whether the user has entered a valid record number before the program deletes the record. If the record number is not valid, the program displays an error message, no record is marked for deletion, and the user is asked to try again.

If only a single record with the requested last name is found on the database file, this record is displayed and the user is asked whether it should be marked for deletion. If the user answers yes (**IF UPPER(Maybe) = "Y"**), the record is marked for deletion.

```
************************************* MailDel.prg
*-------- Delete data for mail management system.
SET TALK OFF
CLEAR
USE Mail INDEX Names

*------------------- Ask for record or exit.
More = .T.
DO WHILE More
   CLEAR
   Search = SPACE(20)
   @ 10,2 SAY "Enter last name of person to delete "
   @ 12,2 SAY "or <--' to exit " ;
   GET Search
   READ
   *----- If no name entered, done.
   IF Search = " "
      More = .F.
      LOOP
   ENDIF (no name entered)

   *------ Try to find requested record.
   Search = UPPER(TRIM(Search))
   SEEK Search

   *---- Make sure record exists.
   IF .NOT. FOUND()
      @ 20,0 CLEAR
      ? "Can't Find",Search
      ?? CHR(7)
      WAIT "Press any key to try again..."
      LOOP
   ENDIF (not found)

   *-- If found, count and display.
   COUNT WHILE UPPER(LName) = Search TO HowMany
   IF HowMany > 1
      CLEAR
      SEEK Search
      DISPLAY LName, FName WHILE ;
      UPPER(LName) = Search
      Recno = 0
      @ 23,2 SAY "Delete which one (by record number) " ;
      GET Recno PICTURE "9999"
      READ
      IF Recno <= RECCOUNT() .AND. Recno > 0
         DELETE RECORD Recno
      ELSE
         @ 20,0 CLEAR
         @ 22,1 SAY "No such record: "+STR(Recno,4)
         ? CHR(7)
         WAIT "Press any key to try again..."
      ENDIF (valid recno)
   ELSE
      SEEK Search
      CLEAR
      DISPLAY LName, FName, Address
      Maybe = " "
      @ 23,1 SAY "Delete this record? (Y/N) ";
      GET MayBe PICTURE "!"
      READ
      IF UPPER(Maybe) = "Y"
         DELETE
```

**FIGURE 11.7:** A sample program for allowing users to pinpoint records to delete. The user can also decide when to pack the database and is given the opportunity to undelete records that are marked for deletion before they are permanently deleted. If the user does not pack the database, the records that are marked for deletion can be hidden from printed displays with the SET DELETED ON command.

```
      ENDIF (maybe)
   ENDIF (howmany)
ENDDO (More)

*-- Final double-check before permanent deletion.
YorN = " "
CLEAR
@ 5,1 SAY "Permanently remove records marked for deletion now? "
@ 7,1 SAY "(Process may take a few minutes to complete...)";
GET YorN PICTURE "!"
READ
IF YorN # "Y"
   RETURN
ENDIF (YorN)

*-- Count how many records marked for deletion
*-- and store in memory variable No_Dels.
? "Counting... Please wait."
COUNT FOR DELETED() TO No_Dels

Permiss = "N"
DO WHILE Permiss = "N" .AND. No_Dels > 0
   CLEAR
   ?
   DISPLAY LName, FName, Address FOR DELETED()
   ?
   Permiss = " "
   @ 23,5 SAY "Ok to delete all these? (Y/N) " ;
   GET Permiss PICTURE "!"
   READ
   *--- If not OK to delete all, find out which.
   IF Permiss # "Y"
      RecNo = 0
      @ 20,0 CLEAR
      @ 23,5 SAY "Recall which one (record number): ";
      GET RecNo PICT "99999"
      READ
      IF Recno > 0 .AND. Recno <= RECCOUNT()
         GOTO RecNo
         IF DELETED()
            RECALL
            No_Dels = No_Dels - 1
         ENDIF (deleted)
      ELSE
         @ 20,0 CLEAR
         @ 22,1 SAY "No such record: "+STR(RecNo,4)
         ? CHR(7)
         WAIT
      ENDIF (recno)
   ENDIF (permiss # y)
ENDDO (permiss and No_dels)

*--- Pack and return
SET TALK ON
PACK
SET TALK OFF
RETURN
```

**FIGURE 11.7:** A sample program for allowing users to pinpoint records to delete. The user can also decide when to pack the database and is given the opportunity to undelete records that are marked for deletion before they are permanently deleted. If the user does not pack the database, the records that are marked for deletion can be hidden from printed displays with the SET DELETED ON command (continued).

## Letting the User Decide When to Pack

On a large database, packing can be very slow, so the user should have some control over when packing takes place. In applications where disk capacity is not a problem, the system might never need to pack records. Instead, the overall application system can use the SET DELETED ON command to hide records that have been marked for deletion from printed reports.

In the routine identified by the comment * – **Final double-check before permanent deletion**, the sample program in Figure 11.7 presents the option to pack the database when the user has finished selecting records to delete. If the user decides against packing the database at this moment, the routine simply returns control to the calling program.

If the user decides to pack the database, the program first counts how many records are marked for deletion (**COUNT FOR DELETED( ) TO No_Dels**). Then the routine proceeds with the packing process. First, however, it gives the user a chance to recall records that have been marked for deletion. The number stored in the No_Dels variable is used in this process, as discussed in the next section.

## Offering a Chance to Undelete Records

If your application allows the user to pack a database, you might want to offer the user an opportunity to recall records that have been marked for deletion before they are permanently removed from the database file. To do so, you'll need a loop that displays all records marked for deletion and gives the user a chance to recall any of those records.

The program shown in Figure 11.7 demonstrates a routine to provide the user with this chance. As long as the user does not give permission to delete records (Permiss = "N") and there are records marked for deletion on the database (No_Dels > 0), the DO WHILE Permiss = "N" loop at the end of the program displays all records marked for deletion and gives the user an opportunity to recall any record by typing in its record number.

When the user gives permission to permanently remove all records from the database file, the last routine packs the database (and any active index files), showing its progress along the way by temporarily setting the TALK parameter on.

# COMMANDS FOR EDITING AND DELETING RECORDS

The programming techniques above provide some general tips on how to present editing and deleting options to the users of a custom application. The remainder of this chapter discusses the technical details of the individual commands used for editing and deleting records.

## The EDIT Command

EDIT presents a full-screen display of data in a record and allows the user to make changes or mark the record for deletion.

### SYNTAX

**EDIT [<scope>] [FIELDS <field names>];**
**[WHILE <condition>];**
**[FOR <condition>]**

where <scope> is one of the dBASE scope commands (such as RECORD, NEXT, ALL, or REST), <field names> are the names of fields to include (if a format file is not in use), and <condition> is any valid query condition.

### USAGE

EDIT allows multiple records to be edited on a full-screen display. If a format file is not activated with a SET FORMAT command, EDIT will create a simple screen for editing data. The cursor-control keys that EDIT supports are similar to those used by the APPEND command. They are presented in Table 11.1.

If multiple related database files are open, EDIT displays data from the currently selected database, unless a format file with -> aliases specifies fields from the related database file. Generally, the format file should display fields from the nonselected database (using SAY), rather than give the user editing power with the GET command.

If a format file is not in use, pressing the F1 key toggles a help menu on and off.

Any active index files are automatically updated when data are changed on the editing screen. Any inactive index files will need to be updated with the REINDEX or INDEX ON command when editing is complete.

Typing Ctrl-U while a record is displayed by the EDIT command acts as a toggle for deleting and undeleting records.

EDIT will access and display records that are already marked for deletion only if the SET DELETED OFF parameter is in effect. Records that are marked for deletion are displayed with the letters Del in the status bar (or at the top of the screen).

If you attempt to edit a record that is marked for deletion and SET DELETED is on, the record will be invisible to EDIT, and the command will be ignored. Furthermore, if you scroll in EDIT when SET DELETED is on, records that are marked for deletion will not appear.

| KEY | ALTERNATE | EFFECT |
| --- | --- | --- |
| Return | | Finishes data entry in one field and moves cursor to next field |
| F1 | | Toggles help menu on and off (if no format file is in use) |
| NumLock | | Toggles between numbers and arrow keys on numeric keypad |
| → | Ctrl-D | Moves cursor right one character |
| ← | Ctrl-S | Moves cursor left one character |
| Home | Ctrl-A | Moves cursor to previous word, start of field, or previous field, depending on cursor's current position |
| End | Ctrl-F | Moves cursor to next word, end of field, or start of next field, depending on cursor's current position |
| PgUp | Ctrl-R | Scrolls to previous page or record, if any |
| PgDn | Ctrl-C | Scrolls to next page or record, if any; otherwise, exits EDIT mode |
| ↑ | Ctrl-E | Moves cursor to previous field |
| ↓ | Ctrl-X | Moves cursor to next field |
| Ins | Ctrl-V | Toggles insert mode on and off |
| Del | Ctrl-G | Deletes character at cursor |
| Backspace | | Moves cursor to left, erasing character |
| Ctrl-T | | Deletes word to right |
| Ctrl-Y | | Deletes all characters to right |
| Ctrl-U | | Marks record for deletion |
| Esc | Ctrl-Q | Aborts last entry and exits EDIT mode (if a memo field is being entered, aborts current entry and returns to EDIT screen) |
| Ctrl-End | Ctrl-W | Saves entry and exits EDIT mode |
| Ctrl-PgDn | Ctrl-Home | Edits a memo field |
| Ctrl-PgUp | Ctrl-End | Saves a memo field and returns to EDIT screen |

**TABLE 11.1:** Command Keys Used with the EDIT and CHANGE Commands

## EXAMPLES

The command

**EDIT RECORD 22**

edits record number 22 on the database currently in use. The commands

**LOCATE FOR LName = "Miller"**
**EDIT WHILE LName = "Miller"**

locate the first record with the name Miller in the LName field and allow the user to scroll through and edit records with Miller in the LName field. As soon as the user attempts to scroll past the Millers, control is returned to the dot prompt or the next command in the command file.

The commands

**USE Customer**
**EDIT FOR CustNo = 1002**

allow the user to edit the record with the number 1002 in the CustNo field of the Customer database.

The commands

**USE Charges INDEX Date**
**EditDate = CTOD("01/01/87")**
**SEEK EditDate**
**EDIT WHILE Date = EditDate**

use the Charges database with an index file named Date (which in this example is presumably indexed on a field named Date with the date data type). The SEEK command positions the record pointer to the first record with 01/01/87 in the Date field and allows the user to scroll through records with that date.

## TIPS

Use the EDIT command to allow users to edit multiple records. For more control over the user's changes, use the READ command with a format file or @...SAY...GET commands in a program to allow the user to edit one record at a time. Generally, EDIT is not a compilable command. Programmers who wish to compile their applications will need to use READ to allow users to edit records.

## SEE ALSO

BROWSE
READ
SET FORMAT

## The CHANGE Command

CHANGE is identical to EDIT. See EDIT above.

## The BROWSE Command

BROWSE displays a full-screen, spreadsheet-like display of database records for editing.

### SYNTAX

**BROWSE [FIELDS <field names>] [LOCK <columns>];**
**[WIDTH <characters>] [FREEZE <field name>] [NOFOLLOW];**
**[NOAPPEND] [NOMENU]**

where <field names> are the names, in order, of fields to include in the display, <columns> is the number of fields on the left of the screen that will not scroll as the user pans to the right, <characters> is a number representing the maximum width of all columns, and <field name> is the name of the only field that can be edited. The FIELDS, LOCK, WIDTH, FREEZE, NOFOLLOW, NOAPPEND, and NOMENU options are discussed in Table 11.2 below.

### USAGE

BROWSE provides a spreadsheet-like interface for editing data. It displays 17 records at once, with as many fields as will fit across the screen. Command keys for editing and scrolling are virtually identical to those used with the EDIT command (shown in Table 11.1). In addition, Ctrl-← and Ctrl-→ pan the display of fields horizontally across the screen. The F10 key toggles the BROWSE menu bar on and off.

If you scroll the highlight past the bottom of the screen, you will be given the opportunity to add new records.

Any active index files are updated automatically by BROWSE. Furthermore, changing any data in an indexed field immediately re-sorts the BROWSE screen. If the NOFOLLOW option is used in the command line, however, the highlight will not follow the edited record to its new position.

#### COMMAND LINE OPTIONS

The optional portions of the BROWSE command line are summarized in Table 11.2.

| COMMAND LINE OPTION | EFFECT |
|---|---|
| FIELDS | Specifies the names and order of fields to display on the BROWSE screen. Each field name must be separated by a comma. |
| LOCK | Specifies the number of columns to be locked into place on the BROWSE screen. When the user pans to the right, locked columns remain in place on the screen. |
| FREEZE | Specifies the name of the only field that can be edited, even though all other fields are displayed. |
| NOFOLLOW | Normally, if a database file is indexed when the BROWSE command is issued, changing an indexed field automatically re-sorts the database and the BROWSE screen, moving the highlight to the new record position. However, if NOFOLLOW is issued in the BROWSE command, the highlight stays in the same general position after the screen is re-sorted, rather than following the record to its new position on the screen. |
| NOMENU | Prevents the user from having access to the menu bar with the F10 key. |
| WIDTH | Specifies the largest width for any field. Any fields that are narrower than the specified width can be scrolled with the ←, →, Home, and End keys on the BROWSE screen. |
| NOAPPEND | Prevents the user from adding records to the database through the BROWSE screen. |

**TABLE 11.2:** Command Line Options for BROWSE

### Menu Bar Options

The menu at the top of the BROWSE screen, displayed by pressing F10, presents several options for managing the highlight and BROWSE display. These are summarized in Table 11.3.

## EXAMPLES

The command below displays the LName, FName, CustNo, and Amount fields (in that order) from the database currently in use:

```
BROWSE FIELDS LName, FName, CustNo, Amount ;
       FREEZE Amount NOAPPEND
```

| MENU OPTION | CAPABILITY |
|---|---|
| Top | Moves the highlight to the first record in the database file or the first record in the current index order |
| Bottom | Moves the highlight to the last record in the database file or last record in the current index order |
| Lock | Lets you specify the number of columns on the left of the screen to lock into place; panning with Ctrl-← and Ctrl-→ scrolls through unlocked columns only |
| Record No. | Lets you specify a record number to move the highlight to |
| Freeze | Lets you enter the name of a single field to edit data in; all other columns only display data |
| Find | Allows you to enter a value to search for in the indexed field (this option appears only if the database is indexed when the BROWSE command is issued) |

**TABLE 11.3:** Top-Menu Options in the BROWSE Mode

Only the Amount field can be edited, and new records cannot be added to the database file.

The commands below display all fields from the Master database for editing, leaving the two leftmost fields on the screen while the user pans to the right:

```
USE Master INDEX PartNo
BROWSE LOCK 2 NOFOLLOW NOMENU WIDTH 15
```

If the user changes an indexed field, the highlight stays in its current position on the screen (where the record was before automatic re-sorting). The user cannot call up the top menu, and no column occupies more than 15 spaces in the screen.

## TIPS

The BROWSE command with the FIELDS and FREEZE options is particularly useful for presenting a checklist of items to work with on the screen. For example, the command

```
BROWSE FIELDS LName,FName,Address,Paid_Yet;
          FREEZE Paid_Yet WIDTH 20
```

displays the fields LName, FName, Address, and Paid_Yet on the screen, but only the Paid_Yet field can be edited. Nevertheless, the other fields provide useful information for making decisions about how to mark the Paid_Yet field. The

WIDTH portion ensures that the combined four fields do not take up more than 80 character positions on the screen.

When using BROWSE to add new records to a database, pressing PgDn to move to the next new record might make the previous record seem to disappear. (Even though the record cannot be seen, it is still on the database file.) Using ↓ rather than PgDn to move to the next new record will avoid the problem altogether.

### SEE ALSO

EDIT
READ

## The REPLACE Command

REPLACE places new data into a database field.

### SYNTAX

**REPLACE <scope> <field name> WITH <data>;**
**[,<field name> WITH <data>...];**
**[WHILE <condition>] [FOR <condition>]**

where <scope> is a scope command (RECORD, ALL, NEXT, REST), <field name> is the name of the field receiving the new data, <data> is the new data being placed into the field, and <condition> is any valid query condition.

### USAGE

To place a literal data item or data stored in a memory variable directly into a database field, use REPLACE without a scope or query condition. For example, the command

**REPLACE Date_Sold WITH CTOD("12/31/87")**

places the date 12/31/87 directly into a field named Date_Sold. For global replacements, use a scope or query condition. For example, the command

**REPLACE ALL Amount WITH Amount*1.05 FOR Vendor = "ABC"**

increases the Amount field by 5 percent for all records that have the code ABC in the field named Vendor.

The data types on both sides of the WITH command must be the same (that is, you can't replace character data with numeric data). Use the functions to convert data types, if necessary, as discussed in Chapters 15, "Managing Data, Records, and Files," and 17, "dBASE Functions."

If an index file is active and you attempt to perform a global replacement on one of the key fields in the index file, the records will be re-sorted immediately after each individual field replacement. Chances are that this will result in only some of the records being replaced. For this reason, it is best not to perform global REPLACE commands on indexed fields. Instead, perform the replacements without the index file active, then use the SET INDEX and REINDEX commands to activate and update the index files.

If you attempt to replace data in a nonexistent record (for example, when the pointer is at the EOF( ) position), dBASE will not generate an error message. Instead, the command simply does nothing. Make sure the record pointer is at the correct position or issue an APPEND BLANK command, so that the data go into the database.

## EXAMPLE

A single REPLACE command can update several fields at once, as long as the total command line width does not exceed 254 characters. In the example below, the PartNo, Invoice_No, Clerk, and Customer fields are updated simultaneously in the new blank record:

```
APPEND BLANK
REPLACE PartNo WITH MPartNo, ;
        Invoice_No WITH MInvoice, ;
        Clerk WITH MClerk, ;
        Customer WITH MCustomer
```

This technique of including several WITH statements in a single REPLACE command is much faster than using multiple REPLACE commands to perform the same task.

## TIPS

Using REPLACE with the APPEND BLANK command to add records to a database file provides good programmer control over what goes into the database. The REPLACE and APPEND BLANK combination can be used effectively in compiled applications as well. See Chapter 10, "Adding New Data," for some examples.

## SEE ALSO

APPEND BLANK
READ

## The DELETE Command

DELETE marks a record or group of records for deletion.

### SYNTAX

**DELETE <scope> [WHILE <condition>] [FOR <condition>]**

where <scope> is one of the scope commands (RECORD, ALL, NEXT, REST), and <condition> is any valid query condition.

### USAGE

The DELETE command marks a record (or records) for deletion. DELETE affects only the currently selected database file, even if multiple related database files are in use. Records marked for deletion can be hidden from access with the SET DELETED ON command or removed permanently with the PACK command. Records that are marked for deletion can be undeleted with the RECALL command. The DELETED( ) function is true (.T.) when the record pointer is at a record number that is marked for deletion.

The LIST and DISPLAY commands display an asterisk to the left of records that are marked for deletion. The APPEND, EDIT, CHANGE, and BROWSE commands display Del for records that are marked for deletion, either at the top of the screen or on the status bar if SET STATUS in on.

If the record pointer is at the end of the file (EOF( )) when DELETE is executed, the command has no effect.

Global deletions are allowed with the scope and FOR/WHILE commands. For example, the command

**DELETE ALL FOR Paid**

deletes all records that have .T. in the logical field named Paid.

The commands

**GO BOTTOM**
**SKIP −19**
**DELETE REST**

delete the last 20 records from the currently active database.

### EXAMPLE

The commands below attempt to find the database record with 1002 in the indexed field:

**USE Master INDEX Master**
**FindIt = 1002**

**SEEK FindIt**
**DELETE**

If found, the record is marked for deletion.

### TIPS

Using SET DELETED ON to hide records that are marked for deletion is much faster than issuing a PACK command after every deletion.

The FOR DELETED( ) condition accesses only records that are marked for deletion, as long as SET DELETED is off. For example, the command **LIST FOR DELETED( )** displays all records that are marked for deletion when the SET DELETED parameter is off.

The ZAP command is equivalent to but much faster than the DELETE ALL and PACK combination of commands.

Be sure to read about the APPEND FROM command (Chapter 10, "Adding New Data") and the COPY command (Chapter 15, "Managing Data, Records, and Files") for the unique and varied ways in which these commands treat records that are marked for deletion.

### SEE ALSO

DELETED( )
PACK
RECALL
SET DELETED
EDIT
BROWSE
ZAP
APPEND FROM

## The RECALL Command

RECALL reinstates a record that has been marked for deletion with the DELETE command or with Ctrl-U in the APPEND, EDIT, CHANGE, or BROWSE command.

### SYNTAX

**RECALL [<scope>] [WHILE <condition>] [FOR <condition>]**

where <scope> is a dBASE scope command such as RECORD, ALL, NEXT, or REST, and <condition> is any valid query condition.

#### USAGE

To recall a single record, position the pointer to that record and issue the RECALL command. Optionally, use the RECALL RECORD command to specify a particular record (**RECALL RECORD 5**).

To recall several records, use the scope or FOR/WHILE commands. Note that RECALL ALL has no effect if the SET DELETED parameter is on. For safety's sake, it is best to set the SET DELETED command off before issuing a RECALL command.

Even if multiple related database files are in use, RECALL affects only the currently selected database file.

#### EXAMPLES

The command below reinstates records marked for deletion that have February 1987 dates in the Exp_Date field and .T. in the field named Renewed:

```
RECALL ALL FOR MONTH(Exp_Date) = 2 .AND. ;
               YEAR(Exp_Date) = 1987 .AND. ;
               Renewed
```

(Exp_Date is assumed to be the date data type and Renewed the logical data type.)

#### TIPS

Use the LIST (or DISPLAY ALL) FOR DELETED( ) and RECALL commands in your applications to allow users to double-check deleted records before packing a database. The sample program presented earlier in this chapter (Figure 11.7) presents a technique for this.

#### SEE ALSO

DELETED( )
DELETE
SET DELETED
PACK

## The PACK Command

PACK permanently removes records that have been marked for deletion from the database.

## SYNTAX

**PACK**

## USAGE

The PACK command removes records that were marked for deletion, compresses the remaining records into the space those records occupied, and reclaims the disk space occupied by the deleted records.

Only active index files are properly updated during a PACK command. Inactive index files will need to be rebuilt using the REINDEX or INDEX ON command.

Note that the DIR command might still show the original number of records for the database until the database is closed. The RECCOUNT( ) function, however, will display the correct number of records immediately.

When SET TALK is on, the screen displays an odometer of the number of records that are not deleted, as well as odometers of any index files being updated automatically.

PACK affects only the currently selected database file. Any related database files in use are unaffected by the PACK command.

## EXAMPLES

The commands

```
USE Charges INDEX CustNo, Dates
SET TALK ON
PACK
SET TALK OFF
```

permanently remove all records marked for deletion from the Charges database, display the progress, and automatically update the CustNo and Dates index files.

## TIPS

Instead of using a time-consuming PACK command to permanently delete records marked for deletion from a database file, an application program can use SET DELETED ON to hide these records from all displays and calculations.

## SEE ALSO

DELETE
RECALL

ZAP
DISKSPACE( )

## The ZAP Command

ZAP permanently removes *all* records from an active database file but leaves the database structure intact.

### SYNTAX

**ZAP**

### USAGE

ZAP has the same effect as the commands

**DELETE ALL**
**PACK**

but it is much faster. All records are irretrievably deleted from the database file currently in use. The disk space previously occupied by the records is reclaimed. Any active index files are updated automatically.

If SET SAFETY is on, dBASE asks for permission before removing all the records from the database. If SET SAFETY is off, all records are deleted immediately.

### EXAMPLES

In the example below, all the records from the Charges database are appended to the bottom of the database file named History. Then ZAP removes all records from the Charges database. The SET SAFETY OFF command prevents dBASE from asking permission before zapping all the records in Charges.

**SET SAFETY OFF**
**USE History**
**APPEND FROM Charges**
**USE Charges**
**ZAP**

### TIPS

Use ZAP to clear out monthly transaction files after updating.

**SEE ALSO**

DELETE
PACK
SET SAFETY

## SUMMARY

This chapter discussed several basic commands for editing and deleting database records, as well as programming techniques that give the user the power to delete and reinstate records selectively.

*For more information on using format files with the EDIT and CHANGE commands:*

- Chapter 8, "Managing Screen Displays"

*For more information on locating records to delete in a database:*

- Chapter 13, "Searching a Database"

*For more information on scope commands:*

- Chapter 15, "Managing Data, Records, and Files"

*For more examples of the use of REPLACE, DELETE, UPDATE, and other commands in this chapter in conjunction with master-file/transaction-file updating:*

- Chapter 16, "Managing Multiple Database Files"

*For additional information on the FOUND( ), DELETED( ), RECCOUNT( ), EOF( ), and DISKSPACE( ) functions discussed in this chapter:*

- Chapter 17, "dBASE Functions"

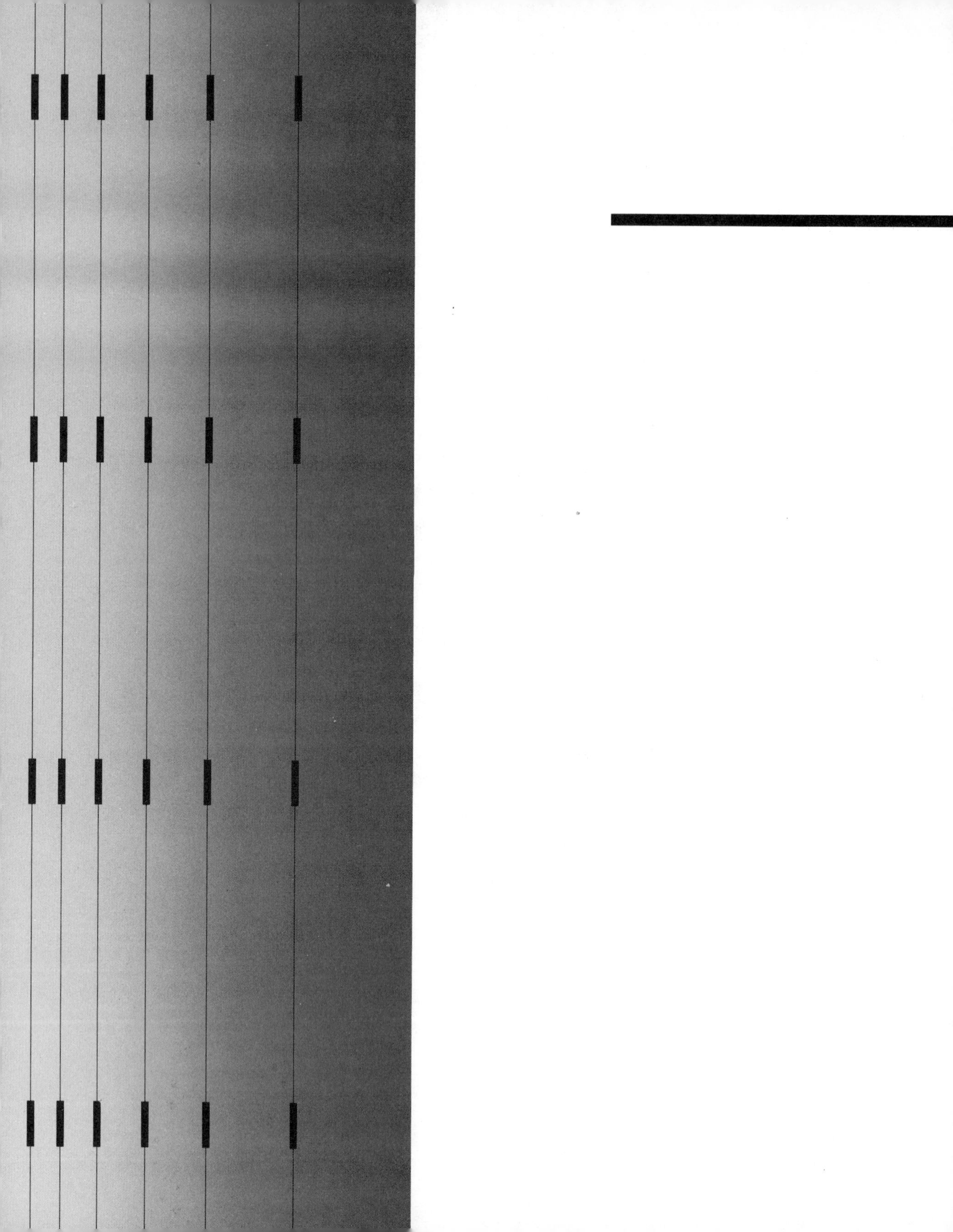

CHAPTER 12

# SORTING AND INDEXING

# SORTING AND INDEXING

In database management, the term *sorting* means to put the records on the database into some meaningful order, such as alphabetically by name, chronologically by date, or perhaps numerically by some amount. This is not to be confused with searching, or *querying,* which involves accessing only records that meet some criterion.

There are four ways to sort database records in dBASE III PLUS:

1. Use the dBASE SORT command to sort the database physically before displaying records.
2. Use the INDEX ON (or REINDEX) command to index the database before displaying the records.
3. Use the LOCATE and INSERT commands to keep the database in sorted order.
4. Use active index files to keep the database in sorted order.

This chapter will discuss the advantages and disadvantages of each of these sorting methods.

## COMPARING THE FOUR DATABASE SORTING TECHNIQUES

Table 12.1 compares the speed of the four database sorting techniques. The processing times assume that the database being sorted has 10,000 records on it and that all sorting takes place on an IBM AT with an 8 Mhz clock. If you are using an IBM PC with floppy disks, your sorting times will be about three or four times longer. Faster computers, such as those with the 80386 processor, will take half as long or less. The comparisons assume that two sort orders are required. Clearly, the use of active index files is by far the fastest. The database used in this example and in the following explanations is named Mail and has the structure shown in Figure 12.1.

| METHOD USED | SORTING TIME |
|---|---|
| SORT command | 1855.8 seconds |
| INDEX ON command | 319.8 seconds |
| LOCATE and INSERT commands | 373.8 seconds |
| APPEND with active index files | 1.0 second |

**TABLE 12.1:** Comparison of Times Required to Maintain Two Sort Orders after Entering Records onto a Database

```
Structure for database: Mail.dbf

Field  Field Name  Type       Width    Dec

    1  Mr_Mrs      Character      4
    2  FName       Character     15
    3  MI          Character      2
    4  LName       Character     20
    5  Company     Character     40
    6  Address     Character     25
    7  City        Character     20
    8  State       Character      5
    9  Zip         Character     10
   10  Country     Character     12
   11  Phone       Character     10
   12  Phone_Ext   Character      4
   13  Hire_Date   Date           8
   14  Salary      Numeric       12      2
   15  Paid_Yet    Logical        1
```

**FIGURE 12.1:** The structure of the Mail database used for sorting comparisons in this chapter. Sorting times assume that the database has 10,000 records on it and that all processing is on an IBM AT with an 8 Mhz clock.

# Using the SORT Command to Sort

If you were to append a record to your database (with the APPEND command) and re-sort it using SORT commands, it would take about 31 minutes to complete both sorts. In the case of the Mail database, the two sort orders are name and zip code. The following commands sort the Mail database:

**SORT ON LName, FName /C TO NameOrd**
**SORT ON Zip TO ZipOrder**

## Using the INDEX Command to Sort

If you were to add a record to your database (with the APPEND command) and then create index files for displaying the records in sorted order, the total processing time for both sorts would be about 5.3 minutes. The following commands index the Mail database:

```
INDEX ON UPPER(LName + FName) TO NameOrd
INDEX ON Zip TO ZipOrder
```

## Using the LOCATE and INSERT Commands to Sort

You can maintain a single sort order on your database by using the LOCATE command to find the proper position for the new record to add and then using the INSERT BEFORE command to insert the new record. For example, if the Mail database were already sorted into zip code order, you could use the commands below to insert a new record into its proper sort position:

```
LOCATE FOR Zip > = "91234"
INSERT BEFORE
```

The time required for dBASE to adjust all records varies, depending on where the insertion takes place. A worst-case situation on the 10,000 record database (where the record is inserted near the top of the file) takes over six minutes.

## Sorting Automatically

If your database already has index files, you can just leave them active while adding the new records. dBASE automatically re-sorts any active index files, and it does so quickly. For example, if the NameOrd and ZipOrder index files have already been created using the INDEX ON command, the commands below will add a new record and automatically re-sort both files:

```
USE Mail INDEX NameOrd,ZipOrder
APPEND
```

There will be about a one-second delay between each added record to instantly re-sort the index files.

As long as the NameOrd index is listed first, any commands that display data will do so in alphabetical order by name. To display records in zip code order, simply reverse the order of the index files in the USE command (or use the SET INDEX or SET ORDER commands discussed in Chapter 18, "Setting Parameters"). Commands that display records always use the order specified by the first-listed index file.

Even though the processing times support the use of active index files for maintaining sort orders, there are situations where it may not be the preferred method. For one, dBASE allows a maximum of seven index files to be active at once. If your application requires more than seven sort orders, the additional orders will need to be maintained by one of the other techniques.

A second situation where active index files might not be the preferred sorting technique is when the database becomes very large, and there are several active index files. The delay between records while entering and editing records may become quite long in such a situation. If this occurs, you may want to leave the index files inactive while entering and editing records. Then, when all of the data entry or editing is complete, use REINDEX to update the index files. Chapter 10, "Adding New Data," shows several examples of using REINDEX after entering new records.

# MANAGING INDEX FILES

dBASE does not automatically keep track of all index files and keep them updated. It is up to the programmer to keep index files from becoming corrupted by making sure that all index files are active whenever database records are added, changed, or deleted. To do so, use the INDEX command in the USE command when opening the database, or use the SET INDEX command.

For example, assuming you've already used the INDEX ON command to create the index files NameOrd and ZipOrder for the Mail database (set up in Figure 12.1), either of the commands below will open (activate) both index files with the Mail database:

**USE Mail INDEX NameOrd,ZipOrder**

or

**USE Mail**
**SET INDEX TO NameOrd,ZipOrder**

Any commands that alter data, including APPEND, INSERT, EDIT, CHANGE, BROWSE, READ, DELETE, and PACK, will automatically update *both* index files.

The first listed index file, NameOrd in this example, is the *master* or *controlling* index file. Any command that displays records will use the sort order determined by the master index file. Furthermore, the SEEK and FIND commands work only with the master index file.

If you create an index file with the INDEX ON command and then forget to activate that index file before altering data with an APPEND, EDIT,

CHANGE, READ, or some other command, the original index file will be corrupted. Before using it again, you will have to rebuild it using INDEX ON or REINDEX.

You must be especially careful that your application program does not corrupt index files. Once you decide which index files will be used regularly throughout a system, you must make sure that those index files are *always* active when the user is adding, changing, or deleting data. Otherwise, the end user will have repeated problems with corrupted index files, and you will get a lot of phone calls.

## Presenting Sort Options to the User

In many applications, you will want to present a simple menu of options to the user for selecting a sort order in which to display data. This frees the user from having to know anything at all about the various dBASE commands and syntax involved in sorting. Figure 12.2 shows a sample routine that presents such a menu and sets up the sort order accordingly. Note that in the example, only the NameOrd and ZipOrder index files are assumed to exist already. If the user opts to sort by date, a temporary index file named Temp.ndx is created on the spot. If the user selects the original (unsorted) order, all index files are closed.

After the user selects a menu option and the DO CASE clause sets up the appropriate sort order, any commands that display records (LIST, DISPLAY, REPORT) or any DO WHILE loop with @ or ? commands will display records in the order chosen by the user. The sample program shows where these commands would be placed.

Before passing control back to the calling program, this program reactivates the NameOrd and ZipOrder index files. This is so future commands that add, edit, or delete data on the database file will also keep these two index files up to date. In this example, the date order is rarely used. Therefore, the programmer decided to have the system create the date index "on-the-fly" as needed.

## Complex Indexing Expressions

A thorough understanding of data types and data type conversions is essential to successful indexing. This section presents techniques for converting and combining data types in indexing expressions.

### Indexing Character Fields

To index a database by a character expression, you should convert all letters to uppercase (in the index file only) so that upper- and lowercase distinctions do not affect the sort order. Use the UPPER function to do so. The example below

```
*********************************** SortMenu.prg
*----------- Display a menu of sorting options.
USE Mail INDEX NameOrd,ZipOrder
CLEAR
TEXT
               Select a Sort Order

              1. Alphabetical by name

              2. Zip code for bulk mailing

              3. Chronological by date hired

              4. Original unsorted order

ENDTEXT
SortOpt = 0
@ 22,10 SAY "Select an option (1-4) ";
        GET SortOpt PICTURE "@Z 9" RANGE 1,4
        READ

CLEAR
DO CASE

   *-------- Name order.
   CASE SortOpt = 1
        SET ORDER TO 1
   *-------- Zip code order.
   CASE SortOpt = 2
        SET ORDER TO 2
   *-------- Date order (needs to be created).
   CASE SortOpt = 3
        SET SAFETY OFF
        CLOSE INDEX
        @ 10,10 SAY "Please wait a moment..."
        SET TALK ON
        INDEX ON Hire_Date TO Temp
        SET TALK OFF
        CLEAR
   *-------- Original, unsorted order.
   CASE SortOpt = 4
        CLOSE INDEX

ENDCASE

*******************************************
* Any data displayed here, by any command *
* or routine, will be displayed in the    *
* requested order.                        *
*******************************************

*----- Reactivate original index files.
USE Mail INDEX NameOrd,ZipOrder

RETURN
```

**FIGURE 12.2:** This sample routine allows the user to select a sort order from a menu. Note that before passing control back to the calling program, this sample routine reinstates the index files that are maintained automatically by the custom application.

creates an index file named NameOrd by combining the last and first name and converting them to uppercase:

**INDEX ON UPPER(LName + FName) TO NameOrd**

To use a SEEK or FIND command with this index file, the value being searched for must be in uppercase, as in the examples below:

```
FIND SMITH

LookFor = "Smith"
SEEK UPPER(LookFor)
```

## Indexing Numeric Fields

If a file is to be indexed on a single numeric field, there is no need to convert the numeric data to another data type. For example, in the command below, CustNo is assumed to be a numeric field:

```
INDEX ON CustNo TO CustNumb
```

If, however, you wish to combine numeric fields or combine numeric data with character data, the numbers must be converted to character strings. In the example below, both ProdNo and Unit_Price are numeric fields, but because they are combined in the indexing expression, both must be converted to character strings:

```
INDEX ON STR(ProdNo,4) + STR(Unit_Price,9,2);
         TO AnyFile
```

If you did not convert the fields above to character strings, dBASE would still accept the expression. However, rather than sorting items into part number order and then by unit price within part number, the index file would contain the sum of the part number and unit price fields on each record (i.e., ProdNo + Unit_Price).

To combine a numeric field with a character field, convert the number to a character string using the STR function. The command line below sorts records by last and first names, and then by total sale within each name:

```
INDEX ON UPPER(LName + FName) + STR(Tot_Sale,9,2);
         TO AnyFile
```

## Indexing Date Fields

If a date is the only field in an index file, there is no need to convert it. For example, the command

```
INDEX ON Hire_Date TO AnyFile
```

will properly place the dates on a database file into chronological order, even if dates outside the twentieth century have been entered with the SET CENTURY parameter on.

To combine multiple dates or combine dates with other data types in the indexing expression, you'll need to use the DTOC (date-to-character) function to convert the date data to character data. Doing so directly, however, has one major negative effect: it sorts the dates by months, and by years within months. Hence, January 1987 will be listed before February 1986.

There are two ways around this problem. The first is to use the SET DATE ANSI command to change the data format from mm/dd/yy to yy.mm.dd. In the commands below, the data will be sorted in proper date order, with names alphabetized within identical dates:

**SET DATE ANSI**
**INDEX ON DTOC(Hire_Date) + UPPER(LName) TO AnyFile**

To look up a date in this index file with the SEEK or FIND command, you must perform the same conversion. The commands in Figure 12.3 present an example of using SEEK to find a date stored in a variable named Search.

The routine involves several steps, because the date to search for is first entered as a plain character string in the familiar mm/dd/yy format. Then the CTOD function and SET DATE ANSI command convert that string to the date data type in the ANSI format. However, because the index file contains the character equivalent of the ANSI date, the SEEK DTOC(Search) command also converts its ANSI format date to character data.

Incidentally, to convert the routine above to one capable of handling four-digit centuries, be sure to use the SET CENTURY ON command before creating the

```
*-- Initialize date as eight characters.
MDate = SPACE(8)
*------- Ask for date in mm/dd/yy format.
SET DATE AMERICAN
@ 10,10 SAY "Enter date to search for ";
        GET MDate PICTURE "99/99/99"
READ
*----------- Convert date to ANSI format.
Search = CTOD(MDate)
SET DATE ANSI
*---- Seek character string of ANSI date.
SEEK DTOC(Search)
```

**FIGURE 12.3:** A small routine demonstrating a technique that allows a user to locate a particular date in an index file. The routine assumes that the database was indexed after a SET DATE ANSI command was issued to convert the date to yy.mm.dd format, and the date was also converted to the character data type.

index file. Then change the command **MDate = SPACE(8)** to **MDate = SPACE(10)**, and change the **PICTURE "99/99/99"** command to **PICTURE "99/99/9999"**.

The second way to sort dates that must be converted to character strings is to use the STR, YEAR, DAY, and MONTH functions to rearrange the date. The commands below create an index file with the dates properly sorted and names alphabetized within identical dates:

```
SET DATE AMERICAN
INDEX ON STR(YEAR(Hire_Date),4) + ;
         STR(MONTH(Hire_Date),2) + ;
         STR(DAY(Hire_Date),2) + ;
         UPPER(LName) TO AnyFile
```

The date is stored in the index file in the format "19870131" (where the date is January 31, 1987).

To seek or find an item in this index file, the data entered by the user must be in the same format as the date in the index file. The routine in Figure 12.4 shows an example where the user enters a date in mm/dd/yy format, and the routine converts it to yyyymmdd format.

## Indexing Logical Fields

Technically speaking, you cannot index directly on a logical field. However, you can use the IIF function to convert the logical data type to the character data

```
*-- Initialize date as eight characters.
MDate = SPACE(10)
*----- Ask for date in mm/dd/yyyy format.
SET DATE AMERICAN
@ 10,10 SAY "Enter date to search for ";
        GET MDate PICTURE "99/99/9999"
READ
*------------ Convert to date data type.
AmDate = CTOD (MDate)
*- Convert to yyyymmdd character string.
Search = STR(YEAR(AmDate),4)+;
         STR(MONTH(AmDate),2)+;
         STR(DAY(AmDate),2)
SEEK Search
```

**FIGURE 12.4:** A sample routine that allows the user to enter a date to search for in an index file. In this example, centuries are included in the dates, and the date is converted to a character string in yyyy/mm/dd format in the index file. Therefore, this routine also converts the date that the user wants to locate into a character string in yyyy/mm/dd format.

type in the index file, as below:

```
INDEX ON IIF(Paid_Yet,"YES","NO ") TO AnyFile
```

This assumes that the Paid_Yet field is the logical data type, and it results in an index file in which the .F. values in the Paid_Yet field will appear before the .T. values. Note that the "NO " value is padded with an extra space to keep the index key of uniform width.

To process only records with .T. in the Paid_Yet field, you could use an algorithm like the one below:

```
FIND YES
DO WHILE Paid_Yet
     <commands>
     SKIP
ENDDO
```

To display all records with .F. in the Paid_Yet field, you could use the routine below:

```
FIND NO
LIST WHILE .NOT. Paid_Yet
```

To combine a logical field with others using the IIF function, be sure all expressions result in character strings. For example, to index on the logical field Paid_Yet and the character field LName, enter a command like the one below:

```
INDEX ON IIF(Paid_Yet,"YES","NO ") + UPPER(LName);
             TO AnyFile
```

Again, a search string with the FIND or SEEK command must match this format to be successful, as shown in the routine below:

```
MPaid = .F.
MLName = "Jones"
Search = IIF(MPaid,"YES","NO ") + UPPER(MLName)
SEEK Search
```

## Descending Index Sorts

INDEX does not offer a simple toggle for descending sort orders, but you can index on a negative or inverse expression to achieve the same result. For example, for a descending index based on a numeric Salary field, place a minus sign in front of the field name, as in the command below:

```
INDEX ON -Salary TO AnyFile
```

In the AnyFile index file, records will be displayed in descending salary order.

If you want to combine the numeric field with another type of field, you'll need to use an inverse, rather than a negative, number when converting the number to a character string. In the example below, each salary is subtracted from a large number, converted to character data, and then linked to the LName field in the index key:

**INDEX ON STR(999999999 – Salary) + UPPER(LName) TO AnyFile**

The result is an index sorted in descending salary order, with last names listed alphabetically within each identical salary.

To index in descending order by date, subtract the date from a large date such as 12/31/1999. The command below presents an example:

**INDEX ON CTOD("12/31/1999") – Hire_Date TO AnyFile**

If you need to combine the date with another field, place the entire expression inside an STR (number-to-string) function, as shown in the command below:

**INDEX ON STR(CTOD("12/31/1999") – Hire_Date) + ;**
**UPPER(LName) TO AnyFile**

As usual, you'll need to make sure that a SEEK or FIND expression performs the same conversion. For example, to locate the first record with the date January 1, 1986 in the Date_Hired field, you would need to use the expression

**SEEK STR(CTOD("12/31/1999") – CTOD("01/01/1986"))**

There is no simple way to index a character field in descending order. The best you can do is index on the negative ASCII code value, as shown below:

**INDEX ON –ASC(LName) TO Names**

Unfortunately, the –ASC(LName) expression operates only on the first letter of the name. Therefore, even though all the Zs will be listed before the Ys, the names beginning with Z might not be in proper reverse alphabetical order (e.g., Zastro might be listed before Zygoat).

If for some reason you want to display an entire database file in reverse order (from last record to first), you can index on the negative value of the record number, as below:

**INDEX ON –RECNO( ) TO Backward**

## COMMANDS TO SORT AND INDEX

The remainder of this chapter discusses the SORT, INDEX, and REINDEX commands in more detail. To make complete use of index files, however, be sure to read Chapter 13, "Searching a Database," as well. The FIND and SEEK commands discussed there work only with active index files.

## The SORT Command

SORT copies records from the current database to a new database in a specified sort order.

### SYNTAX

**SORT <scope> TO [<file name>] ON <field> [/A] [/C] [/D];**
**[, <additional fields...> [/A] [/C] [D] ];**
**[WHILE <condition>] [FOR <condition>]**

where <scope> is a valid scope option such as NEXT or REST, <file name> is the name of the file to store the sorted records on, <field> is the name of the primary sort field, <additional fields> are optional fields separated with commas, and <condition> is any valid query condition.

### USAGE

Up to 10 fields can be included in the sort. Fields should be listed from left to right in order of importance. For example, the command

**SORT ON LName, FName, City TO Alpha**

puts records into last name order and then into first name order within identical last names. Within identical last and first names, records are sorted by city.

Records must be sorted to a separate, unopened database file with the SORT command. A database file cannot be sorted to itself. The newly created database will have the .dbf extension unless you provide another one.

If SET SAFETY is on and you attempt to sort to an existing database file, dBASE will ask for permission to overwrite the existing file. If SET SAFETY is off, dBASE will automatically overwrite the existing file.

The /A, /C, and /D options can be used with each field name. /A specifies ascending order (small to large), and /D specifies descending order (large to small). If no order is specified, ascending order is used. The /C toggle ignores upper- and lowercase distinctions. Two options can be combined for a single field, as in the LName field below:

**SORT ON LName/AC, Amount/D TO NewFile**

The sort order above will produce a sort order with names from the LName field in ascending order (ignoring case distinctions), and the numeric Amount field in descending order, as below:.

**Adams 9999.99**
**ADAMS 876.54**
**Adams 34.56**
**Baker 1234.11**
**BAKER 12.11**
**Baker –123.45**

SORT does not support memo fields or logical fields. Similarly, substrings and other expressions are not allowed with field names.

### EXAMPLES

The commands below create a database file named DateOrd that contains records with the year 1987 in the Hire_Date field:

```
USE Mail
SORT ON Hire_Date/D, LName/AC, FName/AC TO DateOrd;
     FOR YEAR(Hire_Date) = 1987
```

The records on DateOrd.dbf are listed in descending order by date (from December 31, 1987 to January 1, 1987), with names listed in ascending alphabetical order within each date. Upper- and lowercase distinctions are ignored.

### TIPS

For a much faster way to organize database records, see the INDEX command.

The SORT command cannot reliably sort databases with more than 32,000 records.

### SEE ALSO

INDEX

## The INDEX Command

INDEX creates an index file for rapid sorting and searching.

### SYNTAX

**INDEX ON <field expression> TO <file name> [UNIQUE]**

where <field expression> specifies the indexing key and <file name> is the name of the index file to build.

## USAGE

An INDEX command does not physically alter the order of the database file, so each record retains it original record number. Instead, INDEX creates a smaller file that is conceptually similar to the index in a book. The index file contains the keys, in sorted order, and the record numbers (just as a book index contains topics in sorted order and page numbers). When you display records with an index file active, dBASE uses the order specified in the index file.

The INDEX ON command creates a new index file with the name specified to the right of the TO command. dBASE supplies the default extension .ndx.

The *key* (or the field to be indexed) can be a single field or any combination of fields, as long as the combined width does not exceed 100 characters and the expression evaluates to a single data type. You cannot index on memo fields, nor can you index directly on logical fields.

The INDEX ON command only creates index files; it does not guarantee that the index files will be properly maintained. It is the programmer's responsibility to maintain index files by ensuring that all index files are active whenever database records are added, edited, or deleted by the user. To activate existing index files, use the INDEX option in the USE command, as in the example below, where Datafile is the name of the database file, and the IndFile files are names of existing index files:

**USE DataFile INDEX Indfile1,IndFile2,IndFile3,IndFile4**

The SET INDEX command also opens index files for a database. The commands below are equivalent to the USE command above:

**USE DataFile**
**SET INDEX TO Indfile1,IndFile2,IndFile3,IndFile4**

Up to seven index files can be opened simultaneously. The first index file is the master, or controlling, index file. It is this index file that determines the sort order of the data being displayed, and it is also the only index file in which a SEEK or FIND command will operate.

Failure to include an index file in a USE or SET INDEX command will cause the missing index file to be corrupted the next time records are added, changed, or deleted. The index file must be rebuilt with either the INDEX ON or REINDEX commands.

The UNIQUE option deletes duplicate records from the index file. For example, if you entered the command

**INDEX ON UPPER(State) TO AnyFile UNIQUE**
**LIST**

you would see only one record from each state (in alphabetical order, of course).

The effect of the UNIQUE option is identical to that of the SET UNIQUE command.

### EXAMPLE

The command

```
USE Charges
INDEX ON PartNo TO ChrgNx1
INDEX ON Date_Sold TO ChrgNx2
```

creates two index files named ChrgNx1 and ChrgNx2. The first contains the PartNo field, and the second contains the Date_Sold field.

The command below opens the Charges database and activates the ChrgNx1 and ChrgNx2 index files:

```
USE Charges INDEX ChrgNx1,ChrgNx2
```

Any command that displays records will display them in PartNo order. Any commands that modify the database will automatically update both the ChrgNx1 and ChrgNx2 index files.

### TIPS

The DISPLAY STATUS command displays all currently active index files as well as their key expressions.

Never use TRIM( ), LTRIM( ), or RTRIM( ) in an index key expression; doing so disrupts the sort order and produces key expressions of varying widths.

Be sure to read about the SEEK and FIND commands in Chapter 13, "Searching a Database," to take full advantage of the high-speed performance of index files.

### SEE ALSO

USE
REINDEX
FIND
SEEK
SET INDEX
SET ORDER

## The REINDEX Command

REINDEX rebuilds corrupted index files.

#### SYNTAX

**REINDEX**

#### USAGE

Index files that are not active when records on a database are added, changed, or deleted will become corrupted and unreliable. To rebuild the index files, open the database file and all index files, and issue a REINDEX command.

#### EXAMPLES

The commands below rebuild the corrupted NameOrd and ZipOrder index files for the Mail database:

```
USE Mail INDEX NameOrd, ZipOrder
REINDEX
```

#### TIPS

You might want to include a routine in custom applications that allows the user to rebuild corrupted index files without any assistance. (See Chapter 23, "Foreign and Damaged Files.")

#### SEE ALSO

INDEX

## SUMMARY

This chapter discussed numerous techniques for displaying database records in sorted order. The INDEX command, which is the one generally used for maintaining sort orders, was the primary focus. Index files are also invaluable for searching for data, as Chapter 13 discusses.

*For more information on the FIND and SEEK commands for searching index files:*

- Chapter 13, "Searching a Database"

*For more information on manipulating data types:*

- Chapter 15, "Managing Data, Records, and Files"

*For a discussion of the UPPER, STR, DTOC, CTOD, and other functions:*

- Chapter 17, "dBASE Functions"

*For discussions of the SET INDEX and SET ORDER commands:*

- Chapter 18, "Setting Parameters"

*For more technical information on the structure and size of index files:*

- Chapter 23, "Foreign and Damaged Files"

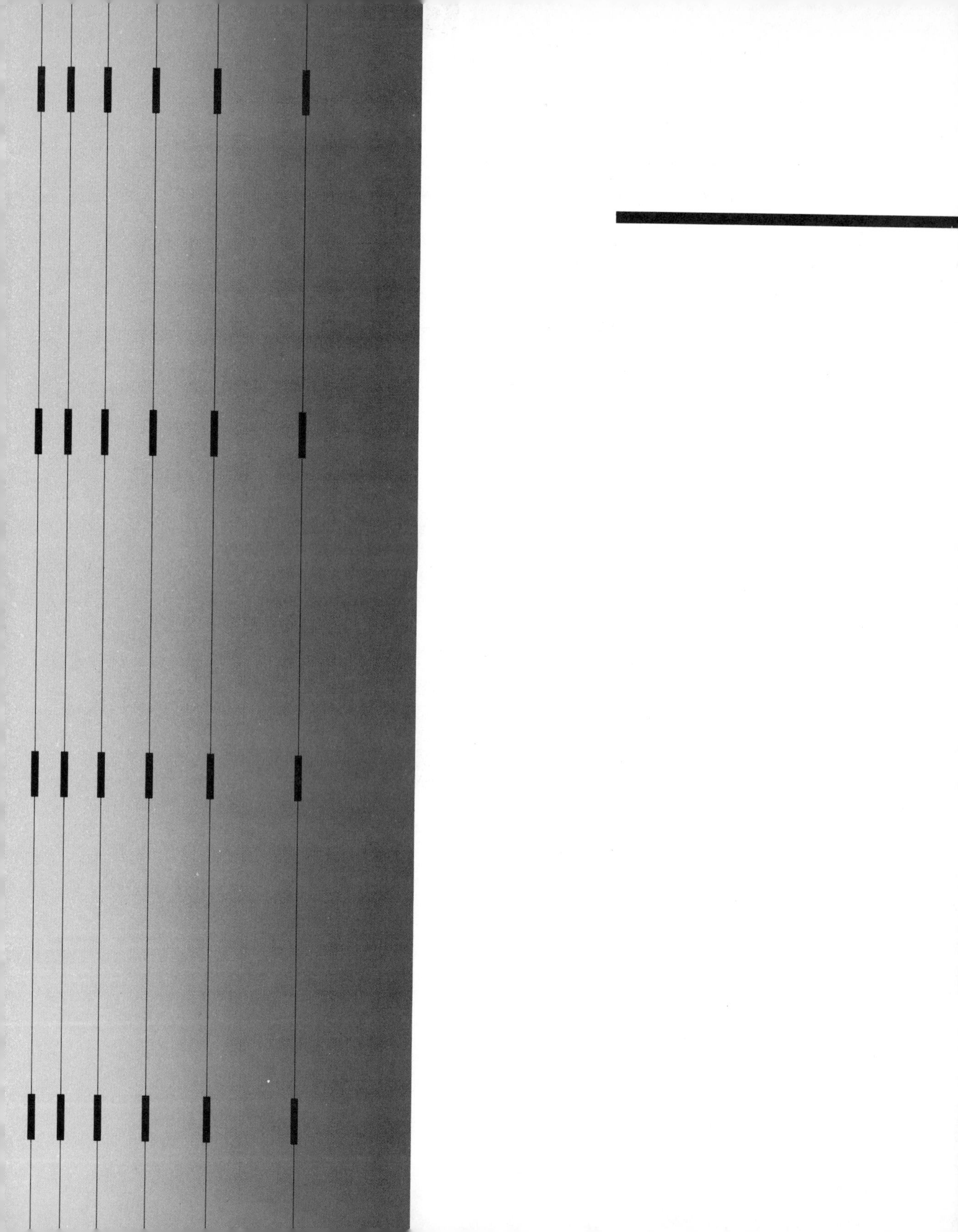

# SEARCHING A DATABASE

# SEARCHING A DATABASE

dBASE offers many techniques for searching, or *querying,* a database, including the LOCATE, FIND, and SEEK commands, the SET FILTER and MODIFY QUERY commands, and the FOR, WHILE, and various scope options that can be used with commands that display or copy data. This chapter discusses these various commands as they pertain to the programmer and custom applications.

## SEARCHING FOR A SINGLE RECORD

The three commands generally used for locating a particular record are LOCATE, FIND, and SEEK. The LOCATE command searches the actual disk file for a value you specify, while FIND and SEEK search an index file.

As you can see in Table 13.1, LOCATE is much slower than either the FIND or SEEK command. Furthermore, while increasing the number of records to search by a factor of ten has a major impact on the LOCATE command, it has no noticeable effect on FIND or SEEK. However, if the field you are searching is not indexed, you have to use the LOCATE command to search for specific records. (All time measurements for the table were taken on an IBM AT with an 8 Mhz clock.)

## Using LOCATE

The LOCATE command can locate a single record that matches any search criteria. LOCATE does not require any index files, but it will use the order specified by the index file when locating the first record that matches the search criterion you specify.

| LOOKUP TECHNIQUE | 1,000th RECORD | 10,000th RECORD |
|---|---|---|
| LOCATE | 6 seconds | 74 seconds |
| FIND/SEEK | 1 second | 1 second |

**TABLE 13.1:** Lookup Times for the LOCATE Command versus the FIND/SEEK Commands

LOCATE does not actually display any data. Instead, it just positions the record pointer to the first record in the database that matches the search criteria. To view the data LOCATE finds, you can use the DISPLAY command. To edit the data LOCATE finds, you can use the EDIT command, or the READ command with a format file.

The general syntax for the LOCATE command is

**LOCATE FOR <condition>**

where the condition is any valid dBASE search criterion. For example, the command below attempts to position the record pointer to the first record in the currently open database that has Miller in the field named LName.

**LOCATE FOR LName = "Miller"**

When you enter this command, dBASE starts at the top of the database file and reads each record until it finds the one with Miller. If the command finds such a record, it stops processing with the record pointer at that record. If it does not find a record with Miller in it, it stops processing with the record pointer at the end-of-file (EOF( )) position.

The LOCATE command supports all of the dBASE operators. Therefore, a command such as

```
LOCATE FOR UPPER(LName) = "SMITH" .AND. ;
           (State = "CA" .OR. State = "NY")
```

will find the first record with Smith in the LName field and either California or New York in the State field.

## Using FIND or SEEK

If the file is indexed and the index file is active, you can search the master (first-listed) index file using either the FIND or SEEK command. Both FIND and SEEK are very fast, because they search a binary tree structure stored in RAM. Neither command, however, can support relational operators (such as <, >, #) or logical operators (such as .AND. or .OR.).

In the commands below, the NameOrd index file was created with the command **INDEX ON UPPER(LName + FName) TO NameOrd**. Because NameOrd is the first-listed index file in the USE command, the FIND command can attempt to find the name Miller in the NameOrd index file:

```
USE Mail INDEX NameOrd, ZipOrder
FIND MILLER
```

The SEEK command also searches for data in an index file, but it can be used with memory variables and functions. For example, in the routine below, the

SEEK command attempts to find the name MILLER in the index file. The name Miller is stored in the memory variable named LookFor, and the UPPER function converts Miller to uppercase:

```
USE Mail INDEX NameOrd,ZipOrder
LookFor = "Miller"
SEEK UPPER(LookFor)
```

## SEARCHING FOR GROUPS OF RECORDS

There are several basic techniques for isolating groups of records. First, the FOR and WHILE options can be used with many commands that display and copy data to isolate records that meet some criterion. The dBASE commands listed in Table 13.2 allow the use of the FOR and WHILE options to specify search criteria.

For example, the command below counts how many records have "CA" in a field named State:

```
COUNT FOR State = "CA" TO HowMany
```

The command below displays records that have the number 1001 in the PartNo field and the current date in the field named Date_Sold, using a report format named AnyRep:

```
REPORT FORM AnyRep FOR PartNo = 1001 .AND. ;
                    Date_Sold = DATE( )
```

(For the exact syntax of these commands refer to the command index at the back of the book).

| | | |
|---|---|---|
| APPEND FROM* | DISPLAY | REPLACE |
| AVERAGE | EDIT | REPORT FORM |
| CHANGE | JOIN | SORT |
| COPY TO | LABEL FORM | SUM |
| COUNT | LIST | TOTAL |
| DELETE | LOCATE | |
| *Supports only the FOR option | | |

**TABLE 13.2:** Commands That Support the FOR and WHILE Options

Both the FOR and WHILE options support all dBASE operators and functions and allow search criteria of any complexity (as long as the entire command line length does not exceed 254 characters). The FOR and WHILE options are perhaps the most commonly used searching techniques in dBASE.

The SET FILTER command (and related MODIFY QUERY command) define a query condition and hide all records that do not match that criterion. These records are hidden from all dBASE commands until the filter is removed. The SET FILTER and MODIFY QUERY commands offer some ease of use to the programmer, but they are slower than FOR and WHILE.

Other commands identify the *scope* of a search in a database (e.g., RECORD, ALL, NEXT, REST). These, however, deal with groups of adjacent records on a database file, not necessarily records that meet some general search condition. Chapter 15, "Managing Data, Records, and Files," discusses these scope conditions in more detail.

To help you determine the most efficient technique for displaying (and analyzing) records that meet a search criterion, the rest of this section compares four techniques: FOR, SET FILTER, LOCATE and CONTINUE, and FIND and WHILE. The following examples show how efficiently each approach can display 100 records out of 10,000 in the sample Mail database (whose structure is shown in Figure 13.1). The Mail database has an index file named NameOrd, which was created with the command

**INDEX ON UPPER(LName + FName) TO NameOrd**

```
Structure for database: Mail.dbf

Field  Field Name  Type       Width    Dec

    1  Mr_Mrs      Character      4
    2  FName       Character     15
    3  MI          Character      2
    4  LName       Character     20
    5  Company     Character     40
    6  Address     Character     25
    7  City        Character     20
    8  State       Character      5
    9  Zip         Character     10
   10  Country     Character     12
   11  Phone       Character     10
   12  Phone_Ext   Character      4
   13  Hire_Date   Date           8
   14  Salary      Numeric       12      2
   15  Paid_Yet    Logical        1
```

**FIGURE 13.1:** Structure of the Mail database. Searching times in this section were calculated using a database with this structure and 10,000 records. 100 records (spaced exactly 100 records apart) had Miller in the LName field. Each technique displayed all the Millers in the database. In one example, the NameOrd index file was used, which was based on the key expression UPPER(LName + FName).

The goal of the search is to display all records that have Miller in the LName field. Of the 10,000 records on the database, exactly 100 have Miller in the LName field. These are spaced exactly 100 records apart. The processing times were calculated on an IBM AT with an 8 Mhz clock and a 30 MB hard disk. Table 13.3 summarizes the searching times for the four techniques.

## The FOR Approach

Probably the most common technique used to isolate groups of records is the FOR option used with dBASE commands that access multiple database records. This method is generally the first one dBASE users learn (because it is the easiest and can be used without index files and without any programming).

For example, suppose you want to display all records in the Mail database that have Miller in the LName field. The commands below will do the trick:

```
USE Mail
LIST FOR LName = "Miller"
```

This technique uses the brute-force method of moving the record pointer to the top of the database, reading each and every record on the database file, and rejecting those that do not have Miller in the LName field. Hence, it requires 10,000 disk accesses to display 100 records. The time required is about 1 minute and 32 seconds.

The FOR option always uses this technique to access records that meet some search criterion, regardless of the command you use with FOR (e.g., REPORT, COPY, APPEND FROM, EDIT, and so forth). While using the FOR option is certainly not the fastest technique for isolating a group of similar database records, it is one of the most flexible, because it does not require the use of index files and can be used with any fields in the database.

| TECHNIQUE | PROCESSING TIME |
|---|---|
| LIST FOR | 92 seconds |
| SET FILTER | 94 seconds |
| LOCATE...CONTINUE | 134 seconds |
| FIND...WHILE | 34 seconds |

**TABLE 13.3:** Comparison of Searching Times for the Four Searching Techniques

## The SET FILTER Approach

The SET FILTER command defines a filter to be used by all subsequent dBASE commands. For example, to isolate the Millers in the Mail database with SET FILTER, the commands below are used:

```
USE Mail
SET FILTER TO LName = "Miller"
LIST
```

This command, like FOR, requires that every record in the database be accessed and compared to the filter condition. Those that do not meet the filtering criteria are ignored. Processing time using this technique is about 1 minute and 34 seconds.

## The LOCATE and CONTINUE Approach

The LOCATE and CONTINUE commands can be used with a DO WHILE loop to display all records that meet a search criterion, as in the example below:

```
USE Mail
LOCATE FOR LName = "Miller"
DO WHILE .NOT. EOF( )
     DISPLAY
     CONTINUE
ENDDO
```

This technique also accesses every record in the database file and thus requires 10,000 disk accesses to display the 100 records with Miller in the LName field. Because the time required to process the DO WHILE loop adds to the time required to access the disk, the processing time for this technique is 2 minutes and 14 seconds.

## The FIND and WHILE Approach

If the field that you are searching is indexed, you can use a combination of the FIND (or SEEK) and WHILE commands to display records that meet a search criterion. This approach is very fast because it uses the following steps:

1. The FIND (or SEEK) command looks up the first record that matches the search criterion in the master index file. This requires no disk accesses.
2. Because the data in the index file are always in sorted order, the WHILE condition can display records as long as the search condition exists in the key field. Each displayed record requires one disk access.

3. When the pointer encounters a record that does *not* match the search criterion, there are no more records available that match that criterion. (Because the data are always in sorted order in the index file, those with matching keys are naturally grouped together.) Therefore, once all the records that match the search criterion are displayed, no more disk accesses are necessary.

Using the FIND and WHILE approach with the Miller example on the Mail database requires exactly 100 disk accesses to display 100 Millers. The other 9,900 disk accesses that the FOR, SET FILTER, and LOCATE methods require never occur, so this searching method is the fastest.

The commands below demonstrate how to display all the Millers using FIND and WHILE:

```
USE Mail INDEX NameOrd
FIND MILLER
LIST WHILE LName = "Miller"
```

This technique requires 25 seconds to display the 100 Millers. Of course, it can be used only on indexed fields, and it is usually impossible to index all the fields in a database file. Nonetheless, you should always try to index fields that are sorted and searched frequently in an application.

# Searching for Multiple Fields

How you perform searches with multiple fields depends on the sort order (or index order) of the records in the database. If the data are in random order, you'll need to use the slower FOR (or LOCATE...CONTINUE or SET FILTER) commands to search the database. However, if the records are indexed on the main field of interest or both fields of interest, you can use the faster WHILE approach, or a combination of WHILE and FOR.

## Using FOR

Regardless of the command you use with the FOR option, it will always check all records in the database file for records that match the search criteria. (Actually, if FOR is combined with a scope or WHILE condition, this changes. But for the time being we'll focus on the FOR condition alone.)

If the fields you want to search are not indexed, you have to use the FOR command. For example, Figure 13.2 shows how the command

```
LIST FOR CustNo = 1002 .AND. MONTH(Date) = 3
```

```
              CustNo        CustName        Date
miss ─────────►1001          Smith         02/01/87
miss ─────────►1003          Jones         03/01/87
miss ─────────►1002          Jackson       01/01/87
miss ─────────►1001          Smith         03/01/87
miss ─────────►1003          Jones         02/01/87
match ────────►1002          Jackson       03/01/87
miss ─────────►1001          Smith         03/01/87
match ────────►1002          Jackson       03/01/87
miss ─────────►1003          Jones         01/01/87
```

**FIGURE 13.2:** How dBASE searches the database in response to the command LIST FOR CustNo = 1001 .AND. MONTH(Date) = 3. Every record is checked, from top to bottom, but only those that match the search criteria are displayed. This example requires nine disk accesses to display two records.

accesses data. The lines labeled "miss" are disk accesses that did not display any data on the screen. Those labeled "match" are records that matched the search criteria and were displayed on the screen.

## Using WHILE

You can use the WHILE technique to access records as long as the database is indexed on the same fields being searched and the fields in the index key expression are listed in the same order as the search criterion fields.

For example, if you wish to use WHILE to access all records for customer number 1002 in the month of March (CustNo = 1002 .AND. MONTH(Date) = 3), the database *must* be indexed on the CustNo and Date fields (in that order), as in the command below:

**INDEX ON STR(CustNo,4) + DTOC(Date) TO AnyFile**

Once the index order is established, you can use FIND or SEEK to locate the first record matching the search critera and then a WHILE command to access remaining records. The commands below demonstrate the series of commands required:

```
* - - Open database with appropriate index file.
USE Charges INDEX CustDate
* - - Search string must match index format.
MCust = 1002
MDate = CTOD("03/01/87")
Search = STR(MCust,4) + DTOC(MDate)
SEEK Search
LIST WHILE CustNo = MCust .AND. Date = MDate
```

In this case, only the records matching both the CustNo and Date criteria are accessed, and only two disk accesses are required, as Figure 13.3 demonstrates. This technique is the fastest.

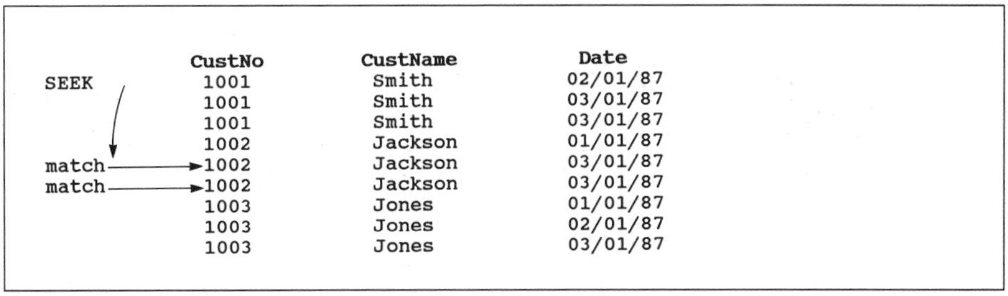

```
              CustNo       CustName        Date
SEEK          1001         Smith          02/01/87
              1001         Smith          03/01/87
              1001         Smith          03/01/87
              1002         Jackson        01/01/87
match ------->1002         Jackson        03/01/87
match ------->1002         Jackson        03/01/87
              1003         Jones          01/01/87
              1003         Jones          02/01/87
              1003         Jones          03/01/87
```

**FIGURE 13.3:** How dBASE searches the database in response to the SEEK and WHILE combination for accessing customer number 1002's March transactions. The SEEK command quickly positions the record pointer to the first record that matches the search criteria, and then the WHILE command accesses only that record and any others that also match the criteria.

When using a combination of the SEEK and WHILE commands, it is important to remember that only the fields that are actually in the index need to match the format of the fields in the index file. This important topic is discussed in the section entitled "Using FIND and SEEK Successfully" below.

## Combining WHILE and FOR

If the database is indexed only on the primary field of interest, you can use a FIND or SEEK command to locate the first matching record, a WHILE option to limit the search to records that match the primary search criterion, and a FOR option to isolate records that match the secondary search criterion.

The commands below show an example, assuming that the open database file is indexed only on the CustNo field:

**USE Customer INDEX CustNo**
**FIND 1002**
**LIST WHILE CustNo = 1002 FOR MONTH(Date) = 3**

Note that the FIND command quickly locates customer number 1002 in the index file. Then the WHILE condition limits the disk accesses to customer 1002. The FOR condition further specifies March dates. Only three disk accesses are required to show March transactions for customer 1002 in this process, as shown in Figure 13.4. While not as efficient as using a WHILE condition for both fields, it is certainly an improvement on using the FOR condition for both fields.

## Using SEEK and DO WHILE

The FIND and SEEK commands can also be used in combination with a DO WHILE loop to locate the first record in a database matching a search criterion

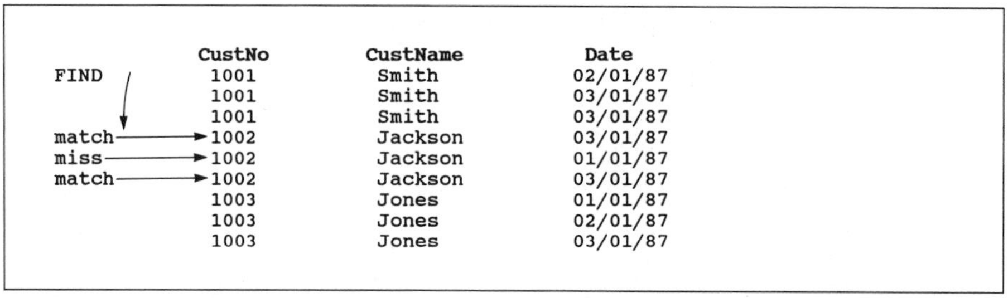

```
                 CustNo       CustName       Date
FIND   |         1001          Smith        02/01/87
       |         1001          Smith        03/01/87
       v         1001          Smith        03/01/87
match---------->1002          Jackson      03/01/87
miss----------->1002          Jackson      01/01/87
match---------->1002          Jackson      03/01/87
                 1003          Jones        01/01/87
                 1003          Jones        02/01/87
                 1003          Jones        03/01/87
```

**FIGURE 13.4:** How dBASE searches the database in response to the FIND, WHILE, and FOR combination of commands for displaying March transactions for customer 1002. The FIND command quickly positions the record pointer to the first record with customer number 1002. The WHILE option accesses only records within customer number 1002. The FOR condition, in turn, limits the actual display to records with dates in March. This technique uses three disk accesses.

and then process all records that match the search criterion. As a precaution, the DO WHILE loop should include a .NOT. EOF( ) condition.

For example, the routine below locates the first record with number 1005 in the CustNo field (assuming, of course, the Charges database is indexed on the CustNo field). Then the DO WHILE loop displays every record for customer number 1005 on a multiple-line report:

```
USE Charges INDEX CustNo
LookFor = 1005
SEEK LookFor
DO WHILE CustNo = LookFor .AND. .NOT. EOF( )
    ? CustNo, TRIM(Fname),LName
    ? Address
    ? TRIM(City) + ", " + State,Zip
    ?
    ?
    SKIP
ENDDO
```

## Searching for Ranges

Index files with the WHILE command can help pull out *ranges* of data from the database. For example, to create a database of individuals whose names begin with the letters M through P, you could use the commands

```
USE Mail
COPY TO Temp FOR LName > = "M" .AND. LName < = "P"
```

This technique is fairly slow and can be accelerated considerably with a technique such as the one below:

**USE Mail INDEX NameOrd**
**FIND M**
**COPY TO Temp WHILE LName < = "P"**

There is one danger in using index files to search for the lowest value in a range, however. If there is no record to match the lowest value, no records at all will be accessed. (Because you cannot use the < = and > = operators, there is no way to use FIND or SEEK to find the first value that is at or above the lowest cutoff point.)

You can design programs, however, that will "decide" whether to use the faster SEEK...WHILE combination of commands or the slower (though perhaps necessary) FOR option. For example, the @ commands in Figure 13.5 ask the user to enter starting and ending dates for a range of dates to display, and the STORE commands convert the user's entries to the date data type.

The SEEK command then attempts to find a date to match the start date in the active HireDate index file (which presumably uses the Hire_Date field as the key expression). If a date matching the start date is found in the index file, the IF clause uses the faster WHILE approach to display the rest of the records in the range. If a date matching the start date cannot be found, the slower, though necessary in this case, FOR technique is used.

```
*-------------------- Indexed on date data type.
USE Mail INDEX HireDate
CLEAR
STORE "        " TO Start,Finish
@ 10,2 SAY "Enter start date " ;
  GET Start PICTURE "99/99/99"
@ 12,2 SAY "Enter ending date " ;
  GET Finish PICTURE "99/99/99"
READ
*********** Convert character dates to date types.
STORE CTOD(Start) TO Start
STORE CTOD(Finish) TO Finish
SEEK Start
*----- Decide whether to proceed with SEEK approach
*----- or revert to the slower, safer FOR approach.
IF FOUND()
    LIST WHILE Hire_Date <= Finish
ELSE
    LIST FOR Hire_Date >= Start .AND. Hire_Date <= Finish
ENDIF
```

**FIGURE 13.5:** A routine to search for a range of dates in a database indexed on a date field named Hire_Date. In this routine, the starting and ending dates to search for are entered by the user and stored in memory variables named Start and Finish. The SEEK command attempts to find a date matching the start date. If a matching date is found, the WHILE approach is used to display all records within the range of dates. If SEEK cannot find a record to match the start date, the slower FOR approach is used.

## SEARCHING FOR THE CLOSEST MATCH

As an alternative to deciding between a WHILE or FOR approach to solving a problem, a program can use a routine to search for the closest match if it can't find an exact match. The SEEK and FIND commands are designed to find only exact matches to the specified search criterion. However, with a little programming, you can write a routine that allows SEEK to find a record that most closely matches a specific value. All you need to do is have the routine slightly change the value you are looking for each time the SEEK fails.

For example, the routine in Figure 13.6 allows the user to enter a customer number. If that number cannot be found, the DO WHILE .NOT. FOUND( ) loop increments the number by one and continues its search.

If the field of interest is the date data type and the database file is indexed on that field, you can allow the user to enter a date and then add (or subtract) a day from that date until SEEK finds the closest matching date. The routine in Figure 13.7 presents an example.

To locate the nearest matching character string, you can shorten the length of the character string with each pass through the DO WHILE .NOT. FOUND( ) loop, as in Figure 13.8.

If you prefer to spread your closest-value search in two directions, you can search for both the next highest value and the next lowest value within the DO WHILE .NOT. FOUND( ) loop. The routine in Figure 13.9 presents an example using the date data type.

In some applications, you may want to put an upper limit on the number of attempts allowed the DO WHILE .NOT. FOUND( ) loop. (As these examples stand, some could run forever if no match at all was found.) Here is a sample

```
*---------- Indexed on numeric CustNo field.
USE Charges INDEX CustNo
Search = 0
@ 2,2 SAY "Enter search number " ;
  GET Search PICT "9999"
READ

SEEK Search
DO WHILE .NOT. FOUND()
   Search = Search + 1  && Next highest number.
   @ 20,1 SAY "Seeking "+STR(Search,4)
   SEEK Search
ENDDO
? "Located ",CustNo, "at record ",RECNO()
```

**FIGURE 13.6:** A routine that uses the SEEK command to find the first record that most closely matches (but is greater than) the number entered by the user. Each time the SEEK command fails, the DO WHILE loop increments the number to search for by one. If this algorithm could be expressed in a single SEEK command, it would be something like SEEK Search > = CustNo.

loop that limits the DO WHILE loop to 100 attempts:

```
Tries = 0
SEEK Search
DO WHILE .NOT. FOUND( ) .AND. Tries < 100
      Search = Search + 1    && next day
      Tries = Tries + 1      && next attempt
      @ 20,1 SAY "Seeking " + DTOC(Search)
      SEEK Search
ENDDO
```

```
*---------------------- Indexed on a date field.
USE Charges INDEX Date
Search = SPACE(8)
@ 2,2 SAY "Enter search date " ;
  GET Search PICT "99/99/99"
READ

Search = CTOD(Search)
SEEK Search
DO WHILE .NOT. FOUND()
   Search = Search + 1  && next day.
   @ 20,1 SAY "Seeking "+DTOC(Search)
   SEEK Search
ENDDO
? "Located ",Date, "at record ",RECNO()
```

**FIGURE 13.7:** A routine that uses the SEEK command to locate the date that most closely matches the date requested by the user. If the exact date cannot be found, the DO WHILE loop increments the date being searched for by one day until a matching date is found. The routine will find the date that is closest to, and greater than, the requested date.

```
*------------------ Indexed on a character field.
USE Charges INDEX PartCode
Search = SPACE(12)
@ 2,2 SAY "Enter search string " ;
  GET Search PICT "@!"
READ

Search = TRIM(Search)
SEEK Search
DO WHILE .NOT. FOUND()
   Search = LEFT(Search,LEN(Search)-1)
   @ 20,1 SAY "Seeking "+Search+SPACE(10)
   SEEK Search
ENDDO
? "Located ",Part_No, "at record ",RECNO()
```

**FIGURE 13.8:** A routine that uses the SEEK command to locate the character string that most closely matches the character string entered by the user. If the exact string cannot be found, the DO WHILE loop shortens the string by one character until a matching string is found.

```
*---------- Indexed on date field.
USE Charges INDEX Date
CLEAR
Search = SPACE(8)
@ 2,2 SAY "Enter search date " ;
  GET Search PICT "99/99/99"
READ
Search = CTOD(Search)
STORE Search TO Lower,Higher
SEEK Search
DO WHILE .NOT. FOUND()
   Lower = Lower - 1
   SEEK Lower
   IF .NOT. FOUND()
      Higher = Higher + 1
      SEEK Higher
   ENDIF
ENDDO

? "Closest match: ",Date, "at record ",RECNO()
```

**FIGURE 13.9:** A routine that uses the SEEK command to locate the date that most closely matches the date requested by the user. If the exact date cannot be found, the DO WHILE loop both increments and decrements the date being searched for by one day, until a matching date is found. The routine will find the date that is closest to the date requested, whether it be an earlier or later date. (In the event of a tie, the later date is selected in this example.)

Of course, the more commands you put between the DO WHILE and ENDDO commands, the longer the search will take. In the examples above, the @ command within the DO WHILE .NOT. FOUND( ) loop acts only as an odometer to show its progress. This command can be removed if you prefer.

# Using FIND and SEEK Successfully

It is important to keep in mind that the fields in the index file do not necessarily "look like" the fields in the database record. Furthermore, the programmer must be very careful about handling the widths of lookup fields in index files. This section discusses important guidelines for searching for data with the FIND and SEEK commands.

## Matching Data Type and Format

It is essential that the data in the FIND or SEEK command *always* match the data type and format of the index key expression. For example, the command

**INDEX ON UPPER(LName) TO Names**

places all last names in uppercase *in the index file only.* Therefore, to list all the Smiths on this database, you would use the commands

```
FIND SMITH        && uppercase for index file only
LIST WHILE LName = "Smith"
```

or

```
LookFor = "Smith"
SEEK UPPER(LookFor)      && uppercase for index file only
LIST WHILE LName = LookFor
```

Note that the uppercase equivalent is used only with the FIND and SEEK commands, as these are the only commands that actually look at data inside the index file. All other commands look at data in the database file.

Similarly, if you convert a number to a character string in an index file, as in the example below, any FIND or SEEK command must also look for STR(CustNo,4,0):

```
INDEX ON STR(CustNo,4,0) + DTOC(Date) TO AnyFile
```

However, other commands will still just refer to CustNo, as below:

```
INPUT "Enter customer number to look for " TO LookUp
SEEK STR(LookUp,4,0)      && convert to match index
LIST WHILE CustNo = Lookup
```

If Date is an index field and you've converted it to a character string for indexing, the FIND or SEEK data must be a character string in the same format, (Chapter 12, "Sorting and Indexing," shows numerous examples of indexing on date fields.)

## Matching Field Lengths

If you wish to search for more than one field in an index file, the lengths of the fields in the search string must match the lengths of the fields in the index file expression exactly (except for the last field, which can be shorter if the SET EXACT parameter is OFF). Some examples will demonstrate.

Referring back to the Mail database structure in Figure 13.1, you can see that the LName field is 20 characters wide, and the FName field is 15 characters wide. So when you create an index file with a command such as

```
INDEX ON UPPER(LName + FName) TO AnyFile
```

the index file contains last names padded to a length of 20 characters and first names padded to a length of 15 characters, as below:

**"ADAMS ANDY "**
**"BAKERSVILLE CHARLES "**
**"CARLSON DAVID "**

Provided that the SET EXACT parameter is off, any search for a last name only (in uppercase) will work correctly. Any search for a last name padded to a length of 20 characters and any portion of a first name will also work correctly. Just about any other match will be inaccurate.

Table 13.4 shows examples of FIND and SEEK searches that will match Andy Adams' name in the index file, as well as searches that will not. If you compare the examples character for character with the contents of the index file, you'll quickly see why some match and others do not (the nonmatching examples are either the wrong case or try to match a letter with a blank space).

In a program, you should convert a user's response to a prompt into a format that matches the format of the index file. To ensure proper widths, use the SPACE function to predefine field widths (to match database widths exactly) and the GET command to read in the user's request (GET always uses the predefined width).

| | ENTRY SEARCHED FOR | SUCCESS OF SEARCH |
|---|---|---|
| **Contents of index file** | "ADAMS ANDY " | |
| **FIND and SEEK searches** | "ADAMS ANDY " | match |
| | "ADAMS ANDY" | match |
| | "ADAMS A" | match |
| | "ADAMS " | match |
| | "ADAMS" | match |
| | "Adams" | no match |
| | "ADAMS ANDY" | no match |
| | "ADAMS " | no match |

**TABLE 13.4:** Examples of Character Strings that Match and Do Not Match an Index Expression

Figure 13.10 shows a simple example. The database is indexed on the expression **INDEX ON UPPER(LName + FName)**. The LName field in the database is 20 characters wide, and FName is 15 characters wide. The SPACE( ) functions predefine these exact widths, and the GET...READ commands ask for a last and first name to search for.

If you imagine all possible entries that a user might make into the sample algorithm in Figure 13.10, you'll see that all follow the format of the index file. The rightmost field (FName in this example) can be trimmed of trailing blanks because the total expression in the search variable can be shorter than the key field expression. (If this sounds confusing, refer back to Table 13.3 for examples of matching and nonmatching expressions.)

If for some reason you have a hard time visualizing the format of the data in an index file, just use a LIST command with the database in use and an expression that exactly matches the index expression. For example, if your database is indexed with the command

**INDEX ON UPPER(LName + FName) + STR(Amount,12,2) TO Abc**

the command below will show you how the data look in the index file, and how, in turn, your search data needs to look:

**LIST UPPER(LName + FName) + STR(Amount,12,2)**

For more information on combining fields in indexing expressions, see Chapter 12, "Sorting and Indexing."

```
****************** Search two fields in index expression.
USE Mail INDEX NameOrd

MLast = SPACE(20)    && exact width of database field.
MFirst = SPACE(15)   && exact width of database field.
@ 10,10 SAY "Enter last name for search " GET MLast
@ 12,10 SAY "Enter first name or initial " GET MFirst
READ

*-------- Build string for SEEK command now.
Search = UPPER(MLast)
*-------- Add first name only if not a blank.
IF MFirst # " "
   Search = Search + UPPER(TRIM(MFirst))
ENDIF (not blank)

SEEK Search
```

**FIGURE 13.10:** Algorithm showing the proper technique for building a search string in an index expression involving both the last and first names. The SPACE( ) function predefines variable widths to match the database field widths. The GET...READ combination of commands maintains these widths, regardless of the user's entry. The Search variable is then built from the uppercase equivalent of the last name plus the first name (if any).

# GIVING THE USER SEARCHING POWER

This section demonstrates programming techniques that allow a novice user to quickly locate a particular record in a database. Each of the examples uses a SET FORMAT and EDIT command to allow the user to edit the located record. In lieu of using these commands, you can use @...SAY or ? commands to display the record on the screen or a REPORT FORM <file name> NEXT 1 command to display the individual record using a report format.

You can also display multiple records that match the search criterion using the WHILE option with commands such as LIST, DO WHILE, DISPLAY, EDIT, DELETE, and so forth. The individual chapters on editing, deleting, and printing reports provide further examples of these techniques.

## Looking Up a Single Field

Typically, you'll want your users to be able to enter a value to search for and then be able to quickly access the record they requested, whether for editing or for display. To provide this capability in a database that is indexed on the field the user is searching, display a prompt on the screen asking the user for the value to search for. Store the user's entry in a memory variable, and use the SEEK command to attempt to find the matching record.

Figure 13.11 shows a program that asks the user to enter a name to search for and then attempts to find that name in the NameOrd index file. If the name is not found, an error message is displayed. If the name is found, it is displayed on the screen ready for editing. The program is designed to keep asking for new records to locate until the user leaves the prompt for entering names blank.

In Figure 13.11, the NameOrd index contains the expression **UPPER(LName)**. The index expression can contain other fields to the right of LName, for example, UPPER(LName + FName) or UPPER(LName) + DTOC(Date).

## Looking Up Multiple Fields

In applications that use large database files, a single data item may not be sufficient for locating a particular record. For example, if you allow the user to enter only a last name to search on a database with 50,000 names on it, the user may have to spend considerable time finding the exact record. After all, if the user requests to look up Smith on a large database, he or she may have to search through 100 Smiths to locate the requested record.

To give the user the power to quickly locate data using more than one field to identify a record, all the appropriate fields must be in the master index file; and

```
****************************************** Search1.prg.
USE Mail INDEX NameOrd

Searching = .T.
DO WHILE Searching

   *------------- LName field is 20 characters wide.
   CLEAR
   MemLname = SPACE(20)
   @ 10,2 SAY "Enter last name of person to look for ";
     GET MemLname
   READ

   *---- If nothing entered, exit.
   IF MemLName = " "
      Searching = .F.
      LOOP
   ENDIF

   *------------- Try to find that person.
   SEEK UPPER(MemLname)

   IF FOUND()
      SET FORMAT TO MailScr
      EDIT
      CLOSE FORMAT
   ELSE
      @ 22,0 CLEAR
      ? CHR(7),"Can't find",MemLname
      WAIT
   ENDIF

ENDDO
*--- end of program.
```

**FIGURE 13.11:** This program asks the user for the last name of an individual to edit and attempts to find that individual with a SEEK command. The NameOrd index file is built on the expression **UPPER(LName)**.

the search data that the user enters must exactly match the data types, formats, and widths of the fields in the index file.

Figure 13.12 shows a program that allows a user to enter a last name to search for, or a last and first name (or even a last name and a first initial). It uses the techniques discussed above in the section entitled "Using FIND and SEEK Successfully" to properly format the user's entry for an accurate lookup.

In this example, the NameOrd index file begins with the expression **UPPER(LName + FName)**. Other keys can be included in the expression to the right of this first expression.

If you prefer to display all records that match the user's search request in this example, you can use the Search variable in a WHILE condition. In this case, however, Search has already been converted to uppercase, so the fields being compared must also be converted to uppercase. For example, to print a report named MailList.frm of all names that match the entered name, replace the commands

**SET FORMAT TO MailScr**

```
************************************** Search2.prg
USE Members INDEX NameOrd, ZipOrder

*------------------- Set up loop for editing.
More = .T.
DO WHILE More
    CLEAR
    Mem_LName = SPACE(20) && Same as database field width.
    Mem_FName = SPACE(15) && Same as database field width.
    @ 10,5 SAY "Last name  :" GET Mem_LName
    @ 12,5 SAY "First name :" GET Mem_FName
    @ 14,1 SAY "** Enter name of person to edit **"
    READ

    *------- Exit if no last name entered.
    IF Mem_LName = " "
        More = .F.
        LOOP
    ENDIF

    *------- If name entered, create search string.
    Search = UPPER(Mem_LName)
    IF Mem_FName # " "
        Search = Search + TRIM(UPPER(Mem_FName))
    ENDIF

    *------- Try to find that individual.
    SEEK Search

    *------- If found, edit.  Otherwise, warn user.
    IF FOUND()
        SET FORMAT TO MailScr
        EDIT RECNO()
        CLOSE FORMAT
    ELSE
        @ 22,5 SAY "Not found!"
        ? CHR(7)
    ENDIF

ENDDO (while More)
```

**FIGURE 13.12:** A sample program that allows a user to enter a last name and optionally a first name to locate a particular record for editing. In this example, the index expression for the NameOrd index file is **UPPER(LName + FName).**

> **EDIT RECNO( )**
> **CLOSE FORMAT**

with a command such as

> **REPORT FORM MailList WHILE UPPER(LName + FName) = ;**
> **Search**

In lieu of REPORT FORM MailList, you can substitute any command that supports WHILE (as listed in Table 13.2) or even a DO WHILE...ENDDO loop with several commands in between.

## Searching One of Several Index Files

In some situations, you might need rapid access to either of two fields. For example, in a customer database, you might want operators to quickly locate customers by either customer number or name. In such an application, you'll need two separate index files, one based on the customer number and the other on the customer name. Then the program will need to decide which index file to search, based on the user's entry.

The sample program in Figure 13.13 shows a technique that offers this kind of rapid searching. In this example, the CustNo index file was created with the command

**INDEX ON CustNo TO CustNo**

and the CustName index file was created with the command

**INDEX ON UPPER(LName + FName) TO CustName**

The program assumes that each customer has a unique customer number, but it does not assume that each customer has a unique name. Therefore, if the user enters a customer name rather than a number, the program first displays all individuals with that last name, along with their customer numbers, as in Figure 13.14. Furthermore, the program asks for the customer number, to make sure that the proper customer is accessed.

Note the use of the SET ORDER command in the sample program in Figure 13.13. The logic of the program is such that if the user entered a name, the second listed index file (CustName in this example) would first be made the master index (using SET ORDER TO 2) so that it can be searched. If the user entered a customer number, the command SET ORDER TO 1 tells dBASE to search the first listed index file (CustNo).

This program operates on the assumption that the CustNo field is numeric and the LName field is character. The program is able to determine whether a name was entered by checking whether the first character of the user's request is a letter A or greater (using the command IF ASC(LOOKUP) > = 65).

In some cases, it might not be so easy to distinguish whether a user entered a name or a code (for example, in an inventory system where the part numbers are character data, such as A-1121-03). There are two ways around this. First, the IF clause can check for *any* character that might provide a clue. For example, if only part numbers contain dashes, the command **IF .NOT. "-" $ LookUp** would indicate that a name was entered.

A second technique is to present two prompts on the screen: one that asks for a code and one that asks for a name. Then the program can determine what the user entered by seeing which prompt was filled and which was left blank.

```
*************************************** Search3.prg
*-------- Allows quick lookup using two index files.
SET TALK OFF
SET HEADING OFF

USE Customer INDEX CustNo,CustName
CLEAR

*------- Set up loop for validating customer code.
*------- Enter customer number or last name and scan for it.
Exiting = .F.
DO WHILE .NOT. Exiting

   Valid = .F.
   DO WHILE .NOT. Valid

      * --------- Get customer name or number.
      Lookup=SPACE(20)
      @ 15,5 SAY "Enter customer code or last name:" GET Lookup
      @ 17,5 SAY "Press Return to exit."
      READ

      * ----------- If nothing entered, exit.
      IF Lookup = " "
         Valid = .T.
         Exiting = .T.
         LOOP
      ENDIF (lookup is blank)

      * ------------ Look up by name, if name entered.
      IF ASC(LOOKUP) >= 65
         Lookup = UPPER(TRIM(Lookup))
         SET ORDER TO 2
         SEEK Lookup

         *------- If found, display customers with that name.
         IF FOUND()
            M_CustNo = 0
            CLEAR
            @ 6,0 SAY "Number Last Name      First Name    Address"
            ?
            DISPLAY OFF WHILE UPPER(LName) = Lookup;
            CustNo,LName, FName, Address
            @ 22,2 SAY "Enter customer number: ";
            GET M_CustNo PICTURE "9999"
            READ
            Lookup = STR(M_CustNo,4)
            CLEAR
         ELSE (if name not found)
            @ 22,0 CLEAR
            ? CHR(7),"Not found!",Lookup
         ENDIF (name not found)
      ENDIF (name entered)

      * ----------- Look up by customer number.
      IF VAL(Lookup) > 0
         M_CustNo = VAL(Lookup)
         SET ORDER TO 1
         SEEK M_CustNo

         *------- If found, continue, else ask again.
         IF FOUND()
            Valid = .T.
         ELSE
            @ 22,0 CLEAR
            ? CHR(7),"Not found!",Lookup
         ENDIF (not eof)
```

**FIGURE 13.13:** This program allows the user to enter either a customer number or a customer name. If the user enters a number, the program searches the customer number index file. If the user enters a name, the program searches the customer name index.

```
      ENDIF (number entered)
   ENDDO (valid)
   IF .NOT. Exiting
      *---- At this point, can use any command (and optionally
      *---- a custom screen) to display customer data.
      EDIT RECNO()
      CLEAR
   ENDIF
ENDDO (exiting)
```

**FIGURE 13.13:** This program allows the user to enter either a customer number or a customer name. If the user enters a number, the program searches the customer number index file. If the user enters a name, the program searches the customer name index (continued).

```
Number Last Name      First Name     Address
1007   Smith          Albert         123 A St.
1132   Smith          Joanna         P.O. Box 1201
2312   Smith          Cyrus          3232 Challenger Rd.
4110   Smith          Susita         1086 Wotan St.

Enter customer number:
```

**FIGURE 13.14:** The program in Figure 13.13 allows the user to enter either a customer name or a customer number to locate a particular record. If the user enters a customer name, the program displays all individuals with the requested last name and asks for the customer number, as shown in this figure. This technique ensures that the correct customer will be accessed.

## Using SEEK with Multiple Databases

When using the SELECT command to switch among open database files, only the currently selected database's master index file can be searched with a FIND or SEEK command. The PosEntry program (Figure 10.21 in Chapter 10, "Adding New Data") demonstrates a technique for using SEEK with multiple database files.

## Finding a Record with LOCATE

If the fields you wish to search are not indexed, you can use a LOCATE command in much the same way you would use SEEK, but the process will be considerably slower if the database is large.

Figure 13.15 demonstrates a program that locates a record based on the last and first name entered by the user. LOCATE is easier to use than SEEK, because conversions are not necessary to make the user's entry match the indexing key ( just to play it safe, however, everything is done in uppercase in this example).

## Presenting a Query Form to the User

To give users complete querying (searching) capability on all the fields in a database with the full range of dBASE operators and functions at their disposal, you can use the dBASE MODIFY QUERY command within your program. MODIFY QUERY presents a full-screen, menu-driven display for entering search criteria and then automatically sets up a filter condition to hide all records that do not match the specified search criteria. (If you are not already familiar with the MODIFY QUERY command, see the reference section at the end of this chapter.)

To give your user access to the MODIFY QUERY screen, you can set up a prompt that asks whether the user wants to display all the records in the database or define a filtering (or query) condition to isolate particular records. If the user

```
************************************** Search4.prg
USE Mail
More = .T.
DO WHILE More
    CLEAR
    Mem_LName = SPACE(20) && same width as database field.
    Mem_FName = SPACE(15) && same width as database field.
    @ 10,5 SAY "Last name  :" GET Mem_LName
    @ 12,5 SAY "First name :" GET Mem_FName
    @ 14,1 SAY "** Enter name of person to edit **"
    READ

    *------- Exit if no last name entered.
    IF Mem_LName = " "
        More = .F.
        LOOP
    ENDIF

    *------- If name entered, create search string.
    IF Mem_FName = " "
       LOCATE FOR UPPER(LName) = UPPER(Mem_LName)
    ELSE
        LOCATE FOR UPPER(LName) = UPPER(Mem_LName);
        .AND. UPPER(FName) = TRIM(UPPER(Mem_Fname))
    ENDIF

    *------- If found, edit.  Otherwise, warn user.
    IF FOUND()
        SET FORMAT TO MailScr
        EDIT RECNO()
        CLOSE FORMAT
    ELSE
        @ 23,5 SAY "Not found!"
        ? CHR(7)
    ENDIF

ENDDO (while More)
```

**FIGURE 13.15:** This program uses a LOCATE command to find a particular record in the database. No index files are required, because LOCATE searches the database file directly. This program allows the user to search for a last name only or a last name and first name (or first initial).

opts to define a filtering condition, have the program execute the MODIFY QUERY command, as shown in the routine in Figure 13.16.

If no records match the user's query request, the EOF( ) condition is set to true when the record pointer is at the top of the database file. Therefore, in Figure 13.16, the GO TOP command and IF EOF( ) clause warn the user when his query results in an empty file.

After the program prints the report, you'll want a line in the program that reads **SET FILTER TO** to deactivate the filter that MODIFY QUERY activated and regain access to all records.

This technique allows the user to reuse the same query form (named Mail.qry) repeatedly. If you prefer to have the user start with a new query form each time, erase the query form *after* printing the report and deactivating the query, as below:

```
SET FILTER TO
IF FILE("Mail.qry")
     ERASE Mail.qry
ENDIF
RETURN     && end of program.
```

If you would prefer that the user have the opportunity to build a library of query forms and assign names to each one for future use, you can use a routine like the one in Figure 13.17, shown below:

```
DIR *.QRY
QFile = SPACE(8)
@ 22,1 SAY "Enter a new name for the query form"
```

```
*------------------ Present Query form if user requests
CLEAR
AllNone = " "
@ 5,2 SAY "Print (A)ll records, or (Q)uery"
@ 7,2 SAY "[Enter A or Q] " GET AllNone PICT "!"
READ
IF AllNone = "Q"
   MODIFY QUERY Mail
   *---Make sure that some records meet the criterion.
   GO TOP
   IF EOF ()
      CLEAR
      ? "Warning... no records match search criterion!"
      ?
      WAIT
   ENDIF (eof)
ENDIF
```

**FIGURE 13.16:** A routine that asks whether the user wishes to display all records in a database file or define a filtering (query) condition to display only certain records. If the user opts to query the database, the routine accesses the dBASE MODIFY QUERY screen.

```
@ 23,1 SAY "or reuse an existing form from above "
@ 23,40 GET QFile
READ
IF QFile # "  "
    MODIFY QUERY &QFile
    <etc...>
ENDIF (qfile)
```

Figure 13.17 shows an entire report-printing program that includes the query capability. This program also includes options for the user to select sort orders, as discussed in Chapter 12, "Sorting and Indexing."

```
**************************************** MailRep
*  Set up sort orders and search conditions,
*    then print the appropriate report.
SET TALK OFF
SET SAFETY OFF
SET BELL OFF
USE Mail
CLEAR
@ 1,1 SAY "Report Options"
@ 2,0 SAY REPLICATE("_",80)
?
TEXT
               1. Directory
               2. Mailing labels
               3. MailMerge file
               X. None (return to Main Menu)
ENDTEXT
MChoice = " "
@ 24,1 SAY "Enter choice " GET MChoice PICT "!"
READ

IF MChoice = "X"
    RETURN
ENDIF

*------------------- Ask about sort order.
CLEAR
@ 1,1 SAY "Sort Options"
@ 2,0 SAY REPLICATE("_",80)
?
TEXT
               1. Last name
               2. Zip code
               3. Date Hired
               4. Original order

ENDTEXT
SChoice = 0
@ 24,1 SAY "Enter choice " GET SChoice PICTURE "9"
READ

*------------------- Set up appropriate sort order.
DO CASE
     CASE SChoice = 1
          SET INDEX TO NameOrd
```

**FIGURE 13.17:** This sample program for printing reports presents report and sorting options to the user, as well as an option to fill in a query form for filtering records. The program uses several techniques discussed both in this chapter and in Chapter 12, "Sorting and Indexing."

```
     CASE SChoice = 2
          SET INDEX TO ZipOrder
     CASE SChoice = 3
          CLEAR
          ? "Please wait a moment..."
          SET TALK ON
          INDEX ON Hire_Date TO Temp
          SET TALK OFF
     CASE SChoice = 4
          CLOSE INDEX

ENDCASE
*--- Let user create query form, or reuse an old one.
CLEAR
AllNone = " "
@ 5,2 SAY "Print (A)ll records, or (Q)uery "
@ 7,2 SAY "[Enter A or Q] " GET AllNone PICT "!"
READ
IF AllNone = "Q"
   CLEAR
   DIR *.QRY
   QFile = SPACE(8)
   @ 22,1 SAY "Enter a new name for the query form"
   @ 23,1 SAY "or reuse an existing form from above "
   @ 23,40 GET QFile
   READ
   IF QFile # " "
      MODIFY QUERY &QFile
      *--- Make sure that some records meet the criterion.
      GO TOP
      IF EOF()
         CLEAR
         ? "Warning... no records match search criterion!"
         ?
         WAIT
      ENDIF (eof)
   ENDIF (qfile)
ENDIF (allnone)

*------------------- Print report based on previous MChoice.
CLEAR
STORE " " TO Printer, PMacro

@ 15,5 SAY "Send data to printer? (Y/N) " GET Printer PICT "!"
READ
IF Printer = "Y"
     PMacro = "TO PRINT"
     WAIT "Prepare printer, then press any key to continue..."
ENDIF

*------- Leave out records marked for deletion.
SET DELETED ON

CLEAR
DO CASE
   CASE MChoice = "1"
        REPORT FORM Director &PMacro
   CASE MChoice = "2"
        LABEL FORM ThreeCol &PMacro
   CASE MChoice = "3"
        DO MailMrge

ENDCASE
```

**FIGURE 13.17:** This sample program for printing reports presents report and sorting options to the user, as well as an option to fill in a query form for filtering records. The program uses several techniques discussed both in this chapter and in Chapter 12, "Sorting and Indexing" (continued).

```
*------------------- Done.  Return to main menu.
IF Printer = "Y"
    EJECT
ENDIF
SET DELETED OFF
SET FILTER TO  &&-- end filter condition.
*------ Reactivate all index files.
USE Mail INDEX NameOrd,ZipOrder
WAIT "Press any key to return to menu..."
RETURN
```

**FIGURE 13.17:** This sample program for printing reports presents report and sorting options to the user, as well as an option to fill in a query form for filtering records. The program uses several techniques discussed both in this chapter and in Chapter 12, "Sorting and Indexing" (continued).

## A Simpler Query Technique with SET FILTER

If you are writing applications for users who find the MODIFY QUERY technique too complex, your program can present a simple menu with individual fields to search on instead of the MODIFY QUERY form. While the simplified menu is extremely easy to use, it lacks flexibility, because the user cannot search on multiple fields.

The routine in Figure 13.18 displays a menu of fields to search on. When the user selects a field (such as State), the prompt displays a message such as

**Search for what state?**

and allows the user to type in a value to search for (such as CA). When reports are printed, only records matching the search criterion (State = CA in this example) are displayed.

The basic logic of the routine allows the user to select a field to search (from the menu inside the TEXT...ENDTEXT commands). Based on that selection, a DO CASE clause asks for the appropriate value to search for, then creates a SET FILTER command to limit the displayed records to those requested by the user. (For more information on the SET FILTER command, see Chapter 18, "Setting Parameters.")

As with the MODIFY QUERY command, a GO TOP command is used after the SET FILTER command to move the record pointer. Also, after the report has been printed, a SET FILTER TO command with no condition terminates the filter condition.

## Commands for Searching and Querying

The remainder of this chapter discusses individual commands used for locating specific records or groups of records, based on values stored in the database fields. Scoping techniques for managing records based on record number are discussed in Chapter 15, "Managing Data, Records, and Files."

```
*** Simplified query routine to replace MODIFY QUERY.
USE Mail
CLEAR
TEXT
              Select a field to search on

                   1. Last name
                   2. Company
                   3. City
                   4. State
                   5. Date hired
                   6. None: display all records
ENDTEXT
QChoice = 0
@ 20,5 SAY "Enter choice (1-5) " GET QChoice PICT "9"
READ

FiltCond = " "
@ 21,1
DO CASE
   CASE QChoice = 1
        ACCEPT "Search for what last name? " TO FiltCond
        SET FILTER TO UPPER(LName) = UPPER(FiltCond)
   CASE QChoice = 2
        ACCEPT "Search for what company? " TO FiltCond
        SET FILTER TO UPPER(Company) = UPPER(FiltCond)
   CASE QChoice = 3
        ACCEPT "Search for what city? " TO FiltCond
        SET FILTER TO UPPER(City) = UPPER(FiltCond)
   CASE QChoice = 4
        ACCEPT "Search for what state? " TO FiltCond
        SET FILTER TO UPPER(State) = UPPER(FiltCond)
   CASE QChoice = 5
        FiltCond = SPACE(8)
        @ 22,1 SAY "Search for what date? " ;
          GET FiltCond PICT "99/99/99"
        READ
        SET FILTER TO Hire_Date = CTOD(FiltCond)
ENDCASE

*--- Make sure that some records meet the criterion.
GO TOP
IF EOF()
   CLEAR
   ? "Warning... no records match search criterion!"
   ?
   WAIT
ENDIF (eof)

***************************************************
* Can print any reports here, as in the MailRep   *
* program in Figure 13.7.                         *
***************************************************

SET FILTER TO  && remember to deactivate filter when done.
RETURN
```

**FIGURE 13.18:** A simpler query technique that allows a user to select a single field to search on from a menu. Then the user can enter a value to search for, and the SET FILTER command filters the database to "hide" records that do not match the user's query request.

## The FIND Command

FIND quickly finds a value in an index file and sets the record pointer to that record.

### SYNTAX

**FIND <literal>**

where <literal> is the value to look for in the index file.

### USAGE

FIND locates an item in the master index file for the current database. If the FIND command is successful, the record pointer will be at the first record that matches the value being searched for. If FIND is not successful, the FOUND( ) function is set to .F. and the EOF( ) function is set to .T. (until some other command moves the record pointer). If the SET TALK parameter is on, an unsuccessful search displays the message **No Find**.

FIND does not support functions or operators. For example, neither expression below is valid:

**FIND UPPER("Smith")**
**FIND CustNo > 100**

If the value to be searched for is stored in a memory variable, a macro is required, as below:

**LookFor = "SMITH"**
**FIND &LookFor**

FIND works only with the master index file. By default, the first-listed index file in the USE or SET INDEX command is the master index file. However, the SET ORDER command can make any of several index files the master index file.

If SET EXACT is off, only the leftmost characters need to match for the search to be successful. For example, **FIND J** will find the first record beginning with the letter J (e.g., Jackson). If SET EXACT is on, only a character-for-character match will be successful (e.g., J will match only the letter J, not Jackson or Jones).

FIND will locate a record that is marked for deletion only if the SET DELETED parameter is set off. FIND will not find a record that is hidden by a SET FILTER or MODIFY QUERY condition.

If the index file contains several keys, the field widths and formats of both the data being searched for and the key expression of the index file must match exactly. FIND cannot locate characters embedded within the index expression (that is, you cannot use the $ operator with FIND).

#### EXAMPLES

Given that the DateOrd index file was created using the command

**INDEX ON STR(CustNo,4) + DTOC(Date_Sold) TO DateOrd**

and DateOrd is the master index file, as below,

**USE Charges INDEX DateOrd,Name**

the command

**FIND 1001**

will search for a record with customer number 1001.

#### TIPS

For programmers, the SEEK command provides more flexibility than the FIND command when locating data through index files. Be sure to read the section above called "Using FIND and SEEK Successfully" for tips on searching for multiple-key expressions.

#### SEE ALSO

SEEK
INDEX
SET INDEX
SET ORDER
SET EXACT

## The SEEK Command

SEEK quickly locates data in an index file. It accepts both memory variables and expressions in its syntax.

#### SYNTAX

**SEEK <expression>**

where <expression> is literal data enclosed in quotation marks, the name of a memory variable containing the value to search for, or an expression defining the format of the value to search for.

## USAGE

SEEK locates an item in the master index file for the current database. If the SEEK command is successful, the record pointer will be at the first record that matches the value being searched for. If SEEK is not successful, the FOUND( ) function is set to .F. and the EOF( ) function is set to .T. (until some other command moves the record pointer). If the SET TALK parameter is on, an unsuccessful search displays the message **No Find**.

SEEK works only with the master index file. By default, the first-listed index file in the USE or SET INDEX command is the master index file. However, the SET ORDER command can make any of several index files the master index file.

If SET EXACT is off, only the leftmost characters need to match for the search to be successful. For example,

```
LookFor = "B"
SEEK LookFor
```

will find the first record beginning with the letter B (for example, Baker). If SET EXACT is on, only a character-for-character match will be successful (that is, there will be a match only if one of the records contains only the letter B, but there will be no match for Baker or Bueller).

SEEK will find a record that is marked for deletion only if the SET DELETED parameter is set off. SEEK will not find a record that is hidden by a SET FILTER or MODIFY QUERY condition.

If the index file contains several keys, the field widths and formats of both the data being searched for and the key expression of the index file must match exactly. SEEK cannot locate characters embedded within the index expression (that is, you cannot use the $ operator with SEEK).

You can use SEEK to create expressions that allow the search data to match the format of the key expression in the index file. For example, if an index file was created with the expression

```
INDEX ON UPPER(LName) + STR(Amount,9,2) TO AnyFile
```

the commands below will search for data in the index file using the proper format:

```
LName = "Smith"
Amount = 123.45
SEEK UPPER(LName) + STR(Amount,9,2)
```

## EXAMPLE

Given that an index file was created with the expression **UPPER(LName + FName)**, the commands below will search for the name MILLER in the index file:

**LookFor = "Miller"**
**SEEK UPPER(LookFor)**

### TIPS

Make sure that the format and length of the expression in the SEEK command matches the format and length of the index key expression, as discussed in the section above called "Using FIND and SEEK Successfully." See Chapter 12, "Sorting and Indexing," for more examples of complex INDEX expressions and matching SEEK commands.

### SEE ALSO

FIND
INDEX
SET INDEX
SET ORDER
SET EXACT

## The LOCATE Command

LOCATE finds the first record in a database file that matches a search criterion.

### SYNTAX

**LOCATE <scope> [FOR <condition>] [WHILE <condition>]**

where <scope> specifies the number of records and <condition> is any valid search condition.

### USAGE

The LOCATE command finds the first (or next) record in a database file that matches the condition specified in the FOR or WHILE portion of the command. LOCATE searches the disk file directly rather than an index file, so it can be used with any fields or combination of fields. LOCATE supports all dBASE functions and operators.

If LOCATE fails to find a matching record, the EOF( ) function is set to .T. and the FOUND( ) function is set to .F.. If the SET TALK parameter is on and LOCATE fails to find a matching record, the screen will display the message **End of LOCATE scope**.

LOCATE will find records that are marked for deletion only if the SET DELETED command is off. LOCATE will not find records hidden by a SET FILTER or MODIFY QUERY condition.

The CONTINUE command can be used with LOCATE to find the next record that matches the search condition.

#### EXAMPLE

The command

**LOCATE FOR UPPER(LName) = "SMITH" .AND.;**
**Amount > 1000**

will locate the first record in the database with Smith in the LName field and an amount greater than 1000 in the Amount field.

#### TIPS

For faster searches, use the FIND or SEEK command with an active index file.

#### SEE ALSO

CONTINUE
FIND
SEEK
INDEX

## The CONTINUE Command

CONTINUE resumes a search that was first initiated by a LOCATE command, beginning at the next record in the database file.

#### SYNTAX

**CONTINUE**

#### USAGE

The CONTINUE command searches the remaining records in the database (or those specified in the scope condition of the LOCATE command) for the next record matching the search criterion. If no record is found, the EOF( ) condition is set to .T. and the FOUND( ) condition is set to .F.. If the SET TALK parameter is on when no more records match the search criterion, the screen displays the message **End of LOCATE scope**.

CONTINUE will find records that are marked for deletion only if the SET DELETED command is off. CONTINUE will not find records hidden by a SET FILTER or MODIFY QUERY condition.

### EXAMPLES

The routine below displays all records that have Smith in the LName field:

```
LOCATE FOR LName = "Smith"
DO WHILE .NOT. EOF( )
     ? TRIM(FName),LName
     ? Hire_Date
     ?
     CONTINUE
ENDDO
```

### TIPS

CONTINUE works only with the LOCATE command. It cannot be used with FIND or SEEK to locate the next matching record.

### SEE ALSO

LOCATE
FIND
SEEK

## The MODIFY QUERY/CREATE QUERY Commands

MODIFY QUERY and CREATE QUERY both present a full-screen menu that allows a user to specify searching criteria in an interactive, menu-driven fashion.

### SYNTAX

**MODIFY QUERY <file name>**

or

**CREATE QUERY <file name>**

where <file name> is the name of the query file to which dBASE adds the .qry extension.

## USAGE

Both the CREATE QUERY and the MODIFY QUERY commands call up the menu for defining search conditions shown in Figure 13.19. The arrow keys move the highlight across the top menu and up and down within the pull-down menus. Pressing Return while a pull-down menu option is highlighted selects that option.

Up to seven expressions for searching the database can be defined on the Set Filter menu. These can be joined with .AND., .OR., or .NOT. operators. They can also be grouped with parentheses using the Nest menu.

After filling in the query form, selecting Save saves the query form for future use and also automatically initiates the filter condition defined in the query form. The **SET FILTER TO** command, with no additional parameter, deactivates the filter condition.

The **SET FILTER TO FILE <file name>** command activates a previously defined query file without displaying the MODIFY QUERY form. The file

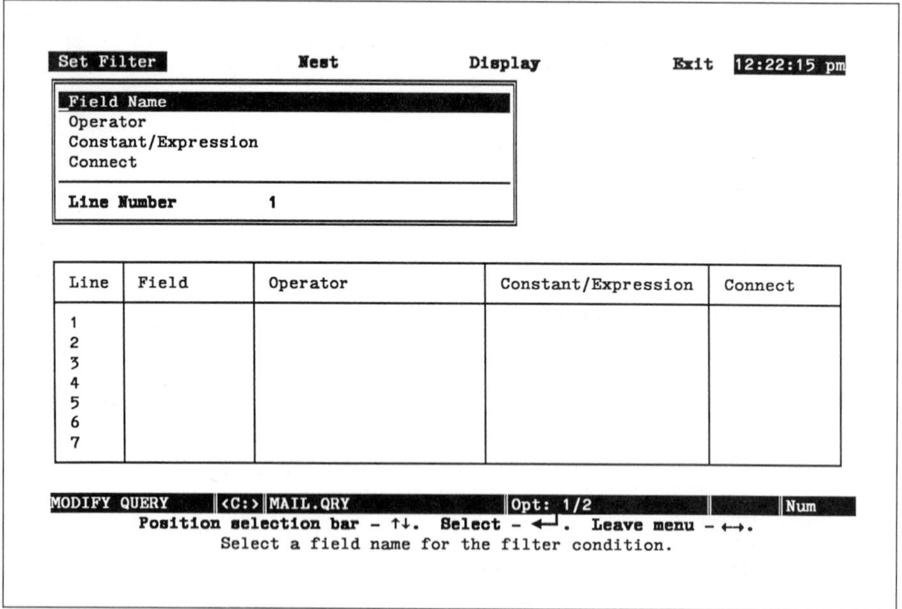


**FIGURE 13.19:** A blank MODIFY QUERY screen ready to accept input from the user. The arrow keys move the highlight across the top menu items and up and down within the pull-down menus. Up to seven search criteria can be defined and linked with .AND., .OR., or .NOT. operators.

name in this example must be the name of an existing and valid query form file. (dBASE assumes the .qry file name extension.)

The menu options on the MODIFY QUERY menu options are summarized below.

## The Set Filter Menu

This menu actually defines the filter condition and must be used before either the Nest or Display options are accessed. The Field Name option displays a submenu of field names in the currently selected database file. The Operator option displays a list of dBASE operators and a brief description of each. These will vary depending on the data type of the current field. The Constant/Expression option waits for the user to enter a value to search for. If the data type of the current field is character, the expression must be enclosed in quotation marks or brackets. If the current data type is date, a CTOD function is necessary (i.e., CTOD("12/31/87")). To use the name of another field in the expression, press F10 rather than type in an expression. The Backspace key can be used to make corrections.

The Connect option links the current field with the next field to be entered using a logical operator. An operator must be entered before moving to the next field.

The Line Number option lets you move to any existing condition in the Set Filter menu. To insert a new line before an existing line, bring the existing line to the Set Filter menu and press Ctrl-N. To delete a line, bring the line to the Set Filter menu and type Ctrl-U.

## The Nest Menu

The Nest menu lets you place parentheses around any existing lines. This allows you to be more specific about the meaning of a search criterion. For example, the condition

**LName = "Jones" .AND. State = "CA" .OR. State = "NY"**

is somewhat ambiguous. However, with the addition of parentheses, the condition clearly specifies "Jones in either CA or NY", as below:

**LName = "Jones" .AND. (State = "CA" .OR. State = "NY")**

The Start option places a left parenthesis at the left of the line you specify. The End option places a right parenthesis to the right of the line you specify.

### THE DISPLAY MENU

This option lets you perform a quick test of the filter condition defined on the Set Filter menu. Selecting this option displays the first record in the database file (if any) that matches the condition. Pressing PgUp and PgDn scrolls through additional records that match the criterion.

### THE EXIT MENU

To exit from the MODIFY QUERY form, you must select this menu. The Save option saves the query form in a file with the .qry extension. This option also activates the filter criterion immediately. The Abandon option exits the query form without saving or activating the filter condition.

## EXAMPLES

The commands

**USE Mail**
**MODIFY QUERY State**

call up the MODIFY QUERY screen for the Mail.dbf database. If a query file named State.qry already exists, its contents are displayed on the screen. If State.qry does not already exist, a blank query form is displayed and then created when the user selects Exit and Save from the top menu.

## TIPS

To activate a previously defined query condition without bringing up the MODIFY QUERY screen, use the command **SET FILTER TO FILE <file name>**, where <file name> is the name of the existing query file.

To deactivate a query filter, enter the command **SET FILTER TO**.

If the record pointer is at a record that does not match the filter criteria when the query condition is saved, the results may be inaccurate. To ensure that a MODIFY QUERY filter condition works properly, use a command to move the record pointer immediately after the MODIFY QUERY command. A simple GO TOP command, or GO BOTTOM followed by a GO TOP command, will do the trick.

To determine whether any records in a database file match the filter condition, move the record to the top of the file and check for an EOF( ) condition, as below:

**MODIFY QUERY AnyFile**
**GO TOP**
**IF EOF( )**

```
    ? "No records match filter condition!"
ENDIF
```

The MODIFY QUERY screen is a powerful technique for providing end users with full querying capability in a custom application. However, at the time of this writing, no dBASE compilers support the command.

**SEE ALSO**

SET FILTER

## SUMMARY

This chapter discussed numerous techniques for locating and filtering database records. Many other techniques in dBASE also define groups of records to access. Other examples of searching for database records appear in the chapters listed below.

*For additional information on using searching commands to print reports:*

- Chapter 9, "Printing Formatted Reports"

*For techniques on locating data in separate, related database files for data verification:*

- Chapter 10, "Adding New Data"

*For additional information on locating specific records to edit in a database file:*

- Chapter 11, "Editing and Deleting Records"

*For additional examples of indexing expressions and matching SEEK conditions:*

- Chapter 12, "Sorting and Indexing"

*For tips on using searching techniques while calculating values:*

- Chapter 14, "Calculating Numbers"

*For scoping techniques for specifying groups of adjacent database records:*

- Chapter 15, "Managing Data, Records, and Files"

*For information on using SET FILTER for querying;*

- Chapter 18, "Setting Parameters"

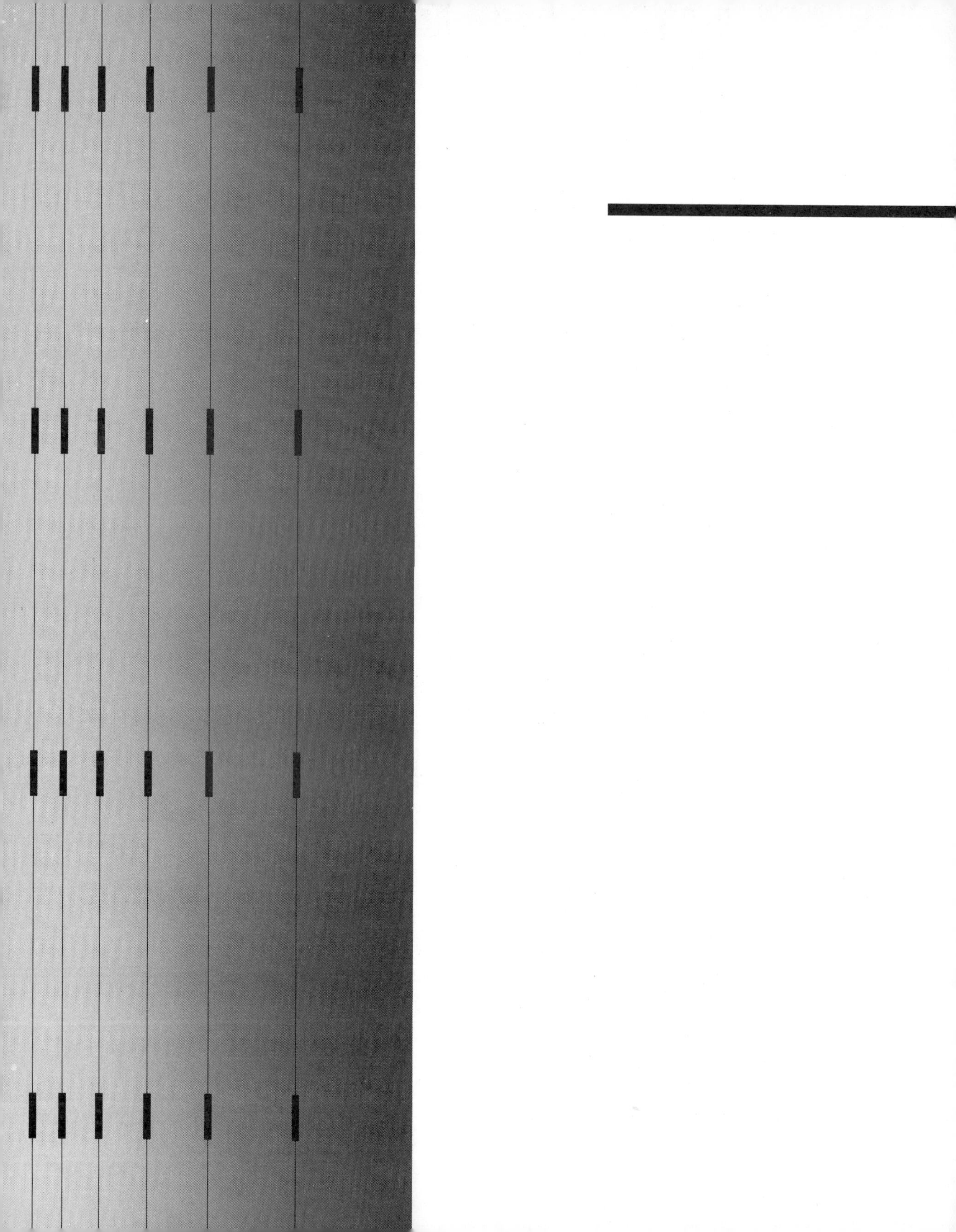

# CALCULATING NUMBERS

# Calculating Numbers

This chapter focuses on commands and techniques that calculate sums and averages in database files. These techniques are useful in nearly all databases that include numbers. For example, in a sales database you might want to calculate total sales for a given product or the average monthly sales for individual sales personnel. Some techniques for performing these calculations are discussed in the beginning of the chapter. The specific commands are discussed in the reference section.

Chapter 9, "Printing Formatted Reports," discusses techniques for displaying totals and subtotals in formatted reports. Chapter 24, "Algorithms to Extend dBASE," discusses techniques for more advanced statistical calculations, such as variance and standard deviation.

## Programming Techniques for Sums and Averages

The SUM and AVERAGE commands are virtually identical, except for the obvious difference that SUM calculates totals and AVERAGE calculates averages. Either command can be used in a program to perform calculations on database files. Both commands support the FOR and WHILE options and can therefore be used to perform calculations on records that meet some search criterion.

You can add programs to your applications that give the user an easy means of performing sums and averages in fields in a database file.

The Charges database file with the structure shown in Figure 14.1 will demonstrate a programming technique that provides the user with an easy means of calculating sums and averages. Figure 14.2 shows a simple command file that allows a user to calculate sums and averages for the Charges database file. Using some of the techniques discussed in Chapter 13, "Searching a Database," the user can opt to print the sum and average for all records or only those that meet a certain query criterion.

```
Structure for database: Charges.dbf

Field  Field Name  Type       Width    Dec
    1  CustNo      Numeric        4
    2  Invoice_No  Numeric        6
    3  Part_No     Character      5
    4  Qty         Numeric        4
    5  Unit_Price  Numeric        9      2
    6  Date        Date           8
```

**FIGURE 14.1:** Structure of the Charges database file used in the SumAvg program shown in Figure 14.2. The sum and average calculated by that program are based on the extended price, calculated as the quantity times the unit price (Qty * Unit_Price).

```
******************************** SumAvg.prg
USE Charges
CLEAR
TEXT

     This program calculates sums and averages of
      quantity, unit price, and extended prices
   (quantity X unit price) on the Charges database.

 Calculate for (A)ll records, or a particular (Q)uery?

ENDTEXT
AllNone = " "
@ 17,2 SAY "[Enter A or Q] " GET AllNone PICT "!"
READ
IF AllNone = "Q"
   MODIFY QUERY SumAvg
   Message = "query condition"
ELSE
   Message = "all records"
ENDIF (allnone)

*------------------- Print calculations based on choice.
SET DELETED ON    && Leave out records marked for deletion.
SET TALK ON

*---------------- Perform calculations.
SUM Qty * Unit_Price TO TotSale
AVERAGE Qty * Unit_Price TO AvgSale
COUNT TO NoSale

*---------------- Display results.
SET TALK OFF
CLEAR
@ 12,20 SAY "Total sales for &Message "+STR(TotSale,12,2)
@ 14,20 SAY "Average sales for &Message " + STR(AvgSale,12,2)
@ 16,20 SAY "Tally for "+LTRIM(STR(NoSale))+" records"

SET DELETED OFF
SET FILTER TO
@ 22,1
WAIT
RETURN
```

**FIGURE 14.2:** A program that allows the user to calculate the sum and average of the extended price in the Charges database file. The user can opt to perform that calculation on all records in the database or only on those records that match a specified query criterion.

The COUNT command displays the number of records in the database that are not "hidden" by a MODIFY QUERY or SET FILTER command. It can also be used to count the number of records that meet a searching criterion.

For example, the command

**COUNT FOR CustNo = 1001 TO HowMany**

counts how many records in the database file have the number 1001 in the field named CustNo. It stores the result in the numeric field named HowMany.

In the sample program in Figure 14.2, the simple command **COUNT TO NoSale** counts how many records match the user's filter criteria and stores the result in a memory variable named NoSale. Later in the program an @ command displays the results of the count.

Note that the RECCOUNT( ) function always displays the *total* number of records in a database file. Therefore, you need not use the COUNT command to count the total number of records in a database file.

## Using Complex Expressions in Calculation Commands

Like all dBASE commands that act on entire database files, you can use complex expressions with the calculation commands. For example, suppose a database of sales transactions contains the fields PartNo, Qty, Unit_Price, and Tax, where Tax is a logical field and the others are numeric. The command below can calculate the total sales for all the records in the database file and add 6 percent tax to those that have .T. in the Tax field:

**SUM (Qty * Unit_Price) * IIF(Tax,1.06,1) TO TotSale**

The command below calculates the average sales transaction for part number 1001, including the tax (if any), and stores its result in a variable named AvgSale:

```
AVERAGE (Qty * Unit_Price) * IIF(Tax,1.06,1) ;
         FOR PartNo = 1001 TO AvgSale
```

## Commands Used for Calculating Numbers

The rest of this chapter discusses the individual commands you can use to perform calculations on numeric fields and to count the number of records that meet some search criterion. Chapter 24, "Algorithms to Extend dBASE," includes custom procedures to perform more advanced calculations, such as variance and standard deviation. Chapter 11, "Editing and Deleting Records," shows some practical uses for the COUNT command.

## The AVERAGE Command

AVERAGE calculates the average (arithmetic mean) of a numeric field.

### SYNTAX

**AVERAGE <expressions> <scope> [WHILE <condition>];**
**[FOR <condition>] [TO <memory variables>]**

where <expressions> are field names or expressions of numeric fields, <scope> is a dBASE scope option, <condition> is a valid query condition, and <memory variables> are names of memory variables to store the results in.

### USAGE

The AVERAGE command calculates the average of a numeric field or fields. Up to five field names or expressions, separated by commas, can be included. If no field names or expressions are specified, all fields are averaged.

If the TO portion of the command is used, there must be a memory variable name for each field name or expression. If the SET TALK parameter is on, the results of the calculations are displayed on the screen. If SET TALK is off, no results are displayed, so the TO portion with memory variable names is required to provide access to the results.

Records hidden by a SET FILTER, MODIFY QUERY, or SET DELETED ON command are not included in the calculation.

### EXAMPLES

The command

```
AVERAGE Ext_Price TO AvgPrice
```

calculates the average of the numeric field Ext_Price and stores the result in a numeric memory variable named AvgPrice.

The command

```
AVERAGE Unit_Price, (Qty * Unit_Price) ;
        FOR PartNo = "A-111" TO AvgUnit,AvgSale
```

calculates the average of the Unit_Price field and the average of the Unit_Price field multiplied by the Qty field for records with A-111 in the PartNo field. The average of the Unit_Price field is stored in the memory variable AvgUnit, and the average of the products of Qty times Unit_Price is stored in the AvgSale memory variable.

To display the results of the calculations above, use @ or ? as shown below:

**? AvgUnit,AvgSale**

### TIPS

It is faster to use several fields or expressions in a single AVERAGE command than to use several separate AVERAGE commands. That is, the command

**AVERAGE Sale,Salary TO AvgSale,AvgSalary**

will run twice as fast as the commands

**AVERAGE Sale TO AvgSale**
**AVERAGE Salary TO AvgSalary**

If the field used in a FOR condition is indexed, use the faster SEEK and WHILE conditions for maximum speed, as below:

```
USE Sales INDEX PartNo
Search = "A-111"
SEEK Search
AVERAGE (Qty*Unit_Price) WHILE PartNo = Search ;
        TO AvgTotSale
```

### SEE ALSO

SUM
COUNT

## The COUNT Command

COUNT counts how many records meet a search criterion.

### SYNTAX

**COUNT <scope> [WHILE <condition>] [FOR <condition>];**
**[TO <memory variable>]**

where <scope> is a dBASE scope option, <condition> is a valid query condition, and <memory variable> is the name of a memory variable to store the result in.

## USAGE

The COUNT command tallies the number of records in the database field that match a search criterion. If SET TALK is off, no results are displayed, so the TO portion with a memory variable name is required to provide access to the results of the tally.

Records hidden by a SET FILTER, MODIFY QUERY, or SET DELETED ON command are not included in the tally.

## EXAMPLES

The command

**COUNT FOR LName = "Smith" TO SmithNumb**

counts how many individuals in the database have the last name Smith and stores this number in a variable named SmithNumb. To view the results of the tally, use @ or ? to display the results, as below:

**? SmithNumb**

## TIPS

The RECCOUNT( ) function displays the total number of records in a database immediately. However, RECCOUNT( ) cannot be used to determine how many records meet a search criterion or how many records remain after the SET DELETED, SET FILTER, or MODIFY QUERY commands hide records from view.

If the field used in a FOR condition is indexed, it is faster to use the SEEK and WHILE conditions, as below:

```
USE Sales INDEX PartNo
Search = "A-111"
SEEK Search
COUNT WHILE PartNo = Search TO HowMany
```

## SEE ALSO

RECCOUNT( )
AVERAGE

## The SUM Command

SUM calculates the sum of numeric fields.

### SYNTAX

**SUM <expressions> <scope> [WHILE <condition>];**
**[FOR <condition>] [TO <memory variables>]**

where <expressions> are field names or expressions of numeric fields, <scope> is a dBASE scope option, <condition> is a valid query condition, and <memory variables> are names of memory variables to store the results in.

### USAGE

Up to five field names or expressions, separated by commas, can be included in the SUM command. If no field names or expressions are listed, all numeric fields are summed. If the TO portion of the command is used, there must be a memory variable name for each field name or expression, each separated by a comma. If the SET TALK parameter is on, the results of the calculation are displayed on the screen immediately. Otherwise, the results are not displayed and therefore must be stored in memory variables to be accessible.

Records that are hidden by a MODIFY QUERY, SET FILTER, or SET DELETED ON command are not included in the calculation.

### EXAMPLES

The command

```
SUM Age TO TotAge
```

calculates the sum of the numeric field Age and stores the result in a numeric memory variable named TotAge.

The command

```
SUM (Qty * Unit_Price, Tax ;
    FOR CustNo = 1010 TO TotSale, TotTax
```

calculates the sum of the Unit_Price field multiplied by the Qty field, and the sum of the Tax field, for records with 1010 in the CustNo field. The sum of the (Qty * Unit_Price) expression is stored in the memory variable named TotSale, and the sum of the Tax field is stored in the TotTax memory variable.

To view the results of the calculations above, use @ or ? to display the results, as below:

```
? TotSale,TotTax
```

### TIPS

It is faster to use several fields or expressions in a single SUM command than to use several separate SUM commands. That is, the command

```
SUM Sale,Salary TO TotSale,TotSalary
```

will run twice as fast as the commands

```
SUM Sale TO TotSale
SUM Salary TO TotSalary
```

If the field used in a FOR condition is indexed, use the faster SEEK and WHILE conditions for maximum speed, as below:

```
USE Sales INDEX CustNo
Search = 1010
SEEK Search
SUM (Qty*Unit_Price) WHILE CustNo = Search ;
     TO TotSale
```

### SEE ALSO

TOTAL
REPORT FORM
UPDATE
AVERAGE

## The TOTAL Command

TOTAL creates a new database with totals of numeric fields summarized by a key field or expression.

### SYNTAX

```
TOTAL ON <key expression> TO <file name> [<scope>];
         [FIELDS <field names>] [WHILE <condition>];
         [FOR <condition>]
```

where <key expression> is the expression representing the field for grouping, <file name> is the name of the file to copy totaled records to, <scope> is a scoping option, <field names> are names of fields to include in the total, and <condition> is any valid search condition.

## USAGE

Use the TOTAL command to create a database containing a single record for each unique value in a particular field in the original database. The numeric fields in the summary database contain the totals of numeric values in the original database file. The database is assumed to be on the current disk drive and directory unless otherwise specified in the file name.

The database must be sorted or indexed on the field or expression of interest (i.e., the <key expression>). Using TOTAL with an improperly indexed or sorted database will not generate an error message. Instead, the command will produce an incomplete summary database.

The structure of the generated summary database file is identical to the structure of the original database, except that memo fields are not copied.

Records that are hidden by a MODIFY QUERY, SET FILTER, or SET DELETED ON command are not included in the totals.

If the SET SAFETY parameter is on, dBASE asks for permission before overwriting a file with the name specified in the TO portion of the command. If SET SAFETY is off, dBASE automatically overwrites the named file.

## EXAMPLE

The sample database in Figure 14.3 is named Sales and is indexed on the PartNo field.

To calculate how many of each item in the database were sold, you could enter the commands below:

**USE Sales INDEX PartNo**
**TOTAL ON PartNo TO SaleSumm FIELDS Qty**

When the TOTAL command completes its job, the SaleSumm.dbf file will contain a summary of the Sales database file, with a single record for each unique part number in the Sales database file. Figure 14.4 shows the contents of the SaleSumm database file generated by the TOTAL command in this example.

```
Record#  PartNo Qty Unit_Price Date_Sold
      1  A-111    5      10.00 01/31/87
      2  A-111    5      10.00 03/31/87
      3  B-222    1     100.00 01/01/87
      4  B-222    1     100.00 10/02/87
      5  C-333   10      50.00 01/01/87
```

**FIGURE 14.3:** Contents of the sample Sales database file. Before totaling, this file is indexed on the PartNo field.

```
Record#  PartNo Qty Unit_Price Date_Sold
      1  A-111   10      10.00 01/31/87
      2  B-222    2     100.00 01/01/87
      3  C-333   10      50.00 01/01/87
```

**FIGURE 14.4:** Contents of the SaleSumm database file generated by the TOTAL command. Note that the Qty field in each record is the sum of all the Qty fields in the Sales database file for each particular part number. The Unit_Price field, however, is not totaled, because this field was not included in the FIELDS portion of the TOTAL command.

Note that the Qty field in the SaleSumm file contains the total of the Qty fields for each part number in the Sales file. The Unit_Price field is not totaled, however, because it was not included in the FIELDS portion of the TOTAL command.

### TIPS

The TOTAL command can be used in place of the summary report option in the MODIFY REPORT command to generate summary totals.

### SEE ALSO

MODIFY REPORT
SUM
AVERAGE
UPDATE

## SUMMARY

This chapter discussed the commands that you can use to calculate totals and averages on numeric fields. For additional information on performing calculations, see the chapters below:

*For techniques on printing formatted reports of totals, subtotals, and summarized totals:*

- Chapter 9, "Printing Formatted Reports"

*For practical uses of the COUNT command:*

- Chapter 11, "Editing and Deleting Records"

*For performing more advanced statistical and financial calculations:*

- Chapter 24, "Algorithms to Extend dBASE"

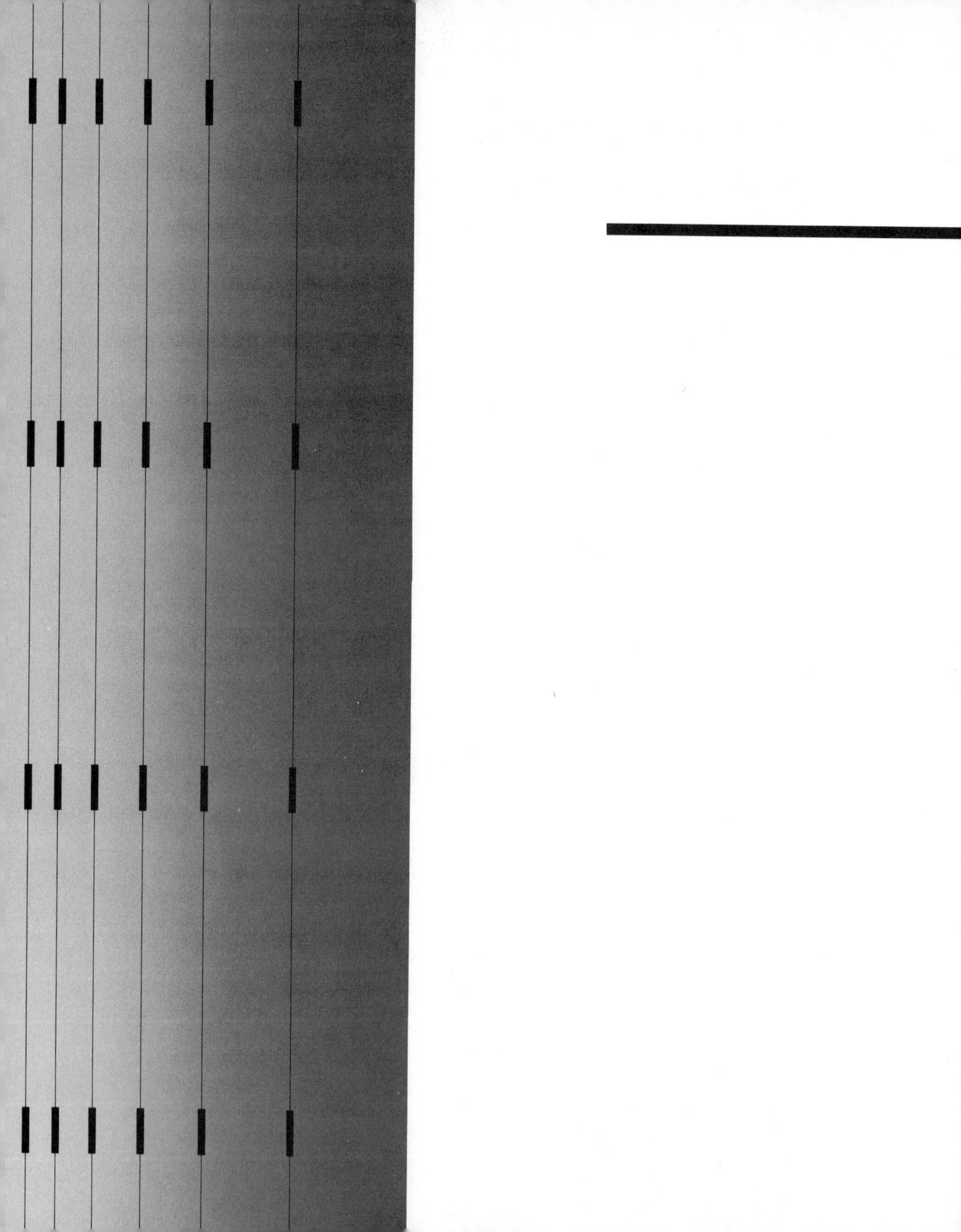

CHAPTER 15

# Managing Data, Records, and Files

# Managing Data, Records, and Files

his chapter discusses general techniques for handling dBASE data. The discussions focus on data at three different levels:

1. Handling individual data elements such as fields and memory variables
2. Processing individual records and groups of records in a database file
3. Managing entire files, including the creation, modification, and deletion of entire files

The reference section of the chapter covers the commands you need for managing data at all three levels.

## Managing Individual Data Elements

At the most basic level, the programmer needs to have complete control over individual items of data, whether they are stored as characters, numbers, dates, logical expressions, or memos. This first section discusses general techniques for handling each of these data types.

### Managing Character Data

The character data type stores any textual information up to 254 characters. In addition to the typical names and addresses that are always stored as character data, pseudo numbers with embedded hyphens (such as telephone numbers and zip codes) are stored as the character data type. As long as these pseudo numbers are of uniform width, they will be sorted and indexed properly even when stored as character strings.

## COMPARING CHARACTER STRINGS

All of the dBASE relational operators can be used to compare character strings, but you need to be careful of upper- and lowercase distinctions. The sections below show how dBASE compares character strings.

***Case Comparisons*** Two strings that have the exact same letters, in the exact same case, are identical. If the case varies, however, the strings are not identical. Lowercase letters are always alphabetically larger than equivalent uppercase letters, because of the ASCII code sequence. (Appendix D shows a complete ASCII chart.)

The UPPER( ) and LOWER( ) functions eliminate any problems caused by case differences by converting all letters to uppercase or lowercase automatically. For example, the command

**? UPPER("AbC") = UPPER("abc")**

evaluates to true, because the uppercase equivalents for AbC and abc are identical. Similarly, the command below converts the contents of the LName field in each record to uppercase before comparing it to the name SMITH. Therefore, the command successfully displays all Smiths, regardless of whether the letters stored in the field are upper- or lowercase.

**LIST FOR UPPER(LName) = "SMITH"**

***Effects of SET EXACT on String Comparisons*** When the SET EXACT parameter is off, which is the default state, dBASE considers two strings to match if the characters on the right side of the expression match the leading characters on the left side of the expression. For example, the first expression below evaluates to true because the letters on the right side, ABC, are the first three letters of ABCDEFG. The LIST command will display Smith, Smithsonian, Smithberry, and any other name beginning with the letters Smi:

**SET EXACT OFF**
**? "ABCDEFG" = "ABC"**
**LIST FOR LName = "Smi"**

The commands below, however, have a different effect altogether:

**SET EXACT ON**
**? "ABCDEFG" = "ABC"**
**LIST FOR LName = "Smi"**

The first expression is false because EXACT requires that both sides of the expression be identical, character for character. The LIST command will list only people whose last names are literally Smi, if any.

Notice that the command below also evaluates to false, even though SET EXACT is off:

```
SET EXACT OFF
? "ABC" = "ABCDEFG"
.F.
```

This is because the longer of the two character strings is on the right side of the expression.

Note that the SET EXACT command affects only the character data type.

## Concatenating Strings

Character strings can be linked with either the plus or the minus operator. When the plus operator is used, trailing blanks are included in the concatenation unless they are trimmed. The comma operator automatically places a blank space between strings. Be forewarned, however, that the comma operator can be used only in commands that display data (such as LIST and DISPLAY), not in commands that store data (such as STORE, REPLACE, or =) or in the @...SAY command.

The examples below demonstrate the results of various techniques to concatenate two character strings. Notice that the initial width of the LName variable is 20 characters, and FName is 15 characters.

```
LName = "Jones               "
FName = "Jason          "

? FName,LName
Jason           Jones

? TRIM(FName),LName
Jason Jones

? FName + LName
Jason          Jones

? FName - LName
JasonJones

? TRIM(FName) + " " + LName
Jason Jones
```

One character can be stuffed inside another using the STUFF( ) function, as shown in the commands below:

**Target = "I want here."**
**Bullet = "this word "**
**? STUFF(Target,8,0,Bullet)**

The ? command displays the message

**I want this word here.**

The STUFF( ) function placed the character string stored in the variable named Bullet inside the character string named Target, starting at the eighth character in Target and overwriting zero characters.

Table 15.1 summarizes the character string operators.

## FINDING EMBEDDED STRINGS

To find out whether a string is embedded in another string, or to find the exact location of the string, use the $ (embedded in) operator or the AT( ) function. The examples below illustrate how to find embedded strings:

**Big = "Now is the time for all good men."**
**Small = "time"**
**? Small $ Big**
**.T.**

Because "time" is in the larger string, the expression evaluates to true.

**? "ALL" $ UPPER(Big)**
**.T.**

| OPERATOR | DESCRIPTION | EXAMPLE |
|---|---|---|
| + | Concatenates two strings | "A " + "B" = "A B" |
| – | Concatenates two strings, subtracting any blanks | "A " – "B" = "AB" |
| $ | Checks whether the contents of the first string are also in the second string | "A" $ "AB" = .T. |

**TABLE 15.1:** Operators Used with Character Strings

Because ALL is in the uppercase equivalent of the larger string, this expression is also true.

```
? AT("TIME",UPPER(Big))
12
```

The command above returns 12 because TIME begins at the twelfth character in the uppercase equivalent of Big.

To display or copy a portion of a string from within a larger string, use the SUBSTR( ) function. The command

```
? SUBSTR(Big,12,4)
```

returns the word "time", because it is a substring beginning at the twelfth character, and it is 4 characters long.

The commands below demonstrate how a single character string can be treated as a small array, from which an item of data can be plucked out with an expression. The memory variable Months contains a three-letter abbreviation for each month in the year. Each abbreviation, in turn, is three characters long:

```
Months = "   JanFebMarAprMayJunJulAugSepOctNovDec"
```

To view the three-letter abbreviation for a particular month, use the actual month multiplied by 3 as the starting point for the substring, and 3 as the length, as in the example below:

```
? SUBSTR(Months,MONTH(DATE( ))*3,3)
Apr
```

In this case, the current date (produced by DATE( )) fell in the month of April. The MONTH( ) function returned 4, which multiplied by 3 produced 12, the position in Months where the Apr string began. (Of course, this is only an example. The CMONTH( ) function can return the month of a date more directly. See Chapter 17, "dBASE Functions.")

## Combining Character and Noncharacter Data

When combining character string data with other data types (as is required by the @ and STORE commands and the assignment operator ( = )), the other data types must first be converted to character data. Table 15.2 lists the functions used to convert noncharacter data to character data.

In the examples below, Date is the date data type, IsPaid is the logical data type, and Amount is the numeric data type. Each example represents a valid technique for combining character data with other data types. The commands

```
Amount = 999.99
@ 2,1 SAY "You win " + LTRIM(STR(Amount,12,2)) + " dollars!"
```

| FUNCTION | DATA TYPE | EXAMPLE |
|---|---|---|
| STR | Numeric | STR(Amount,12,2) |
| DTOC | Date | DTOC(AnyDate) |
| IIF | Logical | IIF(IsTrue,"Y","N") |

**TABLE 15.2:** Functions that Convert Various Data Types to Character Strings

produce

**You win 999.99 dollars!**

(The LTRIM function trims leading blanks off any size number to make it fit well in the text.) The commands

```
Date = DATE( )
IsPaid = .F.
Part = "Balance was"
Msg = Part + IIF(IsPaid," "," not ") + "paid on " + DTOC(Date)
```

produce a variable named Msg containing the string

**Balance was not paid on 04/30/87**

(assuming that the system date is April 30, 1987).

### Internal Storage of Character Data

If you want to interface dBASE with other languages, you will need to know that dBASE stores character strings in memory using hexadecimal ASCII codes followed by a null character. For example, the name Smith would be stored as shown below:

```
53H  6DH  69H  74H  68H  00H
 S    m    i    t    h   NUL
```

## Managing Numeric Data

The numeric data type stores real numbers used for numeric calculations. dBASE maintains about 16 places of accuracy (excluding the decimal point). Both integer and decimal numbers are stored in the numeric data type.

| OPERATOR | DESCRIPTION | EXAMPLE |
|---|---|---|
| ^ | Exponentiation | 4^2 = 16 |
| * | Multiplication | 7*3 = 21 |
| / | Division | 10/5 = 2 |
| + | Addition | 7+3 = 10 |
| – | Subtraction | 10–3 = 7 |

**TABLE 15.3:** Basic Arithmetic Operators for Numbers

## MATHEMATICAL OPERATORS

The mathematical operators used to manage numbers are listed in Table 15.3. The operators are listed in their order of precedence, but parentheses can be used to group operations and assign precedence. For example, while the equation

```
? 100 + 10 * 2
```

produces 120, the equation

```
? (100 + 10) * 2
```

produces 220, because the parentheses force the addition to take precedence over the multiplication.

If a calculation yields asterisks rather than the number you expected, the expression did not produce a valid result. Invalid results can be caused by numbers that do not fit in the field size allotted (for example, trying to squeeze 12345.67 into a field defined as 4 digits with 2 decimal places). Numbers that are between 0 and 1 need space for the zero in front of the decimal place. Negative numbers need a space for the minus sign. Division by zero also yields an invalid result. Also, function arguments that are out of the acceptable range produce invalid results (for example, attempting to find the square root of a negative number).

## COMPARING NUMBERS

Numbers can be compared using the relational operators <, >, =, #, <>, >=, and <=. Comparisons are accurate to about 13 digits. The arithmetic operators take precedence over the relational operators, so all calculations are performed before comparisons. For example, the expression

```
? 27^(1/3) > 10/5
```

results in .T. (true), because 3, which is the cube root of 27, is greater than 2, the quotient of 10 divided by 5.

### Combining Numbers with Character Strings

To concatenate numbers to character strings for use in the @, INDEX, STORE, and other commands, use the STR function. For example, if the numeric variable Amount is 123.45, the command

**INDEX ON LName + STR(Amount,12,2) TO AnyFile**

will produce a proper key expression containing the LName and Amount fields for the index file.

For display purposes, you might want to trim off leading zeros left by the STR function. Use the LTRIM function to do so, as in the example below:

**@ 1,1 SAY "You won " + LTRIM(STR(Amount,12,2)) + " dollars!"**

Do not, however, use LTRIM within INDEX expressions, as doing so will cause unequal field lengths in the index file, which in turn causes faulty indexing.

### Formatting Numbers

The PICTURE command and TRANSFORM function allow you to define various formats for displaying numbers. See Chapter 8, "Managing Screen Displays," and Chapter 9, "Printing Formatted Reports," for formatting techniques using PICTURE and TRANSFORM, as well as Chapter 17, "dBASE Functions," for a discussion of TRANSFORM and other functions that can be used to manipulate numeric data.

### Internal Storage of Numbers

If you need to know how dBASE stores numbers internally, a brief description is included here. dBASE uses the IEEE long real floating point representation. Each number uses 64 bits (8 bytes) of memory. Each number contains a sign bit ( + or −), a significand (representing the significant digits of the number), and an exponent, which multiplies the significand by a power to yield a correct binary (decimal) point in the final result.

## Managing Date Data

The date data type is used to store dates in mm/dd/yy or mm/dd/yyyy format. The SET DATE command allows several alternative date formats, as summarized in Table 15.4.

If the year is entered as two digits (e.g., 87), the twentieth century is assumed. If you use dates before or after the twentieth century (e.g., 1492), use the SET CENTURY ON command with any date format to include the century.

| SET DATE COMMAND OPTION | FORMAT |
|---|---|
| AMERICAN | mm/dd/yy |
| ANSI | yy.mm.dd |
| BRITISH | dd/mm/yy |
| ITALIAN | dd-mm-yy |
| FRENCH | dd/mm/yy |
| GERMAN | dd.mm.yy |

**TABLE 15.4:** Date Format Options for the SET DATE Command

## DATE ARITHMETIC

Dates can be added and subtracted to determine the number of days between two dates or to pinpoint a date in the future. For example, assuming that the system date (DATE( )) is 4/29/87, the expression

**? DATE( ) + 20**

returns the date 20 days in the future:

**05/19/87**

The expression

**? DATE( ) – 20**

produces 04/09/87—the date 20 days in the past.

Notice that adding or subtracting a number and a date automatically produces a date. If you subtract two dates, you'll get a number showing how many days fall between the two dates. For example, the expression

**? DATE( ) – CTOD("04/01/87")**

produces the number of days between the current date (April 29) and April 1st:

**28**

The expression

**? DATE( ) – CTOD("04/30/87")**

displays the number of days between the current date (April 29) and the next day:

**–1**

Later dates are larger than smaller dates in date arithmetic. To help keep the positive and negative results of date arithmetic straight in your mind, just remember that today's date is equal to yesterday's date plus one day ( + 1), and today's date is equal to tomorrow's date minus one day ( − 1).

Date arithmetic can come in handy when accessing database records. For example, the command

**LIST FOR DATE + 90 > = DATE( ) .AND. .NOT. Paid**

displays all records with dates from 90 or more days ago that have an .F. in the logical field named Paid.

## COMPARING DATES

Dates can be compared using the relational operators >, <, =, #, <>, > =, < =. A date that is greater than another date (>) is actually later, and a date that is smaller than another date (<) is actually earlier. For example, the expression

**? CTOD("01/01/87") > CTOD("12/31/86")**

results in true (.T.) because January 1, 1987 is greater (later) than December 31, 1986.

You must be careful when comparing a valid date to a blank date. For example, suppose that the current database has a field named Date_Paid, and you enter the command

**APPEND BLANK**

The new record contains a blank date ("  /  /  "). Assuming that the current date (04/29/87 in this example) is compared to this blank date, the following expressions produce the following results:

**? DATE( ) > = Date_Paid**
**.F.**

**? DATE( ) < = Date_Paid**
**.F.**

As the results indicate, the blank date is neither greater than, less than, nor equal to the current date.

To remedy this situation, you can use the DTOC function to convert both dates in the expression to character data. In that case, any nonblank date is greater than the blank date (and neither less than nor equal to it).

### Combining Dates with Characters

To combine dates with character strings in memory variables or for display with the @ command, use the DTOC (date-to-character) function. For example, the command below displays the prompt **Today's date is** followed by the current date:

```
@ 1,1 SAY "Today's date is " + DTOC(DATE( ))
```

If you are using the date as part of an index key expression, you will probably want to make sure that the year is evaluated first. See Chapter 12, "Sorting and Indexing," for tips.

The CTOD (character-to-date) function converts character data to date data. For example, the commands below create a character field that is eight characters wide. After the user enters a value and presses Return, the CTOD function converts the user's entry to the date data type:

```
DeadLine = SPACE(8)    && Start with 8-character string.
@ 2,2 SAY "Enter date " GET DeadLine PICTURE "99/99/99"
READ
DeadLine = CTOD(DeadLine)    && Convert string to date.
```

Instead of using a blank character date, you can use the current system date as the suggested date. That way, there is no need to use CTOD to convert the character entry to the date data type. The routine below shows an example:

```
DeadLine = DATE( )         && Starts as current date.
@ 2,2 SAY "Enter date " GET DeadLine PICTURE "99/99/99"
READ
* -- DeadLine is still the date data type here.
```

Chapter 17, "dBASE Functions," discusses many other important functions for managing dates.

### Internal Storage of Dates

Dates are stored internally as numbers and are treated as numbers for all calculations and comparisons. Each date uses eight bytes of memory. The range of acceptable dates is approximately 01/01/100 to 12/31/32676.

## Managing Logical Data

The logical data type can have only one of two values, true or false. Generally, true is expressed as .T. and false is expressed as .F.. In some situations when data are entered directly from the screen, other values are acceptable, as discussed throughout this section.

## Storing Logical Data

To store data directly to a logical memory variable or database field, you must use the .T. and .F. syntax. For example, the command below stores the value .F. in a logical field named IsReady:

**IsReady = .F.**

The command below stores .T. in the logical field PaidYet:

**REPLACE PaidYet WITH .T.**

You can also use expressions to store values to logical fields. For example, the command

**IsOver90 = (Date( ) – Date_Due) > = 90**

stores .T. in the IsOver90 variable if the current date minus the Date_Due variable is greater than or equal to 90. If the difference between the two dates is less than 90 days, the variable IsOver90 receives the value .F..

## Logical Picture Templates

If you use an @...SAY...GET command to allow a user to enter logical data into a database field or memory variable, you can use a picture template to determine what is and is not an acceptable entry. For example, the commands below ask the user to enter a value for the logical field ToPrinter:

```
ToPrinter = .F.
@ 10,5 SAY "Print the report? ";
   GET ToPrinter PICTURE "L"
READ
```

The PICTURE "L" component allows only the logical entries T, t, Y, or y for true and F, f, N, or n for false. Any lowercase entry is automatically converted to uppercase on the screen.

The alternative PICTURE "Y" component accepts only Y or y for true and N or n for false. Lowercase letters are automatically converted to uppercase.

The PICTURE commands can also be used with the SAY command. For example, the command below assumes that the field or variable named Taxable contains logical data. In this example, the screen displays either T or F (for true or false).

**@ 10,10 SAY Taxable PICTURE "L"**

In the example below the command displays Y if the Taxable field contains .T. and N if the Taxable field contains .F..

**@ 10,10 SAY Taxable PICTURE "Y"**

## Comparing Logical Data

Logical data require a somewhat different syntax than other data types when used in expressions. Rather than using an operator with an expression on each side, (like State = "CA"), you need only use the name of the logical field or memory variables (and the optional .NOT. operator to indicate false values).

For example, the command

**LIST FOR .NOT. Paid_Yet**

displays all records that have .F. in the field named Paid_Yet. The command

**IF IsReady**

is the same as saying **IF IsReady = .T.**. In a DO CASE clause, you could use a command such as

**CASE IsInStock**

to specify records with .T. in the IsInStock field.

To include multiple logical fields or variables in an expression, use .AND., .OR., and .NOT., as in the command below, which displays records that have .T. in the IsReady logical field and .F. in the PaidYet field:

**LIST FOR IsReady .AND. .NOT. PaidYet**

## Combining Logical Data with Character Data

There is no way to combine the logical data type with character data directly. However, you can use the IIF function to select a character string to combine based on the value in the logical field or variable. For example, the commands below print the message **$123.45 is paid.** if the logical Paid_Yet field is true. Otherwise, the message **$123.45 is not paid.** is displayed:

**@ 1,1 SAY "$123.45 is" + IIF(Paid_Yet," "," not ") + "paid."**

You can use the IIF function to include logical data in expressions for commands such as INDEX and TOTAL as well. In that case, you want to be sure that both .T. and .F. produce character fields of the same length. (The fields within an index file expression must be of the same length, or the index will be inaccurate.) The command below pads the word No with an extra blank to make it the same width as the word Yes:

```
INDEX ON IIF(Paid_Yet,"Yes","No ") + DTOC(Date) TO AnyFile
```

This command produces an index file in which the records with .F. in the Paid_Yet field appear first, ordered by date. You can also use the IIF command when defining report columns in the MODIFY REPORT report generator. For example, if you define the contents of a column such as

```
IIF(Tax,"Y","N")
```

the column will display Y in records where Tax is .T. and N in records where Tax is .F.

## Using Logical Data for Large Expressions

You can use logical variables to shorten complex searching expressions that would otherwise extend beyond the 254-character limit. For example, note how long the IF command below is:

```
IF LName = "Smithsonian" .AND. City = "San Diego" ;
  .AND. Paid_Yet .AND. MONTH(Due_Date) = 4 ;
  .AND. Amount >= 1200 .AND. Terms = 30
```

This long expression could be broken into several lines, which would in turn shorten the IF clause, as shown below:

```
Part1 = (LName = "Smithsonian" .AND. City = "San Diego")
Part2 = (Paid_Yet .AND. MONTH(Due_Date) = 4)
Part3 = (Amount >= 1200 .AND. Terms = 30)

IF Part1 .AND. Part2 .AND. Part3
```

You can, of course, break up the parts of the expression in any way you like. The important point is that you can create IF conditions that extend beyond the 254-character limit by using a few logical variables.

## Internal Storage of Logical Data

In memory, logical fields are stored as hexadecimal numbers occupying a single byte: 00H for .F. and 01H for .T.. In database files, logical fields are stored using the single-byte ASCII hexadecimal values for the letters T and F. That is, .T. is stored as 54H, and .F. is stored as 46H.

## Managing Memo Data

Technically, memo fields are not actually a separate data type, because they contain character data. However, because there are rules that are unique to memo fields, they really need to be treated as a unique type.

A single memo field can contain up to 5,000 characters if you are using the MODIFY COMMAND editor. If you are using an external word processor, such as WordStar, the only limit is the word processor's limit (which is generally far beyond 5,000 characters).

Because of their large size, memo fields are valuable for storing long passages of text in a record, such as notes about telephone conversations with prospective customers or historical information about employees.

### Entering and Editing Memo Data

When entering or editing data in a database file, the screen will show only a small highlight with the word Memo in place of the contents of the memo field. To enter or edit data in the field, move the highlight to the memo field and type Ctrl-PgDn or Ctrl-Home. The MODIFY COMMAND editor (or any editor you may have selected in the Config.db file) will present its usual screen and allow you to enter or edit information in the memo field. When you are done entering memo data, type Ctrl-PgUp or Ctrl-End to return to the append or edit screen.

If you use custom screens for entering and editing data, keep in mind that @...GET commands for memo fields work only if they are stored in a format file and activated with a SET FORMAT command. An @...SAY...GET command stored directly in a command file and executed with a DO command can neither display nor read memo field data.

### Displaying Memo Fields

If you use a LIST or DISPLAY command to view database data, only the word Memo will appear in place of the memo field, unless you specify the name of the memo field in the command. For example, the command below displays the LName, FName, and Notes fields, even if Notes is a memo field.

**LIST FName, LName, Notes**

The MODIFY REPORT and REPORT FORM commands will display memo field data. Just define the memo field as the contents for any report column while designing the report with MODIFY REPORT. The column width you select on the Columns menu Width setting will be the one used in the report.

For example, suppose you want to include a memo field named Notes on a report to be printed by the REPORT FORM command. You also want to add the heading Comments to this report column and limit the width of the column to 30 characters. To do so, use MODIFY REPORT and define the report column on the Columns menu as shown below:

| | |
|---|---|
| **Contents** | **Notes** |
| **Heading** | **Comments** |
| **Width** | **30** |
| **Decimal places** | |
| **Total this column** | |

The memo field will be displayed on the printed report, word-wrapped within the defined 30-character column width.

## Controlling Memo Field Widths

The SET MEMOWIDTH command lets you control the width of a memo field displayed with the LIST, DISPLAY, or ? command. For example, entering the command

**SET MEMOWIDTH TO 20**

sets the width for memo fields to 20 characters. Ensuing commands that display data (except REPORT FORM) will use this predefined width. The entire memo field will be word-wrapped within this 20-character width.

## Sorting, Searching, and Memo Fields

Memo fields cannot be searched in a database file, nor can they be used in key expressions for indexing or sorting a database. For example, in a database with a memo field named Notes, all of the following commands are illegal and will generate only an error message:

**INDEX ON Notes TO AnyFile**
**SORT ON LName, Notes TO AnyFile**
**LOCATE FOR "anxious" $ Notes**

If you want to store information in long character fields but also want to be able to search those fields, consider using a few character fields within the 254-character width limit in lieu of a memo field.

For example, if you include three character fields named Long1, Long2, and Long3 on a database file and assign each a width of 254 characters, you have 762 characters of note-taking space. To find records that have a particular word in one these fields, you could enter a command such as

```
LIST FOR "anxious" $ Long1 .OR. ;
         "anxious" $ Long2 .OR. ;
         "anxious" $ Long3
```

The word-wrap procedure presented in Chapter 24, "Algorithms to Extend dBASE," will help you format these long character fields on the screen or printer.

# MANAGING DATABASE RECORDS

Previous chapters have discussed techniques for entering, editing, sorting, searching, and displaying database records on formatted reports. This section is concerned only with rudimentary (though useful) techniques for manipulating the record pointer and adjacent groups of records in the database file.

## Positioning the Record Pointer

The GO, GOTO, and SKIP commands allow you to position the record pointer to a particular record in the database file. The GO and GOTO commands are interchangeable. These commands are summarized in Table 15.5.

The effects of GO, SKIP, and other commands on the record pointer and beginning- and end-of-file conditions in an unindexed database are summarized in Table 15.6. In the table, x and y are numbers ( −x and −y are negative numbers). RECNO( ) is the record number, BOF( ) is the beginning-of-file condition, and EOF( ) is the end-of-file condition. (These correspond to the actual dBASE functions used to detect these conditions.) Multiple commands displayed on a single line are separated by colons.

| COMMAND | EFFECT |
|---|---|
| GO TOP | Moves record pointer to first database record or first record in index order |
| GO BOTTOM | Moves record pointer to last database record or last record in index order |
| GOTO <record> | Moves record pointer to the specified record number |
| SKIP <n> | Moves record pointer <n> number of records (can be + or −) |

**TABLE 15.5:** Commands that Move the Database Record Pointer

Of the commands shown in Table 15.6, the two that generate an error message attempt to skip too far. Attempting to skip back two records from the top of the file tries to move above the beginning of the file (BOF( )) to record number −1, which does not exist. Skipping twice past the last record attempts to move the pointer beyond the end of the file (EOF( )), which also causes an error.

If no index file is active, GO TOP always moves the pointer to record 1. GO BOTTOM moves the record pointer to the last record in the database file. SKIP moves the record pointer in the record number order (if the record pointer is on record 10 and you issue a SKIP −1 command, the record pointer will be on record 9).

If an index file is active, the order specified in the index file will determine how the GO TOP, GO BOTTOM, and SKIP commands operate. For example, if the database is indexed on names, GO TOP will position the record pointer to the alphabetically "smallest" name (e.g., Aardvark). GO BOTTOM will position the record to the alphabetically largest name (e.g., Zzyyxx). SKIP will move the record pointer in alphabetical order (e.g., from Carlson to Carlton).

The GOTO command is not at all affected by index files. For example, the commands

```
GOTO 20
DISPLAY
```

will display record number 20 on the screen, regardless of any index files in use.

| COMMAND | BOF( ) | RECNO( ) | EOF( ) | ERROR? |
|---|---|---|---|---|
| GO TOP | .F. | 1 | .F. | No |
| GO TOP: SKIP −x | .T. | 1 | .F | No |
| GO TOP: SKIP −x: SKIP −y | .T. | 1 | .F. | Yes |
| GO TOP: SKIP −x: SKIP y | .F. | y + 1 | .F. | No |
| GO BOTTOM | .F. | last | .F. | No |
| GO BOTTOM: SKIP x | .F. | last + 1 | .T. | No |
| GO BOTTOM: SKIP x: SKIP y | .F. | last + 1 | .T. | Yes |
| GO BOTTOM: SKIP x: SKIP −y | .F. | last − y + 1 | .F. | No |
| LOCATE (found record) | .F. | varies | .F. | No |
| LOCATE (not found) | .F. | last + 1 | .T. | No |
| LIST* | .F. | last + 1 | .T. | No |

* Same conditions exist for other commands that access all records, such as COPY, SUM, AVERAGE, COUNT, REPORT, and REPLACE.

**TABLE 15.6:** Effects of GO, SKIP, and Other Commands on Record Number, End-of-File, and Beginning-of-File Conditions for Unindexed Databases

## Scope Options

The dBASE III PLUS *scope options* allow you to manipulate sequential groups of records in a database file. The scope options are listed in Table 15.7.

The commands that support scope options are listed in Table 15.8, along with the default scope that the command uses. The default scope need not be specified in the command. For example, the command **DISPLAY** will display a single record. Therefore, its default is RECORD. The command **LIST** will display

| SCOPE OPTION | MEANING | EXAMPLE |
|---|---|---|
| RECORD | A single record | DELETE RECORD 2 |
| ALL | All records | DISPLAY ALL |
| NEXT | Group of records, starting with the current record | COPY NEXT 20 |
| REST | All remaining records, starting with the current record | LIST REST |

**TABLE 15.7:** Scope Options for Specifying Records to Manipulate

| COMMAND | DEFAULT SCOPE |
|---|---|
| AVERAGE | ALL |
| CHANGE | RECORD |
| COPY TO | ALL |
| COUNT | ALL |
| DELETE | RECORD |
| DISPLAY | RECORD |
| LABEL FORM | ALL |
| LIST | ALL |
| LOCATE | RECORD |
| RECALL | RECORD |
| REPLACE | RECORD |
| REPORT FORM | ALL |
| SORT | ALL |
| SUM | ALL |
| TOTAL | ALL |

**TABLE 15.8:** Commands that Support Scope Options

all records, so its default setting is ALL. Note, however, that the scope options always take a back seat to the FOR and WHILE searching options, as discussed below.

## EFFECTS OF FOR AND WHILE ON SCOPES

When used with the FOR and WHILE options, the scope conditions take on a meaning that can best be thought of as "taking into consideration...". For example, the command

```
DISPLAY ALL FOR State = "CA"
```

will look at all the records in the database, but it will display only those that have CA in the State field. The commands

```
GOTO 20
LIST FOR State = "CA" NEXT 20
```

will list all records between record 20 and record 40 that have CA in the State field. The commands

```
GOTO 900
REPLACE ALL Date_Paid WITH DATE( ) ;
                      FOR Date_Paid = CTOD("  /  /  ") REST
```

will put the current system date into the Date_Paid field for those records between record 900 and the end of the file that have blank Date_Paid fields.

A scope for a single record will also take a back seat to a FOR or WHILE condition. For example, the command

```
DISPLAY RECORD 3 FOR .NOT. DELETED( )
```

will display record number 3 only if it has not been marked for deletion.

## EFFECTS OF INDEX FILES ON SCOPE OPTIONS

The scope options always follow the order specified by the current master index file, if any. Therefore, if you open a database with a command such as

```
USE Mail INDEX NameOrd
```

where the NameOrd index is based on the expression **UPPER(LName + FName)**, the commands

```
SEEK Miller
LIST NEXT 20
```

will display the first Miller in the database and the next 20 records in alphabetical order by name (regardless of the record number order). If ZZyyxx is the alphabetically largest last name on the database, the following commands will list all records with last names between Miller and ZZyyxx (inclusive), regardless of their record numbers:

```
USE Mail INDEX NameOrd
SEEK Miller
LIST REST
```

#### Using NEXT to Pause the Screen

The NEXT option can be handy for developing routines that pause after every screenful of information. For example, when you display a report form on the screen, it will whiz by quickly, unless you can start and stop the scrolling with Ctrl-S.

To place a built-in page pause in a command like REPORT, use a DO WHILE .NOT. EOF( ) loop with a NEXT option inside the loop. In this example, the report displays 20 records and then pauses for the user to press a key before displaying the next 20 records. This process continues until all the records in the database file have been displayed.

```
DO WHILE .NOT. EOF( )
    REPORT FORM <AnyRep> NEXT 20
    ?
    WAIT
    SKIP
ENDDO (eof)
```

## Managing Database Files

The third level of handling data discussed in this chapter is the ability to manage entire files of information. This includes creating, opening, viewing, modifying the structure of, copying, and deleting entire files.

### Creating Database Files

To create a new database file from scratch, enter the command CREATE at the dot prompt. The screen will display an empty form for entering field names, their data types, widths, and the number of decimal places (for numeric data only). Table 15.9 shows the keys that control the cursor and screen as you enter the database structure. Figure 15.1 shows a sample database structure defined

| KEY | ALTERNATE | EFFECT |
|---|---|---|
| Return | | Finishes data entry in one field and moves cursor to next field |
| F1 | | Toggles help menu on and off |
| Num Lock | | Toggles numbers/arrow keys on numeric keypad |
| → | Ctrl-D | Moves cursor right one character |
| ← | Ctrl-S | Moves cursor left one character |
| Ctrl-→ | Ctrl-B | Pans to the right |
| Ctrl-← | Ctrl-Z | Pans to the left |
| Home | Ctrl-A | Moves cursor to previous word, start of field, or previous field, depending on cursor's current position |
| End | Ctrl-F | Moves cursor to next word, end of field, or start of next field, depending on cursor's current position |
| PgUp | Ctrl-R | Scrolls to previous page, if any |
| PgDn | Ctrl-C | Scrolls to next page, if any |
| ↑ | Ctrl-E | Moves cursor to previous field |
| ↓ | Ctrl-X | Moves cursor to next field |
| Ins | Ctrl-V | Toggles insert mode on/off |
| Del | Ctrl-G | Deletes character at cursor |
| Backspace | | Moves cursor to left, erasing character |
| Ctrl-T | | Deletes word to right |
| Ctrl-Y | | Deletes all characters to right |
| Ctrl-U | | Deletes field |
| Esc | Ctrl-Q | Aborts current structure and exits CREATE/ MODIFY STRUCTURE mode |
| Ctrl-End | Ctrl-W | Saves current structure and exits CREATE/ MODIFY STRUCTURE mode |

**TABLE 15.9:** Control Keys Used with CREATE and MODIFY STRUCTURE

on the CREATE screen. Type Ctrl-W or Ctrl-End to save the structure. Unless you specifically assign a file-name extension to the database file, dBASE automatically assigns the extension .dbf.

Field names can be a maximum of ten characters long. Avoid using commands as field names. If you were to assign the field name Next to a field in the database and later enter the command LIST Next, dBASE would consider it an

```
                                                   Bytes remaining:   3802

 CURSOR  <-- -->  |    INSERT     |    DELETE      |  Up a field:     ↑
  Char:     ← →   |  Char:   Ins  |  Char:    Del  |  Down a field:   ↓
  Word: Home End  |  Field:  ^N   |  Word:    ^Y   |  Exit/Save:    ^End
  Pan:     ^← ^→  |  Help:   F1   |  Field:  ^U    |  Abort:         Esc

    Field Name   Type      Width  Dec          Field Name  Type      Width  Dec

 1  MR_MRS       Character    4             9  ZIP         Character   10
 2  FNAME        Character   15            10  COUNTRY     Character   12
 3  MI           Character    2            11  PHONE       Character   10
 4  LNAME        Character   20            12  PHONE_EXT   Character    4
 5  COMPANY      Character   40            13  HIRE_DATE   Date         8
 6  ADDRESS      Character   25            14  SALARY      Numeric     12    2
 7  CITY         Character   20            15  PAID_YET    Logical      1
 8  STATE        Character    5            16  NOTES_      Memo        10

CREATE          |<C:>|MAIL                  |Field: 16/16       |       |Num
                           Enter the field name.
Field names begin with a letter and may contain letters, digits and underscores
```

**FIGURE 15.1:** Sample database defined on the dBASE CREATE screen. Each field is assigned a name, a data type, and a width. The numeric field also requires a setting for the number of decimal places (in the column labeled Dec).

error, because NEXT is a command used with LIST, and it requires a number (e.g., LIST NEXT 5 means "display the next five records").

## Opening and Closing Database Files

If you want to open an existing database file so you can manipulate its contents, enter the USE command followed by the name of the database file. If you do not include an extension on the file name, dBASE assumes the default extension .dbf.

You can open multiple database files simultaneously using the SELECT command, as discussed in Chapter 3, "Database Design." You can also open database files with active index files, as discussed in Chapter 12, "Sorting and Indexing."

To close all open database files, enter the command

**CLOSE DATABASES**

To close a database file in a particular work area, select that area and enter the

USE command without a file name, as below:

```
SELECT C
USE
```

The command **CLEAR ALL** also closes all open database files.

Note that when entering and editing records, some records will be held in a buffer temporarily before being stored on disk. If the computer were shut off at this time, the data in the buffer would be lost. Therefore, it is a good idea to close database files occasionally in any custom application.

## Viewing and Modifying Database File Structures

To view the structure of a database file, open that file and enter the command **DISPLAY STRUCTURE**. To prevent screen pauses, use the command **LIST STRUCTURE**. To display the file structure on the printer, use the command **LIST STRUCTURE TO PRINT**.

To alter the structure of a database file (even if it already has data stored in it), open the file and enter the command **MODIFY STRUCTURE**. The file structure will appear on a screen similar to the one shown in Figure 15.2. You can use the arrow keys to move the cursor and make changes. Instructions and error messages will appear at the bottom of the screen as you work. Table 15.9 shows the keys that control the cursor as you modify the database structure.

*Note:* Never change both the name and the width of a field simultaneously on the MODIFY STRUCTURE screen. Doing so will cause all data for that field to be lost. Instead, change the field name only, and save the new structure. Then enter the MODIFY STRUCTURE command again, change the width of the field, and save the new structure once again.

## Copying Files

dBASE offers three different techniques for copying files: COPY TO, COPY FILE, and COPY STRUCTURE. Regardless of the version of COPY that you use, the *source file* (the one being copied) will always overwrite any existing file that has the same name as the *target file* (the one being copied to). You cannot use the COPY command to combine the contents of two files. If the target file name does not already exist, dBASE will first create a new file with that name and then perform the copy.

The COPY TO version of the COPY command can be used only with database files. This command copies the database file currently in use to a new file. For example, the commands below copy the contents of a database file named

```
                                                    Bytes remaining:   3802

 CURSOR  <-- -->  |     INSERT     |    DELETE     | Up a field:     ↑
  Char:     ← →   | Char:   Ins    | Char:    Del  | Down a field:  ↓
  Word: Home End  | Field:  ^N     | Word:    ^Y   | Exit/Save:      ^End
  Pan:     ^← ^→  | Help:   F1     | Field:   ^U   | Abort:          Esc

     Field Name  Type       Width  Dec           Field Name  Type       Width  Dec

  1  MR_MRS      Character      4            9   ZIP         Character     10
  2  FNAME       Character     15           10   COUNTRY     Character     12
  3  MI          Character      2           11   PHONE       Character     10
  4  LNAME       Character     20           12   PHONE_EXT   Character      4
  5  COMPANY     Character     40           13   HIRE_DATE   Date           8
  6  ADDRESS     Character     25           14   SALARY      Numeric       12    2
  7  CITY        Character     20           15   PAID_YET    Logical        1
  8  STATE       Character      5           16   NOTES       Memo          10

MODIFY STRUCTURE |<C:>|MAIL                  |Field: 1/16        |      |Num
                            Enter the field name.
Field names begin with a letter and may contain letters, digits and underscores
```

**FIGURE 15.2:** The structure of the Mail database on the screen ready for editing. The bottom lines provide instructions as you work. Pressing F1 toggles the menu at the top of the screen on and off. Ctrl-N inserts a new field, and Ctrl-U deletes an existing field. Table 15.9 lists the control keys used in MODIFY STRUCTURE.

Mail.dbf to a file named MailBak.dbf:

**USE Mail**
**COPY TO MailBak**

When the copying is complete, the Mail.dbf and MailBak.dbf database files are identical. If a file named MailBak.dbf already existed before the COPY command was issued, that file was completely overwritten by the new MailBak database file.

The COPY FILE version of the COPY command can be used to copy any file, including nondatabase files. With this version of the COPY command, you must include the file-name extensions for both the source and target files. For example, to copy a screen painter file named AddRecs.scr to a screen painter file named EdRecs.scr, you would use the following command:

**COPY FILE AddRecs.scr TO EdRecs.scr**

The COPY STRUCTURE command copies only the structure of a database file (not any of the records) from the source file to the target file. For example, the commands below copy the structure of the Mail database file to a new file named

MailStru.dbf:

```
USE Mail
COPY STRUCTURE TO MailStru
```

When the copying is complete, MailStru.dbf contains the same structure as Mail.dbf, without any records.

## Deleting Files

The dBASE ERASE command will delete any file from the current directory. This command requires a complete file name, including the extension. For example, the command below erases a dBASE database named Temp.dbf:

```
ERASE Temp.dbf
```

Once erased with this command, a file can be recovered only by using a special utility program, such as Norton Utilities.

Note that a currently open file cannot be erased. You must first issue the appropriate CLOSE command to close the file and then issue the ERASE command.

## Renaming Files

The dBASE RENAME command can be used to change the name of any file. This command requires full file names, including extensions. Unlike the COPY command, RENAME will not overwrite an existing file. For example, the following command attempts to change the name of the Mail.dbf database to Customer.dbf:

```
RENAME Mail.dbf TO Customer.dbf
```

If the Customer.dbf database does not already exist on the current drive and directory, the command will successfully change the name of Mail.dbf to Customer.dbf. If a file named Customer.dbf already exists on the currently logged drive and directory, the command will generate an error message and both files will remain intact with their original file names.

## Viewing Database File Names

The DIR command displays the names of database files on the currently logged disk drive and directory. You can also use DIR to view other types of files by using the standard DOS wild cards (ambiguous file names), where ? stands for any single character and * stands for any group of characters. For example, the command

**DIR *.NDX**

displays all index files with the default extension .ndx. The command

**DIR My*.PRG**

displays all .prg (program) files that begin with the letters My.

## Using Multiple Disk Drives

The SET DEFAULT command specifies the disk drive where dBASE is to look for all files (excluding dBASE itself and its overlays). SET DEFAULT affects all commands that use and create files, such as USE, MODIFY REPORT, REPORT FORM, and so forth.

If you develop an application that runs on an IBM PC, you will probably want to store all of the files for the application on drive B. The command below will tell dBASE to look on drive B for all application files:

**SET DEFAULT TO B**

As an alternative to the SET DEFAULT command, you can place the command

**DEFAULT = B**

in the Config.db file so that dBASE will look to the disk in drive B from the moment it is loaded.

If some of the files for an application are stored on two or more drives, SET DEFAULT will not help, because it specifies a drive to search for all files. Instead, you'll need to specify the drive with each file name. For example, the commands below open the Mail database on drive B and print the report named Director.frm stored on drive A:

**USE B:Mail**
**REPORT FORM A:Director**

For more on the SET DEFAULT command, see Chapter 18, "Setting Parameters." For more information on the Config.db file, see Appendix C, "Configuring dBASE III PLUS."

## Managing Directories

The DOS MKDIR (or MD) command lets you divide a disk (usually a hard disk) into separate directories to help organize data. The dBASE SET PATH command lets you list path names for dBASE to search when trying to locate a file. However, dBASE will always search the currently logged directory for a file before checking the directories listed in the SET PATH command. For example, after executing the commands below, dBASE will first search the current directory for the Master.dbf database:

```
SET PATH TO C:\AcctRec,D:\AcctPay\APData
USE Master
```

If dBASE cannot find the file, it will then search the directory named AcctRec on drive C. If the Master database is not to be found on that directory, dBASE will search the directory and path named \AcctPay\APData on drive D.

Note that the SET PATH command affects only *searches* for files. Any commands that create files will continue to do so on the currently logged directory. Chapter 18, "Setting Parameters," discusses the SET PATH command in more detail.

## Commands Used in Data Handling

This chapter has presented general techniques for handling data at the field (or variable), record, and file levels. The remainder of this chapter discusses the specific commands involved in the handling of data in more detail.

## The CREATE Command

CREATE allows you to define a structure for a new database file.

### SYNTAX

**CREATE <file name> [FROM <structure extended>]**

where <file name> is the name of the new database file to create. The FROM option uses a special "structure-extended" file created with the COPY STRUCTURE EXTENDED command, as discussed under the COPY command.

### USAGE

The new file is created on the currently logged drive and directory unless otherwise specified. The extension .dbf is added to the file name you specify, unless you add your own extension. The USE command, which opens existing database files, also assumes the .dbf extension.

A database file name can be up to eight characters in length (excluding the extension). Never use the letters A through J alone as database file names, as dBASE will confuse these with the SELECT A through SELECT J commands. The file names Abcdefgh.dbf and AA.dbf are both valid, but the file name A.dbf is not.

Each database field name can be up to ten characters in length. Field names must begin with a letter and should not be the same as any command or even a valid abbreviation of a command. (Technically, dBASE will *allow* field names that are the same as a command, but it will sometimes handle them wrong, causing your program to behave unpredictably.) The only punctuation allowed in field names is the underscore (_) character. Examples of valid and invalid field names are listed in Table 15.10.

Each field must be assigned one of the five data types (character, numeric, date, logical, or memo) by typing the initial letter of the data type. Date and memo fields are assigned widths automatically. You must assign widths to the other data types. You must also assign a number of decimal places to the numeric data type.

Error messages and instructions for managing the cursor are displayed at the bottom of the screen displayed by CREATE. In addition, pressing the F1 key toggles a help menu on and off. The cursor cannot be scrolled beyond an incompletely or improperly defined field.

Up to 128 fields can be entered into a database structure. Use the PgUp and PgDn keys to scroll from page to page of field names. Table 15.9 earlier in the chapter lists all of the keys used with CREATE.

## CREATE FROM

The CREATE FROM command copies a "structure-extended" file back to a standard database structure. (See the COPY command for a definition and example of a structure-extended file.) For example, the following commands copy the fields from the Mail database to a database file named TempFile:

**USE Mail**
**COPY TO TempFile STRUCTURE EXTENDED**

| VALID FIELD NAME | INVALID FIELD NAME | WHY INVALID |
|---|---|---|
| Over90 | 90Past | Begins with a number |
| Date_Paid | Date:Paid | Includes a colon |
| Case_No | Case | Same as a command (acceptable, but risky) |
| Rest_Time | Rest | Same as a scope option |

**TABLE 15.10:** Valid and Invalid Field Name Examples

```
USE TempFile
BROWSE
PACK        && Remove any fields marked for deletion.
CREATE NewMail FROM TempFile
LIST STRUCTURE
```

The TempFile database has its fields in structure-extended format. The BROWSE command allows the user to change field definitions or even to add or delete fields, in much the same fashion as MODIFY STRUCTURE. The PACK command removes any records that were marked for deletion, then the CREATE FROM command creates a new file named NewMail.dbf with the database structure in the TempFile database. The LIST STRUCTURE command displays the fields in this new database file.

### EXAMPLES

The following command lets you define a new database file named MyDate.dbf on the currently logged disk drive and directory:

```
CREATE MyData
```

### TIPS

If you use the COPY STRUCTURE EXTENDED and CREATE FROM commands together, you can give your users the same power to modify a database structure that they get with the MODIFY STRUCTURE command, while maintaining more program control over the user's changes than you have with MODIFY STRUCTURE.

### SEE ALSO

COPY
APPEND

## The CLEAR Command

CLEAR provides many basic functions depending on the optional second part of the command.

### SYNTAX

**CLEAR [ALL] [FIELDS] [GETS] [MEMORY] [TYPEAHEAD]**

## USAGE

When used by itself, CLEAR clears the screen. It can also be used to clear a portion of the screen. For example, the command

```
@ 12,0 CLEAR
```

clears only the bottom half of the screen (row 12, column 0, to the bottom of the screen). Chapter 8, "Managing Screen Displays," provides additional examples.

CLEAR ALL closes all open files, including database, index, format, catalog, and memo files. It also erases all memory variables and sets the work area back to 1. Chapter 6, "Memory Variables," provides additional examples.

CLEAR FIELDS releases the settings specified in a SET FIELDS TO command and automatically issues a SET FIELDS OFF command. See Chapter 16, "Managing Multiple Database Files," for examples.

CLEAR GETS releases GET commands on the screen from access through the READ command. This command has no effect on the data stored in fields or memory variables. Chapter 8, "Managing Screen Displays," discusses this command in more detail.

CLEAR MEMORY releases all memory variables, both public and private (unlike RELEASE ALL, which releases only private variables). See Chapter 6, "Memory Variables," for additional details.

CLEAR TYPEAHEAD empties the typeahead buffer, ensuring that no old keystrokes affect new commands that accept data (such as READ, ACCEPT, WAIT, and so forth). Chapter 19, "Event Processing and Error Trapping," discusses this command in more detail.

## EXAMPLES

Consider the commands below:

```
CLEAR
UserName = SPACE(30)
@ 10,10 SAY "Enter your name ";
     GET UserName
READ

@ 20,2 SAY "Hello, " + UserName + "..."
?
CLEAR TYPEAHEAD
WAIT
```

The first CLEAR command clears the screen. The first @...SAY...GET combination waits for the user to type in his name. The second @...SAY combination displays a message with the user's name. The CLEAR TYPEAHEAD command deletes any extraneous keystrokes beyond the allowable length of the UserName variable from the typeahead buffer, so that they will not affect the WAIT command. The WAIT command displays the prompt **Press any key to continue** and waits for the user to press any key.

### TIPS

See the discussion of the various versions of the CLEAR commands in the chapters mentioned above for more details and examples of these commands.

### SEE ALSO

CLOSE
@...SAY...GET
RELEASE
SET FIELDS
SET VIEW
SET TYPEAHEAD

## The CLOSE Command

CLOSE closes the type of file specified, emptying any buffers and ensuring that the closed file is up to date. Each time a file is closed the number of simultaneously open files is reduced by one.

### SYNTAX

**CLOSE [ALL] [ALTERNATE] [DATABASES] [FORMAT] [INDEX];**
**[PROCEDURE]**

### USAGE

The CLOSE command allows you to close files that are no longer needed for immediate use. Closing a file reduces the number of currently open files, so CLOSE can be used to avoid the **Too many files are open** error message. Furthermore, you can use CLOSE in conjunction with commands that will work only with closed files (such as ERASE, MODIFY, SELECT, USE, and others), to close a particular file before issuing the command.

The CLOSE command allows you to close either all open files or only specific types of files, as discussed below.

## EXAMPLES

The following command closes all open files but has no effect on memory variables:

**CLOSE ALL**

To close only the open database, index, and format files, enter the command

**CLOSE DATABASES**

The next command closes all open index files in the currently selected work area:

**CLOSE INDEX**

To close an open format file in the currently selected work area, enter the command

**CLOSE FORMAT**

To close an open procedure file, use the command

**CLOSE PROCEDURE**

The command below closes an open alternate file, ensuring that all recorded text is stored on the file:

**CLOSE ALTERNATE**

The command **CLOSE ALL** closes all of the above files.

## TIPS

Remember, CLOSE DATABASES closes *all* open database, index, and format files. To close only the database, index, and format files in a particular work area, select that work area and issue a USE command without a file name, as below:

**SELECT J**
**USE**

## SEE ALSO

CLEAR
INDEX
SET INDEX

SET FORMAT
SET PROCEDURE
SET ALTERNATE
SELECT
USE

## The COPY Command

COPY makes a copy of an existing file on disk.

### SYNTAX

**COPY [TO <new file name> <scope>] [FIELDS <field list>];**
**[WHILE <condition>] [FOR <condition>];**
**[TYPE <file type>] [FILE] [STRUCTURE];**
**[STRUCTURE EXTENDED]**

where <new file name> is the name of the copy, <scope> is any valid scope option, <field list> is a list of field names delimited by commas, <condition> is any valid search criterion, and <file type> is a foreign file definition. The [FILE], [STRUCTURE], and [STRUCTURE EXTENDED] options are alternate versions of the COPY command.

### USAGE

This section discusses each of the four versions of the COPY command independently.

#### COPY TO

This command copies the currently selected database file to a new database file with the same structure, or at least a portion of the structure. If the file the records are being copied to already exists, dBASE asks for permission before overwriting the existing file *only* if the SET SAFETY parameter is on. If SET SAFETY is off, the file is overwritten automatically.

Unless otherwise specified, all records are copied to the new file. If SET DELETED is on, records that are marked for deletion are not copied. If SET DELETED is off, records that are marked for deletion are copied. If a SET FILTER condition is in effect, only records that meet the filter criteria are copied. If an index file is in use, the records on the copied database file will be in the sort order specified by the index file. The FIELDS option limits the copy to particular fields. For example, the command

**COPY TO Summary FIELDS CustNo, LName, FName, Address**

copies only the four listed fields to a database file named Summary. If the FIELDS option is omitted from the command, all fields are copied.

The WHILE and FOR options limit the records copied to those that meet a search criterion. For example, the commands below copy only records in which the LName field begins with the letters A through M:

```
COPY TO A:Half FOR LName > = "A" .AND. LName < = "M"
```

The name of either file in the COPY command can be stored in a memory variable and treated as a macro. For example, the commands below ask the user for the name of the file to copy and the name of the file to copy it to. The COPY command then uses these file names accordingly:

```
ACCEPT "Enter name of file to copy " TO FromFile
ACCEPT "Enter name of file to copy to " TO ToFile
COPY &FromFile TO &ToFile
```

## COPY FILE

The COPY FILE command copies *any* file to a new file. You must include file-name extensions with both file names in the command. For example, the command

```
COPY FILE MyProg.prg TO A:MyProg.bak
```

copies the command file named MyProg.prg to a file named MyProg.bak on drive A.

If the SET SAFETY parameter is on, COPY FILE will ask for permission before overwriting an existing file. Otherwise, it automatically overwrites the existing file.

COPY FILE is faster than COPY TO if you wish to copy an entire database file. However, unlike the COPY TO command, COPY FILE does not automatically copy memo field (.dbt) files, so you'll need to copy these separately. Furthermore, COPY FILE does not support the FOR, WHILE, or FIELDS options.

## COPY STRUCTURE

The COPY STRUCTURE command copies only the structure of a database to a new file, not the records. Like the COPY TO command, COPY STRUCTURE allows you to limit the copy to particular fields. For example, the commands below create an empty database named Summary, which includes only the CustNo, Amount, and Posted fields from the Charges database. Then the APPEND FROM command copies all the records that have .F. in the Posted field into this new structure:

```
USE Charges
COPY STRUCTURE TO Summary FIELDS CustNo,Amount,Posted
USE Summary
APPEND FROM Charges FOR .NOT. Posted
```

## COPY STRUCTURE EXTENDED

The COPY <file> STRUCTURE EXTENDED command creates a new database with four fields named Field_Name, Field_Type, Field_Len, and Field_Dec. Each record in this new file defines a single field in the file it was copied from. For example, note the structure of the Mail database file below:

```
Structure for database: Mail.dbf
Field  Field Name  Type        Width  Dec
    1  Mr_Mrs      Character       4
    2  FName       Character      15
    3  MI          Character       2
    4  LName       Character      20
    5  Company     Character      40
    6  Address     Character      25
    7  City        Character      20
    8  State       Character       5
    9  Zip         Character      10
   10  Country     Character      12
   11  Phone       Character      10
   12  Phone_Ext   Character       4
   13  Hire_Date   Date            8
   14  Salary      Numeric        12    2
   15  Paid_Yet    Logical         1
   16  Notes       Memo           10
** Total **                      199
```

The commands below will create a structure-extended file of the Mail database. The name of the new file is StruFile.dbf:

```
USE Mail
COPY TO StruFile STRUCTURE EXTENDED
```

The following commands open the new StruFile database and display its structure, as shown:

```
USE StruFile
LIST STRUCTURE
```

```
Structure for database: StruFile.dbf
Field  Field Name  Type       Width  Dec
    1  Field_Name  Character     10
    2  Field_Type  Character      1
    3  Field_Len   Numeric        3
    4  Field_Dec   Numeric        3
** Total **                      18
```

If you list the contents of the new structure file, you'll see that it contains a single record for each field in the original Mail database, as shown below:

```
Record#  Field_Name  Field_Type  Field_Len  Field_Dec
      1  Mr_Mrs          C              4          0
      2  Fname           C             15          0
      3  MI              C              2          0
      4  Lname           C             20          0
      5  Company         C             40          0
      6  Address         C             25          0
      7  City            C             20          0
      8  State           C              5          0
      9  Zip             C             10          0
     10  Country         C             12          0
     11  Phone           C             10          0
     12  Phone_Ext       C              4          0
     13  Hire_Date       D              8          0
     14  Salary          N             12          2
     15  Paid_Yet        L              1          0
     16  Notes           M             10          0
```

In an application, you could allow a user to modify this database structure, using common error-trapping techniques to maintain some control over the modifications. This gives users access to the power of the MODIFY STRUCTURE command while at the same time maintaining some control over the way they use it.

You can create a new database file from the structure-extended file using the CREATE FROM command. For example, the commands below create a new database named Temp.dbf from the StruFile.dbf database and copy the records from the Mail database into the Temp database. Then the RENAME command changes the name of Temp.dbf to Mail.dbf. The end result is that Mail.dbf has a new structure that includes any changes that might have been made to the StruFile database:

```
CREATE Temp FROM StruFile
USE Temp
```

```
APPEND FROM Mail
CLOSE DATABASES
ERASE Mail.dbf
RENAME Temp.dbf TO Mail.dbf
```

## EXAMPLES

The commands below copy the database file Mail.dbf to three smaller files named Part1, Part2, and Part3. The routine demonstrates a technique for storing a large database file from a hard disk onto smaller files on floppies.

```
USE Mail
? "Place Part 1 disk in drive A"
WAIT
COPY TO A:Part1 FOR LName < = "J"
? "Place Part 2 disk in drive A"
WAIT
COPY TO A:Part2 FOR LName > = "K" .AND. LName < = "S"
? "Place Part 3 disk in drive A"
WAIT
COPY TO A:Part3 FOR LName > = "T"
```

The following command copies the memo field file Mail.dbt to a backup file named MailMemo.bak:

```
COPY FILE Mail.dbt TO MailMemo.bak
```

## TIPS

If you need to copy all the records in a database file, the COPY FILE command will do the job more quickly than the COPY TO command. COPY TO is used to export data to non-dBASE formats. Chapter 23, "Foreign and Damaged Files" discusses this topic in detail.

## SEE ALSO

APPEND
FROM
CREATE
MODIFY STRUCTURE
RENAME

# The RENAME Command

RENAME changes the name of a file on disk.

## SYNTAX

**RENAME <old file name> TO <new file name>**

where <old file name> is the complete name of the file to rename, and <new file name> is the complete new name for the file.

## USAGE

RENAME requires the use of file-name extensions in both the original and new file names. The current disk drive and directory are assumed on both file names, unless otherwise specified. The RENAME command does *not* search paths specified in the DOS PATH or dBASE SET PATH commands.

If a database file that contains a memo field is being renamed, the associated .dbt file must be renamed separately.

The new file name must be unique to the currently logged drive and directory. If another file with the specified new file name already exists, an error message is displayed and both files remain as they were. An open file cannot be renamed. Use the appropriate version of the CLOSE command to close an open file before renaming it.

Unlike the DOS RENAME command, the dBASE RENAME command does not support the wild-card characters ? or *.

## EXAMPLES

The command below changes the name of the MyProg.cmd file to MyProg.prg:

```
RENAME MyProg.cmd TO MyProg.prg
```

The command below changes the name of the Archive.dbf database on the BookData directory on drive C to LastYear.dbf:

```
RENAME C:\BookData\Archive.dbf TO C:\BookData\LastYear.dbf
```

The commands below physically sort the Mail database to a file named Temp, then change the name of the sorted temporary database to Mail.dbf:

```
USE Mail
SORT ON LName,FName TO Temp
CLOSE DATABASES
```

```
ERASE Mail.dbf
RENAME Temp.dbf TO Mail.dbf
```

### TIPS

To take advantage of the DOS RENAME wild-card characters, use the syntax ! RENAME or RUN RENAME. For example, the command below changes the names of all files that have the extension .bak to the same file names with the extension .bck:

```
RUN RENAME *.BAK *.BCK
```

### SEE ALSO

COPY

## The DIR Command

DIR displays the names of files on the directory.

### SYNTAX

**DIR <drive> <path> <wild card>**

where <drive> and <path> are the disk drive and path, and <wild card> is an optional ambiguous file name.

### USAGE

If no drive, path, or wild card is included in the command, DIR displays the names of database (.dbf ) files only. For each database file, it displays the number of records, date of last update, and file size (in bytes). DIR also shows the number of files displayed, the total number of bytes that the files occupy, and the number of bytes remaining on the disk drive. If there are more files than will fit on the screen, DIR pauses before each screenful and displays the message **Press any key to continue**.

Use a wild card in the DIR command to display nondatabase files. In the wild card, ? matches any single character and * matches any group of characters. When displaying nondatabase files, the file sizes and latest update dates are not displayed.

### EXAMPLES

The command

**DIR *.prg**

displays the names of all program (.prg) files on the currently logged drive and directory.

The command

**DIR B:\dbdata*.db?**

displays the names of files on the dbdata directory of drive b that begin with the letters "db" in the file extension (e.g., .dbf and .dbt files).

The commands below store a copy of the disk directory in a text file named DirFile.txt:

```
SET ALTERNATE TO DirFile.txt
SET ALTERNATE ON
DIR *.*
CLOSE ALTERNATE
```

### TIPS

The LIST FILES command displays the directory without screen pauses. The syntax LIST FILES LIKE <wild card> also supports ambiguous file names (e.g., LIST FILES LIKE *.prg).

To use the DOS DIR command or a similar utility program from within dBASE, use the RUN or ! command, as below:

**RUN DIR *.prg**

### SEE ALSO

LIST
DISPLAY

## The DISPLAY Command

DISPLAY displays the contents of a database record.

### SYNTAX

```
DISPLAY [<scope>] [<fields/expressions>];
        [WHILE <condition>] [FOR <condition>] [OFF];
        [TO PRINT]
```

where <scope> is a scope option, <fields/expressions> is a list of field names and/or expressions separated by commas, and <condition> is a valid search condition.

## USAGE

The DISPLAY command alone shows a single record from the database file. If a scope option such as ALL, NEXT, or REST is included, the command will display several records. The FOR and WHILE options limit the display to records that match a search criterion. The OFF option suppresses display of the database record numbers. The TO PRINT option directs output to the printer. To direct output to a text file, use the SET ALTERNATE command.

The contents of a memo field are not displayed unless the name of the field is specifically requested in the fields/expressions list. For example, the command **DISPLAY LName, FName, Notes** displays the contents of the memo field named Notes. The default width for memo fields is 50 characters, though this can be changed with the SET MEMOWIDTH command.

If the output of the DISPLAY command is more than 20 lines long, the command will pause after each 20 lines and wait for a key to be pressed to continue.

Field names or expressions are listed above the data if the SET HEADING parameter is on. If SET HEADING is off, only the data are displayed.

If the record pointer is already at EOF( ) when the DISPLAY command is entered, the screen shows nothing (or only field names if SET HEADING is on).

DISPLAY can also be used to show information other than the contents of databases. Examples are listed below.

## EXAMPLES

The command below prints the CustNo, Qty, and Unit_Price fields, as well as the product of the Unit_Price field multiplied by the Qty field, adding 6 percent tax only if the Tax field is .T.. Only records that have 1001 in the CustNo field are included in the display. Record numbers are not included:

```
DISPLAY ALL CustNo, Qty, Unit_Price,;
        IIF(Tax,(Qty*Unit_Price)*1.06,Qty*Unit_Price) ;
        FOR CustNo = 1001 OFF TO PRINT
```

Variations of the DISPLAY command are listed below. Note that all of the commands below support the TO PRINT option, which channels output to the printer, and the SET ALTERNATE command, which channels output to a file.

The command

```
DISPLAY HISTORY LAST 10
```

shows the last ten commands entered at the dot prompt. The optional LAST portion of the command limits the display to ten lines. LAST can be used to specify any number of records to list from the history file, provided it does not exceed the default value of 20 commands or the value specified in the SET HISTORY command. See SET HISTORY and SET DOHISTORY in Chapter 18, "Setting Parameters," for additional information on history files.

The command

**DISPLAY MEMORY**

displays the names of existing memory variables.

The command

**DISPLAY STATUS**

shows the current status of numerous dBASE parameters, including active work areas, names and aliases of open database and index files, index file expressions, database relations, open memo file names, the current directory search path, the default disk drive, the print destination, current settings of SET commands, and function key assignments. Chapter 7, "Debugging Commands and Techniques," discusses this command in more detail.

The command

**DISPLAY STRUCTURE**

displays the structure of the currently selected database file.

### TIPS

LIST is virtually the same command as DISPLAY, but it does not pause for a keypress every 20 lines.

### SEE ALSO

LIST
MODIFY REPORT
REPORT FORM

## The LIST Command

LIST displays the contents of all database records.

### SYNTAX

**LIST [<scope>] [<fields/expressions>];**
**[WHILE <condition>] [FOR <condition>] [OFF];**
**[TO PRINT]**

where <scope> is a scope option, <fields/expressions> is a list of field names and/or expressions separated by commas, and <condition> is a valid search condition.

## USAGE

When used without additional options, LIST displays every record in the database file. If a scope option such as RECORD, NEXT, or REST is included, the display is limited to the number of records specified in the scope condition. The FOR and WHILE options limit the display to records that match a search criterion. The OFF option suppresses the display of the database record numbers. The TO PRINT option directs output to the printer. To direct output to a text file, use the SET ALTERNATE command.

Unlike the DISPLAY command, LIST does not pause for a keypress after every 20 lines.

The contents of memo fields are not displayed by the LIST command unless specifically requested in the fields/expressions list. For example, the command **LIST LName, FName, Notes** displays the contents of the memo field named Notes. The default width for memo fields is 50 characters, though this can be changed with the SET MEMOWIDTH command.

Field names or expressions are displayed above the data if the SET HEADING parameter is set on. If SET HEADING is off, only the data are displayed.

Like DISPLAY, LIST can also be used to show information other than the contents of databases. Examples are listed below.

## EXAMPLES

The command below prints the CustNo, Qty, and Unit_Price fields, and the product of the Unit_Price field multiplied by the Qty field, adding 6 percent tax only if the Tax field is .T.. Only records that have 1001 in the CustNo field are included in the display. Record numbers are not included in the display:

```
LIST CustNo, Qty, Unit_Price,;
     IIF(Tax,(Qty*Unit_Price)*1.06,Qty*Unit_Price) ;
     FOR CustNo = 1001 OFF TO PRINT
```

The command below lists the records numbered 15 through 19, because the GOTO command positions the record pointer to record 15, and the NEXT 5 option in the LIST command limits the display to the current record plus the next four records (for a total of five records):

```
GOTO 15
```

**LIST NEXT 5**

Variations of the LIST command are listed below. Note that all of the commands below support the TO PRINT option, which channels output to the printer, and the SET ALTERNATE command, which channels output to a file.

The command

**LIST HISTORY LAST 5**

shows the last five commands entered at the dot prompt. (See SET HISTORY in Chapter 18, "Setting Parameters," and SET DOHISTORY in Chapter 7, "Debugging Commands and Techniques," for additional information on history files.)

The command

**LIST MEMORY**

displays the names of existing memory variables.

The command

**LIST STATUS**

shows the current status of numerous dBASE parameters, including active work areas, names and aliases of open database and index files, index file expressions, database relations, open memo file names, the current directory search path, the default disk drive, the print destination, current settings of SET commands, and function key assignments. Chapter 7, "Debugging Commands and Techniques," discusses this command in more detail.

The command

**LIST STRUCTURE**

displays the structure of the currently selected database file.

## TIPS

DISPLAY is virtually the same command as LIST, except that it pauses for a keypress after every 20 lines.

## SEE ALSO

DISPLAY
MODIFY REPORT
REPORT FORM

## The ERASE Command

ERASE deletes a file from the directory.

### SYNTAX

**ERASE <file name>**

where <file name> is the complete name of the file, including the extension.

### USAGE

Unless otherwise specified, ERASE searches only the currently logged drive and directory for the file to erase. Furthermore, ERASE does not search the path defined in a dBASE SET PATH or DOS PATH command. Therefore, to erase the file named Archive.dbf on the DBDATA directory on drive C, you would need to enter the following command:

```
ERASE C:\DBDATA\Archive.dbf
```

An open file cannot be erased. Use the appropriate CLOSE command to close the file before erasing.

If the name of the file to be erased is stored in a memory variable, use macro substitution in the ERASE command, as below:

```
FileName = "Archive.bak"
ERASE &FileName
```

Unlike DOS, the dBASE ERASE command does not support ambiguous file names (wild-card characters). For example, you *cannot* use a dBASE command like the one below to erase all files with the .bak extension:

```
ERASE *.bak
```

Issuing such a command only displays the error message **File does not exist**.

Erasing a file that includes a memo field does not automatically erase the associated .dbt (memo field) files. These have to be erased separately.

The command **DELETE FILE** is identical to the ERASE command.

### EXAMPLES

The commands below erase the Mail.dbf database and its memo field file from the disk in drive B:

```
ERASE B:Mail.dbf
ERASE B:Mail.dbt
```

### TIPS

To use wild-card characters in an ERASE command, use the RUN or ! command to access the DOS ERASE command. For example, the command below erases all files with the extension .bak from the directory named DBPROGS on drive C:

**RUN ERASE C:\DBPROGS*.bak**

### SEE ALSO

CLOSE
DELETE

## The GO/GOTO Commands

Both GO and GOTO position the pointer to a specified record number or position in the database file.

### SYNTAX

The GO and GOTO commands support the following syntaxes:

**GO TOP**
**GOTO TOP**
**GO BOTTOM**
**GOTO BOTTOM**
**GO <recno>**
**GOTO <recno>**

where <recno> is the number (or an expression that evaluates to a number) of the record to move the record pointer to.

### USAGE

GO and GOTO can be used interchangeably. The TOP and BOTTOM options move the record pointer to the first or last record in the database file, or the first and last records as determined by the currently active index file. The GO or GOTO commands with a specified number always send the record pointer to the record with that number; they are unaffected by index file ordering.

You can also position the pointer to a particular record just by entering that number (alhough this is rarely used in command files). For example, entering the number 10 at the dot prompt and pressing Return is equivalent to entering the command **GOTO 10** or **GO 10**.

The record number can be calculated in an expression, as in the example below, where the pointer is moved seven records down from the current record position:

```
GOTO (RECNO( ) + 7)
```

If the record number is stored as a character string, use a macro, as in the example below:

```
MoveTo = "22"
GOTO &MoveTo
```

Attempting to go to a record that does not exist causes the **Record out of range** error. This same error will occur even when the record exists on the database file but not in the currently active index file. This is a fairly common error that occurs whenever you add or delete records from a database file without making sure that all the appropriate index files are active. Use the REINDEX or INDEX ON commands to rebuild the index files. (If you get this error message, you have to first find the routine that allows the records to be added or deleted without updating the index files and then fix the problem at that point.)

### EXAMPLES

The command below moves the record pointer to the top of the database file before the DO WHILE .NOT. EOF( ) loop begins processing:

```
GO TOP
DO WHILE .NOT. EOF( )
    <commands...>
    SKIP
ENDDO (not eof )
```

### TIPS

The GO and GOTO commands can position the record pointer to a record that is marked for deletion, even if the SET DELETED parameter is on. For example, the commands below will still display record number 3, even though the record is hidden from most other commands:

```
DELETE RECORD 3
SET DELETED ON
GOTO 3
DISPLAY
```

#### SEE ALSO

SKIP
SET DELETED
RECNO( )

## The MODIFY STRUCTURE Command

MODIFY STRUCTURE allows you to change the structure of an existing database file.

#### SYNTAX

**MODIFY STRUCTURE**

#### USAGE

The MODIFY STRUCTURE command allows you to move the cursor freely and change the field names, data types, widths, and decimal places on any existing field name. You can also add new fields or delete existing fields. The control keys used in MODIFY STRUCTURE are summarized in Table 15.9 earlier in the chapter.

Take care not to change both the name of a field and its width during a single session. Doing so will likely lead to data loss. Instead, use MODIFY STRUCTURE to change the name of the field and save the new database structure immediately. Then use MODIFY STRUCTURE again to change the width of the field and again save the new structure immediately.

#### EXAMPLES

The commands

**USE Mail**
**MODIFY STRUCTURE**

bring the structure of the Mail database to the screen ready for editing.

#### TIPS

If you change your mind about a new database structure or become confused during the process, use Ctrl-Q or Esc to abandon the changes and retain the original structure.

### SEE ALSO

CREATE

## The SKIP Command

SKIP moves the record pointer a specified number of records from its current position.

### SYNTAX

**SKIP <number>**

where <number> is the number of records to move the pointer (or an expression that calculates that number).

### USAGE

If the database file in use is indexed, SKIP moves the record pointer in the order defined by the index file expression. If the database is not indexed, SKIP moves the record pointer sequentially, based on record numbers.

The SKIP command alone moves the pointer forward one record. To move the record pointer backward, you must include a minus sign and a number.

Any expression can be used in the SKIP command, as long as that expression evaluates to a numeric value.

If the pointer is at the last database record and you issue a SKIP command, the pointer moves beyond the last record, and the EOF( ) condition becomes true. Attempting to SKIP past EOF( ) will generate the error message **End of file encountered**. Attempting to move the record pointer above the first record will generate the error message **Beginning of file encountered**.

### EXAMPLES

The command below moves the pointer forward ten records:

**SKIP 10**

This command moves the record pointer back one record:

**SKIP -1**

This command calculates the number of records to skip using a complex expression and memory variables named Cols and Rows:

**SKIP (((Cols - 1)*Rows) - 1)* -1**

The commands below skip ten records, even though the CharVar memory variable stores its data as the character data type:

```
CharVar = "10"
SKIP &CharVar
```

In lieu of the macro in the example above, you can use the VAL function, as below:

```
SKIP VAL(CharVar)
```

### TIPS

SKIP is used almost universally within DO WHILE .NOT. EOF( ) loops to ensure that the pointer advances one record with each pass through the loop.

### SEE ALSO

GO/GOTO
DO WHILE
BOF( )
EOF( )
RECNO( )

## SUMMARY

This chapter discussed many techniques for handling dBASE data at three different levels:

1. Individual data elements stored in fields or memory variables
2. Individual records and groups of records stored in database files
3. Entire database files

References to related topics are listed below.

*To learn techniques for creating and manipulating memory variables:*

- Chapter 6, "Memory Variables"

*To learn more about the role of the DISPLAY and LIST commands in debugging:*

- Chapter 7, "Debugging Commands and Techniques"

*To learn techniques for displaying data on formatted reports:*

- Chapter 9, "Printing Formatted Reports"

*For a discussion of index files and sorting techniques:*

- Chapter 12, "Sorting and Indexing"

*For information on searching for records based on some specific value or a common characteristic:*

- Chapter 13, "Searching a Database"

*To learn more about the dBASE functions, such as BOF( ), EOF( ), and RECNO( ):*

- Chapter 17, "dBASE Functions"

*For explanations of the various dBASE SET commands:*

- Chapter 18, "Setting Parameters"

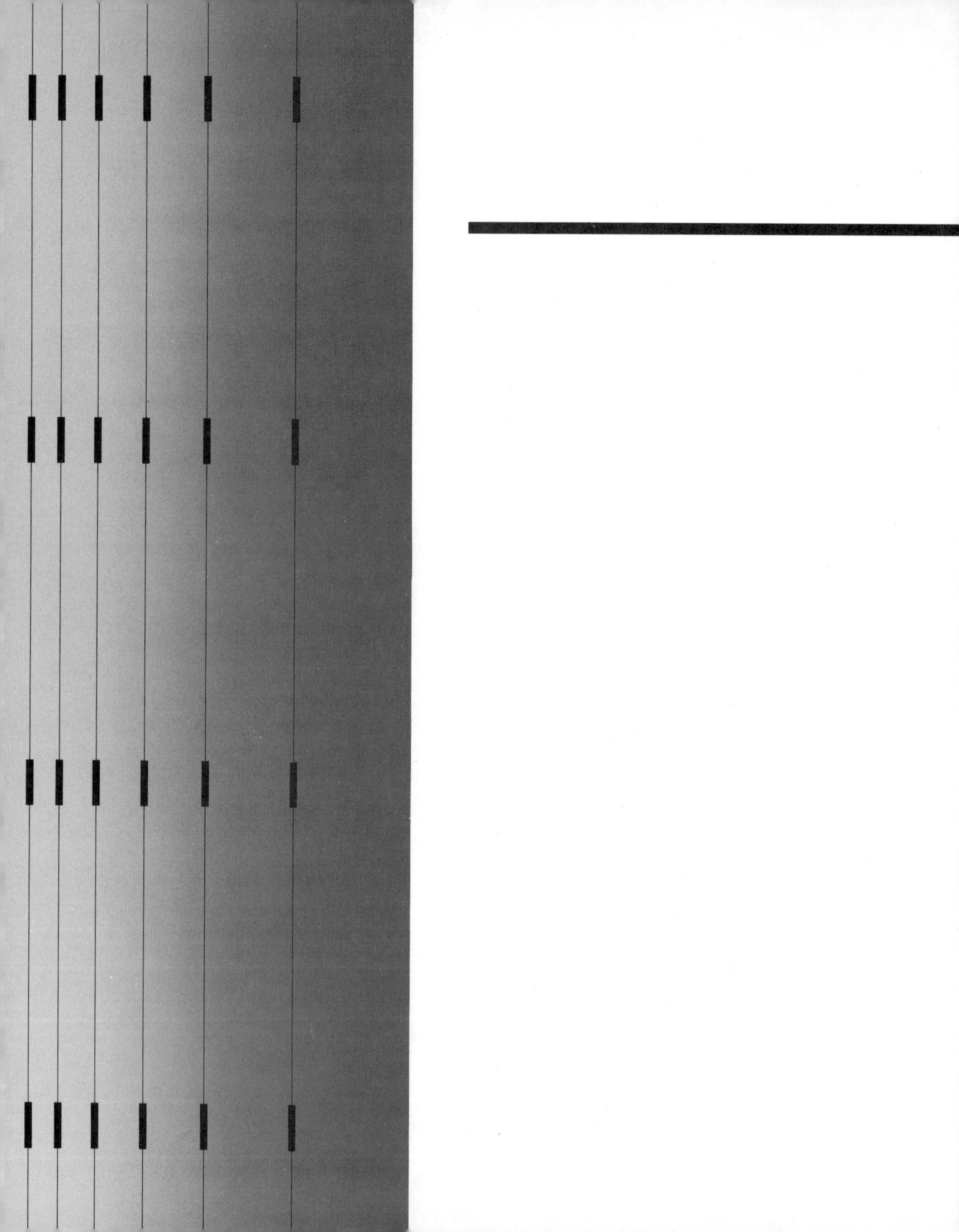

# MANAGING MULTIPLE DATABASE FILES

# Managing Multiple Database Files

This chapter discusses programming techniques for managing multiple database files. It focuses on programming techniques that are commonly used in business applications. Techniques for updating a master file from a transaction file are discussed in detail, as are techniques for analyzing and displaying data in many-to-many relationships.

## Updating Techniques

Updating is a very common technique used in business applications, particularly inventory and bookkeeping systems. In inventory systems, updating is used to change current in-stock, on-order, and other quantities based on recent sales, orders, and shipments received. In bookkeeping or accounting systems, updating plays the role of posting transactions or calculating current balances based on recent charges and payments.

Updating is generally used with the master-file/transaction-file relationship between files. The master file maintains the current quantities or balances, and the transaction files record individual transactions. For example, suppose the small master inventory called Master contains the records listed in the top part of Figure 16.1 (notice that there are 10 of each item currently in stock). The middle database in Figure 16.1, named Sales, contains three records. Notice that two part number A-111s and one part number B-222 have been sold. After performing an update, the Master database would contain the information shown at the bottom of Figure 16.1.

There are now eight baseball bats in stock, because two were sold, and nine baseball mits in stock, because one was sold. The Sales database still contains the sales.

There are two different updating techniques: *batch updating* and *immediate updating;* they are discussed in the sections below.

```
PartNo    PartName              In_Stock       ReOrder
A-111     Baseball bats           10              50
B-222     Baseball mits           10              50
C-333     Tennis rackets          10              20

======================================================

PartNo    Qty_Sold              Date_Sold
A-111        1                  06/01/87
B-222        1                  06/01/87
A-111        1                  06/02/87

======================================================

PartNo    PartName              In_Stock       ReOrder
A-111     Baseball bats            8              50
B-222     Baseball mits            9              50
C-333     Tennis rackets          10              20
```

**FIGURE 16.1:** The effects of updating on a sample master file in a master-file/transaction-file relationship. The top listing shows the contents of the Master database before updating. The middle listing shows the contents of a transaction file named Sales. The bottom listing shows the contents of the Master file after updating. Quantities of items in stock have been reduced by the quantities specified in the Sales database.

## Batch Updating

*Batch updating* is a good method to use when the master file needs to be updated only periodically. For example, an accounts receivable system might update all customers' current balances at the end of each month.

dBASE provides the built-in UPDATE command for batch updating. To use the UPDATE command, you need to open both the master file (the one being updated) and the transaction file. The two databases must have a key field identical in name, data type, and size. The key field on the master database must be unique to every record. Otherwise, only the first of every duplicate will be acted on. To maximize the speed of the update, both database files should be indexed (or sorted) on the key field.

There is more to updating than issuing a single UPDATE command, however. First, the programmer must make certain that no record is ever updated more than once. Second, the programmer must ensure that no record is ever skipped over during an update. To accomplish this, the programmer can either flag fields as having been updated or actually store updated transactions on a separate history file.

## Flagging Updated Records

To update transactions onto a master file and leave them in the original file, each record in the transaction file must have a field that indicates whether the transaction has been posted. The full series of steps required to update a field named CurrChrg (for current charge) in a master database file named ARCust from a transaction file named ARChrg are outlined below. The example assumes that the field named Posted on the ARChrg database contains .F. if the transaction has not been updated. Once the transaction has been updated, the Posted field is set to .T. to flag the record as having been updated.

First, copy all the nonposted transactions from the ARChrg file to a temporary file, as below:

```
USE ARChrg
COPY TO Temp FOR .NOT. Posted
```

Next, use the UPDATE command to perform the actual update from the Posted file. In this example, the field named CustNo is the common field relating ARCust to ARChrg. Both ARCust and ARChrg are indexed on the CustNo field. The REPLACE expression in the UPDATE command increments the CurrChrg field in the ARCust database by the Charge amount in the Temp database:

```
SELECT A
USE ARCust
SELECT B
USE Temp

SELECT A
UPDATE ON CustNo FROM Temp;
        REPLACE CurrChrg WITH CurrChrg + B->Charge
```

After the update has taken place, the Posted field needs to be set to .T. in all records in the ARChrg database, as in the commands below:

```
CLOSE DATABASES
USE ARChrg
REPLACE ALL Posted WITH .T.
```

Of course, any new records added to the ARChrg database must be initialized with the value .F. in the Posted field. (Typically, the user would have no access to this field; the programs would control the content for the Posted field automatically.)

This technique of flagging updated records has one drawback: the transaction file will grow indefinitely. If the application will involve thousands of transactions, the file might become so large as to slow down overall processing considerably. An alternative to flagging updated transactions is discussed below.

### TRANSFERRING POSTED TRANSACTIONS TO A HISTORY FILE

As an alternative to flagging updated records on the transaction file, you can copy the updated transactions to a separate history file. The history file will have the same structure as the original transaction file, though it may have fewer fields if the application does not require a history of all data.

There are three steps involved in performing an update with history files. First, the actual update needs to be performed, as in the example below, where the ARCust database is updated from the ARChrg database:

```
SELECT A
USE ARCust
SELECT B
USE ARChrg

SELECT A
UPDATE ON CustNo FROM Temp;
          REPLACE CurrChrg WITH CurrChrg + B->Charge
```

Next, all of the records from the ARChrg file must be added to the bottom of the existing history file. In the example below, the name of the history file is ARHist:

```
CLOSE DATABASES
USE ARHist
APPEND FROM ARChrg
```

The next step is to remove all of the updated transactions from the current transactions file (ARChrg in this example), as shown below:

```
USE ARChrg
SET SAFETY OFF
ZAP
SET SAFETY ON
```

At this point, new transactions can be added to the empty ARChrg file. The ARCust database contains the total current charges for each customer, and the ARHist file still records individual charge transactions for each customer.

## Batch Updating Example

Figure 16.2 shows three database files named MastInv, InvSold, and InvRecvd, which hold all the data for an inventory application. The PartNo field is the common field relating all three databases, and each database is indexed on this field. The MastInv file maintains a record for each item in stock, including the quantity of each item in stock. The InvSold database holds a single record for

```
Structure for database: MastInv.dbf

Field  Field Name   Type       Width Dec   Description

    1  PartNo       Character      5       Part number
    2  Title        Character     20       Part name
    3  Qty          Numeric        4       Quantity in stock
    4  Pur_Price    Numeric        9   2   Purchase price
    5  Reorder      Numeric        4       Reorder point
    6  On_Order     Numeric        4       Quantity on order
    7  Location     Character      5       Warehouse location
   11  Date         Date           8       Last shipment received

================================================================

Structure for database: InvSold.dbf


Field  Field Name   Type       Width Dec   Description


    1  PartNo       Character      5       Part number
    2  Invoice_No   Numeric        6       Invoice number
    3  Clerk        Character     12       Clerk name
    4  Customer     Character     12       Customer name
    5  Qty          Numeric        4       Quantity sold
    6  Price        Numeric        9   2   Selling price
    7  Date         Date           8       Date sold

================================================================

Structure for database: InvRecvd.dbf

Field  Field Name   Type       Width Dec  Description

    1  PartNo       Character      5       Part number
    2  Qty          Numeric        4       Quantity sold
    3  Cost         Numeric        9   2   Purchase price
    4  Date         Date           8       Date received
    5  Vendor       Character     25       Vendor name
```

**FIGURE 16.2:** Sample database file structures for an inventory management system. The PartNo field is the common field relating all three files. Each database is indexed on this field. The program in Figure 16.3 demonstrates a technique for updating the MastInv inventory file from the InvSold and InvRecvd transaction files.

each sales transaction, and the InvRecvd database holds a single record for each new shipment received.

The SalHist and PurHist files are identical in structure to the InvSold and InvRecvd files and are used to store transactions that have already been updated.

Figure 16.3 shows a sample program that updates the MastInv inventory file from both the InvSold and InvRecvd database files. The expression **REPLACE Qty WITH Qty – B->Qty** in the UPDATE command subtracts the sales quantities in the InvSold database file from the in-stock quantities in the MastInv database file. Then the sales transactions are copied to the bottom of the SalHist history file, and the InvSold file is purged of its records.

In the second UPDATE command, newly received items listed on the InvRecvd file are added to the in-stock quantities using the expression

**REPLACE Qty WITH Qty + B->Qty**. The Date field in the MastInv database is replaced with the Date field in the InvRecvd database using the expression **REPLACE ... Date WITH B->Date**. The purchase price is changed to reflect the latest purchase price, using the expression **REPLACE ... Pur_Price WITH B->Cost**. Finally, the on-order quantity is reduced by the amount

```
****************************************** Updater.prg
*-- Update the MastInv file from InvSold and InvRecvd.
SET SAFETY OFF
@ 5,5 SAY "Updating from the InvSold file..."

*-------- All index files based on PartNo.
SELECT A
USE MastInv INDEX MastInv
SELECT B
USE InvSold INDEX InvSold

*------- Update from the InvSold file.
SELECT A
UPDATE ON PartNo FROM InvSold;
   REPLACE Qty WITH Qty - B->Qty

*-- Copy all updated transactions to SalHist file.
CLOSE DATABASES
USE SalHist
APPEND FROM InvSold
USE InvSold INDEX InvSold
ZAP

*- Now perform the update from the InvRecvd file.
@ 10,5 SAY "Updating from the New Stock file....."
SELECT A
USE MastInv INDEX MastInv
SELECT B
USE InvRecvd INDEX InvRecvd

*------- Update Qty from the InvRecvd file.
SELECT A


UPDATE ON PartNo FROM InvRecvd;
   REPLACE Qty WITH Qty + B->Qty,;
   Date WITH B->Date,;
   Pur_Price WITH B->Cost,;
   On_Order WITH On_Order - B->Qty

*-- Copy posted transactions to PurHist.
CLOSE DATABASES
USE PurHist
APPEND FROM InvRecvd
USE InvRecvd INDEX InvRecvd
ZAP

*------- Update and transfer complete.
CLOSE DATABASES
RETURN
```

**FIGURE 16.3:** The Updater program, which updates the MastInv database from current transactions in the InvSold and InvRecvd database files (shown in Figure 16.2). To ensure that no records are included in the update more than once, this program stores all updated (posted) transactions on separate history files after updating is complete and then empties the current transaction files.

received in the current order using the expression **REPLACE ... On_Order WITH On_Order – B->Qty** in the UPDATE command.

When the second UPDATE command is finished, the updated new-stock transactions are appended to the PurHist history file and erased from the NewStock current transactions file.

## Immediate Updating

The second technique for updating a master file from transactions is *immediate updating,* in which the master file is updated as soon as the transaction is completed. This technique is useful for an inventory system where users must know the exact quantity in stock at any given moment, as well as when a new shipment is due to arrive.

There is no specialized command in dBASE to handle immediate updating. Instead, the programmer needs to open both the master and transaction files and subtract the quantity ordered from the quantity in stock.

For example, Figure 16.4 shows the structures for two database files named Master and Orders. If you wish to automatically update the In_Stock field on

```
Structure for database: Master

Field  Field Name  Type       Width Dec Description

    1  PartNo      Character      5       Part number
    2  PartName    Character     20       Part name
    3  In_Stock    Numeric        4       Quantity in stock
    4  Unit_Price  Numeric        9   2   Unit selling price
    5  Taxable     Logical        1       Taxable?
    6  Reorder     Numeric        4       Reorder point
    7  On_Order    Numeric        4       Quantity on order
    8  Backorder   Numeric        4       Quantity backordered
    9  Rec_Date    Date           8       Date shipment received

=================================================================

Structure for database: Orders

Field  Field Name  Type       Width Dec Description

    1  PartNo      Character      5       Part number
    2  Invoice_No  Numeric        5       Invoice number
    3  Clerk       Character      5       Clerk name
    4  Customer    Character     20       Customer name
    5  Qty         Numeric        4       Qty ordered
    6  Price       Numeric        9   2   Selling price
    7  Date_Sold   Date           8       Date sold
    8  BOrder      Logical        1       Back order?
```

**FIGURE 16.4:** Structures of the Master and Orders database files used in the examples of immediate updating. The PartNo field is the common field linking the two database files, and the Master database file is indexed on this field. During immediate updating, quantities entered into the Qty field of the Orders database are immediately subtracted from the In_Stock quantities of the Master database.

the Master file each time an order is entered onto the Orders database, both database files must be open, and the common field (PartNo in this example) needs to be indexed in the Master file.

To have both database files open simultaneously, use SELECT commands as below:

```
SELECT A
USE Master INDEX Master
SELECT B
USE Orders
```

In the program for entering orders, the user enters a part number (in a memory variable named PartNumb in this example), and the program then verifies that the part number exists, as in the small routine below:

```
SELECT A
SEEK PartNumb
```

Assuming that a matching part number can be found, the user can then enter the quantity to be ordered. For the sake of example, suppose the user enters this value into a memory variable named Quantity. To subtract this quantity from the quantity in stock (while the Master database is still selected), use a simple expression, as below:

```
REPLACE In_Stock WITH In_Stock – Quantity
```

Depending on the sophistication and requirements of the application, you will probably want to provide more capability than simply subtracting the ordered quantity from the quantity in stock, as discussed in the larger example that follows.

## Immediate Updating Example

In most applications involving immediate updating of a database, you'll want to provide feedback if an order exceeds the in-stock quantity, so that the person placing the order can decide whether to proceed with the order.

A prime example would be a business that accepts orders over the telephone. When the customer places the order, the operator can key in the order immediately. If the customer's request exceeds the quantity in stock, the operator's screen displays a warning and additional information (such as when the stock will be replenished) to help the customer decide whether to proceed with the order. If the customer decides to proceed, the order is entered into the Orders database, to be fulfilled at a later time.

The Instant program shown in Figure 16.5 and the accompanying procedure named InvProc shown in Figure 16.6 demonstrate a system with immediate updating and backordering capabilities.

```
********************************** Instant.prg
*  Point-of-sale data-entry program for Orders
*  database.

SET STATUS OFF
SET PROCEDURE TO InvProc
CLOSE DATABASES
SET TALK OFF
SET HEADING OFF

*- Get last-used invoice number from the bottom of
*- the Orders file, and store in MInvoice.
USE Orders
GO BOTT
MInvoice = Invoice_No
*------- Open Master and Orders files.

SELECT A
USE Master INDEX Master

SELECT B
USE Orders
SET RELATION TO PartNo INTO Master

*- Next transaction will begin below
*- the last record in StartTrans.
StartTrans = RECCOUNT()+1

*------- Set up loop for displaying invoice forms.
Again = "Y"
DO WHILE Again = "Y"

   *------- Set up top portion of invoice on the screen.
   CLEAR
   MInvoice = MInvoice + 1      && Increment invoice number.
   STORE SPACE(20) TO MClerk, MCust

   MTotal = 0

   *------- Get heading information for the invoice.
   @ 1,2 SAY DATE()
   @ 1,30 SAY "Invoice number: " + STR(MInvoice,5)
   @ 2,2 SAY "Clerk " GET MClerk
   @ 2,35 SAY "Customer " GET MCust
   @ 3,0 SAY REPLICATE("_",80)
   ? "  Part #  Name",SPACE(20)
   ?? "Qty   Price         Total"
   READ

   *------- Set up loop for each item on the invoice.
   Row = 7
   Adding = .T.
   DO WHILE Adding
      PartNumb = Space(5)
      OK = .F.


      *- Loop for various validity checks on line item.
      DO WHILE .NOT. OK
         BOrder = .F.             && Back order flag.
         SplitOrder = .F.         && Split order flag.
         Quantity = 0             && Quantity ordered.

         *------- Ask for part number.
         PartNumb = SPACE(5)
         @ Row,2 GET PartNumb
```

**FIGURE 16.5:** The Instant.prg command file, which instantly updates the Master database as transactions are added to the Orders database. (Much of this program is based on the PosEntry program shown in Chapter 10, "Adding New Data.") The program displays a warning when an order exceeds in-stock quantities and also automatically handles backorders.

```
READ

*------ Make sure part number exists.
PartNumb = UPPER(TRIM(PartNumb))
SELECT A
SEEK PartNumb

*------- Decide next step based on
*------- existence of part number.
DO CASE

   *---- No part number was entered.
   CASE LEN(PartNumb) = 0
        OK = .T.
        Adding = .F.
        LOOP

   *---- Part number does not exist.
   CASE .NOT. FOUND()
        @ Row,10 SAY "No such part!!!"
        OK = .F.

   *- Part number does exist, so display
   *- part name and unit price, and ask
   *- for quantity ordered.
   CASE FOUND()
        @ Row,10 SAY PartName
        @ Row,35 GET Quantity PICT "@Z 999"
        @ Row,40 SAY Unit_Price
        READ

        *--- Perform immediate update based
        *--- on in_stock and ordered quantities.
        DO CASE

           *-- No quantity entered, retry entry.
           CASE Quantity = 0
                LOOP

           *--- Normal entry, adjust In_Stock qty.
           CASE Quantity <= In_Stock
                REPLACE In_Stock WITH In_Stock - Quantity

           *-- In_Stock quantity is zero.  Ask
           *-- about backordering.
           CASE In_Stock = 0
                YN = " "
                DO BackOrder WITH YN
                IF YN = "Y"
                   BOrder = .T.

                   REPLACE BackOrder WITH BackOrder + Quantity
                ELSE
                   @ Row,0 CLEAR
                   LOOP
                ENDIF (yn=y)

           *-- Qty ordered exceeds in stock qty.
           CASE Quantity > In_Stock
                YN = " "
                DO BackOrder WITH YN
                IF YN = "Y"
                   SplitOrder = .T.
                   Qty1 = In_Stock
```

**FIGURE 16.5:** The Instant.prg command file, which instantly updates the Master database as transactions are added to the Orders database. (Much of this program is based on the PosEntry program shown in Chapter 10, "Adding New Data.") The program displays a warning when an order exceeds in-stock quantities and also automatically handles backorders (continued).

```
                  Qty2 = Quantity - In_Stock
                  REPLACE BackOrder WITH BackOrder + ;
                          (Quantity - In_Stock), ;
                          In_Stock WITH 0
               ELSE
                  @ Row,0 CLEAR


                  LOOP
               ENDIF (yn=y)

         ENDCASE (update cases)

         *---- Display line item total and increment
         *---- invoice total.
         Item_Price = Unit_Price
         @ Row,50 SAY Quantity * Item_Price;
         PICT "##,###.##"
         MTotal = MTotal + (Quantity * Item_Price)
         OK = .T.

         *------- Add a blank record to the TempInv file,
         *------- and fill in the fields.
         IF SplitOrder
            Quantity = Qty1
         ENDIF (splitorder)
         SELECT B

         APPEND BLANK
         REPLACE Date_Sold WITH DATE()
         REPLACE Clerk WITH MClerk
         REPLACE Invoice_No WITH MInvoice
         REPLACE Customer WITH MCust
         REPLACE PartNo WITH PartNumb
         REPLACE Qty WITH Quantity
         REPLACE Price WITH Item_Price
         REPLACE BOrder WITH M->BOrder

         *------------ If order was split in half,
         *------------ add second part of order as
         *------------ a backorder record.
         IF SplitOrder
            APPEND BLANK
            REPLACE Date_Sold WITH DATE()
            REPLACE Clerk WITH MClerk
            REPLACE Invoice_No WITH MInvoice
            REPLACE Customer WITH MCust

            REPLACE PartNo WITH PartNumb
            REPLACE Qty WITH Qty2
            REPLACE Price WITH Item_Price
            REPLACE BOrder WITH .T.
         ENDIF (splitorder)

   ENDCASE (part number cases)
ENDDO (while checking for valid part numbers)

*----------- Increment screen row number.
Row = Row + 1
*----------- Scroll screen if at row 17.
IF Row >= 17
   @ 24,1
   ?
   Row = 16
```

**FIGURE 16.5:** The Instant.prg command file, which instantly updates the Master database as transactions are added to the Orders database. (Much of this program is based on the PosEntry program shown in Chapter 10, "Adding New Data.") The program displays a warning when an order exceeds in-stock quantities and also automatically handles backorders (continued).

```
        ENDIF (row)
        ENDDO (while still adding transactions to invoice)


        *------- Display grand total, and pause before next invoice.
        @ Row+2,40 SAY "Total: "
        @ Row+2,50 SAY MTotal PICT "$#,###.##"
        Pinvoice = "Y"
        @ 23,2 SAY "Print invoice? (Y/N) ";
        GET Pinvoice PICT "!"
        READ

        *------ Print invoice, readjust StartTrans.
        IF Pinvoice = "Y"
           SET PRINT ON
           ? "Date: ", DATE()
           ? "Invoice number: ",STR(MInvoice,5)
           ? "Customer: ",MCust,SPACE(20)
           ?? "Clerk: ",MClerk
           ? REPLICATE("_",80)
           ?
           SELECT B
           GOTO StartTrans


           *- Can use REPORT FORM ... PLAIN below to print line items
           *- to improve formatting and pagination on printed invoice.
           DISPLAY OFF PartNo,A->PartName,Qty,Price,Qty*Price REST
           ?
           ?
           ? " Total: ",SPACE(36),TRANSFORM(MTotal,"$###,###.##")
           EJECT
           SET PRINT OFF
           StartTrans = RECCOUNT()+1
        ENDIF (pinvoice)
        *------------ Ask about doing another transaction.
        CLEAR
        @ 23,2 SAY "Do another transaction? (Y/N) ";
        GET Again PICT "!"
        READ

     ENDDO (while user does not request to exit)

     *------- Close databases and update Orders File.
     CLOSE DATABASES


     CLEAR
     ? "Updating transaction file, please wait..."
     SET TALK ON
     USE Orders INDEX Orders
     REINDEX
     SET TALK OFF
     CLOSE DATABASES
     RETURN
```

**FIGURE 16.5:** The Instant.prg command file, which instantly updates the Master database as transactions are added to the Orders database. (Much of this program is based on the PosEntry program shown in Chapter 10, "Adding New Data.") The program displays a warning when an order exceeds in-stock quantities and also automatically handles backorders. (continued)

The Instant.prg command file is based on the PosEntry program originally described in Chapter 10, "Adding New Data." As you may recall, PosEntry is a point-of-sale data-entry program that allows the user to enter sales transactions into a database file. The Instant program uses the Master and Orders database

```
********************************** InvProc.prg
* Inventory system procedure file.
*
PROCEDURE BackOrder
   PARAMETERS YN
   ? CHR(7)
   @ 18,0 CLEAR
   @ 18,0 SAY REPLICATE ("_",80)
   @ 19,2 SAY "Quantity in stock "+STR(In_Stock,4)
   @ 20,2 SAY "Quantity on order "+STR(On_Order,5)
   @ 21,2 SAY "Expected arrival date "+ DTOC(Rec_Date)
   @ 23,2 SAY "Proceed with order? (Y/N) " GET YN PICT "!"
   READ
   @ 18,0 CLEAR
RETURN
```

**FIGURE 16.6:** A small procedure used by the Instant program to show the status of items that a customer wishes to order but are not in stock. The procedure shows the quantity in stock, the amount on order, and the expected arrival date of the most recent order. The procedure also asks whether to proceed with the order.

files described in Figure 16.4. The Master file is indexed on the PartNo field using the command **INDEX ON PartNo TO Master**.

The main difference between Instant and PosEntry is the DO CASE clause near the middle of the program, which handles the immediate updates. This CASE clause begins with the following comments and command:

```
* - - Perform immediate update based
* - - on in_stock and ordered quantities.
DO CASE
```

If the operator does not enter any quantity to order, the transaction is simply ignored by the first CASE statement, as shown below:

```
* - No quantity entered, retry entry.
CASE Quantity = 0
      LOOP
```

If the quantity to be ordered is less than or equal to the quantity in stock, the amount ordered is subtracted from the quantity in stock, as shown below:

```
* - Normal entry, adjust In_Stock qty.
CASE Quantity < = In_Stock
      REPLACE In_Stock WITH In_Stock - Quantity
```

If the customer orders an item for which there is none in stock, the following CASE clause presents the backordering information and asks whether the user wishes to proceed with the transaction (via the BackOrder procedure). If the customer decides to proceed, the order proceeds normally, and the backorder quantity for the item in the Master file is increased by the amount of the order. The BOrder variable is flagged as .T., thus marking the transaction as a backorder.

(This .T. value is later transferred to the BOrder field in the Orders database.) If the customer does not proceed with the order, the LOOP command simply bypasses the current transaction.

```
* – In_Stock quantity is zero. Ask
* – about backordering.
CASE In_Stock = 0
    YN = " "
    DO BackOrder WITH YN
    IF YN = "Y"
        BOrder = .T.
        REPLACE BackOrder WITH BackOrder + Quantity
    ELSE
        @ Row,0 CLEAR
        LOOP
    ENDIF (yn = y)
```

Also built into the Instant program is the ability to split an order into two separate orders if the order exceeds the quantity in stock. For example, suppose the customer orders 25 of part number A-111, but only 10 are in stock. The routine below will split the order so that the 10 are shipped immediately, and the remaining 15 are placed on backorder:

```
* – Qty ordered exceeds in stock qty.
CASE Quantity > In_Stock
    YN = " "
    DO BackOrder WITH YN
    IF YN = "Y"
      SplitOrder = .T.
      Qty1 = In_Stock
      Qty2 = Quantity – In_Stock
      REPLACE BackOrder WITH BackOrder + ;
                  (Quantity – In_Stock), ;
                  In_Stock WITH 0
    ELSE
      @ Row,0 CLEAR
      LOOP
    ENDIF (yn = y)

ENDCASE (update cases)
```

Note that with this technique, any orders (or parts of orders) that could not be filled immediately because of insufficient quantities in stock have a .T. in the BOrder field in the appropriate record in the Orders database. You will probably want to create two different programs for fulfilling orders: one for orders that are ready to go (BOrder = .F.) and another for old orders when there were too few items in stock to fill the order immediately (BOrder = .T.).

For a more thorough understanding of the entire Instant program, review Chapter 10, "Adding New Data."

## CALCULATING ACROSS DATA FILES

When you store the unit price for each item on a master inventory file and individual transactions on a transaction file, you can still calculate totals for transactions by "borrowing" the unit price from the master file.

To do so, open both the transaction file and the master file, and set up a relationship based on a common part number (or other common field) pointing from the transaction file into the master file. Then use the SUM command with the transaction file while pointing to the unit price in the master file. The following example will demonstrate this technique.

Suppose you have a database named Master that contains, among other things, the part number (PartNo) and unit price (Unit_Price) for each item in your stock. In addition, you have a database named Orders that contains (among other fields) the part number (PartNo) and quantity ordered (Qty) of each order transaction. Even though the Orders database does not include a Unit_Price field, you can calculate the total sales for the orders by setting up a relationship based on the common PartNo field and borrowing the Unit_Price field from the Master database, as in the routine below:

```
SELECT A
USE Orders
SELECT B
USE Master INDEX Master

SELECT A
SET RELATION TO PartNo INTO Master
SUM (Qty * B->Unit_Price) TO Tot FOR PartNo = "A-111"
```

Chapter 9, "Printing Formatted Reports," includes a similar technique for calculating totals using two databases, displaying the results on a formatted report.

## "BACKWARD" UPDATING

The UPDATE command provides a quick way for changing the data in a master file based on the contents of a transaction file. But it works in only one direction: updating the "one" side of the relationship from the "many" side of the relationship.

To copy data from the "one" side of the relationship onto the "many" side of the relationship, you need to open both files and set up a relationship, based on the key field, that points from the "many" side into the "one" side. Then you can use a REPLACE command to copy the appropriate values from the "one" side into the "many" side.

For example, suppose the Master database in this example includes, among other fields, a field named PartNo and a field named Unit_Price. A second database, named Orders, includes the PartNo field and also contains a field Unit_Price, but the Unit_Price field is empty on the Orders database. How do you copy the appropriate unit price for each order transaction into the Orders database?

The routine below shows how this is done. First, the database files are opened (with the Master index based on the PartNo field), and the relationship is set up appropriately:

```
SELECT A
USE Master INDEX Master
SELECT B
USE Orders

SET RELATION TO PartNo INTO Master
REPLACE ALL Unit_Price WITH A->Unit_Price
```

This technique fills in all the Unit_Price fields on the Orders database with the appropriate values from the Master file. (The PosEntry program in Chapter 10, "Adding New Data," demonstrates a technique for performing this kind of transfer one record at a time, during data entry.)

## TECHNIQUES FOR MANY-TO-MANY RELATIONSHIPS

Chapter 3, "Database Design," demonstrates two designs using many-to-many relationships: one for scheduling and one for exploded inventories. This next section explores techniques for displaying reports and extracting information from databases that have already been set up in a many-to-many fashion.

### Printing Schedules with Three Database Files

The simplest form of a many-to-many relationship is the scheduling database composed of three database files: two containing actual data and a third serving as a linking file. Figure 16.7 shows a typical example, using databases named Students, SCLink, and Courses. As the arrows in the figure show, the SCLink file contains key fields relating to both the Students and Courses database files.

```
Structure for database: Students.dbf

Field Name  Type       Width Dec  Description

StudentID   Numeric        5        Student number
LastName    Character     10        Last name
FirstName   Character     10        First name
Address     Character     20        Address
City        Character     20        City
State       Character      2        State
Zip         Character      5        Zip code
Phone       Character     13        Phone number


Structure for database: SCLink.dbf

Field Name  Type       Width      Description

StudentID   Numeric        5        Student number
CourseID    Character      5        Course number

Structure for database: Courses.dbf

Field Name  Type       Width Dec  Description

CourseID    Character      5        Course number
CourseName  Character     10        Course name
Room No     Character      5        Room number
Teacher     Character     20        Instructor name
```

**FIGURE 16.7:** Three databases related in a many-to-many fashion for a typical scheduling database. The SCLink database contains records that list students and the courses in which each student is enrolled.

To print a list of students and their courses, or a list of courses and the enrolled students, you need an algorithm that follows the basic structure shown below:

```
SELECT A
USE <main file of interest>
SELECT B
USE <linking file, indexed on main field of interest>
SELECT C
USE <third file>

SELECT A
SET RELATION TO <linking file>
SELECT B
SET RELATION TO <third file>

SELECT A
GO TOP
DO WHILE .NOT. EOF( )
    ? <record from main file of interest>
```

```
    SELECT B
    LIST <records that match key field in main file>
    SELECT A
    SKIP
ENDDO
```

The Students program in Figure 16.8 shows a more specific example using the database structures shown in Figure 16.7. It lists all the students and their classes, producing the report shown in Figure 16.9. The index expression for Students is based on the StudentID field; the expression for the SCLink index file

```
**************************************** Students.prg
SET HEADING OFF
SET TALK OFF
SET STATUS OFF
*------------------- Open all three files.
SELECT A
*------- Indexed on the StudentID field.
USE Students INDEX Students

SELECT B
*------- Indexed on the StudentID field.
USE SCLink INDEX LinkStud

SELECT C
*------- Indexed on the CourseID field.
USE Courses INDEX Courses

*------------------ Set up relationships.


SELECT A
SET RELATION TO StudentID INTO SCLink
SELECT B
SET RELATION TO CourseID INTO Courses
*------------------ Print the report.
SELECT A
GO TOP
DO WHILE .NOT. EOF()
   *--------------- Print student data.
   ? StudentID,TRIM(LastName)+", "+FirstName
   ? SPACE(5),Address,City,Zip
   ? REPLICATE("-",80)
   SELECT B
   *--------------- List student's courses.
   ? " Course No.  Name        Room      Teacher"
   LIST WHILE StudentID = A-> StudentID;
        SPACE(5),CourseID,C->CourseName,;
        C->Room_No,"   ",C->Teacher OFF
   ?

   ?
   SELECT A
   SKIP
ENDDO (eof)
```

**FIGURE 16.8:** A program that prints a report listing all students and their courses (as in the example shown in Figure 16.9). The index expression for Students is based on the StudentID field; the expression for the SCLink index file is also the StudentID field; and the index expression for the Courses index file is the CourseID field.

is also the StudentID field; and the index expression for the Courses index file is the CourseID field.

Figure 16.10 shows a program named Courses that prints a list of all courses the school offers, as in the example shown in Figure 16.11. Under every course, the report lists the student number, name, and address of each student enrolled in that course. Note the key expressions used in the index files and for defining the relationships in that sample program. The Courses and SCLink databases are both indexed on the CourseID field. The Students database is indexed on the StudentID field. The CourseID field relates the Courses database into the SCLink database, and the StudentID field relates the SCLink database into the Students database.

Both the Students and Courses programs follow the basic algorithm defined earlier in this section. If you would like to add heading, pagination, and other niceties to the printed reports, use the techniques discussed in Chapter 9, "Printing Formatted Reports."

## Printing Schedules with Four Database Files

Some scheduling applications require four or more database files. Printing reports from such database files often requires some tricky index files and SET RELATION commands. An example will best demonstrate techniques for printing reports from such a database, because there really are no hard-and-fast rules to follow. However, you should be able to extrapolate examples from these figures that you can incorporate in similar applications of your own.

Figure 16.12 shows the structures of the four database files used in the example in this section. The arrows in the figure show the fields used to relate

```
10004 Davis, David
      P.O. Box 123          San Diego            92024
-------------------------------------------------------------------
 Course No.  Name        Room      Teacher
       A-111 English     ENG-1     Watson
       B-222 Spanish     LNG-4     Holmes
       C-333 Greek       LNG-7     Moriarty
       D-444 Math        MAT-4     Einstein

10005 Edwards, Eddie
      6789 Grape St.        Encinitas            92123
-------------------------------------------------------------------
 Course No.  Name        Room      Teacher
       A-111 English     ENG-1     Watson
       B-222 Spanish     LNG-4     Holmes
       C-333 Greek       LNG-7     Moriarty
       D-444 Math        MAT-4     Einstein
```

**FIGURE 16.9:** Sample report printed by the Students program shown in Figure 16.8. Each student's name and address is displayed, as well as all courses the student is enrolled in.

```
***************************************** Courses.prg
SET TALK OFF
SET HEADING OFF
*------------------------------ Open all three files.
SELECT A
*----- Indexed on the CourseID field.
USE Courses INDEX Courses

SELECT B
*----- Indexed on the CourseID field.
USE SCLink INDEX LinkCour

SELECT C
*----- Indexed on the StudentID field.
USE Students INDEX Students

*------------------------------ Set up relationships.


SELECT A
SET RELATION TO CourseID INTO SCLink
SELECT B
SET RELATION TO StudentID INTO Students
*------------------------------ Print report.
SELECT A
GO TOP
DO WHILE .NOT. EOF()
   ? "Course: ",CourseID,CourseName
   ?? "Room No.:",Room_No,"  Instructor: ",Teacher
   SELECT B
   *---- List students enrolled in this course.
   LIST WHILE CourseID = A->CourseID;
        SPACE(5),StudentID,C->LastName,C->FirstName,C->Address OFF
   ?
   ?
   SELECT A
   SKIP
ENDDO (eof)
```

**FIGURE 16.10:** A program that prints a report listing all courses and the students enrolled in each course (as in the example shown in Figure 16.11). The index expression for Courses is based on the CourseID field; the expression for the SCLink index file is also the CourseID field; and the index expression for the Students index file is the StudentID field.

```
Course:  A-111 English   Room No.: ENG-1   Instructor:  Watson
       10002 Baker       Bobbi      345 B st.
       10003 Carlson     Carla      345 C st.
       10004 Davis       David      P.O. Box 123
       10005 Edwards     Eddie      6789 Grape St.


Course:  C-333 Greek     Room No.: LNG-7   Instructor:  Moriarty
       10001 Adams       Angela     123 A st.
       10002 Baker       Bobbi      345 B st.
       10003 Carlson     Carla      345 C st.
       10004 Davis       David      P.O. Box 123
       10005 Edwards     Eddie      6789 Grape St.
```

**FIGURE 16.11:** Sample report printed by the Courses program shown in Figure 16.10. Each course is displayed, as well as names and addresses of students enrolled in each course.

```
Structure for database: Students.dbf

Field Name  Type        Width Dec  Description

StudentID   Numeric         5        Student number
LastName    Character      10        Last name
FirstName   Character      10        First name
Address     Character      20        Address
City        Character      20        City
State       Character       2        State
Zip         Character       5        ZIP code
Phone       Character      13        Phone


Structure for database: SCLink2.dbf

Field Name  Type        Width Dec  Description

StudentID   Numeric         5        Student number
CourseID    Character       5        Course number
Section     Numeric         2        Section number


Structure for database: Sections.dbf

Field Name  Type        Width Dec  Description

Section     Numeric         2        Section number
CourseID    Character       5        Course number
Teacher     Character      15        Instructor name
Room_No     Character       5        Room number


Structure for database:  Course2.dbf

Field Name  Type        Width Dec  Description

CourseID    Character       5        Course number
CourseName  Character      10        Course name
Units       Numeric         1        Semester units
```

**FIGURE 16.12:** Four sample databases comprising a database used to manage an academic enrollment schedule. The arrows show the fields used to link the database files. All of the common (linking) fields are indexed.

the files. The Students database holds a record for each student, and the SCLink2 database lists all the students and every course and section in which each student is enrolled.

Because the school offers several sections of each course, the section and course information is split into two files (to avoid redundant data). Information specific to each course is stored on the Course2 database. Information specific to a given section of a course is stored on the Sections database.

The tricky problem in a situation such as this is getting the SET RELATION pointers and the contents of the index files right. Basically, you need to make sure that each database has at least one field that can relate it to the next lower database in a series of SET RELATION commands. This may require that a database be indexed on two or more fields. For example, the Sections database in this application is indexed on both the Section and CourseID fields. If it were indexed on Section alone, there would be no way of telling to which course the section number referred.

Once you are certain that information from the highest-level file (Students in this example) can be traced to individual records in lower-level files (Sections and Course2 in this example) through the index files and SET RELATION commands, you can develop a report to print the data in any format you want.

Figure 16.13 shows a sample program capable of printing a list of students and the sections and courses in which each is enrolled. Note carefully the key

```
************************************************ Student2.prg
SET TALK OFF
SET STATUS OFF
SET HEADING OFF
SELECT A
*----------- Indexed on StudentID.
USE Students INDEX Students

SELECT B
*----------- Indexed on StudentID.
USE SCLink2 INDEX SCLink2

SELECT C
*----------- Indexed on STR(Section,1)+CourseID.
USE Sections INDEX Sections

SELECT D
*----------- Indexed on CourseID.
USE Course2 INDEX Course2

SELECT A
SET RELATION TO StudentID INTO SCLink2
SELECT B
SET RELATION TO STR(Section,1)+CourseID INTO Sections
SELECT C
SET RELATION TO CourseID INTO Course2

SELECT A
GO TOP
DO WHILE .NOT. EOF()
   ? StudentID,LastName,FirstName
   ? SPACE(5),Address,City,Zip
   ? REPLICATE("-",70)
   SELECT B
   ? "Course #     Name     Section    "
   ?? "Instructor       Room # "
   LIST OFF WHILE StudentID = A->StudentID;
        SPACE(5),CourseID,D->CourseName,Section,;
        "    ",C->Teacher,C->Room_No

   ?
   ?
   SELECT A
   SKIP
ENDDO (eof)
CLOSE ALL
```

**FIGURE 16.13:** The Student2 program, which displays a schedule of students and the courses in which they are enrolled from four databases comprising a schedule of students, courses, and sections of courses. The structures of the database files used in this program are displayed in Figure 16.12.

expressions of the index files (shown in comment lines) and the fields used within the SET RELATION commands to define the relationships.

Figure 16.14 shows a sample display from the Student2 program. As you can see, for each student there is a list of the course number, course section, course name, and other relevant information. Some of the course information is taken from the Sections database, and some of it (the course name) is taken from the Course2 database. In the program itself, the C-> alias points into the Sections database, and D-> points into the Course2 database.

If you want to list the individual students enrolled in each section of each course, you have a slightly trickier problem on your hands. You need a pointer going from each section into each course, and then from there into the SCLink2 database (and finally into the Students database). However, because the Course2 database does not have a Section field, the SET RELATION command has to "stretch" the section field from the Sections database to the SCLink2 database, as shown below (and in the Course2 program shown in Figure 16.15).

```
SELECT A
SET RELATION TO CourseID
SELECT B
SET RELATION TO CourseID + STR(A->Section,1) INTO;
                        SCLink2
```

```
10001 Adams      Angela
      123 A St.            San Diego            92122
-----------------------------------------------------------------------
Course #       Name    Section    Instructor         Room #
       B-222 Spanish     1        Adams              BAM-1
       C-333 Greek       2        Keller             LAN-3


10002 Baker      Bobbi
      345 B St.            San Diego            12345
-----------------------------------------------------------------------
Course #       Name    Section    Instructor         Room #
       A-111 English     2        Jones              ENG- 2
       B-222 Spanish     2        Baker              LNG- 2
       C-333 Greek       1        Albertson          LNG- 7


10003 Carlson    Carla
      345 C St.            La Mesa              98765
-----------------------------------------------------------------------
Course #       Name    Section    Instructor         Room #
       A-111 English     1        Smith              ENG-1
       B-222 Spanish     1        Adams              LNG-1
       C-333 Greek       1        Albertson          LNG-7
```

**FIGURE 16.14:** A sample report printed from a scheduling database with four files. The student information comes from the Students database, the students enrolled in each section come from the SCLink2 database, and the information about each course and section of each course come from the Sections and Course2 databases.

Figure 16.15 shows the entire Course2 program, which prints a list of students enrolled in each section of each course. Note the key expressions used in each index file, as listed in the program comments.

Figure 16.16 shows a sample report printed by the Course2 program. The course information is from the Sections and Course2 database files, the list of

```
***************************************** Course2.prg
SET STATUS OFF
SET TALK OFF
SET HEADING OFF
*-- Open database and index files.
SELECT A
*--  Indexed on CourseID+STR(Section,1).
USE Sections INDEX CourSec
SELECT B
*--  Indexed on CourseID.
USE Course2 INDEX Course2
SELECT C
*--  Indexed on CourseID+STR(Section,1).
USE SCLink2 INDEX SCLink3
SELECT D
*--  Indexed on StudentID.
USE Students INDEX Students

*---------- Set up relationships.

SELECT A
SET RELATION TO CourseID INTO Course2
SELECT B
*---- Need to "stretch" from Sections database here.
SET RELATION TO CourseID+STR(A->Section,1) INTO SCLink2
SELECT C
SET RELATION TO StudentID INTO Students
*--------- Print the report.
SELECT A
GO TOP
DO WHILE .NOT. EOF()
   ? "Course: "+CourseId,B->CourseName
   ?? "Section: ",Section
   ? SPACE(9),"Room: ",Room_No,"Instructor: ",Teacher
   ? REPLICATE("-",70)
   SELECT C
   ? "  Student #    Student Name        Address"
   *--- List individual students.
   LIST WHILE CourseID+STR(Section,1) =;

              A->CourseID+STR(A->Section,1);
              SPACE(5),StudentID,D->FirstName,;
              D->LastName,D->Address OFF
   ?
   SELECT A
   SKIP
ENDDO (eof)
CLOSE ALL
```

**FIGURE 16.15:** The Course2 program, which prints a list of students enrolled in each section of each course, using the database structures shown in Figure 16.12. Note the SET RELATION commands and the key expressions in the index files, which use the section number from the Sections database and the course number from the Course2 database to define the relationship between the Course2 and SCLink2 databases.

students enrolled in each section is supplied by the SCLink2 database, and individual student information comes from the Students database file.

## Reports for Exploded Inventories

Another common application of the many-to-many relationship is the exploded inventory, as was originally discussed in Chapter 3, "Database Design." The database structures used for the exploded inventory example are shown in Figure 16.17. Figure 16.18 shows how one can trace which components are used to manufacture which products through the key fields in the three files. Note that the Qty_Used field in the Linker database tells how many of each component are required in each manufactured product.

The field named Required in Linker.dbf is used as a working field later. The user does not need to fill in any data in this field. Instead, a program will use this field to hold quantities as it performs its work.

```
Course: A-111 English   Section:   1
          Room:  ENG-1 Instructor:  Smith
-----------------------------------------------------------------------
  Student #     Student Name        Address
       10003 Carla      Carlson     345 C St.
       10004 David      Davis       P.O. Box 123
       10005 Eddie      Edwards     6789 Grape St.
       10010 Mandy      Miller      3434 Banana St.

Course: A-111 English   Section:   2
          Room:  ENG-2 Instructor:  Jones
-----------------------------------------------------------------------
  Student #     Student Name        Address
       10001 Angela     Adams       123 A St.
       10002 Bobbi      Baker       345 B St.
       10006 Freddie    Fredrix     P.O. Box 123

Course: B-222 Spanish   Section:   1

          Room:  LNG-1 Instructor:  Adams
-----------------------------------------------------------------------
  Student #     Student Name        Address
       10001 Angela     Adams       123 A St.
       10003 Carla      Carlson     345 C St.
       10004 David      Davis       P.O. Box 123
       10005 Eddie      Edwards     6789 Grape St.
```

**FIGURE 16.16:** Sample list of students enrolled in each section of each course. The data is derived from the database structure shown in Figure 16.12. This report is printed by the Course2 program shown in Figure 16.15.

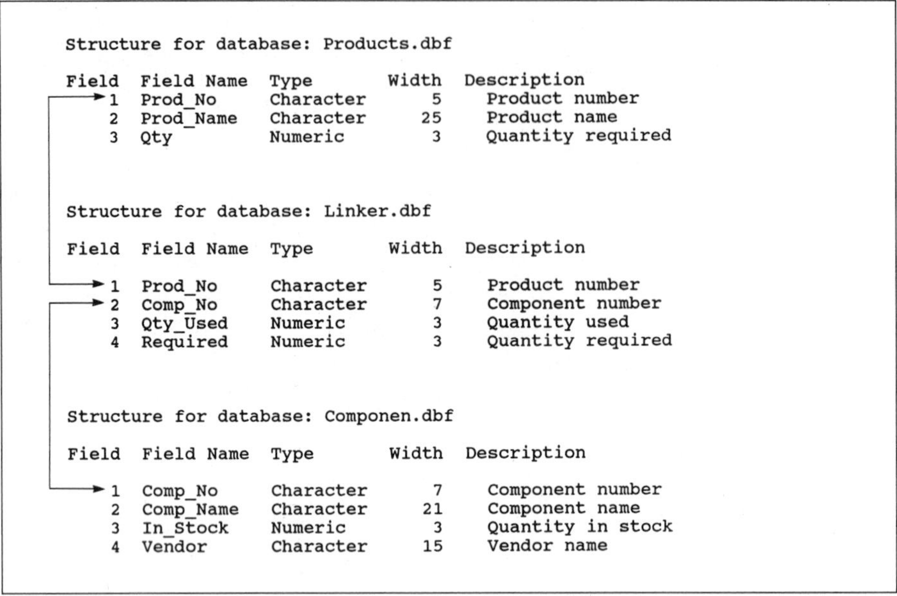

```
Structure for database: Products.dbf

Field  Field Name  Type       Width  Description
    1  Prod_No     Character      5    Product number
    2  Prod_Name   Character     25    Product name
    3  Qty         Numeric        3    Quantity required


Structure for database: Linker.dbf

Field  Field Name  Type       Width  Description

    1  Prod_No     Character      5    Product number
    2  Comp_No     Character      7    Component number
    3  Qty_Used    Numeric        3    Quantity used
    4  Required    Numeric        3    Quantity required


Structure for database: Componen.dbf

Field  Field Name  Type       Width  Description

    1  Comp_No     Character      7    Component number
    2  Comp_Name   Character     21    Component name
    3  In_Stock    Numeric        3    Quantity in stock
    4  Vendor      Character     15    Vendor name
```

**FIGURE 16.17:** The structures of the Products, Linker, and Componen databases in the exploded inventory application. Prod_No is the key field linking Products to Linker, and Comp_No is the key field relating the Componen database to the Linker database. The Qty_Used field in the Linker database defines the number of each component required to manufacture each product. The Required field in the Linker database is used only as a working field by the programs.

```
                                         Linker Database:

                                          Prod_No Qty Comp_No
                                          A-123    1  TT-1234
Products Database:                        A-123    1  VV-1234      Componen Database:
                                          A-123    2  YY-1234
Prod_No Prod_Name                         A-123    2  ZZ-1234      Comp_No    Comp_Name
A-123   Personal Computer 1000            B-123    1  TT-1234      TT-1234    80286 microprocessor
B-123   Personal Computer 2000            B-123    1  UU-1234      UU-1234    Color monitor
C-123   Business Computer 3000            B-123    2  YY-1234      VV-1234    Monochrome monitor
                                          B-123    2  ZZ-1234      WW-1234    Hard disk
                                          C-123    1  TT-1234      YY-1234    Floppy controller
                                          C-123    1  UU-1234      ZZ-1234    Floppy disk drive
                                          C-123    1  WW-1234
                                          C-123    1  YY-1234
                                          C-123    1  ZZ-1234
```

**FIGURE 16.18:** Sample data in the exploded inventory databases, with arrows showing how one can find which components and how many of each component are required to manufacture each product.

## DETERMINING INVENTORY REQUIREMENTS

One of the most common questions you'll ask in an exploded inventory database is, If you want to produce *x* amount of each product, how many of each component will you need? Before you can answer this question, you'll need to create a database to store the answer. In this example, this new database is named Needed and has the structure shown in Figure 16.19.

As you can see, Needed.dbf contains only the fields necessary to determine which components are needed (Comp_No) and how many of each component is required (the Required field). To organize (sort) the data in the Needed database by Comp_No, you can create an index file named Needed using the commands

**USE Needed**
**INDEX ON Comp_No TO Needed**

Next, fill in the Qty field on the Products database with the amount of each product you wish to produce. Assuming that you want to produce five of each product, fill in the Qty field on the Products database as below:

| Record# | Prod_No | Prod_Name | Qty |
|---|---|---|---|
| 1 | A-123 | Personal Computer 1000 | 5 |
| 2 | B-123 | Personal Computer 2000 | 5 |
| 3 | C-123 | Business Computer 3000 | 5 |

Next, you need to open the various files. First, open the Linker database and the LinkProd index file (LinkProd.ndx is based on the Prod_No field in Products.dbf):

**SELECT A**
**USE Linker INDEX LinkProd**

Then open the Products database with the Products index file (which is also built on the Prod_No field):

**SELECT B**
**USE Products INDEX Products**

```
Structure for database: Needed.dbf

Field Name  Type       Width  Dec  Description
Comp_No     Character      7       Component number
Required    Numeric        3       Quantity required
```

**FIGURE 16.19:** The Needed database, which will store the results of calculations to determine inventory requirements in the exploded-inventory application.

Next make sure that the working field named Required in the Linker database is 0, to ensure that any "old" data are eliminated:

```
SELECT A
REPLACE ALL Required WITH 0
```

The next step is to define the relationship between Linker and Products, as below, and make sure the pointer is at the top of the Linker database:

```
SET RELATION TO Prod_No INTO Products
GO TOP
```

Now the Required field on Linker.dbf needs to be incremented by its current value plus the quantity required to manufacture a given product (i.e., **Required + (Qty_Used * B->Qty)).** The Qty value comes from the Products database, hence the B-> in front of the Qty field name. The command to do all of the necessary replacements is simply

```
REPLACE ALL Required WITH Required + (Qty_Used * B->Qty)
```

At this point, the Linker database contains the number of each component that is required to manufacture each product, based on product number. However, for added convenience, you can create a summarized total based on component number rather than product number. To do so, switch to the LinkComp index file (which uses Comp_No as the key expression), and total the database on the Comp_No field, displaying the calculations in the temporary database named Temp:

```
USE Linker INDEX LinkComp
TOTAL TO Temp ON Comp_No
```

Now you can read these summarized data into an empty Needed database as shown below. In the process, you can eliminate components that are not required at all by specifying that only records with a Needed value greater than zero be read in, as below:

```
USE Needed INDEX Needed
ZAP
APPEND FROM Temp FOR Required > 0
```

To show the results (that is, the components needed to produce five of each product), simply enter the LIST command, which displays the results below:

| Record# | Comp_No | Required |
|---|---|---|
| 1 | TT-1234 | 15 |
| 2 | UU-1234 | 10 |
| 3 | VV-1234 | 5 |

| | | |
|---|---|---|
| 4 | WW-1234 | 5 |
| 5 | YY-1234 | 25 |
| 6 | ZZ-1234 | 25 |

If you want to see more information about each required component, set up a relationship between the Needed database and the Componen database, and list the fields that you want to see. Here is an example:

```
SELECT 1
USE Needed INDEX Needed
SELECT 2
USE Componen INDEX Componen
SELECT 1
SET RELATION TO Comp_No INTO Componen
LIST Comp_No,B->Comp_Name,B->In_Stock,Required OFF
```

The resulting display shows the component number, the component name, the quantity in stock of each component, and the number of components required to manufacture the products:

| Comp_No | B->Comp_Name | B->In_Stock | Required |
|---|---|---|---|
| TT-1234 | 80286 microprocessor | 500 | 15 |
| UU-1234 | Color monitor | 500 | 10 |
| VV-1234 | Monochrome monitor | 500 | 5 |
| WW-1234 | Hard disk | 500 | 5 |
| YY-1234 | Floppy controller | 500 | 25 |
| ZZ-1234 | Floppy disk drive | 500 | 25 |

## Updating in an Exploded Inventory

Taking the above information a step farther, you can answer the next important question that arises in exploded inventories: "Assuming that I manufacture five of each product and use the necessary components, how many of each component will I have left in stock?"

At this point, you have a basic updating problem to solve. All you need to do is subtract the quantity required to manufacture the products (stored in the Needed.dbf file) from the in-stock quantities in the Componen database. To perform this feat, enter the commands below:

```
CLOSE DATABASES
SELECT 1
```

```
USE Componen INDEX Componen
SELECT 2
USE Needed INDEX Needed
SELECT 1

UPDATE ON Comp_No FROM Needed ;
        REPLACE In_Stock WITH In_Stock - B->Required
LIST Comp_No,Comp_Name,In_Stock
```

The LIST command displays the results shown below; namely the quantity of each component remaining in stock after the components are used to manufacture the products:

| Comp_No | Comp_Name | In_Stock |
|---|---|---|
| TT-1234 | 80286 microprocessor | 485 |
| UU-1234 | Color monitor | 490 |
| VV-1234 | Monochrome monitor | 495 |
| WW-1234 | Hard disk | 495 |
| YY-1234 | Floppy controller | 475 |
| ZZ-1234 | Floppy disk drive | 475 |

Figure 16.20 shows all of the steps necessary to determine the inventory requirements and update the component database accordingly, combined into a single command file.

```
****************************************** Needed.prg
* Determines how many of each component is required
* to build all the products specified in the Qty field
* of the Products database.

*----------- Open the Linker file with Prod_No index file.
SELECT 1
USE Linker INDEX LinkProd
*-------------- Open the Products file with Prod_No index.
SELECT 2
USE Products INDEX Products
*------------------- Set Required field in Linker to zero.
SELECT 1
REPLACE ALL Required WITH 0
*------------------------- Set up Prod_No as common field.
SET RELATION TO Prod_No INTO Products
GO TOP
*--- Update each record in Linker by quantity in Products.
REPLACE ALL Required WITH Required + (Qty_Used * B->Qty)
*--------------- Create a totaled database named Temp.dbf.
```

**FIGURE 16.20:** This program lists all the steps required to determine the number of components needed to manufacture a given number of products and update the components database accordingly, in a typical exploded-inventory application. This program uses the database structures shown in Figure 16.17.

```
SET SAFETY OFF
USE Linker INDEX LinkComp
TOTAL TO Temp ON Comp_No
*----- Read summarized data from Temp.dbf into Needed.dbf.
USE Needed INDEX Needed
ZAP
APPEND FROM Temp FOR Required > 0
*------------------------------------ Show parts needed.
LIST
CLOSE DATABASES

*-------- Optionally, show component name with other data.
SELECT 1
USE Needed INDEX Needed
SELECT 2
USE Componen INDEX Componen
SELECT 1
SET RELATION TO Comp_No INTO Componen
LIST Comp_No,B->Comp_Name,B->Vendor,B->In_Stock,Required
CLOSE DATABASES
*  The next routine demonstrates how to subtract the "needed"
*  quantities in Needed.dbf from the In_Stock quantities in
*  Componen.dbf (which assumes that the components in the
*  Needed.dbf database have already been "consumed").
SELECT 1
USE Componen INDEX Componen
SELECT 2
USE Needed INDEX Needed
SELECT 1
UPDATE ON Comp_No FROM Needed ;
  REPLACE In_Stock WITH In_Stock-B->Required
LIST Comp_No,Comp_Name,In_Stock
RETURN
```

**FIGURE 16.20:** This program lists all the steps required to determine the number of components needed to manufacture a given number of products and update the components database accordingly, in a typical exploded-inventory application. This program uses the database structures shown in Figure 16.17 (continued).

## COMMANDS FOR MANAGING MULTIPLE DATABASE FILES

For the programmer, the SET RELATION command discussed in Chapter 3, "Database Design," is probably the easiest and most efficient technique for defining relationships among database files. However, dBASE also offers alternative techniques in the MODIFY VIEW and JOIN commands. These alternative commands are included in this chapter mainly as general reference, in case you come across them while modifying another programmer's work, or if you want to experiment with them in your own work.

The UPDATE command, demonstrated earlier in this chapter, is also discussed below. Remember, you can use the UPDATE command only for batch updating. In some cases, you'll want to use other programming techniques (discussed earlier in this chapter) to perform immediate updating of database files.

## The CREATE VIEW/MODIFY VIEW Commands

The CREATE VIEW and MODIFY VIEW commands establish links among database files and store the parameters for setting up the relationship within a view (.vue) file. The two commands are equivalent.

### SYNTAX

**CREATE VIEW/MODIFY VIEW <file name>;**
**[FROM ENVIRONMENT]**

where <file name> is the name of the view file to create or modify.

### USAGE

The CREATE VIEW and MODIFY VIEW commands (without the FROM ENVIRONMENT option) present a full-screen, menu-driven environment for defining the relationships among database files. Once the relationships are defined, the necessary parameters to establish the relationships are stored in the view file. CREATE VIEW creates a new view file, and MODIFY VIEW alters an existing view file.

The default extension that dBASE provides for the view file name is .vue. The view file will contain all of the necessary elements to open the work areas, database files, and index files for the relationship, as well as the necessary relationship definitions. In addition, you can define a filter criterion, fields, and a format file for the view.

The full-screen, menu-driven approach to defining relationships between multiple databases presents the screen shown in Figure 16.21. Options from the main menu at the top of the screen can be selected by moving the highlight with the arrow keys. Each top-menu item, when highlighted, displays a pull-down menu. Options within a pull-down menu are selected by moving the highlight to the option and pressing Return. The ← and → keys will always exit a submenu and return you to the higher-level menu. Individual menu items are discussed below.

### THE SET UP MENU

The Set Up menu displays a list of all database files on the currently logged drive and directory. Databases to be included in the view can be selected (and unselected) by highlighting them and pressing Return. As soon as you select a database file, the screen displays a list of all index file names on the current drive and directory. You can select index files for the database using the same method of highlighting and pressing Return. A triangle appears to the left of database and index file names selected for the view.

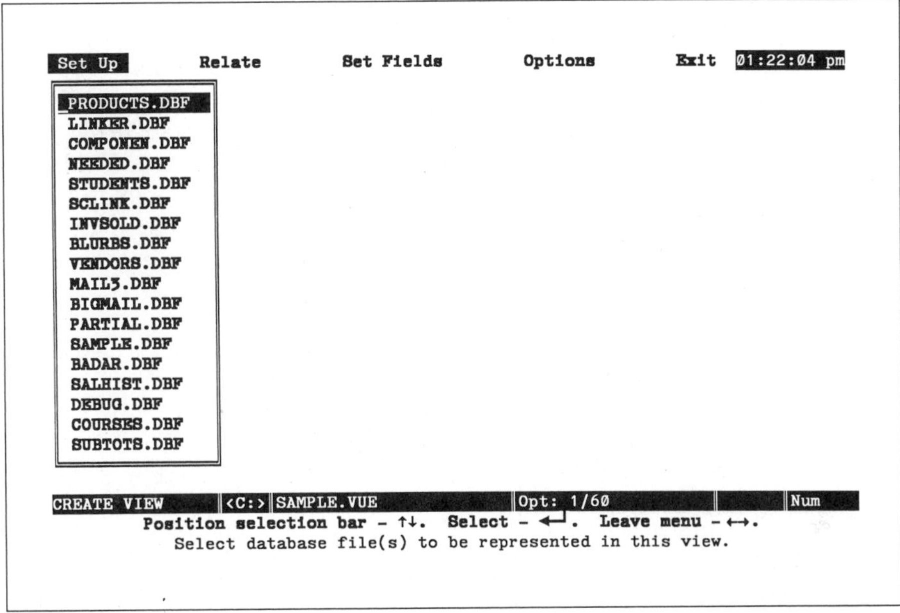


**FIGURE 16.21:** The CREATE/MODIFY VIEW screen for defining database relationships in a menu-driven manner. Each top-menu item has a pull-down menu associated with it. Menu items can be highlighted by using the arrow keys; they are selected by pressing the Return key. Instructions and error messages are displayed at the bottom of the screen.

## THE RELATE MENU

Once the database and index files are selected for a view, the Relate menu displays the names of the selected database files and allows you to select fields from each database to define relationships. When you select a database file from the Relate menu, the screen displays remaining database files that you can set a relationship into. When you select the database file to set the relationship into, the screen asks that you name the expression relating the two files. You can press F10 for a list of field names to base the relationship on and select any field by highlighting it and pressing Return.

The relationships that you define will all be linked. Therefore, if you select three database files for the view, you must define a relationship from the first into the second and from the second into the third. As you define relationships from one file to the next, dBASE displays the relationships on the action line near the bottom of the screen.

### THE SET FIELDS MENU

After the relationships are defined, the Set Fields menu lets you select fields from the database files to display. When you select this menu, it displays the names of all database files in the view file. Selecting a database file name displays a list of all fields in that database. All fields are initially marked with a triangle for display. To exclude a field from display, move the highlight to the field name and press Return. Fields without the triangle on the left are hidden while the view file is in effect. You can include as many or as few fields in the display as you wish.

### THE OPTIONS MENU

The Options menu presents two options, Format and Filter. The Format option lets you select an existing format file that is automatically opened when the view file is opened. Typically, you'll want to create the view, then save it. Then use the screen painter to create a format file for the view. After the format file is complete, use the MODIFY VIEW command to edit the existing view. Then select the Format option from the top menu. The screen will display a list of format file names. Select the format file that you designed for the current view.

The Filter option allows you to define a Filter criterion for selecting records that should be displayed in the view. If no filter is specified, all records are accessible through the view. If a filter condition such as **State = "CA"** is defined, only records with CA in the State field are included in the view file.

### THE EXIT MENU

The Exit menu presents the Save and Abandon options. The Save option saves the current view in the view file and automatically activates the view. The Abandon option abandons the currently defined view, does not save the current view in the view file, and does not activate the view.

## CREATE VIEW FROM ENVIRONMENT

The alternative syntax **CREATE VIEW <file name> FROM ENVIRONMENT** creates a view file from the relationships that have already been determined in a series of SELECT, USE, and SET RELATION commands. This form of the command does not present a full-screen menu-driven technique for defining the view. The example below demonstrates the use of this alternative syntax for the CREATE VIEW command.

Note that the FROM ENVIRONMENT parameter is used only with CREATE VIEW, not with MODIFY VIEW. However, once a view has been created with the CREATE VIEW <file name> FROM ENVIRONMENT command, that view can be altered using MODIFY VIEW <file name>.

## EXAMPLES

In the series of commands below, the CREATE VIEW command stores all the parameters necessary to set up the relationship defined in the previous commands in a file named InvView.vue:

```
SELECT A
USE Master INDEX Master
SELECT B
USE Orders
SELECT A
SET RELATION TO PartNo INTO Master

CREATE VIEW InvView FROM ENVIRONMENT
```

In the future, the single command

```
SET VIEW TO InvView
```

can be used in place of the SELECT, USE, and SET RELATION commands to open the files and set up the relationship.

The command

```
CREATE VIEW InvView
```

allows you to define a view file named InvView.vue using the menu-driven approach.

## TIPS

For programmers, the SET RELATION command offers a much more convenient and flexible method for setting up relationships among files.

## SEE ALSO

SET RELATION
SET VIEW
SET FIELDS

## The JOIN Command

JOIN merges the contents of two database files into a new, third database file.

### SYNTAX

**JOIN WITH <alias> TO <file name> FOR <condition>;**
**[FIELDS <field list>]**

where <alias> is the name of the database file, alias, or work area of the file being combined with currently selected database files, <file name> is the name of the new file being created, <condition> is any valid search criterion that selects what will go in the merged file, and <field list> is an optional list of field names to include in the new file.

### USAGE

Both files to be joined must be open simultaneously. If the FIELDS option is not included, all fields from both database files are included in the newly created file.

### EXAMPLES

The commands below create a database file named BigFile consisting of the FName and LName fields from the Customer database and the Charge and Date fields from the Charges database.

```
SELECT A
USE Customer
SELECT B
USE Charges
SELECT A

JOIN WITH B TO BigFile FOR CustNo = B->CustNo ;
     FIELDS FName, LName, B->Charge, B->Date
```

### TIPS

JOIN is a very slow command that is difficult to use. It also generates very large files. Anything that JOIN has to offer can be accomplished much more quickly, easily, and efficiently with a SET RELATION command.

### SEE ALSO

SET RELATION
SELECT

## The UPDATE Command

UPDATE changes the contents of one database file based on the contents of another database file.

### SYNTAX

**UPDATE ON <key field> FROM <fromfile>;**
**REPLACE <field> WITH <expression>;**
**[<additional fields WITH expressions>], [RANDOM]**

where <key field> is the common field relating the two database files, <fromfile> is the name of the outside file containing the data used in the update, <field> is the name of a field to be changed, <expression> is the change to perform, and <additional fields WITH expressions> are additional fields and expressions in the update.

### USAGE

UPDATE is typically used to update values in a master file based on data stored in a transaction file. Both the master and transaction file must be open, and they must have a common field. Any field names from the transaction file must be preceded with an alias (B->).

Both files should be indexed on the key field that relates the two files. If only the master file (the one being updated) is sorted or indexed, the RANDOM option must be included at the end of the UPDATE command. When RANDOM is used with an unindexed file, the update will usually take more time.

### EXAMPLES

In this example, the master database named MastFile, indexed on the PartNo field, contains the records shown at the top of Figure 16.22. A transaction file called TranFile, which is also indexed on the PartNo field, contains the three sales transactions shown in the middle of Figure 16.22. To subtract the quantities sold from the quantities in stock, replace the Last_Sale field with the date of the last sale, and increment the Ytd_Sold field by the quantity sold for each part number, enter the commands below:

```
SELECT A
USE MastFile INDEX MastFile
SELECT B
USE TranFile INDEX TranFile
```

```
Contents of Master.dbf before updating:

Record#  PartNo PartName      In_Stock Last_Sale Ytd_Sold
      1    1111 Apples              10 12/31/87       100
      2    2222 Bananas             10 12/31/87        50

=========================================================

Contents of TranFile database:

Record#  PartNo Qty_Sold Date_Sold
      1    1111        1    02/01/87
      2    1111        5    02/02/87
      3    2222        5    03/01/87

=========================================================

Contents of Master.dbf after updating:

Record#  PartNo PartName      In_Stock Last_Sale Ytd_Sold
      1    1111 Apples               4 02/02/87       106
      2    2222 Bananas              5 03/01/87        55
```

**FIGURE 16.22:** Effects of updating a master database file with the command **UPDATE ON PartNo FROM TranFile REPLACE In_Stock WITH In_Stock – B->Qty_Sold, Last_Sale WITH B->DateSold, Ytd_Sold WITH Ytd_Sold + B->Qty_Sold.** The top listing shows the Master file before the update. The middle listing shows the contents of the Tranfile database. The bottom listing shows the contents of the Master database file after the update.

```
SELECT A
UPDATE ON PartNo FROM TranFile ;
        REPLACE In_Stock WITH In_Stock - B->Qty_Sold, ;
        Last_Sale WITH B->Date_Sold, ;
        Ytd_Sold WITH Ytd_Sold + B->Qty_Sold
```

When the command is finished, the MastFile database contains the data shown at the bottom of Figure 16.22. Notice that the expression **REPLACE In_Stock WITH In_Stock – B->Qty_Sold** subtracted 6 units from the In_Stock quantity for part 1111 and 5 units from the In_Stock quantity for part number 2222. The second expression, **REPLACE...Last_Sale WITH B->Date_Sold**, replaced the Last_Sale dates with the dates in the Date_Sold field in the TranFile database. The last listed date for part number 1111 (02/02/87) is the one that remained in the MastFile database.

In the MastFile database, the Ytd_Sold field was incremented by six for part number 1111 and by five for part number 2222 because of the UPDATE expression **REPLACE...Ytd_Sold WITH Ytd_Sold + B->Qty_Sold**.

The key field, PartNo, matched the quantities and dates in the TranFile database to the appropriate records in the MastFile database to ensure that the update was accurate.

### TIPS

Be sure to read up on programming techniques for updating discussed earlier in this chapter for information on avoiding accidental multiple updates.

### SEE ALSO

SET RELATION
SELECT

## SUMMARY

This chapter discussed numerous commands and techniques for managing multiple database files, especially programming techniques that are particularly relevant to a variety of business applications. These techniques include both batch and immediate updating, printing scheduling reports from many-to-many related databases, and techniques for analyzing data in exploded-inventory databases, also related in a many-to-many fashion. Related topics are discussed in the chapters listed below:

*For additional information on designing applications with multiple database files:*

- Chapter 3, "Database Design"

*For techniques on printing formatted reports from multiple related database files:*

- Chapter 9, "Printing Formatted Reports"

*For techniques on entering records onto transaction files and sharing data across two related files:*

- Chapter 10, "Adding New Data"

*For information on the SET VIEW, SET FIELDS, and other SET commands:*

- Chapter 18, "Setting Parameters"

# PART 5

# *THE PROGRAMMING ENVIRONMENT*

This part discusses the general commands, functions, and techniques that control the dBASE environment under which your program is running. The commands, functions, and techniques discussed here allow you to refine your application and its interface with the user to add that extra touch of professional polish to the finished product.

Chapter 17 discusses the dBASE functions, which allow you to modify and control individual items of data, whether they are stored in memory variables or fields. (Chapter 1, "Overview of the dBASE Language," provides a brief summary of dBASE functions grouped by the type of data on which they operate.)

Chapter 18 covers all of the dBASE SET commands and includes techniques that allow users to set up your application on their own computers without any knowledge of dBASE III PLUS. These commands allow you to determine many environmental aspects of your application, such as the colors displayed on the screen, the manner in which searches are performed, whether the bell sounds automatically, and so forth.

Chapter 19 discusses event processing and error trapping. These techniques allow you to refine your application further by making it respond to errors and user interruptions with helpful, descriptive messages instead of just "crashing" back to the dBASE dot prompt.

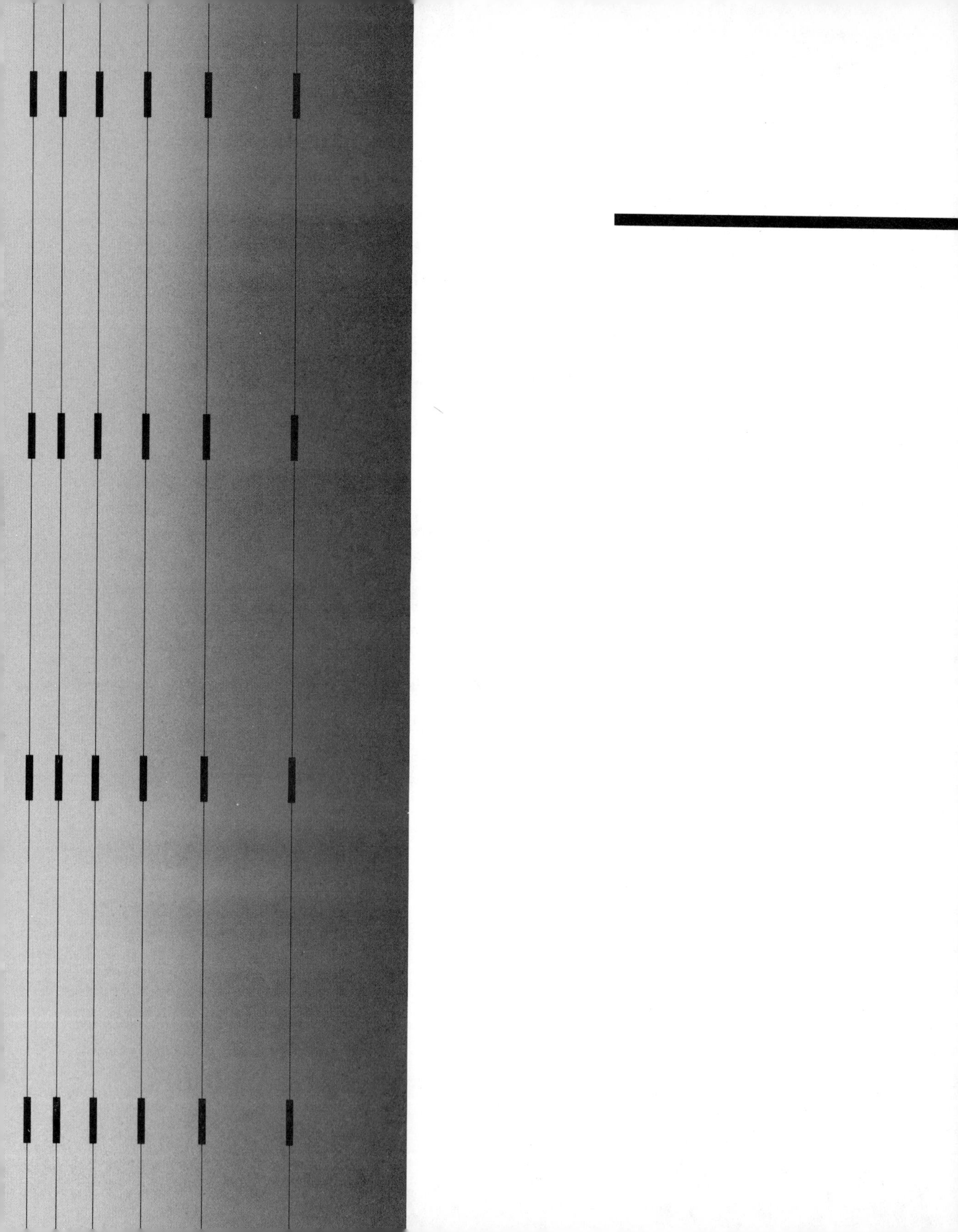

# dBASE Functions

# dBASE FUNCTIONS

dBASE functions are used in conjunction with dBASE commands to perform operations on individual items of data. When discussing functions, the term *argument* refers to the data that the function operates upon, which is always stored inside parentheses. For example, in the expression **? UPPER(LName)**, the variable LName is the argument to the UPPER( ) function.

All functions return some value. The data type of the value returned depends on the individual function.

Functions that do not accept arguments still require the use of the parentheses. For example, the DATE( ) function accepts no argument but still requires the use of empty parentheses, as in the command **? DATE( )**.

## PROGRAMMING TECHNIQUES USED WITH FUNCTIONS

Functions are used in conjunction with a command, usually to modify or refine the item of data the command is accessing. For example, the command **SEEK Search** with no function searches an index file for whatever data item is stored in the memory variable named Search. With the addition of the UPPER( ) function, the SEEK command can be refined to search for only the uppercase equivalent of the data stored in the Search variable, as in the command *SEEK UPPER(Search)*.

Remember that every line in a program and every line entered at the dot prompt must begin with a command. Any function that is used without a command will return the error message **Unrecognized command verb**.

Functions can be used freely in the MODIFY REPORT and MODIFY LABEL screens to refine the data printed in a column. For example, when designing the line to print the city, state, and zip codes on a mailing label, you can use the TRIM( ) function, as below, to display the line in the format **San Diego, CA 92122**:

**TRIM(City) + ", " + State + " " + Zip**

In general, you can use functions to operate on any data item, be it a field, memory variable, or literal data. Just remember that when writing programs or entering commands at the dot prompt, functions can be used only within the command lines. The examples provided in this chapter and throughout the book demonstrate common uses of functions with commands.

You can get some quick help on any dBASE function by entering the HELP command followed by the function name directly at the dot prompt. For example, the command **HELP TRIM** will display information about the TRIM( ) function.

# The dBASE III PLUS Functions

The rest of this chapter discusses the functions available in dBASE III PLUS (version 1.1). The functions used only in networking environments are referenced in this chapter but are discussed thoroughly in Chapter 20, "Networking and Security." For easy reference, the functions are listed in alphabetical order. Table 1.7 in Chapter 1, "Overview of the dBASE Language," lists the functions by category according to the type of data they operate upon and the type of operation they perform.

## The & (Macro Substitution) Function

The ampersand (&) allows a character string stored in a memory variable to be substituted into a command line.

### SYNTAX

**&<variable>**

where <variable> is the name of a memory variable containing a character string.

### USAGE

This function substitutes the contents of the memory variable following the & symbol so that dBASE III PLUS evaluates the contents of the character variable instead of interpreting it literally.

### EXAMPLES

Macro substitution is most often used to insert a variable into a command line where dBASE expects to find literal information. For example, the commands below tell dBASE to open a database file named MyData.dbf:

```
FileName = "MyData"
USE &FileName
```

Without the use of the & macro symbol above, dBASE would have attempted to open a database file named FileName.dbf.

The macro substitution function can also be used to insert one character string within another. For example, the variable RetKey below contains graphic symbols to represent the Return key on IBM keyboards. The ACCEPT command beneath it displays the prompt **Enter name, then press ↵.**

```
RetKey = CHR(17) + CHR(217)
ACCEPT "Enter name, then press &RetKey " TO AnyVar
```

### TIPS

Remember that dBASE III PLUS is expecting the name of a memory variable containing a character string following the macro symbol. See Chapter 6, "Memory Variables" for more information on macro substitution.

## The ABS( ) Function

ABS( ) yields the absolute value of a numeric expression.

### SYNTAX

**ABS(<number>)**

where <number> is any number, numeric expression, or variable.

### USAGE

The absolute value function converts negative numbers to positive. It has no effect on positive numbers.

### EXAMPLES

To find the positive difference between two numbers, regardless of the order in which the subtraction occurs (larger number minus smaller number, or vice versa), perform the subtraction inside the ABS argument, as the steps below demonstrate:

```
STORE 12 TO first
STORE 18 TO second
? ABS(first - second)
     6

? ABS(second - first)
     6
```

Both ? expressions above yield a positive result.

### TIPS

To prevent the square root function (SQRT) from attempting to operate on a negative number, use the ABS function inside the argument to the SQRT function, as below:

**? SQRT(ABS(AnyNumber))**

### SEE ALSO

SQRT( )

## The ACCESS( ) Function

ACCESS( ) returns the access level (1–8) of the user, based on the user profile established in the PROTECT program. See Chapter 20, "Networking and Security," for details.

## The ASC( ) Function

ASC returns the ASCII code value of the leftmost character of any character string.

### SYNTAX

**ASC(<character>)**

where <character> is any character data, character expression, or a variable containing character data.

### USAGE

ASC( ) accepts any character string and returns the decimal ASCII code number for that character string. If the argument is longer than one character, ASC returns the ASCII code for the first character only.

### EXAMPLES

Each of the commands below store the number 42 in a variable named AsciiVal, because 42 is the ASCII number for the asterisk character.

**AsciiVal = ASC("*")**

```
? AsciiVal
     42

AsciiVal = ASC("* - - - comment")
? AsciiVal
     42

AnyText = "* this is anytext"
AsciiVal = ASC(AnyText)
? AsciiVal
     42
```

### TIPS

Appendix D, "ASCII Codes and Symbols," lists all the ASCII codes and characters.

### SEE ALSO

CHR( )

## The AT( ) Function

Known as the substring search function, AT( ) returns the starting position of one character string within another character string.

### SYNTAX

**AT(<character1>,<character2>)**

where <character1> is the value to search for and <character2> is the string to be searched. Either argument can be an expression that results in a character string or the name of a memory variable containing a character string.

### USAGE

The AT( ) function searches the second character string for the starting position of the first character string (or the substring expression). If no starting point is found, a zero (0) is returned.

### EXAMPLE

The commands below return the number 14, because the B in Bob starts at the fourteenth character in the memory variable FNames.

```
FNames = "JoeLarrySteveBobFrank"
? AT("Bob",FNames)
    14
```

### TIPS

The AT function combined with the SUBSTR function can be used to remove the extension from a file name in order to create another file name with the same first name but a new extension. For example, the command below creates a file name with the same first name as the database currently in use and the extension .txt. If the database currently in use is C:Master.dbf, the variable TxtFile will contain C:Master.txt.

```
TxtFile = SUBSTR(DBF( ),1,AT(".",DBF( )) - 1) + ".txt"
```

### SEE ALSO

SUBSTR( )
LEFT( )
RIGHT( )

## The BOF( ) Function

BOF( ) determines whether the beginning-of-file marker has been reached.

### SYNTAX

**BOF( )**

### USAGE

If the record pointer has been moved to the beginning-of-file marker (which is before the first record in a database), the function will yield a logical true (.T.); otherwise, it will return a logical false (.F.).

### EXAMPLE

The commands below demonstrate that the beginning-of-file marker is located one record before the first record in a database file.

```
USE AnyFile INDEX AnyIndex
```

```
? BOF( )
     .F.

SKIP  -1
? BOF( )
     .T.
```

### TIPS

To skip backwards through a database file from the last record to the first, use the construction below:

```
USE <AnyFile> INDEX <AnyIndex>
GO BOTTOM
DO WHILE .NOT. BOF( )
     <commands>
     SKIP -1
ENDDO
```

### SEE ALSO

EOF( )

## The CDOW( ) Function

Referred to as the character day of week function, CDOW( ) returns the name of the day of the week (i.e., Monday, Tuesday, etc.) from the date passed to the function.

### SYNTAX

**CDOW(<date>)**

where <date> is any data of the date data type.

### USAGE

The argument must be the date data type. The day of the week returned is the character data type.

### EXAMPLE

The example below shows how to figure out what day of the week U.S. Independence Day will fall on in 1988.

```
Holiday = CTOD("07/04/88")    && initializes date
```

```
? Holiday
    07/04/88                    && returns date expression

? CDOW(Holiday)
    Monday                      && perfect! (long weekend)
```

### TIPS

To convert a date in mm/dd/yy format to a format such as Monday, October 19, 1987, use the expression in the example below:

```
Date = CTOD("10/19/87")
FullDate = CDOW(Date) + ", " + CMONTH(Date) + " ";
           + LTRIM(STR(DAY(Date),2)) + ;
           ", " + LTRIM(STR(YEAR(Date)))
```

### SEE ALSO

DOW( )
DAY( )
CTOD( )
CMONTH( )
YEAR( )

## The CHR( ) Function

CHR( ) returns the ASCII character for a number.

### SYNTAX

**CHR(<number>)**

where <number> is any number, numeric expression, or numeric variable.

### USAGE

CHR( ) returns the ASCII character assigned to the number (0–255) in the argument. This function can be used to display graphics and other special-effects characters found on most printers and monitors. The function sends ASCII code values for keyboard characters and for characters that have no keyboard equivalents.

ASCII characters in the range of 0 to 128 are standard on most printers and monitors. The extended ASCII character set, in the range of 129 to 255, will vary on different screens and printers.

## EXAMPLE

The command **? CHR(7)** causes the computer to beep.

Figure 17.1 shows a sample program, named ASCII.prg, that displays all the ASCII characters assigned to numbers 0–255. The output from the ASCII program is shown in Figure 17.2. Note that the ASCII character assigned to each number appears to the right of the number. For example, ASCII character 3 (or CHR(3)) is a heart.

```
************************************* ASCII.prg
*--------------------- Display ASCII characters.
SET TALK OFF
CLEAR
Row = 1
Counter = 0
*--- Set up loop for 256 characters.
DO WHILE Counter < 256
   Col = 0
   *--- Set up loop for individual rows.
   DO WHILE Col <= 72 .AND. Counter < 256
      @ Row,Col SAY STR(Counter,3)+" "+CHR(Counter)
      Col = Col + 6
      Counter = Counter + 1
   ENDDO (col and counter)
   Row = Row + 1
ENDDO (counter <= 256)
RETURN
```

**FIGURE 17.1:** The ASCII.prg program, which uses the CHR( ) function to display the ASCII characters 0–255. The output from this program is shown in Figure 17.2.

```
  Ø     1 ☺   2 ☻   3 ♥   4 ♦   5 ♣   6 ♠   7 •   8 ◘   9 ○  1Ø ◙  11 ♂  12 ♀
 13 ♪  14 ♫  15 ☼  16 ►  17 ◄  18 ↕  19 ‼  2Ø ¶  21 §  22 ▬  23 ↨  24 ↑  25 ↓
 26 →  27 ←  28 ∟  29 ↔  3Ø ▲  31 ▼  32    33 !  34 "  35 #  36 $  37 %  38 &
 39 '  4Ø (  41 )  42 *  43 +  44 ,  45 -  46 .  47 /  48 Ø  49 1  5Ø 2  51 3
 52 4  53 5  54 6  55 7  56 8  57 9  58 :  59 ;  6Ø <  61 =  62 >  63 ?  64 @
 65 A  66 B  67 C  68 D  69 E  7Ø F  71 G  72 H  73 I  74 J  75 K  76 L  77 M
 78 N  79 O  8Ø P  81 Q  82 R  83 S  84 T  85 U  86 V  87 W  88 X  89 Y  9Ø Z
 91 [  92 \  93 ]  94 ^  95 _  96 `  97 a  98 b  99 c 1ØØ d 1Ø1 e 1Ø2 f 1Ø3 g
1Ø4 h 1Ø5 i 1Ø6 j 1Ø7 k 1Ø8 l 1Ø9 m 11Ø n 111 o 112 p 113 q 114 r 115 s 116 t
117 u 118 v 119 w 12Ø x 121 y 122 z 123 { 124 ¦ 125 } 126 ~ 127 ⌂ 128 Ç 129 ü
13Ø é 131 â 132 ä 133 à 134 å 135 ç 136 ê 137 ë 138 è 139 ï 14Ø î 141 ì 142 Ä
143 Å 144 É 145 æ 146 Æ 147 ô 148 ö 149 ò 15Ø û 151 ù 152 ÿ 153 Ö 154 Ü 155 ¢
156 £ 157 ¥ 158 ₧ 159 ƒ 16Ø á 161 í 162 ó 163 ú 164 ñ 165 Ñ 166 ª 167 º 168 ¿
169 ⌐ 17Ø ¬ 171 ½ 172 ¼ 173 ¡ 174 « 175 » 176 ░ 177 ▒ 178 ▓ 179 │ 18Ø ┤ 181 ╡
182 ╢ 183 ╖ 184 ╕ 185 ╣ 186 ║ 187 ╗ 188 ╝ 189 ╜ 19Ø ╛ 191 ┐ 192 └ 193 ┴ 194 ┬
195 ├ 196 ─ 197 ┼ 198 ╞ 199 ╟ 2ØØ ╚ 2Ø1 ╔ 2Ø2 ╩ 2Ø3 ╦ 2Ø4 ╠ 2Ø5 ═ 2Ø6 ╬ 2Ø7 ╧
2Ø8 ╨ 2Ø9 ╤ 21Ø ╥ 211 ╙ 212 ╘ 213 ╒ 214 ╓ 215 ╫ 216 ╪ 217 ┘ 218 ┌ 219 █ 22Ø ▄
221 ▌ 222 ▐ 223 ▀ 224 α 225 ß 226 Γ 227 π 228 Σ 229 σ 23Ø µ 231 τ 232 Φ 233 Θ
234 Ω 235 δ 236 ∞ 237 φ 238 ε 239 ∩ 24Ø ≡ 241 ± 242 ≥ 243 ≤ 244 ⌠ 245 ⌡ 246 ÷
247 ≈ 248 ° 249 · 25Ø · 251 √ 252 ⁿ 253 ² 254 ■ 255
```

**FIGURE 17.2:** Output from the ASCII.prg program shown in Figure 17.1. The ASCII character to the right of each number is the character assigned to that number. For example, ASCII code number 3 displays a heart.

### TIPS

See Appendix D, "ASCII Codes and Symbols," for a complete list of ASCII characters and codes.

### SEE ALSO

ASC( )

## The CMONTH( ) Function

CMONTH( ) returns the name of the month (i.e., January, February) from a date passed to the function.

### SYNTAX

**CMONTH(<date>)**

where <date> is any data of the date data type.

### USAGE

The date passed to the function must be a memory variable, a field, or the system date function. The value returned is always the month name as a character string.

### EXAMPLE

The commands below display the system date and the month for the system date:

```
? DATE( )          && system date is set to New Year's Eve Day, 1989
    12/31/89

? CMONTH(DATE( ))
    December
```

### TIPS

The expression below displays the current system date in the format October 31, 1987:

```
? CMONTH(DATE( )) + " " + LTRIM(STR(DAY(DATE( )),2)) + ;
", " + LTRIM(STR(YEAR(DATE( ))))
```

**SEE ALSO**

MONTH( )
DAY( )
DATE( )
CDOW( )
DATE( )
DAY( )

## The COL( ) Function

The COL( ) function returns the current cursor column position.

**SYNTAX**

**COL( )**

**USAGE**

The COL( ) function is commonly used for relative addressing on the screen. For example, the expression **@ 6,COL( ) + 2** moves the cursor two columns to the right of its current position.

The COL( ) function accepts no argument; it only returns a numeric value.

**EXAMPLE**

The following routine creates five highlighted bars in the fifth row of the screen. Each bar will be ten spaces wide and separated from the previous bar by five spaces. Also note the condition of the DO WHILE loop. Each time the loop is executed, the current cursor position is tested with the COL( ) function.

```
Blanks = SPACE(10)
Row = 5
DO WHILE COL( ) < 70
     @ Row,COL( ) + 5 GET Blanks
ENDDO
CLEAR GETS
```

**SEE ALSO**

ROW( )
PROW( )
PCOL( )

## The CTOD( ) Function

CTOD( ) converts a character variable in date format to the date data type.

### SYNTAX

**CTOD(<character>)**

where <character> is any character data in a format resembling a valid date.

### USAGE

The character expression that is passed to the function must be in the date format currently determined by the SET DATE and SET CENTURY commands.

### EXAMPLE

When dBASE is in its default date format (SET DATE AMERICAN), the following command will convert the character string 12/31/87 to the date data type:

```
Date = CTOD("12/31/87")
```

When a different date format is specified, as in the command **SET DATE ANSI**, the character string must resemble that format (that is, yy.mm.dd), as below:

```
Date = CTOD("87.12.31")
```

### TIPS

To have dBASE display a blank date on the screen for the user to fill in and also automatically check the validity of that date, you can use the series of commands below:

```
Date = CTOD("00/00/00")
@ 10,5 SAY "Enter date " GET Date
READ
```

### SEE ALSO

SET DATE
DTOC( )

## The DATE( ) Function

DATE( ) returns the DOS system date.

### SYNTAX

**DATE( )**

### USAGE

The DATE( ) function always returns the system date as the dBASE date data type. The format of the system date can be changed by the SET CENTURY and SET DATE commands.

### EXAMPLE

The commands below display the current system date as a default entry and allow the user to change that date:

```
DatePaid = DATE( )
@ 12,5 SAY "Enter date paid " GET DatePaid
READ
```

### TIPS

To change the DOS system date from within dBASE, use the command **RUN DATE**.

### SEE ALSO

SET CENTURY
SET DATE
RUN

## The DAY( ) Function

DAY( ) returns the numeric value of the day of the month from a date.

### SYNTAX

**DAY(<date>)**

where <date> must be the date data type.

### USAGE

The date passed to the DAY( ) function must be a memory variable, a field, or the system date of the date data type.

### EXAMPLE

The commands below store the number 15 to the variable X, because the date falls on the fifteenth day of the month:

```
Date = CTOD("12/15/88")
X = DAY(Date)
```

### SEE ALSO

CDOW( )
DOW( )

## The DBF( ) Function

DBF( ) returns the name of the currently selected database file.

### SYNTAX

**DBF( )**

### USAGE

The character string returned by DBF( ) contains the current drive designator with the file name, but it does not include the current directory. A null string is returned if no database file is in use in the current work area.

### EXAMPLE

The series of commands below illustrate values returned by the DBF( ) function:

```
USE AnyFile
? DBF( )
     C:AnyFile.dbf
CLOSE DATABASES
? DBF( )
                   && null string is returned
```

### TIPS

To isolate the drive designator and file name, minus the extension, of the database file currently in use, use the AT( ) and SUBSTR( ) functions with the DBF( ) function, as in the series of commands below:

```
USE AnyFile
? SUBSTR(DBF( ),1,AT(".",DBF( )) - 1)
    C:AnyFile
```

### SEE ALSO

AT( )
FIELD( )
LUPDATE( )
NDX( )
RECCOUNT( )
RECSIZE( )

## The DELETED( ) Function

DELETED( ) returns a logical true (.T.) if the current record has been marked for deletion; otherwise, it returns a logical false (.F.).

### SYNTAX

**DELETED( )**

### USAGE

From within programs, you can use the DELETED( ) function as a condition for including or excluding records that are marked for deletion during any process that accesses multiple records, such as LIST, SUM, COUNT, REPORT, and others. Also, during debugging, records can be checked to determine their deletion status.

### EXAMPLE

The command below lists records that have been marked for deletion:

```
LIST FOR DELETED( )
```

#### SEE ALSO

SET DELETED

## The DISKSPACE( ) Function

DISKSPACE( ) returns the number of bytes available on the specified drive.

#### SYNTAX

**DISKSPACE( )**

#### USAGE

This function can be useful in routines that involve backing up data to floppy disks by ensuring that the target disks have sufficient room for the file transfer.

Checking the available disk space is also recommended when attempting a SORT command on a floppy disk. SORT requires twice the disk space of the size of the file being sorted. Otherwise, a disk-full error will occur.

#### EXAMPLE

Assuming that you need a minimum of 25K to sort a database file, you might use the following routine before sorting:

```
FileSize = 25000
IF DISKSPACE( ) > FileSize * 2
     SORT ON Name,Date TO NewFile
ELSE
     ? "Not enough room on disk!"
ENDIF
```

#### SEE ALSO

GETENV( )
RECCOUNT( )

## The DOW( ) Function

DOW( ) returns a number that indicates the day of the week.

### SYNTAX

**DOW(<date>)**

where <date> is the date data type.

### USAGE

The date passed to the function must be the date data type. The value returned is a number between 1 and 7, with Sunday being 1, Monday being 2, and so forth. For example, the command below returns the number 6, because Christmas in 1987 falls on a Friday:

**? DOW(CTOD("12/25/87"))**

### EXAMPLE

You can use the DOW( ) function to view records with dates that fall on a certain day of the week. For example, the command below lists all records with dates that fall on a weekend (assuming that the Date field is the date data type):

**LIST FOR DOW(Date) = 1 .OR. DOW(Date) = 7**

### SEE ALSO

CDOW( )
DAY( )

## The DTOC( ) Function

Known as the date-to-character function, DTOC( ) converts any date to a character string.

### SYNTAX

**DTOC(<date>)**

where <date> is any data of the date data type.

### USAGE

The conversion of a date to a character expression is sometimes necessary when you would like to enter a data item as a date expression (to take advantage of the date input validation features) and retain the date as a character field in the database file.

Also, it can be advantageous to index a file on a concatenated expression, which requires joining several character strings to create the key. If one of these joined expressions is a date field, you must first convert it to character format so that it can be a part of the key.

### EXAMPLE

To enter a data item as a date and retain it in the database file as a character field, use a technique like the following:

```
USE AnyFile
Mdate = DATE( )
@ 10,5 SAY "Enter date" GET Mdate
READ
REPLACE XDate WITH DTOC(Mdate)
```

If, on the other hand, you would like to store the data item as a date field in the database file and use the field as part of the index key, you might create the index file based on the following key expression:

```
USE AnyFile
INDEX ON AcctNumb + DTOC(TranDate) TO AnyIndex
```

### TIPS

See Chapter 12, "Sorting and Indexing," and Chapter 15, "Managing Data, Records, and Files," for additional information on sorting dates.

### SEE ALSO

CTOD( )
SET CENTURY

## The EOF( ) Function

EOF( ) determines whether the end-of-file marker (beyond the last record in a database file) has been reached.

### SYNTAX

**EOF( )**

### USAGE

If the record pointer has been moved to the end-of-file marker, the function will yield a logical true (.T.); otherwise, it will return a logical false (.F.). The end-of-file marker is at the first record position beneath the last record (RECCOUNT( ) + 1).

### EXAMPLE

The example below shows that the end-of-file marker is located one record after the last record in a database file.

```
USE AnyFile INDEX AnyIndex
GO BOTTOM
? EOF( )
      .F.

SKIP
? EOF( )
      .T.
```

### TIPS

Commands that act on all the records in a database file (such as LIST, REPORT, and REPLACE ALL) always leave the record pointer at the EOF( ) position. If you need to perform a DO WHILE .NOT. EOF( ) loop after one of these commands, be sure to reposition the record pointer back to the top of the file, as shown below:

```
REPLACE ALL Price WITH Price * 1.10
GO TOP          && reposition pointer.
DO WHILE .NOT. EOF( )
      <any commands>
      SKIP
ENDDO
```

### SEE ALSO

DO WHILE
BOF( )
FOUND( )

## The ERROR( ) Function

ERROR( ) returns the number corresponding to the error that triggered an ON ERROR condition.

## SYNTAX

**ERROR( )**

## USAGE

When an ON ERROR condition is in effect and an error triggers the condition, the ERROR( ) function contains a number that corresponds to the error. (The MESSAGE( ) function will contain the actual error message.)

## EXAMPLE

The command below tells dBASE to pass control to a program or procedure named ErrProcs when an error occurs:

**ON ERROR DO ErrProcs**

The ErrProcs procedure file (or command file) can then include a DO CASE clause to respond to various types of errors, as shown in Figure 17.3.

## TIPS

See Chapter 19, "Event Processing and Error Trapping," for a complete discussion of error trapping.

## SEE ALSO

ON ERROR
MESSAGE( )

```
*********************************** ErrTrap.prg
*----- Sample procedure to trap common errors.
PROCEDURE ErrProcs
   @ 19,0 CLEAR
   @ 19,0 TO 19,79 DOUBLE
   ? CHR(7)
   DO CASE

    CASE ERROR() = 4  && EOF() encountered.
       ? "End of file encountered unexpectedly."
       ? "Will try to repair. Please wait."
       *-- If index file open, may be corrupted.
       IF NDX() # " "
          REINDEX
       ENDIF
       RETRY
```

**FIGURE 17.3:** A procedure file that can respond to a variety of errors trapped by an ON ERROR condition. The ERROR( ) function contains a number representing the error that occurred, which this routine uses to respond to the error.

```
      CASE ERROR() = 114  && Damaged index file.
         ? "Damaged index file!"
         ? Please wait while rebuilding..."
         REINDEX
         RETRY

       CASE ERROR() = 6  && Too many files open.
         ? "Check the Config.db file on your root"
         ? "directory, as discussed in the manual."
         CANCEL
         CLOSE ALL
         ON ERROR

       CASE ERROR() = 29  && File inaccessible.
         ? "Disk directory is full, or an illegal"
         ? "character appears in file name!"
         ? "Check file name and directory, then try again."

       OTHERWISE   && Unknown error: display dBASE message.
         ? "Unexpected error in program..."
         ? MESSAGE()
         WAIT "Press Esc to abort, any key to continue..."

   ENDCASE
 RETURN
```

**FIGURE 17.3:** A procedure file that can respond to a variety of errors trapped by an ON ERROR condition. The ERROR( ) function contains a number representing the error that occurred, which this routine uses to respond to the error (continued).

## The EXP( ) Function

EXP( ) returns the value of the constant e raised to the power specified in the argument. It represents the inverse of the LOG( ) function.

### SYNTAX

**EXP(<number>)**

where <number> is any number, numeric expression, or numeric variable.

### USAGE

The EXP( ) function uses the constant e, which is approximately equal to 2.7182818285. The number passed to the function is the value of the exponent (x in the expression $e^x$).

### EXAMPLE

Note the varying accuracy of the values returned by the EXP( ) function below:

```
SET DECIMALS TO 2          && the default
? EXP(1)
     2.72
```

**? EXP(1.000)**
**2.718**

**? EXP(1.0000000)**
**2.7182818**

#### TIPS

The number of decimal places passed to the function determines the number of decimal places passed back in the result. To control the number of decimals returned, use the SET DECIMALS and SET FIXED commands.

#### SEE ALSO

LOG( )
SET DECIMALS
SET FIXED

## The FIELD( ) Function

FIELD( ) returns the field name that corresponds to its numeric position in the file structure of the active database file.

#### SYNTAX

**FIELD(<number>)**

where <number> is any number, numeric expression, or numeric variable.

#### USAGE

In a database file, the first field is number 1, or FIELD(1). The largest possible field is number 128, or FIELD(128).

If you pass a number to the function that is greater than the number of fields in the database file, the function will return a null string.

#### EXAMPLE

Assuming that the database MyFile has a field named AcctNumb as the first field and CustName as the eighth field, the commands below produce the results shown:

**USE MyFile**

```
? FIELD(8)
     CUSTNAME

? FIELD(1)
     ACCTNUMB
```

The routine below will count how many fields there are in the currently active database and store the result in a memory variable named No_Fields:

```
USE &AnyFile
No_Fields = 0
DO WHILE LEN(TRIM(FIELD(No_Fields + 1))) > 0
     No_Fields = No_Fields + 1
ENDDO
```

### TIPS

The DISPLAY STRUCTURE command displays the names of all fields in the currently selected database file.

### SEE ALSO

DBF( )
NDX( )
RECCOUNT( )

## The FILE( ) Function

FILE( ) returns a logical true (.T.) if the file name passed to the function is found; otherwise, it returns a logical false (.F.).

### SYNTAX

**FILE(<file name>)**

where <file name> is the file name used as a string or the name of a variable containing the name of the file to search for.

### USAGE

There are a few rules to note regarding the use of the FILE( ) function. First of all, if the file name passed to the function is not contained in a memory variable, it must be enclosed in single quotes, double quotes, or brackets. Second, you must include the file extension in the file name. And third, you must explicitly state the drive or directory if it is different from the default drive or directory.

#### EXAMPLE

The example below ensures that a specific transaction file exists before attempting to use it. TranStru.dbf is an empty database that is used to create identical databases as needed. If Tran0714.dbf does not exist as the program executes, the database file is created by copying the structure of TranStru.dbf to Tran0714.dbf.

```
IF .NOT. FILE("Tran0714.dbf")
    USE TranStru
    COPY STRUCTURE TO Tran0714
ENDIF
USE Tran0714
```

#### TIPS

The FILE( ) function will search only the path specified in the dBASE SET PATH command, not the path specified in the DOS PATH command.

#### SEE ALSO

DIR
SET PATH

## The FKLABEL( ) Function

FKLABEL( ) returns the name assigned to the function key specified by the numeric argument.

#### SYNTAX

**FKLABEL(<number>)**

where <number> is any number, numeric expression, or numeric variable.

#### USAGE

While most keyboards use the standard names F1, F2, F3, and so forth for function keys, others use different names. The FKLABEL( ) function returns the label that appears on the user's keyboard.

FKLABEL( ) can access only programmable function keys. Therefore, on terminals that use the F1 key as the Help key (because there is no dedicated Help key), the smallest programmable function key is number 2. Also, because F2 is the first programmable function key in this case, the function FKLABEL(1) actually refers to the F2 key. The largest programmable function key number is returned by the FKMAX( ) function.

## EXAMPLE

The commands below display the prompt **Press F2 to Exit,** assuming the user's keyboard uses F2 as the label for function key number 1. If the label for function key number 1 is "User 1", then the prompt displays the message **Press User 1 to Exit**.

```
SET FUNCTION 2 TO "QUIT;"
Prompt = "Press " + FKLABEL(1) + " to exit"
@ 2,1 SAY Prompt
```

## TIPS

You can build prompts with the FKLABEL( ) function that display the commands assigned to various function keys, using function key labels that match the user's keyboard. Doing so will ensure that the user presses the appropriate key to run the commands. Figure 17.4 shows a routine that creates the custom function key prompt.

```
***************************************** FuncKeys.prg
*--- Create a prompt for function keys, using function
*--- key names that match the user's keyboard.
CLEAR
SET TALK OFF
Opt1 = "SKIP 1"
Opt2 = "SKIP -1"
Opt3 = "GO TOP"
Opt4 = "GO BOTTOM"

Counter = 1
PLine = " "
DO WHILE Counter <= 4
   Sub = STR(Counter,1)
   SET FUNCTION (&Sub + 1) TO Opt&Sub +";"
   PLine = PLine + FKLABEL(Counter)+ ;
    " = " + Opt&Sub + "    "
   Counter = Counter + 1
ENDDO

*--- At any time, the command below
*--- displays function key assignments.
@ 20,1 SAY PLine
```

**FIGURE 17.4:** A routine named FuncKeys that creates a prompt showing the user the tasks assigned to various function keys. The program will place function key names that match the user's keyboard into the prompt.

After the DO WHILE loop in the FuncKeys routine builds the PLine variable, the last line in the program displays the contents of this variable on the screen. On a standard IBM keyboard, the names of the function keys and the commands they issue would be displayed as below. (You could use the ? or @ command at any time within a program to display these function key assignments.)

```
F2 = SKIP 1   F3 = SKIP -1   F4 = GO TOP   F5 = GO BOTTOM
```

### SEE ALSO

FKMAX( )
SET FUNCTION

## The FKMAX( ) Function

FKMAX( ) returns the maximum number of programmable function keys on the terminal in use.

### SYNTAX

**FKMAX( )**

### USAGE

The largest number that can be assigned to the special function keys in dBASE III PLUS for most ordinary IBM PC/XT/AT computers is 9. (F1 is not reassignable on computer terminals that do not have a separate Help key, because dBASE dedicates that key to Help.)

### EXAMPLE

The DO WHILE loop below repeats once for each programmable function key available on the current keyboard and waits for a command string to be assigned to each key:

```
SET TALK OFF
KeyNo = 1
DO WHILE KeyNo < = FKMAX( )
     Prompt = "Enter command for" + FKLABEL(KeyNo) + " Key"
     ACCEPT Prompt TO String
     SET FUNCTION FKLABEL(KeyNo) TO String
```

```
        KeyNo = KeyNo + 1
    ENDDO
    * - - Show function key assignments when done.
    LIST STATUS
```

### TIPS

When writing applications that will be used on many different computers, you may want to assign the most important function key commands to the smallest-numbered function keys. That way, if a particular computer does not have all of the function keys that your application offers, only the least important ones will be excluded. (For this same reason, your application should offer function keys only as a secondary means of performing a task.)

### SEE ALSO

FKLABEL( )
SET FUNCTION

## The FLOCK( ) Function

FLOCK( ) determines whether a file is locked. If the file is not already locked, FLOCK( ) locks the file if possible. See Chapter 20, "Networking and Security," for details.

## The FOUND( ) Function

FOUND( ) determines whether commands that searched for a particular record found that record.

### SYNTAX

**FOUND( )**

### USAGE

FOUND( ) tests whether the previous SEEK, LOCATE, CONTINUE, or FIND command was successful. It returns a logical true (.T.) if the search was successful. Otherwise it returns a logical false (.F.).

Use the FOUND( ) function to determine what action is to occur next after the SEEK, LOCATE, CONTINUE, or FIND command has been issued.

### EXAMPLE

The following routine illustrates how the FOUND( ) function can be used in a simple validation process:

```
USE AnyFile INDEX LNames
Search = SPACE(20)
@ 5,5 SAY "Enter name to look for  " GET Search
READ
SEEK UPPER(Search)
IF FOUND( )
     DISPLAY
ELSE
     ? "Can't find that name!"
ENDIF
```

### TIPS

As soon as another command (such as SKIP or GOTO) moves the record pointer away from the record found by the SEEK, LOCATE, CONTINUE, or FIND command, the FOUND( ) function will return .F..

### SEE ALSO

LOCATE
CONTINUE
SEEK
FIND

## The GETENV( ) Function

GETENV( ) returns the contents of a DOS environmental variable.

### SYNTAX

**GETENV(<character>)**

where <character> is a DOS environmental variable.

### USAGE

GETENV( ) returns a character string containing the setting or definition of the environmental variable specified by the character argument. The argument can be a literal string, a string variable, or a string expression. If the argument does not match a DOS environmental variable, the function returns a null string.

### EXAMPLE

The command below displays the DOS PATH setting:

**? GETENV("PATH")**
**C:\ROOT**

The command below displays the drive and directory where the DOS command processor (Command.com) is stored:

**? GETENV("COMSPEC")**
**C:\COMMAND.COM**

Note that these are only general examples. Your system may not return the same environmental settings.

### SEE ALSO

OS( )
VERSION( )

## The IIF( ) Function

IIF( ) is known as the immediate if function; it offers an alternative method to the standard IF...ENDIF structure in creating a conditional expression.

### SYNTAX

**IIF(<expression>,<return this>,<else return this>)**

where <expression> is any expression that yields a .T. or .F. result, <return this> is the value returned if <expression> evaluates to .T., and <else return this> is the value returned if <expression> evaluates to .F..

### USAGE

If the logical expression is true, the first data item is returned. If the logical expression is false, the second data item is returned. If either data item is an executable expression (such as a formula), the expression is executed as well. The two data items to the right of the logical expression must be of the same data type.

Note that IIF( ) cannot be used to execute dBASE commands. To execute commands based on a conditional expression, use the IF...ELSE...ENDIF commands.

### EXAMPLE

The command below, whether used in a program or a MODIFY REPORT or MODIFY LABEL column, calculates the extended price with 6 percent tax added if a logical variable named Tax is true. Otherwise, it displays the extended price without tax added:

**IIF(Tax,(Qty*UPrice)*1.06,Qty*UPrice)**

### TIPS

To prevent a number from being divided by 0 (which would create a divide overflow situation), you can use the following expression:

**IIF(y = 0,0,x/y)**

To include a logical field in an index key expression, use IIF to convert .T. to Yes and .F. to No. Be sure that both Yes and No are three characters long, as below:

**INDEX ON IIF(Paid,"YES","NO ") TO LogIndex**

Remember too that IIF can be used in MODIFY REPORT and MODIFY LABEL report columns and in all commands that access multiple records, such as LIST, COUNT, REPLACE, SUM, and so forth.

### SEE ALSO

IF...ELSE...ENDIF

## The INKEY( ) Function

INKEY( ) returns an integer that corresponds to the ASCII code of the most recent key pressed by the user.

### SYNTAX

**INKEY( )**

### USAGE

The INKEY( ) function accepts input from the keyboard at any time during an operation and is often used in programming for branching. The integer value returned by INKEY( ) is the ASCII value (in decimal) of the key pressed. The special nonprinting keys return the integer values shown in Table 17.1. If no key is pressed, INKEY( ) has a value of zero. The range of INKEY( ) values extends from 0 to 255.

If you want your program to save the value of INKEY( ), you should store the value in a memory variable immediately, as in the second example below.

## EXAMPLE

The command below prints a report until the user presses any key to interrupt the report:

**REPORT FORM AnyRep WHILE INKEY( ) = 0**

The routine shown in Figure 17.5 gives the user ten seconds to press a key and shows the clock ticking while the program waits. If the user does not press a key, control is returned to the calling program. Note that the program uses the expression X = INKEY( ) to store the keypress as soon as it occurs.

| KEY PRESSED | EQUIVALENT KEY | INKEY( ) VALUE |
|---|---|---|
| → | Ctrl-D | 4 |
| ← | Ctrl-S | 19 |
| ↑ | Ctrl-E | 5 |
| ↓ | Ctrl-X | 24 |
| Ctrl-→ | Ctrl-B | 2 |
| Ctrl-← | Ctrl-Z | 26 |
| PgUp | Ctrl-R | 18 |
| PgDn | Ctrl-C | 3 |
| Ctrl-PgUp | Ctrl- - | 31 |
| Ctrl-PgDn | Ctrl- ^ | 30 |
| Ins | Ctrl-V | 22 |
| Del | Ctrl-G | 7 |
| Home | Ctrl-A | 1 |
| End | Ctrl-F | 6 |
| Home | Ctrl-] | 29 |
| End | Ctrl-W | 23 |

**TABLE 17.1:** Keypresses and Their INKEY( ) Values

```
*--- Set up finish time (ten seconds from now).
SET TALK OFF
Done = VAL(RIGHT(TIME(),2))+10
Done = (IIF(Done<60,Done,Done-60))

CLEAR
@ 10,10 SAY "Press any key to proceed"
@ 12,10 SAY "(You have ten seconds)"

*- Loop until seconds = Done or a key is pressed.
X = 0
DO WHILE VAL(RIGHT(TIME(),2)) # Done .AND. X = 0
   @ 1,70 SAY TIME()
   X = INKEY()
ENDDO
*--- If no key pressed, return.
IF X = 0
   RETURN
ENDIF
*--- Display key press (if any).
@ 21,1 SAY STR(X,3)+"  "+CHR(X)
```

**FIGURE 17.5:** This sample routine waits ten seconds for the user to press any key. If the user does not press a key within ten seconds, the program returns control to the calling program. If the user does press a key within ten seconds, the program immediately begins processing beneath the ENDIF command. In this example, the program simply displays the value stored in INKEY( ) and the equivalent ASCII character.

### TIPS

While INKEY( ) is in effect, the ← and Ctrl-S keys will still be interpreted as commands to stop and start scrolling, unless the SET ESCAPE parameter is off.

Appendix D, "ASCII Codes and Symbols," lists all the ASCII characters and their numeric codes.

### SEE ALSO

ON KEY
READKEY( )

## The INT( ) Function

Known as the integer function, INT( ) converts any numeric expression to an integer by truncating all digits after the decimal place.

### SYNTAX

**INT(<number>)**

where <number> is any number, numeric expression, or numeric variable.

#### USAGE

The INT( ) function truncates the decimal portion of a number, without rounding, as the sample command below demonstrates:

```
? INT(3.9999)
     3
```

#### EXAMPLE

You can use INT( ) to determine whether a number is odd or even by using the commands

```
IF INT (x/2) = x/2
     ? "Number is even."
ELSE
     ? "Number is odd."
ENDIF
```

This can be useful if you want to filter out or display every odd or even record in a database.

#### SEE ALSO

ROUND( )
MOD( )

## The ISALPHA( ) Function

ISALPHA( ) determines whether the first character in a string is a letter.

#### SYNTAX

**ISALPHA(<character>)**

where <character> is any character data, character expression, or a variable containing character data.

#### USAGE

An alpha character is any upper- or lowercase letter (A–Z). If the argument begins with a letter, ISALPHA( ) returns .T.. Otherwise, ISALPHA( ) returns .F..

### EXAMPLE

The commands below return .F., because the Address variable begins with a number:

```
Address = "123 Oak Tree Lane"
? ISALPHA(Address)
    .F.
```

The commands below return .T., because Address begins with a letter:

```
Address = "P.O. Box 1234"
? ISALPHA(Address)
    .T.
```

### TIPS

The VAL( ) function can detect strings that begin with numeric characters and can also store those numeric characters in a variable or field of the numeric data type.

### SEE ALSO

ISLOWER( )
ISUPPER( )
LOWER( )
UPPER( )
VAL( )

## The ISCOLOR( ) Function

ISCOLOR( ) a logical true (.T.) if the computer is currently using a color video card. ISCOLOR( ) returns a logical false (.F.) if the computer is using a monochrome video card.

### SYNTAX

**ISCOLOR( )**

### USAGE

By using the ISCOLOR( ) function to determine whether a program is running on a color or monochrome video card, you can customize the colors or monochrome attributes according to your tastes. This determination is usually made at the beginning of a program.

**EXAMPLE**

The routine below represents the typical method of setting the video attributes:

```
IF ISCOLOR( )
     SET COLOR TO GR/B,W/R,GR
ELSE
     SET COLOR TO W +
ENDIF
```

**TIPS**

Some computers require that you enter the SET COLOR ON command before accepting the colors defined in the SET COLOR TO command.

**SEE ALSO**

SET COLOR

## The ISLOWER( ) Function

ISLOWER( ) returns a logical true (.T.) if the character expression passed to the function begins with a lowercase letter; otherwise it returns a logical false (.F.).

**SYNTAX**

**ISLOWER( )**

**USAGE**

ISLOWER( ) returns .T. only if the first character in the argument is a lowercase letter (a–z). The commands below demonstrate the value returned by ISLOWER( ) under different conditions:

```
MemVar = "12345"
? ISLOWER(MemVar)
     .F.

MemVar = "ABCDE"
? ISLOWER(MemVar)
     .F.

MemVar = "aBCDE"
? ISLOWER(MEMVAR)
     .T.
```

### SEE ALSO

ISALPHA( )
ISUPPER( )
LOWER( )
UPPER( )

## The ISUPPER( ) Function

ISUPPER( ) returns a logical true (.T.) if the argument begins with an uppercase letter; otherwise it returns a logical false (.F.).

### SYNTAX

**ISUPPER( )**

### USAGE

An uppercase alpha character is any uppercase letter (A–Z). The commands below return different values for ISUPPER under different situations:

```
MemVar = "12345"
? ISUPPER(MemVar)
    .F.

MemVar = "ABCDE"
? ISUPPER(MemVar)
    .T.

MemVar = "abcde"
? ISUPPER(MemVar)
    .F.
```

### SEE ALSO

ISALPHA( )
ISLOWER( )
LOWER( )
UPPER( )

# The LEFT( ) Function

LEFT( ) returns a specified number of characters, starting from the leftmost character.

## SYNTAX

**LEFT(<character>,<number>)**

where <character> is any data of the character data type, and <number> is an expression yielding a number.

## USAGE

The numeric expression in the argument defines how many characters are to be extracted from the left side of the character expression. LEFT( ) simulates the SUBSTR( ) function with a starting position of 1.

## EXAMPLE

To extract the seven leftmost characters from a character expression, type

```
? LEFT("abcdefghijklm",7)
     abcdefg
```

## TIPS

If the numeric expression is larger than the length of the character expression, the whole character string is returned. If the numeric expression is zero or negative, a null string is returned.

When combined with the AT( ) function, LEFT( ) can isolate the leftmost characters up to a particular character. For example, the commands below display only the first name, Hobart, from the name stored in the variable FullName:

```
FullName = "Hobart Frisbee"
? LEFT(FullName,AT(" ",FullName))
     Hobart
```

## SEE ALSO

AT( )
LTRIM( )
RIGHT( )
RTRIM( )
STUFF( )
SUBSTR( )
TRIM( )

## The LEN( ) Function

Referred to as the length function, LEN( ) returns length of a character string.

### SYNTAX

**LEN(<character>)**

where <character> is any character data, character expression, or a variable containing character data.

### USAGE

The character string being measured can be stored in any character memory variable or field. The length of a null string is zero.

### EXAMPLE

The LEN( ) function can be used as a conditional test for branching:

```
CustName = SPACE(20)
@ 5,15 SAY "Enter name" GET CustName
*- - - - If no name entered, return to calling program.
IF LEN(TRIM(CustName)) = 0
     CLOSE DATABASE
     RETURN
ENDIF
```

Note that the length of a string that has been trimmed is usually less than the length to which it was initialized.

### TIPS

To view the lengths of character strings in all the records in a particular field, you can list only the length of the field, as below:

```
LIST LEN(TRIM(Company))
```

If you watch the numbers as they go by on the screen, you'll be able to determine the width of the longest string in the field.

### SEE ALSO

STUFF ( )
STRU( )
SUBSTR( )

## The LOCK( ) Function

LOCK( ) determines whether a record is locked. If the record is not already locked, LOCK( ) locks the record if possible. See Chapter 20, "Networking and Security," for details.

## The LOG( ) Function

LOG( ) returns the natural logarithm of the number passed to it.

### SYNTAX

**LOG(<number>)**

where <number> is any number, numeric expression, or numeric variable.

### USAGE

As you may recall from mathematics, the natural logarithm has a base of e (the mathematical constant approximately equal to 2.7182818285). In the following equation, y is the numeric expression passed to the function, and x is the number returned by the function:

$$e^x = y$$

### EXAMPLE

The command below displays the natural logarithm of 2.71828:

```
? LOG(2.71828)
      1.00000
```

### TIPS

The number of decimal places passed to the function determines the number of decimal places passed back in the result. To control the number of decimals returned, use the SET DECIMAL and SET FIXED commands.

### SEE ALSO

EXP( )
SET DECIMALS
SET FIXED

## The LOWER( ) Function

LOWER( ) converts any character expression to lowercase.

### SYNTAX

**LOWER( )**

### USAGE

The commands below show how the LOWER( ) function operates on a character string containing uppercase letters, lowercase letters, and numbers:

```
Address = "123 Abalone Way APT #32"
? LOWER(Address)
     123 abalone way apt #32
```

### EXAMPLES

If a user enters all values into a field such as FName in uppercase and you want to convert them all to mixed case (with only a single leading uppercase letter), use a routine like the one below:

```
USE AnyFile
REPLACE ALL FName WITH UPPER(LEFT(FName,1)) + ;
                  LOWER(RIGHT(FName,LEN(FName) - 1))
```

### SEE ALSO

ISALPHA( )
ISLOWER( )
ISUPPER( )
LTRIM( )
UPPER( )

## The LTRIM( ) Function

LTRIM( ) removes leading blanks from a character string.

### SYNTAX

**LTRIM( ) (<char>)**

where <char> is any character data, character expression, or a variable containing character data.

#### USAGE

This function removes leading blanks from a character string such as those created by the STR( ) function.

#### EXAMPLE

The series of commands below demonstrates how the LTRIM( ) function can be used to combine character data with data originally stored as a number:

```
Amount = 1234.56
? "You won " + LTRIM (STR(Amount,9,2)) + " dollars!"

You won 1234.56 dollars!
```

#### TIPS

The LTRIM( ) function can be used to concatenate numbers to memory variable names, thereby creating arrays. Chapter 6, "Memory Variables," provides examples of creating arrays.

#### SEE ALSO

STR( )
TRIM( )
RTRIM( )

## The LUPDATE( ) Function

LUPDATE( ) returns the date, as the date data type, of the last update of the currently selected database file.

#### SYNTAX

**LUPDATE( )**

#### USAGE

The LUPDATE( ) function is useful for controlling processes that should not be done more than once a day or that perhaps should be done at least once a day. In either case, simply compare the current date to the date returned from the function to satisfy the condition of executing the process. (Keep in mind that the date returned by the function is a date expression.)

**EXAMPLE**

The LUPDATE( ) function can be used effectively in a database file backup routine. Use the **IF LUPDATE( ) # DATE( )** expression as a condition for backing up the file, as below:

```
USE AnyFile
IF LUPDATE( ) # DATE( )
     DO <backup procedure>
ENDIF
```

## The MAX( ) Function

MAX( ) returns the larger of two numeric expressions.

**SYNTAX**

**MAX(<number1>,<number2>)**

where both <number1> and <number2> are numbers or expressions that result in numeric values.

**USAGE**

The MAX( ) function determines the higher of two numeric expressions. A practical use of the MAX( ) function is to establish a lower limit (or floor) to a numeric expression, or to find the highest value in a numeric field, as in the examples below.

**EXAMPLES**

The routine below calculates and displays an overhead cost using either 10 percent or the value stored in the field named Overhead, whichever is higher:

```
LIST "Total with overhead = ",Cost * MAX(.10,Overhead)
```

The routine below displays the largest value in a numeric field named Amount:

```
USE AnyFile
Largest = 0
DO WHILE .NOT. EOF( )
     Largest = MAX(Largest,Amount)
     SKIP
     ENDDO
? Largest
```

#### SEE ALSO

MIN( )

## The MESSAGE( ) Function

MESSAGE( ) returns the error message describing the error that triggered an ON ERROR condition.

#### SYNTAX

**MESSAGE( )**

#### USAGE

The MESSAGE( ) function returns a character expression that identifies the error that has occurred. You can store the error message to a variable, display it immediately as is, or even display another message that may help to clarify the error to the user (if it occurs within a program).

#### EXAMPLE

In the ErrProcs procedure shown in Figure 17.3, the OTHERWISE condition displays the error message that triggered an ON ERROR condition if none of the preceding CASE clauses traps the error.

#### SEE ALSO

ERROR( )
ON ERROR

## The MIN( ) Function

MIN( ) returns the lower value of two numeric expressions.

#### SYNTAX

**MIN(<number1>,<number2>)**

where <number1> and <number2> are either numbers or expressions that result in numeric values.

### USAGE

MIN( ) returns the smaller of two numeric arguments passed to it. It can be used to place a ceiling (maximum value) on a value or to locate the smallest value in a numeric field, as the examples below demonstrate.

### EXAMPLE

The command below calculates interest on a field named Cost, using either 6 percent or the value stored in the field named TaxAmt, whichever is smaller:

```
LIST "Total with tax =  ",Cost * MIN(.06,TaxAmt)
```

The routine below determines the smallest value in a numeric field named Amount and stores that value in a variable named Smallest:

```
USE AnyFile
Smallest = Amount
DO WHILE .NOT. EOF( )
     Smallest = MIN(Smallest,Amount)
     SKIP
ENDDO
? Smallest
```

### SEE ALSO

MAX( )

## The MOD( ) Function

MOD( ) returns the remainder of the division of the numbers specified in the argument. This remainder is referred to in mathematics as the *modulus*.

### SYNTAX

**MOD(<number1>,<number2>)**

where <number1> is the dividend and <number2> the divisor. <number 1> and <number 2> are either numeric values or expressions that result in numeric values.

### USAGE

The sign of the result, the remainder of the division, is the same as the sign of the divisor.

In the examples below, the MOD( ) function returns different values based on the numbers passed to it:

```
? MOD(3, -2)
    -1

? MOD( -3,2)
    1

? MOD( -3,0)
    -3

? MOD( -1,3)
    2
```

## EXAMPLES

If you use the INT( ) function in combination with the MOD( ) function, you can calculate conversions of units. For example, the steps below convert 422 inches to feet:

```
i = 422
inches = MOD(i,12)
feet = INT(i/12)

? i, "inches = ",feet, "feet", inches, "inches"
    422 inches = 35 feet 2 inches
```

To convert seconds to larger increments of time, use the series of commands demonstrated in Figure 17.6. The routine begins with the number of seconds stored in the variable named Start. Then a series of INT( ) and MOD( ) operations breaks down the number of seconds into days, hours, minutes, and the remaining seconds.

The MOD( ) function can also be used to determine whether a number is evenly divisible by some other number. For example, the IF command below acts only on numbers that are evenly divisible by 10:

```
IF MOD(X,10) = 0
```

The command below deletes every other record (those evenly divisible by two) in a database file:

```
DELETE FOR MOD(RECNO( ),2) = 0
```

```
*------------ Convert seconds to days, hours, minutes.
SET TALK OFF
CLEAR
Store 0 TO Seconds,Minutes,Hours,Days

INPUT "Enter number of seconds to convert " TO Start
Seconds = MOD(Start,60)
Minutes = INT(Start/60)
If Minutes >= 60
   Hours = INT(Minutes/60)
   Minutes = MOD(Minutes,60)
ENDIF
IF Hours >= 24
   Days = INT(Hours/24)
   Hours = MOD(Hours,24)
ENDIF
?
? Start,"seconds converts to..."
?
? Days,"Days"
? Hours,"Hours"
? Minutes,"Minutes"
? Seconds,"Seconds"
```

**FIGURE 17.6:** This routine converts seconds to larger increments of time. The initial number of seconds is stored in the variable named Start. Then a combination of INT( ) and MOD( ) operations breaks down the number of seconds into days, hours, minutes, and the remaining seconds.

### SEE ALSO

INT( )
TIME( )

## The MONTH( ) Function

MONTH( ) returns the number of the month in the date expression passed to the function.

### SYNTAX

**MONTH(<date>)**

where <date> is the date data type.

### USAGE

The date expression must be a memory variable, a field, or the system date function. The value returned is a number between 1 and 12, inclusive, where 1 is January, 2 is February, and so forth. For example, the command below displays the month number of the system date:

**? MONTH(DATE( ))**

### EXAMPLE

You can use the MONTH( ) function to select employees from a database whose birthdays fall in the current month, as shown below:

```
USE Employee
CurrMonth = MONTH (DATE( ))    && or Substitute desired month
DO WHILE .NOT. EOF( )
    If CurrMonth = MONTH (BDAY)
        ? FName, LName, Age
    ENDIF
    SKIP
ENDDO
```

### SEE ALSO

CMONTH( )
DAY( )
YEAR( )

## The NDX( ) Function

NDX( ) returns the name of the index file corresponding to the number passed to the function.

### SYNTAX

**NDX(<number>)**

where <number> is an integer value between 1 and 7.

### USAGE

The number is the position of the index file in the index file list in the currently selected work area. If no index files are open, the function returns a null string. The number returned is always between 1 and 7, because only 7 index files can be open at a time.

The steps below illustrate how the function works:

```
USE Mail INDEX Names, Zips, Dates

? NDX(3)
    C:Dates.ndx
```

```
? NDX(1)
     C:Names.ndx

? NDX(4)
                    && null string is returned
```

### EXAMPLE

The example below displays the names of all index files that are connected to the open database. This can be used in a program where all the index files are displayed and the user is given a choice of which ones to make active.

```
I = 1
DO WHILE (I < = 7) .AND. " " # NDX (I)
     ? NDX (I)
     I = I + 1
ENDDO
```

### TIPS

The DISPLAY STATUS command lists the names and key expressions for all currently active index files.

### SEE ALSO

DBF( )
SET INDEX
SET ORDER

## The OS( ) Function

OS( ) returns the name of the operating system currently in use.

### SYNTAX

OS( )

### USAGE

The OS( ) function returns the name and version number of the operating system currently in use. It is generally used within an IF clause to perform different commands under different operating systems, thereby allowing you to make your applications portable to a variety of computers.

### EXAMPLE

The general structure of the IF clause below can be used to perform different commands under the DOS and UNIX operating systems:

```
SET EXACT OFF
IF OS = "DOS"
     <do these commands>
ENDIF
IF OS( ) = "UNIX"
     <do these commands>
ENDIF
```

### SEE ALSO

GETENV( )
VERSION( )

## The PCOL( ) Function

PCOL( ) returns the current column position of the print head on the printer.

### SYNTAX

**PCOL( )**

### USAGE

The PCOL( ) function is usually used for relative addressing on printed output. The location of the next printed row is therefore dependent on the location of the current row. You can store the value of PCOL( ) to a memory variable.

### EXAMPLE

When printing reports with @...SAY commands and SET DEVICE TO PRINT, PCOL( ) allows you to define spaces between columns without specifying exact column locations, as below:

```
@ PROW( ),1 SAY Name
@ PROW( ),PCOL( ) + 5 SAY Address
@ PROW( ),PCOL( ) + 5 SAY TRIM(City) + ",  " + State,Zip
```

### TIPS

You can use the PCOL( ) and PROW( ) functions to find out whether the paper in the printer is at the beginning of a new page, as in the IF clause below. If it is not, an EJECT command ejects the current page in the printer:

```
IF PROW( ) > 0 .OR. PCOL( ) > 0
     EJECT
ENDIF
```

### SEE ALSO

PROW( )
COL( )
ROW( )

## The PROW( ) Function

Referred to as the printer row function, PROW( ) returns the current row position of the print head on the printer.

### SYNTAX

**PROW( )**

### USAGE

The PROW( ) function is usually used for relative addressing on printed output. This means that the location of the next row to be printed is dependent on the current row. You can store the value of PROW( ) to a memory variable.

### EXAMPLE

The commands below use relative printer addressing to print a double-spaced report on the printer using the @...SAY command and SET DEVICE TO PRINT:

```
USE AnyFile
SET TALK OFF
SET DEVICE TO PRINT
DO WHILE .NOT. EOF( )
     @ PROW( ) + 2,1 SAY Name
     @ PROW( ),PCOL( ) + 5 SAY Address
     SKIP
ENDDO
```

### TIPS

You cannot use negative numbers in relative addressing with the PROW( ) function. The printer's platen can only scroll forward.

As shown in the PCOL( ) function above, you can use PROW( ) to determine whether an EJECT is required to start printing on a new page.

### SEE ALSO

PCOL( )
COL( )
ROW( )

## The READKEY( ) Function

READKEY( ) returns an integer corresponding to the key that was pressed to exit a full-screen command (i.e., APPEND, BROWSE, CHANGE, CREATE, EDIT, INSERT, MODIFY, or READ). The READKEY( ) function also indicates whether changes were made to the data during the full-screen command.

### SYNTAX

**READKEY( )**

### USAGE

Depending on the value returned by READKEY( ), you can determine what to do next after the user exits from one of the full-screen commands.

READKEY( ) returns one of two possible values for a single keypress, depending on whether any data on the screen were altered. If no changes were made to the data, READKEY( ) has a value between 0 and 36. If any field on the screen was changed, the READKEY( ) value is increased by 256.

To make programs easier to read, you can create variable names for the READKEY( ) values and use these names in your program instead of numbers. Table 17.2 lists some suggested variable names for READKEY( ) values, along with the values returned by READKEY( ) when the user leaves a full-screen operation.

### EXAMPLE

In the routine below, the value 15 (which means the user typed past the end of the last field on the screen) is assigned to the variable named RK_Filled. If the user types past the end of the screen without making any changes, the routine

| SUGGESTED VARIABLE NAME | READKEY( ) CODE | UPDATE CODE | KEY PRESSED | INTERPRETATION |
|---|---|---|---|---|
| RK_Bakchr | 0 | | Ctrl-H<br>Ctrl-S<br>←<br>Backspace | Backward one character |
| RK_Forchr | 1 | 257 | Ctrl-D<br>→<br>Ctrl-L | Forward one character |
| RK_Bakwrd | 2 | 258 | Ctrl-A<br>Home | Backward one word |
| RK_Forwrd | 3 | 259 | Ctrl-F<br>End | Forward one word |
| RK_Bakfld | 4 | 260 | Ctrl-E<br>↑<br>Ctrl-K | Backward one field |
| RK_Forfld | 5 | 261 | Ctrl-J<br>Ctrl-X<br>↓ | Forward one field |
| RK_Bakscr | 6 | 262 | Ctrl-R<br>PgUp | Backward one screen |
| RX_Forscr | 7 | 263 | Ctrl-C<br>PgDn | Forward one screen |
| RK_Bakpan | 8 | 264 | Ctrl-Z<br>Ctrl-← | Pan left |
| RK_Forpan | 9 | 265 | Ctrl-B<br>Ctrl-→ | Pan right |
| RK_Delete | 10 | 266 | Ctrl-U | Delete something |
| RK_Insert | 11 | 267 | Ctrl-V | Insert something |
| RK_Quit | 12 | 268 | Ctrl-Q<br>Esc | Terminate without save |
| Return key | 13 | not used | | |
| RK_Write | 14 | 270 | Ctrl-W<br>Ctrl-End | Terminate with save |
| RK_Filled | 15 | 271 | Ctrl-M<br>(past end) | Filled; typed past end |
| RK_Return | 16 | 272 | Return<br>(at start) | APPEND, MODIFY STRUCTURE, MODIFY REPORT |

**TABLE 17.2:** Suggested Variable Names for READKEY( ) Values

| SUGGESTED VARIABLE NAME | READKEY( ) CODE | UPDATE CODE | KEY PRESSED | INTERPRETATION |
|---|---|---|---|---|
| RK_Menu | 33 | 289 | Ctrl-Home<br>Ctrl-] | Menu display toggle |
| RK_Zomout | 34 | 290 | Ctrl-PgUp<br>Ctrl- - | Zoom out |
| RK_Zomin | 35 | 291 | Ctrl-PgDn | Zoom in |
| RK_Help | 36 | 292 | Ctrl- ^<br>F1 | Help function keys |
| RK_Update | | 256 | Ctrl-H<br>Ctrl-S<br>Backspace | Backward one character |

**TABLE 17.2:** Suggested Variable Names for READKEY( ) Values (continued)

simply skips to the next record. If the user made changes to the record and then typed past the end of the screen, the routine presents a prompt that allows the user to make further changes by pressing ↑.

```
RK_Filled = 15
SET FORMAT TO AnyScrn
READ
IF READKEY( ) = RK_Filled
    SKIP
ENDIF
IF READKEY = RK_Filled + 256
    Decide = " "
    @ 22,1 SAY "Press up arrow to make more changes ";
        GET Decide
    READ
ENDIF
```

To determine whether the contents of a memory variable on the screen were changed during the full-screen command and to replace a field if changes occurred, use the following lines within a program:

```
IF READKEY( ) = RK_Write + 256      && key = 270
    REPLACE Field1 WITH MField1, Field2 WITH MField2
ENDIF
```

## TIPS

See Chapter 8, "Managing Screen Displays," for an additional example of the READKEY( ) function.

#### SEE ALSO

INKEY( )
ON KEY
READ

## The RECCOUNT( ) Function

RECCOUNT( ) returns the total number of records in the currently selected database file.

#### SYNTAX

**RECCOUNT( )**

#### USAGE

The RECCOUNT( ) function returns the total number of records in a database file without moving the record pointer. This includes all records, regardless of the number of deleted records or the status of the SET FILTER command. If the database is empty, a zero is returned.

#### EXAMPLE

In many applications, it is useful to move sequentially forward and/or backward through a database file. To display a status notice that tells you which record you are viewing out of how many records in the file, you could use the following command:

```
@ 5,55 SAY "Record " + STR(RECNO( ),5) + ;
" of " + STR(RECCOUNT( ),5)
```

#### TIPS

The value of RECCOUNT( ) is taken directly from the database file header, as discussed in Chapter 23, "Foreign and Damaged Files." Its value is displayed by the DISPLAY STATUS command.

#### SEE ALSO

RECNO( )
RECSIZE( )

## The RECNO( ) Function

RECNO( ) returns the number of the record currently in use.

### SYNTAX

**RECNO( )**

### USAGE

If there are no records in the database file, RECNO( ) returns 1 and EOF( ) returns .T.. If the record pointer is moved past the last record in a nonempty database file, RECNO( ) returns the last RECNO( ) value plus 1. If the record pointer is moved backward beyond the first record in a nonempty database file, RECNO( ) returns 1.

### EXAMPLE

The commands below locate the first record with the name Jones in the LName field and display the record number for that record:

```
Use Mail INDEX Names
FIND Jones
IF FOUND( )
      ? "Jones is at record  ",RECNO( )
ELSE
      ? "Can't find Jones"
ENDIF
```

### TIPS

To sort a database from the largest record number to the smallest, use the command

```
INDEX ON  -RECNO( ) TO Backward
```

RECNO( ) is not stored anywhere on the database file; it is calculated by the record's physical position in the file.

### SEE ALSO

RECCOUNT( )

## The RECSIZE( ) Function

RECSIZE( ) returns the number of bytes used by a single record in the currently selected database file.

### SYNTAX

**RECSIZE( )**

### USAGE

Use the RECSIZE( ) function with the RECCOUNT( ) and DISKSIZE( ) functions if you would like to calculate the total disk space required to back up a given database file to floppy disks.

### EXAMPLE

Assuming that you know the number of fields in the database you would like to back up, you can calculate the header size for a dBASE III PLUS database file as follows:

```
FieldCount = X          &&(where X is the number of fields)
HeadSize = 32 * FieldCount + 35
```

### TIPS

You can use the RECSIZE( ) function to copy large database files from a hard disk to several floppy disks, as shown in the example below:

```
USE AnyFile
FieldCount = X      &&(where X is the number of fields)
HeadSize = 32 * FieldCount + 35
NumRecs = (DISKSPACE( ) – HeadSize))/RECSIZE( )
WAIT "Insert disk in drive A, then press any key..."
DO WHILE .NOT. EOF
     COPY NEXT NumRecs TO A:AnyFile
     ? "Change floppy disk in drive A, then..."
     WAIT
     SKIP
ENDDO
CLOSE DATABASES
```

The COPY command will use only the integer part of the NumRecs number.

RECSIZE( ) is stored in the database file header and can be viewed with the DISPLAY STATUS command. See Chapter 23, "Foreign and Damaged Files," for more information on the dBASE database file header.

### SEE ALSO

DISKSPACE( )
RECCOUNT( )

## The REPLICATE( ) Function

REPLICATE( ) repeats a character string a specified number of times.

### SYNTAX

**REPLICATE(<character>,<number>)**

where <character> is the character or character string to repeat and <number> is a number or numeric expression defining how many times to repeat that character pattern.

### USAGE

The REPLICATE( ) function returns a character expression consisting of <number> repetitions of <character>. The maximum length of the string is 254 characters.

### EXAMPLE

To place a row of double lines across the top of a report, use the command

**@ 4,0 SAY REPLICATE(" = ",80)**

To display a bright, solid bar across the screen, enter the command

**? REPLICATE(CHR(219),80)**

### TIPS

To create an underline the width of the screen that can be used throughout an application, use a command like the one below:

**ULine = REPLICATE("_",80)**

Once defined, the command **? ULine** displays the entire underline.

#### SEE ALSO

SUBSTR( )

## The RIGHT( ) Function

RIGHT( ) returns a specified number of characters starting from the rightmost point in a character expression.

#### SYNTAX

**RIGHT(<character>,<number>)**

where <character> is any character string or expression, and <number> is a number or numeric expression that specifies the number of characters to return.

#### USAGE

The numeric expression in the argument defines the number of characters to extract from the right side of the character expression. If the numeric expression is less than 1, a null string is returned. If the numeric expression is greater than the length of the character expression, the entire character expression is returned.

#### EXAMPLE

The routine below pads any number stored in the variable named X with sufficient leading zeros to give the number an exact width of 15 characters.

```
Leader = "000000000000000"
INPUT "Enter a number  " TO X

? RIGHT(Leader + LTRIM(STR(X,16,2)),15)
```

#### SEE ALSO

LEFT( )
LTRIM( )
STUFF( )
SUBSTR( )
RTRIM( )
TRIM( )

## The RLOCK( ) Function

RLOCK( ) determines whether a record is locked. If the record is not already locked, RLOCK( ) locks the record if possible. See Chapter 20, "Networking and Security," for details.

## The ROUND( ) Function

ROUND( ) rounds a number to the nearest decimal place specified.

### SYNTAX

**ROUND(<number1>,<number2>)**

where <number1> is the number to round, and <number2> is the number of decimal places to round to.

### USAGE

The ROUND( ) function rounds the first number to the number of decimal places specified by the second number. If the second number is negative, the function begins rounding into the integer portion of the number, as shown in the examples below.

### EXAMPLES

The series of commands below demonstrate the various effects of the ROUND( ) function on the number 12.3456:

```
? ROUND(12.3456,3)
    12.3460

? ROUND(12.3456,2)
    12.3500

? ROUND(12.3456,1)
    12.3000

? ROUND(12.3456,0)
    12.0000

? ROUND(12.3456,-1)
    10.0000

? ROUND(12.3456,-2)
    0.0000
```

### TIPS

This function is useful when you are comparing two numbers to see if they are equivalent, particularly in an IF...ENDIF clause. For example, the result of a calculation can be compared to another number to test for equivalence. To avoid small differences that are due to insignificant digits, compare the rounded values.

```
Value1 = 5.00
IF ROUND(Value2/Value3 * 2.34,2) = ROUND(Value1,2)
    <do commands>
ENDIF
```

Note that ROUND( ) determines only the number of places to round to—it does not affect the number of decimal places actually displayed. To control the number of decimals actually displayed, use SET DECIMALS and SET FIXED.

### SEE ALSO

SET DECIMALS
SET FIXED
INT( )

## The ROW( ) Function

The ROW( ) function returns the current row position of the cursor on the screen.

### SYNTAX

**ROW( )**

### USAGE

The ROW( ) function is commonly used for relative addressing on the screen. For example, the expression **@ ROW + 2,5** refers to two rows below the current row (and the fifth column).

You can also store the value of ROW( ) to a memory variable.

### EXAMPLE

The routine in Figure 17.7 creates ten variables named Var1 through Var10 each ten spaces wide. The DO WHILE loop displays these variables on the

```
*----------- Create and display ten blank variables
*----------- on the screen for entering data.
SET TALK OFF
CLEAR
Counter = 1
@ 3,5 SAY ""
DO WHILE Counter <= 10
   Sub = LTRIM(STR(Counter,2))
   Var&Sub = SPACE(10)
   @ ROW()+2,5 GET Var&Sub
   Counter = Counter + 1
   Sub = LTRIM(STR(Counter,2))
   Var&Sub = SPACE(10)
   @ ROW(),20 GET Var&Sub
   Counter = Counter + 1
ENDDO
READ
LIST MEMORY
```

**FIGURE 17.7:** This routine creates ten memory variables named Var1 through Var10, and displays them as prompts in five rows of two columns. The READ command reads in values for the prompts, and then LIST MEMORY displays them. The ROW( ) function inside the DO WHILE loop controls the row position on the screen for the prompts.

screen, in two columns and five double-spaced rows, for data entry. After filling in the prompts, the LIST MEMORY command displays the values entered.

### SEE ALSO

PROW( )
COL( )
PCOL( )

## The RTRIM( ) Function

RTRIM( ) removes trailing blanks from a character expression.

### SYNTAX

**RTRIM(<character>)**

where <character> is any character data, character expression, or a variable containing character data.

### USAGE

The RTRIM( ) function is equivalent to the TRIM( ) function.

#### SEE ALSO

LEFT( )
LTRIM( )
RIGHT( )
TRIM( )

## The SPACE( ) Function

SPACE( ) creates a character string composed of a specified number of blanks.

#### SYNTAX

**SPACE(<number>)**

where <number> is any number, numeric expression, or variable smaller than 254.

#### USAGE

SPACE( ) creates a character string containing a specified number of blank spaces. SPACE( ) is usually used to initialize character memory variables.

#### EXAMPLE

Assuming that the LName field in a database has a width of 20, the routine below allows a user to enter a last name to search for and store that entry in a memory variable named Search. The user's entry cannot exceed 20 characters.

```
USE Mail INDEX LNames
Search = SPACE(20)
@ 10,5 SAY "Enter name to search for ";
    GET SEARCH READ
SEEK UPPER(TRIM(Search))
```

#### TIPS

Using SPACE rather than delimited blanks makes programs more readable, as shown by the equivalent commands below:

```
Search = "                    "
Search = SPACE(20)
```

#### SEE ALSO

REPLICATE( )

# The SQRT( ) Function

SQRT( ) returns the square root of the number passed to the function.

### SYNTAX

**SQRT(<number>)**

where <number> is a positive number, an expression resulting in a positive number, or the name of a variable containing a positive number.

### USAGE

The SQRT( ) function returns a number with either the default number of decimals or the number of decimal places in the expression, whichever is larger.

### EXAMPLE

The commands below calculate and display the square root of 3213.56:

```
Numb = 3213.56
? SQRT(Numb)
   56.69
```

### TIPS

Attempting to take the square root of a negative number produces an execution error, as shown below:

```
Numb = -81
? SQRT(Numb)
***Execution error on SQRT( ) : Negative.
```

To prevent these errors, use the ABS function to convert the argument to a positive number, as below:

```
? SQRT(ABS(Numb))
    9.00
```

### SEE ALSO

ABS( )
SET DECIMAL
SET FIXED

## The STR( ) Function

STR( ) converts any numeric expression into a character string.

### SYNTAX

**STR(<number>,[<length>],[<decimal>])**

where <number> is the number to convert, <length> is the length of the converted number, and <decimal> is the number of decimal places in the number, if any.

### USAGE

The length parameter sets the total length of the character expression (including any decimals, the decimal point itself and the minus sign), and the decimal parameter sets the number of decimal places to be included. If either <length> or <decimal> is omitted, dBASE uses the default length of 10 and the default of 0 decimal places.

If you specify a smaller length than there are digits to the left of the decimal point in the numeric expression, dBASE returns asterisks in place of the number. If you specify fewer decimals than are in the numeric expression, dBASE III PLUS rounds the result to the specified number of decimal places.

### EXAMPLE

The series of commands below demonstrate the effect of the STR function, using various arguments, on the number 1234.56:

```
Number = 1234.56

? STR(Number)
      1235                  (10 characters wide, 0 decimals)

? STR(Number,7,2)
1234.56                     (7 characters wide, 2 decimals)

? STR(Number,8,3)
1234.560                    (8 characters wide, 3 decimals)

? STR(Number,15,1)
          1234.6            (15 characters, 1 decimal)

? STR(Number,4,2)
1235                        (4 characters only, decimals don't fit)
```

### TIPS

The STR( ) function is usually used to combine numeric data with character data. To prevent leading blanks in the converted number from appearing in the character string, use the LTRIM function with the STR function, as below:

**Prize = 100.00**
**Prompt = "You have won " + LTRIM(STR(Prize)) + "dollars!"**

The command **? Prompt** then displays **You have won 100 dollars!**.

To further refine the number that is combined with the character string, you can use TRANSFORM( ) instead of STR, as in the series of commands below:

**Prize = 1000000.00**
**Format = "999,999,999.99"**
**Convert = TRANSFORM(Prize,Format)**
**Prompt = "You have won " + LTRIM(Convert) + " dollars!"**

After this series of commands, the command **? Prompt** displays **You have won 1,000,000.00 dollars!**.

STR( ) can also be used define an exact column width for displaying numbers in printed reports.

### SEE ALSO

LTRIM( )
TRANSFORM( )
VAL( )

## The STUFF( ) Function

STUFF( ) combines two character expressions to produce a third character expression.

### SYNTAX

**STUFF(<character1>,<number1>,<number2>,<character2>)**

where <character1> is the target string, <character2> is the string being inserted, <number1> identifies the character position at which <character2> will be stuffed into <character1> and <number2> identifies how many (if any) characters in <character1> will be deleted or overwritten.

### USAGE

Essentially, the STUFF( ) function lets you stuff the second expression into the first expression. The first number describes where to stuff the second expression into the first, and the second number determines how many characters are overwritten in the first expression. If the second number is zero or negative, no characters in the target string are overwritten.

### EXAMPLE

The commands below demonstrate examples of the outcome of various STUFF( ) operations with two strings named Target and Bullet.

```
Target = "This is a long sentence"
Bullet = "<inserted>"

? STUFF(Target,5,0,Bullet)
     This<inserted> is a long sentence

? STUFF(Target,5,0," " + Bullet)
     This <inserted> is a long sentence

? STUFF(Target,6,4,Bullet)
     This <inserted> long sentence
```

If the string being inserted is a null, STUFF removes characters from the target string, because the overwritten characters are replaced by nothing, as in the example below:

```
Bullet = ""
? STUFF(Target,6,3,Bullet)
     This a long sentence
```

### SEE ALSO

LEFT( )
RIGHT( )
SUBSTR( )

## The SUBSTR( ) Function

Known as the substring function, SUBSTR( ) extracts a smaller string from a larger string.

## SYNTAX

**SUBSTR(<character>,<number1>,[<number2>])**

where <character> is the character string, <number1> is the starting location for the substring, and <number2> is the length of the substring.

## USAGE

The first numeric expression is the starting point of the string to be extracted. The optional second numeric expression signifies how many characters will be extracted; if it is omitted, SUBSTR( ) will extract the maximum number of characters remaining in the character string.

## EXAMPLE

In the simple example below, SUBSTR( ) displays DOG, a three-character substring beginning at the sixth character:

```
String = "YOUR DOG HAS FLEAS"
? SUBSTR(String,6,3)
     DOG
```

The next example is more complex, and it shows how one might use numeric variables with the SUBSTR( ) function:

```
Week = "   Monday   Tuesday   Wednesday   Thursday   Friday   "
CLEAR
? "Week Days"
? "---------"
Day = 1
DO WHILE Day < = 5
     ? SUBSTR(Week,Day*9 - 1,9)
     STORE Day + 1 TO Day
ENDDO
```

The routine produces the following display:

```
Week Days
---------
Monday
Tuesday
Wednesday
Thursday
Friday
```

### TIPS

To isolate single characters, use 1 as the second numeric expression. Doing so allows you to analyze and manipulate the characters in a string independently. The sample routine below uses such a technique to print any character string backwards:

```
ACCEPT "Enter any character string " TO String
?
Point = LEN(String)
DO WHILE Point > 0
     ?? SUBSTR(String,Point,1)
     Point = Point - 1
ENDDO
```

### SEE ALSO

AT( )
LEFT( )
RIGHT( )
STUFF( )

## The TIME( ) Function

TIME( ) returns the system time as a character string.

### SYNTAX

**TIME( )**

### USAGE

TIME( ) returns a character string in the format hh:mm:ss (i.e., 12:55:01). Because TIME( ) is returned as a character string, you cannot do time arithmetic directly. Instead, you must convert individual portions to numbers and manipulate the values as numbers.

### EXAMPLE

To time-stamp a printed display, use the command **? TIME( )** in the report heading. To include the time on a report printed by the REPORT FORM command, use the option **HEADING TIME( )** in the REPORT FORM command.

### TIPS

To convert the value TIME( ) returns to seconds for calculating the elapsed time between two events, use the formula

```
Seconds = VAL(LEFT(TIME( ),2))*3600 + ;
          VAL(SUBSTR(TIME( ),4,2))*60 + ;
          VAL(RIGHT(TIME( ),2))
```

For example, to calculate the amount of time dBASE takes to print a particular report, you could use this algorithm:

```
Start = VAL(LEFT(TIME( ),2))*3600 + ;
        VAL(SUBSTR(TIME( ),4,2))*60 + ;
        VAL(RIGHT(TIME( ),2))

USE AnyFile REPORT FORM AnyRep TO PRINT

Finish = VAL(LEFT(TIME( ),2))*3600 + ;
         VAL(SUBSTR(TIME( ),4,2))*60 + ;
         VAL(RIGHT(TIME( ),2))

? "That took " + LTRIM(STR(Finish – Start)) + " seconds"
```

To convert seconds back into hours and minutes, use the technique demonstrated in the MOD( ) function.

### SEE ALSO

MOD( )
DATE( )

## The TRANSFORM( ) Function

TRANSFORM( ) offers picture formatting features of numeric or character expressions without using the @...SAY command.

### SYNTAX

**TRANSFORM(<data>,<format>)**

where <data> is the item to be formatted, and <format> is the format to use.

## USAGE

TRANSFORM extends picture formatting to commands such as ?, ??, DISPLAY, LABEL, LIST, and REPORT. The first argument can be a numeric or character variable. The second argument is a template, or the name of a variable containing the template, that defines the format.

Table 17.3 lists the picture functions that you can use with the TRANSFORM function. As with the PICTURE command, these function characters must be preceded by an @ sign. Table 17.4 lists the individual picture template characters that can be used in TRANSFORM functions. Table 17.5 displays examples of the output of various TRANSFORM functions.

| SYMBOL | DATA TYPE | EFFECT IN TRANSFORM |
|---|---|---|
| @( | N | Displays negative number in parentheses |
| @B | N | Left-justifies a number |
| @C | N | Displays CR (credit) after positive number |
| @X | N | Displays DB (debit) after negative number |
| @Z | N | Displays a zero as a blank space |
| @! | C | Displays all letters in uppercase |
| @R | C | Inserts template characters into displayed data |
| @S<n> | C | Displays the left <n> characters of data |

**TABLE 17.3:** Picture Functions Used in TRANSFORM( )

| SYMBOL | DATA TYPES | EFFECT IN TRANSFORM |
|---|---|---|
| X | C | Displays any character |
| ! | C | Displays all letters in uppercase |
| 9 | N | Displays digit locations |
| # | N | Same as 9 |
| $ | N | Displays leading dollar signs if space permits |
| * | N | Displays leading asterisks if space permits |
| , | N | Displays comma if digits are present on both sides |

**TABLE 17.4:** Picture Template Characters Used in TRANSFORM( )

| TRANSFORM OUTPUT | DISPLAYED |
|---|---|
| TRANSFORM(−123.45,"@(") | ( 123.45) |
| TRANSFORM(−123.45,"@B(") | (123.45 ) |
| TRANSFORM(−123.45,"@X") | 123.45 DB |
| TRANSFORM(123.45,"@C") | 123.45 CR |
| TRANSFORM(0,"@Z") | |
| TRANSFORM("cat","@!") | CAT |
| TRANSFORM("cat","@R X X X") | c a t |
| TRANSFORM("abcdefg","@S3") | abc |
| TRANSFORM(1234567.89,"999,999.99") | 1,234,567.89 |
| TRANSFORM(1234.56,"$999,999.99") | $$$1,234.56 |
| TRANSFORM(1234.567,"*###,###.##") | ***1,234.57 |
| TRANSFORM(−123,"@X 999,999.99") | 123.00 DB |
| TRANSFORM(123,"@CX 999,999.99") | 123.00 CR |

**TABLE 17.5:** Example of Various TRANSFORM( ) Function Formats

## EXAMPLE

To display a list of current costs using the LIST command and formatted output:

```
LIST NEXT 5 TRANSFORM(Price,"999,999.99")
Record#        TRANSFORM(Price,"999,999.99")
     11             999.95
     12          21,995.00
     13           4,995.00
     14           9,995.00
     15         121,000.00
```

Note that either argument in the TRANSFORM function can be a variable, as in the example below:

```
Amount = 12345.67
Format = "999,999,999.99"
?TRANSFORM(Amount,Format)
     12,345.67
```

## TIPS

Remember that TRANSFORM can be used when defining the columns in MODIFY REPORT and MODIFY LABEL.

#### SEE ALSO

@...SAY

## The TRIM( ) Function

TRIM( ) removes trailing blanks from a character expression.

#### SYNTAX

**TRIM(<character>)**

where <character> is any character data, character expression, or a variable containing character data.

#### USAGE

This function removes trailing blanks from a character expression. The trailing blanks are typically those used to pad the string to a width defined in a database field or a predefined width created by a SPACE function before a READ command.

#### EXAMPLE

A common use of the TRIM( ) function is to create the last line on a mailing label. Separate fields usually exist for city, state, and zip, but TRIM( ) allows you to create a single line in the format **Los Angeles, CA 92122,** as the line below demonstrates:

**? TRIM(City) + ", " + TRIM(State) + " " + Zip**

#### TIPS

Never use TRIM( ) in an index key expression, as this produces unequal key lengths within the index file, with unpredictable results.

#### SEE ALSO

LTRIM( )
RTRIM( )

## The TYPE( ) Function

TYPE( ) returns a single character code that indicates the data type of the expression passed to the function.

### SYNTAX

**TYPE(<expression>)**

where <expression> is an expression of any type, or the name of a database field or memory variable enclosed in quotation marks or brackets.

### USAGE

The TYPE( ) function is a test for the existence of an expression, field, or variable; if it does not exist, a U (for undefined) is returned. If the variable does exist, the appropriate data type is returned.

These are the possible data types returned by the function:

C = character
N = numeric
D = date
L = logical
M = memo
U = undefined

### EXAMPLE

Some examples of commands typed at the dot prompt will give you a feel for the TYPE( ) function:

```
STORE 0 TO memvar
? TYPE("memvar")
    N

Name = "Jones"
? TYPE("Name")
    C
```

```
STORE .F. TO Expired
? TYPE("expired")
    L

? TYPE("Today")
    U

? TYPE("DATE( )")
    D

? TYPE("DATE( )") = "D"
    .T.
```

### TIPS

From within a program, you can use the TYPE( ) function to test for the presence of a variable to determine whether a subroutine will be executed:

```
IF TYPE("InpFile") = "U"
    *- - - - InpFile variable does not exist yet.
    *- - - - Call GetIFile to create it.
    DO GetIFile
ENDIF
```

### SEE ALSO

FIELD( )

## The UPPER( ) Function

UPPER( ) converts any lowercase letters in a character expression to uppercase.

### SYNTAX

**UPPER( )**

### USAGE

UPPER converts all lowercase letters in a character string to uppercase. It has no effect on numbers or uppercase letters. It is often used in index file expressions to prevent case distinctions from affecting sort orders and searches.

### EXAMPLE

The commands below demonstrate an example of UPPER:

**Name = "SuSiTa, 123 Apple St."**
**Name = UPPER(Name)**
**? Name**
**SUSITA, 123 APPLE ST."**

### SEE ALSO

ISALPHA( )
ISLOWER( )
ISUPPER( )
LOWER( )

## The VAL( ) Function

Known as the string-to-number function, VAL( ) converts numbers stored as character strings to the numeric data type.

### SYNTAX

**VAL(<character>)**

### USAGE

If the argument contains leading numeric characters followed by nonnumeric characters, VAL( ) returns the leading numeric characters as a number. If the argument consists of leading nonnumeric characters (other than blanks), the function returns a 0. The number of decimals returned by the function is determined by the SET DECIMALS command.

### EXAMPLE

The commands below store the street address number as a numeric variable in a variable called StreetNo and then display that number:

**Address = "34567 Adams St."**
**StreetNo = VAL(Address)**
**? StreetNo**
**34567**

### TIPS

See the TIME( ) function for an example that uses VAL( ) to convert the TIME( ) character string to seconds.

### SEE ALSO

SET DECIMALS
STR( )
TIME( )

## The VERSION( ) Function

VERSION( ) returns a character expression containing the version number of dBASE III PLUS in use.

### SYNTAX

**VERSION( )**

### USAGE

VERSION( ) can be used to make sure that certain commands are used only with the versions of dBASE III PLUS that support the command.

### EXAMPLE

The command below displays the version of dBASE III PLUS in use at the moment:

```
? VERSION( )
     dBASE III PLUS Version 1.1
```

### TIPS

A display of the Ashton-Tate version number and release data is stored in a function named VERSION(1), as shown below:

```
? VERSION(1)
     dBASE III PLUS Version 2.0x100 (07/24/86)
```

### SEE ALSO

OS( )
GETENV( )

## The YEAR( ) Function

YEAR( ) returns the numeric value of the year from a date expression.

### SYNTAX

**YEAR(<date>)**

where <date> is any data of the date data type.

### USAGE

The YEAR( ) function returns a four-digit representation of the year.

### EXAMPLE

The example below displays the year for the current system date:

```
? YEAR(DATE( ))
    1987
```

### TIPS

To combine a date with a character string in an index file, you can convert the date to a character string in yyyymmdd format (so the years take precedence over the months and days in the sort order) using the technique below:

```
INDEX ON STR(YEAR(<date>),4 + STR(MONTH(<date>),2) + ;
         STR(DAY(<date>),2) TO <index file name>
```

### SEE ALSO

MONTH( )
DAY( )
SET CENTURY
INDEX

## SUMMARY

This chapter discussed dBASE III PLUS functions, which are used to manipulate data items or to provide new data items in conjunction with a dBASE command.

*For a summary list of all functions, categorized by the type of service they perform:*

- Chapter 1, "Overview of the dBASE Language"

*For information on using functions to define complex sort orders:*

- Chapter 12, "Sorting and Indexing"

*For examples of using functions to search for information in a database file:*

- Chapter 13, "Searching a Database"

*For additional information on using functions to combine data types:*

- Chapter 15, "Managing Data, Records, and Files"

*For information on the dBASE functions used only in a networking environment:*

- Chapter 20, "Networking and Security"

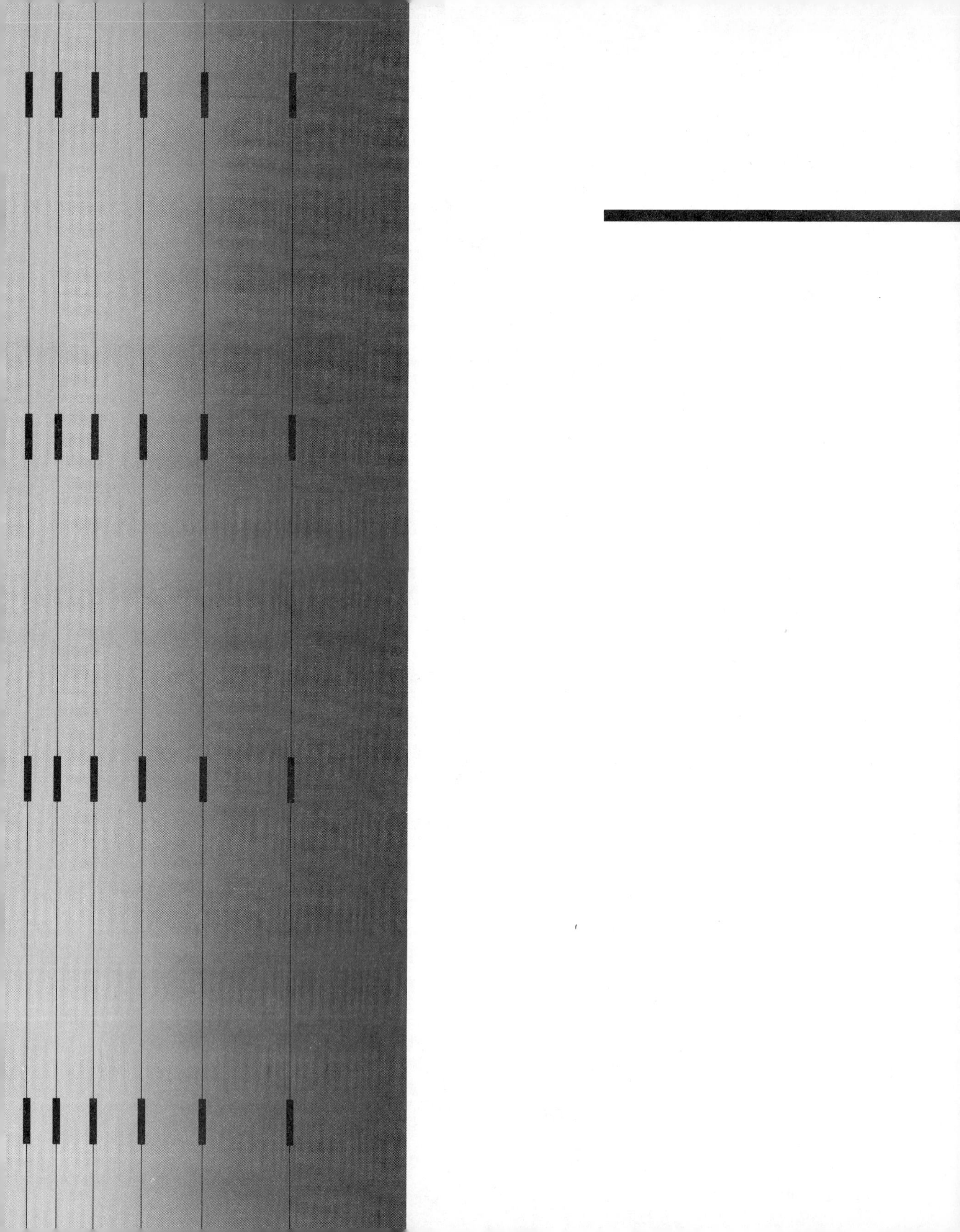

CHAPTER 18

# SETTING PARAMETERS

# Setting Parameters

This chapter covers the commands used to define dBASE environmental parameters. These parameters control numerous global settings that remain in effect throughout the remainder of the current dBASE session (or until another SET command changes the setting). For example, once you define colors for the screen, those colors are used with all commands throughout dBASE. When you define a particular date format, all dates are displayed in that format.

All of the commands used to set these global parameters begin with the word SET. The beginning of this chapter discusses SET commands as they relate to the programmer. The reference section of the chapter discusses most of these SET commands in more technical detail.

## Viewing and Altering Current Settings

The current status of the various SET commands can be viewed with the DISPLAY STATUS or LIST STATUS command. Figure 18.1 shows a listing of the settings dBASE starts with by default.

The settings displayed near the top of the screen are controlled with the commands listed below:

| **Setting** | **Controlling command** |
|---|---|
| File search path | SET PATH |
| Default disk drive | SET DEFAULT |
| Print destination | SET PRINTER |
| Margin | SET MARGIN |

(The current work area is controlled by the SELECT command.)

The programmable function key commands, listed near the bottom of the display, are controlled by the SET FUNCTION command.

The status of the SET PROCEDURE, SET RELATION, and SET ALTERNATE TO commands are displayed only if the commands have already been issued and a parameter has been defined.

```
File search path:
Default disk drive: C:
Print destination:  PRN:
Margin =       0
Current work area =     1

ALTERNATE  - ON    DELETED    - OFF   FIXED      - OFF   SAFETY     - OFF
BELL       - ON    DELIMITERS - OFF   HEADING    - ON    SCOREBOARD - ON
CARRY      - OFF   DEVICE     - SCRN  HELP       - OFF   STATUS     - OFF
CATALOG    - OFF   DOHISTORY  - OFF   HISTORY    - ON    STEP       - OFF
CENTURY    - OFF   ECHO       - OFF   INTENSITY  - ON    TALK       - ON
CONFIRM    - OFF   ESCAPE     - ON    MENU       - ON    TITLE      - ON
CONSOLE    - ON    EXACT      - OFF   PRINT      - OFF   UNIQUE     - OFF
DEBUG      - OFF   FIELDS     - OFF

Programmable function keys:
F2  - assist;
F3  - list;
F4  - dir;
F5  - display structure;
F6  - display status;
F7  - display memory;
F8  - display;
F9  - append;
F10 - edit;
```

**FIGURE 18.1:** The default settings for the dBASE SET commands. These settings are displayed with the DISPLAY STATUS or LIST STATUS command. Some settings, such as PROCEDURE and RELATION, are displayed only if they are active.

The SET command alone also displays the current status of all settings, but it allows you to change the settings. You can redefine the default settings for most of the SET commands in the Config.db file. See Appendix C, "Configuring dBASE III PLUS," for details.

## PROGRAMMING TECHNIQUES WITH SET

As a programmer, you will need to use the SET commands to define basic parameters for your applications. Most applications use the default settings, with these two changes:

**SET TALK OFF**
**SET STATUS OFF**

SET TALK OFF keeps the results of calculations and memory variable storage from cluttering the screen (though SET TALK ON can be used to show the progress of time-consuming commands such as COPY and PACK). You can use SET STATUS OFF inside your applications to delete the status bar from the screen. Doing so gives you more screen space to work with and also keeps the status bar from showing when it is of no value, as when a menu is displayed on the screen.

## Letting the User Define Parameters

When you develop a custom application, you can allow the user to define some parameters, such as the date format and the printer margin. The easiest way to do so is to store the settings for these parameters in a memory file that the user can edit. Then, when the application runs, it first uses these values to define the various settings and then proceeds with normal processing. An example will help demonstrate.

### Creating a Settings File

Assume that you want the user to define settings for the bell, the Return key (the CONFIRM setting), the date format, and the margin. First you must create a memory file to store the settings for these parameters. The commands in the example below create the logical variables MBell and MConfirm, a character variable named MDate, and two numeric variables named DateNo and MMargin. These variables are then stored in a memory variable file named SetUp.mem.

```
STORE .F. TO MBell, MConfirm
MDate = SPACE(8)
DateNo = 1
MMargin = 0
SAVE TO Setup
```

You can just type these commands directly at the dot prompt, because you need to create this setup file only once.

### Creating a User Interface

A program that allows a user to change SET parameter settings should first read in the current parameter settings, then display them on the screen for editing, and finally save the new settings. Figure 18.2 shows a sample program, named SetUp.prg, that demonstrates how to do this using the Setup.mem memory file created in the previous section. Figure 18.3 shows how the SetUp program looks on the screen when executed.

To select a date format, the user only has to enter a number instead of typing the whole format. Then a DO CASE clause stores the appropriate parameter (AMERICAN, ANSI, etc.) in the MDate variable, which will be used later by the actual application program.

In most application programs, the user will probably change these settings only occasionally. Therefore, you might want to include SetUp as an independent program that can be run outside of your application. However, if you

```
*************************************** SetUp.prg.
SET TALK OFF
SET STATUS OFF

*------------ Restore current settings.
CLEAR MEMORY
RESTORE FROM SetUp

*------------ Ask for new settings.
CLEAR
@ 1,0  TO 3,79 DOUBLE
@ 2,22 SAY "Select parameters for the system"
@ 5,2  SAY "Ring bell on filled entries? (Y/N) ";
       GET MBell PICTURE "Y"
@ 7,2  SAY "Require Return key on all entries? (Y/N) ";
       GET MConfirm PICTURE "Y"
@ 9,2  SAY "Enter left margin spaces for printer (0 - 32) ";
       GET MMargin PICTURE "99" RANGE 0,32
@ 11,2 SAY "Select a date format from below (1-6) ";
       GET DateNo PICTURE "9" RANGE 1,6
@ 12,1 TO 16,53
@ 13,2 SAY "1 = AMERICAN  (mm/dd/yy)    4 = ITALIAN  (dd-mm-yy)"
@ 14,2 SAY "2 = ANSI      (yy.mm.dd)    5 = FRENCH   (dd/mm/yy)"
@ 15,2 SAY "3 = BRITISH   (dd/mm/yy)    6 = GERMAN   (dd.mm.yy)"

Done = " "
@ 20,1 TO 22,79 DOUBLE
@ 21,3 SAY "Press "+CHR(24)+" to change, or Return if done ";
       GET Done

READ
*------- Convert date number to command.
DO CASE
   CASE DateNo = 1
        MDate = "AMERICAN"
   CASE DateNo = 2
        MDate = "ANSI"
   CASE DateNo = 3
        MDate = "BRITISH"
   CASE DateNo = 4
        MDate = "ITALIAN"
   CASE DateNo = 5
        MDate = "FRENCH"
   CASE DateNo = 6
        MDate = "GERMAN"
   OTHERWISE
        MDate = "AMERICAN"
ENDCASE
*------ Store appropriate values in memory file.
RELEASE Done
SAVE TO SetUp
```

**FIGURE 18.2:** A program named SetUp that allows the user to select options that define dBASE SET parameters. The program uses the RESTORE command to first read in current settings; then @...SAY...GET and READ commands allow the user to change these settings. The SAVE command then saves the new settings in the memory file.

prefer, you can make the SetUp program available as a menu option within your application. The choice is up to you and depends only on whatever you feel would be easiest for your users.

This setup program example is fairly simple. For applications that will be marketed on a large scale, you might want to use these same techniques to allow users

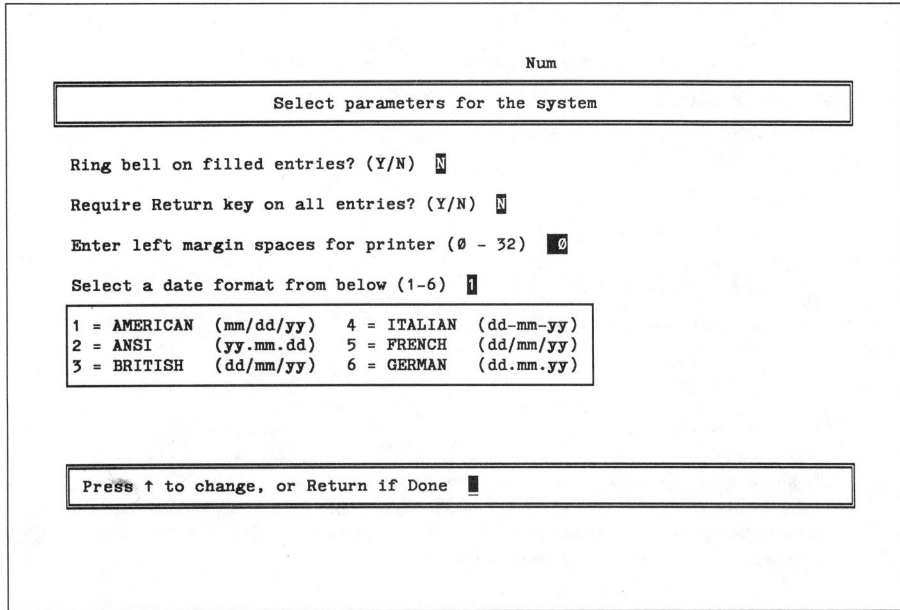


**FIGURE 18.3:** The screen display produced by the SetUp program shown in Figure 18.2. The user can define settings for any of the options displayed. The application program will use these settings in the future.

to define the default disk drive for locating files (SET DEFAULT), file search paths (SET PATH), screen colors (SET COLOR), printer ports (SET PRINTER), and function keys (SET FUNCTION).

## Activating User-Defined Parameters

An application program that supports user-defined parameter settings needs to read in all of the user's settings and apply them to the appropriate SET commands. It should perform this step before any others, so that the correct parameters are set from the start.

Figure 18.4 shows a portion of a sample program, named MainMenu.prg, that reads in the settings previously defined in the SetUp.mem file discussed above. (Presumably, the application main menu is displayed beneath the comment that reads ***----Display main menu.**)

As you can see in the figure, MainMenu starts by setting some fixed parameters that the user cannot alter (TALK and STATUS in this example). Then MainMenu reads in the user's parameters from the SetUp memory file using the RESTORE command.

```
************************************ MainMenu.prg
*-------------- First program run in application.
SET TALK OFF
SET STATUS OFF

*----- Set up user-defined parameters.
RESTORE FROM SetUp
BellStat = IIF(MBell,"ON","OFF")
SET BELL &BellStat
ConfStat = IIF(MConfirm,"ON","OFF")
SET CONFIRM &ConfStat

SET MARGIN TO MMargin
SET DATE &MDate

RELEASE ALL EXCEPT MDate

*--- Display main menu.
<commands...>
```

**FIGURE 18.4:** Portion of an application's main menu program that reads in user-defined parameter settings from a memory file named SetUp.mem. The program uses IIF functions to convert logical values to the words ON and OFF for use with the SET BELL and SET CONFIRM functions. The numeric variable MMargin can be used without any further treatment. The character variable MDate needs to be substituted into the command as a macro.

Because the BellStat and MConfirm variables are stored as logical values (either .T. or .F.), two IIF functions are used to convert these to ON or OFF character strings. These character strings are then substituted into the SET commands as macros (i.e., **SET BELL &BellStat**). The MARGIN setting is initially stored as a number, so it requires no further conversion; it is used directly in the command **SET MARGIN TO MMargin**. Similarly, the MDate value is stored as a character string (**AMERICAN**, for example), so it can be substituted into the SET DATE command as a macro.

Before displaying the main menu, the program releases all the memory variables (except MDate), because they are no longer needed. In this example, the MDate variable, which contains the date format definition, is saved for future use. For example, if this application uses an index file based on dates converted to ANSI format, the program may, at some time, need to switch to ANSI format temporarily to locate a particular date in an index file. To convert back to the user's selected date format after the lookup, the application can use the command **SET DATE &MDate** once again.

## COMMANDS USED TO SET ENVIRONMENTAL PARAMETERS

The remainder of this chapter discusses most of the SET commands used to control dBASE parameters. They are organized alphabetically. The following, specialized SET commands are only referenced in this chapter and are discussed in depth elsewhere in the book: SET RELATION (Chapter 3, "Database Design"); SET PROCEDURE (Chapter 5, "Procedures and Parameters"); SET DEBUG, SET DOHISTORY, SET ECHO, and SET STEP (Chapter 7, "Debugging Commands and Techniques"); and SET FORMAT (Chapter 8, "Managing Screen Displays").

## The SET Command

The SET command, when used alone, displays all current parameter settings and allows them to be changed through a menu.

### SYNTAX

**SET**

### USAGE

SET displays a full-screen, menu-driven technique for viewing and changing current parameter settings. Figure 18.5 shows the screen displayed by the SET command.

The → and ← keys move the highlight across the top-menu options. Each top-menu option has a pull-down menu associated with it. The ↑ and ↓ keys move the highlight through pull-down menu options. Pressing Return selects the currently highlighted item. To toggle the parameter between settings (e.g., from ON to OFF and vice versa), press Return. Additional instructions appear at the bottom of the screen as you work. For more help with a particular item, see the related SET command in this chapter. (For example, for additional information on the CENTURY option, see SET CENTURY.)

### EXAMPLE

At the dot prompt, enter the command

**SET**

to view or alter SET parameters.

### TIPS

The default values for most SET parameters can be redefined in the Config.db file as discussed in Appendix C, "Configuring dBASE III PLUS."

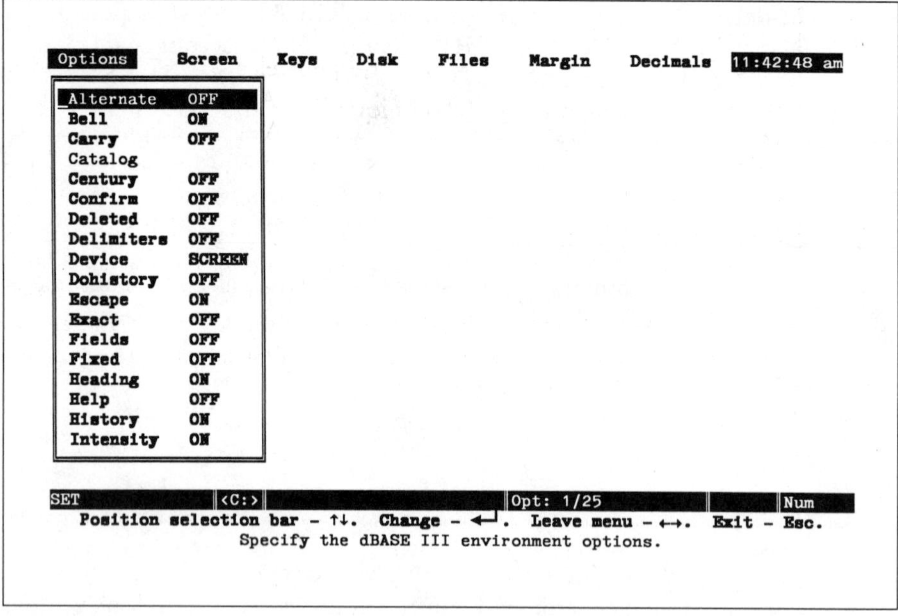


**FIGURE 18.5:** The screen displayed by the SET command, which shows the current status of all environmental parameters. The arrow keys move the highlight across the top-menu options and up and down through items in the pull-down menus. Pressing Return selects the currently highlighted item. Additional instructions appear at the bottom of the screen as you work.

### SEE ALSO

LIST STATUS
DISPLAY STATUS

## The SET ALTERNATE Command

SET ALTERNATE determines whether ensuing screen text is stored on the currently active alternate file.

### SYNTAX

**SET ALTERNATE [OFF][ON]**

where the default is OFF.

### USAGE

The SET ALTERNATE ON command tells dBASE to record all screen entries and displays except the output of @...SAY...GET commands in the currently open alternate file. The SET ALTERNATE OFF command temporarily deactivates the alternate file so that ensuing screen displays are not recorded. The SET ALTERNATE ON command reactivates the file. Once an alternate file is closed, there is no way to add new data to it. (The next SET ALTERNATE TO command to open the file would cause that file to be overwritten.)

Remember that SET ALTERNATE TO <file name> must precede the SET ALTERNATE ON command. Furthermore, the SET ALTERNATE TO <file name> command does not activate the alternate file; it only defines the file name. SET ALTERNATE ON is required to start recording text.

### EXAMPLE

The commands below create an alternate file named Text.txt, open that file, and copy the ? commands and their output in that file. The CLOSE ALTERNATE command then closes the alternate file.

```
SET ALTERNATE TO Text
SET ALTERNATE ON
? SQRT(144)
? "This is only a test."
SET ALTERNATE OFF
CLOSE ALTERNATE
```

### TIPS

There is no way in dBASE to direct @...SAY...GET displays to a file. The REPORT FORM command offers the TO FILE option for storing formatted reports in text files.

### SEE ALSO

SET ALTERNATE TO

## The SET ALTERNATE TO Command

SET ALTERNATE TO creates an ASCII text file to which dBASE can direct output.

#### SYNTAX

**SET ALTERNATE TO [<file name>]**

where <file name> is the name of the text file to create.

#### USAGE

The SET ALTERNATE TO command must be used before the SET ALTERNATE ON command for the text to be created. The text file name will have a .txt extension unless otherwise specified.

Not using the <file name> clause will close the alternate file. (The CLOSE ALTERNATE command also closes the file.)

If a file of the requested name already exists when the SET ALTERNATE TO command is issued, that file will be overwritten when SET ALTERNATE ON activates it.

#### EXAMPLE

The command

**SET ALTERNATE TO AltFile**

creates a text file named AltFile.txt, which will capture screen text when SET ALTERNATE is on.

#### TIPS

Make sure that you close the alternate file when done recording text to ensure that the information is properly saved.

#### SEE ALSO

SET ALTERNATE

## The SET BELL Command

SET BELL determines whether the warning bell sounds when you type beyond the width of a field or enter an invalid data type.

#### SYNTAX

**SET BELL [OFF][ON]**

where the default is ON.

### USAGE

Use SET BELL OFF to prevent the bell from ringing repeatedly on screen displays that include many fields.

### EXAMPLE

In the example that follows, the bell will ring if the user fills any of the memory variables completely. By setting the bell off after the READ command, the bell will not ring when the user answers the yes/no question.

```
STORE SPACE(20) TO Name, Address, City
YesNo = " "
SET BELL ON
@ 5,5 SAY "Enter name:" GET Name
@ 6,5 SAY "Enter address:" GET Address
@ 7,5 SAY "Enter city:" GET City
READ
SET BELL OFF
@ 10,5 SAY "Continue ? " GET YesNo
READ
```

### TIPS

The command ? CHR(7) always causes the bell to ring, regardless of the status of the SET BELL parameter.

### SEE ALSO

SET CONFIRM

## The SET CARRY Command

SET CARRY copies data from the previous record to the next record when using the APPEND or INSERT commands.

### SYNTAX

**SET CARRY [OFF][ON]**

where the default is OFF.

### USAGE

Using the SET CARRY ON command can be beneficial in some data-entry programs where much information is repeated from one record to the next. This command minimizes typing mistakes and accelerates data entry.

The new record that is appended or inserted will not be saved unless some changes are made or a Ctrl-W or Ctrl-End command is entered.

### EXAMPLE

The commands below set the carry option on before data are entered through the custom form MailScr:

```
USE Mail
SET FORMAT TO MailScr
SET CARRY ON
APPEND
```

### TIPS

Chapter 10, "Adding New Data," shows a data-entry routine that allows a user to decide whether to carry data to the next new record on a record-by-record basis.

### SEE ALSO

APPEND
INSERT
READ
SET FORMAT

## The SET CATALOG Command

SET CATALOG determines whether files are added to an open catalog.

### SYNTAX

**SET CATALOG [OFF][ON]**

where the default is OFF. However, using the **SET CATALOG TO <file name>** command automatically sets CATALOG to ON.

### USAGE

If CATALOG is set to ON and is used in conjunction with the SET CATALOG TO command, the open catalog is updated automatically by commands such as CREATE, INDEX, and CREATE/MODIFY REPORT. By issuing the SET CATALOG OFF command, the files used by these commands will not be entered into the catalog.

### EXAMPLE

In the commands below, the Mail database and Names and Zips index files are stored in the MailList catalog, but the Temp index file is not stored in the catalog:

```
SET CATALOG TO MailList
USE Mail
INDEX ON UPPER(LName + FName) TO Names
INDEX ON Zip TO Zips
SET CATALOG OFF
INDEX ON City TO Temp
```

### TIPS

There is a difference between the SET CATALOG TO and the SET CATALOG OFF commands. SET CATALOG TO (without a file name) simply closes the catalog. SET CATALOG OFF keeps the catalog open and lets you use the catalog query clause ("?") to select files from the catalog.

### SEE ALSO

SET CATALOG TO

## The SET CATALOG TO Command

SET CATALOG TO creates and activates a new catalog, activates an existing catalog, or closes an open catalog.

### SYNTAX

**SET CATALOG TO [<file name>]**

where <file name> is the name of the catalog file, with the .cat extension.

## USAGE

Catalog files are used to group the names of files belonging to a particular application into a single file. Though assigned the file-name extension .cat, catalog files are actually dBASE database files.

Using the command **SET CATALOG TO <file name>** opens the catalog file if it exists, or creates it if it doesn't exist, and activates the catalog in the same way that SET CATALOG ON does. The first time you create a catalog file on a directory, dBASE automatically creates a file called Catalog.cat. The names of all future catalog files created on that directory are stored in the Catalog.cat file.

SET CATALOG TO provides you with a way to query a catalog and see a menu of all files related to the database file in use. When the SET CATALOG ON command is used, all files opened or created are added to the catalog. This includes index (.ndx) and report (.frm) files. As new files are added, you are prompted for a descriptive name up to 49 characters to store in the open catalog.

Once a SET CATALOG TO <file name> command is issued, you can use the ?, known as the query clause, in many commands to ask the catalog for a display of all related files.

## EXAMPLE

The commands below open an existing catalog named My_File.cat and check the catalog for existing database, report, and index file names:

```
SET CATALOG TO My_File
USE ?                      && Select a file from the menu
SET CATALOG OFF            && Catalog can still be queried
REPORT FORM ? TO PRINT     && Select a report from the menu
SET INDEX TO ?             && Select an index from the menu
SET CATALOG ON
```

## TIPS

An open catalog counts as an open file and uses the SELECT 10 work area.

The SET CATALOG and SET CATALOG TO commands are of no real value to the dBASE programmer and are generally used only by beginners and occasional dBASE users.

## SEE ALSO

SET CATALOG

## The SET CENTURY Command

SET CENTURY allows the input and display of century prefixes on the year portion of dates.

### SYNTAX

**SET CENTURY [OFF][ON]**

where the default is OFF (indicating that the century cannot be displayed or input).

### USAGE

Using SET CENTURY ON displays a four-digit year. Using SET CENTURY OFF displays a two-digit year and assumes the 20th century.

### EXAMPLE

The commands below accept two dates from the screen—one in mm/dd/yy format and the other in mm/dd/yyyy format:

```
STORE DATE( ) TO mdate1,mdate2
SET CENTURY ON
@ 12,5 SAY "Enter date:" GET mdate1
READ
SET CENTURY OFF
@ 13,5 SAY "Enter date:" GET mdate2
READ
@ 16,5 SAY "First date was " + mdate1
@ 17,5 SAY "Second date was " + mdate2
```

### TIPS

Although SET CENTURY ON displays a four-digit year instead of the usual two-digit year, the database field size is always eight bytes long, because the date is stored internally as a number.

### SEE ALSO

CTOD( )
DATE( )
DTOC( )

## The SET COLOR Command

SET COLOR allows you to change the colors displayed on the screen.

### SYNTAX

**SET COLOR TO [<standard>][,<enhanced>][,<border>];**
**[,<background>]**
**SET COLOR ON/OFF**

where <standard> is the basic dBASE screen, <enhanced> is reversed video, <border> is the screen border, and <background> is the background color setting used only on some monitors.

### USAGE

To display a particular color combination, use the letter codes presented in Table 18.1. In the command, the color of the text comes first, followed by a slash and the background color. For example, **R/W** displays red letters on a white background. The U (underline) and I (inverse) options work only on monochrome monitors.

The <standard> portion of the command affects the usual text display,

| COLOR | CODE |
|---|---|
| Black | N |
| Blue | B |
| Green | G |
| Cyan | BG |
| Red | R |
| Magenta | RB |
| Brown | GR |
| White | W |
| Underline | U (monochrome) |
| Inverse | I (monochrome) |
| Blank | X |
| Blinking | * |
| High intensity | + |

**TABLE 18.1:** Color Codes Used with the SET COLOR Command

including displays by the ?, LIST, REPORT, and SAY commands. The <enhanced> portion of the command affects those characters displayed in reverse video, such as highlighted menu options and data displayed by the GET command. The <border> portion affects the border color (assuming the particular monitor in use has a border). The <background> portion applies to color monitors that can't set the individual background colors for standard and enhanced display. The * symbol for blinking and + character for high intensity work only for foregrounds (the actual typed letters).

Use SET COLOR ON/OFF to switch between color and monochrome screens on computers that have both.

## EXAMPLE

To set standard video with yellow letters on a red background, enhanced video with white letters on a red background, and the border to yellow, type the following from the dot prompt:

**SET COLOR TO GR + /R,W/R,GR +**

To set these same colors on a machine that can't set individual character backgrounds, type the following:

**SET COLOR TO GR + , W, GR + , R**

The commands below display an error message with blinking yellow letters on a red background:

```
ErrMsg = "Invalid entry!"
SET COLOR TO GR + */R
@ 12,35 SAY ErrMsg
```

## TIPS

The X color combination can be used for password entry to make any typed characters invisible.

The Screen menu on the SET command screen allows you to experiment with color combinations and view the results immediately.

The Color program in Figure 18.6 displays all the possible color combinations, including high intensity and blinking, and also shows the color codes used to create each color combination. If you want to see its display on a color monitor, you can key it in and run it.

## SEE ALSO

SET INTENSITY
SET

```
**************************************** Color.prg
*----- Display colors & blinking for color screen.
CLEAR
SET TALK OFF

*---------- Set letters for dBASE III PLUS colors.
X0 = "N"     && Black
X1 = "B"     && Blue
X2 = "G"     && Green
X3 = "BG"    && Cyan
X4 = "R"     && Red
X5 = "RB"    && Magenta
X6 = "GR"    && Brown
X7 = "W"     && White
*-------------------- Display standard foreground.
OutLoop = 0
DO WHILE OutLoop <= 7
   InLoop = 0
   DO WHILE InLoop <= 7
      Letters = "X"+STR(OutLoop,1)
      BGround = "X"+Str(InLoop,1)
      JJ = &Letters + "/" + &BGround
      SET COLOR TO &JJ
      ?? "  "+JJ+ "  "
      InLoop = InLoop + 1
   ENDDO
   OutLoop = OutLoop + 1
ENDDO

*--------------- Display enhanced foreground (+).
OutLoop = 0
DO WHILE OutLoop <= 7
   InLoop = 0
   DO WHILE InLoop <= 7
      Letters = "X"+STR(OutLoop,1)
      BGround = "X"+Str(InLoop,1)
      JJ = &Letters + "+/" + &BGround
      SET COLOR TO &JJ
      ?? "  "+JJ+ "  "
      InLoop = InLoop + 1
   ENDDO
   OutLoop = OutLoop + 1
ENDDO

*--------------- Display blinking foreground (*).
OutLoop = 0
DO WHILE OutLoop <= 7
   InLoop = 0
   DO WHILE InLoop <= 7
      Letters = "X"+STR(OutLoop,1)
      BGround = "X"+Str(InLoop,1)
      JJ = &Letters + "*/" + &BGround
      SET COLOR TO &JJ
      ?? "  "+JJ+ "  "
      InLoop = InLoop + 1
   ENDDO
   OutLoop = OutLoop + 1
ENDDO
*------ Pause before ending program.
SET COLOR TO GR+/B,N/BG,G
WAIT "Press any key when done viewing..."
```

**FIGURE 18.6:** The Color program displays all of the possible color combinations available through the SET COLOR command, including blinking and high intensity.

## The SET CONFIRM Command

Determines whether a user can type beyond the end of a field prompt without pressing the Return key.

### SYNTAX

**SET CONFIRM [OFF][ON]**

where the default is OFF.

### USAGE

With the SET CONFIRM ON command, the Return key must be pressed to finish entering data into any field. When SET CONFIRM is off, filling the field prompt will automatically move the cursor out of the field, even if the Return key is not pressed.

### EXAMPLE

The commands below let the user enter a Y or N character but require that the user also press Return after entering the character:

```
YesNo = .F.
SET CONFIRM ON
@ 23,1 SAY "Return to menu now? ";
    GET YesNo PICTURE "Y"
READ
```

### TIPS

SET CONFIRM ON can be particularly useful during data-entry processes where it is advisable that the user press the Return key before continuing to the next field. Although more keystrokes are required, it allows the user the chance to change the entry before continuing and thus increases data integrity.

### SEE ALSO

@...SAY...GET

## The SET CONSOLE Command

SET CONSOLE turns the screen either off or on for screen display other than @...SAY commands.

### SYNTAX

**SET CONSOLE [OFF][ON]**

where the default is ON.

### USAGE

This command is normally used to turn off the screen so that commands that send a message back to the screen can be handled by other programming techniques and commands. The SET CONSOLE command will not affect output to a printer.

### EXAMPLE

The commands below display the message **Press End to terminate report** on the screen and print a formatted report. The report is displayed only on the printer:

```
SET CONSOLE OFF
@ 2,2 SAY "Press End to terminate report"
REPORT FORM AnyRep WHILE INKEY( ) # 6 TO PRINT
SET CONSOLE ON
```

### TIPS

The SET CONSOLE OFF command can be used when sending special control characters to the printer so that graphic characters are not unintentionally displayed on the screen.

### SEE ALSO

SET PRINT
SET DEVICE

## The SET DATE Command

SET DATE determines the format for date expressions.

### SYNTAX

**SET DATE <format>**

where <format> is any valid dBASE date format.

## USAGE

Regardless of the format used to enter a date, the SET DATE command will display all dates in the specified format. Table 18.2 lists the date formats available.

## EXAMPLE

The series of commands below demonstrate various formats for the date January 1, 1989.

```
Date = CTOD("01/28/89")
? Date
     01/28/89

SET DATE BRITISH
? Date
     28/01/89

SET DATE ANSI
? Date
     89.01.28

SET DATE AMERICAN
? Date
     01/28/89
```

## TIPS

The SET DATE ANSI format can be used to ensure that dates converted to character strings in index files are still properly sorted by years. See Chapter 12, "Sorting and Indexing," for details.

| SETTING | FORMAT |
|---|---|
| AMERICAN | mm/dd/yy |
| ANSI | yy.mm.dd |
| BRITISH | dd/mm/yy |
| ITALIAN | dd-mm-yy |
| FRENCH | dd/mm/yy |
| GERMAN | dd.mm.yy |

**TABLE 18.2:** Formats Used with the SET DATE Command

#### SEE ALSO

DATE( )
INDEX

## The SET DEBUG Command

SET DEBUG determines whether output from SET ECHO ON is sent to the screen or the printer. See Chapter 7, "Debugging Commands and Techniques," for details.

## The SET DECIMALS Command

SET DECIMALS determines the minimum number of decimal places displayed in the results of numeric functions and calculations.

#### SYNTAX

**SET DECIMALS TO <width>**

where <width> is a number representing the number of decimal places to display.

#### USAGE

SET DECIMALS is generally used with the SET FIXED command to determine a fixed number of decimal places when displaying calculation results.

#### EXAMPLE

The commands below demonstrate the result of a calculation first in the default mode and then after defining a decimal width with the SET DECIMALS and SET FIXED commands:

```
? 123.456 * 22.8
     2814.7968

SET DECIMALS TO 2
SET FIXED ON
? 123.456 * 22.8
     2814.80
```

### TIPS

If SET FIXED is not on, SET DECIMALS will not affect multiplication. The SET DECIMALS and SET FIXED commands, as well as the ROUND( ) function, are useful for rounding numbers.

### SEE ALSO

SET FIXED
ROUND( )

## The SET DEFAULT Command

SET DEFAULT selects a disk drive for storing and accessing files.

### SYNTAX

**SET DEFAULT TO <drive>**

where <disk drive> is a letter representing the disk drive. The default is the currently logged drive.

### USAGE

Use the SET DEFAULT command to change the drive used for reading and writing of database, index, memory, procedure, format, and alternate files.

### EXAMPLE

The command below searches the disk in drive B for a database file named MyFile:

```
SET DEFAULT TO B
USE MyFile
```

### TIPS

The colon that usually follows a disk drive name (A:) can be omitted in the SET DEFAULT command.

### SEE ALSO

SET PATH

## The SET DELETED Command

SET DELETED determines whether records marked for deletion are hidden.

### SYNTAX

**SET DELETED [OFF][ON]**

where the default is OFF.

### USAGE

Use the SET DELETED command as a filter on the database to mask out those records marked for deletion. Once the SET DELETED ON command is issued, records that are marked for deletion are invisible to all dBASE commands until a SET DELETED OFF command is issued.

### EXAMPLE

The commands below exclude records that are marked for deletion from the SUM and AVERAGE calculations:

```
SET DELETED ON
SUM Qty * Unit_Price TO TotSale
AVERAGE Qty * Unit_Price TO AvgSale
```

### TIPS

The FOR .NOT. DELETED( ) option can be used as an alternative to SET DELETED to exclude records that are marked for deletion. For example, the command below displays only records that are not marked for deletion, regardless of the SET DELETED setting:

```
LIST FOR .NOT. DELETED( )
```

### SEE ALSO

SET FILTER

## The SET DELIMITERS Command

SET DELIMITERS determines whether delimiters are displayed around data-entry and editing fields.

### SYNTAX

**SET DELIMITERS [OFF][ON]**

where the default is OFF.

### USAGE

The SET DELIMITERS ON command places delimiters around the highlighted entry field displayed by a GET command, as well as around the highlighted fields on the default screens for APPEND, EDIT, and INSERT.

### EXAMPLE

The commands below enclose all data-entry fields in curly braces when an APPEND, EDIT, READ, or INSERT command is issued:

**SET DELIMITERS TO "{ }"**
**SET DELIMITERS ON**

### TIPS

When SET DELIMITERS is off, data-entry fields are displayed in reverse video or highlighting only.

### SEE ALSO

SET DELIMITERS TO

## The SET DELIMITERS TO Command

SET DELIMITERS TO defines the characters that delimit the data-entry and editing fields.

### SYNTAX

**SET DELIMITERS TO [<characters>] [DEFAULT]**

where <characters> are the delimiters to display enclosed in quotation marks, and DEFAULT represents the default colon (:) characters.

### USAGE

Either one or two characters can be specified in the command. If only one character is specified, that character is used on both sides of the field display. If two characters are entered, the first character represents the delimiter on the left side of the field, and the second character represents the delimiter on the right side of the field.

### EXAMPLE

The commands below display square brackets around data-entry fields when an APPEND, EDIT, READ, or INSERT command is issued:

**SET DELIMITERS TO "[]"**
**SET DELIMITERS ON**

### TIPS

No matter what the delimiters are set to, if the SET DELIMITERS OFF command is in effect, no delimiters are used.

### SEE ALSO

SET DELIMITERS
SET INTENSITY
@...SAY...GET
READ

## The SET DEVICE Command

SET DEVICE determines whether the @...SAY command will be displayed on the screen or the printer.

### SYNTAX

**SET DEVICE TO [PRINT] [SCREEN]**

where the default is SCREEN.

### USAGE

The SET DEVICE TO SCREEN command channels all output from @...SAY commands to the screen. SET DEVICE TO PRINT channels all @...SAY command displays to the printer.

### EXAMPLE

The commands below display the message **Hi there...** on the screen and **I'm over here now...** on the printer:

```
@ 10,10 SAY "Hi there..."
SET DEVICE TO PRINT
@ 10,10 SAY "I'm over here now..."
EJECT
SET DEVICE TO SCREEN
```

### TIPS

SET DEVICE TO PRINT channels only @...SAY output to the printer, not @...GET or any other output. To channel other output to the printer, use the SET PRINT ON command or the TO PRINT option with the appropriate command.

Attempting to move up a row when displaying @...SAY commands on the printer will cause a page eject. For example, in the commands below, the line **This is line one** appears on one page and **Tried to skip back a line!** appears on the next page:

```
SET DEVICE TO PRINT
@ 5,1 SAY "This is line one"
@ 4,1 SAY "Tried to skip back a line!"
```

To print both lines on the same page, reverse the order of the two @ commands so @ 4,1 is executed before @ 5,1.

### SEE ALSO

SET PRINT ON
@...SAY

## The SET DOHISTORY Command

SET DOHISTORY determines whether commands from command files are recorded as they are executed. See Chapter 7, "Debugging Commands and Techniques," for details.

## The SET ECHO Command

SET ECHO displays command lines from dBASE III PLUS programs on the screen and/or the printer while running the programs. It is used as a debugging tool by the programmer. See Chapter 7, "Debugging Commands and Techniques," for details.

## The SET ESCAPE Command

SET ESCAPE determines whether the Esc key interrupts processing.

### SYNTAX

**SET ESCAPE [OFF][ON]**

where the default is ON.

### USAGE

If the Esc key is pressed while a program is running and SET ESCAPE ON is in effect, the program stops and the following message is displayed:

**Called from - <file name.prg>**
**Cancel, Ignore, Suspend? (C,I, or S)**

If the Esc key is pressed while executing a command from the dot prompt and SET ESCAPE ON is in effect, the message *** **INTERRUPTED** *** is displayed, and the dot prompt appears.

If the SET ESCAPE OFF command is issued, pressing Esc will not do anything.

### EXAMPLE

The command

**SET ESCAPE OFF**

near the top of an application program prevents the user from being able to interrupt processing by pressing the Esc key.

### TIPS

If you press the Esc key during a program to temporarily stop the processing, you are presented with three options: Cancel, Ignore, and Suspend. If you choose Cancel, the program terminates and returns you to the dot prompt. If you select Ignore, the program resumes immediately. If you select Suspend, you can view memory variables or change the pointers in the database file from the dot prompt and then resume processing by typing RESUME.

You can use the ON ESCAPE command to trap the Esc keypress and direct processing to a procedure to handle the keypress. See Chapter 19, "Event Processing and Error Trapping," for complete details.

#### SEE ALSO

ON ESCAPE

## The SET EXACT Command

SET EXACT determines how a comparison between two character expressions is evaluated.

#### SYNTAX

**SET EXACT [OFF][ON]**

where the default is OFF.

#### USAGE

The SET EXACT OFF command makes a character-by-character comparison between the two character expressions and allows for a match to be made if the shorter string matches the characters on the left side of the longer string.

#### EXAMPLE

The commands below will list all individuals whose last names begin with the letters Black, including Black, Blackwell, Blacksmith, etc.

```
SET EXACT OFF
LIST FOR LName = "Black"
```

The following commands will display only the individuals with the last name Black:

```
SET EXACT ON
LIST FOR LName = "Black"
```

#### TIPS

SET EXACT affects only character-string comparisons.

#### SEE ALSO

TRIM( )
LTRIM( )
RTRIM( )

## The SET FIELDS Command

SET FIELDS allows you to use or ignore the list of fields defined with the SET FIELDS TO command.

#### SYNTAX

**SET FIELDS [OFF][ON]**

where the default is OFF.

#### USAGE

If SET FIELDS is off, all fields of the active database are available for display, entry, and editing. Fields in other files are also available by using their aliases.

If SET FIELDS is on, the fields that are available for display or entry are limited to those listed with the SET FIELDS TO command.

#### EXAMPLE

The commands below "hide" all fields from the currently open database except the CustNo, Qty, Unit_Price, and Date fields:

```
SET FIELDS TO CustNo, Qty, Unit_Price, Date
SET FIELDS ON
```

#### TIPS

SET FIELDS ON allows editing of fields from files beyond the one in the currently selected database file by specifying fields from the unselected database. For example, the commands below open two files and allow editing of two fields from each file:

```
SELECT A
USE Sales
SELECT B
USE Master INDEX Master
```

```
SELECT A
SET RELATION TO PartNo INTO Master
SET FIELDS TO PartNo,B->PartName,Qty,B->Unit_Price
SET FIELDS ON
EDIT
```

### SEE ALSO

SET FIELDS TO
SET VIEW

## The SET FIELDS TO Command

SET FIELDS TO defines a list of fields to be displayed that can be accessed by one or more files.

### SYNTAX

**SET FIELDS TO [<field list>/ALL]**

where <field list> is a list of field names, separated by commas, of fields to include in displays.

### USAGE

SET FIELDS TO only defines fields to be displayed. The field definition is not activated until a SET FIELDS ON command is issued. Additional SET FIELDS TO commands add new field names to the existing field name list. The SET FIELDS TO ALL command makes all fields accessible.

To include fields from a separate, related database file, select that work area with the SELECT command, or use the file's alias with the field names. When the SET FIELDS TO command includes fields from multiple files, all the fields are displayed as though from a single file. However, records can still be appended and inserted only into the currently selected database file. When they are appended or inserted, all fields are accessible from the selected file.

When you use LIST or DISPLAY STRUCTURE with a SET FIELDS ON command in effect, those fields on the field list will have a greater than (>) symbol to the left of the field named.

### EXAMPLE

In the commands below, the SET FIELDS command specifies the PartNo and Qty fields from the Sales database and the PartName, Unit_Price, and Taxable fields from the Master database. The commands beneath the SET FIELDS ON command display data and perform calculations using the five defined fields.

```
SELECT A
USE Sales
SELECT B
USE Master INDEX Master

SELECT A
SET RELATION TO PartNo INTO Master

SET FIELDS TO PartNo,B->PartName,Qty, ;
                  B->Unit_Price, B->Taxable
SET FIELDS ON
LIST            && Displays five fields.
* -- Calculate total sale.
SUM (Qty * Unit_Price) * IIF(Taxable,1.06,1) TO Total
```

### TIPS

Once you've defined a relationship between databases, you can display fields using the alias arrows (i.e., B->) without using the SET FIELDS commands at all. For most programmers this is the preferred method, because it offers more field-by-field control over data being displayed and edited. For more information on multiple database files and database relations, see Chapter 3, "Database Design."

### SEE ALSO

@...GET
MODIFY VIEW
SET VIEW
SELECT
SET RELATION

## The SET FILTER Command

SET FILTER hides records in a database file that do not match a specified condition.

### SYNTAX

**SET FILTER TO [<condition>][FILE<file name>]**

where <condition> is any valid dBASE search criterion, or <file name> is the name of a query (.qry) file created by MODIFY QUERY.

### USAGE

If a condition is given, the SET FILTER command will mask the database so that only those records that meet the condition will be shown. SET FILTER applies only to the database file open in the work area where the command is issued. If several database files are open simultaneously, a separate and unique filter can be set for each work area.

**SET FILTER TO FILE <file name>** reads the filter condition from a query (.qry) file established by the CREATE/MODIFY QUERY command.

**SET FILTER TO** without a condition will turn off the filter on the active database and allow all records to be accessed.

### EXAMPLE

The example below masks the LIST display to show only those records that fit the prescribed condition. In this case, monthly sales commissions must exceed $10,000 to be displayed:

```
USE Salesmen INDEX Sales_name
SET FILTER TO "Mth_Comm >= 10000"
GO TOP
LIST
```

If a MODIFY QUERY command was used to define a filtering condition and the query was saved under the file name Query1, the command below would activate that query without redisplaying the MODIFY QUERY form:

```
SET FILTER TO FILE Query1
```

The command below deactivates any filter condition in the current work area, thereby making all records in the database file accessible once again:

```
SET FILTER TO
```

### TIPS

In programs, the command GO TOP should be used immediately after a SET FILTER command to reposition the record pointer to the top of the newly filtered database. This is because filters are not activated until the record pointer is moved.

### SEE ALSO

CREATE/MODIFY QUERY

## The SET FIXED Command

SET FIXED determines whether numeric data are displayed with a fixed number of decimal places as set by the SET DECIMALS command.

### SYNTAX

**SET FIXED [OFF][ON]**

where OFF is the default value.

### USAGE

IF SET FIXED is on, all numeric values are displayed with the number of decimal places specified in the most recent SET DECIMALS command.

### EXAMPLE

The commands below demonstrate the results of calculations before and after setting the FIXED parameter on.

```
? 123.456 * 456.321
      56335.565376

? 27 ^ (1/3)
      3.00

? 999.9999999 * 10
      9999.9999990

SET DECIMALS TO 2
SET FIXED ON

? 123.456 * 456.321
      56335.57

? 27 ^ (1/3)
      3.00
```

```
? 999.9999999 * 10
      10000.00
```

### TIPS

SET FIXED and SET DECIMALS can be used in lieu of the ROUND( ) function to round numbers.

### SEE ALSO

SET DECIMALS
ROUND( )

## The SET FORMAT Command

SET FORMAT selects a custom format that has been previously stored in a format (.fmt) file. This command is discussed in detail in Chapter 8, "Managing Screen Displays."

## The SET FUNCTION Command

SET FUNCTION allows each function key to be reprogrammed to represent a character expression up to 30 characters long.

### SYNTAX

**SET FUNCTION <key> TO <string>[;]**

where <key> is the name of the function key to program, <string> is the string of up to 30 characters that the key is to type, and the optional semicolon represents a press on the Return key.

### USAGE

The first expression, which identifies the function key, can be numeric or character, depending on whether your terminal has numbered function keys. If you have numbered function keys, use the numeric expression of the key; if your terminal does not have numbered function keys, use a character expression to enter the name of the programmable function key.

The semicolon causes a carriage return to be generated when you press the function key. The semicolon must follow the command and be inside the quotation marks surrounding the string.

Table 18.3 shows the default function key assignments used by dBASE. Any key except F1 can be changed with the SET FUNCTION command.

## EXAMPLE

The following example allows you to run WordStar from the dot prompt so that you need not leave dBASE III PLUS to edit a command file with WordStar:

**SET FUNCTION 10 TO "RUN WS;"**

The command below sets up function key 9 to perform three commands: CLOSE PROCEDURE, CANCEL, and MODIFY COMMAND (the abbreviated versions of the commands are used to fit them into the 30-character limit):

**SET FUNCTION 9 TO "CLOSE PROC;CANCEL;MODI COMM "**

## TIPS

Note that the multiple commands can be chained together in the character expression as long as they do not exceed 30 characters in length. Be sure to put a semicolon between each command.

## SEE ALSO

FKLABEL( )
FKMAX( )

| KEY | DEFAULT VALUE |
|---|---|
| F1 | help; |
| F2 | assist; |
| F3 | list; |
| F4 | dir; |
| F5 | display structure; |
| F6 | display status; |
| F7 | display memory; |
| F8 | display: |
| F9 | append; |
| F10 | edit; |

**TABLE 18.3:** Default Settings for Function Keys

## The SET HEADING Command

SET HEADING determines whether column titles are shown above each field for the DISPLAY, LIST, SUM, and AVERAGE commands.

### SYNTAX

**SET HEADING [OFF][ON]**

where the default is ON.

### USAGE

Normally, the commands DISPLAY, LIST, SUM, and AVERAGE display a column title for each displayed field, memory variable, or expression. When SET HEADING is OFF, the column titles will not be displayed.

### EXAMPLE

In the example below, the LIST command displays field names and expressions above each column, as shown:

```
SET HEADING ON
LIST PartNo,Qty,B->Unit_Price,(Qty*B->Unit_Price)

PartNo  Qty  B->Unit_Price  (Qty*B->Unit_Price)
A-111    1          100.00               100.00
B-222    2          150.00               300.00
```

With HEADING set off, only the actual data are displayed, as below:

```
SET HEADING OFF
LIST PartNo,Qty,B->Unit_Price,(Qty*B->Unit_Price)

A-111    1          100.00               100.00
B-222    2          150.00               300.00
```

### TIPS

The column width will be either the length of the heading or the length of the field, whichever is larger.

#### SEE ALSO

LIST
DISPLAY

## The SET HELP Command

SET HELP determines whether the query **Do you want some help? (Y/N)** appears when a command is incorrectly entered from the dot prompt.

#### SYNTAX

**SET HELP [OFF][ON]**

where the default is ON.

#### USAGE

When you opt for help in response to the error prompt, the HELP screen for the command in the line being executed is displayed regardless of the actual cause of the error.

#### TIPS

Even when SET HELP is OFF, you can still access the dBASE help system directly from the dot prompt. For example, for help on the USE command, enter the command

**HELP USE**

at the dot prompt. (HELP works only if the dBASE Help.dbs file is available on the disk.)

#### SEE ALSO

HELP

## The SET HISTORY Command

SET HISTORY turns the HISTORY feature on and off.

## SYNTAX

**SET HISTORY [OFF][ON]**

where the default is ON.

## USAGE

The HISTORY feature allows commands that have been entered from the dot prompt to be recalled, edited, and executed again. To recall a command, press the ↑ key repeatedly when the dot prompt is displayed until the command you want is displayed. You can use the arrow, Ins, and Del keys to edit the command; press Return to reexecute the command.

## EXAMPLE

The HISTORY feature is useful when you want to create a new index file that resembles the one just created. For example, you might have just created an index file as follows:

**USE My_file**
**INDEX ON Zip + UPPER(LName + FName) TO Index1**

To enter a similar command without retyping, press ↑ until the INDEX command line reappears. Then, using the arrow keys and the Del and Ins keys, you can change the command as in the line below to create the second index file:

**INDEX ON STR(Age,2) UPPER(LName + FName) TO Index2**

## TIPS

The HISTORY command applies only to commands entered at the dot prompt. To include commands from programs in the history file, you must set the DOHISTORY command on.

## SEE ALSO

DISPLAY HISTORY
LIST HISTORY
SET DOHISTORY
SET HISTORY TO

## The SET HISTORY TO Command

SET HISTORY specifies the number of command lines to be stored in the history file.

### SYNTAX

**SET HISTORY TO <number>**

where <number> is the number of lines to include in the history file.

### USAGE

The default value for SET HISTORY TO is 20. The allowable range of commands stored is from 0 to 16,000.

If HISTORY is set to a number that is less than the number of commands currently stored in HISTORY, all stored commands are erased. Otherwise, they are saved, and new commands are appended to the list.

### TIPS

To calculate the amount of memory that HISTORY consumes, add nine bytes to the number of bytes in each command.

### SEE ALSO

SET HISTORY
DISPLAY HISTORY
LIST HISTORY
SET DOHISTORY

## The SET INDEX Command

SET INDEX activates index files for the currently open database file.

### SYNTAX

**SET INDEX TO [<file names>]**

where <file names> is the list of all index files to activate.

#### USAGE

A maximum of seven index files can be opened at once for a given database. The first listed index file is the master index, which determines the sort order of the records in the database. The master index is the only one that can be searched with a SEEK or FIND command. All listed index files are updated automatically when data are changed on the database file.

**SET INDEX TO** by itself closes all the index files for the given database. It has the same effect as the CLOSE INDEX command.

#### EXAMPLE

The command line below causes both the NameOrd and ZipOrd index files to be updated automatically whenever information is added to, changed, or deleted from the Mail database. The NameOrd index determines the sort order and is the only index file that can be searched with SEEK or FIND.

**USE Mail INDEX NameOrd,ZipOrd**

#### TIPS

Note that the SET INDEX TO command merely *opens* existing index files; it cannot be used to *create* new index files.

#### SEE ALSO

CLOSE
INDEX
REINDEX
SET ORDER
USE

## The SET INTENSITY Command

SET INTENSITY determines whether the fields in a database are highlighted in reverse video for full-screen commands such as EDIT and APPEND.

#### SYNTAX

**SET INTENSITY [OFF][ON]**

where the default is ON (indicating that reverse video is normally in effect).

### USAGE

Normally, there are two types of screen attributes: standard and enhanced. When INTENSITY is set ON, the enhanced attributes are displayed in reverse video for full-screen operations. When INTENSITY is set OFF, the standard attribute is used for both standard and enhanced areas.

### EXAMPLE

The commands below allow the user to enter records through a custom screen named CustScre. Entry fields are not displayed in reverse video, but instead are displayed with bracket delimiters.

```
USE AnyFile INDEX AnyIndex
SET FORMAT TO CustScre
SET DELIMITERS TO "[ ]"
SET DELIMITERS ON
SET INTENSITY OFF

APPEND
```

### TIPS

If SET INTENSITY is off, the SET DELIMITERS command should be used to identify the field entry areas on the screen.

### SEE ALSO

SET COLOR
SET DELIMITERS
SET DELIMITERS TO

## The SET MARGIN Command

SET MARGIN adjusts the left margin for all printed output.

### SYNTAX

**SET MARGIN TO <number>**

where <number> is the amount of characters to leave blank in the left margin.

### USAGE

The default value for the printer margin is zero. The SET MARGIN command lets you reset this margin to any number of spaces. SET MARGIN affects only printed output; it has no effect on video display.

### EXAMPLE

The commands below print all records in the Mail database with a left margin of 10 characters.

```
USE Mail
SET MARGIN TO 10
LIST TO PRINT
```

### TIPS

When printing reports with the **REPORT FORM <AnyFile> TO PRINT** command, the left margin setting specified in MODIFY REPORT is added to the SET MARGIN setting.

### SEE ALSO

MODIFY REPORT
SET PRINT

## The SET MEMOWIDTH Command

SET MEMOWIDTH determines the column width of memo field output.

### SYNTAX

**SET MEMOWIDTH TO <number>**

where <number> is the width of the memo field display.

### USAGE

The default width for memo field displays is 50 characters. The SET MEMOWIDTH command can be used to alter this width. Memo fields will be word-wrapped within the specified width. SET MEMOWIDTH affects only LIST, DISPLAY, and ? commands. Note that the Width setting in MODIFY

REPORT is used when printing the report with REPORT FORM, regardless of the SET MEMOWIDTH setting.

#### EXAMPLE

The command below displays fields from the Mail database, including the memo field named Notes. All the entries in the memo field will be word-wrapped in a column that is 35 characters wide.

**SET MEMOWIDTH TO 35**
**LIST LName, FName, Notes**

#### TIPS

See Chapter 24, "Algorithms to Extend dBASE," for a procedure named WordWrap that can word-wrap long fields of the character data type.

#### SEE ALSO

MODIFY REPORT
LIST
DISPLAY

## The SET MENU Command

SET MENU determines whether a cursor-control-key menu appears with full-screen commands.

#### SYNTAX

**SET MENU [OFF][ON]**

where the default setting is ON.

#### USAGE

With SET MENU in its default mode, full-screen commands such as APPEND and EDIT automatically display a menu of cursor-control keys at the top of the screen. With SET MENU OFF, this menu is not automatically displayed. Regardless of the SET MENU command, the F1 key turns the menu display off and on during a full-screen operation.

**EXAMPLE**

The command below suppresses the initial display of cursor-control-key menus on the full-screen displays:

**SET MENU OFF**

**SEE ALSO**

SET HELP

## The SET MESSAGE Command

SET MESSAGE displays a message centered on the bottom of the screen.

**SYNTAX**

**SET MESSAGE TO [<string>]**

where <string> is the message to display.

**USAGE**

The message line will be displayed only if the SET STATUS parameter is on. Messages can be only one line, which is a maximum of 79 characters. The message must be in single quotes, double quotes, or brackets, unless stored in a memory variable.

The command **SET MESSAGE TO** with no message erases the message currently at the bottom of the screen.

**EXAMPLE**

The commands below display the message **Try again!** at the bottom of the screen:

```
SET STATUS ON
SET MESSAGE TO "Try again!"
```

The commands below display the message **Press ↵ to continue...** at the bottom of the screen, then erase the message as soon as the Return key is pressed:

```
RetKey = CHR(17) + CHR(196) + CHR(217)
Msg = "Press " + RetKey + "  to continue..."
```

**SET MESSAGE TO Msg**
**ACCEPT TO RetPress**
**SET MESSAGE TO**

### TIPS

As long as no @...SAY...GET commands use the bottom line of the screen and SET STATUS is on, SET MESSAGE can be used with the READ command and custom screens.

### SEE ALSO

SET STATUS
SET SCOREBOARD

## The SET ODOMETER Command

SET ODOMETER determines how often the odometer is updated during commands that display their progress.

### SYNTAX

**SET ODOMETER TO <number>**

where <number> is the increment that the odometer displays. The default number is 1.

### USAGE

If the SET TALK parameter is on, commands such as COPY, PACK, and APPEND FROM display their progress on an odometer on the screen as they work. Usually, this odometer counts individual records as the command processes them.

You can have the odometer display progress in other increments, such as groups of 10 or 100 records, by assigning the appropriate value with the SET ODOMETER command.

### EXAMPLE

The routine below copies a large file named Biggie to a file named BigCopy. Because the process takes some time, the routine shows the user how many records need to be copied. Because SET TALK is on, COPY will automatically display an odometer of its progress as it copies the records. In this example, the odometer displays the progress in groups of 10 records.

```
USE Biggie
? "Copying " + LTRIM(STR(RECCOUNT( )) + " records..."

SET TALK ON
SET ODOMETER TO 10

COPY TO BigCopy
```

#### TIPS

Displaying the progress of commands that take a long time ensures the user that all is well and the computer is not simply "hung up."

SET ODOMETER is available only in version 1.1 of dBASE III PLUS.

#### SEE ALSO

SET TALK

## The SET ORDER Command

SET ORDER selects any open index file as the master index or removes control from all open index files.

#### SYNTAX

**SET ORDER TO [<number>]**

where <number> is the number of the index file to make into the master. The default number is 1.

#### USAGE

The master index controls the order in which records are displayed in the database and also determines the fields that SEEK and FIND can search. The SET ORDER command lets you change the controlling index to another index file in use so that a new order can be used to move within the database file.

Prior to using the SET ORDER command, you must have already opened a database file and its associated index files with a statement like the following:

```
USE My_file INDEX Ndx1,Ndx2,Ndx3...Ndx7
```

The order of the index files in this statement establishes the original order of what is formally called the index list.

To select the third index file (Ndx3 above) as the new controlling index, you would type **SET ORDER TO 3**. To reselect the first file as the new controlling index, you would type **SET ORDER TO 1**. The number of the chosen index file corresponds to its location in the index list.

dBASE III PLUS limits the number of open index files to 7, so the numeric expression used in the SET ORDER command must be 7 or less.

If you type **SET ORDER TO 0**, none of the index files will be in control, and the record pointer can be moved through the database in physical (or nonindexed) order. Also, the order of the index list is not lost when you type **SET ORDER TO 0**, so the index files can be reactivated afterwards with another **SET ORDER TO 1** command.

### EXAMPLE

The Mail database below is opened with NameOrd as the master index file:

**USE Mail INDEX NamOrd,ZipOrd**

To display records in zip-code order or to SEEK a particular zip code, make ZipOrd the master index file using the command

**SET ORDER TO 2**

### TIPS

After adding new records or packing the database file with the command **SET ORDER TO 0**, you should type **SET ORDER TO 1** and **REINDEX** to ensure that all the index files are properly updated.

SET ORDER is slightly faster than SET INDEX, because it does not have to search the disk for the index files to open.

### SEE ALSO

INDEX
SET INDEX
NDX( )

## The SET PATH Command

SET PATH defines the directory path that dBASE will follow to locate a file that is not found in the current directory.

### SYNTAX

**SET PATH TO [<path list>]**

where <path list> is a list of path names separated by commas or semicolons.

### USAGE

A path directory is a list of directories separated by backslashes and listed in order from the top-level directory to subdirectory levels (i.e., in the \LETTERS \PERSONAL directory, the directory called \PERSONAL is within the \LETTERS directory). A path list is a series of path directories separated by commas or semicolons (i.e., \LETTERS\PERSONAL;\ROUTINES; \EFFECTS includes three path directories).

If dBASE cannot find a file in the current directory, paths listed in the SET PATH command are searched one by one until the file is located.

### EXAMPLE

In the commands below, dBASE attempts to locate the file named Program-.prg on the current directory. If the file is not found, the \LETTERS\PERSONAL directory is searched, then the \ROUTINES directory, and finally the EFFECTS directory.

**SET PATH TO \LETTERS\PERSONAL;\ROUTINES;\EFFECTS**
**DO Program**

### TIPS

Except for the RUN (and equivalent !) command, dBASE does not search the directories established by the DOS PATH command. To mimic the PATH command in dBASE, use the SET PATH command.

The SET PATH command is used only for locating files, never for creating files. All files are created on the current directory.

### SEE ALSO

SET DEFAULT
DIR

## The SET PRINT Command

SET PRINT directs all output that is not formatted with the @...SAY command to the printer and the screen.

#### SYNTAX

**SET PRINT [OFF][ON]**

where the default is OFF.

#### USAGE

SET PRINT ON channels all output to the printer, except output displayed with @...SAY commands. To channel @...SAY displays to the printer, use the SET DEVICE TO PRINT command.

#### EXAMPLE

The ? commands below display their results on the printer:

```
SET PRINT ON
? 27 ^ (1/3)

? SQRT(88)

SET PRINT OFF
```

#### TIPS

Not all printers respond immediately to the screen output. Some printers respond to output only after a second line is printed. To ensure that all output is printed, issue an EJECT command after printing and setting PRINT back off, to empty the print buffer and eject the page from the printer.

#### SEE ALSO

SET DEVICE
EJECT

## The SET PRINTER Command

SET PRINTER selects a DOS device for printer output.

#### SYNTAX

**SET PRINTER TO <device>**

where <device> is a valid DOS device name.

### USAGE

The default printer device is the first parallel port, LPT1. Use SET PRINTER to redirect output to other output devices if available, including both serial and parallel printers. For parallel printers, use **SET PRINTER TO LPT1** or **LPT2** or **LPT3**. For serial printing devices, use **SET PRINTER TO COM1** or **COM2**.

### EXAMPLE

The example presented below shows how you might switch to an alternate serial printer to print a report:

```
SET PATH TO \DOS                  && \DOS contains mode.com
RUN MODE COM1:9600,N,8,1,P        && Set the serial port
SET PRINTER TO COM1               && Select printer port

USE AnyFile
REPORT FORM AnyRep TO PRINT
```

### TIPS

Alternate printers can be especially useful if you need to print labels on one printer, business correspondence on another, and program source code listings on another.

### SEE ALSO

SET PRINT
SET DEVICE
RUN

## The SET PROCEDURE Command

SET PROCEDURE opens a designated procedure file. See Chapter 5, "Procedures and Parameters," for details.

## The SET RELATION Command

SET RELATION links two open database files according to a key expression that is shared by both files. See Chapter 3, "Database Design," for an in-depth discussion.

## The SET SAFETY Command

SET SAFETY provides a degree of protection against overwriting or destroying files.

### SYNTAX

**SET SAFETY [OFF][ON]**

where the default is ON.

### USAGE

When SET SAFETY is ON, warning messages such as the one below occur before an existing file is overwritten or deleted:

**<file name> already exists, overwrite, it? (Y/N)**

When SET SAFETY is OFF, files are deleted or overwritten without any warning.

### EXAMPLE

In the example below, records from the Charges database are copied to a file named Temp. Even if the Temp file already exists, dBASE won't ask for permission before overwriting the file because the SAFETY parameter is set off.

```
SET SAFETY OFF
USE Charges
COPY TO Temp FOR .NOT. Posted
```

### TIPS

Applications programs usually turn the SET SAFETY parameter off, so users do not have to have to respond to this prompt.

### SEE ALSO

COPY
ZAP

## The SET SCOREBOARD Command

SET SCOREBOARD determines whether some dBASE III PLUS messages are displayed.

### SYNTAX

**SET SCOREBOARD [OFF][ON]**

where the default is ON.

### USAGE

When SCOREBOARD is set on and STATUS is set off, scoreboard messages appear on row 0 on the screen. Scoreboard messages include Del to indicate that a record is marked for deletion, Ins when the insert mode is on, the state of the NumLock key, and errors caused by entries that fall outside an acceptable RANGE specification. When SCOREBOARD is set off, none of these scoreboard messages is displayed.

When STATUS is set on, scoreboard messages appear on the status bar and error line (row 22), regardless of the SET SCOREBOARD status.

### EXAMPLE

The commands below prevent scoreboard messages from being displayed on the screen:

```
SET SCOREBOARD OFF
SET STATUS OFF
```

### TIPS

With SET SCOREBOARD OFF, you can use row 0 in @ commands without having the scoreboard messages overwrite your display.

### SEE ALSO

SET STATUS

## The SET STATUS Command

SET STATUS determines whether the status bar is displayed at the bottom of the screen.

### SYNTAX

**SET STATUS [OFF][ON]**

where the default is ON.

### USAGE

When SET STATUS is on, the status bar is displayed at row 22 on the screen. The status bar displays information about the current working environment: the current command, current database in use, current record number, insert/overwrite status, and NumLock status. Row 23 is the error line, and it displays data-entry error messages.

Scoreboard information is also shown on the status bar. This includes current record-deletion status and @...GET error messages. If STATUS is set off and SCOREBOARD is set on, the SCOREBOARD information is displayed on row 0 (at the top of the screen.)

### EXAMPLE

The commands below remove the status bar before displaying a bar graph with a procedure named BarGraph:

**SET STATUS OFF**
**DO BarGraph WITH 0,100,9,"Sample Graph"**

### TIPS

If a format file does not access row 22 on the screen, the status bar can be left on the screen during the use of a SET FORMAT and READ combination of commands.

### SEE ALSO

SET MESSAGE
SET SCOREBOARD

## The SET STEP Command

SET STEP stops the execution of a program after each line of instruction. This command is discussed in detail in Chapter 7, "Debugging Commands and Techniques."

## The SET TALK Command

SET TALK determines whether certain commands display informative messages.

#### SYNTAX

**SET TALK [OFF][ON]**

where the default is ON.

#### USAGE

SET TALK displays the progress of commands that might take a long time but do not otherwise display any data on the screen, for example, the APPEND FROM, COPY, PACK, STORE, AVERAGE, and SUM commands.

#### EXAMPLE

The commands below pack the Charges database and show the progress along the way:

```
SET TALK ON
PACK
SET TALK OFF
```

#### TIPS

Setting TALK on while running programs can be useful for debugging purposes, because it shows some of the activity that takes place as the program is running.

#### SEE ALSO

SET ECHO
SET DEBUG
SET STEP

## The SET TITLE Command

SET TITLE determines whether the catalog file title is displayed.

#### SYNTAX

**SET TITLE [ON][OFF]**

where the default is ON.

#### USAGE

When adding a new file to the catalog, you are normally prompted for a catalog file title. When SET TITLE is off, this prompt is not shown.

#### EXAMPLE

These commands open and activate a catalog file named ThisApp but prevent the catalog title prompts from being displayed.

```
SET CATALOG TO ThisApp
SET CATALOG ON
SET TITLE OFF
```

#### TIPS

Catalogs are generally not used by programmers, hence the topic is given only cursory treatment in this book. See the dBASE manual or an introductory-level text for information on catalogs.

#### SEE ALSO

SET CATALOG

## The SET TYPEAHEAD Command

SET TYPEAHEAD establishes the number of characters that the typeahead buffer holds.

#### SYNTAX

**SET TYPEAHEAD TO <number>**

where <number> is the number of keystrokes that the typeahead buffer will store. The default number is 20 keystrokes.

#### USAGE

A typeahead buffer stores keystrokes that are typed too fast to be processed and then feeds those keystrokes to dBASE when it is ready to accept them. The SET TYPEAHEAD command determines the number of keystrokes that this typeahead buffer will hold. The acceptable range is from 0 to 32,000 characters. SET TYPEAHEAD works only when ESCAPE is set on.

To disallow typeahead keystrokes, use **SET TYPEAHEAD TO 0**. Any keystrokes that are typed faster than dBASE can process them will cause the bell to ring (assuming SET BELL is on). The extra keystrokes will be lost. Note that setting the typeahead buffer to 0 disables the ON KEY command and the INKEY( ) function.

### TIPS

In procedures that are called by an ON ERROR condition, you can use **SET TYPEAHEAD TO 0** immediately to prevent further keystrokes from complicating the error condition. Before returning control to the calling program, use SET TYPEAHEAD again to return to the default value of 20 or to any other number.

### SEE ALSO

INKEY( )
ON
SET BELL
SET ESCAPE

## The SET UNIQUE Command

SET UNIQUE determines whether all records or only records with unique key values are included in an index file.

### SYNTAX

**SET UNIQUE [OFF][ON]**

where the default is OFF.

### USAGE

An index file created with SET UNIQUE ON will contain only unique values within the database. When the field being indexed contains duplicate values, only the first of the duplicate records will be included in the new index file.

Once the index file is created with SET UNIQUE ON, the file will keep its UNIQUE status (even after reindexing.) To create a normal index file of the same name, **SET UNIQUE OFF** must be issued before reindexing.

If you add new records to a database file that is indexed using the UNIQUE status, the records will be stored in the database file as usual, but they will remain hidden from displays if they match the key indexing expression of an existing record.

### EXAMPLE

To view a list of all the unique zip codes in the Mail database, set UNIQUE on and index on the zip code field. Then list the field of interest, as below:

```
USE Mail
SET UNIQUE ON
INDEX ON Zip TO UniqZips

* --- View unique zip codes.
LIST Zip
```

### TIPS

SET UNIQUE can be used to temporarily hide records that have duplicate entries in one or more fields.

An alternative syntax for SET UNIQUE is INDEX ON <key expression> TO <file name> UNIQUE.

### SEE ALSO

INDEX
SET INDEX
REINDEX
USE

## The SET VIEW Command

SET VIEW opens a view (.vue) file created with the CREATE/MODIFY VIEW command.

### SYNTAX

**SET VIEW TO <file name>**

where <file name> is the name of the view file, with the extension .vue.

### USAGE

SET VIEW opens a view file, which in turn opens multiple database files and defines relationships between the files. The view file is created with the CREATE VIEW or MODIFY VIEW command. A single view file can replace a series of SELECT, USE, SET RELATION, SET FIELDS, SET FORMAT, and SET FILTER commands.

#### EXAMPLE

The command below opens a view file named BigPict.vue:

**SET VIEW TO BigPict**

#### TIPS

For programmers, the SELECT, USE, and SET RELATION commands generally offer more control over managing multiple index files. View files are used more often by casual or novice dBASE users.

#### SEE ALSO

MODIFY VIEW
SET FIELDS
SET FILTER
SET FORMAT
SET RELATION

## SUMMARY

This chapter discussed the various SET commands that control environmental and global operating parameters within dBASE. The chapter also discussed ways to develop applications that allow the user to define some of the parameters the application will use. Related topics are discussed in the chapters listed below.

*For information on defining database relations with the SET RELATION command:*

- Chapter 3, "Database Design"

*For information on procedure files and the SET PROCEDURE command:*

- Chapter 5, "Procedures and Parameters"

*For information on the SET commands used in debugging, as well as the DISPLAY STATUS and LIST STATUS commands:*

- Chapter 7, "Debugging Commands and Techniques"

*For information on the SET FORMAT command and custom screens:*

- Chapter 8, "Managing Screen Displays"

*For information on the SET commands used in networks:*

- Chapter 20, "Networking and Security"

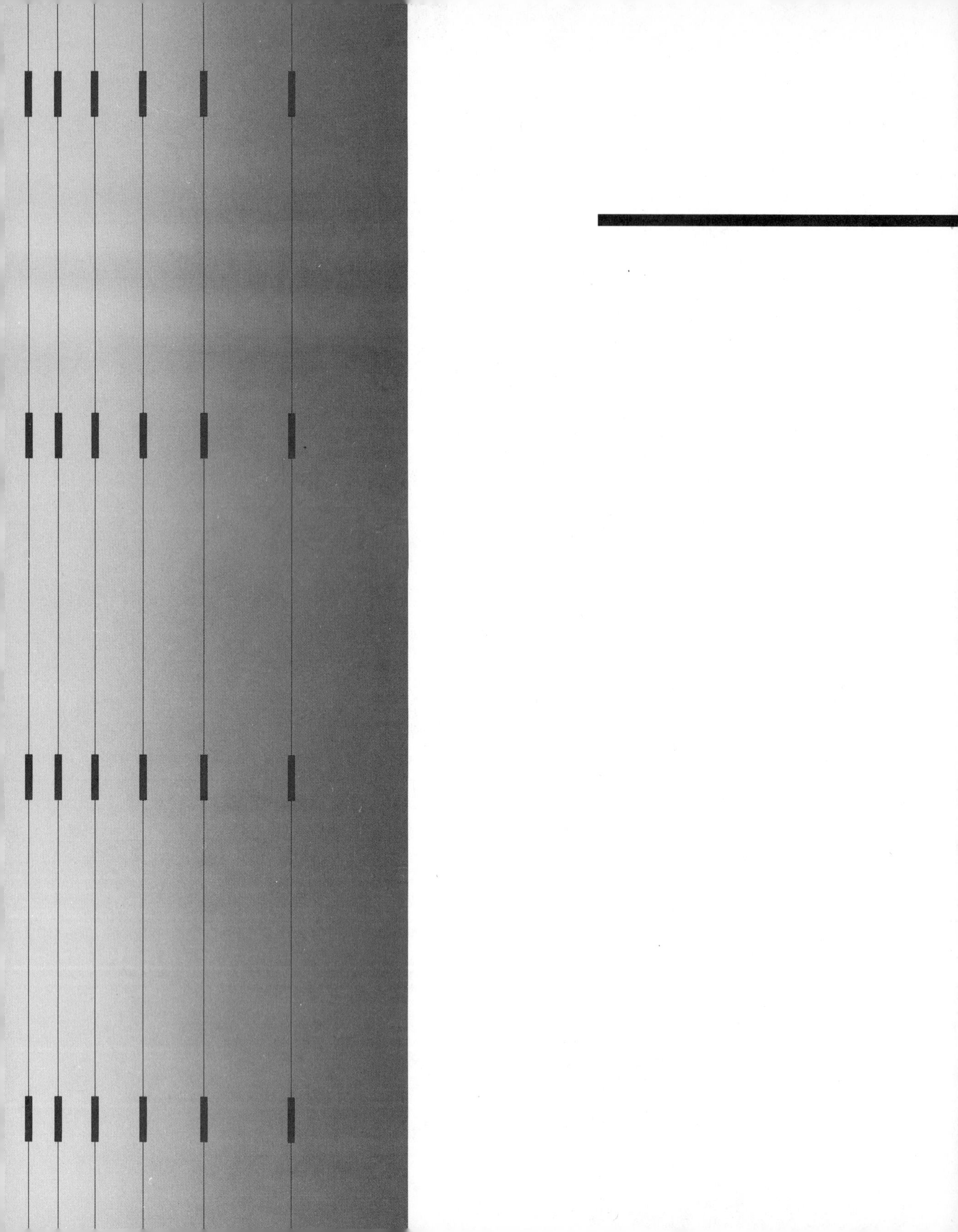

CHAPTER 19

# Event Processing and Error Trapping

# Event Processing and Error Trapping

This chapter discusses the commands and techniques used to incorporate event processing and error trapping into your programs. With these techniques, you can refine applications and provide your users with elegant and informed ways to interrupt long processes and respond to errors, avoiding having your program crash back to the dot prompt.

*Event processing* allows an application program to respond to a keystroke, regardless of the task the program is performing at the time. *Error trapping* allows an application program to detect a dBASE error and prevent the error from causing the entire application system to crash.

The ON command is used for both event processing and error trapping. ON KEY and ON ESCAPE provide the event-processing capabilities, and ON ERROR provides the error-trapping capabilities.

## Event Processing

Usually, you must press the Esc key to interrupt a program while it is running. When you do so, the screen displays the options **Cancel, Ignore, or Suspend?**. If you use event-processing commands, however, you can tailor your programs to respond to other keystrokes to interrupt a program's flow, and you can also change the effects of pressing the Esc key.

### Interrupting Processes with ON KEY

While a program is running, the ON KEY command checks whether a key is pressed and takes some action if it is. Because ON KEY checks for a keypress only between commands (not while a command is actually being executed), it cannot be used to interrupt single commands that might take a long time to complete, such as REPORT FORM or LIST. For this reason, ON KEY is generally used within DO WHILE loops to interrupt the loop.

For example, Figure 19.1 shows a small routine that prints a report from a database using a DO WHILE loop. The ON KEY command allows the user to press any key to interrupt the report. For example, if the paper in the printer is out of alignment, the user can interrupt the report without having to

```
*--- Sample routine allowing the user to
*--- press any key to stop the printer.
SET PROCEDURE TO OnProcs
USE Master

*----------------- Display instructions.
CLEAR
@ 2,1 SAY "Press any key to stop printing..."
*-------------- Set console off, printer on.
SET CONSOLE OFF
SET PRINT ON

*-------------- Set up response to keypress.
ON KEY DO KeyPress
*-------------- Print the report.
DO WHILE .NOT. EOF()
   ? PartNo,PartName,Qty
   SKIP
ENDDO

*---- Disable previous ON KEY.
ON KEY
*--- Set console and printer back to normal.
SET CONSOLE ON
EJECT
SET PRINT OFF
RETURN
```

**FIGURE 19.1:** Sample routine that prints a report using a DO WHILE loop and allows the user to press any key to pause or discontinue printing. If the user presses a key to interrupt printing, the first ON KEY command passes control to the KeyPress procedure (shown in Figure 19.2).

return all the way to the dot prompt. After the report has stopped printing, the user has the choice of realigning the paper and continuing to print or aborting printing altogether.

The sample routine opens a procedure file named OnProcs and a database file named Master. Then it displays the instructions **Press any key to stop printing...** on the screen. Then the console is set off and the printer is set on, so that data from the ? commands in the DO WHILE loop are displayed only on the printer. The command **ON KEY DO KeyPress** tells dBASE to run a procedure named KeyPress (see Figure 19.2) as soon as the user presses any key. Then the DO WHILE loop begins printing the report, which the user can interrupt at any time by pressing any key.

When the report is completely printed, the ON KEY command without any additional parameters (below the ENDDO command in Figure 19.1) deactivates the first ON KEY command, so that future keypresses do not call the KeyPress procedure.

Figure 19.2 shows the procedure named KeyPress, which in this example is stored in a procedure file named OnProcs. The command **Dummy = INKEY( )** clears the keypress that triggered the ON KEY command from the typeahead buffer so that it is not carried over to the READ command later in the routine.

```
********************************** OnProcs.prg
*- Procedure file to respond to ON commands.

*- Responds to ON KEY to abort printing.
PROCEDURE KeyPress
  Dummy = INKEY() && Clear out keypress.
  Abort = .T.
  @ 23,1 SAY "Abort printing? (Y/N)" ;
    GET Abort PICTURE "Y"
    READ
  *- If aborting, set everything back to normal.
  IF Abort
     SET PRINT OFF
     SET CONSOLE ON
     EJECT  && this is optional.
     ON KEY
     RETURN TO MASTER
  ENDIF
RETURN
```

**FIGURE 19.2:** The KeyPress procedure in the OnProcs procedure file. This procedure responds to any key pressed while the DO WHILE loop in Figure 19.1 is printing data. The procedure allows the user to either continue printing the report or abort the process altogether.

The @ command displays the prompt for determining whether to abort printing. The use of @ is important here, because it displays its message on the screen only, even when SET CONSOLE is off and SET PRINT is on.

If the user opts to abort printing (by answering Yes to the **Abort Printing? (Y/N)** prompt), the console is set back on and the printer is set off. If the user tells dBASE to continue printing by typing N, printing resumes. The last ON KEY command, with no additional instructions on the command line, deactivates the previous ON KEY command. Therefore, all keypresses once again behave normally.

The optional EJECT command in the sample procedure ejects the paper currently in the printer. The RETURN TO MASTER command passes control back to the highest-level program in the application, so that control will go back to the main program instead of the place where the interrupt occurred. (This assumes that the program shown in Figure 19.1 is called from another program with a DO command.)

Note that ON KEY responds to the Esc key only if an ON ESCAPE command (discussed below) is not active.

## Interrupting Processes with ON ESCAPE

As you've no doubt noticed by now, any time you press the Esc key while a program is running, dBASE immediately stops processing and displays the options Cancel, Ignore, or Suspend. The ON ESCAPE command allows you to present options of your own in response to the Esc key.

Unlike the ON KEY command discussed above, ON ESCAPE will interrupt a command even while the command is being executed. For this reason, ON ESCAPE is particularly useful for interrupting individual commands that might take a long time to complete, such as LIST or REPORT FORM.

For example, suppose you want the user of your application to be able to interrupt a long REPORT FORM command, in which the output is being sent to the printer. The routine shown in Figure 19.3 is set up to provide this capability. The routine opens a procedure file named OnProcs and a sample data-base file named Master. Then it displays the instructions **Press Esc to stop printing...** on the screen and sets the console off so the report is displayed only on the printer. The **ON ESCAPE DO EscPress** command passes control to a procedure named EscPress (Figure 19.4) if the user presses the Esc key while the report is being printed. (Presumably, the EscPress procedure is stored in the OnProcs procedure file.)

The REPORT FORM command then prints the report. If the user does not interrupt the report, the console is set back on and the previous ON ESCAPE command is disabled once the entire report is printed.

If the user does press the Esc key while the report is printing, the EscPress procedure displays the message **Print job aborted...** on the screen and sets the console back on. The optional **EJECT** command ejects the current page from the printer. Then the **RETURN TO MASTER** command passes control back to the highest-level program in the system.

```
*--- Sample routine allowing the user to
*--- press Esc to stop the printer.
SET PROCEDURE TO OnProcs
USE Master

*----------------- Display instructions.
CLEAR
@ 2,1 SAY "Press Esc to stop printing..."

*-------------- Set the console off.
SET CONSOLE OFF

*-------------- Set up response to keypress.
ON ESCAPE DO EscPress

*-------------- Print the report.
REPORT FORM MastRep TO PRINT

*---- Restore console and disable ON ESCAPE.
SET CONSOLE ON
ON ESCAPE
RETURN
```

**FIGURE 19.3:** Sample routine that allows the user to abort a REPORT FORM printing process by pressing the Esc key. In this example, control is passed to a procedure named EscPress (shown in Figure 19.4) when the user presses Esc.

```
*-- Respond to Esc key.
PROCEDURE EscPress
  @ 23,1 SAY "Print job aborted..."
  EJECT  && this is optional.
  ON ESCAPE
  SET CONSOLE ON
  RETURN TO MASTER
RETURN
```

**FIGURE 19.4:** The EscPress procedure. This procedure is accessed if the user presses Esc while the REPORT FORM command in Figure 19.3 is printing data.

Notice that the EscPress procedure does not give the user the option to resume printing. This is because a RETURN command to pass control back to the calling program would begin processing at the command *after* REPORT FORM, so the report would not be completed. If you used RETRY rather than a RETURN command to pass control back to the calling program, the REPORT FORM command would start printing from the first record in the database file. So there really is no way to ensure that a command interrupted with an Esc key will be able to resume processing at exactly the point that it left off.

As a programmer, you probably will not want your users to have the power to interrupt commands that build files, particularly the UPDATE and INDEX commands. Interrupting these processes will probably cause the files being generated to be corrupted or inaccurate.

## Interrupting Processes with INKEY( )

When preceded by the WHILE .NOT. condition, the INKEY( ) function offers a third technique for interrupting processing. For example, the command

**REPORT FORM MastRep WHILE INKEY( ) # 6**

will print the report named MastRep as long as the user does not press the End key. For more information on the INKEY( ) function, see Chapter 17, "dBASE Functions."

# ERROR TRAPPING WITH ON ERROR

Error trapping is a technique whereby any dBASE error that would normally interrupt a program and display an error message instead performs some command or procedure that you specify. With error trapping, you can prevent programs from crashing and returning to the dot prompt, leaving users in a state of confused panic. Instead of crashing, the error merely displays some helpful information and allows the user to correct the error and go back to what he or she was doing.

The ON ERROR command automatically performs a predefined action whenever a command, whether it appears at the dot prompt or in a program, generates a dBASE error. Typically, you would use ON ERROR in an application to trap easily correctable errors, such as opening corrupted index files or entering an illegal file name.

Whenever an error occurs within dBASE, the dBASE ERROR( ) function receives a numeric value representing that error, and the MESSAGE( ) function receives a character string message that briefly describes the error. Table 19.1 lists all the ERROR( ) numbers and MESSAGE( ) strings in dBASE. (The messages are listed in alphabetical order. For more information on a particular error message, see Appendix A, "Error Messages.")

| ERROR( ) | MESSAGE( ) |
|---|---|
| 24 | ALIAS name already in use |
| 13 | ALIAS not found |
| 72 | ALTERNATE could not be opened |
| 38 | Beginning of file encountered |
| 89 | Cannot erase a file which is open |
| 17 | Cannot select requested database |
| 111 | Cannot write to a read-only file |
| 42 | CONTINUE without LOCATE |
| 44 | Cyclic relation |
| 122 | Data Catalog has not been established |
| 9 | Data type mismatch |
| 131 | Database is encrypted |
| 26 | Database is not indexed |
| 41 | .DBT file cannot be opened |
| 56 | Disk full when writing file: <file name> |
| 103 | DOs nested too deep |
| 4 | End of file encountered |
| 51 | End of file or error on keyboard input |
| 110 | Exclusive open of file is required |

**TABLE 19.1:** ERROR( ) Numbers and MESSAGE( ) Text Generated by the ON ERROR Command

| ERROR( ) | MESSAGE( ) |
|---|---|
| 77 | ***Execution error on +: Concatenated string too large |
| 76 | ***Execution error on −: Concatenated string too large |
| 57 | ***Execution error on CHR( ): Out of range |
| 58 | ***Execution error on LOG( ): Zero or negative |
| 87 | ***Execution error on NDX( ): Invalid index number |
| 88 | ***Execution error on REPLICATE( ): String too large |
| 59 | ***Execution error on SPACE( ): Too large |
| 60 | ***Execution error on SPACE( ): Negative |
| 61 | ***Execution error on SQRT( ): Negative |
| 79 | ***Execution error on STORE: String too large |
| 63 | ***Execution error on STR( ): Out of range |
| 102 | ***Execution error on STUFF( ): String too large |
| 62 | ***Execution error on SUBSTR( ): Start point out of range |
| 75 | ***Execution error on ^ or **: Negative base, fractional exponent |
| 73 | ^ ^ Expected ON or OFF |
| 48 | Field not found |
| 7 | File already exists |
| 1 | File does not exist |
| 49 | File has been deleted |
| 3 | File is already open |
| 108 | File is in use by another |
| 29 | File is not accessible |
| 91 | File was not LOADed |
| 46 | Illegal value |
| 114 | Index damaged. REINDEX should be done before using data |
| 112 | Index expression is too big (220 char maximum) |
| 19 | Index file does not match database |
| 113 | Index interrupted. Index will be damaged if not completed |
| 23 | Index is too big (100 char maximum) |
| 43 | Insufficient memory |
| 66 | Internal error: CMDSET( ): |
| 67 | Internal error: EVAL work area overflow |

**TABLE 19.1:** ERROR( ) Numbers and MESSAGE( ) Text Generated by the ON ERROR Command (continued)

| ERROR( ) | MESSAGE( ) |
|---|---|
| 68 | Internal error: Illegal opcode |
| 65 | Internal error: Unknown command code: |
| 81 | Invalid date (press SPACE) |
| 118 | Invalid DIF character |
| 115 | Invalid DIF File Header |
| 117 | Invalid DIF type indicator |
| 99 | Invalid DOS SET option |
| 11 | Invalid function argument |
| 31 | Invalid function name |
| 106 | Invalid index number |
| 107 | Invalid operator |
| 123 | Invalid printer port |
| 124 | Invalid printer redirection |
| 120 | Invalid SYLK file dimension bounds |
| 121 | Invalid SYLK file format |
| 119 | Invalid SYLK file header |
| 86 | ^_. Keyword not found |
| 54 | Label file invalid |
| 18 | Line exceeds maximum of 254 characters |
| 137 | Maximum record length exceeded |
| 55 | Memory Variable file is invalid |
| 96 | Mismatched DO WHILE and ENDDO |
| 148 | Network server busy |
| 52 | No database is in USE. Enter file name: |
| 47 | No fields to process |
| 14 | No find |
| 93 | No PARAMETER statement found |
| 45 | Not a Character expression |
| 15 | Not a dBASE database |
| 37 | Not a Logical expression |
| 27 | Not a numeric expression |
| 140 | Not a valid PFS file |
| 134 | Not a valid QUERY file |

**TABLE 19.1:** ERROR( ) Numbers and MESSAGE( ) Text Generated by the ON ERROR Command (continued)

| ERROR( ) | MESSAGE( ) |
|---|---|
| 127 | Not a valid VIEW file |
| 82 | ** Not Found ** |
| 101 | Not suspended |
| 39 | Numeric overflow (data was lost) |
| 90 | Operation with Logical field invalid |
| 34 | Operation with Memo field invalid |
| 21 | Out of memory variable memory |
| 22 | Out of memory variable slots |
| 75 | ^ – – – Out of range |
| 30 | Position is off the screen |
| 126 | Printer is either not connected or turned off |
| 125 | Printer not ready |
| 50 | Record file invalid |
| 109 | Record is in use by another |
| 20 | Record is not in index |
| 25 | Record is not inserted |
| 130 | Record is not locked |
| 5 | Record is out of range |
| 33 | Structure invalid |
| 10 | Syntax error |
| 105 | Table is full |
| 53 | There are no files of the type requested in this drive or catalog |
| 6 | Too many files are open |
| 28 | Too many indices |
| 74 | ^ – – – Truncated |
| 92 | Unable to load COMMAND.COM |
| 129 | Unable to LOCK |
| 128 | Unable to SKIP |
| 2 | Unassigned file no. |
| 133 | Unauthorized access level |
| 132 | Unauthorized login |
| 8 | Unbalanced parentheses |
| 104 | Unknown function key |

**TABLE 19.1:** ERROR( ) Numbers and MESSAGE( ) Text Generated by the ON ERROR Command (continued)

| ERROR( ) | MESSAGE( ) |
|---|---|
| 16 | *** Unrecognized command verb |
| 36 | Unrecognized phrase/keyword in command |
| 35 | Unterminated string |
| 95 | Valid only in programs |
| 12 | Variable not found |
| 70 | ** WARNING ** Data will probably be lost. Confirm (Y/N) |
| 94 | Wrong number of parameters |
| 75 | ^ – – –Out of range |
| 74 | ^ – – –Truncated |
| 73 | ^ ^ Expected ON or OFF |
| 86 | ^ – – –Keyword not found |

**TABLE 19.1:** ERROR( ) Numbers and MESSAGE( ) Text Generated by the ON ERROR Command (continued)

Presumably, when you finish writing your application, all the basic syntax bugs will be corrected, so there would be no need for dBASE to respond to every conceivable error. However, if you use error trapping to trap and respond to errors that could occur even after you've fully tested and debugged your application (such as an attempt to use a corrupted index file), you can prevent the system from crashing in the user's hands in such a situation.

Figure 19.5 shows a sample procedure named ErrTrap that attempts to recover from some common errors. A DO CASE clause responds to the ERROR( ) number generated and attempts to deal with the error. In the case of an unrecoverable error, such as when too many files are open, the procedure simply provides instructions and terminates processing with a CANCEL command. In cases where the error is recoverable, such as a disk-full error, the procedure displays instructions for rectifying the problem and then tries again to execute the command that caused the error (via the RETRY command).

The application programs that use the error procedures need only open the procedure file and use ON ERROR once to call the ErrTrap procedure when an error occurs, as in the commands below:

**SET PROCEDURE TO ErrTrap**
**ON ERROR TO ErrTrap**

The ON ERROR command remains active until another ON ERROR command (with no TO clause) is issued.

Keep in mind that the error-trapping procedure shown in Figure 19.5 is only an example. You will probably want to develop specialized error-trapping procedures for your own applications.

```
********************************** ErrTrap.prg
*----- Sample procedure to trap common errors.
PROCEDURE ErrTrap
   @ 19,0 CLEAR
   @ 19,0 TO 19,79 DOUBLE
   ? CHR(7)
   DO CASE

    CASE ERROR() = 4  && EOF() encountered.
       ? "End of file encountered unexpectedly."
       ? "Will try to repair.  Please wait."
       *-- If index file open, may be corrupted.
       IF NDX() # " "
          REINDEX
       ENDIF
       RETRY

     CASE ERROR() = 114  && Damaged index file.
       ? "Damaged index file!"
       ? Please wait while rebuilding..."
       REINDEX

     CASE ERROR() = 6  && Too many files open.
       ? "Check the Config.db file on your root"
       ? "directory, as discussed in the manual."
       CANCEL
       CLOSE ALL
       ON ERROR

     CASE ERROR() = 29  && File inaccessible.
       ? "Disk directory is full, or an illegal"
       ? "character appears in file name!"
       ? "Check file name and directory, then try again."

     CASE ERROR() = 56    && Disk full error.
       ? "That disk is full. Change disks and"
       ? "try again..."
       WAIT
       RETRY

     OTHERWISE   && Unknown error: display dBASE message.
       ? "Unexpected error in program..."
        ? MESSAGE(),"["+LTRIM(STR(ERROR()))+"]"
       WAIT "Press Esc to abort, any key to continue..."

   ENDCASE
RETURN
```

**FIGURE 19.5:** A sample procedure that responds to dBASE errors, displays its own error message, and attempts to recover from the error.

## COMMANDS USED IN EVENT PROCESSING AND ERROR TRAPPING

Only two dBASE commands are actually required for event processing and error trapping: the ON command (in its three different forms) and the RETRY command. These commands are discussed below.

## The ON Command

ON takes a specific action in response to an error or event, regardless of the task dBASE is performing at the moment.

### SYNTAX

**ON KEY <command>**
**ON ESCAPE <command>**
**ON ERROR <command>**

where <command> is the action to take when the event occurs.

### USAGE

The three ON options each respond to a unique situation, as summarized below:

| | |
|---|---|
| ON KEY | Responds to any keypress |
| ON ESCAPE | Responds to the Esc key |
| ON ERROR | Responds to a dBASE error |

The three different versions of the ON command can be active simultaneously within a given program or application.

### ON KEY

ON KEY checks for a keystroke after executing each command in a command file. If a key was pressed while the command was being executed, dBASE performs the action specified in the ON KEY command line.

The keypress that triggers the ON KEY command stays in the keyboard buffer until it is explicitly removed by another command or stored in a memory variable. To remove the triggering keypress from the keyboard buffer, store it in a memory variable using the INKEY( ) function. Figure 19.2 earlier in the chapter shows an example where the command **Dummy = INKEY( )** clears the buffer so that the triggering keypress does not interfere with the GET and READ commands later in the procedure.

The command **ON KEY**, without any additional instruction on the command line, deactivates any previous ON KEY command.

If an ON ESCAPE command is active at the same time that an ON KEY command is active and the SET ESCAPE parameter is on, ON KEY responds to any key *except* the Esc key.

## ON ESCAPE

The ON ESCAPE command responds only to the Esc key, and only if the SET ESCAPE parameter is on. Unlike the ON KEY command, ON ESCAPE is executed immediately, even in the middle of a long process such as REPORT FORM or LIST.

The ON ESCAPE command takes precedence over the ON KEY command when both are active. Therefore, when an ON ESCAPE is active and the SET ESCAPE parameter is on, the ON KEY command responds to any keystroke except the Esc key.

The command **ON ESCAPE**, with no additional instruction on the command line, deactivates any previous ON ESCAPE command.

## ON ERROR

The ON ERROR command responds to any dBASE error by performing the instructions that follow it. For example, the command

**ON ERROR DO ErrCheck**

passes control to a program or procedure named ErrCheck as soon as a dBASE error occurs. The ERROR( ) function receives a numeric value representing the error and the MESSAGE( ) function receives a character string describing the error. (Table 19.1 lists the ERROR( ) and MESSAGE( ) values of the various dBASE errors. The messages are described in more detail in Appendix A, "Error Messages.")

ON ERROR responds only to dBASE errors, not to DOS errors such as inaccessible disk drive or printer requests.

The command **ON ERROR**, without any additional command on the line, deactivates any previous ON ERROR command.

### EXAMPLES

The commands below open a procedure file called OnProcs and set up the ON KEY, ON ESCAPE, and ON ERROR commands to branch to procedures named KeyPress, EscPress, and ErrCheck, respectively:

**SET PROCEDURE TO OnProcs**
**ON KEY DO KeyPress**
**ON ESCAPE DO EscPress**
**ON ERROR DO ErrCheck**

See Figures 19.1 through 19.5 for additional examples of the various ON commands and routines that respond to them.

### TIPS

See the INKEY( ) function in Chapter 17, "dBASE Functions," for another technique that can be used to interrupt processing.

When using ON ERROR to trap errors and a DO CASE clause to respond to errors, always include an OTHERWISE clause to display the error number and message of any errors that do not match any of the errors included in the CASE statements. Otherwise, it will be very difficult to track and correct bugs in programs that are not detected by the DO CASE clause. Figure 19.5 shows an OTHERWISE clause that uses the expression

**? MESSAGE( ),"[" + LTRIM(STR(ERROR( ))) + "]"**

to print the error message and number in the format below:

**End-of-file encountered [4]**

### SEE ALSO

INKEY( )
ERROR( )
MESSAGE( )

## The RETRY Command

RETRY returns control to the calling program and reexecutes the line that was active when the call took place.

### SYNTAX

**RETRY**

### USAGE

Unlike the RETURN command, which passes control back to the *next* line in a calling program, RETRY passes control back to the line that initiated the call and reexecutes that line. RETRY is generally used in conjunction with the ON ERROR command to attempt to reexecute the command that caused the error.

RETRY can be used in command files and procedure files. When used in a command file, it closes the called program when it returns control to the calling program. RETRY also resets the ERROR( ) value back to zero.

## EXAMPLE

The commands below call a procedure named FileErr if an error occurs while trying to rename a file:

```
* – Allow user to rename file,
* – but watch for file name error.
ACCEPT "Enter new name for file " TO NewName
IF .NOT. "." $ NewName
    NewName = NewName + ".dbf"
ENDIF
ON ERROR DO FileErr
RENAME ThisFile.DBF TO &NewName
ON ERROR          &&Deactivate previous ON ERROR.
```

If the name stored in the NewName variable already exists, the ON KEY command passes control to the FileErr procedure with an ERROR( ) value of 7. The FileErr procedure responds by asking the user to enter a new name for the file and attempting to process the RENAME command again. The FileErr procedure is shown below:

```
* – – FileErr procedure: Respond to illegal file name.
IF ERROR( ) = 7
    ? "File name already exists!"
    ? "Reenter file name and try again."
    ACCEPT TO NewName
    RETRY
ENDIF
RETURN
```

## TIPS

Use RETRY to respond to recoverable errors only after allowing the user to take some action to correct the error. For unrecoverable errors such as **Too many files open**, use RETURN to pass control back to the command beneath the line that caused the error, or use CANCEL to terminate processing altogether.

## SEE ALSO

ERROR( )
RETURN

## SUMMARY

This chapter discussed numerous commands and techniques for responding to events and errors that occur while a program or application is running. These techniques allow you to refine the user-interface aspects of your application by providing the user with a graceful means to terminate or interrupt long processes and to respond to errors that might otherwise cause the application to crash.

*For techniques on general error trapping with user-interface commands such as @, ACCEPT, and INPUT:*

- Chapter 4, "Command Files"

*For tips on using PICTURE and RANGE commands to trap errors before they are entered in a database file:*

- Chapter 8, "Managing Screen Displays"

*For additional event-processing techniques to interrupt printed reports:*

- Chapter 9, "Printing Formatted Reports"

*For information on trapping invalid data while entering records into a transaction file:*

- Chapter 10, "Adding New Data"

*For more information on INKEY( ), ERROR( ), MESSAGE( ), and other dBASE functions:*

- Chapter 17, "dBASE Functions"

*For detailed explanations of error messages and possible steps to recover from errors:*

- Appendix A, "Error Messages"

# Part 6

# *Beyond the Programming Environment*

This section discusses programming considerations that extend beyond the basic development of dBASE applications. These topics include networking, compiling, using assembly language subroutines, and interfacing with foreign software systems.

Chapter 20 discusses the basics of using the dBASE ADMINISTRATOR for setting up your dBASE applications on a network, as well as developing security schemes to prevent unauthorized access to confidential or sensitive data. It also presents some programming techniques that are useful in a network environment. (For network installation information, read Appendix B, "Installing dBASE III PLUS.")

Chapter 21 discusses the RunTime+ program that comes with the dBASE III PLUS package, as well as the popular Clipper and Quicksilver compilers. These add-on packages allow you to encrypt your programs so that unauthorized users cannot tamper with them. In addition, the compilers allow your programs to run both much faster and directly from DOS, without the use of dBASE III PLUS.

Chapter 22 covers techniques for accessing assembly language subroutines from within dBASE. This chapter discusses techniques for loading and running assembly language subroutines, as well as passing data to and from the subroutines.

Chapter 23 discusses techniques for exporting data from dBASE databases and importing data to dBASE databases. This chapter also discusses techniques for recovering damaged dBASE files that have become inaccessible to dBASE.

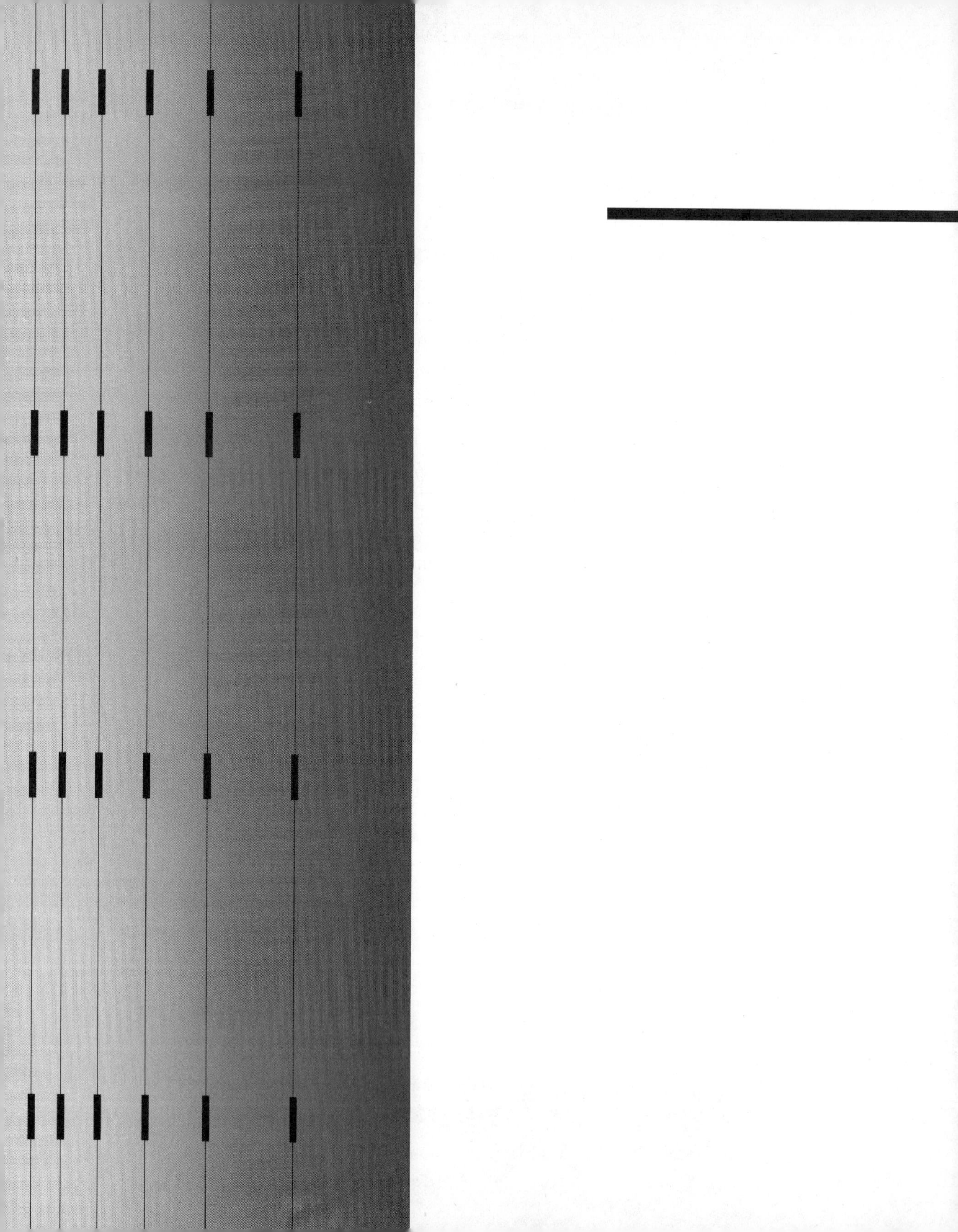

CHAPTER 20

# NETWORKING AND SECURITY

# NETWORKING AND SECURITY

This chapter discusses the networking and security aspects of dBASE III PLUS. These topics are treated together because the multiuser version of dBASE III PLUS (included in your dBASE package as the dBASE ADMINISTRATOR) handles both networking and security, and because the two topics actually go hand in hand. Extensive data security is generally required only on network systems where certain users need to be denied access to private or sensitive information. It is not as important for single-user applications.

This chapter begins with an overview of networks and an explanation of the dBASE ADMINISTRATOR program. Then it discusses security techniques and how to implement a security system with the dBASE PROTECT program. Finally, commands and programming techniques used in developing networking applications are discussed. Commands and functions that are unique to the networking environment are referenced at the end of the chapter.

## RUNNING dBASE ON A NETWORK

Before using dBASE III PLUS on a network, you have to set up a network system with a network package. The local area network, or LAN, is a system of computers that are linked to one another with cables and networking software so they can share information and resources. Figure 20.1 shows a sample network configuration with four computers and two printers. In this configuration, any of the computers can use either of the printers, and the computers can also share information stored in files.

Within the network, at least one computer is designated as the *file server.* The file server manages all communications and access to shared files. Typically, the file server is a large microcomputer with a hard disk and at least 640K RAM. (The term *network driver,* used with some networking packages, is synonymous with file server.)

The individual computers attached to the file server are called *workstations.* These can be smaller microcomputers with only one or two floppy-disk drives. With most networking systems, each workstation needs a minimum of 384K RAM, though in the 3Com network, workstations need 512K. (In some network packages, workstations are referred to as *network nodes.*)

When you install your network using the network software package of your choice, you can designate which computer will be the file server and which ones will be the workstations.

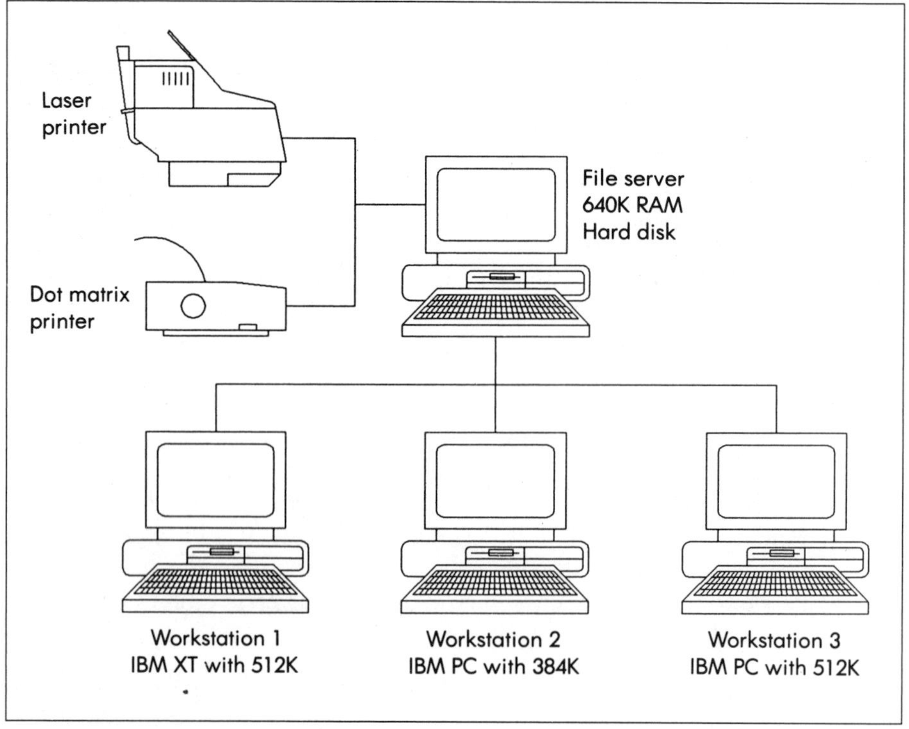


**FIGURE 20.1:** Diagram of a sample local area network (LAN) system. In this network, four computers can share the two printers, all the programs, and data. The computer designated as the *file server* must have the dBASE ADMINISTRATOR installed on it to use dBASE in the network.

## Networks Compatible with dBASE III PLUS

dBASE can be used with the following network programs:

- IBM PC Network (version 1.0)
- IBM PC LAN (version 1.10)
- Novell Advanced Netware/86 (version 1.01)
- 3Com 3 + Share (version 1.0 or 1.01)

The minimal hardware and software requirements for setting up the various dBASE-compatible networks are summarized in Table 20.1. Note that some networks may have additional requirements as products evolve. Refer to your particular network's user's manual for specific instructions on setting it up.

| | IBM PC | Novell | 3Com |
|---|---|---|---|
| **Program** | IBM PC Network or LAN | Advanced Netware /86 | 3+ Share Software |
| **Version** | 1.10 | 1.01 | 1.0, 1.01, 1.1, or 1.2 |
| **File server hardware** | Network adapter card | Network communication card and key cards | 3Com Etherlink or Etherlink Plus card |
| **Workstation hardware** | Network adapter card | Network communication board | 3Com Etherlink or Etherlink Plus card |
| **File server minimum RAM** | 640K | 640K | 640K |
| **Workstation minimum RAM** | Messenger: 640K<br>Receiver: 512K<br>Redirector: 448K<br>General: 384K | 384K | 512K |
| **Minimum file server disk storage** | 1 hard disk<br>1 floppy disk | 1 hard disk<br>1 floppy disk | 1 hard disk<br>1 floppy disk |
| **Minimum workstation disk storage** | None required | None required | None required |

**TABLE 20.1:** Hardware and Software Requirements for a LAN That Supports dBASE

## Installing dBASE ADMINISTRATOR

After you have set up your network system, you have to install the dBASE ADMINISTRATOR on the file server. The dBASE ADMINISTRATOR is the networking version of dBASE III PLUS. Specific instructions for installing dBASE III PLUS on various networks are included in Appendix B, "Installing dBASE III PLUS." Be sure to refer to the appropriate section in the appendix for the instructions specific to your network software.

## Running dBASE ADMINISTRATOR

The command you use to get dBASE up and running on your network depends on the particular network system you are using, as discussed in Appendix B, "Installing dBASE III PLUS." Generally, you'll need to use the command DBA, rather than dBASE, to start multiuser dBASE III PLUS.

Note that single-user and multiuser dBASE III PLUS are completely compatible. If you run programs with networking capabilities in single-user dBASE,

dBASE will simply ignore the networking commands and functions. When you run those same programs in multiuser dBASE (under the dBASE ADMINISTRATOR), the networking commands and functions will be executed.

There is, of course, more to networking than installing the dBASE ADMINISTRATOR and running it, particularly for the dBASE applications programmer. For one, you may need to add levels of security to prevent unauthorized access to vital or sensitive information. Secondly, there are many network programming techniques that you should follow to ensure that your application runs well on the network. These techniques are discussed below.

## USING PROTECT TO PROVIDE NETWORK SECURITY

Unless you implement a security system in a network, all network users will have complete access to all files, including the power to add, view, change, and delete records on any database file. Allowing many people to have this kind of carte-blanche power in an application is likely to result in lost or inaccurate data. To avoid such problems, you can use the PROTECT program to set up a file security system.

The PROTECT program is stored on the Administrator #1 disk that comes with your dBASE III PLUS package, under the file name Protect.exe. You run this program at the DOS level on any disk by entering the command PROTECT at the DOS prompt. However, when you finish running PROTECT, you must copy the dbSystem.db file that it creates onto the directory that contains the dBASE ADMINISTRATOR. (Don't leave PROTECT on this directory, however, because doing so will allow unauthorized users to modify the security scheme.)

When you first run the PROTECT program, a copyright notice appears. Then you can begin developing a security scheme by going through the menus discussed later in this section.

When used with the dBASE ADMINISTRATOR, the PROTECT program offers three types of security, as summarized in Table 20.2.

### Log-In Security

Log-in security prevents unauthorized users from accessing dBASE altogether. Whenever a user on the network attempts to run dBASE, he or she is automatically asked for three items of information, as shown below:

**Enter group name**
**Enter your name**
**Enter password**

The user must enter all three items. For added security, the password does not appear on the screen when typed.

| TYPE OF SECURITY | DEFINES | RESULT |
|---|---|---|
| Login | User names and passwords | Only users who know passwords can access dBASE |
| Access level | Access levels | Limits individuals' power to add, change, view, and delete data |
| Data encryption | User and file group | Encrypts the contents of database files so that only users who have been assigned to a specific group can access the data |

**TABLE 20.2:** Types of Security Offered by PROTECT and the dBASE ADMINISTRATOR

Once the group name, user name, and password are entered, dBASE compares them to the group, user, and password names you've previously defined (through the PROTECT program). If any item is invalid, the user is denied access to dBASE III PLUS. If the entry is valid, the user is immediately assigned an access number, and dBASE is loaded and run (so the user sees the dot prompt or an application program running).

## Access-Level Security

You can control access to database information by using the PROTECT program to define *privileges,* or levels of access to database files and fields. For each user on the network, you can develop a *user profile* that limits the user's freedom in adding, changing, viewing, and deleting information. Within that user profile, you assign an access-level number between 1 and 8, with 1 having the least restrictions and 8 having the most restrictions.

The PROTECT program allows you to combine the various privileges into a single *file privilege scheme.* These privileges affect database and index files only. No other file types, including memo field (.dbt) files, are protected. Access-level security is explained in detail in the section "Defining File Privilege Schemes" later in this chapter.

## Data-Encryption Security

The third level of security is *data encryption,* in which data is encoded so that it cannot be read until it is decoded. As soon as you assign a file privilege scheme to a database file through the PROTECT program, the file is automatically encrypted and given the file-name extension .crp. The original database is still stored under the usual .dbf file-name extension.

To enhance security, you should copy the original .dbf file to a separate floppy disk, then use the DOS or dBASE RENAME command to change the .crp file to the same file name but with the .dbf extension.

Note that the dBASE ADMINISTRATOR also provides the SET ENCRYPTION command, which allows you to decide whether to encrypt copied files. SET ENCRYPTION is discussed in the reference section of this chapter.

You can encrypt program (.prg) files using a program named dBCODE. See Chapter 21, "RunTime+ and the Compilers," for more information on encrypting programs.

Keep in mind that the PROTECT program also allows you to assign database and index files to *groups* representing a particular application. All of the database and index files within a group use the same *encryption key* (a code for encrypting and decrypting files). Files in different groups use different encryption keys. Therefore, users who are granted full access to all files in a particular group can have free access only to the files in that group. They cannot access (decrypt) files outside of the group(s) to which they are assigned.

## The Network Administrator Password

The first step in implementing network security through PROTECT is to assign a password to the network administrator. The term *administrator* refers both to the ADMINISTRATOR program and the person who is in charge of the network system. Generally, at least one person will be in charge of the network (probably the chief dBASE programmer). Throughout this chapter, the dBASE ADMINISTRATOR *program* is referred to in all uppercase letters, and the network administrator *person* is referred to in lowercase letters.

After PROTECT presents its copyright notice, it asks for the administrator password, using a prompt like the one below:

**dBASE ADMINISTRATOR Password Security System**
**Enter administrator password**

The network administrator can now enter a password up to eight characters long; the screen does not display the password when it is typed. *Be sure to write this password down someplace and file it away for safe keeping. If you lose it, you will never again be able to gain access to the security scheme!* After entering the password, the screen asks you to type the password again to verify your first entry. Once you've defined the password, you will need to enter the correct password every time you want to gain access to the security system.

Bear in mind that any person who knows this password will have full access to all database files in the network, because he or she can change file security at any time. Therefore, be sure that only the people in charge of the overall network system know this password.

# Navigating the PROTECT Menus

After you have passed the initial administrator log-in prompt, you'll see the PROTECT menu system for defining network users and file security schemes, as shown in Figure 20.2. This menu system works like all other dBASE full-screen menu-driven systems. The ← and → keys move the highlight across the top menus, and each of these displays a pull-down menu of options. Within each pull-down menu, you can use the ↑ and ↓ keys to highlight menu options and Return to select those menu options. Additional instructions and error messages appear at the bottom of the screen as you proceed.

## DEFINING USER PROFILES

Each user in the network can be assigned a *user profile.* The user profile actually provides all three levels of security discussed earlier. It provides log-in security, because only those people who have user profiles can access dBASE. It provides access-level security, because the access level you assign to users in their profiles determines which files and operations the users can and cannot have access to.

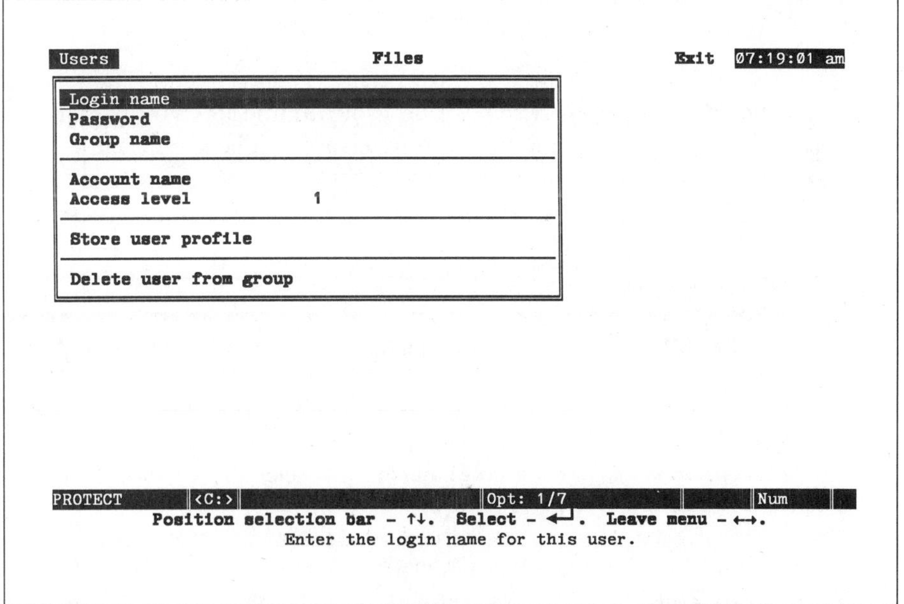


**FIGURE 20.2:** The Users menu on the PROTECT program screen. Use the ← and → keys to move the highlight across the top menu options. Each top menu option displays a pull-down menu of options. Within each pull-down menu, use the ↑ and ↓ keys to highlight individual menu options, and press Return to select a menu option.

Finally, the user profile determines data-encryption security, because the users can decrypt only files that belong to groups to which they are assigned.

Within the PROTECT menu, the Users menu (shown in Figure 20.2) lets you create, change, and delete user profiles; define a group name for each user; and define or change an access level for each user. The access level defines the user's file privileges, as discussed in more detail in the section "Defining File Privilege Schemes" below. You assign the log-in identifications to each user, as summarized in Table 20.3.

***Assigning the Login Name*** The login name is the name the user will enter when first entering dBASE. There is no need for this name to be cryptic; the user's actual first or last name or initials will be sufficient. Up to eight characters are allowed (upper- and lowercase are irrelevant).

***Assigning the Password*** The password should be unique and confidential to each user. Users should select their own passwords, up to 16 characters long. Whenever the user logs on, he or she will have to enter this password. The password will not appear on the screen as it is typed, to prevent curious bystanders from knowing the user's password.

***Assigning the Group Name*** The group name lets you organize users by application (e.g., payroll, accounts receivable). The group name should be an abbreviation, because it is limited to eight characters. Once a group name has been assigned to a database file (under the Files menu), only users with that group name can access the file.

| MENU ITEM | PURPOSE OF CODE | EXPECTED VALUE |
|---|---|---|
| Login name | Identifies individual user | 1– 8 characters |
| Password | User's unique password | 1–16 characters |
| Group name | Matches user to a particular application | 1– 8 characters |
| Account name | Optional additional user identification | 1–24 characters |
| Access level | Access level as defined on the Files menu | 1– 8 (number) |

**TABLE 20.3:** Users Menu Items in PROTECT

To give a user access to more than one application, enter a profile for the user for each group name. For example, if you want Jones to have access to both payroll and accounts receivable, you must define two user profiles for Jones, each with the appropriate group name.

Note that all files in a single group will have the same encryption key, while files in different groups have different encryption keys (PROTECT assigns encryption keys automatically). Therefore, even a user who has full access to all the files in his or her own group (or groups) cannot access files outside that group (or groups).

***Assigning the Account Name*** The optional account name can be up to 24 characters in length. This name is not entered by the user when logging. Instead, it is simply recorded here for future reference by the system manager or programmer. Usually, this name is the user's department (e.g., sales, marketing) or perhaps the name of a project that the user is working on.

***Assigning the Access Level*** The access level you select here can be a number from 1 (most privileges) to 8 (least privileges). This number will correspond to the file access privileges you define on the Files menu. Later when the user logs on, his or her access level will be assigned automatically and stored in the dBASE ACCESS( ) function. Your programs can detect the user's access level simply by accessing the number stored in the ACCESS( ) function. (The ACCESS( ) function is discussed in the section "Network and Security Programming Techniques" later in this chapter.)

***Storing the User Profile*** Once you've defined a user's profile, select the Store user profile option to save it. This will store the user's profile in encrypted form in the file named dbSystem.db.

***Deleting a User*** The Delete user from group option deletes the user profile currently displayed on the screen. Note that if the user is assigned to several groups, his or her profile will be deleted only from the group currently displayed on the screen.

***Changing User Profiles*** Whenever you define the login name, password, and group name on the Users menu, the PROTECT program automatically checks whether that user profile has already been defined. If these three items already match an existing user profile, the rest of the information for that user is automatically displayed on the menu. You can then change any of the existing information. When you are done making changes, select the Store user profile option from the Users menu and the Save or Exit option from the Exit menu.

## DEFINING FILE PRIVILEGE SCHEMES

After you have created the user profiles, you can begin developing the *file privilege schemes*. These schemes let you refine the access-level security of the system by determining exactly which records and fields users are allowed to view, add to, change, and delete.

The Files menu on the PROTECT screen (shown in Figure 20.3) allows you to define or modify file privilege schemes. This menu lets you assign a file to a group, assign up to eight access levels to each file, and assign field access privileges for each file access level. As the figure shows, all file access privileges are initially set to 8, and the field access privilege level is initially set to 1. Each menu option is discussed in the sections below.

***Selecting the File*** The first option on the Files menu, Select new file, allows you to select a database file to assign access levels to. When you press Return to select

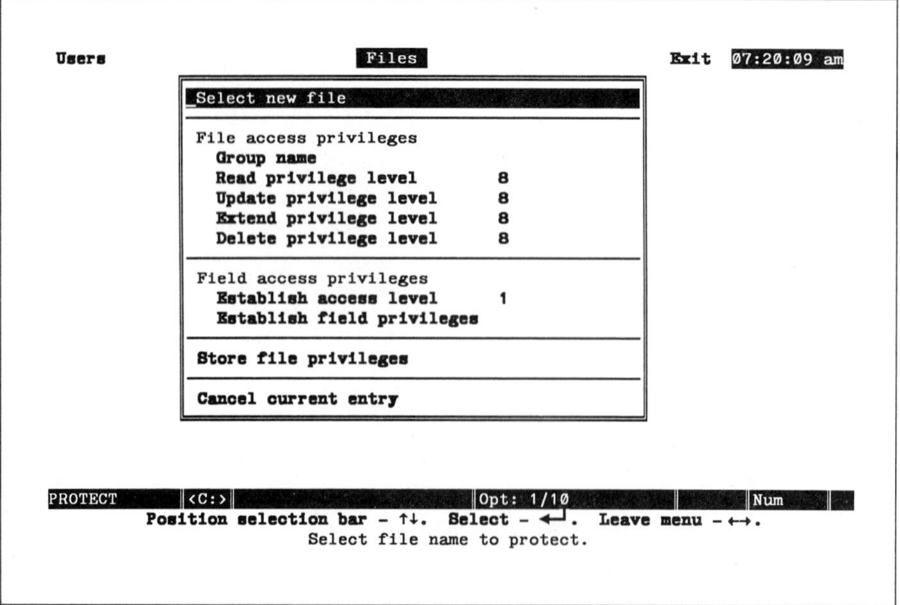


**FIGURE 20.3:** The Files menu on the PROTECT screen. This menu lets you assign a file to a group, assign up to eight access levels to each file, and assign field access privileges for each file access level.

this option, the names of all database files on the current directory appear on a submenu. Use the arrow keys to highlight the database file you wish to work with, and press Return to select that database file. The database file name will appear next to the Select new file menu option, and all remaining changes will affect only that database file.

Note that you can assign access levels for up to ten database files during a single session with PROTECT. After selecting the tenth database file and assigning access privileges to it, move the highlight to the Exit menu option and select Exit or Save. Then, if you want to assign access levels to more files, you can move the highlight back to the Files pull-down menu and select additional database files.

***Assigning the File to a Group*** Under the File access privileges section of the Files menu, the Group name option allows you to assign the currently selected database file to a group name. As discussed earlier, you will probably want to assign the file to a group based on an application, such as accounts receivable or payroll. Users whose profiles match the group name assigned here will be able to access the file. Database files in the same group share the same encryption key. Files in separate groups use different encryption keys to prevent cross-accessing of files assigned to different applications.

***Establishing File Privilege Levels*** The last four items in the File access privileges section of the menu allow you to establish privilege levels for four types of access, as listed below:

| **Access privilege** | **Meaning** |
|---|---|
| Read | User can read (view) the file |
| Update | User can change data in the file |
| Extend | User can add new records to the file |
| Delete | User can delete records from the file |

When assigning privilege levels, use the numbers 1 through 8. Level 1 provides the fullest access (least restrictions), and level 8 provides the least access (most restrictions). The number you assign to each type of privilege determines the extent of file access for each individual user.

For example, if employees Joe Smith and Sandy Beach have an access level of 4, those two users will be able to perform the tasks to which you assign a level of 8, 7, 6, 5, or 4 in this section of the menu. They will *not* be able to perform tasks to which you assign levels of 3, 2, or 1.

Looking at it from another angle, suppose that you assign the access levels shown below for the current database file:

| | |
|---|---|
| Read privilege level | 8 |
| Update privilege level | 6 |
| Extend privilege level | 4 |
| Delete privilege level | 2 |

Any users who have an access level of 1 (as established on their user profiles) will have complete access to the database file, including the ability to read, update, extend, and delete the file. A user with an access level of 7 or 8 could only read the file. A user with an access level of 5 or 6 could read and update the file but not add or delete records from the file.

To fill in the appropriate numbers on the menu, move the highlight to the appropriate menu item and press the Return key. Then either type in the number (1–8) or use the ↑ and ↓ keys to automatically increase or decrease the number. When the correct value is displayed, press the Return key again.

***Establishing Field Privilege Levels*** The section of the Files menu entitled Field access privileges lets you determine which fields are accessible to individual users beyond their overall access to the file. The Establish access level option lets you select an access level for which to define field privileges. For each possible user access level (1–8), you can assign a different set of field access privileges. For example, you could hide a particular field from individuals with an access level of 6 or higher, but display those fields for individuals with an access level of 5 or lower.

After you have selected a field access level to work with, select the Establish field privileges option. A list of all field names appears in a submenu next to the Files menu, with initial FULL access granted to all fields. You can change any of these privileges to match the current access level you are assigning field privileges to. To change a value, move the highlight to that field name and press Return. Each time you press Return, the value is automatically changed to a new value (either R/O or NONE). When the setting you desire is in the field, press the ↑ or ↓ key to move to the next field name. For example, Figure 20.4 shows a sample field list, with privileges assigned for access level 4.

You can assign any one of three access privileges to each field, as summarized below:

| Level | Privileges |
|---|---|
| FULL | User can read and write data in the field |
| R/O | User can read but not write data in the field (i.e., read only) |
| NONE | User can neither read nor write data in the field |

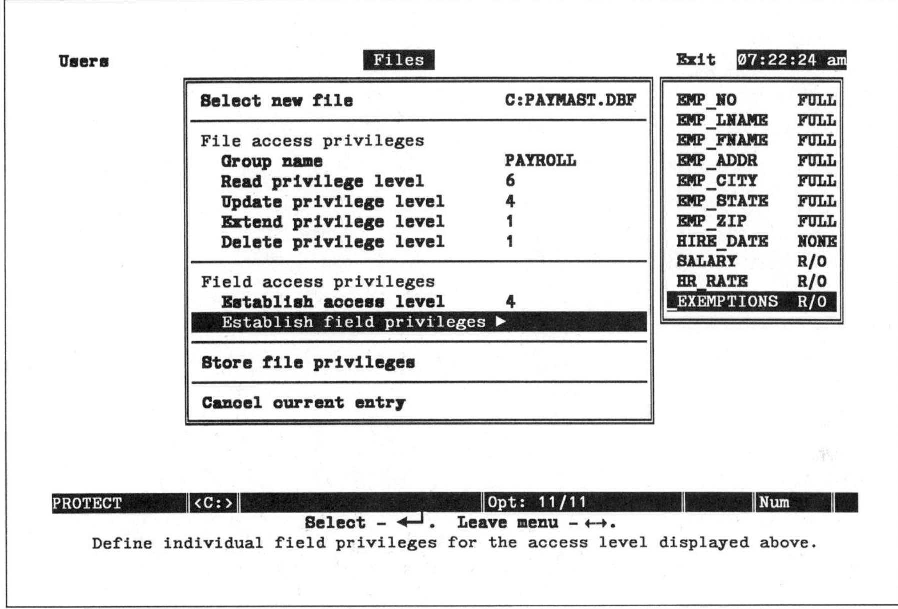


**FIGURE 20.4:** Field names displayed in a submenu and assigned access privileges. FULL privilege allows users at this access level to read and write data in the field. R/O privilege allows users at this access level only to read (view) the data. NONE privilege prevents users at this access level from either viewing or changing the data in the field.

Note, however, that file privileges take precedence over field privileges. If the file privilege states that the user can only read data in the file, a field privilege of FULL makes no sense. Therefore, if the user can only read the file, the only valid field options would be R/O or NONE.

After you have defined the appropriate settings for each field at the current access level, press ← to leave the field name submenu. Then, if necessary, select another file access level to work with (1–8), and repeat the process of assigning FULL, R/O, or NONE access levels for each field for the new file access level. You can continue to do so until field privilege levels are assigned for each file access level.

Note that if you change a field access level from FULL at a given file access level, all corresponding field privileges at more restrictive file access levels are automatically set to NONE, unless you specifically change them. Therefore, it is generally a good idea to work from the least restrictive level (1) to the most restrictive level (8), and review all of your work before saving the file and field definitions.

***Saving the File Privilege Scheme*** When you are satisfied with the file and field privilege scheme for the current database file, select the Store file privileges option from the Files menu. You can then select the Select new file option to begin work with a new database file, or select the Exit option from the top menu to leave PROTECT.

***Changing File Privilege Schemes*** The bottom option on the Files menu, Cancel current entry, lets you delete the file privilege scheme that you are currently working on and start all over again.

If you wish to change a file privilege scheme after you have already saved and tested it, run the PROTECT program again. Select the Select new file option from the Files menu and enter the database file name, just as though you were creating the privilege scheme for the first time. PROTECT will bring up the existing scheme, and you can change it using the usual arrow and Return keys. Remember to store the changes and save your work before exiting PROTECT.

### Exiting PROTECT

The last menu item at the top of the PROTECT screen is Exit. When you select this option, you'll be given three options: Save, Abandon, and Exit.

Selecting the Save option saves all new and modified privilege schemes. The user profiles are saved in a file named dbSystem.db. File privilege schemes are stored in the database file structure. When the file privilege scheme is saved, the associated database file and its index files are automatically encrypted.

Selecting the Abandon option cancels all new or modified user profiles and file privilege schemes. Any previous settings that were defined before the current PROTECT session are restored.

Selecting Exit from the pull-down menu saves any changes and then leaves the PROTECT program and returns you to the DOS prompt.

## Using Security Forms

Before you actually use the PROTECT program to set up a security system, you may want to create some forms to help you work things out on paper. For example, the sample form shown in Figure 20.5 lets you fill in users' login names, passwords, group names, account names (if any), and access levels. This example shows how the form might be filled in for a hypothetical company named ABC Co. Note that several users are assigned to more than one group, because they have access to more than one application. The network administrator (B. King in this example), has assigned herself unrestricted access (1) to all the groups in the entire network system, so that she can have full control over all files.

Figure 20.6 shows a sample form that you can use to help develop a file privilege scheme for a file. It is filled in for a database file named PayMast. Enter the

ABC Company

dBASE ADMINISTRATOR User Profiles

| Employee Name | Login Name | Password | Group Name | Account Name | Access Level | Entered By |
|---|---|---|---|---|---|---|
| B. King | King | Honcho | Payroll | DP | 1 | BK |
| B. King | King | Honcho | Payables | DP | 1 | BK |
| B. King | King | Honcho | Ledger | DP | 1 | BK |
| A. Adams | Abigail | Kitten | Payroll | Personnel | 1 | BK |
| A. Adams | Abigail | Kitten | Payables | Personnel | 1 | BK |
| B. Jones | Bart | Pluto | Payroll | Personnel | 6 | BK |
| C. Smith | Chuck | Banana | Ledger | Finance | 4 | BK |
| K. Watson | Kay | Sky | Payroll | Personnel | 4 | BK |
| K. Watson | Kay | Sky | Ledger | Finance | 4 | BK |
| R. Yokem | Ron | Tree | Payables | Management | 8 | BK |
| R. Yokem | Ron | Tree | Ledger | Management | 1 | BK |
| | | | | | | |
| | | | | | | |
| | | | | | | |

**FIGURE 20.5:** A suggested form for listing user login names, passwords, group names, account names, and access levels. Filling in this form before going online with PROTECT can simplify establishing user profiles. Note that some users are assigned to more than one group, because they need access to more than one application.

file name and group name at the top of the form. For file privileges, you can enter an X at the most restrictive level. For field privileges, you can enter FULL, R/O, or NONE values for each of the eight possible file privilege levels.

The forms can actually serve a dual purpose. Besides giving you a worksheet to plan your overall security scheme, they provide a hard copy of the security scheme for future reference. When you need to add new users to the system, refer to your hard copies of the existing security scheme to help determine access levels for the new users. If the dbSystem.db file on your network becomes corrupted or lost, you can simply copy the backup version of the dbSystem.db file back onto the dBASE ADMINISTRATOR directory of the network system.

As an added precaution, one person should also periodically make unencrypted backup copies of all the database files in the system. This person (presumably the network administrator or the administrator's aide) needs to have full access to the database files and all the fields (an access level of 1, with FULL privileges on every field). This person can then copy files from the hard disk to floppy disks using the commands below:

```
USE <file name>
SET ENCRYPTION OFF
COPY TO A:<file name>
SET ENCRYPTION ON
```

The <file name> above refers to the name of the encrypted database file being copied, and A: assumes that the floppy disk drive is drive A.

File Security Scheme Worksheet

Database file name: PayMast

Group name : Payroll

| File Privilege | <-- Least restrictions | | | | | | Most restrictions -> |
|---|---|---|---|---|---|---|---|
| Access level | 1 | 2 | 3 | 4 | 5 | 6 | 7 | 8 |
| Read | | | | | | | | X |
| Update | | | | X | | | | |
| Extend | X | | | | | | | |
| Delete | X | | | | | | | |

FIELD PRIVILEGES

| Field Name | Access Level 1 | 2 | 3 | 4 | 5 | 6 | 7 | 8 |
|---|---|---|---|---|---|---|---|---|
| Emp-No | F | | | F | | R | | R |
| Emp-LName | F | | | F | | R | | R |
| Emp-FName | F | | | F | | R | | R |
| Emp-Addr | F | | | F | | R | | R |
| Emp-City | F | | | F | | R | | R |
| Emp-State | F | | | F | | R | | R |
| Emp-Zip | F | | | F | | R | | R |
| Hire-Date | F | | | N | | R | | R |
| Salary | F | | | R | | R | | N |
| Hr-Rate | F | | | R | | R | | N |
| Exemptions | F | | | R | | R | | N |

F = FULL R = R/O N = NONE

**FIGURE 20.6:** A sample form for defining a file privilege scheme for a single database file. The file and group name are at the top of the form. File privilege levels 1–8 are listed in the middle of the form. Individual fields on the database and their access levels can be listed near the bottom of the form.

Beyond the basics of creating and maintaining a security system on a network is the need to develop applications that run smoothly on the network system. There are specialized programming commands, functions, and techniques required to develop networked applications, and these are discussed in the sections below.

## Managing Files on the Network

Local area networks pose problems to the programmer that are not encountered in a single-user environment. In particular, the system needs to be designed to prevent *collisions:* situations where two or more users make changes to a database that override or cancel each other out. These collisions might happen at either the file or single-record level.

The dBASE ADMINISTRATOR provides three ways of preventing accidental collisions on a network system:

1. It lets a given user (or workstation) have exclusive use of a file so that no other users can interfere with his or her work.
2. It temporarily locks a file that is otherwise available to several users so that only one person can use it at a time.
3. It locks a single record so that only one user can edit that record.

How and when you use these locking techniques depends on the file-open attribute in use at the moment: exclusive or shared, as discussed below.

## Exclusive Access

When a file is opened for exclusive access, only the user currently working with the file has access to it. By default, dBASE opens most files for exclusive use automatically. There is no need to lock the file or any record in the file, because only a single user has access to the file. However, the default exclusive mode can be overridden with the SET EXCLUSIVE OFF command, which provides shared access to the file.

In most applications, you should use SET EXCLUSIVE OFF only in situations where you are certain that multiple users need access to the file. But for maximum efficiency, there are many cases where you will want several users to access the same file at the same time.

## Shared Access

When SET EXCLUSIVE is off, multiple users on the network can access the same database file simultaneously. When this is the case, file-locking and record-locking techniques are required to prevent collisions among the multiple users. With proper programming techniques (discussed below), you can increase network efficiency by allowing shared access among users most of the time, limiting exclusive access to only those tasks that absolutely require exclusive access.

(*Note:* Only files stored on shared directories as defined at the network level can be shared. See Appendix B, "Installing dBASE III PLUS," or your networking manual, for creating shared directories from the network level.)

Also, keep in mind that once the SET EXCLUSIVE OFF command is issued, *all* files are opened for shared access until a SET EXCLUSIVE ON command resets the opening attribute to exclusive access. As a network programmer, you'll need to keep track of which files are opened for exclusive use and which are not. The following sections will help clarify this issue.

## Default File Access Modes

As mentioned earlier, dBASE opens most files for exclusive access automatically, and an intentional SET EXCLUSIVE OFF command is required to open the file for shared access. However, certain files and commands pose no threat of collision and are therefore automatically opened in shared mode. For example, if two or more users want to print a report using the same report format (.frm) file, there is no threat of the users simultaneously *changing* the report format. Therefore, the report format file can be safely opened for multiple users. Table 20.4 shows the default file modes that dBASE uses for various types of files.

When a file is opened for exclusive use, there is no need to be concerned with locking files and records, because only the current user has access to the database file. Some operations absolutely require exclusive use of the file. These are listed in Table 20.5, along with commands requiring other types of handling in the network. All other operations can be used in shared mode, but the programmer has to use file locking and record locking to prevent collisions. These topics are discussed in the sections below.

## File and Record Locking

Any file that is opened after a SET EXCLUSIVE OFF command is issued is automatically opened in shared mode. Multiple users can access the file at the same time. However, commands that act upon the entire database file require that only a single user have access to a database file at the moment. (That is, even though the file is in shared mode, it needs to be temporarily locked while a particular command is being performed.)

There are three levels of locking in dBASE: automatic file locking, explicit file locking, and explicit record locking, as discussed in the sections below.

### Automatic File Locking

Commands that work on an entire file require that the shared database file be locked for the duration of the command. These commands will automatically attempt to lock the file before performing their tasks. If the command cannot lock the file (because it is locked by another user), dBASE returns the error message **File is in use by another**. If an ON ERROR command is in effect, the ERROR( ) function receives the value 108.

The commands that automatically lock files are listed in Table 20.5, along with commands requiring exclusive use of a file and commands requiring file or record locks. There are numerous programming techniques that you can use to deal with error messages that might be returned by commands that use automatic file locking. These are discussed later in the section "Network and Security Programming Techniques."

| FILE TYPE | COMMAND | DEFAULT OPEN MODE |
|---|---|---|
| Alternate (.txt) | SET ALTERNATE TO | Exclusive |
| Catalog (.cat) | SET CATALOG TO | Shared |
| Command (.prg) | MODIFY COMMAND | Exclusive |
| | DO | Shared |
| Database (.dbf)* | COPY | Exclusive |
| | CREATE | Exclusive |
| | JOIN | Exclusive |
| | SORT | Exclusive |
| | TOTAL | Exclusive |
| | USE | Exclusive |
| | APPEND FROM | Shared |
| | CREATE | Exclusive |
| | CREATE...FROM | Shared |
| | UPDATE | Shared |
| Format (.fmt) | SET FORMAT TO | Shared |
| | MODIFY COMMAND | Shared |
| Index (.ndx) | INDEX | Exclusive |
| | USE | Exclusive |
| | SET INDEX TO | Exclusive |
| Label (.lbl) | CREATE/MODIFY LABEL | Exclusive |
| | LABEL FORM | Shared |
| Memo (.dbt)* | USE <database file> | Exclusive |
| Memory (.mem) | SAVE | Exclusive |
| | RESTORE | Shared |
| Procedure (.prg) | MODIFY COMMAND | Exclusive |
| | SET PROCEDURE | Shared |
| Query (.qry) | CREATE/MODIFY QUERY | Exclusive |
| | SET FILTER | Shared |
| Report (.frm) | CREATE/MODIFY REPORT | Exclusive |
| | REPORT FORM | Shared |
| View (.vue) | CREATE VIEW | Exclusive |
| | MODIFY VIEW | Shared |
| | SET VIEW | Shared |

*Index and memo files are opened in the same access mode as the associated database file.

**TABLE 20.4:** Default File-Open Attributes on a Network

| Commands Requiring Exclusive Use of Files | | |
|---|---|---|
| INSERT [BLANK] | | |
| MODIFY STRUCTURE | | |
| PACK | | |
| REINDEX | | |
| ZAP | | |
| **Commands That Automatically Lock and Unlock Files** | | |
| APPEND [BLANK] | COUNT | REPLACE ALL |
| APPEND FROM | DELETE ALL | SORT |
| AVERAGE | INDEX | SUM |
| BROWSE | JOIN | TOTAL |
| COPY | RECALL ALL | UPDATE |
| COPY STRUCTURE | | |
| **Commands That Require File or Record Locking** | | |
| @...SAY...GET <field name> READ | | |
| REPLACE <a single field> | | |

**TABLE 20.5:** Network Techniques Required for Various Commands

## Explicit File Locking

The explicit file-locking technique allows you to lock a database file temporarily while a particular user makes some change to the file. When the user is finished with his or her task, the file is immediately unlocked.

Explicit file locking is useful in situations where users need locked access only for a short period of time. Other users will have to wait a few seconds before they can access the file. Your application can determine the maximum wait period and provide alternative actions for users who are waiting.

## Explicit Record Locking

Explicit record locking locks only a single record in a database file while a user makes a change to that record. This technique is highly efficient, because other users are locked out of only the single record being changed, not the entire database file.

To use record locking, an application program first locates the record to be changed and sees whether the record is currently unlocked. If the record is unlocked, the program locks the record, then displays the current data on the screen. At this point, no other user on the network can change the data on the screen. The user can then make changes and save them. The new data are stored on the file, and the record is then unlocked so that other users once again have access to it.

## File-Locking Functions

dBASE offers several commands and functions for locking and unlocking files and records. The FLOCK( ) function is used for locking files, and the RLOCK( ), or just LOCK( ), function is used for records. FLOCK( ) and RLOCK( ) behave a little like commands, though they are actually functions.

Both FLOCK( ) and RLOCK( ) first test whether the file or record is already locked. If the file or record is not already locked, the function immediately locks the file or record for the current user and returns the value .T.. If the file or record is already locked and cannot be locked by the current user, FLOCK( ) or RLOCK( ) returns .F. (i.e., you do not have the file or record locked).

The UNLOCK command (not a function) releases a lock on a file or record. Your programs can use the locking functions and UNLOCK command to temporarily lock a shared file (if it is not already locked), allow the current user to make a change, and then quickly unlock the file or record for other users. The simple routine below shows the general logic:

```
USE AnyFile
IF RLOCK( )
      EDIT RecNumb
      UNLOCK
ELSE
      ? "Can't edit - record is locked already!"
ENDIF
```

You'll likely need more sophisticated algorithms than this in an actual application. But the basic logic remains the same for all types of locking.

For every successful lock placed by a user, there should be some command to unlock the file or record to return access to the other users. This can be accomplished by using the UNLOCK command, by locking another file or record, or by issuing a CLOSE, USE, CLEAR ALL, or QUIT command.

## Special Cases of Record Locks: CHANGE and EDIT

The CHANGE and EDIT commands allow records to be edited individually. They also allow the user to scroll up and down through records using the PgUp and PgDn keys. When these commands are used in a network, the user must lock the record before making any changes.

Users can lock and unlock any record displayed on the screen during a CHANGE or EDIT command by typing Ctrl-O. The status bar at the bottom of the screen (or the scoreboard at the top of the screen) displays the message **Record locked** or **Record unlocked**, depending on the current status of the record displayed on the screen. In addition, if the file is in exclusive use, the prompt **exclusive** appears on the screen. The user can view any record (locked or unlocked).

If a record is locked when the user wants to make a change, he or she must wait for the record to be unlocked. Before making a change, the user must then lock the record (with Ctrl-O) from his or her own keyboard before making the change. When done editing the record, the user can type Ctrl-Q or Ctrl-W to finish the editing and unlock the record, scroll to a new record to unlock the record, or type Ctrl-O again to unlock the record.

# NETWORK AND SECURITY PROGRAMMING TECHNIQUES

As discussed above, the RLOCK( ) and FLOCK( ) functions allow shared files to be locked temporarily to prevent collisions, and the UNLOCK command can then be used to make the file or record available to the other users. There are additional commands and functions that you can use in the networking environment to build applications that run smoothly. There are also general programming techniques that you can use reliably, and these are the main focus of this section.

## Limiting Access to Programs and Commands

When a user logs into the network system, his or her access level (as defined in the user profile under the PROTECT program) is stored in the dBASE function ACCESS( ). You can use this ACCESS( ) function to determine which users can access various commands and functions. The easiest way to do this is to determine access levels right inside your menu programs.

Figure 20.7 shows a sample main menu program that controls the programs users can branch to based on the ACCESS( ) function. For example, note that only users with access levels of 1, 2, or 3 can access the AddNew and EditDel programs, while users with access levels of 1 through 6 can access the PrintRep program. The access is controlled by using the IF ACCESS( ) clause to determine the user's access level before branching to a program.

Instead of repeating the IF clause in each CASE statement, you could place the IF clause in a procedure, as shown in Figure 20.8. Then your CASE clauses could use a DO...WITH command to pass the appropriate parameters to the procedure.

```
************************************** MainMenu.prg.
SET TALK OFF
Choice = 0
DO WHILE Choice < 4
   CLEAR
   TEXT
                 Main Menu

              1. Add new records
              2. Edit records
              3. Print Reports
              4. Exit
   ENDTEXT
   @ 20,1 SAY "Enter choice " GET Choice PICT "@Z 9"
   READ

   DO CASE
      CASE Choice = 1
           *--- Only users with access levels <= 3.
           IF ACCESS() <= 3
              DO AddNew
           ELSE
              ? "Sorry -- access denied."
              WAIT
           ENDIF

      CASE Choice = 2
           *--- Only users with access levels <= 3.
           IF ACCESS() <= 3
              DO EditDel
           ELSE
              ? "Sorry -- access denied."
              WAIT
           ENDIF

      CASE Choice = 3
           *--- Only users with access levels <= 6.
           IF ACCESS() <= 6
              DO PrintRep
           ELSE
              ? "Sorry -- access denied."
              WAIT
           ENDIF

   ENDCASE
ENDDO
```

**FIGURE 20.7:** Sample main menu program that presents a menu and waits for the user's selection. Before branching to the appropriate subprogram, an IF clause within each CASE statement determines the user's access level. If the user's access level is greater than a specified cutoff point, access to the subprogram is denied.

For example, to permit access to the AddNew program only for users with an access level of 3 or less, you could call the procedure with the single command

**DO TestFrst WITH "AddNew",3**

The TestFrst procedure will branch to the AddNew program only if the user's access level is less than or equal to 3.

## A File-Locking Procedure

When files are in use in the shared mode and one user has a file or record locked for a given task, other users should not be expected to wait indefinitely for the file or record to be unlocked. Instead, your application should use techniques that attempt to access the file for only a specified period of time, then allow the user to move on to something else and try again later if necessary. This is most easily accomplished with procedures that use DO WHILE loops that attempt to lock the file (again, for the current user) for a certain number of repetitions, then present a message if the access still fails.

Figure 20.9 shows a procedure that attempts to place a lock on a file for a limited period of time. The procedure displays the message **Trying to access file...** while it is attempting to unlock the file. It repeats a loop until either the file is unlocked for the

```
PROCEDURE TestFrst
PARAMETERS ProgName,Required
   IF ACCESS() <= Required
      DO &ProgName
   ELSE
      ? CHR(7)
      @ 20,2 SAY "Access to this function denied."
      ?
      WAIT
   ENDIF
RETURN
```

**FIGURE 20.8:** A procedure that checks the user's access level before passing control to a called program. The ProgName parameter is the name of the program to be called, and the Required parameter is the access level required to run the program.

```
PROCEDURE AccFile
   @ 24,1 SAY "Trying to access file..."

   *----- Try accessing for 100 loops.
   FCount = 1
   DO WHILE FCount <= 100 .AND. .NOT. FLOCK()
      FCount = FCount + 1
   ENDDO (fcount)
   *----- If still not available, present message.
   IF .NOT. FLOCK()
      @ 24,1 SAY "File not available. Try again later!"
   ELSE
      @ 24,1 CLEAR
   ENDIF (not flock())
RETURN
```

**FIGURE 20.9:** A procedure that attempts to lock a file for the time required to complete 100 DO WHILE loops. If the file still cannot be locked by the current user, the procedure displays the message **File not available. Try again later!** before returning control to the calling program.

current user or a counter variable, named FCount in this example, reaches the number 100. (You may want to experiment with different values in place of 100 in your own applications.)

To access this procedure from an application, call it immediately after issuing the command to open the file. When the procedure returns control to the calling program, perform the appropriate command only if the file is still not locked. A typical call to the AccFile procedure shown in Figure 20.9 might look like this:

```
USE AnyFile
DO AccFile      && try to get a lock on the file.
IF FLOCK( )
    <Perform command here...>
    UNLOCK
ELSE
    ? "Attempted command denied..."
ENDIF
```

As shown in the small routine above, the program should unlock the file when the lock is no longer needed, so other users can regain access to the file.

## A Record-Locking Procedure

Like the file-locking procedure discussed in the previous section, record-locking procedures can be used to put a time limit on an attempted record access. Figure 20.10 shows a procedure named AccRec that attempts to access a record for the time required to complete 50 loops. Like the AccFile procedure, it displays the message **Record not available. Try again later!** if the record cannot be accessed and locked for the current user during the allotted time.

```
PROCEDURE AccRec
   @ 24,1 SAY "Trying to access record..."

   *----- Try accessing for 50 loops.
   RCount = 1
   DO WHILE RCount <= 50 .AND. .NOT. RLOCK()
      RCount = RCount + 1
   ENDDO (rcount)
   *----- If still not available, present message.
   IF .NOT. RLOCK()
      @ 24,1 SAY "Record not available. Try again later!"
   ELSE
      @ 24,1 CLEAR
   ENDIF (not rlock())
RETURN
```

**FIGURE 20.10:** A procedure that attempts to lock a record for the time required to complete 50 DO WHILE loops. If the record still cannot be locked by the current user, the procedure displays the message **Record not available. Try again later!** before returning control to the calling program.

A typical use of the AccRec procedure would be when the user has located a particular record and wishes to edit it with a custom screen and READ command, as in the small sample routine shown in Figure 20.11. (The routine assumes the **SET PROCEDURE** command has already opened the appropriate procedure file.)

## Trapping Network Errors

Chapter 19, "Event Processing and Error Trapping," discusses the use of the ON ERROR command to trap an error and respond to it. This same technique can be used to trap errors in network systems and attempt to deal with the error gracefully. You should add a procedure to your network application to respond to the errors **File is in use by another** (108) and **Record is in use by another** (109). A single procedure can respond to either error and attempt to access the locked file or record for a limited period of time.

Assuming that the name of the procedure file that contains procedures for trapping errors is ErrTraps.prg, and the procedure that responds to errors is named ErrTrap, your network will need the commands below somewhere near the top of the main menu program for the application:

**SET PROCEDURE TO ErrTraps**
**ON ERROR DO ErrTrap**

```
USE AnyFile INDEX AnyFile
SET FORMAT TO AnyScreen

LookFor = SPACE(5)
@ 20,2 SAY "Enter part number to edit " ;
  GET LookFor PICTURE "!!!!!"
READ
*------ Try to find that record.
SEEK LookFor

*------ If record found, try to lock it for edit.
IF FOUND()
   DO AccRec
   IF RLOCK()  && if locked, proceed with edit.
      READ
      UNLOCK
   ENDIF
*---- If record not found at all, display error message.
ELSE
   ? "No such record exists!"
ENDIF
```

**FIGURE 20.11:** A sample routine that accesses the AccRec procedure shown in Figure 20.10 to attempt to lock a record and edit it. If the AccRec procedure cannot lock the file, no edit takes place. If the record can be locked, the user can edit it, after which the UNLOCK command immediately frees the record for access by other users.

A sample procedure for responding to the inaccessible-file and inaccessible-record errors is shown in Figure 20.12. (The procedure is shown inside of the procedure file named ErrTraps, which might also include other procedures, including the AccFile and AccRec procedures shown above.)

The procedure makes ten attempts to correct the error. Between each attempt, it pauses for as much time as is required to perform 50 iterations of a DO WHILE loop. If after ten attempts the procedure does not gain access to the file or record, it displays the message **Still can't get access. Try again later...**

The calling program for this procedure needs to initialize the variable named Attempts to zero so that the procedure makes all ten attempts and so that the calling program can detect whether the procedure was successful.

The small routine below shows how the calling program can be set up to use the procedure (assuming the SET PROCEDURE and ON ERROR commands have already been executed):

```
Attempts = 0
USE AnyFile INDEX AnyFile
* -- If Attempts variable reached 10, file/record not accessed.
```

```
********************************** ErrTraps.prg
*----- Sample procedure to trap common errors.
PROCEDURE ErrTrap
   @ 19,0 CLEAR
   @ 19,0 TO 19,79 DOUBLE
   ? CHR(7)

   DO CASE
      CASE ERROR = 108 .OR. ERROR = 109
           @ 19,2 SAY "Trying to access data..."
           *---- Wait a few seconds.
           Timer = 1
           DO WHILE Timer <= 50
              Timer = Timer + 1
           ENDDO
           Attempts = Attempts + 1
           IF Attempts <= 10
              RETRY
           ELSE
              @ 19,2 SAY "Still can't get access."
              @ 21,2 SAY "Try again later..."
              RETURN
           ENDIF

         *---- Additional CASES for ON ERROR may follow...

   ENDCASE
RETURN
```

**FIGURE 20.12:** A sample procedure to trap network errors caused by trying to access a locked file or record. The procedure is called by an **ON ERROR DO ErrTrap** command. The procedure passes time by counting to 50 with an empty DO WHILE loop before trying the RETRY command again. After ten unsuccessful retries, the procedure displays the error message **Still can't get access. Try again later...** and passes control back to the calling program. The calling program must initialize the Attempts variable and respond to its final value.

```
IF Attempts > = 10
    WAIT
    RETURN TO MASTER
ENDIF
* -- Otherwise, proceed with program.
```

The procedure shown in Figure 20.12 will protect against errors caused by programs attempting to skip or go to a record that is in exclusive use by another user. The procedure will also protect against a networking error known as *file deadlock* or *deadly embrace.* A deadly embrace occurs when two users attempt to access the same exclusive files, and a RETRY command (if not limited to a specific number of attempts) keeps trying to access the two files indefinitely.

Figure 20.13 shows programming conditions that lead to a deadly embrace. At one workstation, a program is attempting to access the Master and Charges database in exclusive mode, while at another workstation a program is attempting to access the same two files, in opposite work areas, but also in exclusive mode. The RETRY command that is responding to the error would keep bouncing back and forth between errors indefinitely (as shown by the arrows in the figure), if some limit were not placed on the number of attempts allowed.

Bear in mind that during the initial development, testing, and debugging cycles of your software development, you can use the SUSPEND command within your error-trapping procedure to return temporarily to the dot prompt. When the dot prompt reappears, use the DISPLAY STATUS command to view the status of all open files. In a networking environment, DISPLAY STATUS displays the same information that it does in single-user mode, but it also displays the status of the SET EXCLUSIVE and SET ENCRYPTION parameters, as well as the lock status of any active database files. These will provide additional clues as to the cause of any problems.

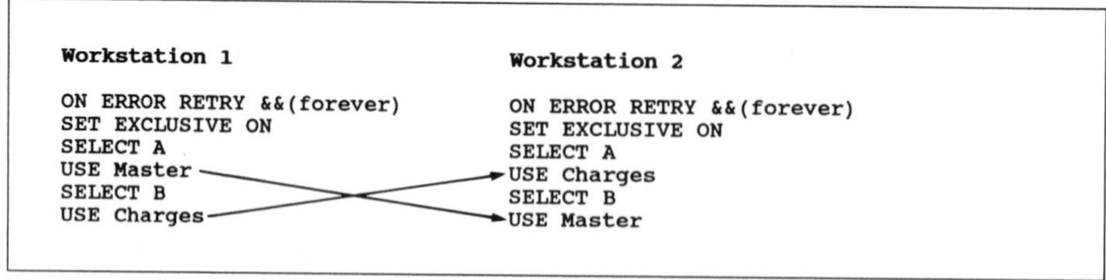


**FIGURE 20.13:** Two workstations attempting to access the same files, in exclusive mode, at the same time. If the ON ERROR condition does not place a limit in the number of RETRY commands that respond to the error, the two programs end up in a *deadly embrace,* bouncing off each other's errors indefinitely.

# Commands That Behave Differently in a Network

This section summarizes commands used in single-user environments that behave differently in network environments. For information on all of the details of the command, see the appropriate reference in the single-user chapters.

## CHANGE/EDIT in a Network

The CHANGE and EDIT commands use the same syntax in a network environment that they do in a single-user environment. There are only two differences in their behavior. In a network environment, the status bar displays the following file or record information, as is appropriate to the file or record being edited:

**Exclusive**
**File Locked**
**Read Only**
**Record Locked**
**Record Unlocked**

If the file currently being edited is in shared mode, the record must be locked before it can be edited.

The second unique feature of the CHANGE/EDIT commands in the network environment is that the user can type Ctrl-O to lock and unlock the record currently on the screen.

## DISPLAY/LIST STATUS in a Network

When used in a network environment, the DISPLAY STATUS and LIST STATUS commands display the lock status of the currently open database file. In addition, the status of the SET ENCRYPTION and SET EXCLUSIVE parameters is displayed.

## SET in a Network

The SET command, with no additional parameters, displays a full-screen menu-driven technique for viewing and altering SET parameters, just as it does in the single-user mode. However, the screen also includes the current settings for the SET ENCRYPTION and SET EXCLUSIVE commands.

## USE in a Network

In a network, you can use the EXCLUSIVE command at the end of a USE command to open a file for exclusive use. This is similar to a SET EXCLUSIVE ON command, but it specifies only the file currently being opened for exclusive use. For example, the command below opens the database file named Charges and the ChrgNo index file for exclusive use:

**USE Charges INDEX ChrgNo EXCLUSIVE**

## SET PRINTER in a Network

SET PRINTER directs printer output to a specific device on the network. On an IBM PC network, the general syntax is

**SET PRINTER TO \\<station name>\<printer name> = ;**
**<destination>**

On a Novell/86 network, the general syntax is

**SET PRINTER TO \\SPOOLER**

To send printed output to a local printer, use the syntax

**SET PRINTER TO <destination>**

To empty the network print spooler and reset the default printer destination, use the syntax

**SET PRINTER TO <printer or device name>**

In the above commands, <station name> is a network-assigned workstation name, <printer name> identifies an IBM network printer, \\SPOOLER identifies a Novell network printer, <printer name> is a network-assigned printer name, and <destination> specifies the installed printer name (e.g., LPT1, LPT2, or LPT3).

For example, the command below directs printed output to the network printer attached to the LPT2 port of the workstation assigned the name Station1:

**SET PRINTER TO \\Station1\PRINTER = LPT2**

The commands below set up a serial laser printer in the COM1 port of the current workstation and send output to that port:

**RUN MODE COM1: 9600,N,8,1,P**
**SET PRINTER TO COM1**

For additional information on naming printers on your own network system, see your network manual. For additional information on the MODE command for defining parameters for devices, see your DOS manual.

# COMMANDS USED ONLY IN NETWORKS

The commands listed in this section are used only in a network environment. They are listed in alphabetical order.

## The DISPLAY USERS Command

DISPLAY USERS identifies workstations on the network that are currently logged into dBASE.

### SYNTAX

**DISPLAY USERS**

### USAGE

DISPLAY USERS lists the network-assigned names of all workstations currently logged into dBASE and places an arrow (>) next to the currently logged user (the workstation that issued the DISPLAY USERS command).

### EXAMPLE

The DISPLAY USERS command might display a list like the one below:

```
Computer Name
_____________
>Station1
 Station4
 Station6
 Station8
```

In this example, the DISPLAY USERS command was issued from the workstation named Station1.

### TIPS

Before uninstalling the dBASE ADMINISTRATOR from the hard disk, use the DISPLAY USERS command to make sure nobody is still logged onto dBASE.

### SEE ALSO

DISPLAY STATUS

## The LOGOUT Command

LOGOUT logs out the current user and logs in a new user.

### SYNTAX

**LOGOUT**

### USAGE

LOGOUT forces a user to log out of the system, then redisplays the initial dBASE ADMINISTRATOR login prompt for a new user to log in. The login prompt waits for the new login name, group name, and password.

LOGOUT closes all open database and related files at the current workstation.

In a single-user system or in a system where no security system has been created with the PROTECT program, the LOGOUT command is ignored.

### EXAMPLES

The main menu program shown in Figure 20.14 acts like any normal menu program, except that when the user opts to exit the menu, the program logs the current user out and brings up a login screen for a new user instead of quitting dBASE or exiting to the dot prompt. (See Figure 20.8 for the TestFrst procedure accessed in this program.)

When the new login screen appears, the new user is given three attempts to log in correctly. If he or she fails to do so within three attempts, the program ends. (Optionally, the user can press Esc to leave the login screen and terminate the program.)

### TIPS

Including a LOGOUT command within a DO WHILE loop ensures that a new user is brought into the same program that the previous user left, rather than just returned to the dot prompt. To prevent a user from automatically accessing the same program that was in effect when the previous user logged out, place the LOGOUT command outside of the loop controlling the main menu.

## The SET ENCRYPTION Command

SET ENCRYPTION determines whether a newly created (or copied) database file is encrypted.

```
******************************************** MainMenu.prg.
SET TALK OFF
NewUser = .T.
DO WHILE NewUser
   Choice = 0
   DO WHILE Choice < 4
      CLEAR
      TEXT
                     Main Menu

                  1. Add new records
                  2. Edit records
                  3. Print Reports
                  4. Exit
      ENDTEXT
      @ 20,1 SAY "Enter choice " GET Choice PICT "@Z 9"
      READ

      DO CASE

         CASE Choice = 1 .
              *--- Only users with access levels <= 3.
              Do TestFrst WITH "AddNew",3

         CASE Choice = 2
              *--- Only users with access levels <= 3.
              DO TestFrst WITH "EditDel",3

         CASE Choice = 3
              *--- Only users with access levels <= 6.
              DO TestFrst WITH "PrintRep",6
      ENDCASE
   ENDDO (Choice < 4)
   LOGOUT   &&--- Log out the current user,
            &&--- and wait for a new one.
ENDDO (newuser)
```

**FIGURE 20.14:** Sample main menu program that presents a menu and waits for the user's selection. When the user opts to exit by selecting menu item number 4, the LOGOUT command logs out the current user and waits for a new user to log in.

## SYNTAX

### SET ENCRYPTION ON/OFF

where the default value is ON in a protected network environment.

## USAGE

After the PROTECT program has been used to set up a security scheme, all database and index files are automatically encrypted so that users who do not have appropriate access levels cannot view the data. Users who log in with an appropriate access level (via the login name, group name, and password) will have access to the file in decrypted form.

To create a decrypted copy of a file for a single-user system or to store on a floppy disk as a backup, use the SET ENCRYPTION OFF command before copying the file. In most situations, only users who have complete access to all database records and fields will be able to make exact copies of files in decrypted form. That's because the copy is limited to the files and fields that the particular user has access to. A user who has no access to certain fields cannot produce a decrypted file that contains those fields.

### EXAMPLES

The routine below makes a decrypted backup copy of a database file, assuming that the user has an access level of 1 or 2. The backup copy of the file is stored on the disk in drive A.

```
IF ACCESS( ) < = 2
    USE Master
    SET ENCRYPTION OFF
    COPY TO A:Master
    SET ENCRYPTION ON
ENDIF
```

Note that a MODIFY STRUCTURE command can be used only with a decrypted file. Therefore, to modify the structure of a database file, you must make a decrypted copy of the file and modify the copied file. Then you can rename the file with the new structure to the original file name, as below:

```
SET ENCRYPTION OFF
USE Master EXCLUSIVE
COPY TO Temp
USE Temp EXCLUSIVE
MODIFY STRUCTURE
ERASE Master.dbf
RENAME Temp.dbf TO Master.dbf
```

### TIPS

All files in a single group share the same encryption key, while files of differing groups have different encryption keys. Therefore, you cannot decrypt a file that is outside of the current group name.

The SET ENCRYPTION OFF command can be used prior to a COPY command with one of the options DELIMITED, SDF, DIF, PSF, SYLK, or WKS to export encrypted files to other software systems.

## The SET EXCLUSIVE Command

SET EXCLUSIVE establishes the file-open attribute for all succeeding USE commands.

### SYNTAX

**SET EXCLUSIVE ON/OFF**

where ON is the default value.

### USAGE

When SET EXCLUSIVE is on, all opened files can be used only by the user that opened the files. Other users will receive the error message **File is in use by another** if they attempt to access the same database file.

When SET EXCLUSIVE is off, the database file is opened in shared mode, and other users on the network will have access to the same database file. In this situation, the programmer needs to use file and record locking to avoid collisions among simultaneous users of the database.

The following commands require exclusive use of the database file: INSERT [BLANK], MODIFY STRUCTURE, PACK, REINDEX, ZAP.

### EXAMPLES

The commands below open the Master database in work area A for shared access by all users and the Charges database in work area B for exclusive use of the current user:

```
SET EXCLUSIVE OFF
SELECT A
USE Master INDEX PartNo
SELECT B
SET EXCLUSIVE ON
USE Charges INDEX ChrgNo
```

### TIPS

In a single-user environment, all files are opened in a SET EXCLUSIVE ON mode. If a SET EXCLUSIVE OFF command is issued in a single-user environment, the command is ignored.

## The UNLOCK Command

UNLOCK releases any currently active file or record lock on a shared file so that other users can have access to that file or record.

#### SYNTAX

**UNLOCK [ALL]**

where the optional ALL parameter releases all current locks in all work areas.

#### USAGE

When one user locks a record or a file to perform an update with the READ or REPLACE command, other users on the network lose access to that file or record. To return access to other users, an UNLOCK command must be issued. (Note, however, that the commands CLOSE, USE, CLEAR ALL, or QUIT will also unlock a file.)

#### EXAMPLES

The commands below attempt to replace data in a single record by first locking the record. If the REPLACE command is successful, the UNLOCK command immediately unlocks the record for use by others:

```
GOTO 21
IF RLOCK( )
     REPLACE Unit_Price WITH Unit_Price * 1.10
     UNLOCK
ELSE
     ? "Can't access record right now..."
ENDIF
```

#### TIPS

Use UNLOCK immediately after an edit is completed to ensure that other users have quick access to the previously locked record or file.

#### SEE ALSO

FLOCK( )
RLOCK( )

## FUNCTIONS THAT WORK ONLY IN A NETWORK ENVIRONMENT

This section lists functions that work only in a network environment. If any of these functions are used in a single-user environment, they are ignored by dBASE.

## The ACCESS( ) Function

ACCESS( ) returns the access level (1–8) of the user, based on the user profile.

### SYNTAX

**ACCESS( )**

### USAGE

To build additional security beyond the basic file protection scheme, you can use the ACCESS( ) function to prevent users from accessing particular programs in the system.

### EXAMPLES

The commands below allow a user to run a program named AddNew only if the user has an access level of 3 or smaller:

```
IF ACCESS( ) < = 3
      DO AddNew
ELSE
      ? "Sorry, you can't do this."
ENDIF
```

Figures 20.7 and 20.8 display a sample program and procedure that use the ACCESS( ) function in a menu program.

### TIPS

To prevent users from modifying programs to change the access-level requirements, use the dBCODE program discussed in Chapter 21, "RunTime+ and the Compilers," to encrypt the command files.

## The FLOCK( ) Function

FLOCK( ) attempts to lock a database file so a single user can make changes and avoid collisions with other users.

### SYNTAX

**FLOCK( )**

#### USAGE

The FLOCK( ) function acts partly as a function and partly as a command. When issued, the FLOCK( ) function attempts to lock the file for the current user. If it is successful, it returns the value .T. and locks the file. If it fails, it returns the value .F. and does not lock the file.

When the file is locked, other users on the network cannot access the file. Instead, they receive the error message **File is in use by another**. If an ON ERROR command is in effect, the ERROR( ) function turns the value 108. The lock remains in effect until an UNLOCK command, or another command that unlocks the file, is issued.

#### EXAMPLES

Figure 20.9 shows a sample routine that attempts to lock a file for a specified period of time. If the attempted lock fails, the procedure suggests that the user try again later.

Figure 20.12 shows an ON ERROR procedure that can respond to a **File is in use by another** error.

#### TIPS

Use FLOCK( ) on operations that involve global editing, such as a REPLACE ALL command or a DO WHILE loop that automatically changes the values in a group of records. When editing a single record with the READ command, use the RLOCK( ) function instead.

#### SEE ALSO

RLOCK( )
UNLOCK

## The RLOCK( ) and LOCK( ) Functions

RLOCK( ) and LOCK( ) attempt to lock a single database record for editing.

#### SYNTAX

**RLOCK( )**
**LOCK( )**

## USAGE

RLOCK( ) and LOCK( ) are identical functions, though RLOCK( ) is preferred because it is clearer in meaning and less likely to be confused with FLOCK( ) by other programmers who work on your programs.

RLOCK( ) is the most efficient way to lock a record for editing, because other users still have access to other records on the file while the record lock is in place.

Though RLOCK( ) is a function, it behaves as a command in some ways because it performs an action. When a user attempts to lock a record, the RLOCK( ) function returns .T. if the record is available for locking and immediately locks the record. If the record is already locked by another user, RLOCK( ) returns .F. and does not lock the record.

If the RLOCK( ) function is successful, no other user can access the record until the record is unlocked. Instead, other users attempting to access that record receive the error message **Record is in use by another**. If an ON ERROR condition is in effect, the ERROR( ) function turns the value 109.

## EXAMPLES

Figure 20.10 shows a sample procedure that attempts to lock a record for a specific period of time. If the locking fails for the duration of the attempt, the procedure suggests that the user try again later.

Figure 20.12 demonstrates an ON ERROR procedure that responds to a **Record is in use by another** error.

## TIPS

Use RLOCK( ) to lock a single record when edits are performed with @...SAY...GET and READ commands or with a REPLACE command that accesses a single record. Use FLOCK( ) to lock an entire file when global edits are required.

## SEE ALSO

FLOCK( )
UNLOCK

## Summary

This chapter discussed the security and networking capabilities of the dBASE ADMINISTRATOR, the multiuser version of dBASE III PLUS. Specific programming techniques for security systems and networks were discussed, along with the commands and functions used in a network environment.

*For additional information on the ON ERROR and RETRY commands:*

- Chapter 19, "Event Processing and Error Trapping"

*For information on encrypting command files to prevent access by unauthorized users:*

- Chapter 21, "RunTime+ and the Compilers"

*For additional information on installing the dBASE ADMINISTRATOR on a particular network system:*

- Appendix B, "Installing dBASE III PLUS"

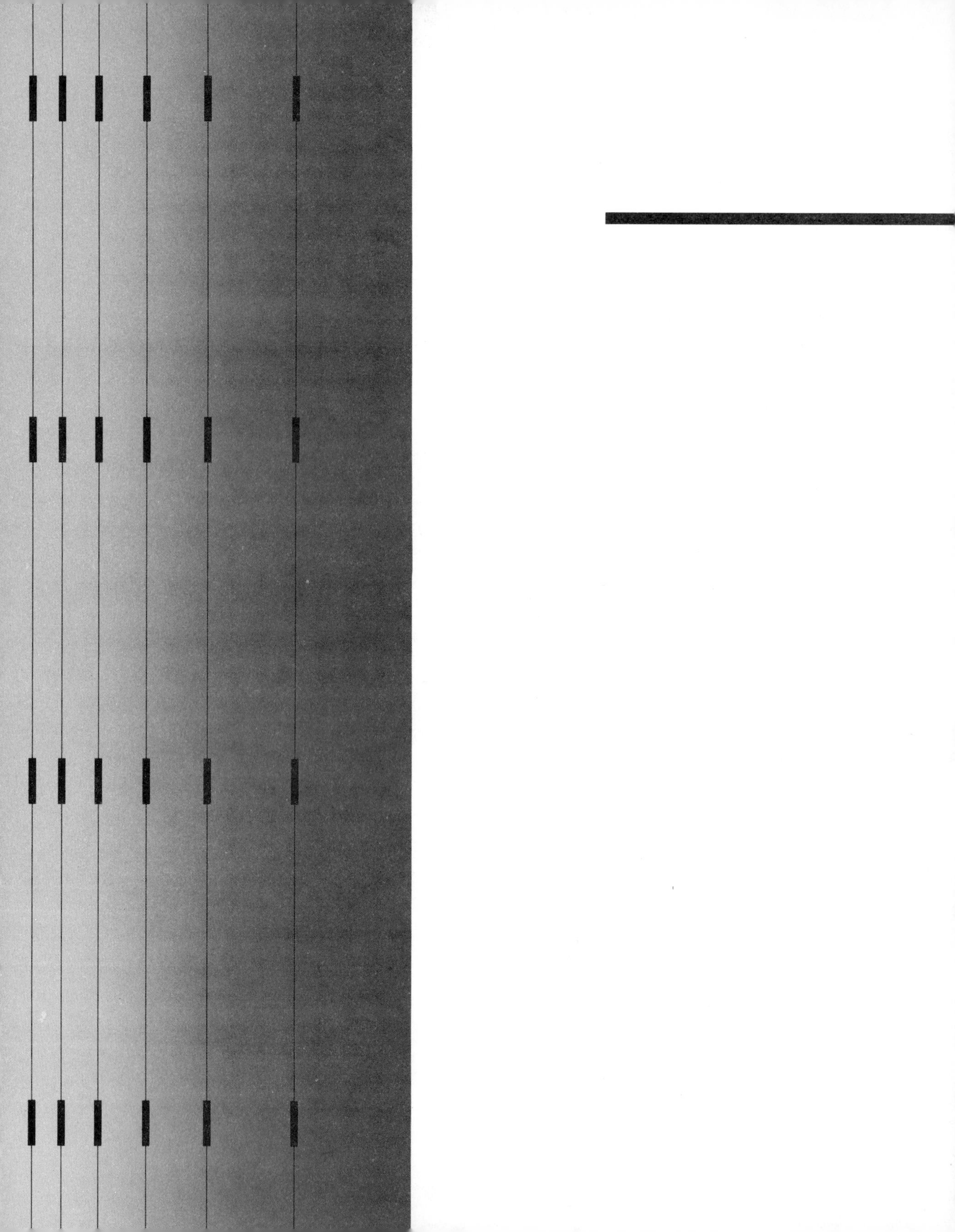

CHAPTER 21

# RunTime+ and the Compilers

# RUNTIME+ AND THE COMPILERS

The topics in this chapter will be of interest to those who are either considering marketing the programs they create or need maximum speed and performance in their custom dBASE III PLUS systems. The chapter discusses two different types of marketing aids: the RunTime+ package provided by Ashton-Tate and the compilers offered by third-party companies.

RunTime+ , which is included in your dBASE III PLUS package, allows you to encrypt your command files, improve their speed slightly, and market your programs to people who do not own dBASE III PLUS. Your customers would need only dBRUN to run your system, which they can buy for less than the dBASE III PLUS package.

The compilers, discussed later in the chapter, allow you to convert your programs to machine language instructions. Your compiled programs will run faster than dBASE programs and will have complete independence from dBASE III PLUS and dBRUN. Your potential customers can run your programs directly from the DOS prompt. (In fact, with the compilers, you don't even need dBASE III PLUS to create the programs.) Also, like RunTime+ , the compilers prevent users from having access to your original programs, thereby preventing unauthorized tampering.

## RUNTIME+

RunTime+ consists of two programs that come with your dBASE III PLUS package: dBCODE and dBLINKER. dBCODE encrypts your command files so that unauthorized users cannot access the original command files (*source code*). dBLINKER can combine several command files (*not* procedure files) into a single large file that is more compact and runs a bit more quickly than standard dBASE III PLUS programs. Command files that are encrypted with dBCODE (and optionally combined with dBLINKER) can be run either from dBASE III PLUS directly or from a separate product named dBRUN III PLUS.

### Creating the RunTime+ Directories

To use dBCODE and dBLINKER, you need to move files around and create new directories. A good understanding of basic DOS file management techniques is a must, but the examples in this chapter explain the use of all the necessary DOS commands. Keep in mind that dBCODE and dBLINKER are run from the DOS prompt, so you need not have dBASE III PLUS running or even available to use these programs.

To simplify using RunTime+, you can create two directories named Source and RunTime on either your hard disk or a blank, formatted disk in drive B. On a hard disk, log onto your root directory and enter these commands from the DOS C> prompt (remember to press Return after typing each command):

**MD\Source**
**MD\RunTime**

On a floppy disk system, log onto drive A and at the DOS A> prompt enter these commands:

**MD B:\Source**
**MD B:\RunTime**

## Copying the Command Files to Encrypt

After you have created directories for storing source code and encrypted files, you need to copy all the files that you want to encrypt to the Source directory. First log onto the Source directory. On a hard disk, enter **CD\Source**. On a floppy disk, enter these commands:

**B:**
**CD\Source**

To help keep track of where you are, enter the command **PROMPT $P$G** at the DOS prompt. The DOS prompt will then show both the currently logged drive and the directory (for example, **C:\Source>** or **B:\Source>**).

Next you need to use the DOS COPY command to copy all the .prg files to the Source directory. You can use wild-card characters to copy all the necessary files and change their names along the way. For example, to copy all of the program (.prg) files from a directory named dBASE onto the Source directory and change the file-name extension to .src automatically, you would enter the command below:

**COPY C:\dBASE*.prg *.src**

On a floppy disk system, you would enter the following command to copy all the .prg files to the floppy disk in drive B, again renaming the .prg files to .src extensions along the way:

**COPY A:*.prg B:*.src**

If you don't want to copy all the programs on the original drive or directory, you have to copy each file individually. For example, the DOS commands below copy the files named Members.prg, AddNew.prg, and Reports.prg to the currently logged Source drive and directory, and then change the names of all the .prg files to .src extensions using a single DOS RENAME command:

**COPY C:\DB\Members.prg**
**COPY C:\DB\AddNew.prg**
**COPY C:\DB\Reports.prg**
**RENAME *.prg *.src**

Incidentally, if you develop a system in the future that you know you are going to encrypt, you can save a little time by naming the files with identical leading characters (for instance, MemMenu.prg, MemAdd.prg, MemRep.prg, MemEdit.prg, MemDup.prg). That way you can use a single command such as

**COPY C:\DB\:Mem*.prg Mem*.src**

to copy and rename all the appropriate files.

When all the necessary .prg files are copied to the Source directory and renamed to .src extensions, you are ready to create a response file.

## Creating a RunTime+ Response File

A *response file* is an ASCII text file that contains the names of the command files to encrypt and link. You can use any word processor (as long as it can produce ASCII text files), a line editor, the dBASE III PLUS MODIFY COMMAND editor, or even the DOS COPY CON command to create this file. The response file must have the extension .rsp, and it must list the root command file (usually the main menu) first. Probably the easiest way to create the response file is to stay logged onto the Source directory and use the DOS COPY CON command, as in the example below, which creates a response file named MemProgs:

**COPY CON MemProgs.rsp**

Then carefully type the names of the command files to encrypt, without the .prg extensions. Be sure to list the root (main menu) program first, as this is the program that will later call all other programs. Also, be sure to press Return after typing in each file name, *including* the last file name. To save the file, press F6 (or Ctrl-Z) after typing all the file names.

If you wanted to encrypt the sample program files named Members, AddNew, and Reports, your screen would look like the example below after creating the response file with the COPY CON command (this list assumes that Members is the main menu program):

**COPY CON MemProgs.rsp**
**Members**
**AddNew**

**Reports**
**^Z**
**1 File(s) copied**

To verify that the .rsp file exists, use the DOS TYPE command to view it, as in the example below:

**TYPE MemProgs.rsp**

You should see the names of the files that you plan to encrypt listed on the screen.

If you use a word processor to create the .rsp file, be sure to copy it to the Source directory and use CD\Source to log onto the Source directory again when done.

## Copying RunTime+

After you have created directories for RunTime+ and copied your source programs to the source directory, you'll need to copy the RunTime+ programs. Find the dBCODE and dBLINKER programs (named DBC.COM and DBL.COM) on your dBASE III PLUS Sample Programs and Utilities disk, and copy them to the Source directory. While still logged onto the Source directory, put the appropriate dBASE III PLUS disk in drive A and enter the following command:

**COPY A:DB?.COM**

You should see the message **2 file(s) copied**. (If you don't see the message, try a different dBASE III PLUS disk in drive A.) When the copy is successful, you're ready to use dBCODE to encrypt the command files. (*Note:* You can actually run DBC and DBL from any disk or directory, but copying them to the source directory, as in this example, helps to simplify matters.)

## Using dBCODE

To run dBCODE from the DOS prompt, enter the command DBC at the DOS prompt. The options (in the form of flags) that you can use with the command to define file and directory names are summarized in Table 21.1. You can see these same options on your screen by entering the command **DBC ?** at the DOS prompt on the Source directory.

The general syntax for the DBC command is

**DBC –c[<copyright file>] –i[<information file>];**
**–o<RunTime directory> –r<response file>;**
**–s<source directory>**

The flags can be typed in any order.

| OPTION | PURPOSE |
|---|---|
| –c | Specifies the name of the text file containing the copyright notice for the programs (with .hdr extension) |
| –i | Generates an information file with .dbg extension |
| –r | Specifies the name of the response file (with .rsp extension) |
| –s | Specifies the name of the directory containing the source files |
| –o | Specifies the name of the directory for output files |

**TABLE 21.1:** Options Available with dBCODE

Typically, you'll use the DBC command with only the following options: –r (with the name of the .rsp file), –s (with the name of the source directory where the files to encrypt are located), and –o (with the name of the RunTime directory where the encrypted files will be stored). If you enter the command DBC without any flags, it will step you through a series of questions that prompt you for the file names and source directory.

Referring back to the example of the MemProgs.rsp response file created in the last section, you would enter the command below to encode the Members, AddNew, and Reports programs:

**DBC –rMemProgs.rsp –s\Source\ –o\RunTime**

Note that there is no space between the flags and their arguments (e.g., –rMemProgs.rsp). There are, however, spaces between each flag. Note also that directory names use the usual DOS backslash characters.

You'll see a copyright notice and the names of files on the screen as the encryption progresses. When done, the DOS prompt will reappear.

The optional copyright header and information files are discussed a little later in the chapter.

## Verifying the Encryption

To verify that the command files have been encrypted after running dBCODE, check the \RunTime directory with the DIR command. (The encrypted files will have the extension .prg.) If you attempt to view one of the encrypted files with the command **TYPE Members.prg**, you'll see either nothing or some nonsensical encrypted code, and nobody will be able to tamper with this code. Your original .prg command files are still on the disk or directory where they were originally created, and copies of them, with .src instead of the original .prg extension, will still be in the source directory.

*Note:* Never copy these encrypted .prg files to the disk or directory that contains your original command files. The encrypted files will overwrite the originals, and even you won't be able to access your original command files! To play it safe, you might want to make extra backups of your command files when working with dBCODE.

Now you could stop at this point and market the encrypted files in this format. You can run these encrypted files with either dBASE III PLUS or dBRUN. However, you might as well go ahead and link the encrypted files into a single file with dBLINKER.

## Using dBLINKER

The dBLINKER program (DBL.com) can combine several programs that have been encrypted with dBCODE into a single file. It also provides several options (in the form of flags) in the command line, as summarized in Table 21.2. Entering the command **DBL ?** displays a summary of the flags. These flags can be used in the command line as follows:

**DBL –c[<copyright file>] –i[<information file];**
**–f<linked file> –p –r<response file>;**
**–s<source directory>**

These flags can be typed in any order.

The optional –c and –i flags allow you to include a copyright notice in your program and generate an information file. These options are discussed later in the chapter. The required –f flag contains the name of the linked file, –r is followed by the name of the response file, and –s is followed by the name of the

| OPTION | PURPOSE |
|---|---|
| –c | Specifies the name of the copyright notice file for the programs (with .hdr extension) |
| –i | Generates an information file with .map extension |
| –f | Specifies the name of the output file containing all linked programs (will have .prg extension) |
| –p | Makes directory prefix significant in file names |
| –r | Specifies the name of the response (.rsp) file containing names of files to link |
| –s | Specifies the name of the source directory containing encrypted files to link |

**TABLE 21.2:** Options Available with dBLINKER

source directory. With −p in effect, the command **DO \DB\AddNew** requires that the \DB directory exists on the target computer. Without the −p flag, the \DB directory refers only to the computer being used to link the files, and the target computer will simply use DO AddNew in the final linked application.

Suppose, for example, that you want to link the three files listed in the MemProgs.rsp response file into a single encrypted file named Mail. The encrypted files are stored on the directory named RunTime. You would enter the command below to link the files (and also to generate the optional information file):

**DBL −rMemProgs.rsp −fMail −s\RunTime\ −i**

Note that there is no space between the flag and its argument (e.g., −fMail). There are, however, spaces between each flag. Note also that the directory name uses the usual DOS backslash characters.

If you enter the command DBL with no flags and no question mark, the screen will ask individually for the names of the linked application file and the files to put into the linked application.

When dBLINKER is finished linking the files, the DOS prompt reappears.

*Note:* dBLINKER cannot link procedure files. If your system uses a procedure file, eliminate its name from the response file before using dBLINKER. The procedure file must be included on the disk that you plan to market, but it must be separate from the linked files. However, the procedure file can be encrypted with dBCODE so that it cannot be read.

To verify the link, you can use the DIR command at the DOS prompt. In the example above, dBLINKER linked all the files into a program named Mail. To verify this, you would enter the command **DIR Mail.*** at the DOS prompt (while still on the Source directory). You should see the file name Mail.prg, in this example, somewhere on the directory. If you attempt to look at the Mail.prg file, you'll see only encrypted code.

## Including a Copyright Notice

You can store a copyright notice inside the programs that are encrypted and linked with dBCODE and dBLINKER. If your users attempt to view or modify the contents of the programs, they will see the copyright notice above the encrypted code.

To include a copyright notice, first store it in a text file with the extension .hdr. The text file can be created with any text editor (including MODIFY COMMAND) or the DOS COPY CON command. For example, the commands below create a copyright notice named MyCopy.hdr using the COPY CON command:

**COPY CON MyCopy.hdr**

**Copyright (c) 1987 ABC Software Company**
**All Rights Reserved**

Press F6 (or Ctrl-Z) after typing the copyright notice to save the file. Use the TYPE command to verify that the file was saved (e.g., **TYPE MyCopy.hdr**).

To include this copyright notice in your encrypted program, use the −c flag with the file name as in the example below:

**DBL −rMemProgs.rsp −fMail −s\RunTime\ −cMyCopy.hdr**

The −cMyCopy.hdr flag in the command line tells RunTime+ to include the copyright notice in the encrypted programs.

## Including an Information File

The −i option with both dBCODE and dBLINKER generates an information file that helps link the encrypted code with the original source code.

### dBCODE Information Files

When used with dBCODE, the −i option generates a file for each source program that has the same name as the source program but the extension .dbg (for debug). This information file contains the name of the original input file and the generated file, and the relationship between the byte location (in hexadecimal) in the encrypted file and the line number in the original source file. Figure 21.1 shows an example.

When you use dBRUN to run the encrypted program, it will display the byte number (rather than the original line number) of any command that generates an error. You can look up that byte number in the information file to locate the line number of the error in the original source code.

### dBLINKER Information Files

When you use the −i option with dBLINKER, it generates an information file with the same name as the linked files but with the extension .map. This file contains the name of the final program containing all the linked files and all files and procedures that are accessed with a DO command. Three types of files are referenced in the dBLINKER information file, as discussed below. Figure 21.2 shows a sample information file generated by dBLINKER.

***Files Defined and Referenced*** Files that are defined and referenced in the dBLINKER information file are files that are included in the linked files and called with a DO command. This section of the information report lists the name

```
Input file: \Source\Members.src

Output file: \RunTime\Members.prg



  BYTE   LINE

    89      1
    94      6
    99      7
    9F      8
    A5      9
    AB     10
    B4     11
    C8     12
    CA     14
    DE     15
    E7     16
    <etc....>
```

**FIGURE 21.1:** An information file generated by the dBCODE –i option. The first two lines show the names and directories of the original source code and the encrypted code. The two columns display the byte number that dBRUN will display when it encounters an error in the generated code. The second column shows the corresponding line number in the original source code.

of the called program (e.g., Reports), the version of dBASE III PLUS used (e.g., 1.1), the byte number in the linked file where the program begins (under the column labeled Offset), and the size of the file (under the column labeled Size). All values are in hexadecimal.

***Files Defined and Not Referenced*** The section of the report entitled Files Defined & NOT Referenced includes any programs within the linked files that are not called with a DO command. Typically, the main menu program for the application will be referenced here, because all lower-level programs will return to this program rather than call it with a DO command. "Dead" programs (those that are never called) are also listed in this section.

This section also displays the name of the linked file, the version of dBLINKER used to link the files, and the offset (starting location) and size of the file within the linked application. All numbers are displayed in hexadecimal.

***Files Referenced and Not Defined*** The section of the report entitled Files Referenced & NOT Defined displays the names of all files outside of the linked applications that are called by DO commands. Typically, this section lists calls to procedures. However, any illegal calls (such as when you misspell a file name or call a nonexistent program) will also be listed in this section.

```
Output File: MAIL.PRG

Files Defined & Referenced:


    Input File      Vs.  Offset    Size

   ADDNEW.PRG       1.1     B36     B2A
   REPORTS.PRG      1.1    1E9F     B48

 *** Count:     2

Files Defined & NOT Referenced:

    Input File      Vs.  Offset    Size

   MEMBERS.PRG      1.1      88     AAD

 *** Count:     1


Files Referenced & NOT Defined:

    Reference           Offset          Reference          Offset

   PROPER.PRG              6E2         PROPER.PRG             939
   PROPER.PRG              995         PROPER.PRG             9DC
   CENTER.PRG             11E0         PROPER.PRG            139B
   PROPER.PRG             142B         PROPER.PRG            15AA
   CENTER.PRG             1950         PROPER.PRG            19CA
   PROPER.PRG             28DB         PROPER.PRG            290A

 *** Count:    12
```

**FIGURE 21.2:** A sample information file, with the .map extension, generated by dBLINKER. Note that all offset and size values are displayed in hexadecimal. The first section lists files in the linked application that are called by a DO command. The second section lists files in the linked application that are not called by a DO command. The third section lists procedures that are called by a DO command but are outside of the linked application.

The Files Referenced & NOT Defined section lists the name of the file called with the DO command and the location (offset, in hexadecimal) of the DO command within the linked files. In the sample report shown in Figure 21.2, you can see that the linked application calls two procedures, named Proper and Center, from 12 different locations within the linked files.

Note that when dBRUN encounters an error in an encrypted and linked application, it displays a description of the error, a trace of the files that led to the error, and offsets in hexadecimal. You may need to do a little hexadecimal arithmetic to locate the exact line of the error; then you can use the information files from both dBCODE and dBLINKER to isolate the offending line. Of course, if you do all of your development and debugging in dBASE III PLUS *before* you encrypt your files, you will probably not have to concern yourself with errors in the encrypted and linked files.

## RunTime+ Limitations

Before using RunTime+ for serious work, make sure you understand its limitations and rules thoroughly, as discussed below.

### Illegal Commands

RunTime+ cannot process the SET, ASSIST, or HELP commands. You can use SET with specific parameters, such as SET COLOR and SET DEFAULT; it is illegal only if it is used without parameters. RunTime+ will, however, ignore the following SET commands:

SET DEBUG
SET DOHISTORY
SET ECHO
SET STEP
SET SUSPEND

### ON Commands

RunTime+ supports the ON KEY, ON ERROR, and ON ESCAPE commands, and these can call either external procedures or programs within the linked application. However, a little extra caution is required. If a linked file is called with an ON command, the called file should reset the ON condition before calling another program. This, however, will not be a concern if the called file or procedure simply returns control to the calling program after responding to the ON condition. Also, RunTime+ cannot support nested ON conditions, such as ON KEY ON ERROR DO <file name>.

### Clause Size Restrictions

You can encrypt and link command files of any size with RunTime+. However, clause commands, such as DO WHILE, IF, and DO CASE, cannot exceed 32K in size. Any clause commands that exceed 32K will need to be reduced, perhaps by moving the commands within the clause to an external file and calling them with a DO command within the clause.

### Macro Restrictions

You cannot use macros as command verbs or as SET parameters. For example, the following sequence is illegal because LIST is a command verb:

**Z = "LIST"**
**&Z LName, FName, Address**

This sequence is illegal because TALK is a SET parameter:

```
Z = "TALK"
SET &Z OFF
```

You can use macros in a DO command only if the file you are calling is *not* linked: it must be external to the linked programs. For example, the sequence

```
ProgNam = "PrintDir"
DO &ProgNam
```

is legal only if PrintDir.prg is external to the linked programs. (It can, however, still be encrypted.)

Because dBCODE must encrypt a command, a macro cannot be used in place of a command. (The macro implies that the command will be different under different circumstances, and therefore dBCODE has no specific command to encode.) This is why commands cannot be replaced by macros in the source program. Also, dBLINKER does not call programs within the linked file by the name you assign but rather uses symbols of its own. This is why the DO <¯o> construction is illegal.

All other uses of macros are legal. For example, the sequence

```
PMacro = "TO PRINT"
REPORT FORM Director &PMacro
```

is legal because "TO PRINT" is neither a command verb (the first word on a line) nor an illegal SET parameter, and it is not used as a file name.

### Procedure Files

As mentioned earlier, procedure files cannot be linked with dBLINKER. They can be encrypted with dBCODE, but they must be excluded from the linking process. Be sure to put a copy of the encrypted procedure file on the distribution disk so that the linked files can find it.

## The dBRUN Program

The dBRUN program, which must be purchased from Ashton-Tate for *each* copy of your application that you sell, is very similar to dBASE III PLUS, except that it can run only encrypted command files. It offers no dot prompt and does not support the SET debugging commands (SET ECHO, SET STEP, SET DEBUG).

When you market your application, your customer will need to have the dBRUN program on his or her disk. To run the application, your customer will need to enter the commands **dBRUN <application>** where <application> is the name of the main menu program for your application.

To allow your user to run your application using a single command, you can name the main menu program dBRUNCmd.prg, which is the file name that dBRUN automatically looks for when first executed. Then you can rename the dBRUN.exe program to some file name that represents your application, such as Members.exe. Then, when your user types in the command MEMBERS, your application will begin running automatically.

Note also that dBRUN supports a configuration file similar to the Config.db file that dBASE III PLUS uses. dBRUN, however, searches for the configuration file named Config.rt. See Appendix C, "Configuring dBASE III PLUS," for more on the dBASE configuration file.

## Preparing Your RunTime+ Application

When the time comes to distribute or market your work, be sure to copy all the associated database (.dbf), index (.ndx), report-format (.frm), label (.lbl), format (.fmt), and any procedure (.prg) files associated with the system to a floppy disk.

To be sure that you haven't forgotten any files or left any bugs in the system, test every feature before you start distributing. Any errors that slip by at this point will certainly come back to haunt you later.

Be sure to include some documentation that explains to the customer how to use the system, as well as instructions for making backups. You should also contact Ashton-Tate about the dBRUN program, so that you can market the product to customers who do not own dBASE III PLUS.

To prepare your encrypted application with dBRUN for prospective customers, you will need to create three floppy disks, one containing the dBRUN program (purchased from Ashton-Tate), a second containing all the program files for your application, and a third containing the database files for your application. In the sections below, these disks are referred to as Customer Disk #1, Customer Disk #2, and Customer Disk #3.

***Customer Disk #1*** You should call the disk with the dBRUN.exe program on it Customer Disk #1. You may want to tell your customers to copy the DOS system tracks (using the DOS SYS command) to this disk if they wish to boot up from this disk (assuming that they are not booting up from a hard disk).

***Customer Disk #2*** Customer Disk #2 should contain all of the encrypted program files for your application, as well as a copy of the dBRUN.ovl file from the dBRUN disk. Use the DOS COPY command to copy dBRUN.ovl from the dBRUN disk to Customer Disk #2. You may also want to rename dBRUN.ovl to dBRUNOvl.bak on Customer Disk #1. Doing so ensures that you keep a copy of the original dBRUN.ovl file on your own disks as a backup.

***Customer Disk #3*** Customer Disk #3 should contain database and index files. Keeping these files on a separate disk ensures the maximum amount of free disk space for the customer to store data. Customer Disk #3 need not contain any of the RunTime+ or dBRUN programs.

### How the Customer Uses dBRUN

In general, your customer will take the following steps to run your encrypted application:

1. Boot up his/her computer using DOS.
2. Enter Customer Disk #1 in drive A and execute the dBRUN program.
3. When prompted, remove Customer Disk #1 from drive A and replace it with Customer Disk #2.
4. Place Customer Disk #3 in drive B.
5. When prompted, press Return to begin running the application.

The exact sequence of steps will vary slightly, depending on the hardware configuration of the customer's computer. For example, if the customer is using a hard disk, you can just have the user copy all the customer disks to a single directory on the hard disk and execute the entire application from the hard disk.

## RunTime+ System Defaults

Table 21.3 lists the default file-name extensions and optional extensions that dBASE III PLUS and RunTime+ support. The examples discussed earlier in this chapter, however, represent file-name extensions that will make it easier to keep track of source, encrypted, linked, response, and copyright header files.

dBRUN will always default to the currently logged drive and directory when searching for files. To alter this, use the SET DEFAULT and SET PATH commands within your application, or use the DEFAULT = and PATH = commands within the Config.rt file.

In addition, RunTime+ automatically resets all function keys to nulls. To redefine the function keys for your application, use the usual SET FUNCTION command within your programs, or use the F<number> = option within the

| | INPUT FILE | | OUTPUT FILE | |
|---|---|---|---|---|
| PROGRAM | DEFAULT | ALLOWED | DEFAULT | ALLOWED |
| dBASE III PLUS | .prg | any | none | any |
| dBCODE | .src | any | .prg | .prg |
| dBLINKER | .prg | any | .prg | any |
| dBRUN | .prg | any | none | any |

**TABLE 21.3:** Default and Allowed File-Name Extensions for dBASE III PLUS and RunTime+

Config.rt file. (The Config.rt file is similar to the Config.db file discussed in Appendix C, "Configuring dBASE III PLUS".)

## dBASE III PLUS Compilers

This section introduces the dBASE III PLUS *compilers,* which offer many advantages to the programmer who is considering marketing his or her software. These advantages are summarized below:

- Better performance. Compiled dBASE programs run up to 20 times faster than dBASE command files (though in most applications, the speed increase will not be quite so dramatic).
- Stand-alone performance. Because a compiled program can be run directly from the DOS prompt, a potential user need not own dBASE III PLUS or dBRUN. The compiled programs are completely independent.
- Program security. Because the compiled version of a dBASE command file contains only machine language commands, unauthorized users cannot access the original dBASE program.
- More power. The compilers include additional commands and functions that the dBASE language does not offer. (However, they generally lack some dBASE commands, such as BROWSE and EDIT.)

At present, there are two compilers available for dBASE III PLUS. One is Clipper, manufactured by Nantucket Corporation in Culver City, California. The other is Quicksilver, manufactured by WordTech Systems in Orinda, California. Both compilers are discussed in the sections that follow.

This compiler information is not intended to replace the reference manuals that each of these compilers provide. Instead, it provides a basic reference to the features and capabilities of compilers in general, and of the Clipper and Quicksilver compilers specifically.

## Comparing dBASE to Assembly Language

Before discussing the compilers, a brief comparison of dBASE and assembly language will emphasize the benefits of compiling dBASE programs. Figure 21.3 shows a dBASE III PLUS command file that can display all the ASCII characters on the screen, with a space between each character. The program occupies about 215 bytes of disk space and takes about 22 seconds to run. However, since you need to have dBASE readily available to run the program, the actual disk space required to run this program is closer to 451,275 bytes (or 440K).

Figure 21.4 shows a program written in assembly language that also shows ASCII characters with blank spaces in between. The left column contains commands for the assembler, the middle column contains the assembly language proper (starting at the mov cx,100h command and ending at the int 20h command), and the lines preceded by semicolons are programmer comments. Although the sample dBASE and assembly programs perform exactly the same task, the assembly language program takes only 1 second to run and occupies only 21 bytes of disk space.

Before you can run the assembly language program, you need to assemble it into machine language by using the IBM ASM or MASM assemblers. Figure 21.5 shows the assembly program after it has been translated into machine language.

The dBASE program must also be translated to machine language by the dBASE III PLUS *interpreter*. The interpreter reads a single line from your dBASE program, checks it for errors, translates it to machine language, and then executes it. It repeats this process for every line in the command file. All these steps take time; hence the program runs relatively slowly.

So the two big advantages of assembly language over dBASE are disk space and speed. The assembly language ASCII program discussed in this example runs about 22 times faster using about 1/20,000th the disk space.

The disadvantage to assembly language, however, is that it is difficult to learn, read, and produce. While dBASE has many English-like commands, such as

```
*----------------------- ASCII.prg
*----------------------- Display all ASCII codes.
SET TALK OFF
Counter = 0
DO WHILE Counter <= 255
   ?? STR(Counter,3),CHR(Counter)+" "
   Counter = Counter + 1
ENDDO (Counter = 0)
```

**FIGURE 21.3:** dBASE III PLUS program to display ASCII codes on the screen. This program takes about 22 seconds to run and occupies about 440K of disk space (including dBASE III PLUS) when not compiled. When compiled, the program takes about 10 seconds to run and occupies about 127K of disk space.

APPEND, EDIT, and UPDATE, assembly language has only very primitive commands, such as mov, int, push, and pop. Assembly language has no built-in commands for managing data files or even screen displays. To produce an assembly language program to perform what dBASE does in a single command (such as INDEX) could take days or even weeks.

## Benefits of Compiling dBASE Programs

To gain the advantages of using assembly language while avoiding the disadvantages, you use a compiler. A compiler takes your command file(s) and makes a copy that is in essence written in assembly language. Like all assembly

```
;------------------------ ASCII.asm
;------------------------ Display all ASCII codes.
prog    segment             ;start of segment
        assume cs:prog      ;assume code segment
        mov cx,100h         ;start counter at 256 dec
        mov dl,0            ;start with 0 ASCII character
next:   mov ah,2            ;call DOS output function
        int 21h             ;call to DOS function
        push dx             ;save last value in dx
        mov dl,20h          ;put in ASCII space
        int 21h             ;call DOS function
        pop dx              ;get back last dx value
        inc dl              ;next ASCII character
        loop next           ;repeat until done
        int 20h             ;return to DOS
prog    ends                ;end of segment
        end                 ;end of assembly
```

**FIGURE 21.4:** Assembly language program to show ASCII characters on the screen. While this program performs exactly the same task as the one shown in Figure 21.3, this program takes only about 1 second to run and occupies only 21 bytes of disk space.

```
B90001
B200
B402
CD21
52
B220
CD21
5A
FEC2
E2F2
CD20
```

**FIGURE 21.5:** Machine language program to show ASCII codes. This program is closer to what the computer actually "sees" when it runs a program. Each "line" in this program is a hexadecimal instruction that the computer can quickly execute.

language programs, the compiled program can be run directly from the DOS prompt.

A compiled program is never quite as efficient as one that is actually written in assembly language. But it's much easier to write a program in dBASE and compile it (using two simple commands) than it is to write a program in assembly language. Therefore, the compiler acts as sort of a compromise between the convenience of dBASE and the efficiency of assembly language.

## THE CLIPPER COMPILER

The Clipper compiler allows you to compile any command file or group of command files from the dBASE .prg to the DOS .exe executable format. Because Clipper is a true *native-code* compiler (which means it generates .exe files that require no further interpretation), significant increases in speed are virtually guaranteed. (The last section in this chapter provides examples of performance improvements.)

To compile a program with Clipper, you need to enter two commands at the DOS prompt. To compile a program named Test1.prg, you would first enter the command **CLIPPER Test1**. Then link the compiled program using the command **PLINK86 FILE Test1**. (PLINK86 is a separate program that comes with Clipper.) You can compile and link groups of command files, procedure files, and *user-defined functions* into a single large file. A user-defined function is similar to a normal dBASE function such as TRIM( ) or RECNO( ), except that you create and define it.

The following sections refer to the Autumn 1986 version of Clipper. Future releases may include additional features.

### Clipper Enhancements to dBASE

Clipper provides more flexibility than dBASE III PLUS in several respects. Clipper allows up to 2048 memory variables, 1024 fields per record, and up to eight children to one parent in a SET RELATION definition (as opposed to one in dBASE). Clipper also provides the capability to add custom help screens, which the user can access by pressing F1.

Clipper enables you to store memo fields in memory variables as long strings, which means you can search and manipulate the memo field. Clipper provides liberal use of macros, including macros as conditions in DO WHILE loops and recursive macros. Macros cannot be used in place of commands (such as USE, LIST, DISPLAY, and so forth).

User-defined functions provide more flexibility than procedures. Chapter 24, "Algorithms to Extend dBASE," discusses a business procedure that can accept parameters such as

**DO Pmt WITH (150000,.16/12,30*12)**

In Clipper, you can easily change this procedure into a user-defined function and treat it as you would any other function, using the syntax

**Payment = PMT(15000,.16/12,30*12)**

or

**? PMT(15000,.16/12,30*12)**

During editing, Clipper allows the user to press Ctrl-U to undo a change. For example, if during editing the user changes the part number A-111 to Z-999, typing Ctrl-U immediately converts the part number back to A-111. Clipper can call assembly language subroutines with up to seven parameters (as opposed to one in dBASE). Clipper can save and restore screens displayed with @ SAY commands, so that they "pop up" on the screen instantly.

The Clipper DECLARE statement allows you to use true arrays in your programs. For example, you could use the array

```
DECLARE Day[7]
Day[1] = "Sunday"
Day[2] = "Monday"
Day[3] = "Tuesday"
Day[4] = "Wednesday"
Day[5] = "Thursday"
Day[6] = "Friday"
Day[7] = "Saturday"
```

Once an array is declared, you can use numbers to access the array elements. For example, **? Day[3]** displays **Tuesday**. If variable XYZ equals 7, the command **? DAY[XYZ]** displays **Saturday**. An array can contain up to 2048 elements.

## Clipper Functions

All the dBASE III PLUS functions are supported by Clipper, though some are supported through an external file you must link into your compiled program. (This is easily achieved through the PLINK86 program included with Clipper.) Some additional functions that are unique to Clipper are listed in Table 21.4.

| FUNCTION | EFFECT |
|---|---|
| ADEL( ) | Deletes an element from an array, moving all lower elements up a notch |
| ADIR( ) | Copies file names on the directory into an array |
| AINS( ) | Inserts an element into the array, moving all lower elements down a notch |
| ALIAS( ) | Returns the alias assigned to a SELECT work area |
| ALLTRIM( ) | Trims both leading and trailing blanks from a character string |
| AMPM( ) | Displays time based on a 12-hour clock with "am" or "pm" |
| ASCAN( ) | Searches for a specific value within an array |
| DAYS( ) | Calculates days based on a number of seconds |
| DBEDIT( ) | Allows full-screen editing of dBASE files |
| DTOS( ) | Converts a date to yyyymmdd format as a character string (e.g., 19861201)—this is very useful for combining dates and character strings in index files |
| ELAPTIME( ) | Calculates elapsed time between two times |
| EMPTY( ) | Returns true (.T.) if a variable or expression is blank or if a logical expression is false |
| FCOUNT( ) | Returns the number of fields in the selected database |
| HARDCR( ) | Returns a string with soft carriage returns converted to hard carriage returns |
| HEADER( ) | Returns the size of the dBASE file header |
| INDEXKEY( ) | Returns the key expression of an index file |
| LENNUM( ) | Returns the length of a number |
| MEMOEDIT( ) | Allows a memo field to be edited on the screen |
| MEMOREAD( ) | Returns the contents of a text file |
| MEMORY( ) | Returns the amount of available memory |
| MEMOTRAN( ) | Returns a string with hard carriage returns converted to semi-colons and soft carriage returns converted to spaces |
| MEMOWRITE( ) | Writes a character string to a text file |
| PCOUNT( ) | Returns the number of parameters passed to a procedure |
| PROCLINE( ) | Returns the line number of the current program or procedure file |
| PROCNAME( ) | Returns the name of the current program or procedure file being executed |
| SECONDS( ) | Converts a time string to seconds |

**TABLE 21.4:** Clipper Functions That Extend the dBASE Language

| FUNCTION | EFFECT |
|---|---|
| SECS( ) | Returns the number of seconds in a time string |
| SETPRC( ) | Sets internal printer row and column positions to specific values |
| SOUNDEX( ) | Returns the Soundex code for a word, which helps find data of similar sound but with different spelling |
| STRZERO( ) | Creates the string equivalent of a number with leading zeros rather than leading blanks |
| TSTRING( ) | Converts seconds to a time string |
| UPDATED( ) | Returns .T. if a value was changed during a READ command |

**TABLE 21.4:** Clipper Functions That Extend the dBASE Language (continued)

## Networking Commands and Functions

The Autumn 1986 version of Clipper offers several networking commands and functions. These are summarized in Table 21.5.

## dBASE Commands Not Supported by Clipper

Table 21.6 lists the dBASE commands not supported by Clipper. Keep in mind that some of this information is likely to change with future releases of Clipper. As discussed below, most of the listed commands are excluded because they are virtually useless in a compiled program.

### Debugging Commands

The dBASE III PLUS debugging commands (such as SET ECHO and SET DEBUG) are not supported by Clipper for two reasons. First, you don't want to compile a program until it is fully tested and debugged. (If it didn't work in dBASE III, it isn't going to work in Clipper.) Second, Clipper has its own debugger to help you debug compiled programs. See your Clipper manual for information on the debugger.

### Create and Modify Commands

Generally, you create and modify database files, format files, report formats, and label formats while you are creating your custom system. Rarely do you include a CREATE or MODIFY command in your finished custom system.

Keep in mind that Clipper does support the DO, REPORT FORM, LABEL

| NETWORKING COMMAND/FUNCTION | EFFECT |
|---|---|
| ADD_REC( ) | Returns true (.T.) if the record was successfully appended, and locks the record |
| FIL_LOCK( ) | Tries to lock the current shared file for a limited time |
| FLOCK( ) | Locks a file to prevent changes by other users |
| NET_USE( ) | Tries to open a file for exclusive or shared use for a limited time |
| NETERR( ) | Returns information about the success of the APPEND BLANK and USE EXCLUSIVE commands on a network |
| NETNAME( ) | Returns the name of the computer in use |
| REC_LOCK( ) | Tries to lock the current record for a limited time |
| RLOCK( ) | Locks a record to prevent changes by other users |
| SET EXCLUSIVE ON/OFF | Controls access to an open database |
| SET PRINTER TO | Directs the printer output to a device or print file |
| UNLOCK [ALL] | Releases the file or record lock in a SELECT area; the ALL option releases all current locks in all work areas |
| USE<file name> EXCLUSIVE | Controls access to an open database file |

**TABLE 21.5:** Clipper Networking Functions

FORM, SET FORMAT, and USE commands, so that the compiled program can access previously created command, report, mailing label, format, and database files. In addition, Clipper provides utilities that allow you to create the various format files, so you do not even have to use dBASE III PLUS to create them.

## Full-Screen Operations

Commands like APPEND, EDIT, BROWSE, and INSERT are not supported, because most systems use custom screens rather than standard dBASE screens. You can use SET FORMAT and READ instead to provide editing capabilities to the user.

| | |
|---|---|
| APPEND* | ON KEY, ESCAPE, ERROR |
| ASSIST | RELEASE MODULE |
| BROWSE | RETRY |
| CHANGE | RETURN TO MASTER |
| CLEAR FIELDS | SET |
| CLEAR TYPEAHEAD | SET CARRY |
| CREATE<FILE NAME>** | SET DATE |
| CREATE/MODIFY LABEL*** | SET DEBUG |
| CREATE/MODIFY QUERY | SET DOHISTORY |
| CREATE/MODIFY REPORT*** | SET ECHO |
| CREATE/MODIFY SCREEN | SET FIELDS |
| CREATE/MODIFY VIEW | SET HEADING |
| DISPLAY/LIST FILES | SET HELP |
| DISPLAY/LIST HISTORY | SET HISTORY |
| DISPLAY/LIST MEMORY | SET MEMOWIDTH |
| DISPLAY/LIST STATUS | SET MENUS |
| DISPLAY/LIST STRUCTURE | SET ORDER |
| EDIT | SET SAFETY |
| EXPORT | SET STATUS |
| HELP | SET STEP |
| IMPORT | SET TITLE |
| INSERT | SET TYPEAHEAD |
| LOAD | SET VIEW |
| MODIFY COMMAND | SET TALK |
| MODIFY STRUCTURE | SUSPEND |

* APPEND FROM and APPEND BLANK are supported.
** CREATE<new file> FROM<old file> is supported.
*** Clipper includes separate programs that provide similar capabilities.

**TABLE 21.6:** dBASE Commands Not Supported by Clipper

## Clipper Index Files

Clipper creates its own index files with the extension .ntx. After creating your database, you can run a special utility included in your Clipper package to create index files directly from the DOS prompt. Also, if a command file contains an

INDEX ON command, Clipper creates the .ntx index file rather than the dBASE .ndx index file.

## Hiding Clipper Commands from dBASE

To work with dBASE programs that contain features unique to Clipper, you must use the PUBLIC Clipper command. You can place the command **PUBLIC Clipper** near the top of any command file. dBASE will create the variable Clipper and assign it the value .F. false. dBASE always initializes public memory variables as false. Then you can place Clipper-specific commands inside IF statements. For example, because dBASE uses .ndx for index file names and Clipper uses .ntx, you could enter a routine as below:

```
PUBLIC Clipper

IF Clipper
     USE MyFile INDEX MyFile.ntx
ELSE
     USE MyFile INDEX MyFile.ndx
ENDIF
```

dBASE III PLUS will use the .ndx file and Clipper will use the .ntx index file, because Clipper always sets the public Clipper variable to true (.T.) when it first encounters it. (It does this *only* with the variable specifically named Clipper.)

## Mimicking APPEND and EDIT in Clipper

Although Clipper does not support dBASE's full-screen APPEND and EDIT commands, Clipper does provide the LASTKEY( ) function, which can be used to build procedures that mimic APPEND and EDIT. (The Clipper LASTKEY( ) function is similar to the dBASE READKEY( ) function discussed in Chapter 17, "dBASE Functions"; it detects the keypress used to exit a full-screen READ command.)

Figure 21.6 shows a couple of sample Clipper procedures that mimic the dBASE APPEND and EDIT commands. To use the procedures in a Clipper-compiled application, replace an APPEND command (after a SET FORMAT command) with DO ClipAppe. For example, if your dBASE application contains the commands

```
USE Orders
SET FORMAT TO OrScreen
APPEND
```

```
*---------------------------------------- ClipProc.prg.
* Clipper procedures to simulate the dBASE EDIT
* and APPEND commands using predefined format (.FMT) files.
*
* Clipper LASTKEY() function is similar to dBASE READKEY(),
*   except that it uses different numbers.  In brief, 27 is Esc,
*   23 is Ctrl-W, 18 is PgUp, 3 is PgDn, and 13 is Return.
*   If user types beyond end of screen, LASTKEY() is the ASCII
*   code for the last character typed (e.g. a number >= 32).

*---------- Mimic the dBASE EDIT command with custom format file.
*---- Record pointer must be set to appropriate record
*---- (using SEEK or LOCATE) before calling this procedure.
PROCEDURE ClipEdit
KeyPress = 0
DO WHILE KeyPress # 27 .AND. KeyPress # 23
   READ
   KeyPress = LASTKEY()
   DO CASE
      *--- Exited screen with PgUp.
      CASE KeyPress = 18 .AND. .NOT. BOF()
           SKIP -1
      *--- Exited screen with PgDn or Return.
      CASE (KeyPress=3 .OR. KeyPress = 13) .AND. RECNO() < RECCOUNT()
           SKIP
      *--- PgDn pressed while bottom record displayed on the screen.
      CASE KeyPress = 3 .AND. RECNO() = RECCOUNT()
           KeyPress = 23
   ENDCASE
ENDDO
CLOSE FORMAT
RETURN

*------ Mimic the dBASE APPEND command with custom format file.
PROCEDURE ClipAppe
KeyPress = 0
APPEND BLANK
DO WHILE KeyPress # 27 .AND. KeyPress # 23
   READ
   KeyPress = LASTKEY()
   DO CASE
      *--- Exited screen with PgUp.
      CASE KeyPress = 18 .AND. .NOT. BOF()
           SKIP -1
      *--- Filled screen or pressed PgDn, but not
      *--  at end of file.
      CASE (KeyPress = 3 .OR. KeyPress >= 32) .AND. RECNO() < RECCOUNT()
           SKIP
      *--- Filled screen at last record, (adding a new record).
      CASE (KeyPress=3 .OR. KeyPress >= 32) .AND. UPDATED()
           APPEND BLANK
           GO BOTT
      *--- Left new record blank, so exit (blank record is still
      *--- in the data file).
      CASE (KeyPress=3 .OR. KeyPress >= 32 .OR. KeyPress= 13);
           .AND. .NOT. UPDATED()
           KeyPress = 27
           * Can use DELETE command here to remove blank record.
   ENDCASE
ENDDO
CLOSE FORMAT
RETURN
```

**FIGURE 21.6:** Clipper procedures to mimic the dBASE APPEND and EDIT commands. The Clipper LASTKEY( ) function is similar to the dBASE READKEY( ) function, which detects the keypress used to exit a full-screen READ command. These procedures use the LASTKEY( ) function to allow the user to scroll through records while editing and appending data.

the Clipper-compiled version could use the commands

```
SET PROCEDURE TO ClipProc
USE Orders
SET FORMAT TO OrScreen
DO ClipAppe
```

For editing, use the same basic technique, but be sure to get the record pointer to the right record before calling the ClipEdit procedure. For example, the dBASE routine

```
USE Orders INDEX LNames
FIND Smith
SET FORMAT TO OrScreen
EDIT RECNO( )
```

would translate to

```
USE Orders INDEX LNames
FIND Smith
SET FORMAT TO OrScreen
DO ClipEdit
```

You can use the usual **PUBLIC Clipper** syntax so that your application still runs under the dBASE interpreter when compiled, as in the example below:

```
PUBLIC Clipper      && - Place near top of main menu program...
* - - - - - - - - - - Editing program.
USE Orders INDEX LNames
FIND Smith
SET FORMAT TO OrScreen
IF Clipper
    DO ClipEdit               && If compiled, use ClipEdit.
ELSE
    EDIT RECNO( )             && If using dBASE, use EDIT.
ENDIF (clipper)
RETURN
```

Note that the Clipper LASTKEY( ) function uses different numbers for keypresses than the dBASE READKEY( ) function.

## THE QUICKSILVER COMPILER

The Quicksilver compiler, manufactured by WordTech systems, was released in the summer of 1986. This latest version, Quicksilver 1.0, of the original dB III Compiler is a true native-code compiler that converts dBASE programs into DOS-executable .exe files. Quicksilver offers several unique features to dBASE programmers, the most impressive of which is probably its "windows," as discussed later in this section.

Quicksilver comes with several optional linkers that allow you to be specific about the type of machine the compiled program will run on. You can select among PC-DOS machines (IBM PC and 100-percent compatibles) and MS-DOS machines (will run on any MS-DOS machine, including the IBM PC). There is also an option that allows the compiled program to use both dBASE II and dBASE III data.

Full compilation is a three-step process. For example, to compile a program named Test1.prg, you enter the command **dB3C Test1.prg**. To link the compiled file into a DOS-executable .exe file, you enter the command **dB3L Test1**.

To maximize the performance of the final compiled program and make it linkable machine code, you can use a single command with the flag –f (for fastest execution) –l (for link). For example, to link the Test1 program you would enter

**QS –f –l Test1**

QS creates several object files, which you then must link using the DOS LINK program.

## Quicksilver Enhancements to dBASE

Quicksilver offers several general features that are not available in dBASE III PLUS. One is the command SET DEVICE TO ALTERNATE. This allows a program to store text printed with @...SAY commands in a file. (dBASE III PLUS allows @...SAY commands to be displayed only on the screen or printer.) Similarly, the SET FEED command allows the programmer to control page ejects sent to the printer by @...SAY commands.

The SET DBF and SET NDX commands allow you to specify drives and directories for database files and index files. Programs and other files can exist on a separate drive or directory.

For more advanced programmers, the BITSET, IN, OUT, and DOSINT commands provide control over low-level functions, such as the speaker or an external port. BITSET returns a .T. if the bit at a specified position is set on. IN returns a single numeric value from a specified port. OUT sends a single value to the specified port. DOSINT allows data to be sent to and read from DOS interrupt vectors.

## Quicksilver Functions

Quicksilver supports most dBASE III PLUS functions and also lets you create your own user-defined functions. Quicksilver offers a few of its own functions as well, as summarized in Table 21.7.

| FUNCTION | EFFECT |
|---|---|
| CEIL( ) | Returns the smallest integer greater than or equal to the entered value |
| FLOOR( ) | Returns the largest integer less than or equal to the entered value |
| IN( ) | Returns a single numeric value from a system port |
| LOG10( ) | Returns the logarithm base 10 of the argument |
| OUT( ) | Sends a single value to a system port |
| SINKEY( ) | Like INKEY( ), this function can capture any keypress, but SINKEY returns the character representation, rather than the ASCII code, of the key pressed |

**TABLE 21.7:** Quicksilver Functions Not Available in dBASE

## Networking Commands and Functions

Quicksilver offers complete networking and file-sharing capabilities. The commands and functions used in Quicksilver networking are summarized in Table 21.8.

## Quicksilver Windows

Unlike simple boxes drawn on screens, Quicksilver offers true windows that can display several different activities simultaneously on different parts of the screen. The Quicksilver windows allow you to develop quick pop-up menus and help screens that can temporarily obscure data and then instantly disappear to return full view of the data. You can also determine any colors and shapes you want for your windows and even move the windows very quickly about the screen.

Quicksilver's windows have a huge visual impact on a custom application. The Quicksilver compiler comes with a program named Demonat, which demonstrates what windows can do. If you decide to purchase Quicksilver, be sure to run the Demonat program. For windowing commands and techniques, see the Quicksilver user's manual.

## Quicksilver Environmental Variables

Quicksilver offers several *environmental variables:* arguments passed from the command line into the executing program. You can pass up to 30 variables in this fashion, named XARG01 through XARG30.

| NETWORKING COMMAND/FUNCTION | EFFECT |
|---|---|
| FLOCK( ) | Locks a database file and returns a .T. or .F. value indicating the status of the lock |
| RESTORE FROM EXCLUSIVE | Recalls memory variables from disk but prevents other users from changing memory variables until they are placed back on disk with the SAVE command |
| LOCK( ) (or RLOCK( )) | Locks a specific record in a database and returns a .T. or .F. indicating the status of the lock |
| RETRY | Returns control to the first line of a program in which an error occurred |
| SAVE | Saves memory variables to a previously created disk file and unlocks that file |
| SET AUTOLOCK | When AUTOLOCK is set on, file and record locking are handled automatically by the network |
| SET DELAY | Sets a time, from 0 to 21,540 seconds, that specifies how long the network will wait before attempting to reaccess a locked file |
| SET EXCLUSIVE | When EXCLUSIVE is off, all files are opened and shared on a network; with exclusive ON, all files are opened in a locked state |
| SET INDEX...SHARED | Activates an index file so that two or more network users can use the index simultaneously |
| SET LASTLOCAL | Allows each workstation in a network to define which drive designators are local (physically attached to the workstation) and which reside on the network file server |
| SET MULTIUSER | When set to off, the MULTIUSER option suspends the operation of the network and ignores attempts to lock files or records |
| SET RETRY | Determines the number of times (from 0 to 65535) that the networker will retry an unsuccessful attempt to lock a record or file |
| SET SUSPEND | Same as SET AUTOLOCK |
| UNLOCK [ALL] | Releases the file or record lock in a SELECT area; the ALL option releases all current locks in all work areas |

**TABLE 21.8:** Quicksilver Networking Commands and Functions

| NETWORKING COMMAND/FUNCTION | EFFECT |
|---|---|
| USE<file> EXCLUSIVE | When EXCLUSIVE is used in the USE command, the file is opened and access is limited to the current user |
| USERNO( ) | Returns the current workstation's number assignment |

**TABLE 21.8:** Quicksilver Networking Commands and Functions (continued)

In addition to the 30 arguments you can define yourself, Quicksilver automatically initializes eight other environmental variables, which are summarized in Table 21.9.

## dBASE Commands Not Supported by Quicksilver

Like the Clipper compiler, Quicksilver does not support interactive (dot prompt) commands or debugging aids. (Quicksilver also has its own debugger.) dBASE commands not supported by Quicksilver are listed in Table 21.10.

The reasons for the exclusion of these commands are discussed in the section "dBASE Commands Not Supported by Clipper."

## Quicksilver Index Files

Index files created and maintained in dBASE III PLUS are completely compatible with Quicksilver index files, and vice versa.

## Hiding Quicksilver Commands from dBASE

To keep dBASE III PLUS from attempting to execute a Quicksilver-specific command, simply precede the command line with the characters *\. dBASE will treat the line as a comment; Quicksilver will ignore the *\ characters and compile the line. For example:

```
*\ SET DEVICE TO ALTERNATE
SET ALTERNATE TO AltFile
SET ALTERNATE ON
```

dBASE III PLUS will ignore the "illegal" SET DEVICE TO ALTERNATE command.

| VARIABLE | EFFECT |
|---|---|
| XARGC | Provides count of passed arguments |
| XCOMMANDLN | Lists arguments specified on the command line |
| XPRINTON | Provides status of printer when compiled program was loaded into RAM |
| XPRINTBUSY | Returns .T. if printer was offline or in use when compiled program was loaded into RAM |
| XCOLOR | Returns .T. if a color monitor is in use; otherwise returns .F. |
| XDRIVE | Contains a character representing the current default drive |
| XCURRDRV | Contains both the current default drive and directory when the program was loaded into RAM |
| XARG00 | Provides name of command used to load the current program into RAM (actually the name of the program itself) |

**TABLE 21.9:** Quicksilver Environmental Variables

### Quicksilver Macro Restrictions

Macros can be used in place of all file names and as conditions in DO WHILE loops. Keywords and commands cannot be stored in macros. For example, the sequence

```
Mac = "ON"
SET FLASH     &MAC
```

is not allowed.

## PERFORMANCE COMPARISONS

Compiling a custom system does not guarantee that the entire system is suddenly going to run at the speed of light. Keep in mind that a compiler basically just preinterprets your command files and stores these already interpreted commands in a separate file. It does not make the hardware operate any faster.

When you compile a program, you can expect major speed improvements in routines that do not access the screen, printer, or disk. (That's because these external devices won't slow down the execution speed.) dBASE III PLUS commands that manage data already in RAM (like SEEK and FIND) are likely to show no apparent improvement in performance when compiled. (Arguably, 0.8 seconds is 20 percent faster than 1.0 second, but few people will notice the 0.2-second difference.)

Processes that are heavily disk bound, such as a LOCATE command, will not show a major improvement in performance. That's because most of the time spent in a LOCATE command goes to physically searching the disk for data. The compiled program cannot speed up the physical movement of the disk drive.

To demonstrate the effect of the compilers, four different programs are compared. The first, named Test1.prg, is shown in Figure 21.7. This program simply displays a starting time, repeats a loop 1000 times, and displays the time when done. Because it does not access the screen or disk, its speed will be most improved when compiled.

| | |
|---|---|
| APPEND* | RESUME |
| ASSIST | SET |
| BROWSE | SET CARRY |
| CHANGE | SET CATALOG |
| CLEAR FIELDS | SET DEBUG |
| CREATE ** | SET DOHISTORY |
| CREATE/MODIFY LABEL*** | SET ECHO |
| CREATE/MODIFY QUERY | SET ENCRYPTION |
| CREATE/MODIFY REPORT*** | SET FIELDS |
| CREATE/MODIFY SCREEN | SET HEADING |
| CREATE/MODIFY VIEW | SET HELP |
| DISPLAY/LIST FILES | SET MENU |
| DISPLAY/LIST HISTORY | SET HISTORY |
| DISPLAY/LIST STATUS | SET MESSAGE |
| DISPLAY USERS | SET PRINTER |
| EDIT | SET SAFETY |
| EXPORT TO TYPE PFS | SET STATUS |
| HELP | SET STEP |
| IMPORT FROM TYPE PFS | SET TITLE |
| INSERT | SET TYPEAHEAD |
| LOAD | SET TALK |
| MODIFY COMMAND | SET VIEW |
| MODIFY STRUCTURE | SUSPEND |

* APPEND FROM and APPEND BLANK are supported.
** CREATE<new file> FROM<old file> is supported.

**TABLE 21.10:** dBASE Commands Not Supported by Quicksilver

The second program, Test2.prg, also repeats a loop 1000 times, but it displays a number on the screen each time through the loop. In this case, the screen slows down the execution of the compiled program, so the performance improvement is not as dramatic as for Test1.prg. (Obviously, a printer would slow things down even more.) Test2.prg is shown in Figure 21.8.

The third program, Test3.prg, attempts to locate the last name Smith in an unindexed database named CTest.DBF. (In this example, Smith was stored at the 1000th record.) Because the primary job of this program is to search the disk for a particular piece of information, one would expect little speed improvement when compiled. Test3.prg is shown in Figure 21.9.

Test4.prg, shown in Figure 21.10, accesses both the screen and disk through a LIST command. The effect of the compiler on the speed of this program is an "averaging" of the Test2 and Test3 programs.

```
*************************************** Test1.prg
*---- Program that accesses no external devices.

SET TALK OFF
? TIME()

Counter = 1
DO WHILE Counter <= 1000
   Counter = Counter + 1
ENDDO

? TIME()
```

**FIGURE 21.7:** The Test1.prg command file. This program uses a DO WHILE loop to count to 1000. It does not access any peripherals, such as the screen or printer. Therefore, this program should show a significant increase in speed when compiled.

```
*************************************** Test2.prg
*-------- Program that accesses only the screen.
SET TALK OFF
StartTime = TIME()

Counter = 1
DO WHILE Counter <= 1000
   ? Counter
   Counter = Counter + 1
ENDDO

? StartTime
? TIME()
```

**FIGURE 21.8:** The Test2.prg command file. Like Test1.prg, this program also counts to 1000, but it displays its progress on the screen. When compiled, this program will show some increase in speed, but not as dramatic an increase as the Test1.prg command file, because the screen accesses will require a small amount of time.

```
*********************************** Test3.prg
*-------- Program that is heavily disk bound.
SET TALK OFF
? TIME()

*-------- Locate the 1,000th record.
USE CTest
LOCATE FOR LName = "Smith"
? RECNO()

? TIME()
```

**FIGURE 21.9:** The Test3.prg command file. This program searches the disk drive for a record with the Smith in a database field called LName. In the examples, Smith happens to be in the 1000th record. Because this program is heavily dependent on the speed of the disk drive, compilation will show little or no improvement.

```
************************************** Test4.prg
*-------- Program that is disk and screen bound.
SET TALK OFF
StartTime = TIME()

*-------- Show 1,000 records on the screen.
USE CTest
LIST LName, FName, Company, Address

? StartTime
? TIME()
```

**FIGURE 21.10:** The Test4.prg command file. This program accesses both the screen and a disk file. The effect of the compiler on the speed of this program is an "averaging" of the Test2 and Test3 programs shown in Figure 21.9 and 21.10.

The actual processing times on an IBM AT 339 with an 8 Mhz clock, 1.5 MB of RAM, and a 30-MB hard disk drive are shown in Table 21.11. (These processing times will differ on other computers.)

The sizes of the files are also shown in Table 21.11. For the dBASE III PLUS row, you need to add 440K if dBASE III PLUS is used to run the program.

As would be expected, Test1.prg shows the most significant improvement when compiled. The 13-second dBASE program was reduced to 3 seconds with Quicksilver and a slim 2 seconds with Clipper.

The screen accessing (with the ? command) in Test2.prg slows down all three versions as expected. However, both the Clipper- and Quicksilver-compiled versions are definitely faster than the dBASE III PLUS version; the Clipper-compiled version is more than twice as fast.

The Test3.prg program, which used the LOCATE command to locate the thousandth record on the database, ran at the same speed regardless of whether

| | Test1 | Test2 | Test3 | Test4 | |
|---|---|---|---|---|---|
| **dBASE III PLUS** | 13<br>256+ | 34<br>256+ | 3<br>256+ | 53<br>256+ | seconds<br>bytes |
| **Clipper compiled** | 2<br>126,944 | 16<br>126,992 | 3<br>127,024 | 35<br>127,056 | seconds<br>bytes |
| **Quicksilver compiled** | 3<br>119,520 | 19<br>119,584 | 3<br>112,096 | 31<br>119,632 | seconds<br>bytes |

**TABLE 21.11:** Comparison of Source and Compiled Code

or not it was compiled. The heavy use of the disk drive overpowered any improvement in speed the compiler might have offered.

Test4.prg, which accesses both the disk and screen, was improved when compiled with Clipper (35 seconds vs. 53 seconds), and improved even more by Quicksilver (31 seconds).

## SUMMARY

This chapter has discussed numerous dBASE add-ons that advanced programmers can use to help market the applications programs they develop. The RunTime+ package, which comes with dBASE III PLUS, lets you encrypt your applications so that they cannot be tampered with by others. If you use RunTime+ your potential customers only need dBRUN, which costs much less than dBASE III PLUS, to run the encrypted applications.

The compilers convert your dBASE applications programs to stand-alone assembly language programs that can be run directly from the DOS prompt, without any help whatsoever from dBASE III PLUS. The compilers also offer significant improvements in processing speed over both dBASE III PLUS and the RunTime+ package.

*For information on the READKEY( ) function and other dBASE functions:*

- Chapter 17, "dBASE Functions"

*For information on dBASE networking commands and functions:*

- Chapter 20, "Networking and Security"

*For information on running assembly language subroutines from within dBASE III PLUS:*

- Chapter 22, "Using Assembly Language Subroutines in dBASE"

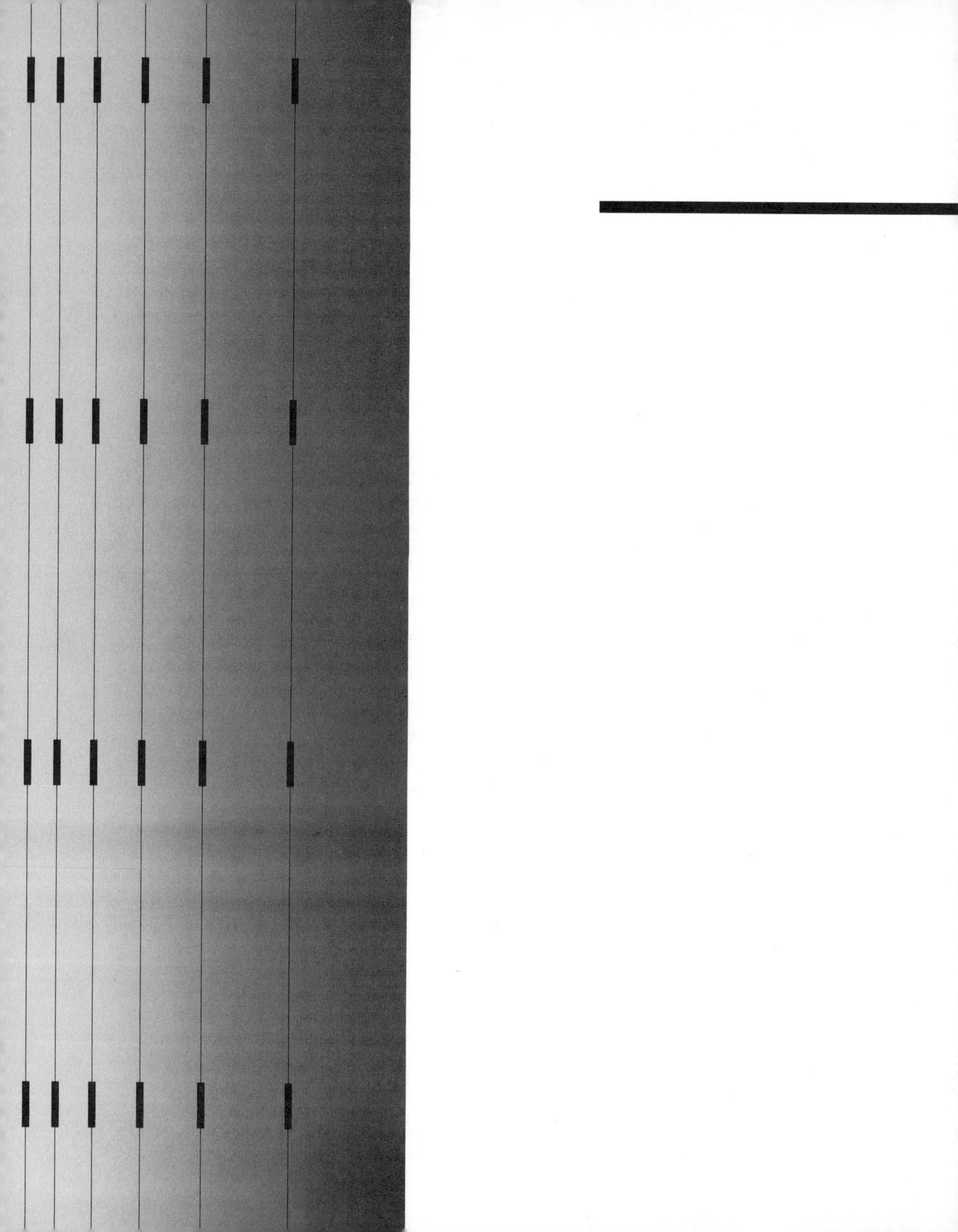

# USING ASSEMBLY LANGUAGE SUBROUTINES IN dBASE

# USING ASSEMBLY LANGUAGE SUBROUTINES IN dBASE

dBASE III PLUS has the ability to call subroutines written in assembly language. This is useful if you want your program to do something that the dBASE language doesn't provide for, or to perform some task at a much faster speed than dBASE can achieve on its own. Some examples of applications for assembly language subroutines include music or sound effects, data logging from special-purpose hardware, specialized mathematical calculations, animated color graphics, high-speed data communication, and control of laboratory experiments.

This chapter is not meant to be a complete tutorial on writing assembly language programs. Instead, it assumes a familiarity with assembly language and with certain hardware features of computers: particularly registers, segments, and stacks. However, the chapter will provide you with enough background to use assembly language subroutines by others in your dBASE programs. A few useful assembler programs are included in the chapter.

## CALLING ASSEMBLY LANGUAGE SUBROUTINES FROM dBASE

LOAD and CALL are the dBASE commands used for interfacing with assembly language. LOAD is used to load an assembly language subroutine into RAM, and CALL is used to execute a previously loaded assembly language subroutine. For example, **LOAD MyProg** loads the assembly language subroutine named MyProg into RAM. Once assembly MyProg has been loaded, the command **CALL MyProg** will execute it.

The CALL command can also pass a character string to the called subroutine, in much the same way that a DO...WITH command can pass a parameter to a procedure. For CALL to pass a parameter to the assembly language subroutine, the subroutine must be designed to make some use of the passed parameter.

For example, suppose the MyProg assembly language subroutine is a communication driver designed to send a string of characters to some device. You could use the dBASE CALL command to pass a parameter to MyProg as follows:

**CALL MyProg WITH "This is the message."**

or

**MsgVar = "This is the message."**
**CALL MyProg WITH MsgVar**

The second approach is the preferred approach for three reasons:

1. MyProg can modify the MsgVar variable and thereby communicate some information back to the dBASE program.
2. Once MsgVar is defined, it can be used repeatedly, which is easier than repeating the literal string many times.
3. MsgVar might be a field name of a database file. In that case the program can select a message by selecting a record from the file. The single CALL statement can then send a variety of messages.

In general, any character-string expression can be used after the WITH portion of the CALL command. However, if your subroutine is going to return some data to your dBASE program, you must use a character-string variable rather than a literal expression. A subroutine that neither requires data from nor returns data to dBASE should be called without the WITH clause.

The RUN command provides another way to execute an assembly language subroutine. The differences between RUN and LOAD/CALL are quite significant. RUN requires a stand-alone program that can be executed by itself from the DOS command line. LOAD/CALL requires a binary file designed for a single, smaller purpose. Stand-alone programs are typically ten to fifty times larger than binary files. Each time RUN is used, the stand-alone program must be loaded from disk, which requires many seconds. A binary file remains in memory after it is loaded and can be called instantly. Also, there is no convenient or rapid method for passing data between dBASE and a stand-alone program, although it can be done using a disk file as an intermediate medium. The WITH clause provides that facility for LOAD/CALL.

## Writing an Assembly Language Module

An assembly language module is basically just a single subroutine that returns with a far return. This is accomplished most easily by making it a FAR procedure. The module can alter almost any of the registers; only the stack pointer and stack segment need to be preserved. Other details will be explained along with the examples.

The following software tools are required to write assembly language subroutines for dBASE:

1. A text editor
2. MASM.exe, the Microsoft or IBM PC assembler
3. LINK.exe, the linker
4. EXE2BIN.exe, which must be used to create the required binary file

Both EXE2BIN.exe and LINK.exe come with your DOS package. The MASM assembler needs to be purchased separately.

All assembly language subroutines must have the file-name extension .asm. This .asm file must then be assembled to produce an object file with the .obj file-name extension. The .obj file, in turn, needs to be converted to a binary (.bin) file. The binary file created by EXE2BIN is the only one that dBASE uses. All this conversion can be done automatically, as explained below.

## Creating Binary Files Automatically

Figure 22.1 shows a DOS batch file called dBSUB.bat that can automate the process of converting .asm assembly language files to the .bin binary file format. If this batch file is in your working directory, you can go from source (.asm) to binary (.bin) format with one command. For instance, if your source file is named Demo.asm, you can type **dBSUB Demo** at the DOS prompt to produce Demo.bin.

## A Simple Assembly Language Subroutine

Figure 22.2 shows an assembly language source file named Demo.asm. While this file is of limited practical value, it demonstrates a basic technique for composing a dBASE assembly language subroutine. In addition, it demonstrates a technique that can be used to manipulate a character string passed to an assembly language subroutine through the dBASE CALL...WITH command.

```
REM ------- dBSUB.bat - usage: dBSUB <file name.asm>
MASM %1 %1;
LINK /m %1, %1, %1;
EXE2BIN %1
```

**FIGURE 22.1:** A simple DOS batch file that converts assembly language source modules with the file-name extension .asm to binary files with the extension .bin. dBASE can load the finished binary file into memory and execute it with the CALL command.

```
; Demo.asm - simple assembly language demo for dBASE
; modifies a string passed by dBASE III+

mdstrng         segment         byte
        assume  cs:mdstrng

modstring       proc    far
        mov     [bx+4], byte ptr 'B'    ; write "BOY" in string
        mov     [bx+5], byte ptr 'O'
        mov     [bx+6], byte ptr 'Y'
        mov     ax, 0       ; test to see if it's ok to destroy DS
        mov     ds, ax
        mov     ax, 0       ; test to see if it's ok to destroy BP
        mov     bp, ax
        ret

modstring       endp

mdstrng         ends
                end
```

**FIGURE 22.2:** Sample assembly language subroutine named Demo.asm, which accepts a character string from dBASE and changes it. This program uses the DS and BX registers to write BOY starting at the fifth character in the string.

Figure 22.3 shows a dBASE program, named Demo.prg, that calls the binary file named Demo.bin. Demo.bin, of course, was built from the Demo.asm source file via the dBSUB batch program shown in Figure 22.1. Once this has been done, Demo.prg can be executed from within dBASE with the usual DO command.

Note that dBASE refers to the module by its file name, not the procedure or code segment names. Because dBASE has not been linked with the .obj file, it knows nothing of the names used in the source code for the module. dBASE knows only the file name. Hence any module that will be used by dBASE must have its first executable statement at the beginning of its code segment (at offset position 00h), as in Figure 22.2. If there are subroutines and data areas in the module, they cannot be at the very beginning.

Note also that there is no stack or data segment, because they are already in use by dBASE. (There will be a warning message from LINK about the absence of a stack segment, which you can safely ignore in this case.) Thus, all memory references must refer to the code segment, because that is the only memory your module knows anything about. You do not know where in memory your module will be loaded, nor do you know which memory in the data segment is being used by dBASE. (The AnyCall.asm program in Figure 22.6 below illustrates a technique to create a scratchpad data area within the code segment.)

However, although the character string passed to the subroutine by dBASE is in a data segment controlled by dBASE, you know exactly where it starts and ends. When your module begins execution, the BX register has been set to the offset of this character string within the segment defined by DS. In other words, DS:BX is a far pointer to the string. The end of the string is marked by a null, or binary zero, byte.

```
*********************************************** Demo.prg
*----- Test the Demo.bin assembly language subroutine.
SET TALK OFF

*------ Load the Demo.bin assembly language subroutine.
LOAD Demo

*------ Create and print sample character string.
dstring = "The cat went to market."
? dstring

*------ Pass sample string to subroutine and show results.
CALL Demo WITH dstring
? dstring
```

**FIGURE 22.3:** A sample program that loads the Demo.bin assembly language subroutine into memory and later calls the subroutine, passing the contents of the dstring memory variable to that subroutine.

The Demo.asm program in Figure 22.2 illustrates some simple manipulation of the character string, but you can do anything you want to it. Demo.asm uses the DS and BX registers to write BOY starting at the fifth character in the string. The DS register is used by default when no segment register is named. [BX + 0] would point to the first character. The word BOY replaces whatever was there initially. Demo should be called with a string of at least seven characters, so that BOY has someplace to go. A shorter string, or the command **CALL Demo** by itself, will cause those three characters to be written to unallocated memory, with unpredictable results.

The last portion of the Demo.asm program is a simple test to see whether dBASE preserves the DS and BP registers. If dBASE did not preserve these registers, these four **mov** commands would cause the program to crash. However, the subroutine runs without a hitch. Therefore, this test shows that dBASE does indeed preserve these registers, and you can alter these registers within any assembly language subroutine that you write.

## AN ASSEMBLY LANGUAGE SUBROUTINE TO PRODUCE A TONE

Figure 22.4 shows an example of an assembly language subroutine named Tone.asm. This subroutine produces a tone; the dBASE program that calls it can specify the duration and frequency of the tone. In an application program, you could use this module to return tones of different pitches and durations for different types of feedback, such as low tones for errors and higher beeps for valid entries. If you were feeling particularly creative, you could even use the module to play music from within a dBASE program. (Although this module uses the speaker as an external device, you could use similar techniques to access any external device.)

The dBASE program Muzik.prg (Figure 22.5) shows how Tone.bin is used. Tone does not return any information (only sound), so there is no harm

```
; TONE.ASM -- Assembly language subroutine to sound a tone.

gate_port       equ     61H     ; PPI device
channel_2       equ     42H     ; timer device channel used for sound
channel_3       equ     43H     ; timer device control channel

code        segment         byte
        assume  cs:code

tone        proc    far
; convert the two numbers in the command string to binary, then push
; them on the stack:
        call atob   ; atob works off the command string using DS:BX
        cmp     dx, 0    ; don't allow a zero to be pushed
        jnz     p1       ; this would only result from a command error
        mov     dx, 1    ; push a 1 instead (very short duration)
p1:     push dx      ; push the first parameter
        inc bx       ; gets to next number's 1st digit
        call atob    ; convert second parameter
        cmp     dx, 0    ; don't allow a zero to be pushed
        jnz     p2       ; this would only result from a command error
        mov     dx, 500 ; push 500 instead (a high note)
p2:     push dx      ; push second parameter

        in      al, gate_port           ; enable sound generation
        or      al, 3
        out     gate_port, al

        mov     al, 0B6H        ; set timer chip to modify sound channel
        out     channel_3, al

        pop     ax              ; retrieve the second parameter
        out     channel_2, al   ; set sound channel for desired frequency
        mov     al, ah
        out     channel_2, al

        mov     ax, 40H         ; change DS to access system tick count
        mov     ds, ax
        mov     cx, ds:[6CH]    ; fetch low word of tick count from 40:6C
        pop     ax              ; retrieve the 1st parameter
        add     cx, ax          ; add it to tick count
tite_loop:                      ; now loop until system tick count reaches
        cmp     cx, ds:[6CH]    ; the computed value in cx
        jnz     tite_loop

        in      al, gate_port   ; disable sound generation
        and     al, 0FCH
        out     gate_port, al

        ret                     ; Return to dBASE.
tone        endp

; routine to convert an ASCII string to a binary number:

atob    proc    near        ; enter here with BX pointing to first digit
        mov     cl, 3       ; to set up shift to multiply by eight
        sub     dx, dx      ; clear result register

; this is the main processing loop of subroutine atob:
mnlup:  mov   al, byte ptr [bx]   ; fetch the next character
        sub     ah, ah            ; clear high byte of ax
```

**FIGURE 22.4:** The Tone.asm assembly language subroutine, which sounds a tone with the frequency and duration determined by a dBASE command string. For example, the command **CALL Tone WITH "36 4000"** produces a tone for two seconds (36 clock ticks) with a frequency of 1,190,000 / 4000 cycles per second.

```
        cmp     ax, '0'         ; test for decimal digit
        jge     notneg          ; We are done if a value is found outside
        ret                     ; the range of 0-9.  Otherwise, we
notneg: cmp     ax, '9'         ; continue the conversion process
        jle     convert
        ret

convert: sub    ax, '0'         ; convert ASCII digit to binary value
        push    ax              ; save value while we multiply, below
; multiply partial result by ten: (fast execution method)
m10:    mov     ax, dx      ; save result register
        shl     dx, cl      ; multiply partial result by eight
        add     dx, ax      ; add previous value
        add     dx, ax      ; add it one last time, 8 + 1 + 1 = 10
        pop     ax          ; retrieve value of the latest character
        add     dx, ax      ; add it to partial result
        inc     bx          ; point to next character
        jmp     mnlup
atob endp

code          ends
                end
```

**FIGURE 22.4:** The Tone.asm assembly language subroutine, which sounds a tone with the frequency and duration determined by a dBASE command string. For example, the command **CALL Tone WITH "36 4000"** produces a tone for two seconds (36 clock ticks) with a frequency of 1,190,000 / 4000 cycles per second. (continued)

```
***************************************** Muzik.prg
*-- dBASE program to play a series of tones using
*-- the Tone.bin assembly language subroutine.

LOAD Tone
CALL Tone WITH "18 1800"
CALL Tone WITH "9 1400"
CALL Tone WITH "18 900"
CALL Tone WITH "9 2700"
CALL Tone WITH "36 3600"
```

**FIGURE 22.5:** Sample dBASE program that loads the Tone.bin assembly language subroutine into memory and calls it with a variety of durations and pitches. Within the single passed parameter, the duration is listed first (18). It is followed by a space and the calculated frequency (1800).

in using a literal string rather than a variable name after the WITH portion of the command.

In Figure 22.5, the first number in the command string is the duration of the tone, in ticks. There are 18.2 system clock ticks per second, so a half-second tone would have a 9 for the first number. The second number controls the frequency. This number specifies the period of the waveform with respect to a 1.19 Mhz clock. If you want a frequency of 880 cycles per second, the second number should be 1,190,000 / 880 = 1352.

Tone begins by converting each number in the command string into a binary value in the DX register and then pushing it on the stack. The subroutine AtoB does most of this work by moving the BX pointer along the string as it does the conversion. The single inc bx instruction between the two calls to AtoB gets the pointer over the intervening space.

After the two numbers are on the stack, the hardware devices are accessed as described briefly in the programmer comments. The duration and frequency values are popped off the stack when they are needed.

Tone does not do any checking of the command string. The conversion routine returns to the calling command whenever a nondigit character is found. If the first character is not a digit, the result of the conversion will be zero. This can happen any time there is a leading space in the command string or a double space between the numbers. Because a zero would cause either a very long tone or an inaudible tone, Tone includes a test that converts a zero to an acceptable value rather than allowing it to be pushed on the stack.

## A Module to Perform a Software Interrupt

Software interrupts are a feature of the Intel 8086 family of microprocessors. In assembly language, a software interrupt is any signal sent by a running program that tells the processor that an event requiring immediate attention has occurred. Software interrupts are used by the MS-DOS, PC-DOS, and IBM ROM software to access services that are available from the processor, such as various video display (cursor size, scrolling), disk (read and write sectors), keyboard (read next character), and communications (send and receive characters) services.

AnyCall.asm, shown in Figure 22.6, is an assembly language module designed to be used by dBASE III PLUS. Its purpose is to perform a software interrupt by interpreting a command string passed to it by dBASE. The command string, an ordinary dBASE character string, tells the routine what interrupt to perform and how to set up the registers prior to the interrupt.

```
; ------------------------------------------------------- AnyCall.asm.
; This routine performs an INT instruction after setting register
; values.  The number of the INT and the register values are taken from
; the command string.  A pointer to the command string is passed to the
; routine by dBASE when it is called.  The string is null terminated.

; The command string looks like this (for example):
; AH=3 AL=1B INT=10

; In general it is any number of assignments separated by spaces, where
; each assignment begins with INT or any of the following register names:

;    AX, AL, AH, BX, BL, BH, CX, CL, CH, DX, DL, DH, SI, DI, ES, DS
;    (you can't use SP or BP or SS)
```

**FIGURE 22.6:** Sample assembly language subroutine that interprets a command string and performs an INT instruction. The routine is designed to be called from dBASE III PLUS with the command CALL AnyCall WITH ComVar where ComVar is a character string variable containing a command.

```
; The numerical values are in hexadecimal.  There must be no spaces on
; either side of the equal sign.  The assignments may be in any order.
; There must be no more than one assignment to any name.
; Only uppercase letters are acceptable.
; If you use AX, don't use AH or AL, and similarly for BX, CX and DX.

code        segment         byte
        assume  cs:code

; Our general strategy here is to find all the equal signs and push the
; values and register ID's on the stack.  This data is then used to
; load the various registers.  The INT data is used to modify the operand
; field of an INT instruction.

anycall     proc    far    ; dBASE passes pointer to command string in DS:BX
        mov  word ptr cs:bx_store, bx    ; preserve original far pointer
        mov     ax, ds                   ; for writing error message in
        mov  word ptr cs:bx_store+2, ax  ; command string if necessary
        mov  word ptr cs:st_store, sp    ; save original stack pointer
        mov  byte ptr cs:intfound, 0    ; initialize this variable
        sub     bp, bp       ; clear bp, will count register assignments

mainlp:             ; scan the string looking for '=' or the null terminator
        cmp      [bx], byte ptr 0          ; have we reached null terminator?
        jz       str_done                  ; if so, then execute the command.
        cmp      [bx], byte ptr '='        ; else, are we at an equal sign?
        jz       got1                      ; if so, process this assignment.
incbx:  inc      bx                        ; else advance pointer to next char
        jmp      mainlp                    ; continue scanning command string

got1:               ; an equal sign has been found
        cmp     [bx-2], byte ptr 'N'    ; detect INT assignment by the 'N'
        jnz      reg_assign          ; if not an INT, its register assignment
        ; maybe its an INT assignment:
        cmp     [bx-3], byte ptr 'I'    ; check that the 'I' is there
        jz      T?
        jmp     erloc
T?:     cmp     [bx-1], byte ptr 'T'    ; check for the 'T'
        jz      int_assign
        jmp     erloc

int_assign:  ; here we modify the INT instruction, filling in the value
        call     htob      ; converts ASCII hex to binary, result in DX
        mov    byte ptr cs:int_ins+1, dl    ; modify the int instruction
        mov    byte ptr cs:[intfound], 1    ; signal that this occurred
        jmp      incbx    ; continue scanning

reg_assign:             ; convert ASCII hex string to binary, push it on stack
        call     htob      ; converts ASCII hex to binary, result in DX
        push     DX        ; push value on stack
        inc      bp        ; increment assignment counter
        ; find position in register name table, push that on stack
        mov      si, offset regnames
matchlp:
        mov      al, [bx-2]    ; fetch first character of pair in cmd. string
        cmp      al, cs:[si]       ; if it matches the table
        jz       char1             ; check the second character, else
        jmp repeat                 ; continue scanning reg. names table

char1:  ; the first character matches, try the second:
        mov      al, [bx-1]        ; fetch the second character
        cmp      al, cs:[si+1]     ; if it matches we have our register!
        jz       match
```

**FIGURE 22.6:** Sample assembly language subroutine that interprets a command string and performs an INT instruction. The routine is designed to be called from dBASE III PLUS with the command CALL AnyCall WITH ComVar where ComVar is a character string variable containing a command. (continued)

```
repeat: add     si, 2             ; no match - advance table pointer
        cmp     si, (offset regnames + 32)    ; end of table?
        jl matchlp               ; if not, continue scanning reg. names table
        sub     bx, 2            ; if so, locate position for error message
        jmp erloc

        ; this is when a match is found:
match:  mov     ax, offset regnames   ; calculate register identifier:
        sub     si, ax                ; subtract starting address
        shr     si, 1             ; divide by 2
        push    si                ; si is position in table
        jmp     incbx             ; continue scanning command string

        ; this is when the end of command string is reached:
str_done:  cmp bp, 0             ; see if any registers were to be loaded
        jnz     regload          ; if so, proceed, else error
        jmp     erloc            ; error reported if no register assignment
regload:
        mov     al, byte ptr cs:[intfound]   ; see if the INT= was handled
        cmp     al, 0                ; this will be nonzero if INT found
        jnz     l0                   ; if so, proceed, else error
erloc:  mov     word ptr cs:[errisat], bx  ; error location
        jmp     errexit              ; error if no INT= was handled

l0:     cmp     bp, 0            ; test bp to see if we're done.
        jnz     n0               ; bp holds register assignment count
        jmp      do_int          ; when its down counted to zero, go to exit

n0:     dec     bp               ; decrement the assignment counter
        pop     ax               ; fetch the next register ID
        cmp     ax, 0            ; if 0 was popped, then get a value for AX
        jnz      n1              ; else check first for a 1, then a 2, etc.
        pop     ax               ; get the new value for AX
        ; Since AX is needed for processing we will store the value in RAM
        ; and restore it just before the final return.
        mov  word ptr cs:al_store, ax     ; store AX there until the end
        jmp     regload

n1:     cmp     ax, 1             ; if 1, get a value for AL
        jnz      n2
        pop     ax
        mov  byte ptr cs:[al_store], al    ; store AL there until the end
        jmp     regload

n2:     cmp     ax, 2
        jnz      n3
        pop     ax                        ; get value for AH
        mov  byte ptr cs:[ah_store], al   ; store AH there until the end
        jmp     regload

n3:     cmp     ax, 3
        jnz      n4
        pop     bx                ; get value for BX
        jmp     regload

n4:     cmp     ax, 4
        jnz     n5
        mov     ah, bh        ; get value for BH
        pop     bx
        mov     bh, ah
        jmp     regload
```

**FIGURE 22.6:** Sample assembly language subroutine that interprets a command string and performs an INT instruction. The routine is designed to be called from dBASE III PLUS with the command CALL AnyCall WITH ComVar where ComVar is a character string variable containing a command. (continued)

```
n5:     cmp     ax, 5
        jnz      n6
        mov     ah, bl          ; get value for BL
        pop     bx
        mov     bh, bl
        mov     bl, ah
        jmp     regload

n6:     cmp     ax, 6
        jnz      n7
        pop     cx                  ; get value for CX
        jmp     regload

n7:     cmp     ax, 7
        jnz      n8
        mov     ah, ch          ; get value for CH
        pop     cx
        mov     ch, ah
        jmp     regload

n8:     cmp     ax, 8
        jnz      n9
        mov     ah, cl          ; get value for CL
        pop     cx
        mov     ch, cl
        mov     cl, ah
        jmp     regload

n9:     cmp     ax, 9
        jnz      nA
        pop     dx                  ; get value for DX
        jmp     regload

nA:     cmp     ax, 0AH
        jnz      nB
        mov     ah, dh          ; get value for DH
        pop     dx
        mov     dh, ah
        jmp     regload

nB:     cmp     ax, 0BH
        jnz      nC
        mov     ah, dl          ; get value for DL
        pop     dx
        mov     dh, dl
        mov     dl, ah
        jmp     regload

nC:     cmp     ax, 0CH
        jnz      nD
        pop     si                  ; get value for SI
        jmp     regload

nD:     cmp     ax, 0DH
        jnz      n14
        pop     di                  ; get value for DI
        jmp     regload

n14:    cmp     ax, 0EH
        jnz      nF
        pop     es                  ; get value for ES
        jmp     regload
```

**FIGURE 22.6:** Sample assembly language subroutine that interprets a command string and performs an INT instruction. The routine is designed to be called from dBASE III PLUS with the command CALL AnyCall WITH ComVar where ComVar is a character string variable containing a command. (continued)

```
nF:     cmp     ax, 0FH
        jnz      n10
        pop     ds                  ; get value for DS
        jmp     regload

n10:    ; software error, shouldn't get here, alter command and return
        jmp errexit

do_int:         ; almost ready to perform the INT, just need to load AX
        mov ax, word ptr cs:[al_store]   ; put desired value in AX
        mov sp, word ptr cs:[st_store]   ; restore stack pointer
int_ins:          ; execute the desired interrupt
        int 0FFH  ; argument to be replaced, assuming INT in command string
        ret       ; return to dBASE III+
errexit:        ; alternate exit path when an error is detected:
        mov    ax, word ptr cs:[bx_store+2]  ; restore original data segment
        mov     ds, ax
        mov     bx, word ptr cs:[errisat]     ; point to error in string
        sub     bx, 4                         ; position pointer 3 bytes
l1:     inc     bx                            ; earlier, but not prior to
        js      l1                            ; start of command string
        mov     [bx], byte ptr 'E'            ; say "ERR" in command string
        mov     [bx+1], byte ptr 'R'
        mov     [bx+2], byte ptr 'R'
        mov sp, word ptr cs:[st_store]   ; restore stack pointer
        ret       ; return to dBASE III+
anycall        endp

; routine to convert an ASCII hexadecimal string to a binary number:
htob    proc    near
        mov     si, bx      ; point si at equal sign
        inc     si          ; point to first digit of value
        mov     cl, 4       ; to set up shift of one hex digit
        sub     dx, dx      ; clear result register
m16:    shl     dx, cl      ; multiply partial result by sixteen
        mov   al, byte ptr [si]  ; fetch the character
        sub     ah, ah
        call    convert           ; convert it to a binary value

        cmp     ax, 0             ; test for reasonable value
        jge     notneg
        mov     word ptr cs:[errisat], si  ; error location
        jmp     errexit
notneg: cmp     ax, 10H
        jl      okval
        mov     word ptr cs:[errisat], si  ; error location
        jmp     errexit

okval:  add     dx, ax            ; add it to partial result
        inc     si                ; advance pointer to next character
        cmp   byte ptr [si], ' '  ; is next char a space or control char?
        jg      m16               ; if not, process the next digit
        ret                       ; if so, done, result in dx

convert:        ; convert hex ASCII digit in AX to a binary value 0-15
        cmp     ax, '9'           ; if the ASCII code is
        jle     le9               ; greater than the code for 9
        sub     ax, 'A'-10        ; then A becomes 10, B is 11, C is 12, etc.
        ret
le9:    sub     ax, '0'     ; otherwise, just subtract the code for zero
        ret
htob endp
```

**FIGURE 22.6:** Sample assembly language subroutine that interprets a command string and performs an INT instruction. The routine is designed to be called from dBASE III PLUS with the command CALL AnyCall WITH ComVar where ComVar is a character string variable containing a command. (continued)

```
; The Data Area - this is in the code segment because we don't have access
; to the dBASE III data segment.

regnames:  db   'AXALAHBXBLBHCXCLCHDXDLDHSIDIESDS'    ; the register names
           ;     0 1 2 3 4 5 6 7 8 9 A B C D E F  (register vs. position)
al_store: db 0        ; temporary storage for AL and AH
ah_store: db 0
bx_store: dw 0, 0     ; to save the original pointer ds:bx
st_store: dw 0        ; to save original stack pointer
intfound: db 0        ; set when the INT instruction is found
errisat: dw 0         ; bx value in command string of detected error, > 0

code         ends

                end
```

**FIGURE 22.6:** Sample assembly language subroutine that interprets a command string and performs an INT instruction. The routine is designed to be called from dBASE III PLUS with the command CALL AnyCall WITH ComVar where ComVar is a character string variable containing a command. (continued)

To illustrate this, Figure 22.7 shows a dBASE program that draws a string of blue happy faces across the screen. This program, CallTest.prg, first locates the file AnyCall.bin and copies it into RAM. Then it stores a command string in a memory variable named ComVar. This command string specifies INT 10 (the ROM BIOS video control interrupt), function 9 (repeat characters), character code 2 (the symbol for a happy face), 4E repetitions, and attribute byte 9, which produces blue characters on a color screen or bold underlined characters on a monochrome screen. All numbers are in hexadecimal.

CopyVar is a copy of ComVar made prior to calling AnyCall. This is done for error-checking purposes. AnyCall checks for correct register names, at least one register assignment, at least one INT assignment, no lowercase letters, at least one space between each assignment, and no spaces next to the equal signs. If an error is found, no INT is performed and ERR is placed in the command string variable just prior to where the error is detected (but not outside of the string). Therefore, if you check ComVar after the call to see if it has changed, you will know whether your command string was acceptable to AnyCall. (Any Call does not check for reasonable values of the numbers or reasonable selection of registers.)

The CALL command in CallTest.prg executes AnyCall, which should display a line of blue happy-face characters. After that the command string is checked for errors. There should not be any unless you change the program and put in an incorrect command string. In that case the before and after command strings will be shown.

```
* Calltest.prg - demonstrates the assembler module ANYCALL

SET TALK OFF
LOAD AnyCall
ComVar = "INT=10 AH=9 AL=2 CX=4E BL=9"
CopyVar = ComVar
CALL AnyCall WITH ComVar
IF CopyVar <> ComVar
    ? ComVar
    ? CopyVar
ENDIF
```

**FIGURE 22.7:** Sample program to load the AnyCall.bin assembly language subroutine and pass a command string to it. The command string (stored in the variable named ComVar) consists of a series of register names followed by equal signs and hexadecimal values to be placed into the registers.

## The Command String for AnyCall

The command string consists of a sequence of two or more assignments. Each assignment consists of a name, an equal sign, and a hexadecimal number, with no intervening blanks. The assignments are separated by spaces. Each assignment can begin with INT or any of the following register names: AX, AL, AH, BX, BL, BH, CX, CL, CH, DX, DL, DH, SI, DI, ES, DS. (You can't use SP, BP, or SS.)

The numeric values must be in hexadecimal. The assignments can be in any order. There must be no more than one assignment to any name. Only uppercase letters are acceptable. If you use AX, don't use AH or AL. If you use BX, don't use BH or BL. The same rule applies to CX and DX. There must be an INT assignment and at least one register assignment.

# DEBUGGING ASSEMBLY LANGUAGE SUBROUTINES

If you know how to use the Debug program or a similar one, you will be able to use it to study the execution of your module when it is called by dBASE. There is one problem, however. You will not know where to place a breakpoint in order to take over control of execution, because your module is not even in RAM when dBASE begins execution, and you do not know where it will eventually be placed.

To solve this problem using Debug, put an INT 3 instruction into your source file near where you think errors might lie, and then compile, link, and convert it to a .bin file as usual. Then type **DEBUG dBASE.exe,** and give the **G** command to the debugger to begin execution of dBASE. Load your module and call it as usual. When the instruction pointer reaches the INT 3 instruction, control will return to the debugger. Now convert the INT 3 instruction to a NOP with the **A** (assemble) command. You are now in control and can proceed as you normally would with a debugger. Don't forget to set a breakpoint within your module before you allow execution to proceed into dBASE again.

This procedure works because INT 3 is the special one-byte software interrupt that is used by all debuggers for breakpoints. When you set a breakpoint with a debugger, it substitutes the opcode for INT 3 at the beginning of the instruction where you requested the breakpoint. The original contents are saved and restored after the break.

# Commands Used with Assembly Language Subroutines

This section discusses the individual commands used to load and call assembly language subroutines from within dBASE. Though usually used within command files, these commands can also be used directly at the dot prompt when first developing and testing your assembly language modules.

## The LOAD Command

LOAD copies an assembly language subroutine into RAM, where it can be executed with a CALL command.

### SYNTAX

**LOAD <file name>**

where <file name> is the name of the assembly language module to load.

### USAGE

LOAD assumes that the assembly language subroutine has been converted to a binary file with the DOS EXE2BIN program, which produces a file with the extension .bin. Up to five assembly language subroutines can be loaded into RAM at once, each with a maximum length of 32,000 bytes.

### EXAMPLES

The commands below load two assembly language subroutines named MyMod1.bin and MyMod2.bin into RAM:

**LOAD MyMod1**
**LOAD MyMod2**

To execute the subroutines, use the commands **CALL MyMod1** or **CALL MyMod2**.

### TIPS

The DISPLAY STATUS and LIST STATUS commands show the names of all assembly language modules currently loaded in RAM.

### SEE ALSO

CALL
RELEASE MODULE
RUN

## The CALL Command

Call executes an assembly language (binary) module that has already been loaded into RAM.

### SYNTAX

**CALL <module name> WITH <parameter>**

where <module name> is the name of the assembly language module, and <parameter> is a character string being passed to the module.

### USAGE

The WITH portion of the CALL command passes the starting address of a character string memory variable stored in RAM. This starting address is stored in the DS:BX register.

The assembly language subroutine can change the contents of the string or shorten the string by replacing some of its characters with zeros, but it cannot increase the length of the string.

### EXAMPLES

The command below calls an assembly language subroutine named MyMod and passes the address of the character string "This is a test" to the module:

**CALL MyMod WITH "This is a test"**

The routine below performs the same task as the one above, but it first stores the character string in a memory variable so that dBASE can easily access that character string again in the future:

```
PassVar = "This is a test"
CALL MyMod WITH PassVar
```

### TIPS

The DISPLAY STATUS and LIST STATUS commands show the names of all assembly language modules currently loaded in RAM.

### SEE ALSO

LOAD
RELEASE MODULE
RUN

## The RELEASE MODULE Command

RELEASE MODULE removes assembly language subroutine from RAM.

### SYNTAX

**RELEASE MODULE <module name>**

where <module name> is the name of an assembly language subroutine in RAM.

### USAGE

If the named module has not already been loaded into RAM, the command simply displays the error message **File was not LOADed.** Unlike the RELEASE command used with memory variables, RELEASE MODULE does not support wild-card characters. For example, you cannot use the command RELEASE MODULE LIKE M* to release all assembly language subroutines that begin with the letter M.

### EXAMPLES

The command below removes an assembly language subroutine named MyMod1 from RAM:

```
RELEASE MODULE MyMod1
```

### TIPS

If a particular application requires more than the maximum five assembly language subroutines, you can use RELEASE MODULE to delete a module from RAM that is not required at the moment. Then use LOAD to load another module in its place.

The DISPLAY STATUS and LIST STATUS commands show the names of all assembly language modules currently loaded in RAM.

### SEE ALSO

LOAD
CALL
RUN

## SUMMARY

This chapter demonstrated some assembly language subroutines and discussed techniques for accessing these subroutines from dBASE. Because assembly language is far too large a topic to cover in depth in a single chapter (or even a single book), this chapter was written for the experienced assembly language programmer.

*For information on running programs outside of dBASE III PLUS using the RUN (or !) command:*

- Chapter 23, "Foreign and Damaged Files"

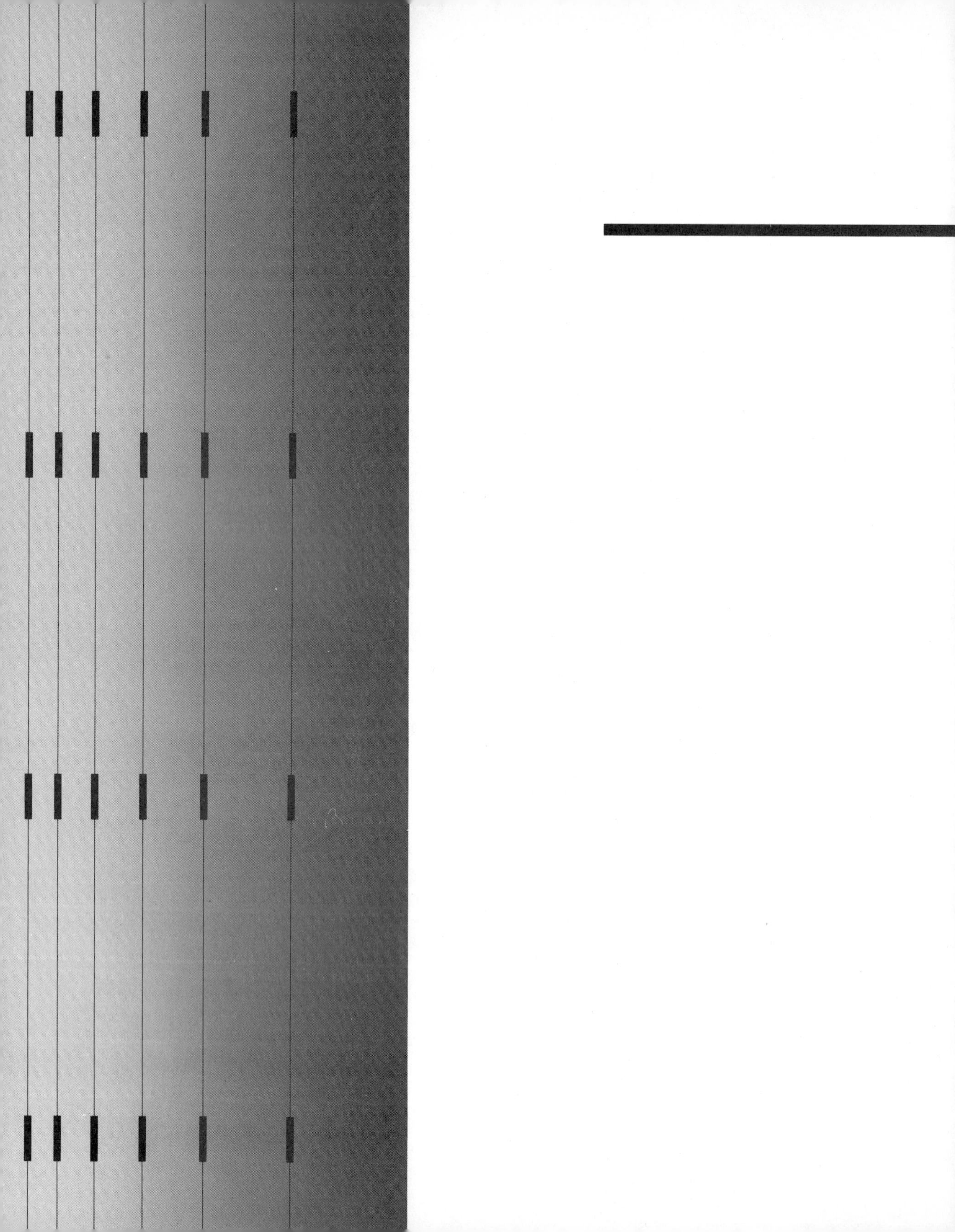

CHAPTER 23

# Foreign and Damaged Files

# Foreign and Damaged Files

This chapter explains how to read information from other software systems into dBASE III PLUS database files, as well as how to export dBASE III PLUS data to these other software systems. It also covers techniques for recovering dBASE files that have been damaged and are thus inaccessible to dBASE.

The RUN command is also discussed; it allows you to run external programs without actually leaving dBASE. When the external program is finished, control is returned to the dBASE dot prompt. The internal structure of dBASE III PLUS database and memo field files is discussed for the benefit of experienced programmers who want to create database files with programs written in C or another language. Knowledge of the dBASE internal structure is also helpful for developing techniques to salvage damaged files. The reference section at the end of the chapter presents the IMPORT, EXPORT, and RUN commands in full detail.

## Interfacing dBASE Data with Other Software Systems

This section discusses the dBASE commands that allow you to interface directly with several other software systems, including PFS:FILE, Lotus 1-2-3, Multiplan, and VisiCalc.

Keep in mind that many software systems, such as Paradox, R:BASE System V, Lotus 1-2-3, Symphony, and Framework, also offer techniques for importing and exporting dBASE files. Therefore, you might want to check the manual of the software system that you want to interface with for alternative techniques.

Most software interfaces use the dBASE COPY TO and APPEND FROM commands to export and import foreign data (excluding the PFS:FILE format, which uses the IMPORT and EXPORT commands). When COPY TO and APPEND FROM are used, you simply add the optional TYPE parameter and one of the format options listed in Table 23.1 to the end of the command to export or import the data.

When using COPY TO and APPEND FROM to import and export data, you can still use the other options that the commands support, such as FOR with the APPEND FROM command and the FOR, WHILE, and FIELDS options that COPY TO supports. In addition, the SET FILTER and SET DELETED commands will still work properly for filling records that are being exported. Note, however, that when exporting files with COPY TO, memo fields are not copied.

| FILE FORMATS | USUAL FILE-NAME EXTENSION | TYPE OF IMPORT/EXPORT |
|---|---|---|
| DIF | .dif | Data Interchange Format used with VisiCalc and some other spreadsheets |
| SYLK | none | Multiplan spreadsheet and Multiplan add-on packages |
| WKS | .wks/.wk1 | Lotus 1-2-3 (including version 2.0) |

**TABLE 23.1:** Spreadsheet File Formats Used with COPY TO and APPEND FROM

## Interfacing with PFS Files

To import a PFS file into dBASE III PLUS, first make sure the PFS file is readily available on the disk in drive B or on your hard disk. Also, be sure to specify the correct drive and directory. For example, to import a PFS file named Accounts stored on drive B, you would enter the command

```
IMPORT FROM B:Accounts TYPE PFS
```

dBASE III PLUS will separate the PFS file into several manageable files: a database file (.dbf), a format file for custom screens (.fmt), and a view file for combining the screen and data files (.vue). Each will have the same first name as the PFS file, but a dBASE III PLUS extension.

To export dBASE data to a PFS file, you must first open the database (.dbf) file with the USE command. Also, if the database to be exported has a custom screen associated with it (a .fmt file), you should activate that screen before exporting, using the SET FORMAT TO command from the dot prompt. The commands in the example below export a database file named MyData.dbf and a format file named MyScreen.fmt to a PFS file named PFSData:

```
USE MyData
SET FORMAT TO MyScreen
EXPORT TO PFSData. TYPE PFS
```

## Interfacing with Spreadsheets

You can interface dBASE III PLUS data with a variety of spreadsheet packages. When exporting database files to a spreadsheet, dBASE places the records and fields into spreadsheet columns and rows.

When importing spreadsheet files, dBASE expects the data being imported to be in columns and rows that can be converted to fields and records. If you attempt to import a spreadsheet file that does not have its data stored in even columns and rows, the format of the imported data will be unpredictable. You may want to first arrange your spreadsheet into even columns and rows that are more easily imported by dBASE.

## Interfacing with VisiCalc

To copy a database file to VisiCalc format, open the database with the USE command and enter the command

**COPY TO <file name> TYPE DIF**

where <file name> is the name of the new file. dBASE will add the extension .dif to the exported file.

To import data from a VisiCalc DIF file into a dBASE database file, you must open the database file and then type the command

**APPEND FROM <file name>.dif TYPE DIF**

This assumes the VisiCalc file is stored with the file-name extension .dif. If the VisiCalc file has a different extension, use that extension in the file name.

## Interfacing with Multiplan

To export data from dBASE to Multiplan spreadsheets, use the SYLK option with the copy command, as below:

**COPY TO <file name> TYPE SYLK**

Again, the file being exported must have been opened with the USE command before the COPY command is issued. The copied file will not have an extension unless you specify one in the <file name> portion of the command.

To import a Multiplan spreadsheet into dBASE, use the command

**APPEND FROM <file name> TYPE SYLK**

If the Multiplan file that you are importing has no extension, use a period after the file name. For example, to import a Multiplan spreadsheet named Accounts on drive B, enter the command

**APPEND FROM B:Accounts. TYPE SYLK**

## Interfacing with Lotus 1-2-3

To copy dBASE data to Lotus 1-2-3 format, use the WKS option with the COPY command, as below:

**COPY TO <file name> TYPE WKS**

The new file will have the extension .wks.

To import Lotus 1-2-3 worksheets into dBASE, use the WKS option with the APPEND FROM command, as below:

**APPEND FROM Accounts.wks TYPE WKS**

Again, be sure to use the B: drive designator on a file name if you are using a floppy disk system. Also, be sure to pay attention to the extension of the file you are importing and to use that extension in the file name of the APPEND FROM command.

### INTERFACING WITH OTHER SPREADSHEET PROGRAMS

Other spreadsheet packages can generally import and export data stored in the structured data format (SDF). See the discussion in the section "Interfacing with ASCII Text Files" for details.

## Interfacing with Word Processors

You can send dBASE reports to word processing systems for further editing or inclusion in other documents. In addition, you can create special data files in dBASE that most word processors can read to print form letters and envelopes. This section discusses some of the basic techniques used for interfacing with word processors, using WordStar as an example.

### SENDING REPORTS TO WORD PROCESSORS

To send a copy of a printed report to a word processor, design your report using the MODIFY REPORT command in dBASE. Then print the report to a disk file with the **TO <file name>** option. You can then load your word processor and read the report into the word processing system.

Here is a typical scenario using the WordStar program as the word processor:

**USE Mail**<br>
**MODIFY REPORT ByName**<br>
**(Define report format)**<br>
**REPORT FORM ByName TO Transfer**<br>
**QUIT**

The **TO Transfer** option with the REPORT FORM command sends a copy of the report to a disk file named Transfer.txt. When you quit dBASE, the A> prompt reappears on the screen. Now you can load WordStar.

Suppose you want to pull the dBASE report into a WordStar document called Manual.txt. At the DOS prompt, enter the command

**WS Manual.txt**

When the document appears on the screen, position the cursor at the place you want the dBASE report to appear. Then press Ctrl-KR. When the WordStar program asks for the name of the file to read, reply with **Transfer.txt**. That's all there is to it. The dBASE report is now in a WordStar document and also in a disk file called Transfer.txt.

Any text file that you create from dBASE using the SET ALTERNATE command can also be read directly into any word processor. Remember that dBASE automatically adds the extension .txt to any alternate file that you create. When writing technical documentation for your application system, you may want to store copies of the output from the LIST STRUCTURE and LIST STATUS commands to read into a word processing document.

## Word Processing Form-Letter Files

Most word processors can read files stored in *ASCII-delimited* format for printing form letters and envelopes. This section discusses general techniques for creating such files, once again using the WordStar program as the sample word processor.

Suppose you want to send a copy of a database file named Mail.dbf, which contains the fields LName, FName, Address, City, State, Zip, and Phone, to a WordStar MailMerge file for printing form letters. After loading dBASE, type **USE Mail**. Then copy the Mail database to an ASCII-delimited data file by typing the command below at the dot prompt:

**COPY TO MM DELIMITED**

This creates a data file called MM.txt, which the MailMerge file can access to create form letters.

Next you have to quit dBASE, load up your word processor, and create your form letter. Figure 23.1 contains a sample form letter called Form.let that can read the dBASE data in the MM.txt file you've just created.

Notice that the Phone field from the original dBASE database was included in the .RV command, even though it is not used in the form letter. This is essential if the Phone field exists in the dBASE file. The number of fields specified in the .RV command must match the number of fields on the data file, regardless of whether each field is used in the form letter. Even if you wanted only the first name for your form letter, you would still have to read in all of the fields. (Of course, you can specify which fields to export to the MailMerge file using the FIELDS option in the COPY TO command.)

```
.DF MM.txt
.RV LName,FName,Address,City,State,Zip,Phone
&FName& &LName&
&Address&
&City&, &State&     &Zip&

Dear &FName&:

How do you like getting these form letters? You
probably wouldn't know the difference if it were
not for my dot-matrix printer.

Sincerely,



Susita Marie Simpson

.PA
```

**FIGURE 23.1:** Sample WordStar MailMerge file capable of printing form letters. The dBASE COPY TO command with the DELIMITED option created an ASCII text file named MM.txt that WordStar can read. The .DF and .RV commands near the top of the letter define the file name and record structure. The field names surrounded by ampersands (&) will be replaced with data from the data file.

After you create and save the form letter, you merely need to merge-print it using the appropriate MailMerge command. That is, select WordStar option M from the WordStar main menu, and when it asks for the name of the file to merge-print, type **Form.let**. A letter for each person in the Mail database will then be printed.

You can combine the resources of dBASE and WordStar to print mailing labels (with a dBASE .lbl file). You can also create a WordStar MailMerge document to print names and addresses directly on envelopes, one envelope at a time. Figure 23.2 is a MailMerge file (named Envel.txt) that will print envelopes from the MM.txt data file.

After you create and save Envel.txt, you can merge-print it in the usual WordStar fashion. However, when the merge-print option asks

**PAUSE FOR PAPER CHANGE BETWEEN PAGES (Y/N)**

be sure to answer Y. Then you can insert each envelope, lining it up so that the print head is where you want the printing to start. The MailMerge option will print one envelope, eject it from the printer, and wait for you to put in the next envelope.

If you want your form letter to go only to certain individuals, you can specify this in your dBASE COPY command. For example, if wanted your form letters to go only to San Diego residents, you would enter the command below:

**COPY TO MM FOR City = 'San Diego' TYPE DELIMITED**

```
.MT 0
.OP
.DF MM.txt
.RV LName,FName,Address,City,State,Zip,Phone

 &FName& &LName&
 &Address&
 &City&, &State&    &Zip&

.PA
```

**FIGURE 23.2:** This small WordStar MailMerge file will print an envelope for each record on the exported dBASE file. Answering Yes to the WordStar "Pause for paper change" prompt before printing will pause printing after each envelope, giving you time to insert a new envelope.

If you already have a MailMerge data file and want to use some dBASE commands to manage it, you can send a copy of it to dBASE. To do so, you need to load up dBASE and create an empty file with the CREATE command. Structure it so that it has the same fields as your MailMerge file. When dBASE asks **INPUT data records now? (Y/N)**, respond with **N**. Then load the newly created database and issue the command

**APPEND FROM MM.dat TYPE DELIMITED**

(assuming the name of the existing MailMerge file is MM.dat). You can now sort your MailMerge file or do whatever you please with it in dBASE III PLUS. To get the dBASE database back into MailMerge-readable form, just load the dBASE file and issue the command

**COPY TO MM.dat DELIMITED**

This will overwrite your existing MM.dat data file with the exported version of the dBASE MM.dbf database.

## Interfacing with ASCII Text Files

Data files that are exported from mainframes and minicomputers, as well as data exported from some microcomputer packages, might come in either of two textual formats: *structured data format (SDF)* or *delimited.* Both of these structures store only textual data, with no header or special codes.

In the SDF format, all fields are of equal length, and each record ends with a carriage-return and linefeed character (ASCII characters 13 and 10). Files in the SDF format are also called *random-access* data files.

Data files stored in the delimited format have fields and records of varying lengths. Each field is separated by a comma (or some other character), character strings are generally enclosed in quotation marks (or other characters), and each record ends with a carriage-return and linefeed character (ASCII characters 13 and 10). Delimited files are sometimes called *sequential files*.

You can view an ASCII text file with the DOS or dBASE TYPE command. The carriage-return and linefeed characters at the end of each record do not appear on the screen. Instead, they cause the cursor to jump to the next line, thereby showing the file with each record beginning at the first column of a new row.

The COPY TO and APPEND FROM commands with the SDF and DELIMITED options are used to import and export ASCII text files. As mentioned earlier, these commands cannot import or export memo fields. Furthermore, APPEND FROM can import dates only in the yyyymmdd (i.e., 19871231) format into dBASE date fields.

Table 23.2 shows several possible ASCII text files that dBASE could import or export using the SDF and DELIMITED options with COPY TO and APPEND, along with the option used to export or import the file type. The top example displays the data before exportation, or after importation, as displayed by a dBASE LIST command. DELIMITED is the most commonly used option, with quotes around the character strings and commas between each field. Note that the data types of the fields are character, numeric, date, and logical, in that order.

The basic techniques discussed in this section allow you to import or export ASCII text files in just about any format. Just remember to view the file to be imported (or the exported file) with the DOS or dBASE TYPE command to make sure you are using the correct format. Also, keep in mind that you can use

| **PARAMETER** | **SAMPLE RECORD FORMAT** |
|---|---|
| dBASE .dbf format | Adams 123.45 01/01/87 .T.<br>Jones −1.00 12/31/87 .F. |
| SDF | Adams 123.4519870101T<br>Jones −1.0019871231F |
| DELIMITED | "Adams",123.45,19870101,T<br>"Jones",−1.00,19871231,F |
| DELIMITED WITH , | ,Adams,,123.45,19870101,T<br>,Jones,,−1.00,19871231,F |
| DELIMITED WITH ; | ;Adams;,123.45,19870101,T<br>;Jones;,−1.00,19871231,F |
| DELIMITED WITH BLANK | Adams 123.45 19870101 T<br>Jones −1.00 19871231 F |

**TABLE 23.2:** COPY TO and APPEND FROM Text File Formats

any character with the DELIMITED WITH option. When exporting encrypted database files from a network that has used the PROTECT program to encode the data, be sure to turn SET ENCRYPTION off before exporting the data from the dBASE file.

## Exporting ASCII Text Files

When you export a file in ASCII text format with the COPY TO command, dBASE automatically adds the extension .txt to the file name you provide, unless you specify another extension. To export a file, first open the dBASE file (in dBASE), then enter the COPY TO command with the appropriate FOR, WHILE, and FIELDS options (if any) and the appropriate TYPE parameter for the format of the exported file. For example, the commands below export the fields PartNo, PartName, Qty, Unit_Price, and Date from a dBASE database file named Master.dbf into a file named Master.txt. Only the records with dates in January are included in the exported file. The exported file is in the delimited format.

```
USE Master
COPY TO Master FIELDS PartNo,PartName,Qty,Unit_Price,Date;
        FOR MONTH(Date) = 1 TYPE DELIMITED
```

## Importing ASCII Text Files

To import ASCII text files, first open a dBASE database structure (with USE or CREATE) that matches the structure of the file being imported. If the file being imported is in SDF format, the field widths in the dBASE file structure must match the field widths of the file to be imported *exactly.* (You might want to use the **dBASE TYPE <file name> TO PRINT** command to create a hard copy of the file to be imported, which will make it easier to count the exact width of each field.)

When using the APPEND FROM command with a TYPE option, dBASE assumes that the foreign file has the extension .txt unless you specify otherwise. If the file to be imported has no extension, use the DOS or dBASE RENAME command to add the extension .txt to the file name before importing it with the APPEND FROM command.

In the example below, the commands open a database file named Master.dbf and read in records from an ASCII text file named Master.txt. In this example, the file to be imported is stored in SDF format.

```
USE Master
APPEND FROM Master.txt TYPE SDF
```

# Recovering Damaged dBASE Files

On rare occasions, dBASE files become damaged or corrupted due to power failures during processing, old equipment, bad disk sectors, or any of a myriad of other mysterious reasons. Once the file is corrupted, all or some of the data in the database file may become inaccessible to dBASE. When this occurs, it is best to think of the data not as lost, but only temporarily stored in a foreign file format that needs to be restructured into a dBASE file. (Of course, if the data were actually deleted and packed, erased, or zapped, it may truly be lost!)

This section discusses some of the more common types of damage that might occur with dBASE database files, along with steps that you can take to recover damaged files.

## Handling a Missing .dbt File

When a database that contains a memo field cannot access the .dbt file that contains the memo fields, dBASE displays the error message

**.DBT file cannot be opened.**

and refuses to open the database.

When this occurs, your first step should be to try to locate the missing .dbt file. Use the **DIR *.dbt** command on all the directories to try to find the file. It will have the same first name as the dBASE .dbf file, unless you've renamed the original .dbf file. In that case, it may have still have the name of the original .dbf file. If you find the .dbt file, copy it to the same drive and directory as the .dbf file (and rename it to the same name as the .dbf file if necessary). If you can do that, your problem is solved.

If you cannot find the .dbt file, you can try to use an unerase program, such as the one that comes with the Norton Utilities, to try to find the .dbt file. Follow the instructions in the manual of that program to unerase the file. If the file is still intact, you should be able to recover it and get everything back in shape.

If the .dbt file is lost forever, you can still recover the data in the .dbf file. To do so, use MODIFY COMMAND or another text editor to create a file with the same first name as the .dbf file but with the extension .dbt. Save this new file (even if it is empty) and get back to the dot prompt. Now you will be able to open the .dbf file with the usual USE command. Of course, all the memo fields will be empty, but at least you'll have regained access to the database (.dbf) file.

## Recovering Erased Files

If you accidentally erase a file with the DOS or dBASE ERASE command, the first thing you should do is stop whatever you are doing. When DOS erases a file, it does not remove it from the disk. Instead, it changes a byte in the file name of the directory, as an indication that the space once occupied by that file can now be overwritten. Therefore, if you subsequently create or save any files, the new data may overwrite the "erased" data, making the old information permanently irretrievable.

Your next step should be to use an unerase program to attempt to bring the file back. There are several unerase programs available on the market, perhaps the most well known being the one that comes with the Norton Utilities software package. When you get your unerase program, follow the instructions in the manual to unerase the file. If a memo field (.dbt) file was erased along with the data file, you'll need to recover that file too.

## Recovering Missing Records

Occasionally, some records in a database file may seem to disappear suddenly from the file. It can be pretty disconcerting to open a database file that you know had 1000 records in it and find that there are suddenly only 10!

Before taking any drastic measures, first check whether there are any legitimate reasons for the records to be missing. Enter the commands SET DELETED OFF and SET FILTER TO at the dot prompt to see whether they were hiding any records. (Use LIST after entering the two SET commands to check the file again.)

If the records are still missing, use the DISPLAY STRUCTURE command to see how many records dBASE actually "thinks" are in the file. If this number is smaller than what you expected, perhaps it is wrong and there are indeed records beyond what the number indicates. To determine whether this is the case, leave dBASE with the QUIT command and use the DOS DIR command to view the size of the database file in question (e.g., **DIR AnyFile.dbf**). The DIR command will tell you the actual number of bytes in the file, as below:

**MAIL DBF 1890816 4-23-87 4:55**

In this example, DOS reports that there are 1,890,816 bytes still in the file (so it is indeed a large file). If the evidence seems to indicate a large discrepancy between the number of records DISPLAY STRUCTURE displays and the size of the file the DOS DIR command displays, the record number counter in the dBASE file header is wrong and needs to be corrected.

To reset the record number pointer to the correct number of records for the database file, you'll need to use the Debug.com program (or an equivalent debugger) that comes with your DOS package. You'll also have to do a little work with hexadecimal numbers, and perhaps some conversions from decimal to hexadecimal and vice versa.

To fix the record counter in the header of a dBASE file, follow these steps:

1. Make a DOS COPY of the database file to work with.

2. Jot down the number of bytes in the file, as displayed by the DOS DIR command.
3. Jot down the "presumed" number of records and the record length, as displayed by the DISPLAY STRUCTURE command.
4. Use Debug to determine the actual number of records in the database file (in hex).
5. Use Debug to place the correct record count in the file header.
6. Save the corrected dBASE file.

The remainder of this section uses a sample database file named Mail.dbf to demonstrate these steps. Mail.dbf should have about 1000 records in it, but the DISPLAY STRUCTURE and LIST commands indicate only 100 records.

Following step 1, use DOS (not dBASE, because dBASE will copy only the first 100 records) to make a copy of the file to work with. (That way, if you make a mistake that makes matters worse, you'll still have your original file.) In this example, you would enter the command

**COPY Mail.dbf Temp.dbf**

to create a copy of the Mail database file named Temp.dbf.

Next, use DIR to display the actual size of the Temp (copied) file. Using the Temp.dbf example, DIR showed the following:

**TEMP DBF 189514 5-25-87 3:20p**

Jot down the number of bytes.

Next, run dBASE and use DISPLAY STRUCTURE to view the number of records in the file and the number of bytes per record, as shown in Figure 23.3.

In the example of Temp.dbf, the following information is known:

| | |
|---|---|
| File size according to DIR: | 189514 |
| Number of records (from DISPLAY STRUCTURE): | 100 |
| Number of bytes per record: | 189 |

A little quick arithmetic indicates that something is wrong, because if you divide the file size by the number of bytes per record, you end up with 1002.72, indicating that there are approximately 1002 records in the file. (This number is approximate because the file header takes up some bytes.)

Now that you know there are records that are not included in the file header's count, it is time to determine the actual number of records in the file and then correct the file header. First, you must look at the file header using the Debug program. (Just copy the Debug.com file from the DOS disk onto the drive and directory that contains the troublesome dBASE file.) For this example, type **DEBUG Temp.dbf** at the DOS prompt. (*Note:* If the file is extremely large, Debug may only show an error message such as **Divide Overflow**. If this occurs, you'll need to use the technique discussed in the section "Salvaging Severely Corrupted Files.")

When Debug is ready, it shows a hyphen on the screen. Type the letter **d**, press Return, and you'll see part of the file header, as in Figure 23.4. The leftmost columns indicate memory locations in hex. You need be concerned only with the number to the right of the colon (e.g., 0100 in 32D9:0100). Your screen may show different numbers to the left of the colon. The :0100 indicates the memory address of the leftmost value on the line.

```
Structure for database: C:Temp.dbf
Number of data records:       100
Date of last update   : 04/23/87

Field  Field Name  Type         Width    Dec

    1  Mr_Mrs      Character        4
    2  FName       Character       15
    3  MI          Character        2
    4  LName       Character       20
    5  Company     Character       40
    6  Address     Character       25
    7  City        Character       20
    8  State       Character        5
    9  Zip         Character       10
   10  Country     Character       12
   11  Phone       Character       10
   12  Phone_Ext   Character        4
   13  Hire_Date   Date             8
   14  Salary      Numeric         12      2
   15  Paid_Yet    Logical          1


** Total **                       189
```

**FIGURE 23.3:** Structure of the Temp.dbf database used in the example of fixing the record number counter in a dBASE III PLUS file header. The number of records in the file is displayed near the top, and the length of each record is displayed beneath the field length definitions.

```
C:\WORK>DEBUG Temp.dbf
-d
32D9:0100  03 57 04 17 64 00 00 00-01 02 BD 00 00 00 00 00   .W..d...........
32D9:0110  00 00 00 00 00 00 00 00-00 00 00 00 00 00 00 00   ................
32D9:0120  4D 52 5F 4D 52 53 00 00-00 00 00 43 03 00 9E 7E   MR_MRS.....C...~
32D9:0130  04 00 00 00 01 00 00 00-00 00 00 00 00 00 00 00   ................
32D9:0140  46 4E 41 4D 45 00 00 00-00 00 00 43 07 00 9E 7E   FNAME......C...~
32D9:0150  0F 00 00 00 01 00 00 00-00 00 00 00 00 00 00 00   ................
32D9:0160  4D 49 00 00 00 00 00 00-00 00 00 43 16 00 9E 7E   MI.........C...~
32D9:0170  02 00 00 00 01 00 00 00-00 00 00 00 00 00 00 00   ................
-_
```

**FIGURE 23.4:** A portion of a dBASE file header as displayed by the Debug d command. The left column indicates the memory address (in hexadecimal) of the first byte on the row. The column after the colon displays the actual byte (in hexadecimal) in each memory location. The rightmost column displays each byte converted to ASCII.

Proceeding to the right, the other memory locations on the line are 0101, 0102, 0103, 0104, 0105, 0106, 0107, 0108, 0109, 010A, 010B, 010C, 010D, 010E, 010F. The next line begins with memory location 0110, as shown by the leading address 32D9:0110.

The values in the center columns are actual hexadecimal values in the file. The column on the right is the ASCII equivalent of each hexadecimal number. (The entire structure of the dBASE header is discussed later in the chapter.)

The information that you are concerned with is in bytes 0104 through 0107, which display the number of records in the database file, in hexadecimal and in reverse sequence. Bytes 0108 and 0109 display the number of bytes in the header, again in hexadecimal and reversed, and bytes 0110 and 0111 display, in hexadecimal and reversed, the number of bytes in each record. For now, you need only jot down the number of bytes in the header, 0201h in this example (it is customary to place an h after hexadecimal numbers to avoid confusion with decimal numbers). Figure 23.5 shows these locations pinpointed on the Debug display.

Now that you have jotted down the size of the dBASE file header (0201h in this example) you can leave Debug by typing the letter q and pressing Return. The DOS prompt will reappear on the screen.

Using whatever means you have available, convert the hexadecimal number of bytes in the header to decimal. There are several software packages that can help you convert decimal numbers to hexadecimal numbers. For example, the SideKick program includes a pop-up calculator that quickly converts hexadecimal to decimal and vice versa and also does calculations in both decimal and hexadecimal. If you do not have SideKick or a similar program handy, you can use the dBASE Hex2Dec and Dec2Hex programs shown in Figures 23.6 and 23.7. When you run the Hex2Dec program, it asks for a number in hexadecimal and displays the decimal equivalent. When you run the Dec2Hex program, it asks for a decimal number and displays the hex equivalent.

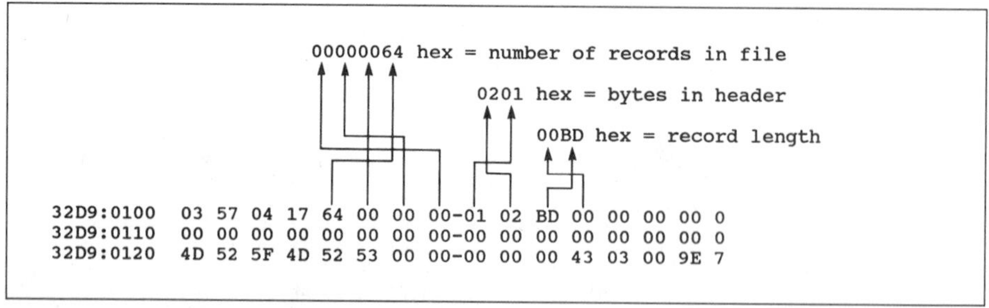


**FIGURE 23.5:** A portion of the Debug display of a dBASE file header, showing the exact locations and values of the number of records in the file, the number of bytes in the header, and the length of each record.

```
******************************************** Hex2Dec.prg.
*------------ Converts decimal integers to hexadecimal.
SET TALK OFF
CLEAR
Entry = SPACE(4)
@ 5,5 SAY "Enter hex number ";
  GET Entry PICT "@!"
READ
HexChar = "123456789ABCDEF"
HexNumb = SPACE(4-LEN(TRIM(Entry)))+TRIM(Entry)

DecNumb = AT(SUBSTR(HexNumb,1,1),HexChar)*4096 +;
          AT(SUBSTR(HexNumb,2,1),HexChar)*256 +;
          AT(SUBSTR(HexNumb,3,1),HexChar)*16 +;
          AT(SUBSTR(HexNumb,4,1),HexChar)

*----------- Print result.
? DecNumb
```

**FIGURE 23.6:** The dBASE program Hex2Dec, which asks for a hexadecimal number and displays the decimal equivalent. This program can accept integer values in the range of 0 to FFFF.

```
********************************************* Dec2Hex.prg.
*----- Converts positive decimal integers to hexadecimal.
SET TALK OFF
CLEAR
Entry = SPACE(5)
@ 5,5 SAY "Enter decimal number  (up to 65535) ";
  GET Entry PICT "99999"
READ
HexChar = "0123456789ABCDEF"
Dec = INT(VAL(Entry))
HexNumb = " "

DO CASE
   CASE Dec <= 15
        HexNumb = SUBSTR(HexChar,Dec+1,1)
   CASE Dec > 15 .AND. Dec <= 255
        HexNumb = SUBSTR(HexChar,INT(Dec/16)+1,1)+;
           SUBSTR(HexChar,(Dec/16.000-INT(Dec/16))*16+1,1)
   CASE Dec >= 256 .AND. Dec <= 4095
        HexNumb = SUBSTR(HexChar,INT(Dec/256)+1,1)+;
           SUBSTR(HexChar,(Dec/256.000-INT(Dec/256))*16+1,1)+;
           SUBSTR(HexChar,(Dec/16.000-INT(Dec/16))*16+1,1)
   CASE Dec >= 4096 .AND. Dec <= 65535
        HexNumb = SUBSTR(HexChar,INT(Dec/4096)+1,1)+;
           SUBSTR(HexChar,(Dec/4096.000-INT(Dec/4096))*16+1,1)+;
           SUBSTR(HexChar,(Dec/256.000-INT(Dec/256))*16+1,1)
          HexNumb = HexNumb+;
           SUBSTR(HexChar,(Dec/16.000-INT(Dec/16))*16+1,1)
ENDCASE
? "Result = ",HexNumb
```

**FIGURE 23.7:** The dBASE program Dec2Hex, which asks for a decimal number and displays the hexadecimal equivalent. The acceptable range of numbers for Dec2Hex is integers in the range of 0 to 65535.

In this case, 0201h converts to 513 decimal. Subtract this number from the total number of bytes in the file, as below:

| | |
|---|---|
| 189514 | Total file size |
| 513 | Total header size |
| 189001 | Total amount of data in file (below header) |

This number tells you how much data is stored in the file beneath the file header. Dividing this number by the length of each record (189 in this example) produces 1000.0053, or simply 1000 rounded off. Therefore, there are actually 1000 records in this database file.

The next step is to convert this number to hex and put it back into the dBASE file header. In this example, 1000 converts to 03E8h. To put 03E8 into the dBASE file header, first enter the command **DEBUG Temp.dbf** at the DOS prompt. When the Debug hyphen appears, enter the letter **d** to view the top of the file header.

Now, the number of bytes in the file must go into bytes 0104 and 0105 on the Debug display. Remember, the number is reversed, so E8 goes into 0104, and 03 goes into 0105. To place the value in 0104, enter the command **e0104** and press Return. DEBUG displays

**32D9:0104 64.**

indicating that byte 0104 currently contains 64. Type E8 and press Return.

To fill in the byte for 0105, enter **e0105**. DEBUG displays

**32D9:0105 00.**

indicating that there is currently 00 in that byte. Type **03** and press Return.

To verify that the numbers were entered, enter the command **-d100** to display a few lines starting at 0100. You'll see the new bytes in 0104 and 0105, as shown below:

**32D9:0100 03 57 04 17 E8 03 00 00-01 02 BD 00 00 00 00 00**

Now save the file by typing in the letter **w** and pressing Return. You'll see the message

**Writing 2E44A bytes**

(the number of bytes will depend on the size of your particular file). Next, type in the letter **q** and press Return to leave Debug.

To test the effects of your change, go into dBASE and open the copied file you worked on (Temp.dbf in this example). Use DISPLAY STRUCTURE and

LIST to verify that all is well. If all your records are back, you can erase your original damaged dBASE file (or better yet, copy it to a backup file name, and then erase it) and rename the corrected temporary file to the original file name.

## Removing Extraneous Characters

Once in a while, a dBASE file may end up with some mysterious, unwanted characters in it that cause the fields to move out of alignment. For example, Figure 23.8 shows the structure of a sample database file named EmpNames.dbf and a display of its contents. As you can see, record number 4 has the extraneous characters ^@&! embedded in the last name Mendez. All fields to the right of these characters and the records beneath are out of alignment and are no longer properly accessible.

Note that if all of the fields in a database file are out of alignment, starting at the first record, and you've recently completed an APPEND FROM <file name> SDF command, the problem is not extraneous characters. Instead, the structure of the database file did not match the structure of the file you appended from. In that case, do not use the procedures discussed below. Instead, inspect the contents of the records in the file, and try to determine which fields are the wrong length. Then zap the current contents of the database file, and use the MODIFY STRUCTURE command to change its structure. Then try

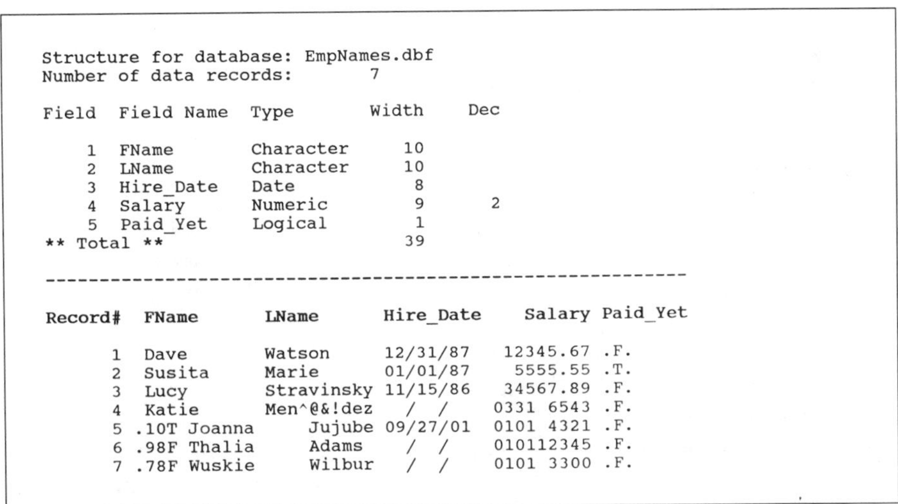

```
Structure for database: EmpNames.dbf
Number of data records:       7

Field  Field Name  Type       Width    Dec

    1  FName       Character     10
    2  LName       Character     10
    3  Hire_Date   Date           8
    4  Salary      Numeric        9      2
    5  Paid_Yet    Logical        1
** Total **                      39

------------------------------------------------------------

Record#  FName      LName      Hire_Date    Salary Paid_Yet

      1  Dave       Watson     12/31/87   12345.67 .F.
      2  Susita     Marie      01/01/87    5555.55 .T.
      3  Lucy       Stravinsky 11/15/86   34567.89 .F.
      4  Katie      Men^@&!dez   /  /    0331 6543 .F.
      5 .10T Joanna     Jujube 09/27/01  0101 4321 .F.
      6 .98F Thalia     Adams    /  /    010112345 .F.
      7 .78F Wuskie     Wilbur   /  /    0101 3300 .F.
```

**FIGURE 23.8:** Structure and contents of the EmpNames database file. As the figure shows, the database has been corrupted because extraneous characters ( ^ @&!) are inserted into the name Mendez. All fields to the right of these extraneous characters have been pushed out of alignment.

the APPEND FROM...TYPE SDF command again. Repeat this process until your database structure correctly matches the structure of the SDF file you are appending from.

In this example, only a few extraneous characters were inserted into the file. In some examples, large blocks of mysterious characters may creep in, but you can still use the techniques discussed here to remove the extraneous characters.

You can use the DOS Debug program to remove the extraneous characters and realign the fields if the file is not exceptionally large. (If the file is too large for Debug, you'll see the error message **Divide Overflow** when you attempt to run Debug. In that case, read the section entitled "Salvaging Severely Corrupted Files" later in this chapter.)

Before using Debug to fix the file, you should try to determine the approximate byte location of the first faulty character. To do so, multiply the record size (shown by the DISPLAY STATUS command) by the number of the record containing the faulty characters (record 4 in this example). Then add 256 (for the 0100 hex starting location of Debug), and convert this number to hexadecimal. (You can use the Dec2Hex program in Figure 23.7 to convert the number.) Using the EmpNames database example, the calculation is as follows:

| | |
|---:|---|
| 39 | (record size) |
| × 4 | (record number) |
| 156 | (bytes from first data item) |
| +256 | (for Debug overhead) |
| 412 | (total bytes from top) |
| 19C | (converted to hexadecimal) |

This is only an approximate location, because it calculates the distance from the first byte of *data* to the error. The dBASE header also occupies some space, which can be determined by multiplying the number of fields by 32 and adding 35 to that result. This calculation, however, is close enough to get you in the ball park.

Next, quit dBASE and use DOS to make a working copy of the file (so that any drastic mistakes do not mess up the original file any more than it is). In this example, you could use the DOS command below to make a copy of the file named EmpTemp.dbf:

**COPY EmpNames.dbf EmpTemp.dbf**

If you have not already done so, you'll need to copy the Debug.com program that came with DOS from the DOS disk to the current drive and directory, using the usual DOS COPY command. Then load the database file into Debug by typing **DEBUG EmpTemp.dbf** at the DOS prompt. Debug will display a hyphen when the file is successfully loaded.

Next, you'll want to display the block of memory addresses near the faulty characters. Use the d command with the calculated hex location of the faulty bytes, rounded down to the nearest tenth (190 instead of 19C in this example), as in the command **d190**. After pressing Return, the addresses beginning at location 019C appear on the screen.

If the faulty record does not appear, enter the d command repeatedly until it does appear. In this example, entering the d command once again was sufficient to bring the faulty record to the screen, as shown in Figure 23.9. (You can see the faulty Men ^ @&!dez name over to the right, in ASCII format.)

Next, you need to determine the exact byte that contains the first faulty character. There is an exact one-for-one correspondence between the hexadecimal memory values and the ASCII values on the screen. Looking in the left column of the line containing Men ^ @&!dez, you can see that the memory locations start at 32D9:0240, but you need be concerned only with the 0240.

The space at the beginning of the line (a space has a hexadecimal ASCII value of 20) is at 240, M is at 241, e is at 242, and n is at 243, so the first faulty character, ^ , is at 244. Indeed, 5E is the hexadecimal number for ASCII character ^ . (Appendix D shows a complete ASCII chart with decimal and hexadecimal values.)

The first good character after the first bad character is d, at memory location 248, with the hexadecimal value of 64. (When doing this in the future, don't

```
C:\WORK>DEBUG EmpTemp.dbf
-d190
32D9:0190  09 02 00 00 01 00 00 00-00 00 00 00 00 00 00 00   ................
32D9:01A0  50 41 49 44 5F 59 45 54-00 00 00 4C 34 00 E7 64   PAID_YET...L4..d
32D9:01B0  01 00 00 00 01 00 00 00-00 00 00 00 00 00 00 00   ................
32D9:01C0  0D 20 44 61 76 65 20 20-20 20 20 20 57 61 74 73   . Dave      Wats
32D9:01D0  6F 6E 20 20 20 20 31 38-38 37 31 32 33 31 20 31   on    18871231 1
32D9:01E0  32 33 34 35 2E 36 37 46-20 53 75 73 69 74 61 20   2345.67F Susita
32D9:01F0  20 20 20 4D 61 72 69 65-20 20 20 20 31 39 38         Marie     198
32D9:0200  37 30 31 30 31 20 20 35-35 35 35 2E 35 35 54 20   70101  5555.55T
-d
32D9:0210  4C 75 63 79 20 20 20 20-20 20 53 74 72 61 76 69   Lucy      Stravi
32D9:0220  6E 73 6B 79 31 39 38 36-31 31 31 35 20 33 34 35   nsky19861115 345
32D9:0230  36 37 2E 38 39 46 20 4B-61 74 69 65 20 20 20 20   67.89F Katie
32D9:0240  20 4D 65 6E 5E 40 26 21-64 65 7A 20 20 20 20 31    Men^@&!dez    1
32D9:0250  39 38 37 30 33 33 31 20-36 35 34 33 32 2E 31 30   9870331 65432.10
32D9:0260  54 20 4A 6F 61 6E 6E 61-20 20 20 20 4A 75 6A 75   T Joanna    Juju
32D9:0270  62 65 65 20 20 20 31 39-38 36 30 31 30 31 20 34   bee   19860101 4
32D9:0280  33 32 31 30 2E 39 38 46-20 54 68 61 6C 69 61 20   3210.98F Thalia
-_
```

**FIGURE 23.9:** The faulty record in the corrupted database displayed on the screen through the DEBUG d command. The faulty name, Men ^ @&!dez, appears in ASCII in the rightmost column of the display.

forget that the memory locations go from 0 to F, e.g., 0240 to 024F, on each line.) So to fix this file, you need to move all of the characters, starting at 248 (the first good character after the bad ones), to the location starting at the first bad character (244 in this example). That way, everything will shift left and overwrite the bad characters and realign all the good ones.

Before you move the characters, you need to determine how many bytes in hex are in the file. This you can determine using the register command (r). If you type r now and press Return, you'll see the information below (plus some more irrelevant information that doesn't fit on the page):

```
AX = 0000   BX = 0000   CX = 0200   DX = 0000   SP = FFEE
DS = 31B8   ES = 31B8   SS = 31B8   CS = 31B8   IP = 0100
```

The BX and CX registers combined (in that order) define the entire size of the file. In this example, the file size is 00000200, or 200 if you trim off the leading zeroes. But because Debug starts at memory location 0100, the actual last byte in the file is at hexadecimal 300 (because 200h + 100h = 300h).

To use the move command, enter m, the starting address of the block to move, the ending address of the block to move, and the location to move the block to. In this example, you want to enter the command

**m 248 300 244**

and press Return.

To verify that the move took place, use the d command to redisplay the address near the original problem. In this example, entering the command **d200** displays the appropriate block of memory. As you can see in Figure 23.10, the ^ @&! characters have been removed from the name Mendez.

To save the corrected file, type w and press Return. You'll see a message, indicating the number of bytes (in hexadecimal) being saved, and the Debug hyphen. Type q and press Return to exit Debug and return to the DOS prompt.

Now you can load dBASE and open the corrected file (EmpTemp.dbf). A LIST command will quickly display the corrected file, as shown in Figure 23.11.

## Salvaging Severely Corrupted Files

In some situations, a file might become so corrupted that dBASE cannot even open the file. This is generally caused by a file header that is corrupted beyond recognition. Before taking any drastic measures to salvage the file, be sure to test the simpler potential problems below.

First, use the dBASE (not DOS) DIR command to see if the faulty file is a dBASE II database file. (The dBASE DIR display will tell you immediately.) If

```
-m248 300 244
-d200
32D9:0200  37 30 31 30 31 20 20 35-35 35 35 2E 35 35 54 20   70101   5555.55T
32D9:0210  4C 75 63 79 20 20 20 20-20 20 53 74 72 61 76 69   Lucy       Stravi
32D9:0220  6E 73 6B 79 31 39 38 36-31 31 31 35 20 33 34 35   nsky19861115 345
32D9:0230  36 37 2E 38 39 46 20 4B-61 74 69 65 20 20 20 20   67.89F Katie
32D9:0240  20 4D 65 6E 64 65 7A 20-20 20 20 31 39 38 37 30    Mendez     19870
32D9:0250  33 33 31 20 36 35 34 33-32 2E 31 30 54 20 4A 6F   331 65432.10T Jo
32D9:0260  61 6E 6E 61 20 20 20 20-4A 75 6A 75 62 65 65 20   anna    Jujubee
32D9:0270  20 20 31 39 38 36 30 31-30 31 20 34 33 32 31 30     19860101 43210
-
-
-
-
-
-
-
-
-
-
-
-
-
-
-_
```

**FIGURE 23.10:** The faulty characters from the name Mendez have been removed from the dBASE file, as displayed in the rightmost column. The Debug move (m) command was used to shift all characters to the right of the faulty characters to the left, overwriting the faulty characters and bringing all other fields back into proper alignment.

| Record# | FName | LName | Hire_Date | Salary | Paid_Yet |
|---|---|---|---|---|---|
| 1 | Dave | Watson | 12/31/87 | 12345.67 | .F. |
| 2 | Susita | Marie | 01/01/87 | 5555.55 | .T. |
| 3 | Lucy | Stravinsky | 11/15/86 | 34567.89 | .F. |
| 4 | Katie | Mendez | 03/31/87 | 65432.10 | .T. |
| 5 | Joanna | Jujubee | 01/01/86 | 43210.98 | .F. |
| 6 | Thalia | Adams | 01/01/87 | 123456.78 | .F. |
| 7 | Wuskie | Wilbur | 01/01/87 | 33000.00 | .T. |

**FIGURE 23.11:** Contents of the EmpTemp database file after removing the extraneous characters from the name Mendez. All fields are now properly aligned and accessible.

that is the case, use the simple dBASE dCONVERT program that came with your dBASE III PLUS package to convert the file to a dBASE III PLUS file.

If the file cannot be opened and dBASE displays the error message **File is not accessible**, the problem is probably a full disk or directory. Exit dBASE and use the DOS ERASE command to erase any unnecessary files from the drive and directory on which the file is located. Then run dBASE again and try to open the file. If the problem was disk or directory space, it will now be solved.

If all else fails, your best bet is to strip the dBASE header off the file completely and create a standard ASCII text file in SDF format of the data in the file. Then you can create a new dBASE file structure for the corrupted file and use the APPEND FROM...TYPE SDF command to read the raw data back into a dBASE file.

To simplify this task, you can use the BASIC program, named dBSave.bas, shown in Figure 23.12. The program will run under the Basica.com interpreter that came with your DOS package. You'll need to type in the program exactly as

```
10 REM -------------------------------- dBSAVE.bas
20 REM -- BASIC program to copy corrupted dBASE
30 REM -- .dbf file to a text file in SDF format.
40 CLS
50 INPUT "Enter name of dBASE file to read (excluding .dbf) ",XFILE$
60 INPUT "How many bytes (characters) per record? ",RECLEN%
70 INPUT "How many records in file? ",FILELEN
80 IFILE$ = XFILE$+".dbf"
90 REM ---- Search for first character of data.
100 OPEN IFILE$ AS 1 LEN=1
110 FIELD #1, 1 AS INFO$
120 MSG$ = "Enter # for first character of data, or 0 to proceed"
130 FOR X% = 1 TO 500
140    GET #1,X%
150    PRINT X%-1;
160    PRINT "-"+INFO$
170    IF X%/20 = INT(X%/20) THEN PRINT MSG$:INPUT FIRST%
180    IF FIRST% <> 0 THEN 200
190 NEXT X%
200 REM -------------- Build text file.
210 OFILE$ = XFILE$ + ".txt"
220 OPEN OFILE$ AS #2 LEN=1
230 FIELD #2, 1 AS CHAR$
240 CLS:COUNTER = 1
250 FOR OL = FIRST% TO (FIRST%+(FILELEN*RECLEN%)) STEP RECLEN%
260     PRINT "Rec "+STR$(COUNTER)+": ";
270     FOR IL% = 1 TO RECLEN%
280         GET #1, OL+IL%
290         LSET CHAR$=INFO$
300         PUT #2
310        PRINT INFO$;
320     NEXT IL%
330     LSET CHAR$=CHR$(13)
340     PUT #2
350     LSET CHAR$=CHR$(10)
360     PUT #2
370     PRINT
380 COUNTER = COUNTER +1
390 NEXT OL
400 CLOSE
410 PRINT:PRINT:PRINT
420 PRINT "The data from "+IFILE$+" are now in "+OFILE$
430 PRINT "in the SDF data format."
440 PRINT:PRINT:PRINT
```

**FIGURE 23.12:** A BASIC program named dBSave.bas that can help you recover a severely damaged dBASE III PLUS data file. This program allows you to locate the first byte of actual data in the file. Then it makes a copy of the data (without the damaged dBASE header) using ASCII text standard data format (SDF). After this program removes the faulty header from the file, you can create a new dBASE database for the file and use the APPEND FROM...TYPE SDF command to read the data into the new dBASE file.

shown in the figure, using any text editor or BASIC. If you use BASIC to type the program, remember to use the **SAVE "dBSave.bas",A** command at the BASIC Ok prompt to save the program. The ,A will save it in ASCII format so you can edit it with a text editor later if you like.

Before using the dBSave program, be aware that it makes a copy of your damaged dBASE file with the same name but the extension .txt. If you already have a file by this name that you wish to keep, you can either rename or copy that file or change line 210 in the dBSave program so that it adds an extension other than .txt to the name of the file it creates.

To use the dBSave program, copy the Basica.com (or Basic.com) program from your DOS disk to the drive and directory containing the damaged file and the dBSave.bas program (if you have not already done so to create the BASIC program). Type **BASIC** or **BASICA** at the DOS prompt, and press Return. Assuming that you've already created the dBSave.bas program, enter the command **RUN "dBSave"** at the BASIC Ok prompt.

The program will first present the following prompt:

**Enter name of dBASE file to read (excluding .dbf)**

Type in the name of the corrupted dBASE file (without the .dbf extension), and press Return. Next, the program will ask

**How many bytes (characters) per record?**

You must enter the exact number of bytes, including the invisible marked-for-deletion character, as displayed by the dBASE DISPLAY STRUCTURE command. If you are not sure of this value, take a reasonable guess. When dBSave creates the text file, you'll be able to refine that guess based on the output of the dBSave program (as discussed later). Enter the number of bytes per record and press Return.

The next question dBSave asks is

**How many records in file?**

If you know exactly how many records were in this file, enter that value and press Return. If you do not know, take a reasonable guess, but aim high. If you guess too high, dBSave will just add blank records to the bottom of the file, or records containing indecipherable information that you can delete later with the dBASE DELETE command.

When you've entered the information above, dBSave will start showing you the contents of the dBASE file, byte by byte, starting at the first byte in the dBASE file header. You want to look for the first byte containing data (*not* field names or anything else that would be stored in the header). The program will display the byte number (in decimal), a hyphen, and the character of each byte, one screenful at a time, along with the prompt

**Enter # for first character of data, or 0 to proceed**

If you do not see the first character of data in the file, just enter 0 and press Return to view the next screenful of information. You may have to repeat this process for several screens of information.

When you see some text that looks like information stored in a record, type in the number to the left of the first character of data, and press Return. For example, Figure 23.13 shows a screen displayed by dBSave, where the field containing the part number C-333 begins at byte number 226. Assuming that this part number marks the first field in the first record of the database file, you would enter 226 as the first byte of data in the file and press Return.

At this point, the screen clears and dBSave begins copying the data from the damaged dBASE file to the .txt file of the same name. dBSave shows the abbreviation Rec and a record number to the left of each record. If your estimate of the record length was wrong, the records will not look right on the screen (the fields will be out of alignment). You can press Ctrl-Break to halt processing if you like. You'll probably be able to figure out how far off your original guess was by the display. Enter the command **RUN** at the BASIC Ok prompt, and try again with a new record length. Repeat this process, if necessary, until you get the record length right.

```
?
 220 -
 221 -
 222 -
 223 -
 224 -

 225 -
 226 - C
 227 - -
 228 - 3
 229 - 3
 230 - 3
 231 - B
 232 - a
 233 - s
 234 - e
 235 - b
 236 - a
 237 - l
 238 - l
 239 -
Enter # for first character of data, or 0 to proceed
?
1LIST  2RUN←  3LOAD"  4SAVE"  5CONT←  6,"LPT1  7TRON←  8TROFF←  9KEY  0SCREEN
```

**FIGURE 23.13:** Output from the first routine in the dBSave.bas program. The column displays the byte number and character in each byte, starting at the first byte in the dBASE header. When the screen displays the first byte of actual data (not information from the file header), enter this number in response to the prompt near the bottom of the screen. In this example, the first byte of data starts at byte 226 (because the first field in the first record contains the part number C-333).

When dBSave appears to have created a valid text file judging by the alignment of fields on the screen, you can exit BASIC by entering the command SYSTEM at the Ok prompt. The DOS prompt will reappear on the screen.

If you like, you can now use any text editor or word processor (in an ASCII text mode) to inspect and change the .txt file created by dBSave. If there were originally extraneous characters in the file that were throwing the fields out of alignment, you can use a text editor or word processor to remove those characters now. In fact, you can edit these data in any way you like as long as you keep all the columns (fields) of information at even widths.

Now you need to go back into dBASE and use the CREATE command to create a dBASE database structure that exactly matches the structure of the SDF file created by dBSave. If you are confused about the exact field widths to specify during the CREATE process, you can use the **dBASE TYPE <file name> TO PRINT** command to print a hard copy of the .txt file that dbSave created. Then just count the number of characters in each field. Note that there are no blank spaces between fields.

After you create the appropriate database structure, enter the command

**APPEND FROM <file name> SDF**

where <file name> is the name of the file that dBSave created (including the .txt extension). All the records from the .txt file will be read into the dBASE file structure, and you'll be back in business. Enter the LIST command to verify that everything is back in shape.

If the field alignment is off when you enter the LIST command, inspect the records and try to determine which field lengths were wrong. Then zap all the records from the file, use MODIFY STRUCTURE to change the database structure, and try the APPEND FROM...SDF command again. You may have to repeat this process a few times to get it right.

## Running External Programs

The RUN and equivalent ! commands let you run external programs from within dBASE. You can use RUN to access DOS utilities such as RENAME, MODE, COUNTRY, ATTRIB, BACKUP, and others. You can also run larger external programs such as word processors and spreadsheets using the RUN command.

If you use an external word processor such as WordStar to write programs, you can quickly access the word processor by using the RUN command at the dBASE dot prompt. For example, either **RUN WS** or **!WS** will call up WordStar.

If you reconfigure your word processor so that it automatically starts in ASCII text mode, you can specify the name of the file you want to edit in the RUN command (assuming your word processor allows file names on the DOS command line). For example, the command below loads the program named

MainMenu.prg in WordStar, ready for editing (the .prg extension is required when using external word processors):

**!WS MainMenu.prg**

When you exit the external program, control returns to the dBASE dot prompt, and all files that were open before the external program was called will still be open.

Note that if you edit a procedure file that is currently open (with SET PROCEDURE) or a command file that is suspended, only the disk version of the file will be edited. The copy of the procedure file or program in RAM will not be affected. To use the edited procedure or command file, you must reissue the SET PROCEDURE command or cancel the program with CANCEL and load the edited file back into RAM with the DO command.

The RUN command requires additional memory beyond the minimum 256K required by dBASE. For additional details on RUN, see the reference section at the end of this chapter.

# THE STRUCTURE OF dBASE DATABASE FILES

It is useful to learn the technical details of the structure of dBASE database files, because this information can help you develop techniques of your own for salvaging damaged files. This section discusses the exact contents of dBASE .dbf and .mem files. For experienced programmers, this information is useful for creating a dBASE database file from scratch, such as when you want to create dBASE database files with programs written in C, Pascal, or another language.

## The Structure of dBASE .dbf Files

Every dBASE database (.dbf) file has a header that tells dBASE the structure, size, and field contents of the data stored in the file. Keep in mind that all values are stored in hexadecimal format (the h following some of the numbers indicates hexadecimal). The records within the database are always stored beneath the header. The actual length of the header will vary, depending on the number of fields in the database file.

### THE MAIN HEADER BYTES

Table 23.3 shows the structure of the first 31 bytes of the header, which is the same structure used in all dBASE .dbf file headers.

Figure 23.14 shows how the entire dBASE header looks when brought to the screen with the Debug program that comes with DOS. (Part of the first record in

| BYTES | CONTENTS | MEANING |
|---|---|---|
| 0 | 1 byte | dBASE III version number: 03h without a .dbt file; 83h with a .dbt file |
| 1–3 | 3 bytes | Date of last update in yymmdd format |
| 4–7 | 32-bit number | Number of records in database file |
| 8–9 | 16-bit number | Number of bytes in file header |
| 10–11 | 16-bit number | Number of bytes per record |
| 12–14 | 3 bytes | Reserved |
| 15–27 | 13 bytes | Reserved for multiuser dBASE |
| 28–31 | 20 bytes | Reserved |
| 32–n | 32 bytes each | Description of each field in the database, as shown in Table 23.4 |
| n + 1 | 1 byte | Field terminator: 0Dh |

**TABLE 23.3:** Structure of a dBASE Database (.dbf) File Header

the database file is also displayed.) Notice that all values are in hexadecimal notation, and in most cases the least significant value precedes the most significant value, as shown back in Figure 23.5.

## Field Descriptor Bytes

Beyond byte 31 of the field header, each group of 32 bytes describes an individual field. The contents of each field descriptor are summarized in Table 23.4.

## Individual Record Storage

The actual data records in a dBASE file begin beneath the last field descriptor. Each record is stored with a single leading byte that contains the marked-for-deletion flag. If the record is not marked for deletion, the byte contains a space (20h). If the record is marked for deletion, the byte contains an asterisk (2Ah). There are no delimiters between fields or terminators at the ends of records.

Table 23.5 shows how the data of various dBASE data types are stored within records. Note that memo fields contain only a pointer into a memo (.dbt) file, and that logical fields can store any valid single-byte entry (e.g., Y,T,F,N), although the data are always displayed as .T. or .F. through the dBASE LIST or DISPLAY commands. When undefined, logical fields store a single question mark (?) character.

At the end of the file, dBASE III PLUS stores an ASCII 26 (Ctrl-Z or 1Ah) character. However, unlike dBASE II, dBASE III PLUS does not consider an

```
C:\WORK>DEBUG Master.dbf
-D 100,250
32D9:0100  03 57 05 19 04 00 00 00-E1 00 27 00 00 00 00 00   .W........'.....
32D9:0110  00 00 00 00 00 00 00 00-00 00 00 00 00 00 00 00   ................
32D9:0120  50 41 52 54 4E 4F 00 00-00 00 00 43 07 00 F2 64   PARTNO.....C...d
32D9:0130  05 00 00 00 01 00 00 00-00 00 00 00 00 00 00 00   ................
32D9:0140  50 41 52 54 4E 41 4D 45-00 00 00 43 0C 00 F2 64   PARTNAME...C...d
32D9:0150  0F 00 00 00 01 00 00 00-00 00 00 00 00 00 00 00   ................
32D9:0160  49 4E 5F 53 54 4F 43 4B-00 00 00 4E 1B 00 F2 64   IN_STOCK...N...d
32D9:0170  04 00 00 00 01 00 00 00-00 00 00 00 00 00 00 00   ................
32D9:0180  55 4E 49 54 5F 50 52 49-43 45 00 4E 1F 00 F2 64   UNIT_PRICE.N...d
32D9:0190  09 02 00 00 01 00 00 00-00 00 00 00 00 00 00 00   ................
32D9:01A0  54 41 58 41 42 4C 45 00-00 00 00 4C 28 00 F2 64   TAXABLE....L(..d
32D9:01B0  01 00 00 00 01 00 00 00-00 00 00 00 00 00 00 00   ................
32D9:01C0  56 45 4E 44 5F 43 4F 44-45 00 00 43 29 00 F2 64   VEND_CODE..C)..d
32D9:01D0  04 00 00 00 01 00 00 00-00 00 00 00 00 00 00 00   ................
32D9:01E0  0D 20 43 2D 33 33 33 42-61 73 65 62 61 6C 6C 20   . C-333Baseball
32D9:01F0  20 20 20 20 20 20 20 20-20 34 20 20 20 20 31 34            4    14
32D9:0200  2E 39 35 54 41 42 41 20-20 42 2D 32 32 32 54 6F   .95TABA  B-222To
32D9:0210  6D 61 74 6F 65 73 20 20-20 20 20 20 20 20 20 20   matoes
32D9:0220  30 20 20 20 20 31 39 2E-39 35 46 41 42 41 20 20   0    19.95FABA
32D9:0230  41 2D 31 31 31 53 6F 63-63 65 72 20 42 61 6C 6C   A-111Soccer Ball
32D9:0240  73 20 20 20 20 20 20 39-20 20 20 20 31 32 2E 30   s      9    12.0
32D9:0250  30                                                0
-_
```

**FIGURE 23.14:** The entire header of a dBASE database file displayed with the **DEBUG d** command. Some database records, stored beneath the header, are also displayed. The left column displays memory locations in hexadecimal, and the middle columns display the contents, in hexadecimal, of each memory location. The right column displays the ASCII equivalent of each hexadecimal value.

| BYTES | CONTENTS | MEANING |
|---|---|---|
| 0–10 | 11 bytes | Name of field, padded with ASCII zeros |
| 11 | 1 byte | Field type, in ASCII (i.e., C, N, L, D, or M) |
| 12–15 | 32-bit number | Field data address set in RAM memory (not useful on disk file) |
| 16 | 1 byte | Length of field (in binary) |
| 17 | 1 byte | Number of decimal places (in binary) |
| 18–19 | 2 bytes | Reserved for multiuser dBASE |
| 20 | 1 byte | Work area identification |
| 21–22 | 2 bytes | Reserved for multiuser dBASE |
| 23 | 1 byte | Flag for SET FIELDS |
| 24–31 | 8 bytes | Reserved bytes |
| 32 | 1 byte | 0Dh terminates field description |

**TABLE 23.4:** Structure of Field Descriptors in dBASE File Headers

| DATA TYPE | HOW STORED |
|---|---|
| Character | ASCII characters |
| Numeric | – . 0 1 2 3 4 5 6 7 8 9 |
| Logical | ? Y y N n T t F f |
| Date | Eight digits in yyyymmdd format (e.g. 19871231 for 12/31/1987) |
| Memo | Ten digits pointing to a .dbt block |

**TABLE 23.5:** Storage of Data Types in dBASE Records

ASCII 26 to be the absolute end of the file. Instead, dBASE III PLUS relies on the number stored in bytes 4–7 of the file header as being the accurate count of records in the file. Any ASCII 26 code embedded in a record above the end of the file is simply displayed as its ASCII character (a → character).

## The Structure of Memo Field (.dbt) Files

dBASE memo fields are stored in a file that is separate from the .dbf data file. This file has the same first name as the .dbf file but the extension .dbt. Data in the .dbt file are stored sequentially in 512-byte blocks.

The first block in the .dbt file is block number zero. The first four bytes of this block represent the header for the .dbt file. This header contains the block number of the next available block for storing a memo field, in hexadecimal format. For example, if the next available block for storing a memo field is number 5500 decimal (157C hexadecimal), the first four bytes of block number zero contain 7C 15 00 00.

Within the .dbf file, the memo field contains a number that points to the appropriate block in the .dbt file that contains the memo for that record. (This number is hidden behind the word Memo that you see when you edit or list a database that has a memo field in it.)

Whenever information in a memo field is changed, the original contents remain in the .dbt file, and the new contents are written in the next available block. (Of course, the number in the .dbf file is changed to point to this new block.) For this reason, memo files can grow to an extremely large size if they are edited frequently. To delete the old, unused memo fields from the memo file and reduce the size of the file, use the dBASE COPY command to copy the .dbf file to a new file name. Only the latest versions of memo fields will be copied to the new .dbt file, thereby reclaiming the space originally used by the old memo fields.

If a memo field extends beyond 512 bytes, the next available block number in block zero is incremented by the appropriate number of bytes. Each memo field within the .dbt file is terminated with two hexadecimal 1A bytes.

# Commands Used for Interfacing with External Files

This section of the chapter discusses only the EXPORT, IMPORT, and RUN commands, which have not been referenced elsewhere in the book. The basic COPY TO command for copying database files is discussed in Chapter 15, "Managing Data, Records, and Files." The APPEND FROM command is discussed in Chapter 10, "Adding New Data."

The commands used with the DOS Debug program are discussed in detail in the DOS manual that comes with your computer. The commands for creating, editing, running, and saving BASIC programs are discussed in the BASIC manual that probably came with your computer.

## The EXPORT Command

EXPORT exports a dBASE database to PFS:FILE format.

### SYNTAX

**EXPORT TO <file name> TYPE PFS**

where <file name> contains the name of the PFS:FILE file to create.

### USAGE

Before using the EXPORT command, the database that you want to export must be open. If you wish to export a copy of the dBASE format (.fmt) file used for entering and editing records, that format file should also be opened with the SET FORMAT TO command.

If SET SAFETY is on, EXPORT will ask for permission before overwriting an existing PFS:FILE file with the same name. If SET SAFETY is off, EXPORT overwrites the existing file automatically.

PFS:FILE files generally have no extension, so you should always follow the name of the file to be created with a single period, as in the example below.

### EXAMPLES

The commands below export a copy of the Mail.dbf database and the MailScr.fmt format file to a PFS:FILE file named PFSMail:

```
USE Mail
SET FORMAT TO MailScr
EXPORT TO PFSMail. TYPE PFS
```

### TIPS

Note that any exported file might exceed the maximum number of fields allowed by the external software package. If this occurs, the external package will probably truncate the fields in the exported database.

### SEE ALSO

COPY TO
IMPORT

## The IMPORT Command

IMPORT copies a PFS:FILE database to dBASE III PLUS format.

### SYNTAX

**IMPORT FROM <file name> TYPE PFS**

where <file name> is the name of the PFS file to import.

### USAGE

The IMPORT command automatically creates three dBASE files from the single imported file: a database (.dbf) file, a format (.fmt) file, and a view (.vue) file. Each of these dBASE files has the same name as the imported file, with the appropriate dBASE extension added.

You can use the SET VIEW TO <file name> command to open the imported file. Doing so automatically opens both the database and the format files. Optionally, you can use the USE and SET FORMAT TO commands to access the imported database and format files.

Because PFS:FILE file names have no extension, you do not use an extension in the IMPORT command. (Of course, if you've purposely added an extension to a PFS file name, that extension must be used in the IMPORT command.)

### EXAMPLE

The command below imports a PFS:FILE database (and screen) named MailList:

**IMPORT FROM MailList TYPE PFS**

### TIPS

As soon as a PFS:FILE database is imported, it is open and ready for use. The DISPLAY STATUS command shows the files that are automatically opened by the IMPORT command.

### SEE ALSO

EXPORT
APPEND FROM

## The RUN and ! Commands

RUN and ! execute an external command or program from within dBASE.

### SYNTAX

**RUN <command>**
**! <command>**

where <command> is the DOS command or the name of the external program to run.

### USAGE

RUN and the equivalent ! command execute an external DOS command or an external program and then return control to the dBASE dot prompt when the external task is done.

RUN requires additional memory beyond the minimum 256K required by dBASE. An additional 17K, plus whatever memory is required by the external program, are necessary. If there is insufficient memory to run the external program, RUN returns the error message **Insufficient memory** and redisplays the dot prompt.

The DOS Command.com file must be on the drive and directory stored in the DOS COMSPEC parameter. In most cases, this is automatic and the programmer need not be concerned. However, if Command.com is not available, the DOS SET command can be used to define the location of Command.com. For example, the DOS command **SET COMSPEC = C:\Command.com** informs DOS that the command processor is stored on the root directory of drive C under the usual file name Command.com.

You can also exit dBASE, temporarily, back to the DOS prompt if you know the location of the DOS Command.com program, or if you have included the drive for the Command.com program in your PATH command. (To determine the drive and directory location of Command.com, you can enter the command **? GETENV("COMMAND.COM")** at the dBASE dot prompt.)

To temporarily exit dBASE to DOS, enter the RUN or ! command with the drive, directory, and Command.com file name. For example, if Command.com is stored on the root directory of drive C (which has no directory name), enter the command **RUN C:\Command**. The DOS prompt will appear on your screen. From here, you can execute *any* DOS command or run any other program. Be forewarned, however, that if you load any memory-resident programs while in DOS, there may not be enough memory to get back into dBASE. If that occurs, you might lose some data. (For that reason, you might want to close all files in dBASE before issuing the **RUN Command** command.)

To return to dBASE from the DOS prompt, enter the command **EXIT** at the DOS prompt.

#### EXAMPLES

The commands below allow the user to reset the DOS system date and time from within dBASE III PLUS:

**RUN Date**
**RUN Time**

#### TIPS

You can use RUN or ! to access an external word processor for editing command files without leaving dBASE.

Keep in mind that some DOS commands, such as PRINT and ASSIGN, remain in memory after being run. On computers with limited memory available, there may not be enough memory left for dBASE to resume processing. When this is the case, these DOS commands should be run outside of dBASE.

## SUMMARY

This chapter discussed numerous techniques for accessing data and programs outside of the dBASE database. It also discussed techniques for salvaging damaged dBASE files by treating them as external files and restructuring them back into dBASE databases.

*For additional information on the APPEND FROM command:*

- Chapter 10, "Adding New Data"

*For more information on the COPY command:*

- Chapter 15, "Managing Data, Records, and Files"

*For information on exporting encrypted database files:*

- Chapter 20, "Networking and Security"

*For information on running assembly language subroutines:*

- Chapter 22, "Using Assembly Language Subroutines in dBASE"

# Part 7

## *Commonly Used Algorithms*

This part presents numerous procedures and programs that you can use to extend dBASE beyond its off-the-shelf capabilities. Most of these routines are written so that they are easy to adapt into your own custom applications.

The statistical procedures offer techniques for calculating the highest and lowest values in a numeric field, variance and standard deviation, correlation coefficient, and frequency distributions.

The business procedures offer techniques for calculating payment on a loan, future value, present value, compound annual growth rate, and base 10 logarithm.

More advanced procedures presented in this section allow you to enhance your applications with bar graphs, light-bar menus, date-to-English translations (e.g., display 1/1/87 as January 1, 1987), and number-to-word translations (e.g., display 1234.56 as ONE THOUSAND TWO HUNDRED THIRTY FOUR AND 56/100).

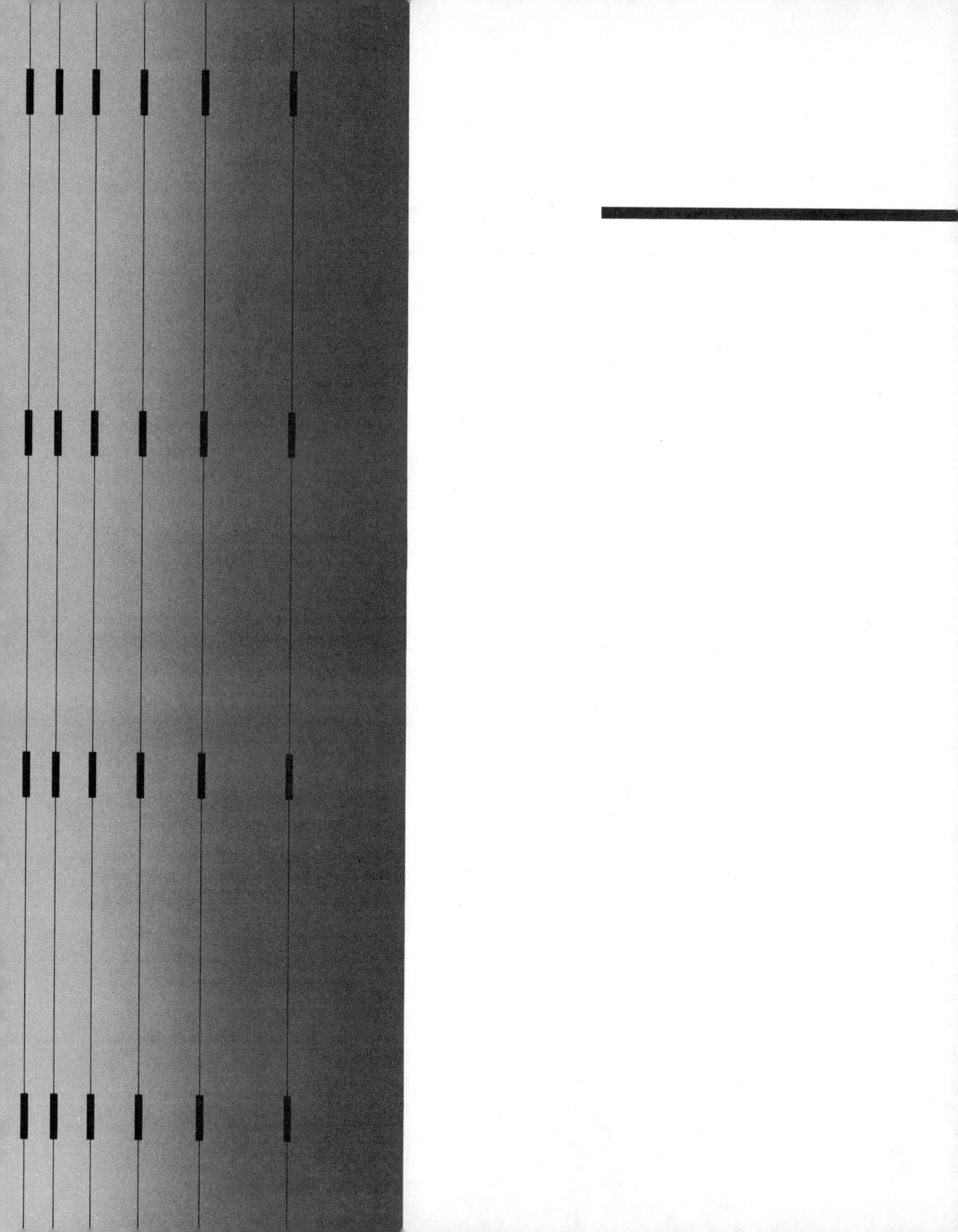

# Algorithms to Extend dBASE

# ALGORITHMS TO EXTEND dBASE

The procedures and programs presented in this chapter are categorized by the type of capability they provide, such as statistical calculations, financial calculations, graphics procedures, and so forth. Each procedure and program description includes a description of the procedure, any public memory variables required, an example of how to use the procedure, and additional information as required.

Most of the algorithms in the chapter are presented as procedures, so that you can quickly put them into your own applications with few or no modifications. For maximum speed in accessing a procedure, you should store all the procedures for an application in a single procedure file and pass data back from the procedures as public variables. (Chapter 5, "Procedures and Parameters," discusses these topics in detail.)

## STATISTICAL CALCULATIONS

The procedures in this section all perform statistical calculations on a field in a database file. By default, each procedure takes into consideration all of the records in the database file when performing the calculation. To hide records that have been marked for deletion from a procedure, precede the procedure call with a SET DELETED ON command. To limit the calculations to records that meet some filtering criterion, precede the procedure call with a SET FILTER or MODIFY QUERY command.

To prevent any extraneous messages from appearing on the screen during calculations, issue the SET TALK OFF command before calling the procedure.

### Largest Value in a Field

The Largest procedure calculates the largest value in a numeric field and stores its results in the public memory variable Largest. The procedure is shown in Figure 24.1.

```
**** Largest procedure finds largest value in a field.
*----------- Requires a public variable named Largest.
PROCEDURE Largest
PARAMETERS FieldName
  GO TOP
  IF EOF()
     ? "No records match filter criteria!"
  ENDIF (eof)
  Largest = &FieldName
  *-------- Find highest value.
  DO WHILE .NOT. EOF()
     Largest = MAX(Largest,&FieldName)
     SKIP
  ENDDO
RETURN
```

**FIGURE 24.1:** The Largest procedure, which finds the largest value in a numeric field. This procedure stores its result in a variable named Largest, which should be declared public before the procedure is called.

## USING THE LARGEST PROCEDURE

To use the Largest procedure, first declare a variable named Largest as public. Open the database file of interest, and call the procedure with the field name (or field expression) in which you wish to find the highest value, using the following general syntax:

**DO Largest WITH <field name>**

where <field name> is the name of the field(s) of interest. The field name should be enclosed in quotation marks or other valid delimiters unless it is stored in a memory variable. The largest value in the specified field(s) will be stored in the variable named Largest.

## EXAMPLES

All of the procedure calls below are performed on a database named Sales, which contains the numeric fields Qty and U_Price. Before any procedure calls are made, the Largest variable should first be declared public:

**SET TALK OFF**
**PUBLIC Largest**
**USE Sales**

The following commands calculate and display the largest value in the numeric field named Qty:

**DO Largest WITH "Qty"**
**? Largest**

These commands calculate and display the largest product of the U_Price field multiplied by the Qty field:

**DO Largest WITH "Qty * U_Price"**
**? Largest**

The commands below hide records that are marked for deletion and limit the calculation to records with part number A-123 in the PartNo field. Note that in this example the name of the field to analyze, U_Price, is stored in a memory variable named FldName:

**SET FILTER TO PartNo = "A-123"**
**FldName = "U_Price"**
**DO Largest WITH FldName**

## Smallest Value in a Field

The Smallest procedure calculates the smallest value in a numeric field and stores its results in the public memory variable Smallest. The Smallest procedure is shown in Figure 24.2.

### USING THE SMALLEST PROCEDURE

To use the Smallest procedure, first declare a variable named Smallest as public. Open the database file of interest, and call the procedure with the field name (or field expression) in which you wish to find the smallest value, using the following general syntax:

**DO Smallest WITH <field name>**

```
** Smallest procedure finds smallest value in a field.
*---------- Requires a public variable named Smallest.
PROCEDURE Smallest
PARAMETERS FieldName
  GO TOP
  IF EOF()
     ? "No records match filter criteria!"
  ENDIF (eof)
  Smallest = &FieldName
  *-------- Find smallest value.
  DO WHILE .NOT. EOF()
     Smallest = MIN(Smallest,&FieldName)
     SKIP
  ENDDO
RETURN
```

**FIGURE 24.2:** The Smallest procedure, which finds the smallest value in a numeric field. This procedure stores its result in a variable named Smallest, which should be declared public before the procedure is called.

where <field name> is the name of the field(s) of interest, enclosed in quotation marks or other delimiters, or the name of a memory variable containing the field name. The smallest value in the specified field(s) will be stored in the variable named Smallest.

**EXAMPLES**

All of the procedure calls below are performed on a database file named Sales, which contains the numeric fields Qty and U_Price. Note that the Smallest variable is declared public before any procedure calls are made:

```
SET TALK OFF
PUBLIC Smallest
USE Sales
```

The following commands calculate and display the smallest value in the numeric field named U_Price:

```
DO Smallest WITH "U_Price"
? Smallest
```

These commands calculate and display the smallest product of the U_Price field multiplied by the Qty field:

```
DO Smallest WITH "U_Price * Qty"
? Smallest
```

The commands below hide records that are marked for deletion and limit the calculation to records with part number B-222 in the PartNo field. Note that in this example the name of the field to analyze, Qty, is stored in a memory variable named FldName:

```
SET FILTER TO PartNo = "B-222"
FldName = "Qty"
DO Smallest WITH FldName
```

# Variance

The Variance procedure measures how much the values in a range cluster around one another. The formula for calculating variance is

$$\text{Variance} = \frac{\Sigma x^2 - \dfrac{(\Sigma x)^2}{N}}{N - 1}$$

where $\Sigma x^2$ is the sum of the squared score values, $(\Sigma x)^2$ is the square of the sum of all the scores, and $N$ is the number of items used in the calculation.

Figuring out variance and standard deviation can be useful for a number of business decisions. For example, suppose a company wants to market a product to customers in the age range of 30 to 35. They are trying to decide whether to buy advertising time on a soap opera or a news show. Looking at a sample of viewers' ages for the two groups shows that both shows have an average viewer age of 32 years, as shown in Figure 24.3.

However, the variance and standard deviation tell another story. Generally speaking, about two thirds of viewers will be within one standard deviation of the mean (or average). Hence, for the news show, two thirds of the viewers will be in the age range of 7 to 57: a large spread. For the soap opera, about two thirds of the viewers will fall in the age range of 26 to 38, a much tighter group and thus a better target audience for the product. The dBASE procedure for calculating variance is shown in Figure 24.4.

## USING THE VARIANCE PROCEDURE

To use the Variance procedure, create a public variable named Variance and open the database file of interest. To exclude records that are marked for deletion from the calculation, enter the SET DELETED ON command. To limit the

```
                     News    Soap Opera

                      20        30
                      60        20
                      10        35
                      10        30
                      45        30
                      55        35
                       5        35
                      15        35
                      60        30
                      70        20
                      10        25
                      55        30
                      21        40
                       5        20
                      15        40
                       5        30
                      36        36
                      63        36
                      75        37
                      10        40

                    ------- -------
           Average    32        32

          Variance 633.14    41.48
Standard deviation  25.16     6.44
```

**FIGURE 24.3:** The two columns in this display represent the ages of viewers of two TV shows, one a soap opera and the other a news show. Though the average ages of both groups is 32 years, the variance and standard deviation measures show that there is less variance in the ages of viewers of the soap opera; hence the ages are clustered more tightly around the average.

calculation to records that meet some search criterion, use the SET FILTER or MODIFY QUERY commands. Then enter the procedure call using the general syntax

**DO Variance WITH <field name>**

where <field name> is the name of the numeric field on which to perform the calculation.

## EXAMPLES

The examples below use a database file named SoapNews, containing data like those shown in Figure 24.3. The database contains two numeric fields named News and Soap. To calculate and display the variance for each of the fields, use the commands below:

**SET TALK OFF**
**USE SoapNews**
**PUBLIC Variance**

**DO Variance WITH "Soap"**
**? Variance**

**DO Variance WITH "News"**
**? Variance**

The field name can be stored in a variable, as below:

**FldName = "News"**
**DO Variance WITH FldName**

```
*----------------- Variance procedure finds the variance.
*---------Requires a public variable named Variance.
PROCEDURE Variance
PARAMETERS FieldName
  GO TOP
  IF EOF()
     ? "No records match filter criteria!"
  ENDIF (eof)
  COUNT TO N
  SUM(&FieldName),(&FieldName^2) TO TOT,TOTSq
  Correction = TOT^2/N
  Variance = (TOTSq-Correction)/(n-1)
RETURN
```

**FIGURE 24.4:** The Variance procedure calculates the variance on a single numeric field. It requires a public variable named Variance to pass its results back to the calling program or dot prompt.

Calculations can be used in place of the field name, as in the example below:

**DO Variance WITH "News*Soap"**

## Standard Deviation

Standard deviation is the square root of the variance (discussed above). Figure 24.3 shows two measures of standard deviation. The formula for calculating standard deviation is

$$\text{Standard Deviation} = \sqrt{\frac{\Sigma x^2 - \frac{(\Sigma x)^2}{N}}{N - 1}}$$

where $\Sigma x^2$ is the sum of the squared score values, $(\Sigma x)^2$ is the square of the sum of all the scores, and $N$ is the number of items used in the calculation. The dBASE procedure for calculating standard deviation is shown in Figure 24.5.

### USING THE STD PROCEDURE

To use the StD procedure, create a public variable named StD and open the database file of interest. To exclude records that are marked for deletion from the calculation, enter the SET DELETED ON command. To limit the calculation to records that meet some search criterion, use the SET FILTER or MODIFY QUERY commands. Then enter the procedure call with the general syntax

**DO StD WITH <field name>**

where <field name> is the name of the numeric field to perform the calculation on.

```
*------- StD procedure finds the standard deviation.
*------------- Requires a public variable named StD.
PROCEDURE StD
PARAMETERS FieldName
  GO TOP
  IF EOF()
     ? "No records match filter criteria!"
  ENDIF (eof)
  COUNT TO N
  SUM(&FieldName),(&FieldName^2) TO TOT,TOTSq
  Correction = TOT^2/N
  Variance = (TOTSq-Correction)/(n-1)
  StD = SQRT(Variance)
RETURN
```

**FIGURE 24.5:** The StD procedure calculates the standard deviation on a single numeric field. It requires a public variable named StD to pass its results back to the calling program or dot prompt.

### EXAMPLES

The examples below use a database file like the one shown in Figure 24.3, which contains two numeric fields named News and Soap. To calculate and display the standard deviation for each of the fields, use the commands below:

```
SET TALK OFF
USE SoapNews
PUBLIC StD

DO StD WITH "Soap"
? StD

DO StD WITH "News"
? StD
```

The field name can be stored in a variable, as below:

```
FldName = "News"
DO StD WITH FldName
```

Calculations can be used in place of the field name, as in the example below:

```
DO StD WITH "News*Soap"
```

## Frequency Distribution

Frequency distribution involves listing unique items in a field and the number of occurrences of each. For example, on a large mailing list database, you might be interested in knowing how many individuals fall within each zip code category. A frequency distribution could tell you how many records contain each unique zip code, as in Figure 24.6. The procedure for displaying the frequency distribution is shown in Figure 24.7.

```
Frequency distribution for Zip_Code:

90001     100
90002      50
90003     125
90004    4561
90007     255
90008      11
99999     543
```

**FIGURE 24.6:** This sample frequency distribution report describes how many records contain each of the unique zip codes in the left column (for example, 100 records have the zip code 90001). This report was printed by the FreqDist procedure shown in Figure 24.7.

```
* FreqDist procedure displays frequency distribution.
PROCEDURE FreqDist
PARAMETERS FieldName
  *- Print title
  ?
  ?  "Frequency Distribution for &FieldName"
  ?
  *- Index on appropiate field.
  INDEX ON &FieldName TO TEMP
  *- Calculate and display distribution.
  GO TOP
  DO WHILE .NOT. EOF()
     Lookup = &FieldName
     COUNT WHILE &FieldName = Lookup TO FreQty
     ? lookup,FreQty
  ENDDO (not eof)

RETURN
```

**FIGURE 24.7:** This procedure displays a frequency distribution of any field in a database file. It requires no public memory variables. It is called with the command **Do FreqDist WITH <field name>** where <field name> is the name of the field on which to perform the calculation.

### USING THE FREQDIST PROCEDURE

The FreqDist procedure requires no public variables, because it displays its results instead of returning a value. You need only open the database of interest and call the procedure with the general syntax

**DO FreqDist WITH <field name>**

where <field name> is the field of interest.

### EXAMPLES

The commands below display a frequency distribution of a field named PartNo in a database named Sales.

**USE Sales**
**DO FreqDist WITH "PartNo"**

For a hard copy of the frequency distribution, just set the printer on before entering the DO...WITH command, as in the example below:

**SET PRINT ON**
**DO FreqDist WITH "Date"**
**SET PRINT OFF**

## Factorials

Factorials, which are used occasionally in statistical calculations, are calculated by decrementally multiplying a number by itself minus one until the number 2 is reached. For example, 5 factorial is 5 × 4 × 3 × 2, or 120. Factorials become very large very quickly, and dBASE can display a number up to a maximum of about 20 factorial. The procedure for calculating factorials (called Fact) is shown in Figure 24.8.

## USING THE FACT PROCEDURE

The Fact procedure calculates a factorial and returns the result in the public variable Fact. Note that a single parameter is passed to procedure, and it must be a number.

To use the Fact procedure, first declare a public variable named Fact, then call the procedure with the general syntax

**DO Fact WITH <number>**

where <number> is any number in the range of about 1 to 20.

## EXAMPLES

The commands below calculate and display the factorial of 10:

```
SET TALK OFF
PUBLIC Fact
DO Fact WITH 10
? Fact
   3628800
```

The number passed to the procedure can be stored in a variable, as below:

```
X = 15
DO Fact WITH X
? Fact
   1307674368000
```

```
*--- Fact procedure calculates factorial of a number.
*------------- Requires a public variable named Fact.
PROCEDURE Fact
PARAMETERS Number
  Fact = Number
  Counter = Number
  DO WHILE Counter > 1
     Counter = Counter - 1
     Fact = Fact * Counter
  ENDDO (Counter > 1)
RETURN
```

**FIGURE 24.8:** The Fact procedure calculates a factorial on any number up to about 20. It returns the results of its calculation in a public memory variable named Fact.

## Correlation Coefficient

The Pearson Product-Moment Correlation Coefficient (r) is used to determine whether there is a relationship between two sets of data. For example, suppose a company creating a new cola performs a taste test and thinks there might be a relationship between age and taste score. The scores and ages are listed in Figure 24.9.

The Pearson r test will tell you whether there is a significant relationship between age and score (or rating) in these data. If the r value is zero, there is no relationship. If the r value is +1.00, there is a perfect relationship (as Age increases, Score also increases evenly). An r of −1.00 indicates a perfect negative relationship (as Age increases, Score decreases evenly). Any values in between indicate the strength of the relationship.

The formula for the Pearson Product-Moment Correlation Coefficient is

$$r = \frac{N\Sigma xy - (\Sigma x)(\Sigma y)}{[N\Sigma x^2 - (\Sigma x)^2][N\Sigma y^2 - (\Sigma y)^2]}$$

where $N$ is the number of items used in the calculation, $\Sigma xy$ is the sum of the products of the paired items, $\Sigma x$ is the sum of the items on one variable, $\Sigma y$ is the sum of the items on the other variable, $\Sigma x^2$ is the sum of the squared items on the $x$ variable, and $\Sigma y^2$ is the sum of the squared items on the $y$ variable.

Figure 24.10 shows the entire procedure, named Pearson, for calculating the correlation.

| Age | Score |
|---|---|
| 38 | 2.1 |
| 54 | 2.9 |
| 43 | 3.0 |
| 45 | 2.3 |
| 50 | 2.6 |
| 61 | 3.7 |
| 57 | 3.2 |
| 25 | 1.3 |
| 36 | 1.8 |
| 39 | 2.5 |
| 48 | 3.4 |
| 46 | 2.6 |
| 44 | 2.4 |
| 39 | 2.5 |
| 48 | 3.3 |

**FIGURE 24.9:** Sample data used with the Pearson procedure, which measures the correlation coefficient, that is, the extent to which the two columns of data are related. In other words, it tests whether there is any relationship between a person's age and his or her score.

## USING THE PEARSON PROCEDURE

To use the procedure, you first need to declare the variable named Pearson as public. Then open the database file of interest, and call the procedure with the names of the numeric fields of interest, using the general syntax

**DO Pearson WITH <field1>,<field2>**

where <field1> and <field2> are the names of the numeric fields on which to perform the calculation.

## EXAMPLE

The example below uses a database named AgeTest, similar to the one shown in Figure 24.9. Note that the commands set the TALK option off, declare the Pearson variable as public, open the database file of interest, perform the calculation, and then display the results.

**SET TALK OFF**
**PUBLIC Pearson**
**USE AgeTest**

```
************** Pearson Product-Moment Correlation
*------ Requires a public variable named Pearson.
PROCEDURE Pearson
PARAMETERS X,Y
  GO TOP
  *-- Get N
  COUNT TO N
  *-- Sum the products and squares.
  SUM (&X * &Y),(&X ^2),&X,(&Y ^ 2),&Y TO ;
      SumProd,TotSqX,TotX,TotSqY,TotY
  SumProdXN = SumProd * N
  TotSqXxN = TotSqX * N
  TotXSq = TotX ^ 2
  TotSqYxN = TotSqY * N
  TotYSq = TotY ^ 2
  TotYxTotX = TotX * TotY
  *-- Get numerator
  RNum = SumProdXN - TotYxTotX
  *-- Subtract squares
  DifSqX = TotSqXxN - TotXsq
  DifSqY = TotSqYxN - TotYSq
  *-- MultiPly differences
  DifDif = DifSqX * DifSqY
  DifRoot = SQRT(DifDif)
  *-- Calculate Pearson R
  Pearson = RNum/DifRoot
RETURN
```

**FIGURE 24.10:** The Pearson procedure used to calculate the Pearson Product-Moment Correlation Coefficient on two fields of numbers. The general syntax for calling the procedure is **DO Pearson WITH <field1>,<field2>**.

**DO Pearson WITH "Age","Score"**
**? Pearson**

The field names can also be stored in variables, as below:

**Field1 = "Age"**
**Field2 = "Score"**
**DO Pearson WITH Field1,Field2**
**? Pearson**

# Financial Calculations

dBASE III has a number of mathematical functions, such as square root and logarithm, for managing numeric data. But for many financial applications, a dBASE user needs specific procedures for calculating financial data. This section provides procedures for performing calculations such as payment on a loan, future value of an investment, present value of an annuity, compound annual growth rate, and logarithm base 10 (used in some financial calculations).

## Payment on a Loan

The formula for calculating the payment on a loan is

**Payment = Principal * Interest / (1 – (1 + Interest) ^ – Term)**

where Principal is the amount of the loan, Interest is the periodic interest rate, and Term is the number of payment periods of the loan. Remember to convert percentages to fractions of one; i.e., 9.3% = .093. The dBASE procedure for calculating the payment on a loan is shown in Figure 24.11.

```
*--------- Pmt procedure calculates payment on a loan.
*--------------- Requires a public variable named Pmt.
PROCEDURE Pmt
PARAMETERS Principal, Interest, Term
     Pmt= Principal * Interest/(1-(1+Interest)^-Term)
RETURN
```

**FIGURE 24.11:** Procedure to calculate the payment on a loan. A public variable named Pmt must be created before calling the procedure with the syntax **DO Pmt WITH <principal>, <interest>, <term>** where <principal> is the loan amount, <interest> is the periodic interest rate, and <term> is the number of equal payments to be made.

### USING THE PMT PROCEDURE

Three parameters are passed to the procedure: Principal, Interest, and Term. The general syntax for calling the Pmt procedure is

**DO Pmt WITH <principal>, <interest>, <term>**

where <principal> is the amount borrowed, <interest> is the periodic interest rate, and <term> is the number of payments to be made. The period of the interest rate must agree with that of the term.

### EXAMPLE

To determine the payment on a loan of $5000 with an interest rate of .00833 per month (10 percent per year) for a period of 12 months, enter the commands below:

```
SET TALK OFF
PUBLIC Pmt
DO Pmt WITH 5000,.00833,12
```

You need not calculate the monthly interest yourself if all you know is the annual percentage rate. Just divide the annual interest rate by 12 in the WITH portion of the DO command. Similarly, if the term is 20 years, you can multiply the term by 12 to automatically calculate the number of months in the WITH portion. For example, to calculate and display the monthly payment on a loan of $168,000 at an annual interest rate of 9.375 percent for a 20-year term, enter the commands

```
DO Pmt WITH 168000,.09375/12,20*12
? Pmt
     1552.29264
```

## Future Value

The formula for calculating the future value of an investment is

**Future value = Payment * ((1 + Interest) ^ Term – 1)/Interest**

where Payment is the payment per period, Interest is the periodic interest rate, and Term is the number of payments. The dBASE procedure for calculating future value is shown in Figure 24.12.

```
*--------------- FV procedure calculates future value.
*---------------- Requires a public variable named FV.
PROCEDURE FV
PARAMETERS Payment,Interest,Term
   FV= Payment * ((1+Interest)^Term-1)/Interest
RETURN
```

**FIGURE 24.12:** Procedure to calculate future value using the general syntax **DO FV WITH <payment>, <interest>, <term>**. Before calling the procedure, a variable named FV should be declared public.

## USING THE FV PROCEDURE

The general syntax for using the FV procedure is

**DO FV WITH <payment>, <interest>, <term>**

where <payment> is the payment per period, <interest> is the periodic interest rate, and <term> is the number of payments. The period of the interest rate must agree with that of the term.

## EXAMPLES

Before calling the procedure, first declare the FV variable as public and set the TALK parameter off, as below:

```
SET TALK OFF
PUBLIC FV
```

Now, suppose you want to calculate and display the future value of an investment of $200.00 per month at 12 percent annual interest for 20 years. Again, the annual interest must be divided by 12 for the proper periodic interest rate, and the years must be multiplied by 12 for the correct number of payments. Enter the commands

```
DO FV WITH 200,.12/12,20*12
? FV
     197851.07
```

To see the future value of regular deposits of $2000 per year at 10 percent annual interest per year for 30 years, enter the commands

```
DO FV WITH 2000,.10,30
? FV
     328988.05
```

## Present Value

The formula for calculating the present value of equal, regular payments on a loan is calculated with the formula

**Present value = Payment * (1 – 1/(1 + Interest) ^ Term)/Interest**

where Payment is the payment per period, Interest is the periodic interest rate, and Term is the number of equal payments. The dBASE procedure for calculating present value is shown in Figure 24.13.

### USING THE PV PROCEDURE

The general syntax for the PV procedure is

**DO PV WITH <payment>, <interest>, <term>**

where <payment> is the amount of each payment made, <interest> is the periodic interest rate, and <term> is the number of equal payments made. The period of the interest rate must agree with that of the term. The result is stored in the public memory variable PV.

### EXAMPLES

Before calling the procedure, first declare the PV variable as public and set the TALK parameter off, as below:

```
SET TALK OFF
PUBLIC PV
```

Now, suppose you can afford to pay $1000 per month on a mortgage. Given that the current interest is 12 percent per year and you are willing to finance the house for 30 years, how much can you afford to borrow? To find out, you would enter the commands

```
DO PV WITH 1000,.12/12,30*12
? PV
```

```
* PV procedure calculates present value of an annuity.
PROCEDURE PV
PARAMETERS Payment, Interest, Term
  PV= Payment * (1-/(1+Interest)^Term)/Interest
RETURN
```

**FIGURE 24.13:** Procedure to calculate present value using the general syntax **DO PV WITH <payment>, <interest>, <term>**. Before calling the procedure, a variable named PV should be declared public.

**97218.33**

As you can see, with these terms you can borrow $97,218.33 for your new house.

## Base 10 Logarithm

The base 10 logarithm might be considered a mathematical rather than a financial calculation. However, the log 10 calculation is required for calculating compound annual growth rate (discussed below), so the procedure is discussed here. The procedure for calculating the base 10 logarithm is shown in Figure 24.14. The calculation is performed by multiplying the natural logarithm by .43429448, rounding for maximum accuracy.

### USING THE LOG10 PROCEDURE

To use the Log10 procedure, declare a variable named Log10 public and then call the procedure with the general syntax

**DO Log10 WITH <number>**

where <number> is the number on which to perform the calculation. The result is stored in the public variable named Log10.

### EXAMPLES

The commands below calculate and display the base 10 logarithm for 128:

```
SET TALK OFF
PUBLIC Log10
DO Log10 WITH 128
? Log10
    2.1072100000
```

```
*--Log10 calculates the base 10 logarithm of a number.
*------------- Requires a public variable named Log10.
PROCEDURE Log10
PARAMETERS Number
  Log10=ROUND(LOG(number)*.43429448,6)
RETURN
```

**FIGURE 24.14:** Procedure to calculate a base 10 logarithm. The procedure requires that a variable named Log10 be declared public. Then the procedure can be called with the general syntax **DO Log10 WITH <number>**. The results of the calculation are stored in the public memory variable named Log10.

## Compound Annual Growth Rate

The formula for calculating compound annual growth rate is

**CAGR = (10 ^ ((Log(Future/Present))/Years)) – 1**

The Log portion of the formula refers to a base 10 logarithm. The Log10 procedure discussed above needs to be accessed by this procedure. To maximize the speed of the calculation, the Log10 and CAGR procedures should be stored in the same procedure file. The procedure that calculates the compound annual growth rate is shown in Figure 24.15.

The compound annual growth rate is calculated by first taking the log of the future value divided by the present value and then using the result in the appropriate formula.

### USING THE CAGR PROCEDURE

The general syntax for accessing the CAGR procedure is

**DO CAGR WITH <present value>, <future value>, <years>**

where <present value> is the amount you wish to invest, <future value> is the amount you wish to have at the end of the period, and <years> is the number of years you are willing to invest the money. The answer is stored in the public memory variable CAGR.

### EXAMPLE

Suppose you have $5000 to invest and you want it to double in 10 years. What interest rate would you need to meet this goal? To find the answer, set the TALK parameter off, declare the Log10 and CAGR variables as public, enter the

```
*------CAGR calculates the compound annual growth rate.
*------Uses Log10 procedure for log base 10.
*------Requires a public variable named CAGR.
PROCEDURE CAGR
PARAMETERS Present, Future, Years
     DO Log10 WITH (Future/Present)
     CAGR=(10^(Log10/Years))-1
RETURN
```

**FIGURE 24.15:** The CAGR procedure for calculating the compound annual growth rate. This procedure needs to access the Log10 procedure. To maximize the speed of the calculation, both the CAGR and Log10 procedures should be stored in a single procedure file. The CAGR procedure requires a public memory variable named CAGR.

procedure call, and display the results, as below (remember, the Log10 procedure must have also been created and the Log10 variable declared public before the CAGR procedure will work correctly):

```
SET TALK OFF
PUBLIC Log10,CAGR
DO CAGR WITH 5000,10000,10
? CAGR
     .07
```

In this example, CAGR is .07, or 7 percent, indicating that you need an interest rate of 7 percent to double your money in 10 years. (*Note:* You can use the SET DECIMALS and SET FIXED commands to fix the number of decimal places returned in the CAGR variable. Also, the DISPLAY MEMORY command will show you the result carried to ten decimal places of accuracy.)

# Graphics Procedures

The procedures in this section allow you to add graphics capabilities to your applications, such as graphics characters and prompts for enhancing screen displays and bar graphs for displaying data.

## Graphics Symbols

The KeySigns procedure, shown in Figure 24.16, will set up special graphics characters for use in your applications. It assigns public variable names to each of the graphics characters.

Note that the procedure begins by declaring the variables Ret, Left, Right, Up, Down, Bullet, Solid, Degrees, Reverse, Blink, and Standard as public. Then it assigns ASCII characters to all but the last three variables. For example, the ASCII code for a left arrow is assigned to the variable Left. (*Note:* These codes may vary; use the ASCII program in Chapter 17, "dBASE Functions," to look up codes for your screen.) The variables Standard, Reverse, and Blink are assigned codes to be used in conjunction with the SET COLOR command.

### USING THE KEYSIGNS PROCEDURE

To use the KeySigns procedure, enter the command **DO KeySigns**. You won't see anything happen before the dot prompt reappears. However, if you enter the command **DISPLAY MEMORY** to view memory variables, you'll see that you have some new variables to work with.

```
*-------- Set up symbols and colors in variables.
PROCEDURE KeySigns
  PUBLIC Ret, Left, Right, UP, Down, Bullet, ;
  Solid, Degrees, Reverse, Blink, Standard

  Ret = CHR(17)+CHR(196)+CHR(217)
  Left = CHR(27)
  Right = CHR(26)
  UP = CHR(24)
  Down = CHR(25)
  Bullet = CHR(249)
  Solid = CHR(219)
  Degrees = CHR(248)
  *---- SET COLOR macros
  Standard = "GR+/B,W+/R,BG"
  Reverse = "0/7+"
  Blink = "W+*"
RETURN
```

**FIGURE 24.16:** The KeySigns procedure stores graphics characters and SET COLOR commands in public memory variables. Once defined, you can access these special codes and characters within your application by using the memory variable names assigned.

### EXAMPLES

You can use the ? command to display individual graphics symbols. For example, to see a left arrow, enter the command **? Left**.

You can use the symbols as macros embedded in other character strings. For example, the command below shows the Ret symbol (←┘) in a prompt displayed with an @...SAY command:

**@ 12,5 SAY "This symbol, &Ret, is the Return key"**

The symbols for Standard, Blinking, and Reverse must always be used as macros with the SET COLOR command, as in the commands below:

**SET COLOR TO &Blink**
**SET COLOR TO &Reverse**
**SET COLOR TO &Standard**

## Bar Graphs

This section discusses a procedure for displaying simple bar graphs. The program can comfortably display up to about 12 columns of data on an 80-column-wide screen, though you can display many more columns on a printer with wide paper or in compressed print mode. Figure 24.17 shows the entire bar graph procedure.

```
****************************************** BarGraph.prg
* procedure to plot data on bar graph.  Data to be
* plotted must be assigned in calling program using
* variable names Col1, Col2, Col3, etc. X-axis
* titles must also be assigned using variable names
* Title1, Title2, Title3, etc.
*------------------------------------------------------
* Passed parameters are:
* Title     : Title to appear at top of graph
* No_Col    : Number of columns in graph
* Col_Width : Width of each bar in graph
* Lr        : Lowest Y-axis value
* Hr        : Highest Y-axis value

PROCEDURE BarGraph
PARAMETERS Title,No_Col,Col_Width,Lr,Hr
SET TALK OFF
SET STATUS OFF
CLEAR
? "Working..."

*------------------- Pad titles and create bottom line.
Counter=1
TWidth=Col_Width-2
BLine=SPACE(6)
DO WHILE Counter <= No_Col
   Sub=LTRIM(STR(Counter,2))
   Title&Sub=SUBSTR(Title&Sub,1,TWidth)+;
    SPACE(TWidth-LEN(Title&Sub))
   BLine=BLine+Title&Sub+SPACE(2)
   Counter=Counter+1
ENDDO (counter)

*------------- Pad title for centering.
Title=SPACE((((Col_Width*No_Col)+5)/2)- ;
      (LEN(TRIM(Title))/2))+Title

      *********************************************
      *     Display graph on screen         *
      *********************************************
*--------- Assign graphics characters for screen.
XChar=CHR(196)
YChar=CHR(179)
BChar=CHR(219)

*-- Create Y-axis, X-axis, and bar for screen graph.
Line=SPACE(1)+YChar
XLine="  "+REPLICATE(XChar,No_Col*Col_Width)
Bar=" "+REPLICATE(BChar,Col_Width-1)

*------------------ Draw graph background.
CLEAR
@ 0,0 SAY Title

*------------------ Draw Y-axis.
?
BCount=0
Cntr=1
DO WHILE Cntr<21
   Left=SPACE(5)
IF (((Cntr-1)/4=INT((Cntr-1)/4)).OR.Cntr=1).AND.Cntr<20
         Left=STR(Hr-((BCount/5)*Hr),5)
         BCount=BCount+1
   ENDIF (cntr-1)
   ? Left+Line
   Cntr=Cntr+1
ENDDO (while <21 lines printed)
```

**FIGURE 24.17:** The BarGraph procedure can draw simple bar graphs on the screen and most printers. Figures 24.19 and 24.22 show sample graphs printed by the procedure.

```
*--- Draw X-axis and bottom line.
? STR(Lr,5)+XLine
? '  '+BLine

*------- Set up outer loop for drawing bars (OLoop).
ColPos=7
Div=(Hr-Lr)/10
OLoop=1
DO WHILE OLoop <= No_Col
   VName='Col'+LTRIM(STR(OLoop,2))
   @ 21,ColPos SAY ' '
   Col=2* &VName/Div
   Row=21
   *-------------- Draw bars on screen.
   DO WHILE Col > 0
      @ Row,ColPos SAY Bar
      Row=Row-1
      Col=Col-1
   ENDDO (while Col > 0)
   ColPos=ColPos+Col_Width

   OLoop=OLoop+1
ENDDO  (OLoop)

*---------------- Ask about printed copy of graph.
@ 23,0 SAY " "
WAIT "Press any key..."
CLEAR
WAIT 'Send graph to printer? (Y/N) ' TO YN

     *********************************************
     *  Display graph on printer, if requested   *
     *********************************************

*- If printed graph not requested, exit.
IF UPPER(YN) # 'Y'
   RETURN
ENDIF (upper yn)
CLEAR
? "Working..."
*------------------- Set up printer graphics characters.
XChar=CHR(45)
YChar=CHR(124)
BChar=CHR(35)

*------- Create X-axis, bar, and blanks for printed graph.
XLine=REPLICATE(XChar,(No_Col*Col_Width)-1)
Bar=REPLICATE(BChar,Col_Width-1)
Blanks=SPACE(Col_Width-1)

*------- Center title on printer graph.
CLEAR
SET PRINT ON
? Title
?
*--------- Start graph loops.
LCount=1
CCount=1
BCount=0
*--------- Build printed graph line (GLine).
DO WHILE LCount<21
   GLine = SPACE(5)+YChar
   IF (((LCount-1)/4=INT((LCount-1)/4)).OR.LCount=1).AND.LCount<20
        GLine=STR(Hr-((BCount/5)*Hr),5)+YChar
        BCount=BCount+1
   ENDIF (lcount)
```

**FIGURE 24.17:** The BarGraph procedure can draw simple bar graphs on the screen and most printers. Figures 24.19 and 24.22 show sample graphs printed by the procedure (continued).

```
      DO WHILE CCount<=No_Col
         VName='Col'+LTRIM(STR(CCount,2))
         GLine = IIF(LCount>20-(2*(&VName/Div)),GLine+Bar,GLine+Blanks)+' '
         CCount=CCount+1
      ENDDO (for ccount)
      *------- Print graph line (GLine) and proceed thru loop.
      ? GLine
      CCount=1
      LCount=LCount+1
   ENDDO    (lcount)
   c
   *------------- Print bottom titles and X-axis.
   ? STR(Lr,5)+" "+XLine
   ? ' '+BLine
   EJECT
   SET PRINT OFF
   RETURN
```

**FIGURE 24.17:** The BarGraph procedure can draw simple bar graphs on the screen and most printers. Figures 24.19 and 24.22 show sample graphs printed by the procedure (continued).

## USING THE BARGRAPH PROCEDURE

To use the BarGraph routine, you must first assign data to memory variables for plotting. These data can be calculated directly from data in a database, as shown in the Examples section below. The number values to be plotted must be stored in variables named Col1, Col2, Col3, etc. The titles at the bottom of each bar must be assigned as character data to variables named Title1, Title2, Title3, etc. The commands below show an example:

**Col1 = 20**
**Title1 = "1985"**
**Col2 = 55**
**Title2 = "1986"**
**Col3 = 67.54**
**Title3 = "1987"**
**Col4 = 100**
**Title4 = "1988"**

Once these variables are assigned values, you can call the BarGraph procedure using the following syntax:

**DO BarGraph WITH <graph title>,<number of columns>, ;**
**<column width>, <lowest Y-axis value>, ;**
**<highest Y-axis value>**

where <graph title> is the title printed on the graph, <number of columns> is the number of data items being plotted, <column width> is the width you want for each bar on the graph, <lowest Y-axis value> is the smallest number on the Y-axis, and <highest Y-axis value> is the highest value on the Y-axis.

## EXAMPLES

The command below places the title **Sample Graph** over the bar graph and plots 4 columns, each 15 characters wide, with 0 as the lowest Y-axis value and 100 as the highest Y-axis value:

**DO BarGraph WITH "Sample Graph",4,15,0,100**

Presumably, the variables Col1, Col2, Col3, Col4, and Title1, Title2, Title3, and Title4 have already been assigned data prior to calling the BarGraph routine.

Figure 24.18 shows a sample command file named EZGraf that accesses the BarGraph routine. Note that 12 columns of data, Col1–Col12, and 12 column

```
*************************************** EZGraf.prg

*-- Sample program to call the BarGraph routine.
SET TALK OFF

*-- Define graph data
*-- Must use variable names Col1, Col2, Col3,...
*-- Titles use Title1, Title2, Title3,... as shown:
Col1 = 5
Title1 = "Jan"
Col2 = 10
Title2 = "Feb"
Col3 = 15
Title3 = "Mar"
Col4 = 25
Title4 = "APr"
Col5 = 35
Title5 = "May"
Col6 = 40
Title6 = "Jun"
Col7 = 50
Title7 = "Jul"
Col8 = 60
Title8 = "Aug"
Col9 = 70
Title9 = "Sep"
Col10 = 80
Title10 = "Oct"
Col11 = 90
Title11 = "Nov"
Col12 = 100
Title12 = "Dec"

*-- Define graph parameters
GTitle = "Sample Graph"
Columns = 12
Col_Width = 6
Lowest = 0
Highest = 100
*-- Display the bar graph (with option for printed graph).
DO BarGraph WITH GTitle,Columns,Col_Width,Lowest,Highest

*-- All done.
RETURN
```

**FIGURE 24.18:** Sample command file for plotting a bar graph. This sample program uses data stored in 12 memory variables, named Col1 to Col12, to display the bar graph shown in Figure 24.19.

titles, Title1–Title12, are first assigned data as memory variables. The variables GTitle (graph title), Columns (number of columns), Col_Width (column width), Lowest (lowest Y-axis value), and Highest (highest Y-axis value) are also assigned values and are passed to the BarGraph routine through the DO...WITH command. Figure 24.19 shows how the resulting bar graph appears on the screen. Press any key after viewing the graph, and the screen will ask whether you want a printed copy of the graph. Answer Y if you want to print the bar graph.

More often than not, you will probably want to plot data directly from a database. That way, you can easily add, change, and delete data on the database and then replot the new data. When creating your own dBASE applications, you can include the BarGraph procedure as a menu selection, so users can experiment with different values in database fields and view the effects of those experiments simply by selecting an option from a menu.

Figure 24.20 shows a sample database named Sales2.dbf. Note that the Date column contains dates throughout the year 1986. Though the sample database contains only 16 records, there really is no limit to the size of the database you can use.

Figure 24.21 shows a sample command file named GrafTest, which calculates the total sales (Qty * U_Price) for each quarter from the Sales2 database. The

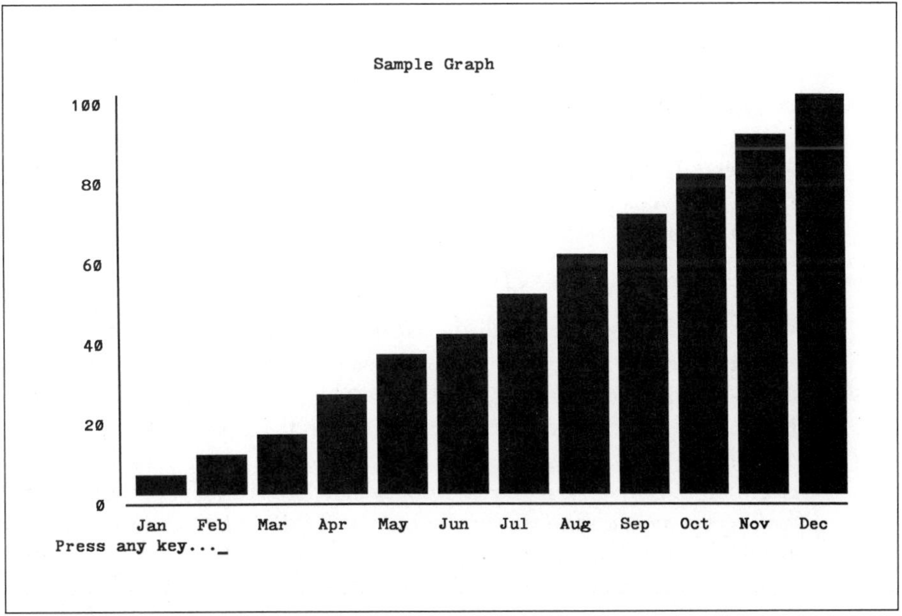


**FIGURE 24.19:** Sample bar graph created by the BarGraph procedure shown in Figure 24.17 and the EZGraf command file shown in Figure 24.18.

| Record# | PartNo | PartName | Qty | U_Price | Date |
|---|---|---|---|---|---|
| 1 | A-123 | MicroProcessor | 100 | 55.55 | 01/01/86 |
| 2 | B-222 | Laser Engine | 2 | 1234.56 | 02/01/86 |
| 3 | C-333 | Color Terminal | 5 | 400.00 | 02/01/86 |
| 4 | D-444 | Hard Disk | 25 | 500.00 | 03/02/86 |
| 5 | E-555 | Disk Controller | 50 | 200.00 | 04/15/86 |
| 6 | F-666 | Graphics Board | 20 | 249.00 | 05/15/86 |
| 7 | G-777 | Modem | 5 | 249.00 | 05/15/86 |
| 8 | H-888 | SemiDisk | 25 | 600.00 | 06/15/86 |
| 9 | A-123 | MicroProcessor | 10 | 55.55 | 07/30/86 |
| 10 | B-222 | Laser Engine | 8 | 1234.56 | 07/31/86 |
| 11 | A-123 | MicroProcessor | 10 | 55.00 | 08/30/86 |
| 12 | E-555 | Disk Controller | 25 | 200.00 | 09/01/86 |
| 13 | E-555 | Disk Controller | 100 | 180.00 | 10/01/86 |
| 14 | F-666 | Graphics Board | 5 | 200.00 | 11/01/86 |
| 15 | A-123 | MicroProcessor | 20 | 50.00 | 11/15/86 |
| 16 | H-888 | SemiDisk | 15 | 600.00 | 12/15/86 |

**FIGURE 24.20:** Sample Sales2 database used by the GrafTest and GTest2 command files (Figures 24.21 and 24.23) to calculate and display data on bar graphs.

SUM commands used to calculate the data include FOR commands that limit each sum to a range of data reflecting each quarter in the year. These calculated values are stored in the variables Col1 through Col4. The Title1 through Title4 variables are also assigned data in the program.

Because it is not possible to know in advance the upper range for the Y-axis on the graph when plotting data based on calculations, the GrafTest program calculates the upper Y-axis value through a series of MAX functions and some rounding. The calculated highest Y-axis value is stored in a memory variable named YTop.

The last line of the program, shown below, plots the bar graph with the title **Quarterly Data from Sales**, using four columns of 15 characters each with 0 as the lowest Y-axis value and the current contents of the YTop variable as the highest Y-axis value:

**DO BarGraph WITH "Quarterly Data from Sales",4,15,0,YTop**

Figure 24.22 shows the resulting bar graph as it appears on the screen.

In the interest of maximizing both speed and flexibility, the BarGraph program has no built-in error-trapping capabilities, so it is up to you to ensure that reasonable data is passed to the program. For example, if the highest value to be plotted on a graph is 1234 and the specified highest value on the Y-axis is 1000, the program will likely bomb. Similarly, if you attempt to plot 12 columns, each 10 characters wide, you'll get a mess on the screen, because 12 × 10 is 120 and the screen is only 80 characters wide. You must take into consideration that the numbers to the left of the Y-axis take up 5 characters of space, and the axis itself takes up a column. Therefore, the product of the number of columns and the column width should not exceed 72. The column titles must be sized accordingly, too.

```
************************************ GrafTest.prg
*-- Test BarGraph procedure using Sales database.
CLEAR
? "Working..."
SET TALK OFF

*--- Sample.dbf includes the numeric fields Qty and U_Price.
USE Sales2

*--- Sum data for plotting (must use subscripted names
*--- such as Col1, Col2... Title1, Title2...)

*--- Store first quarter total in Col1 variable.
SUM (Qty*U_Price) FOR Month(Date) <= 3 TO Col1
Title1 = "1st Quarter"

*--- Store second quarter total in Col2 variable.
SUM (Qty*U_Price) FOR Month(Date) >= 4 .AND. MONTH(Date) <= 6 TO Col2
Title2 = "2nd Quarter"

*--- Store third quarter total in Col3 variable.
SUM (Qty*U_Price) FOR Month(Date) >= 7 .AND. MONTH(Date) <= 9 TO Col3
Title3 = "3rd Quarter"

*--- Store fourth quarter total in Col4 variable.
SUM (Qty*U_Price) FOR Month(Date) > 9 TO Col4
Title4 = "4th Quarter"

*--- Determine highest value for highest Y-axis value (YTop).
YTop = 100
YTop = MAX(Col1,YTop)
YTop = MAX(Col2,YTop)
YTop = MAX(Col3,YTop)
YTop = MAX(Col4,YTop)

*---- Round highest Y-axis value upwardly.
Digits = LEN(LTRIM(STR(YTop,12,0)))
Zeroes = REPLICATE("0",Digits-3)
Roundup = YTop + VAL("5"+Zeroes)
YTop = ROUND(Roundup,-1*(Digits-2))
*----- Turn off status bar and set up colors.
SET STATUS OFF
IF ISCOLOR()
   SET COLOR TO W+/B+,GR+/N,R+
ENDIF (iscolor)
CLEAR

*-------------- Send parameters to BarGraph routine.

DO BarGraph WITH "Quarterly Data from Sales",4,15,0,YTop

*-------------- All done.
RETURN
```

**FIGURE 24.21:** The GrafTest program calculates and plots data from the sample Sales2 database. The program calculates the total sales (Qty * U_Price) for each quarter and displays these data on a bar graph using the BarGraph procedure. The highest value on the Y-axis range is calculated and stored in a variable named YTop.

If you attempt to plot very large numbers, your data may overflow the 5-digit maximum for numbers along the Y-axis. You can rectify this situation by dividing all data to be plotted by some constant. Figure 24.23 shows a modified version of the GrafTest program, which divides each of the values to be plotted

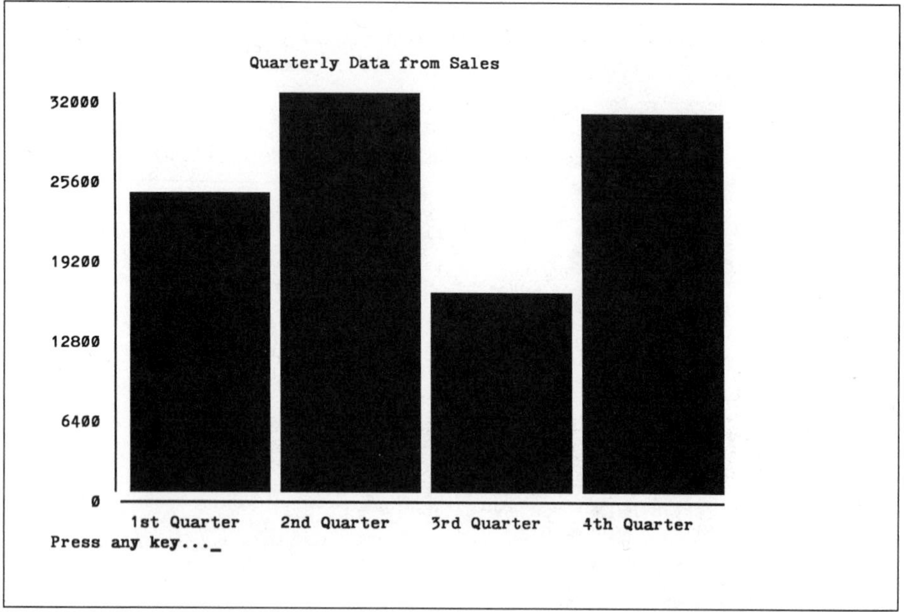


**FIGURE 24.22:** Sample graph printed by the GrafTest program shown in Figure 24.21. The data plotted are total quarterly sales from the Sales2 database shown in Figure 24.20. The BarGraph procedure was called to print the graph.

(Col1–Col4) by 100 prior to calculating the highest range on the graph and printing the graph.

Dividing data to be plotted might make a better-looking graph anyway, because the data along the Y-axis will not be so "literal." Because dBASE has no high-resolution capability, plotted data are rounded to the nearest row. So rounding will probably not have an effect on the appearance of the graph.

## Customizing the BarGraph Procedure

The BarGraph procedure can be customized to accommodate various screens and printers. The routine below assigns ASCII codes to graphics characters drawn on the screen. XChar is the character used to draw the X-axis (bottom line), YChar is the character used to draw the Y-axis, and BChar is the character used to draw the bar:

```
* - - - - Assign graphics characters for screen.
XChar = CHR(196)
YChar = CHR(179)
BChar = CHR(219)
```

```
************************************ GTest2.prg
*-- Test BarGraph procedure using Sales database.
CLEAR
? "Working..."
SET TALK OFF

*--- Sample.dbf includes the numeric fields Qty and U_Price.
USE Sales2

*--- Sum data for plotting (must use subscripted names
*--- such as Col1, Col2... Title1, Title2...)

*--- Store first quarter total in Col1 variable.
SUM (Qty*U_Price) FOR Month(Date) <= 3 TO Col1
Title1 = "1st Quarter"
Col1 = Col1/100

*--- Store second quarter total in Col2 variable.
SUM (Qty*U_Price) FOR Month(Date) >= 4 .AND. MONTH(Date) <= 6 TO Col2
Title2 = "2nd Quarter"
Col2 = Col2 / 100

*--- Store third quarter total in Col3 variable.
SUM (Qty*U_Price) FOR Month(Date) >= 7 .AND. MONTH(Date) <= 9 TO Col3
Title3 = "3rd Quarter"
Col3 = Col3/100

*--- Store fourth quarter total in Col4 variable.
SUM (Qty*U_Price) FOR Month(Date) > 9 TO Col4
Title4 = "4th Quarter"
Col4 = Col4/100

*--- Determine highest value for highest Y-axis value (YTop).
YTop = 100
YTop = MAX(Col1,YTop)
YTop = MAX(Col2,YTop)
YTop = MAX(Col3,YTop)
YTop = MAX(Col4,YTop)

*---- Round highest Y-axis value upwardly.
Digits = LEN(LTRIM(STR(YTop,12,0)))
Zeroes = REPLICATE("0",Digits-3)
Roundup = YTop + VAL("5"+Zeroes)
YTop = ROUND(Roundup,-1*(Digits-2))

*----- Turn off status bar and set up colors.
SET STATUS OFF
IF ISCOLOR()
   SET COLOR TO W+/B+,GR+/N,R+
ENDIF (iscolor)
CLEAR

*-------------- Send parameters to BarGraph routine.
DO BarGraph WITH "Quarterly Data from Sales",4,15,0,YTop

*-------------- All done.
RETURN
```

**FIGURE 24.23:** Modified version of the GrafTest program, which divides all of the values to be plotted by 100 to decrease the size of the numbers plotted to the left of the Y-axis.

You may have to modify these values for a better-looking bar graph on your particular screen.

The routine below, embedded in the middle of the BarGraph program, assigns ASCII characters for use on the printed copy of the graph:

```
* - - - - - - - - - - Set up printer graphics characters.
XChar = CHR(45)
YChar = CHR(124)
BChar = CHR(35)
```

These may have to be changed for a better-looking printed graph on your particular printer.

## How BarGraph Processes Data

One of the tricks when developing a procedure like BarGraph is finding a way to pass an unknown number of parameters to the procedure. As you may recall, the PARAMETERS statement requires a fixed number of parameters. But BarGraph needs to be flexible enough to handle bar graphs with different numbers of parameters (i.e., a graph with any number of columns).

The BarGraph procedure uses pseudo arrays to handle an unknown number of data elements. The parameter passed as No_Col tells the procedure how many bars of data are to be displayed. Because the data to be displayed are already stored in pseudo arrays (e.g., Col1, Col2, Col 3,... and Title1, Title2, Title 3,...), BarGraph can use loops to process as many items of data as are required.

For example, the first routine to pad titles to the proper width for each column uses a DO WHILE loop that repeats as long as the Counter variable is between 1 and the number of columns in the graph (No_Col), as shown below:

```
* - - - - - - - - - - Pad titles and create bottom line.
Counter = 1
TWidth = Col_Width - 2
BLine = SPACE(6)
DO WHILE Counter < = No_Col
```

Next, the variable Sub is assigned the character equivalent of the number Counter, with leading blanks removed:

```
Sub = LTRIM(STR(Counter,2))
```

Within the loop, which repeats once for each column in the graph, the routine pads (or truncates) each title to the appropriate width for the column, as shown below:

```
Title&Sub = SUBSTR(Title&Sub,1,TWidth) + ;
            SPACE(TWidth - LEN(Title&Sub))
```

**BLine = BLine + Title&Sub + SPACE(2)**
**Counter = Counter + 1**
**ENDDO (Counter)**

The Sub variable is added to the word Title as a macro. Therefore, as Counter increases so does Sub, and with each pass through the loop a different title is acted upon (Title1, Title2, Title3, etc.).

The **DO WHILE <variable> < = No_Col** loop is used in several places throughout the BarGraph procedure to process all of the data that has been defined for display on the graph.

# STRING-MANIPULATION PROCEDURES

The string-manipulation procedures operate on character data. The Center procedure automatically centers a line of text. The WordWrap procedure can word-wrap character strings up to 254 characters long, within margins you specify. It will break lines of text only between words. The proper case procedures convert text to proper case, with either only the first letter capitalized or the first letter in each word capitalized. The multiple-column-report procedure will display a report with data in a "telephone-directory" format, where the fields are alphabetized on multiple columns on each page.

## Automatic Centering

The Center procedure automatically centers a string of characters on the screen or printer; it is shown in Figure 24.24.

### USING THE CENTER PROCEDURE

The procedure expects two parameters: Title (the string to be centered) and RM (right margin). The general syntax for calling the procedure is

**DO Center WITH <string>,<right margin>**

```
*----------- Center procedure centers any string.
PROCEDURE Center
PARAMETERS Title,RM
  Pad = SPACE((RM/2)-(LEN(TRIM(Title))/2))
  ? Pad + TRIM(Title)
RETURN
```

**FIGURE 24.24:** The Center procedure centers any character string on the screen or printer. The general calling syntax for the procedure is **DO Center WITH <string>,<right margin>**.

where <string> is the character string to be centered and <right margin> is the right margin to be used in calculating where to center the string.

Immediately after the procedure is called, the character string will be displayed, centered on the screen or printer within the right margin you specify. (Precede the procedure call with SET PRINT ON to send the string to the printer.) The string is always printed on the current screen or printer row.

### EXAMPLES

To center the words **Hello There** on an 80-column screen, you would enter the command

**DO Center WITH "Hello There",80**

Either parameter or both can be variables, as in the commands below:

**Title = "Accounts Receivable Aging Report"**
**Margin = 80**
**DO Center WITH Title, Margin**

## Word Wrapping

The WordWrap procedure can format any character string up to 254 characters long within margins you specify. (WordWrap does not work with memo fields.) To fit the long string within the margins, WordWrap breaks the string at spaces between words. Figure 24.25 shows the WordWrap procedure.

### USING THE WORDWRAP PROCEDURE

The WordWrap procedure is called with the general syntax

**DO WordWrap WITH <string>,<left margin>,<right margin>;**
**<lines>**

where <string> is the name of the memory variable or field containing the long character string to be formatted, <left margin> and <right margin> are the left and right margins to use when wrapping the string, and <lines> is a variable that keeps track of the number of lines printed. Be sure SET TALK is off before calling the procedure.

### EXAMPLES

Suppose you have a field named Abstract in a database that you want to display, word-wrapped, on the screen or printer with a left margin of 5 and a right margin of 50. You would simply call the WordWrap procedure with the

```
************************ Word-wrap long strings.
PROCEDURE WordWrap
PARAMETERS String, Left, Right, LF
  PRIVATE Temp
  Temp = String
  Length = LEN(TRIM(Temp))
  *-------------------- Set up loop through string.
  DO WHILE Length > Right-Left
     Place = Right-Left

     *-- Find blank nearest right margin (Place).
     DO WHILE SUBSTR(Temp,Place,1) # " "
        Place = Place - 1
     ENDDO (until blank space found)

     *-- Print Portion, and assign rest to Temp.
     ? SPACE(Left)+LTRIM(LEFT(Temp,Place-1))
     Temp = SUBSTR(Temp,Place=1,Length-Place)
     Length = LEN(TRIM(Temp))
     LF = LF + 1
  ENDDO      (while length > margin)
  *------ Print remainder of Temp, then return.
  ? SPACE(Left) + LTRIM(Temp)
  LF = LF + 1
RETURN
```

**FIGURE 24.25:** The WordWrap procedure can word-wrap any character string up to 254 characters long within the margins specified. The procedure also keeps track of the number of lines printed in a variable named LF.

appropriate parameters, as below:

**SET TALK OFF**
**DO WordWrap WITH Abstract,5,50,0**

When the procedure is done, the character string in Abstract will be neatly displayed on the screen, with a left margin of 5 spaces and a right margin of 50.

A practical application of the WordWrap procedure would be printed reports that display a long character field. Figure 24.26 shows the structure of a hypothetical database with a long field named Abstract that consists of 250 characters.

Figure 24.27 shows a sample command file named TestWrap that prints a formatted report from the Library database. The sample command file also keeps track of the number of lines printed on each page, using the variable LF. This variable is passed to the WordWrap procedure in the **DO WordWrap WITH Abstract,8,68,LF** command. Passing LF to the WordWrap procedure in this fashion ensures that lines printed during the word-wrap are also included in this line counter.

The TestWrap program also includes a routine for ejecting the page when 55 or more lines have been printed (starting at the comment * – – **If 55 or more lines printed…**). This routine ensures even page breaks with a title printed at the top of each page.

Figure 24.28 shows two sample records printed from the Library database using the TestWrap command file. The general techniques used in TestWrap can easily be used to print long fields from any database.

```
Structure for database: Library.dbf

Field  Field Name  Type       Width     Dec

    1  Author      Character     30
    2  Title       Character     60
    3  pub         Character     40
    4  Location    Character     40
    5  Pages       Character     10
    6  Abstract    Character    250
** Total **                     430
```

**FIGURE 24.26:** The structure of a database named Library, which contains a character field named Abstract that is 250 characters long. The program in Figure 24.27 uses this database and the WordWrap procedure to print a report with the long abstracts neatly displayed on the screen.

```
**************************************** TestWrap.prg
*- Test WordWrap procedure with Library data.
SET TALK OFF
*--- Open database
USE Library

*-- Print heading.
SET PRINT ON
? "                         Reference Listing"
?
*-- Start LineFeed Counter.
LF = 2

*-- Loop through database.
GO TOP
DO WHILE .NOT. EOF()
   ? "Author:     ",Author
   ? "Title :     ",Title

   ? "Publisher: ",TRIM(Pub)+", "+Location
   ?
   ? "Abstract:  "
   *--- Increment LineFeed counter (LF).
   LF = LF + 5
   *--- Print abstract with margins of 10 and 68.
   DO WordWrap WITH Abstract,8,68,LF
   ?
   LF = LF + 1

   *----- If 55 or more lines printed, start on
   *----- new page, print heading, and reset LF.
   IF LF >= 55
      EJECT
      ? "                       Reference Listing"
      ?
      LF = 2
   ENDIF
   *---- Skip to next record and continue loop.
   SKIP

ENDDO
SET PRINT OFF
EJECT
CLOSE PROCEDURE
RETURN
```

**FIGURE 24.27:** A sample program that uses the WordWrap procedure to wrap the long Abstract field in the Library database shown in Figure 24.26. Figure 24.28 shows a couple of records displayed by this program.

```
                        Reference Listing

Author:      Simpson, Alan
Title :      Advanced Techniques in dBASE III PLUS
Publisher:   SYBEX, Alameda, CA

Abstract:
        This book presents numerous techniques for designing and
        developing custom systems written in dBASE III PLUS.
        Includes mailing list, inventory, and accounts receivable
        systems.  Also discusses maximizing speed of custom systems.

Author:      Simpson, Alan
Title :      Understanding dBASE III PLUS
Publisher:   SYBEX, Alameda, CA

Abstract:
        Written for the novice computer user, this book discusses
        general techniques for creating, sorting, searching,
        formatting, and editing data through dBASE III PLUS.
        Provides an introduction to developing custom systems with
        command files.
```

**FIGURE 24.28:** Sample output from the TestWrap program shown in Figure 24.27. The WordWrap procedure, shown in Figure 24.25, was used to format the long Abstract field on the report.

# Proper Case in Character Strings

The two procedures in this section can convert any character strings to proper case. The Proper procedure converts the first letter to uppercase and all following letters to lowercase. For example, if a variable named Test1 contains the character string **this WaS a BIt of a MeSs**, the command **DO Proper WITH Test1** converts the contents of the Test1 variable to **This was a bit of a mess**.

The FullProp procedure converts the first letter of each word to uppercase and all others to lowercase. For example, if the variable Test2 contains **DR. ADAM P. JONES**, the command **DO FullProp WITH Test2** converts the contents of the Test2 variable to **Dr. Adam P. Jones**. Figure 24.29 shows both the Proper and FullProp procedures.

## USING THE PROPER AND FULLPROP PROCEDURES

The Proper and FullProp procedures use similar calling syntaxes:

**DO Proper WITH <character>**
**DO FullProp WITH <character>**

where <character> is the name of the variable containing the character string to perform the operation on.

## EXAMPLES

Before you can call the Proper or FullProp procedures, you must open the ProProcs procedure file:

**SET PROCEDURE TO ProProcs**

The commands below show the technique for converting a character string stored in a variable named Test1 to proper case (using the Proper procedure):

**Test1 = "THIS WAS ALL UPPERCASE"**
**DO Proper WITH Test1**
**? Test1**
**This was all uppercase**

The commands below demonstrate the technique for converting the character string stored in a variable named Test2 to proper case using the FullProp procedure:

**Test2 = "this was all lowercase"**
**DO FullProp WITH Test2**
**? Test2**
**This Was All Lowercase**

```
************************************* ProProcs.prg
******************** Capitalize first letter only.
PROCEDURE Proper
PARAMETERS String
      String = UPPER(LEFT(String,1)) + ;
      LOWER(RIGHT(String,LEN(String)-1))
RETURN

********** Capitalize first letter of every word.
PROCEDURE FullProp
PARAMETERS String
String = UPPER(LEFT(String,1)) + ;
 LOWER(RIGHT(String,LEN(String)-1))
BSearch = 1
CapSpot = 1
DO WHILE BSearch > 0
   BSearch = AT(" ",SUBSTR(String,CapSpot,;
   LEN(TRIM(String))-CapSpot))

   IF BSearch > 0
      CapSpot = BSearch + CapSpot
      String = STUFF(String,CapSpot,1,;
      UPPER(SUBSTR(String,CapSpot,1)))
   ENDIF
ENDDO (bsearch)
RETURN
```

**FIGURE 24.29:** The Proper and FullProp procedures used for converting character strings to proper case. Both procedures are stored in a single procedure file named ProProcs.prg.

Note that the data being converted must be stored in a memory variable. If the data are stored in a field, they must be stored in a memory variable before calling the procedure. In the example below, the contents of the fields named FName and LName are stored in a variable named FullName, then passed to the FullProp procedure:

```
FullName = TRIM(FName) + " " + LName
DO FullProp WITH FullName
```

The Proper and FullProp procedures do not create new variables. Instead, the converted string is stored in the same variable that was used to pass the character string. Hence, after entering the above commands, the converted character string is stored in the variable named FullName. To view the converted string, use a ? or @ command, as below:

```
? FullName
@ 10,10 SAY FullName
```

## Multiple-Column Reports

The ColRept procedure discussed here can print data in three or more columns on each page (as in a phone book). In the example shown in Figure 24.30, page 1 lists last names beginning with the letters A through O, and page 2 lists last names beginning with P through Z.

The ColRept. procedure, shown in Figure 24.31, can get data from any dBASE database into multiple-column format. The program allows you to

```
-------------------------------------------

Adams          Franklin       Kellerman
Baker          Gomer          Lambert
Carlson        Harris         Morris
Davis          Iglew          Nautach
Edwards        Johnson        Orasco

          Page number:  1

-------------------------------------------

Peterson       Trible         Xavier
Quincy         Ungulat        Young
Rasputin       Vista          Zeppo
Schumack       Walters

          Page number:  2
```

**FIGURE 24.30:** Basic format of a report printed by the ColRept procedure shown in Figure 24.31. Note that the alphabetical listing resembles a telephone directory, with names beginning with the letters A through O alphabetized on page 1, and names beginning with letters P through Z appearing on page 2. The alphabetization was achieved by using an index file.

```
****************************************** ColRept.prg
* Prints data in alphabetical order divided into
* columns on a page.  Assumes database file is
* open and indexed if necessary.

PROCEDURE ColRept
PARAMETERS Cols,Rows,ColWidth,FieldNam

*--------- Make a copy of the database to be printed.
SET SAFETY OFF
GO TOP
COPY TO Temp

*--------- Pad for an even number of records.
USE Temp
DO WHILE MOD(RECCOUNT(),Cols) # 0
   APPEND BLANK
ENDDO
GO TOP

*--------- Page counter and number of items
*---------printed are initialized below.
PgCount = 1
Printed = 0

*--------- Outermost loop counts records printed.
SET PRINT ON
DO WHILE Printed < RECCOUNT()
   OnThisPage = MIN(Rows*Cols,RECCOUNT()-Printed)
   Rows = MIN(Rows,(OnThisPage/Cols))
   ThisRow = 1
   *-------- Middle loop controls rows.
   DO WHILE ThisRow <= Rows .AND. Printed <= RECCOUNT()
      ThisCol = 1
      ? LEFT(&FieldNam,ColWidth)+ ;
        SPACE(MAX(0,ColWidth-LEN(&FieldNam)))
      Printed = Printed + 1
      *------- Inner loop controls columns.
      DO WHILE ThisCol < Cols .AND. Printed <= RECCOUNT()
         SKIP Rows
         ?? LEFT(&FieldNam,ColWidth)+ ;
            SPACE(MAX(0,ColWidth-LEN(&FieldNam)))
         ThisCol = ThisCol + 1
         Printed = Printed + 1
      ENDDO (columns)
      ThisRow = ThisRow + 1
      SKIP (((Cols-1)*Rows)-1) * -1
   ENDDO (rows)
   ?
   ?  "Page number: ",PgCount
   EJECT
   PgCount = PgCount + 1
   SKIP ((Cols-1)*Rows)
ENDDO (records)
*--------------------- Done printing report.

SET PRINT OFF
CLOSE DATABASES
ERASE Temp.dbf
RETURN
```

**FIGURE 24.31:** The ColRept procedure lets you display data from one or more fields in a multiple-column report like the one shown in Figure 24.30. The procedure lets you specify the number of columns and rows on each page, the width of each column, and the contents of each column.

define the number of columns on each page, the number of rows on each page, and the width of each column.

## USING THE COLREPT PROCEDURE

The general syntax for calling the ColRept procedure is

**DO ColRept WITH <columns>,<rows>,<column width>;**
**<contents>**

where <columns> is the number of columns to print on the page, <rows> is the number of lines per page, <column width> is the width of each column, and <contents> is the name of the field or field expression defining the contents of each column.

## EXAMPLES

Assume you have a database named NameList that has a field called LName containing last names. You want the names displayed in three columns, with 50 lines (rows) per page and a width of 20 characters per column.

Your first step is to ensure that the names are in alphabetical order. If an index file specifying this order does not exist, you can create one using the commands

```
USE NameList
INDEX ON LName TO NameList
```

When the sort order is set up, you just run the ColRept procedure with the appropriate parameters, as shown below:

```
DO ColRept WITH 3,50,20,"LName"
```

The ColRept program takes over from there and prints the report you want. Note that in the WITH portion of the command, 3 is the number of columns per page, 50 is the number of lines per page, 20 is the width of each column, and LName is the name of the field being printed on the report.

You can combine two or more fields in a single column of the report. For example, suppose the NameList database contains the fields LName and FName. To ensure a proper sort order, the database is indexed with the command

```
INDEX ON LName + FName TO NameList
```

To print a two-column report with 55 lines per page and 35 characters per column that displays the LName and FName fields with a space between the names, call the ColPrint procedure with the command

```
DO ColRept WITH 2,55,35,"TRIM(LName) + ' ' + FName"
```

You can also use numeric data in the report if you convert the numbers to character strings using the dBASE STR function. The command below prints the fields named LName and Number on a three-column report, with 45 lines per page and a width of 20 characters per column:

**DO ColRept WITH 3,45,20,"LName + STR(Number,3,2)"**

Similarly, you can include dates in the report as long as you use the DTOC function to convert date data to the character data type, as in the command

**DO ColRept WITH 2,55,35,"DTOC(Date) + ' ' + LName"**

## TRANSLATION PROCEDURES

The date translation procedure presented here can convert dates in mm/dd/yy format to the more formal December 31, 1987 format. The number translation procedure can convert a number, such as 123.45, to English words, such as ONE HUNDRED TWENTY THREE AND 45/100. This procedure is useful for writing checks.

Chapter 17, "dBASE Functions," includes some additional techniques for converting the dBASE TIME( ) function to seconds and for calculating elapsed time between two events. See the MOD( ) and TIME( ) functions in that chapter for examples.

### Translating Dates to English

The TransDat procedure shown in Figure 24.32 translates dBASE III date data from the mm/dd/yy format to English (e.g., December 31, 1987). TransDat uses the parameter PDate and the public variable Eng_Date.

```
********************** Translate date to English.
*------- Make Eng_Date public in calling program.
PROCEDURE TransDat
PARAMETERS PDate
  PDay = STR(DAY(PDate),IIF(DAY(PDate)<10,1,2))
  Eng_Date = CMONTH(PDate) + " " + PDay + ", " ;
    + STR(YEAR(PDate),4)
RETURN
```

**FIGURE 24.32:** The TransDat procedure converts dates in dBASE mm/dd/yy format to the more formal December 31, 1987 format. The procedure stores the converted date in a public variable named Eng_Date.

### USING THE TRANSDAT PROCEDURE

The TransDat procedure requires that you predefine a public memory variable named Eng_Date. The general syntax for calling the TransDat procedure is

**DO TransDat WITH <date>**

where <date> is any date item or the name of a variable containing a date item of the dBASE date data type.

### EXAMPLES

To convert and display the dBASE system date in the more formal English format, you could use the commands below:

```
PUBLIC Eng_Date
DO TransDat WITH DATE( )
? Eng_Date
```

You can also convert a character string to the date format within the procedure call, as below:

```
DO TransDat WITH CTOD("12/31/87")
```

Optionally, you can store the data in a variable and then pass the variable name, as below:

```
T_Date = CTOD("12/31/87")
DO TransDat WITH T_Date
```

## Translating Numbers to Words

The TransNum procedure translates a dollar amount (for example, 1234.76) to English (for example, ONE THOUSAND TWO HUNDRED THIRTY FOUR AND 76/100), which is useful when writing a program that prints checks. TransNum can translate any number up to 999,999.99 to its proper English equivalent.

First, the procedure will need to have access to all of the unique English equivalents for numbers. For convenience, you can store these on a memory file named English.mem. To create the English.mem file, type in the English.prg command file shown in Figure 24.33. Then run the program, and it will create the English.mem memory file for you.

After running the English.prg command file, check to make sure it ran correctly by typing in the command **RESTORE FROM English**. Then type **DISPLAY MEMORY**. You should see all of the English words stored to memory variables. Each memory variable name begins with the letter U and ends with

```
**************************************** English.prg
* Sets up memory file for storing English equivalents.

CLEAR
? "Creating English.mem memory file..."
?
SET TALK ON
CLEAR MEMORY

U = " "
U1 = "ONE"
U2 = "TWO"
U3 = "THREE"
U4 = "FOUR"
U5 = "FIVE"
U6 = "SIX"
U7 = "SEVEN"
U8 = "EIGHT"
U9 = "NINE"
U10 = "TEN"
U11 = "ELEVEN"
U12 = "TWELVE"
U13 = "THIRTEEN"
U14 = "FOURTEEN"
U15 = "FIFTEEN"
U16 = "SIXTEEN"
U17 = "SEVENTEEN"
U18 = "EIGHTEEN"
U19 = "NINETEEN"
U20 = "TWENTY"
U30 = "THIRTY"
U40 = "FORTY"
U50 = "FIFTY"
U60 = "SIXTY"
U70 = "SEVENTY"
U80 = "EIGHTY"
U90 = "NINETY"

*----- Save all variables to English.mem file.
SAVE TO English
CLEAR
?
?
? "English.mem now has English words for numbers."
SET TALK OFF
```

**FIGURE 24.33:** The English.prg command file, used to create memory variables containing all the unique names for numbers in English. The English.mem memory file that this program creates is used by the TransNum procedure to translate numbers to words.

the number that it represents (for example, U20 is "Twenty", U9 is "Nine", and so forth). Figure 24.34 shows the results of the commands **RESTORE FROM English** and **DISPLAY MEMORY**.

Creating these English variables solves several problems right away. For example, to see the English equivalent for the number eleven, you merely need to enter the command **? U11,** and dBASE displays **ELEVEN**. To see the English equivalent for 99, enter the command **? U90,U9** and dBASE displays **NINETY NINE**.

Of course, you can't store English equivalents for every possible number, but you can build long English translations from the elements in the memory variables. The TransNum procedure, shown in Figure 24.35, performs just this task.

```
U           pub   C   " "
U1          pub   C   "ONE"
U2          pub   C   "TWO"
U3          pub   C   "THREE"
U4          pub   C   "FOUR"
U5          pub   C   "FIVE"
U6          pub   C   "SIX"
U7          pub   C   "SEVEN"
U8          pub   C   "EIGHT"
U9          pub   C   "NINE"
U10         pub   C   "TEN"
U11         pub   C   "ELEVEN"
U12         pub   C   "TWELVE"
U13         pub   C   "THIRTEEN"
U14         pub   C   "FOURTEEN"
U15         pub   C   "FIFTEEN"
U16         pub   C   "SIXTEEN"
U17         pub   C   "SEVENTEEN"
U18         pub   C   "EIGHTEEN"
U19         pub   C   "NINETEEN"
U20         pub   C   "TWENTY"
U30         pub   C   "THIRTY"
U40         pub   C   "FORTY"
U50         pub   C   "FIFTY"
U60         pub   C   "SIXTY"
U70         pub   C   "SEVENTY"
U80         pub   C   "EIGHTY"
U90         pub   C   "NINETY"
   28 variables defined,       209 bytes used
  228 variables available,    5791 bytes available
```

**FIGURE 24.34:** Memory variables restored from English.mem. The memory variables were created and saved to disk by the English.prg command file shown in Figure 24.33.

```
*************************************** TransNum.prg
* Make Eng_Num variable public in calling program.
* Must have access to English.mem variables.

PROCEDURE Transnum
PARAMETERS Amount

*---------- Set up memory variables.
Counter = 1
Start = 1
String = STR(Amount,9,2)
Eng_Num = " "

*-------- Loop through thousands and hundreds.
DO WHILE Counter < 3

   *------ Split out hundreds, tens, and ones.
   Chunk = SUBSTR(String,Start,3)
   Hun = SUBSTR(Chunk,1,1)

   Ten = SUBSTR(Chunk,2,2)
   One = SUBSTR(Chunk,3,1)
```

**FIGURE 24.35:** The TransNum procedure converts numbers such as 1234.56 to words such as ONE THOUSAND TWO HUNDRED THIRTY FOUR AND 56/100. It uses the English.mem memory file, shown in Figure 24.34, to aid in the translation.

```
      *------ Handle hundreds portion.
      IF VAL(Chunk) > 99
         Eng_Num = Eng_Num + U&Hun + ' HUNDRED '
      ENDIF (chunk > 99)

      *------ Handle second two digits.
      T = VAL(Ten)
      IF T > 0

         DO CASE
            *-- Handle even tens and teens.
            CASE (INT(T/10.0)=T/10.0).OR. ;
                 (T>9.AND.T<20)
                 Eng_Num = Eng_Num + U&Ten

            *-- Handle greater than 10, but not evenly divisible.
            CASE T > 9 .AND. (INT(T/10.0)#T/10.0)
                 Ten = SUBSTR(Ten,1,1) +'0'
                 Eng_Num = Eng_Num + U&Ten+' '+U&One

            *-- Handle less than 10.
            CASE T < 10
                 Eng_Num = Eng_Num + U&One

         ENDCASE
      ENDIF (T > 0)

      *-- Add "Thousand" if necessary.
      IF Amount > 999.99 .AND. Counter = 1
         Eng_Num = Eng_Num +' THOUSAND '
      ENDIF (need to add "thousand")

      *-- Prepare for pass through hundreds.
      Start = 4
      Counter = Counter + 1

   ENDDO (while counter < 3)

   *----- Tack on cents.
   IF INT(Amount) > 0
      Eng_Num = Eng_Num + " AND "
   ENDIF

   Eng_Num = Eng_Num + SUBSTR(String,8,2)+"/100"

   *-------- End procedure.
   RETURN
```

**FIGURE 24.35:** The TransNum procedure converts numbers such as 1234.56 to words such as ONE THOUSAND TWO HUNDRED THIRTY FOUR AND 56/100. It uses the English.mem memory file, shown in Figure 24.34, to aid in the translation (continued).

## USING THE TRANSNUM PROCEDURE

Once the TransNum.prg and English.mem files are created, you need to perform three steps to use the procedure:

1. Call in the English memory variables.
2. Declare the Eng_Num variable as public.

3. Call the procedure with the general syntax

   **DO TransNum WITH <number>**

   where <number> is the number, or the name of a variable containing the number, to be converted to English.

**EXAMPLES**

The commands below load the English.mem memory variables, declare the public variable Eng_Num, call the TransNum procedure with the number 345.67, and then display the result:

```
RESTORE FROM English ADDITIVE
PUBLIC Eng_Num
DO TransNum WITH 12345.67
? Eng_Num
    THREE HUNDRED FORTY FIVE AND 67/100
```

If you prefer, you can pass the number to be translated as a variable. For example, the commands below assign a number to the variable X, then translate and display the number:

```
STORE 555.55 TO X
DO TransNum WITH X
? Eng_Num
    FIVE HUNDRED FIFTY FIVE AND 55/100
```

# LIGHT-BAR MENUS

As a programmer, you are probably familiar with the pull-down menus used in dBASE commands such as MODIFY REPORT and MODIFY LABEL. These menus display a highlight, or light-bar, that you can move up and down through menu items with the ↑ and ↓ arrows. To select a menu item, you move the highlight to that menu item and press the Return key.

## The LiteBar Procedure

The LiteBar procedure discussed in this section lets you add light-bar menus to your applications. The menu created allows the user to select menu items either by highlighting and pressing Return or by entering the menu option number. Figure 24.36 displays a sample light-bar menu created by the LiteBar procedure. The LiteBar procedure is stored in a procedure file named Menu.prg, which is shown in Figure 24.37.

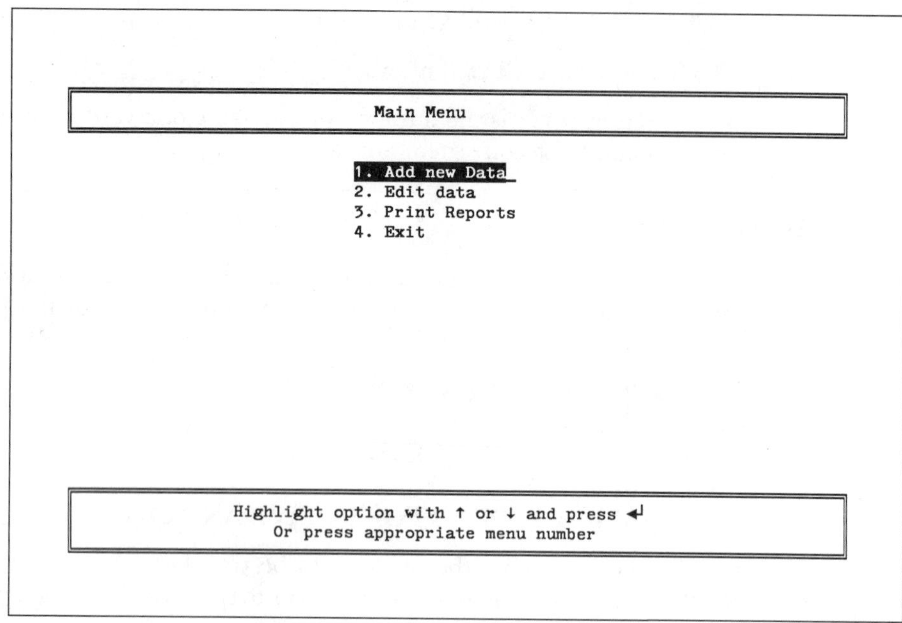


**FIGURE 24.36:** A sample light-bar menu displayed by the LiteBar procedure in Figure 24.37. The user can select a menu option by moving the highlight with the ↑ or ↓ keys and pressing Return when the menu item is highlighted. The user may also just type in the number to the left of the menu item.

## USING THE LITEBAR PROCEDURE

To use the LiteBar procedure, you need to open the Menu procedure file in the calling program. The calling program must also create a memory variable named Choice, which will be used to branch to a calling program based on the user's menu choice. (If the LiteBar procedure is to be called from subprograms, these subprograms should include the **PRIVATE Choice** command to prevent submenu selections from affecting higher-level menu selections.)

Each program that calls the LiteBar procedure needs to define menu options using variables named Opt1, Opt2, Opt3, to Opt9. Then the program can call the LiteBar procedure with the general syntax

**DO LiteBar WITH <options>,<menu title>**

where <options> is the number of options to display on the menu, and <menu title> is the title to be displayed above the menu.

## EXAMPLES

The program in Figure 24.38, MainMenu, uses the LiteBar procedure to display menu items (stored in memory variables Opt1 to Opt4). Note that the

```
*
************************************************** Menu.prg
*--- procedure to display a light-bar menu for up to 9 menu
*--- options.  Menu options should be stored as "Opt" plus
*--- subscript:  Opt1, Opt2,... Opt9
PROCEDURE LiteBar
PARAMETERS OpNo,MenuTitle
   *------------------------- Display the menu title.
   CLEAR
   Row = 5
   @ 1,1 TO 3,78 DOUBLE
   @ 2,32 SAY MenuTitle

   *--------------------- Display menu instructions.
   @ 21,1 TO 24,78 DOUBLE
   @ 22,18 SAY "Highlight option with using "
   @ 22,40 SAY CHR(24)+" or "+CHR(25)+" and press ";
     +CHR(17)+CHR(217)
   @ 23,22 SAY "or press appropriate menu number"

   *------------------ Paint menu options on screen.
   @ 4,30
   Row=5
   DO WHILE Row-4<=OpNo
      Sub= STR(Row-4,1)
      Opt&Sub = IIF(Val(Opt&Sub)=0,STR(Row-4,1)+". "+Opt&Sub,Opt&Sub)
      @ Row,30 SAY Opt&Sub
      Row=Row+1
   ENDDO (row)

   *------------- Initialize memory variables.
   Opt=1
   Sub="1"
   Sel=0

   *--------------- Reverse-video on option 1.
   @ 5,30 GET Opt1
   CLEAR GETS

   *----------- Loop for selecting menu options.
   Choice = 0
   DO WHILE Choice=0
      Sel=0
      *-- Wait for keypress.
      DO WHILE Sel=0
         Sel=INKEY()
      ENDDO (Sel)

      *----- Arrow key pressed.
      IF Sel=24.OR.Sel=5
         @ Opt+4,30 SAY Opt&Sub
         Opt=IIF(Sel=24,Opt+1,Opt-1)
         Opt=IIF(Opt>OpNo,1,Opt)
         Opt=IIF(Opt<1,OpNo,Opt)
         Sub=STR(Opt,1)
         @ Opt+4,30 GET Opt&Sub
         CLEAR GETS
         LOOP
      ENDIF

 *--------- Number pressed.
      IF Sel>=49.AND.Sel<49+OpNo
         Choice=Sel-48
      ENDIF (number pressed)
```

**FIGURE 24.37:** The Menu.prg procedure file, which contains the LiteBar procedure for displaying light-bar menus. The procedure is called with the general syntax **DO LiteBar WITH <options>,<title>** where <options> is the number of items in the menu and <title> is the title that appears above the menu.

```
         *-- Return key pressed.
         IF Sel=13
            Choice=Opt
         ENDIF (Return key)
      ENDDO
   RETURN
   *----------- End of LiteBar procedure.
```

**FIGURE 24.37:** The Menu.prg procedure file, which contains the LiteBar procedure for displaying light-bar menus. The procedure is called with the general syntax **DO LiteBar WITH <options>,<title>** where <options> is the number of items in the menu and <title> is the title that appears above the menu (continued).

```
****************************************** MainMenu.prg
* Accesses the LiteBar procedure with four menu options.
SET TALK OFF
SET PROCEDURE TO Menu

*----------- Prepare loop for this menu.
Options = 4
Choice = 0
DO WHILE Choice # Options

   *-- Set up options and menu title.
   Opt1 = "Add new data"
   Opt2 = "Edit data"
   Opt3 = "Print reports"
   Opt4 = "Exit"
   Options =4
   ThisTitle = "Main Menu"

   *---- Display light-bar menu of options.
   SET COLOR TO GR+/B,W+/BR,G
   CLEAR
   DO LiteBar WITH Options, ThisTitle

   DO CASE

      CASE Choice = 1
           @ 19,1 SAY "You selected option #1"
           WAIT

      CASE Choice = 2
          @ 19,1 SAY "You selected choice # 2"
          WAIT

      CASE Choice = 3
           DO PrinMenu

      ENDCASE

ENDDO
CLEAR
? "You exited by selecting choice # 4"
CLOSE PROC
```

**FIGURE 24.38:** This program displays the main menu for an application, using the LiteBar procedure to allow the user to select menu items by highlighting and pressing Return. Note that the program defines menu options as Opt1, Opt2, and so forth, as required by the LiteBar procedure.

LiteBar procedure is called with four options to display (Options = 4) and the title Main Menu (ThisTitle = "Main Menu").

The PrinMenu.prg program in Figure 24.39, which is called by the MainMenu program in Figure 24.38, also calls the LiteBar procedure with nine menu

```
*************** PrinMenu.prg
PRIVATE Choice

* Submenu to test LiteBar procedure with 9 menu options.

*------- Set up menu options.
Opt1 = "Customer List"
Opt2 = "Form Letters"
Opt3 = "Mailing Labels"
Opt4 = "Invoices"
Opt5 = "Monthly Summary"
Opt5 = "Aging Report"
Opt6 = "History by Account Number"
Opt7 = "History by Date Range"
Opt8 = "History by Part Number"
Opt9 = "Return to main menu"

*----------- Prepare loop for this menu.
Options = 9
Choice = 0
DO WHILE Choice # Options

   *-- Set up number of options and menu title.
   Options = 9
   ThisTitle = "Print a Report"

   *---- Display light-bar menu of options.
   SET COLOR TO GR+/R,BG+/W,B+
   CLEAR
   DO LiteBar WITH Options, ThisTitle

   DO CASE

      CASE Choice = 1
           *---- Do something
      CASE Choice = 2
           *---- Do Something
      CASE Choice = 3
           *---- Do something
      CASE Choice = 4
           *---- Do Something
      CASE Choice = 5
           *---- Do something
      CASE Choice = 6
           *---- Do Something
      CASE Choice = 7
           *---- Do something
      CASE Choice = 8
           *---- Do Something
   ENDCASE
ENDDO

*----- When exit selected, return to main menu with Choice reset.
Choice = 0
RETURN
```

**FIGURE 24.39:** The PrinMenu program is called by the MainMenu program shown in Figure 24.38. This menu also uses the LiteBar procedure to display the nine menu items stored in the variables Opt1 through Opt9. To prevent the Choice variable created in this program from affecting the Choice variable in the MainMenu program, the variable is declared as private in this program.

items (Opt1 through Opt9). Note that this program declares Choice as a private memory variable, as shown near the top of the listing.

When using dBASE III PLUS on an IBM PC, the light-bar menu will probably be too sluggish for practical use. But if you compile the program or use it on an AT, it is fast enough.

Note that in the main menu the menu options are defined inside the DO WHILE loop. On the submenu, the menu options are defined outside the loop. In your application, you should define the menu options (using the names Opt1, Opt2, Opt3, and so forth) inside the DO WHILE loop for displaying the menu on all menus except the bottommost level (a menu that does not call any lower-level menus).

# A Debugging Tool

The two biggest impediments to the debugging process are lack of proper indentations, which make it difficult to see "chunks" of logic in a program at a glance, and missing ENDDO, ENDIF, and ENDCASE commands, which dBASE III is incapable of telling you about. This section discusses a command file that can put proper indentations into any command file and also inform you of any missing or extraneous ENDIF, ENDDO, or ENDCASE commands.

## The Debug Program

The Debug program uses a database named Debug.dbf, which has the structure shown in Figure 24.40.

You'll need to use the dBASE CREATE command to create this database before using the Debug command file. Notice that the file contains only one field named Line, which is 254 characters wide. When the Debug program is run, each record in this database will contain a command line from the command file. After creating the Debug.dbf database file, you'll need to create the Debug command file, as shown in Figure 24.41.

```
Structure for database: Debug.dbf
Field  Field Name  Type        Width    Dec
    1  Line        Character     254
** Total **                      255
```

**FIGURE 24.40:** Structure of the Debug.dbf database used by the Debug program to aid in the debugging process. Note that the database has only a single field named Line.

```
******************************************** Debug.prg
*-  Test for unmatched clauses in command files,
*-  and correct indentations.
*-  Requires the Debug.dbf database.
SET TALK OFF
SET EXACT OFF
SET SAFETY OFF
CLEAR

*------------------------ Make sure Debug.dbf is available.

IF .NOT. FILE("Debug.dbf")
   ? CHR(7)
   ? "Sorry, can't find the Debug.dbf database on this drive."
   ?
   ? "COPY Debug.dbf to this drive, then try again."
   ?
   ? "Exiting the debugger..."
   ?
   CANCEL
ENDIF (no file)

*------- Get name of program to debug.
FileName = SPACE(14)
@ 5,5 SAY "Enter name of command file to analyze"
@ 7,5 SAY "The .prg extension is assumed unless you"
@ 8,5 SAY "specify otherwise (e.g. MyProg.cmd)."
@ 10,5 SAY "The currently logged drive is assumed "
@ 11,5 SAY "unless you specify otherwise (e.g. B:MyProg)"
@ 13,5 GET FileName
READ

CLEAR
? "Working..."

*------- Add .prg extension if necessary.
IF .NOT. "." $(FileName)
   FileName = TRIM(FileName) + ".prg"
ENDIF

*------- Make sure file exists.
IF .NOT. FILE(FileName)
   ? CHR(7)

   ?
   ? "Sorry, can't find a file named "+UPPER(FileName)
   ?
   ? "Exiting the debugger..."
   ?
   CANCEL
ENDIF

*------- Store FileName without extension to FName.
FileName = UPPER(FileName)
FName = SUBSTR(FileName,1,AT(".",FileName)-1)

*------- Pull a copy of the program into Debug.dbf.

CLOSE DATABASES
USE Debug
ZAP
APPEND FROM &FileName SDF
GO TOP

*------- Start counters for clause commands.
```

**FIGURE 24.41:** The Debug command file can help debug a program by informing you of any unbalanced clauses (missing ENDDO, ENDIF, or ENDCASE commands) and by putting proper indentations into the command file being debugged.

```
STORE 0 TO Indent, Amt, DoWhile, NewIf, DoCase, ;
           CEndDo, CEndIf, CEndCase, PCount

*------- Loop through each line of the command file.

DO WHILE .NOT. EOF()
   MemVar = TRIM(Line)
   *------ Peel off leading blanks
   MemVar = LTRIM(MemVar)

   *------- Set flags to false.
   STORE .F. TO Increase, Decrease, NewElse, ;
                NewCase, NewText

   *------- Check for clause commands and
   *------- handle counters and indents.
   DO CASE

      CASE UPPER(Memvar) = "DO WHIL"
           DoWhile = DoWhile + 1
           Amt = 3
           Increase = .T.

      CASE UPPER(Memvar) = "IF "
           NewIf = NewIf + 1
           Amt = 3
           Increase = .T.

      CASE UPPER(Memvar) = "DO CASE"
           DoCase = DoCase + 1
           Amt = 8
           Increase = .T.

      CASE UPPER(Memvar) = "CASE" .OR. Memvar = "OTHE"
           NewCase = .T.

      CASE UPPER(Memvar) = "ENDD"
           CEndDo = CEndDo + 1
           Indent = Indent - 3

      CASE UPPER(Memvar) = "ENDI"
           CEndIf = CEndIf + 1
           Indent = Indent - 3

      CASE UPPER(Memvar) = "ENDC"

           CEndCase = CEndCase + 1
           Indent = Indent - 8

      CASE UPPER(Memvar) = "ELSE"
           NewElse = .T.

      CASE UPPER(Memvar) = "TEXT"
           NewText = .T.

      *------- Note calls to another programs.
      CASE UPPER(MemVar) = "DO " .OR. ;
           UPPER(MemVar) = "SET PROC" .OR. ;
           UPPER(MemVar) = "CALL" .OR. ;
           UPPER(MemVar) = "LOAD "
           PCount = PCount + 1
           PSub = LTRIM(STR(PCount,3))
           PCall&Psub = TRIM(MemVar)

    ENDCASE
```

**FIGURE 24.41:** The Debug command file can help debug a program by informing you of any unbalanced clauses (missing ENDDO, ENDIF, or ENDCASE commands) and by putting proper indentations into the command file being debugged (continued).

```
*------- Add new Indent to line.
REPLACE Line WITH SPACE(MAX(Indent,0)) + MemVar

*------- If command was "ELSE", unindent the one line.
IF NewElse
   Indent = Indent - Amt
   REPLACE Line WITH SPACE(MAX(Indent,0)) + MemVar
   Indent = Indent + Amt
ENDIF

*------- If command was a CASE or OTHERWISE, unindent.
IF NewCase
   Indent = Indent - 5
   REPLACE Line WITH SPACE(MAX(Indent,0)) + MemVar
   Indent = Indent + 5
ENDIF

*------- If remaining lines to be indented,
*------- increase Indent.
IF Increase
   Indent = Indent + Amt
ENDIF
    REPLACE Line WITH TRIM(Line)
    ? TRIM(Line)

    *------- Don't modify anything in
    *------- TEXT...ENDTEXT block.


    IF NewText
       SKIP
       DO WHILE .NOT. "ENDT" $ (UPPER(Line))
          ? TRIM(Line)
          SKIP
       ENDDO
    *------- Otherwise, skip to next line.
    ELSE
       SKIP
    ENDIF (NewText)

 ENDDO (while not eof)

 *------- Store original command file
 *------- with .old as the extension.
 Oldname = FName + ".old"
 IF FILE(Oldname)
    ERASE &Oldname
 ENDIF

 RENAME &FileName TO &Oldname

 *------- Copy new version of program
 *------- to original FileName.
 COPY TO &FileName DELIM WITH BLANK
 CLOSE DATABASES

 *------- Display command file stats.
 CLEAR
 ToPrint = " "
 WAIT "Send statistics to printer? (Y/N) " TO ToPrint
 ToPrint = UPPER(ToPrint)
 IF ToPrint = "Y"
    SET PRINT ON
 ENDIF

 CLEAR
```

**FIGURE 24.41:** The Debug command file can help debug a program by informing you of any unbalanced clauses (missing ENDDO, ENDIF, or ENDCASE commands) and by putting proper indentations into the command file being debugged (continued).

```
Whoops = "  <--- Whoops!  Unmatched pair."
? "Command file statistics for: "+FileName
?

*------- Print DO WHILE...ENDDO stats.
? "DO WHILE statements  :", DoWhile
? "ENDDO statements     :", CEndDo
IF DoWhile # CEndDo
  ?? Whoops
ENDIF
?

*------- Print IF...ENDIF stats.
? "IF statements        :", NewIf
? "ENDIF statements     :", CEndIf


IF NewIf # CEndIf
   ?? Whoops
ENDIF
?

*------- Print DO CASE...ENDCASE stats.
? "DO CASE statements   :", DoCase
? "ENDCASE statements   :", CEndCase
IF DoCase # CEndCase
   ?? Whoops
ENDIF
?
? "Calls to other programs:"
Row = 14
IF PCount = 0
   ?? " None"
ELSE
   ?
   Counter = 1
   DO WHILE Counter <= PCount
      PSub = LTRIM(STR(Counter,3))
      ? PCall&PSub
      Counter = Counter + 1
      Row = Row + 1

IF ToPrint = "Y" .AND. Row > 56
         EJECT
         Row = 1
      ENDIF (Printer)
      IF ToPrint # "Y" .AND. Row > 21
         ?
         WAIT
         ?
         Row = 2
      ENDIF (screen)
   ENDDO (counter)
ENDIF (pcount = 0)

*------- Print closing statements.
?
? "The original command file is now stored under &OldName"
?
? "The modified, indented version is stored under &FileName"

IF ToPrint = "Y"
   SET PRINT OFF
   EJECT
ENDIF (to Print)
```

**FIGURE 24.41:** The Debug command file can help debug a program by informing you of any unbalanced clauses (missing ENDDO, ENDIF, or ENDCASE commands) and by putting proper indentations into the command file being debugged (continued).

## USING THE DEBUG PROGRAM

Before using the program, put Debug.dbf, Debug.prg, and the command file that you want to debug on the same disk drive and directory. Then simply enter the command **DO Debug** at the dBASE dot prompt. The screen will ask that you enter the name of the command file to debug, as below:

**Enter name of command file : :**

If the file that you want to debug already has the extension .prg, you can type just the name without the extension. Otherwise, specify the extension in the file name. The screen will display the prompt

**Working...**

and then each line of the command file as it puts in the proper indentations.

Next, the program displays a count of all commands that involve clauses and points out any unmatched DO WHILE...ENDDO, IF...ENDIF, and DO CASE...ENDCASE pairs. The screen also lists all calls to other programs with the DO, SET PROCEDURE, and LOAD commands. Furthermore, the debugged command file will have proper indentations. The example below demonstrates.

## EXAMPLE

Figure 24.42 displays a test program named Testdbug.prg before it was run through the Debug program.

After running the Testdbug.prg command file through the Debug program, the screen displays the information shown in Figure 24.43.

At this point, you could edit the new program and add the missing ENDCASE clause. Unfortunately, the debugger can't tell you where to put the ENDCASE command; only a human programmer can decide that!

If you wish to have Debug reindent the program lines to take into consideration the new ENDCASE command, just enter the **DO Debug** command again, and specify Testdbug as the command file.

After Debug makes its second pass through the Testdbug command file and informs you that there are no more unmatched clause commands, use the dBASE TYPE or MODIFY COMMAND command to see how the command file looks with proper indentations. Figure 24.44 shows the Testdbug.prg command file after the Debug program cleaned it up.

Notice that all the proper indentations are put in, and all commands are capitalized. There may still be other errors in the program, because Debug looks only for unmatched clauses. But most other errors are the type that dBASE will spot immediately and inform you of at the dot prompt.

```
********************************* Testdbug.prg
*--------------------- Test the Debug.prg program.
SET TALK OFF

*--------- Display menu and get user's choice.
Choice = 0
DO WHILE Choice # 5
   CLEAR
   TEXT

            Membership System Main Menu

                1. Add new members
                2. Print membership information
                3. Change/delete data
                4. Check for duplicates

                5. Exit membership system

   ENDTEXT
   @ 12,22 SAY "Enter choice (1-5) " GET Choice
   READ

   *------------ Branch to appropriate program.
   DO CASE

      CASE Choice = 1
           DO AddNew

      CASE Choice = 2
           DO Reports

      CASE Choice = 3
           DO EditDel

      CASE Choice = 4
           SET PROCEDURE TO GenProcs
           DO DupCheck WITH "Zip + Address + LName"
           CLOSE PROCEDURE

        ENDDO (while choice < 5)
        CLOSE DATABASES
        QUIT
```

**FIGURE 24.42:** Sample program, named Testdbug, before running it through the debugging program. Notice the random indentations used in the program.

For safety's sake, don't use the Debug program on a real command file until the Debug program itself is fully tested and debugged. Your best bet is to make a test program simply for working with Debug.prg. Once the test program is created, make a copy of it with the command **COPY FILE Test.prg TO Test.bak**. Then, when you run the Debug program, enter Test as the name of the program to debug. If the Debug program bombs, you can just correct your error and enter the **DO Debug** command again. You can get your original command file back by entering the commands

**ERASE Test.prg**
**RENAME Test.bak TO Test.prg**

(for this example).

```
                                                   Num
Command file statistics for: TESTDBUG.PRG

DO WHILE statements  :         1
ENDDO statements     :         1

IF statements        :         0
ENDIF statements     :         0

DO CASE statements   :         1
ENDCASE statements   :         0  <--- Whoops!  Unmatched pair.

Calls to other programs:

DO AddNew
DO Reports
DO EditDel
SET PROCEDURE TO GenProcs
DO DupCheck WITH "Zip + Address + LName"

The original command file is now stored under TESTDBUG.OLD

The modified, indented version is stored under TESTDBUG.PRG
```

**FIGURE 24.43:** Screen displayed after running the Testdbug program through the debugging tool. Note that the screen points out a missing ENDCASE command. The screen also lists all calls to other programs, as well as the names of the debugged (properly indented) command file and the original command file.

Keep in mind that the Debug program calculates the amount of indentation based on the commands in the program you are debugging. Therefore, if the program is missing an ENDDO, ENDIF, or ENDCASE command, the indentations will be inaccurate in the newly indented program. An inaccurate indentation may point out the exact spot in a program where the missing ENDIF, ENDCASE, or ENDDO command belongs.

You can run any command file through the Debug program as many times as you wish. However, each time you do, the program stored with the .old filename extension will represent the latest debugged program, rather than the original .prg program.

```
********************************** Testdbug.prg
*--------------------- Test the Debug.prg program.
SET TALK OFF

*--------- Display menu and get user's choice.
Choice = 0
DO WHILE Choice # 5
   CLEAR
   TEXT

            Membership System Main Menu

                1. Add new members
                2. Print membership information
                3. Change/delete data
                4. Check for duplicates

                5. Exit membership system

   ENDTEXT
   @ 12,22 SAY "Enter choice (1-5) " GET Choice
   READ

   *------------ Branch to appropriate program.
   DO CASE

      CASE Choice = 1
           DO AddNew

      CASE Choice = 2
           DO Reports

      CASE Choice = 3
           DO EditDel

      CASE Choice = 4
           SET PROCEDURE TO GenProcs
           DO DupCheck WITH "ZiP + Address + LName"
           CLOSE PROCEDURE
   ENDCASE

ENDDO (while choice < 5)
CLOSE DATABASES
QUIT
```

**FIGURE 24.44:** The Testdbug command file after adding the missing ENDCASE command and running it through the debugging tool again. Notice that all the random indentations in the original program have now been replaced by proper indentations.

## SUMMARY

This chapter presented some handy routines that you can use to expand on the built-in capabilities that dBASE offers. As mentioned earlier, you'll probably want to store these routines (with the exception of the Debug program) as procedures within procedure files, so that they can be called quickly and easily from within your own applications.

Topics related to those discussed in this chapter are discussed elsewhere, as summarized below:

*For a general discussion on creating and using procedures and procedure files:*

- Chapter 5, "Procedures and Parameters"

*For a general discussion of pseudo arrays:*

- Chapter 6, "Memory Variables"

*For general debugging commands and techniques:*

- Chapter 7, "Debugging Commands and Techniques"

*For examples of routines that convert the TIME( ) function to other units of time, see the MOD( ) and TIME( ) functions in*

- Chapter 17, "dBASE Functions"

*For information on extending dBASE capabilities through the use of assembly language subroutines:*

- Chapter 22, "Using Assembly Language Subroutines in dBASE"

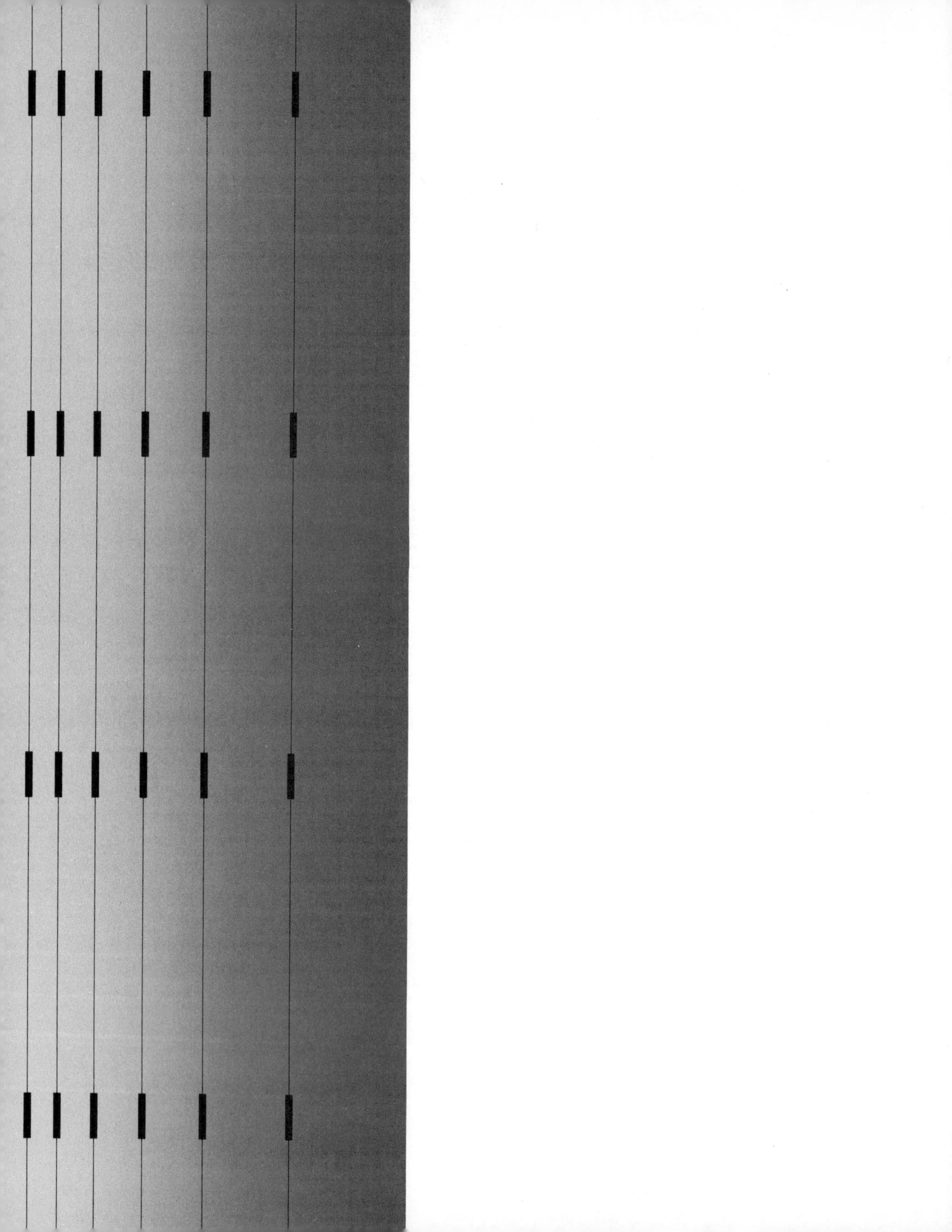

# Error Messages

This appendix lists all dBASE error messages. The first section lists all messages and descriptions in alphabetical order by the first word. The second section lists error messages in numeric order according to the value returned by the ERROR( ) function.

## Alphabetical Listing of Error Messages

This section lists all dBASE III PLUS error messages and their meanings. If the error returns a number in the ERROR( ) function in response to an ON ERROR condition, that number is displayed in brackets. If the error occurs only under certain circumstances such as networking or installation, those circumstances are also displayed in brackets.

Some error messages may mean different things under different circumstances. When that is the case, the dBASE III PLUS single-user error message is displayed first, and other situations are displayed in brackets following the description of the situation.

Some error messages begin with a file or field name, as below:

*****YourPrg.prg not found!**

These error messages are alphabetized under the first keyword after the file name. (In the example above, the error message is alphabetized under **not found!**) Similarly, messages that display leading characters such as *** or ^ are alphabetized by the first word to the right of the symbols.

**A DBF file in view is not in current directory**

A database file specified in a view (.vue) file is not on the current drive or directory. Perhaps the file has been renamed or erased, or the dBASE SET PATH command does not extend the file search to the appropriate directory.

**A Memo field cannot be selected**

During a full-screen operation you attempted to select or enter a memo field when it was not appropriate to do so. The operation may be invalid on memo fields.

**ALIAS name already in use**

[24] You attempted to use a database file that is already open. This error also occurs if you try to use two or more database files with the same first name but different extensions. If the latter is the cause of the problem, use the ALIAS command in the USE command to assign a unique ALIAS name to each database file.

**ALIAS not found**

[13] You attempted to use a SELECT area outside the range of A–J (or 1–10) or an alias that has not been defined by a SELECT command.

**ALTERNATE could not be opened**

[72] The ALTERNATE file specified in the Config.db file cannot be opened because of an invalid file name or insufficient space on the directory. See the error message **File is inaccessible** for handling full directories.

**At least one file must be in use for this operation**

Before accessing the Options menu in CREATE VIEW or MODIFY VIEW, at least one database file must be opened.

**Beginning of file encountered**

[38] You have attempted to position the record pointer above record number 1.

**Cannot erase a file which is open**

[89] You have attempted an ERASE or DELETE FILE command on a file that is currently open in dBASE. Close the file and attempt the ERASE command again.

**Cannot have subgroups without groups**

You attempted to define a subtotal grouping in MODIFY REPORT without first defining a grouping for totals.

**Cannot locate dBASE system files on disk**

[IDLAN] While installing dBASE ADMINISTRATOR on a network, the dBASE system files from ADMINISTRATOR Disk #1 could not be found on the specified drive and directory.

**Cannot locate SIGNON.COM on disk.**

[IDLAN] The IDLAN program could not locate the Signon program on the current drive and directory.

**Cannot select requested database**

[17] The work area specified is outside the range of A–J (or 1–10).

**Cannot write to a read-only file**

[111] You attempted to write to a file that is opened for read-only access. On a single-user system (and some networks), this attribute is set through the DOS ATTRIB command. The same DOS ATTRIB command needs to be used to make the file available for read-write status (using the –R option in ATTRIB).

**Check network drive specification**

[ADMINISTRATOR STARTUP] The dBASE ADMINISTRATOR and DBNETCTL.300 files could not be located on the network file server. You need to specify the correct drive and directory and set the correct DOS PATH command to locate the appropriate directory.

**Command not recognized!**

The command you've requested in HELP does not exist.

***** <input file name> contains no code!**

[RUNTIME+] The program being encrypted with dBCODE contains no commands.

**CONTINUE without LOCATE**

[42] The CONTINUE command is only valid after a LOCATE command. Using Cont or Continue as a variable name can cause this error. Use a different variable name.

**Control file cannot be processed**

[ADMINISTRATOR STARTUP] The DBA.ctl file in the directory called DBNETCTL.300 is damaged or missing.

**Control file LOCK failure**

[ADMINISTRATOR STARTUP] An internal error occurred when checking the DBA.ctl file.

**Control file name not found**

[ADDUSER] The ADDUSER program cannot find the DBA.ctl file in the DBNETCTL.300 directory. The file is missing or damaged. You may need to uninstall the dBASE ADMINISTRATOR and then reinstall it.

**Cyclic relation**

[44] You attempted to set a relation from one file back into the same file, forming a cyclic relation. For example, if you set a relation from A into B and B into C and then C into A, a cyclic relation error occurs. Use the SET RELATION TO command with no parameters to disconnect the relationships.

**Data Catalog has not been established**

[122] You attempted to use a query symbol (?) in a command before opening a catalog file with the SET CATALOG TO command.

**Data type mismatch**

[9] You attempted to combine conflicting data types in a single operation. Occurs when you attempt to combine different data types in a single string or index file; when you attempt to REPLACE, SEEK, or FIND with the wrong data type; or when you attempt to sort on a logical or memo field. See Chapter 15, "Managing Data, Records, and Files," for information on combining data types.

**Database is encrypted**

[131] You attempted to open a database file in single-user dBASE that was encrypted in the multiuser mode, or you attempted to open a database file in multiuser mode for which you have no access. An authorized user can make unencrypted copies of database files using the SET ENCRYPTION OFF and COPY commands.

**Database is not indexed**

[26] You attempted a FIND, SEEK, SET RELATION, or UPDATE command on a database file with no active index files. Use the INDEX command to create the appropriate index file, or use the USE...INDEX command to open the index file.

**dBASE ADMINISTRATOR already exists in the destination drive. Please uninstall your old version first.**

[INSTALL/UNINSTALL] An attempt was made to install the dBASE ADMINISTRATOR on a drive or directory that already has the ADMINISTRATOR on it. You need to UNINSTALL the ADMINISTRATOR before reinstalling it.

**dBASE ADMINISTRATOR has not been initialized. Please run IDLAN.**

[INSTALL/UNINSTALL] You must run the IDLAN program before using the dBASE ADMINISTRATOR. The serial number that IDLAN requests is on the dBASE System Disk #1 label.

**dBASE ADMINISTRATOR installation has been aborted**

[INSTALL/UNINSTALL] A previously installed version of the dBASE ADMINISTRATOR was found while attempting to reinstall the ADMINISTRATOR. The first installed copy needs to be uninstalled before reinstalling.

*****dBCODE: Illegal option <illegal option>**

[RUNTIME+] An invalid flag was entered on the dBCODE command line. The flag is ignored.

*****dBLINKER: illegal option <illegal option>**

[RUNTIME+] An invalid flag was entered on the dBLINKER command line. The flag is ignored.

**.DBT file cannot be opened**

[41] There is no .dbt file for the memo field in this database. See Chapter 23, "Foreign and Damaged Files," for recovery procedures.

**Disk full when writing file: <file name>**

[56] The disk was filled while trying to write data to it.

**DOs nested too deep**

[103] The maximum number of 20 nested DO commands was exceeded.

**Empty structure will not be saved**
You exited a CREATE or MODIFY STRUCTURE operation without defining any fields for the database. The empty structure file is not saved.

**End of file encountered**
[4] When using APPEND FROM, UPDATE, or USE, this error is caused by an invalid database file structure. When using FIND or SEEK, this message occurs when the index file is corrupted or damaged. Use REINDEX to rebuild the index file. When using MODIFY REPORT, MODIFY LABEL, REPORT FORM, or LABEL FORM, this error is caused by an incomplete format file structure or an incomplete database file structure. When using SKIP, an attempt was made to move the record pointer past the end of the file.

**End of file or error on keyboard input**
[51] The file used to simulate keyboard input, from the DOS SET command, is corrupted.

*****End of input found prematurely on file <input file name> – input line**
[RUNTIME+] dBCODE encountered an invalid program or bad disk sector while trying to encrypt a source file.

*****ENDCASE unexpected in file <file name> – input line<line number>**
[RUNTIME+] An ENDCASE command that is not preceded by a DO CASE command was encountered while encrypting a command file. The command is ignored.

*****ENDDO unexpected in file <file name> – input line <line number>**
[RUNTIME+] An ENDDO command that is not preceded by a DO WHILE command was encountered while encrypting a command file. The command is ignored.

*****ENDIF unexpected in file <file name> – input line <line number>**
[RUNTIME+] An ENDIF command that is not preceded by an IF command was encountered while encrypting a command file. The command is ignored.

**Error in HELP system**
The Assist.hlp file, used to display help messages in the dBASE Assistant, is missing from the current drive or directory.

**Errors: <count>**
[RUNTIME+] Displays the number of errors encountered while dBCODE was encrypting a file.

**Exceeded report print width. Press any key to continue**
When designing a report format in MODIFY REPORT, the total width of the fields specified in the Columns menu exceeds the page width specified on the Options menu.

**Excess header lines lost**
When entering a report or column heading in MODIFY REPORT, the number of semicolons in the heading created a header that would require more than four lines to print. All text beyond the fourth semicolon is ignored.

**Exclusive open of file is required**
[110] [ADMINISTRATOR EXECUTION] An attempt to perform an INSERT [BLANK], MODIFY STRUCTURE, PACK, REINDEX, or ZAP command was issued on a database file that is not in exclusive use on a network. Use the SET EXCLUSIVE or USE...EXCLUSIVE command to open the file for exclusive use before reattempting the command.

**Exclusive use on database is required**
[110] You attempted to perform an operation requiring exclusive use of the database file. Use the SET EXCLUSIVE or USE...EXCLUSIVE command to open the file for exclusive use before reattempting the command.

*****Execution error on + : Concatenated string too large**
[77] You attempted to create a character string that is more than 254 characters long while joining two strings with +.

*****Execution error on – : Concatenated string too large**
[76] You attempted to create a character string that is more than 254 characters long while joining two strings with –.

*****Execution error on ^ or ** : Negative base, fractional exponent**
[78] You attempted to raise a negative number to a power between 0 and 1.

*****Execution error on CHR( ) : Out of range**
[57] The argument to the CHR( ) function was outside the acceptable range of 0 to 255.

*****Execution error on LOG( ) : Zero or negative**
[58] You attempted to use a negative number or zero as the argument to the LOG function.

*****Execution error on NDX( ) : Invalid index number**
[87] You attempted to use a number outside the range of 1–7 in an NDX( ) function.

*****Execution error on REPLICATE( ) : String too large**
[88] The REPLICATE( ) function attempted to create a character string longer than 254 characters.

*****Execution error on SPACE( ) : Too large**
[59] The SPACE( ) function attempted to create a character string longer than 254 characters.

*****Execution error on SPACE( ): Negative**
[60] The argument to a SPACE( ) function was a negative number.

*****Execution error on SQRT( ) : Negative**
[61] You attempted to take the square root of a negative number. You can use the ABS function to convert the argument to a positive number.

*****Execution error on STORE : String too large**
[79] You attempted to store a character string longer than 254 characters to a memory variable.

*****Execution error on STR( ) : Out of range**
[63] The STR function attempted to create a character string longer than 19 characters, or the decimal portion of the converted number is too large for the width specified. The decimal portion cannot exceed the length minus 2.

*****Execution error on STUFF( ) : String too large**
[102] The STUFF( ) function attempted to create a string that exceeds the 254-character limit.

*****Execution error on SUBSTR( ) : Start point out of range**
[62] A SUBSTR( ) function attempted to access a starting point that is longer than the entire character string.

**^ ^ Expected ON or OFF**
[73] You set an ON/OFF parameter in Config.db to some value other than ON or OFF. The command is ignored.

*****Fatal error: can't open file <input file name>**
[RUNTIME+ ] An input file that was verified during a dBCODE command disappeared.

**Field name already in use**
While using CREATE or MODIFY STRUCTURE, you attempted to use the same field name more than once.

**Field not found**
[48] You attempted to freeze a field that does not exist in BROWSE.

**Field type must be C, N, D, L or M**
While using CREATE or MODIFY STRUCTURE, a character other than C, N, D, L, or M was entered as the data type.

**File already exists**
[7] You attempted to rename a file to a file name that already exists. The file is not renamed.

**File does not exist**

[1] You attempted to locate or open a file that does not exist on the current drive and directory or in the SET PATH search path.

**File is already open**

[3] You attempted to open a file that is already open.

**File is in use by another**

[108] [ADMINISTRATOR EXECUTION] You attempted to open a file that is in exclusive use by another user.

**File is not accessible**

[29] You attempted to create a file with an invalid file name character ( +, ", <, >, ?, *, [, ]), or you attempted to create or access a file on the disk that has a full directory. (The maximum number of files on a double-sided, double-density disk is 112.) Erase any unnecessary files before reattempting the command. [IDLAN] IDLAN cannot access the files on ADMINISTRATOR Disk #1. The disk may be damaged.

**File too large, some data may be lost**

You've gone beyond the 5000-character limit in the MODIFY COMMAND editor. If the file was loaded into the MODIFY COMMAND editor inadvertently, be sure to abort the file with Ctrl-Q or the Esc key.

**File was not LOADed**

[91] You attempted to load a binary file that cannot be located or contains zero bytes, or you attempted to call or release a module that was not loaded.

**HELP text not found**

The Help.dbs file is not on the same drive or directory as the dBASE.ovl file, so help is not available.

**Illegal character data length**

A character field length in a structure-extended file is not within the acceptable range of 1 to 254 characters.

*****Illegal character – ignored – input line <line number>**

[RUNTIME+] An illegal character in a command file was ignored during encryption. Most likely, the illegal character is one that was inadvertently inserted by a word processor.

*****Illegal command macro (&) in file <input file name> input line <line number>**

[RUNTIME+] dBCODE cannot encrypt files that contain command lines beginning with the macro (&) symbol.

*****Illegal condition in ON statement in file<input file name>input line<n>**
[RUNTIME+ ] An ON command in the file being encrypted is missing a condition or contains an invalid condition.

**Illegal data length**
The width you specified for a field of the character data type is not within the acceptable range of 1 to 254.

**Illegal Decimal length**
The number of decimal places you specified for the numeric data type is not in the acceptable range of 0 to 15.

*****Illegal DO statement in file <input file name> – input line <line number>**
[RUNTIME+ ] A DO command in the file being encrypted was not followed by a WHILE or CASE command or a file name.

**Illegal field name**
The structure-extended file contains a field name with illegal characters in it.

**Illegal field type**
The structure-extended file contains an invalid data type (must be C, N, D, L, or M).

**Illegal Numeric data length**
You specified a length for a number that is outside the acceptable range of 1 to 19.

*****Illegal RunTime+ SET option in file <input file name> – input line <number>**
[RUNTIME+ ] The file being encrypted contains an invalid SET command or a SET command without a parameter.

**Illegal value**
[46] During a full-screen SET operation, you attempted to enter an invalid number for the decimals or margin settings.

**Improper data type in subsubtotal expression**
The REPORT format has a logical or memo field in the subsubtotal expression.

**Improper data type in subtotal expression**
The REPORT format has a logical or memo field in the subtotal expression.

**Index damaged. REINDEX should be done before using data**
[114] You attempted to use an index file that has been corrupted or previously aborted with the Esc key or an ON condition. Use REINDEX to rebuild the index file.

**Index expression is too big (220 char maximum)**
[112] The total number of characters used to define an index expression exceeds the maximum width of 220 characters. (This error message refers to the literal key expression as entered in the INDEX command, rather than the resulting index key.) Remove any unnecessary blanks, if possible, from the INDEX ON command line to reduce the size of the expression.

**Index file does not match the database**
[19] You attempted to use an index file that does not include the same fields as the database file in use. The index file most likely belongs to another database file, or a MODIFY STRUCTURE command removed a field used in the index file key expression.

**Index interrupted. Index will be damaged if not completed.**
[113] An INDEX operation was aborted with the Esc key or an ON condition. If the operation is aborted, the index file will be corrupted and will need to be recreated later.

**Index is too big (100 char maximum)**
[23] The result of the key expression in an INDEX command produced a key that exceeds the maximum 100-character length of index files. If you attempt to index on a long character string (or strings), use the LEFT( ) function to limit the number of characters in the key expression.

***** <input file name> is a duplicate!**
[RUNTIME+] The file being encoded by dBCODE or dBLINKER has the same name as another encrypted program.

***** <input file name> is not a dBCODE III file!**
[RUNTIME+] The file being linked with dBLINKER has not been encrypted with dBCODE yet. USE dBCODE to encrypt the file before using dBLINKER.

**Insert impossible**
In MODIFY REPORT, you attempted to insert a field, but the maximum number of fields (24) has already been reached.

**Insufficient dynamic memory for contents window**
Your computer does not have enough RAM memory to display the Contents menu in MODIFY REPORT.

**Install terminated**
[INSTALL/UNINSTALL] You terminated the installation process by typing Ctrl-C, or the wrong disk is in the drive, or the DBA.com and DBA.lod files cannot be located on the disk.

**Insufficient memory**

[43] You attempted to run dBASE on a computer with less than 256K. Or, you attempted to execute more than 128 GET commands without issuing a CLEAR or CLEAR GETS command. Or, you attempted to run an external program requiring more than the amount of memory remaining (the TEDIT and WP commands in Config.db can also cause this error). Or, you attempted to load a binary file that is larger than the amount of memory available.

**Insufficient memory to display fields**

Your computer does not have enough main memory to display the pull-down menu requested.

**Internal error: CMDSET( ):**

[66] The dBASE III PLUS program is damaged. Make a new copy. If you still get the error, contact Ashton-Tate software support.

**Internal error: EVAL work area overflow**

[67] You attempted to use an expression that is too complex and may not be possible.

**Internal error: Illegal opcode**

[68] The dBASE III PLUS program is damaged. Make a new copy. If you still get the error, contact Ashton-Tate software support. The error might also be caused by an extremely complex expression with 150 terms or more.

**Internal error: Unknown command code**

[65] The dBASE III PLUS program is damaged. Make a new copy. If you still get the error, contact Ashton-Tate software support.

*****INTERRUPTED *****

You interrupted processing by pressing the Esc key.

**Invalid date (press SPACE)**

[81] The date that you entered is not a valid date. Press the space bar and try again.

**Invalid DIF character**

[118] The DIF file being imported contains an invalid character, possibly inserted by a word processor.

**Invalid DIF File Header**

[115] You attempted to import a DIF file that has an invalid header.

**Invalid DIF type indicator**

[117] The data type specified in a DIF file is invalid.

**Invalid DOS SET option**

[99] An invalid DOS SET command was attempted.

**Invalid drive letter specified. Install is aborted.**
[INSTALL/UNINSTALL] The drive specified during installation does not exist.

**Invalid drive name**
[ADDUSER] The floppy disk drive specified when using the ADDUSER program is invalid or missing.

**Invalid function argument**
[11] The argument in a function is the wrong data type for that function.

**Invalid function name**
[31] The function you attempted to use does not exist. Check your spelling.

**Invalid index number**
[106] You attempted to use the SET ORDER TO command for an index file that is not in the list of open index files, or you specified a number outside the range of 0 to 7.

**Invalid network id, please check and try again**
[ADDUSER] The drive specified was invalid.

**Invalid operator**
[107] You attempted to use an operator that cannot be used with the current data types, such as attempting to multiply two character strings.

**Invalid printer port**
[123] The printer port specified in a SET PRINTER TO command does not exist. Ports must be valid DOS names, such as LPT1, LPT2, COM1, COM2, and so forth, as determined by the operating system.

**Invalid printer redirection**
[124] [ADMINISTRATOR EXECUTION] The printer you specified in a SET PRINTER TO \\ command does not exist on the network.

**Invalid serial number**
[IDLAN] The serial number you entered does not match the format of the serial number printed on System Disk #1. [ADDUSER] The floppy disk inserted to add or remove a user does not have a valid serial number.

**Invalid SYLK file dimension bounds**
[120] You attempted to import a SYLK file that contains data items outside of the bounds specified in the SYLK file. Recreate the SYLK file, if possible, and try again.

**Invalid SYLK file format**
[121] You attempted to import a SYLK file that is corrupted or was not created by Multiplan.

**Invalid SYLK file header**
[119] You attempted to import a SYLK file that is corrupted or was not created by Multiplan. The file header is invalid.

**Invalid system disk**
[ADDUSER] The disk that you are using for adding or removing a user is not a valid dBASE disk.

**^ - - - Keyword not found**
[86] The keyword in the Config.db file is invalid.

**Label file invalid**
[54] The label file specified in a LABEL FORM or MODIFY LABEL command is corrupted or not recognized as a label file.

**Line exceeds maximum width of 254 characters**
[18] The maximum command line width of 254 characters has been exceeded. If possible, decrease the line length by removing blank spaces between operators.

**Load failed**
[ADMINISTRATOR STARTUP] The files in the DBNETCTL.300 directory could not be read.

**LSeek failed for count file**
[ADDUSER] The ADDUSER program could not read or write to the DBA.ctl file in the DBNETCTL.300 directory. You may have specified the wrong drive, or the DBA.ctl file may be corrupted. You may need to uninstall, then reinstall, the dBASE ADMINISTRATOR.

**Max number of fields already reached**
The database file you are attempting to create or modify has already reached the maximum of 128 fields.

**Maximum network users reached (xx) Please try later**
[ADMINISTRATOR STARTUP] The maximum number of users allowed on the network are already logged in. (xx) displays this number.

**Maximum record length exceeded**
[137] A CREATE or MODIFY STRUCTURE command attempted to create a structure with more than the maximum 4000 characters per record.

**Memory allocation error**
[ADMINISTRATOR STARTUP] When starting the dBASE ADMINISTRATOR, an internal error occurred during execution of the DBA.com program. Check the network requirements for installed memory.

**Memory Variable file is invalid**
[55] An attempt to restore data from an invalid (corrupted) memory (.mem) file was made.

**Mismatched DO WHILE and ENDDO**

[96] An ENDDO command for which there was no corresponding DO WHILE command was encountered in a program. There must be one, and only one, ENDDO command for every DO WHILE command.

*****Missing (',",or]) – inserted (EOL) – input line <line number>**

[RUNTIME+ ] An opening or closing quotation mark or bracket is missing from the command file being encrypted. Correct the error in the source file before reattempting to encrypt the file.

**Network drive not supplied**

[ADMINISTRATOR STARTUP] The network drive must be specified in the #DF = portion of the command used to start the dBASE ADMINISTRATOR. Or, possibly, the DBNETCTL.300 directory could not be found.

**Network load failure**

[ADMINISTRATOR STARTUP] A corrupted dBASE ADMINISTRATOR program or DBNETCTL.300 directory was found. You may need to uninstall and reinstall the dBASE ADMINISTRATOR.

**Network server busy**

[148] [ADMINISTRATOR EXECUTION] Too much traffic on the network; the file server cannot process the number of tasks requested. Some dBASE commands may not have been executed correctly. You should quit dBASE and reboot the network.

**No database is in USE. Enter file name:**

[52] An attempt to perform a file operation was attempted but no database file was in use. Enter the name of the database file and press Return.

**No fields of the type required are present**

When attempting to access a fields submenu in a full-screen operation, dBASE could not find any fields of the type required in the current database structure or the SET FIELDS list.

**No fields to process**

[47] An attempt was made to sum or average a database file that has no numeric fields.

**No find**

[14] A FIND or SEEK command could not find the data you were looking for. (The FOUND( ) function is set to .F., and EOF( ) is set to .T..) This message appears only if SET TALK is on.

**No PARAMETER statement found**

[93] You attempted to call a procedure or program with a DO...WITH command, but the called procedure or program contained no PARAMETERS command.

**No room for heading**
The heading exceeded the maximum width for the column during a CREATE or MODIFY REPORT command.

**Not a Character expression**
[45] You used a numeric, date, memo, or logical data type where the character data type is required.

**Not a dBASE database**
[15] You attempted to use a damaged dBASE file or an external file that was not created by dBASE III or dBASE III PLUS. See Chapter 23, "Foreign and Damaged Files," for help.

**Not a Logical expression**
[37] You attempted to use a character, date, numeric, or memo data type where a logical expression is required.

**Not a numeric expression**
[27] You attempted to use a character, date, logical, or memo data type where a numeric data type is required.

****Not a RunTime file**
[RUNTIME+] dBRUN attempted to access a procedure file that has not been encrypted with dBCODE.

**Not a valid PFS file**
[140] An attempt was made to import a file that was not stored in PFS format.

**Not a valid QUERY file**
[134] The query (.qry) file is corrupted or contains an invalid condition. The file may need to be erased and recreated with the CREATE QUERY command.

**Not a valid VIEW file**
[127] The view (.vue) file specified in a SET VIEW or MODIFY VIEW command has been corrupted. The file may need to be erased and recreated with the CREATE VIEW command.

**Not enough disk space for sort**
The disk does not have enough room to sort the database file. There must be enough space on the disk for three copies of the database being sorted, because dBASE creates a temporary file for sorting, as well as the final sorted database file.

**Not enough memory**
[IDLAN] There is not enough memory available to run the IDLAN program. Either the computer has less than 256K RAM, or memory resident programs are consuming too much memory. Possibly, the system is not recognizing all of the installed memory.

**Not enough records to sort**

An attempt was made to sort a database file with fewer than two records in it.

**** Not Found ****

[82] You attempted to find an item of data that does not exist in the file. This occurs while using the FIND option in BROWSE.

***** <copyright file name> not found!**

[RUNTIME+] The copyright header file for an encrypted program was not found during dBCODE or dBLINKER operations. Program will be encoded without the copyright notice.

***** <input file name> not found!**

[RUNTIME+] The file to encrypt or link with dBCODE or dBLINKER cannot be found on the specified drive and directory.

**not readable**

You entered the DIR command while dBASE was unable to read the file.

**Not suspended**

[101] You attempted to use the RESUME command for a command file that was not suspended.

**Numeric overflow (data was lost)**

[39] The number created by an operation or in a REPLACE or TOTAL command is too large to be stored in the field or variable. The size of the field or variable needs to be increased.

**Open failed for count file**

[ADDUSER] The ADDUSER program could not open the DBA.ctl file in the DBNETCTL.300 directory, because someone else is running the ADDUSER program, because the file cannot be found, or because file-access restrictions have been set.

**Operation with Logical field invalid**

[90] You attempted to sort or index on a logical field. (The IIF function can be used to convert the logical field to a character data type equivalent.)

**Operation with Memo field invalid**

[34] An attempt was made to sort, index, or search a memo field or to store a memo field to a memory variable. None of these operations is allowed with memo fields.

**Original count cannot be added or subtracted**

[ADDUSER] You cannot use System Disk #1 to add a new user if it was already used to install the dBASE ADMINISTRATOR. When removing a user, you cannot reduce the count to zero unless the dBASE ADMINISTRATOR is uninstalled.

**Out of memory variable memory**

[21] You exceeded the 6000-byte limit of memory space allocated for memory variables. The limit can be changed using the MVARSIZ command in the Config.db file (see Appendix C, "Configuring dBASE III PLUS").

**Out of memory variable slots**

[22] You have attempted to store more than the maximum of 256 memory variables. You can use RELEASE to release memory variables that are no longer needed and reclaim those slots.

**^ - - - Out of range**

[75] A value outside the acceptable range was specified in a Config.db file command (see Appendix C, "Configuring dBASE III PLUS").

**Please set all files to Read/Write mode before continuing**

[IDLAN] Some of the files on ADMINISTRATOR Disk #1 are not set for read/write access, or the disk has a write-protect tab on it.

**Please use the dBASE III PLUS System Disk #1 to run the installation. Install is aborted.**

[INSTALL/UNINSTALL] You attempted to begin the installation with the wrong disk. Use the System Disk #1 to install.

**Position is off the screen**

[30] An @ command attempted to display data outside the range of 0 to 24 rows or 0 to 79 columns.

*****Premature end of input on file <input file name> – input line <line number>**

[RUNTIME+] dBCODE tried unsuccessfully to encrypt a command file that was invalid or stored on a damaged disk.

***** .prg file not generated *****

[RUNTIME+] Fatal error while using dBCODE or dBLINKER prevented the creation of a .prg file. (This message usually follows a more descriptive error message.)

**Printer is either not connected or turned off**

[126] You issued a SET PRINTER command to a port that does not have a printer on it.

**Printer not ready**

[125] An attempt was made to print data, but the printer was off, offline, or in some other way not ready to accept the output. You can try to rectify the error and run the command again, or just abort the command.

**Product loader cannot be opened**

[ADDUSER] The DBA.com file cannot be opened by ADDUSER. The file may be corrupted, not in the DOS SET PATH list, or not available for read/write access.

**Product loader cannot be read**

[ADDUSER] The ADDUSER program cannot read the DBA.com file, possibly because the file is corrupted.

***Ran out of memory on file <file name>**

[RUNTIME+] A file buffer could not be reserved while trying to encrypt a file.

***Read error on file <input file name> – input line <line number>**

[RUNTIME+] dBCODE or dBLINKER encountered an invalid file or damaged disk sector.

**Read failed for count file**

[ADDUSER] The ADDUSER program could not open the DBA.ctl file in the DBNETCTL.300 directory, because someone else is running the ADDUSER program, because the file cannot be found, or because file-access restrictions have been set.

**Read failed for Serialization**

[ADDUSER] ADDUSER cannot read the serial number from the floppy disk. The disk may be defective.

**Record is in use by another**

[109] [ADMINISTRATOR EXECUTION] An attempt was made to access a record that is locked by another user on the network.

**Record is not in index**

[20] An attempt was made to go to a record that does not exist in the index file. The index file may need to be rebuilt using the REINDEX or INDEX ON command.

**Record is not inserted**

[25] An INSERT operation was aborted before the record was inserted into the database file.

**Record is not locked**

[130] [ADMINISTRATOR EXECUTION] You attempted to edit a record that is not locked. If using EDIT or CHANGE, type Ctrl-O to lock/unlock the record. (The record must be locked before editing.)

**Record is out of range**

[5] You attempted to go to a record that has a record number larger than the number of records in the file (shown by RECCOUNT( )). If an index file is in

use, it may be corrupted. Use REINDEX to rebuild the index file. If you think the database file might be damaged, see Chapter 23, "Foreign and Damaged Files," for recovery procedures.

**Records do not balance (program error)**
The dBASE III PLUS program is damaged. Make a new copy. If you still get the error, contact Ashton-Tate software support.

**Report file invalid**
[50] The file specified in a MODIFY REPORT or REPORT FORM command is not a valid report (.frm) file. The file may need to be erased and rebuilt with the CREATE REPORT command.

*****Source - output filename conflict - file <.prg input file name>**
[RUNTIME+] When encrypting command files with dBCODE, the input and output file names will be the same, so the process is aborted. Rename the source file so that it has some extension other than .prg.

**Structure invalid**
[33] A CREATE FROM command attempted to build a file from an invalid structure-extended file. CREATE FROM can read only files that were created with a COPY...STRUCTURE EXTENDED command.

**Syntax error**
[10] The command entered does not conform to the syntax required, or a keyword in the command line is misspelled.

**Syntax error in [contents] [field] [group] [subgroup] expression**
While creating a REPORT or LABEL format, the expression used to define the column, field, group, or subgroup was invalid. A field name may have been misspelled, or data types may have been mixed illegally. If the database file structure was modified and fields were renamed or deleted, the report (.frm) or label (.lbl) file may refer to a field name that no longer exists. If possible, use MODIFY LABEL or MODIFY REPORT to correct the error. Otherwise, you may need to erase the report or label file and rebuild it with CREATE REPORT or CREATE LABEL. Also, a blank report column can cause this error. In MODIFY REPORT, check the Locate menu for any blank column definitions (they may be at the bottom), and delete them with Ctrl-U.

**Table is full**
[105] You attempted to load more than five binary files. You can use RELEASE MODULE to selectively delete binary files from memory that are no longer needed.

**The disk has already been added to the network**

[ADDUSER] Users cannot be added with System Disk #1, which was used for the original installation, or from a dBASE ACCESS disk that has already been used to install the maximum number of users.

**The HELP file is not available**

The Assist.hlp file, used to display help messages in the dBASE Assistant, is not on the same drive or directory as dBASE.ovl.

**There are no files of the type requested in this drive or catalog**

[53] You've attempted to view all the files of a particular type, such as .dbf files, but there are no files of that type on the current disk or directory.

**This copy has already been initialized**

[IDLAN] The IDLAN disk in use has already been successfully initialized.

**This field must contain a valid dBASE expression**

Invalid field names or invalid operators were entered in an expression while using MODIFY REPORT or MODIFY QUERY.

**This is not the latest version of dBASE**

[IDLAN] You are attempting to copy the IDLAN program onto a disk containing an old version of dBASE, or the ADMINISTRATOR Disk #1 is defective.

**This must be a valid dBASE expression**

While entering an expression in MODIFY LABEL, you entered an invalid field name or operator or attempted to combine two data types incorrectly.

**This string must not contain any semicolons**

You entered a semicolon while entering a report title. Semicolons cannot be entered on the page title four-line window in MODIFY REPORT.

**Too many characters in REPORT**

The parameters in the MODIFY REPORT command that you specified exceed the maximum 1440 character limit.

**Too many files are open**

[6] The maximum number of files open has been reached. Either a total of 15 files is already open, or the Config.sys file on the boot-up disk does not specify the Files = 20 setting.

**Too many indices**

[28] You attempted to open more than the maximum of seven index files in a USE or SET INDEX command.

**Too many merge steps**

The dBASE III PLUS program is damaged. Make a new copy. If you still get the error, contact Ashton-Tate software support.

**Too many sort key fields**
You specified more than the maximum of ten key fields in a SORT command.

**Total label width exceeds maximum allowable size**
The LABEL FORM format exceeds the maximum width of 250 columns.

**^ - - - Truncated**
[74] The line in the Config.db file was too long and was therefore was truncated.

**Two files must be in use in order to set a relation**
An attempt was made to define a relationship between database files, but only one database file is open.

**Unable to load COMMAND.COM**
[92] The DOS Command.com file is required for the RUN command or to issue a command specified in a Config.db TEDIT or WP option. The Command.com file needs to be on the root directory of the boot-up drive, or the drive specified in the DOS COMSPEC setting. The dBASE command **? GETENV-("COMSPEC")** displays the location of the Command.com file.

**Unable to LOCK**
[129] [ADMINISTRATOR EXECUTION] You attempted to lock a record that was in use by another when you pressed Ctrl-O. Wait for the other user to unlock the record.

***** Unable to open response file <response file name>**
[RUNTIME+] The response file specified in a dBCODE or dBLINKER command line could not be located. Either the file name is misspelled or it is lacking the appropriate extension.

**Unable to SKIP**
[128] [ADMINISTRATOR EXECUTION] An attempt was made to skip to a record that is locked by another user.

**Unassigned file no.**
[2] The dBASE III PLUS program is damaged. Make a new copy. If you still get the error, contact Ashton-Tate software support.

**Unauthorized access level**
[133] [ADMINISTRATOR EXECUTION] You attempted to access a field or file for which you have not been granted access privileges.

**Unauthorized duplicate**
An attempt was made to run a copy of copy-protected dBASE III PLUS which has already been installed on another computer. [ADMINISTRATOR STARTUP] The DBA.lod file cannot be found in the dBASE ADMINISTRATOR directory.

**Unauthorized login**
[132] [ADMINISTRATOR EXECUTION] After three attempts, you were still unable to enter a valid login sequence. Access is denied.

**Unbalanced parenthesis**
[8] An expression contains an unequal number of open and closed parentheses. In MODIFY QUERY, you added or removed one parenthesis without adding or removing the opposing parenthesis. All expressions must contain an equal number of open and closed parentheses.

**Unknown function key**
[104] The function key specified in a SET FUNCTION command does not exist.

**Unknown SCEDIT( ) return code**
[2] The dBASE III PLUS program is damaged. Make a new copy. If you still get the error, contact Ashton-Tate software support.

*****Unrecognized command in file <input file name> – input file line <line no.>**
[RUNTIME+] dBCODE does not recognize a command in the source file.

*****Unrecognized command verb**
[16] The first word in a command line is not a valid dBASE command or may be misspelled.

**Unrecognized phrase/keyword in command**
[36] A command contains a phrase or keyword that is not valid for the command, is out of place, or is perhaps misspelled.

**Unsupported path given**
You attempted to create a database file with ..\ specified as the path name.

**Unterminated string**
[35] A character string literal is missing a quotation mark, apostrophe, or bracket. You need to put in the closing quotation mark, apostrophe, or bracket.

**Valid only in programs**
[95] At the dot prompt you entered a command that is valid only in programs, such as DO WHILE, DO CASE, IF, TEXT, LOOP, SUSPEND, ENDDO, CASE, OTHERWISE, ENDCASE, ENDIF, or ENDTEXT.

**Variable not found**
[12] The field or variable name does not exist as a field on the currently selected database file, nor as a memory variable name. Perhaps it is misspelled,

the memory variable has been released, or the wrong database file is in use. Use the DISPLAY STRUCTURE and DISPLAY MEMORY commands to view the names of current memory variables and fields.

**** WARNING ** Data will probably be lost. Confirm (Y/N)**
[70] Occurs when you select Abort in response to a disk-full error. If possible, put another disk in the drive and enter N to retry.

**** WARNING ** Report form empty**
You exited REPORT FORM without first defining any fields for the report to display.

*****Write error on file <output file name> – input line <line number>**
[RUNTIME+ ] The disk is full or damaged.

**Write failed for count file**
[ADDUSER] The ADDUSER program could not write to the DBA.ctl file on the DBNETCTL.300 directory, because the file was used by somebody else or because of access restrictions that were set previously.

**Wrong number of parameters**
[94] An attempt was made to pass the wrong number of parameters to a procedure or command file. The number of parameters passed must match the number of parameters specified in the PARAMETERS command.

**You entered the command incorrectly. The correct syntax is:**
[INSTALL/UNINSTALL] The syntax you used to run the INSTALL or UNINSTALL command was incorrect. The screen displays the proper syntax.

**You must enter a serial number**
[IDLAN] The serial number printed on the System Disk #1 label must be entered.

**You must enter at least two characters**
[IDLAN] The company name specified in the IDLAN program must contain at least two characters.

**Your System disk has missing files. Install is aborted**
[INSTALL/UNINSTALL] The current drive does not contain all the necessary files for completing the installation.

## Error Messages by ERROR( ) Number

When an ON ERROR condition is in effect, an error will store a number in the dBASE ERROR( ) function and the error message in the MESSAGE( ) function. This section lists the error messages associated with each error, in numeric order by ERROR( ) number. Refer to the alphabetical listing of error messages above for more details on a particular error message.

| Error Number | Error Message |
|---|---|
| 1 | File does not exist |
| 2 | Unassigned file no. |
| 3 | File is already open |
| 4 | End of file encountered |
| 5 | Record is out of range |
| 6 | Too many files are open |
| 7 | File already exists |
| 8 | Unbalanced parenthesis |
| 9 | Data type mismatch |
| 10 | Syntax error |
| 11 | Invalid function argument |
| 12 | Variable not found |
| 13 | ALIAS not found |
| 14 | No find |
| 15 | Not a dBASE database |
| 16 | *** Unrecognized command verb |
| 17 | Cannot select requested database |
| 18 | Line exceeds maximum width of 254 characters |
| 19 | Index file does not match the database |
| 20 | Record is not in index |
| 21 | Out of memory variable memory |
| 22 | Out of memory variable slots |
| 23 | Index is too big (100 char maximum) |
| 24 | ALIAS name already in use |
| 25 | Record is not inserted |
| 26 | Database is not indexed |

27 Not a numeric expression
28 Too many indices
29 File is not accessible
30 Position is off the screen
31 Invalid function name
33 Structure invalid
34 Operation with Memo field invalid
35 Unterminated string
36 Unrecognized phrase/keyword in command
37 Not a Logical expression
38 Beginning of file encountered
39 Numeric overflow (data was lost)
42 CONTINUE without LOCATE
43 Insufficient memory
44 Cyclic relation
45 Not a Character expression
46 Illegal value
47 No fields to process
48 Field not found
50 Report file invalid
51 End of file or error on keyboard input
52 No database is in USE. Enter file name:
53 There are no files of the type requested in this drive or catalog
54 Label file invalid
55 Memory Variable file is invalid
56 Disk full when writing file: <file name>
57 ***Execution error on CHR( ) : Out of range
58 ***Execution error on LOG( ) : Zero or negative
59 ***Execution error on SPACE( ) : Too large
60 ***Execution error on SPACE( ): Negative
61 ***Execution error on SQRT( ) : Negative
62 ***Execution error on SUBSTR( ) : Start point out of range
63 *** Execution error on STR( ) : Out of range
65 Internal error: Unknown command code

| | |
|---|---|
| 66 | Internal error: CMDSET( ): |
| 67 | Internal error: EVAL work area overflow |
| 68 | Internal error: Illegal opcode |
| 70 | ** WARNING ** Data will probably be lost. Confirm (Y/N) |
| 72 | ALTERNATE file could not be opened |
| 73 | ^ ^ Expected ON or OFF |
| 74 | ^- - -Truncated |
| 75 | ^- - -Out of range |
| 76 | ***Execution error on – : Concatenated string too large |
| 77 | ***Execution error on + : Concatenated string too large |
| 78 | ***Execution error on ^ or ** : Negative base, fractional exponent |
| 79 | ***Execution error on STORE : String too large |
| 81 | Invalid date (press SPACE) |
| 82 | ** Not Found ** |
| 86 | ^- - -Keyword not found |
| 87 | ***Execution error on NDX( ) : Invalid index number |
| 88 | ***Execution error on REPLICATE ( ) : String too large |
| 89 | Cannot erase a file which is open |
| 90 | Operation with Logical field invalid |
| 91 | File was not LOADed |
| 92 | Unable to load COMMAND.COM |
| 93 | No PARAMETER statement found |
| 94 | Wrong number of parameters |
| 95 | Valid only in programs |
| 96 | Mismatched DO WHILE and ENDDO |
| 99 | Invalid DOS SET option |
| 101 | Not suspended |
| 102 | ***Execution error on STUFF( ): String too large |
| 103 | DOs nested too deep |
| 104 | Unknown function key |
| 105 | Table is full |
| 106 | Invalid index number |
| 107 | Invalid operator |

| | |
|---|---|
| 108 | File is in use by another |
| 109 | Record is in use by another |
| 110 | Exclusive use on database is required |
| 110 | Exclusive open of file is required |
| 111 | Cannot write to a read-only file |
| 112 | Index expression is too big (220 char maximum) |
| 113 | Index interrupted. Index will be damaged if not completed. |
| 114 | Index damaged. Reindex should be done before using data. |
| 115 | Invalid DIF File Header |
| 117 | Invalid DIF type indicator |
| 118 | Invalid DIF character |
| 119 | Invalid SYLK file header |
| 120 | Invalid SYLK file dimension bounds |
| 121 | Invalid SYLK file format |
| 122 | Data Catalog has not been established |
| 123 | Invalid printer port |
| 124 | Invalid printer redirection |
| 125 | Printer not ready |
| 126 | Printer is either not connected or turned off |
| 127 | Not a valid VIEW file |
| 128 | Unable to SKIP |
| 129 | Unable to LOCK |
| 130 | Record is not locked |
| 131 | Database is encrypted |
| 132 | Unauthorized login |
| 133 | Unauthorized access level |
| 134 | Not a valid QUERY file |
| 137 | Maximum record length exceeded |
| 148 | Network server busy |

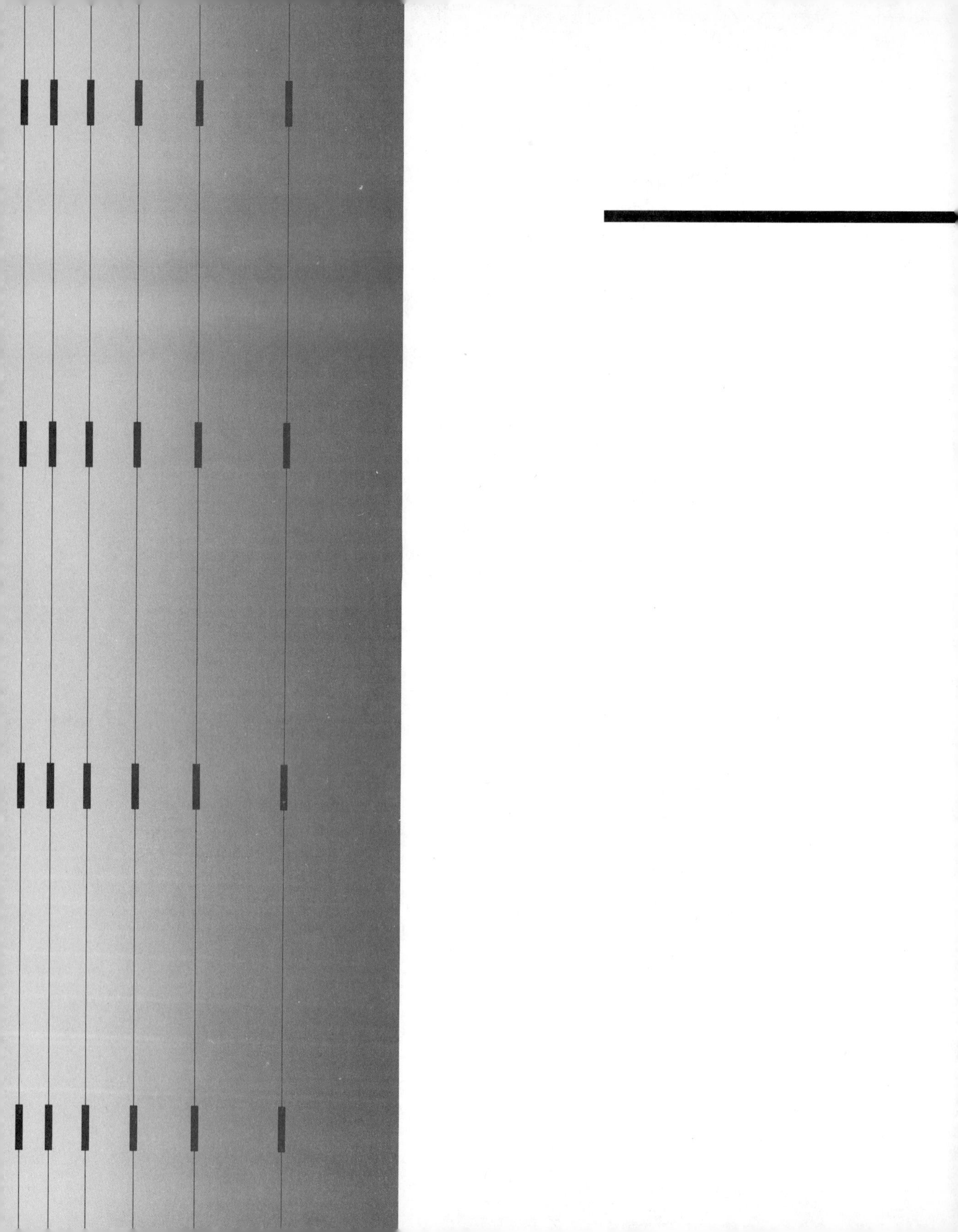

# INSTALLING dBASE III PLUS

# INSTALLING dBASE III PLUS

This appendix first discusses the steps required to install dBASE III PLUS on a single-user system, and then it covers installation for networking systems. Be sure to turn to the appropriate section of the chapter for your own computer configuration.

## INSTALLING SINGLE-USER dBASE III PLUS

This section discusses the steps required to install dBASE III PLUS version 1.1 on a single-user computer. Note that the steps for installing dBASE on a computer with only 256K RAM are different than those required for computers with more memory, as discussed below.

### Running the ID Program

Before you can use dBASE III PLUS, you must run the ID program on System Disk #1 to "tag" your copy of dBASE with your serial number, company name, and personal name. First, boot up your computer in the usual fashion so that the DOS prompt appears on the screen.

Next, write down the serial number on System Disk #1. Place the dBASE III PLUS System Disk #1 in drive A, and make A the current drive (by entering the command **A:** and pressing Return).

Enter the command **ID** and press Return. Type in your serial number (from the System Disk #1 label), company name, and personal name, as requested on the screen.

### Installing on a Hard Disk

If your computer has a hard disk, follow the instructions in this section. You'll need at least 700K of space available on your hard disk to install dBASE III PLUS. If your computer has only 256K memory, turn to the section entitled "Computers with 256K RAM" below.

## Creating the Config.sys File

Before installing dBASE III PLUS, you should check the root directory (the one that your computer boots from) for the existence of the Config.sys file. If you enter the command

**TYPE Config.sys**

at the DOS prompt and a Config.sys file exists, you'll see its contents. Otherwise, you'll see the error message **File not found**.

If there is no Config.sys file on your hard disk root directory, place the dBASE III PLUS System Disk #1 in drive A of your computer, then copy the file named Config.sys to your hard disk, as below:

**COPY A:Config.sys**

If you do have a file named Config.sys on your root directory already, check whether it has the commands

**FILES = 15**
**BUFFERS = 20**

If it does not, change it so it contains the two lines shown above.

## Installing dBASE

Before installing dBASE III PLUS version 1.1 on your hard disk, you should uninstall any previous version of dBASE that you might have on your disk. Use the UNINSTAL program that came with the previous version to do so.

To install dBASE on its own directory, create the directory, if necessary, and log onto that directory. The commands below demonstrate how to do this using a sample directory named DB:

**MD\DB**
**CD\DB**

If you would like DOS to display the name of the directory that you are logged onto to help you keep track of where you are, enter the command **PROMPT $P$G** at the DOS prompt. Then place the dBASE III PLUS System Disk #1 in drive A. Log onto drive A by typing **A:**. You should see the A> prompt on your screen.

Enter the **INSTALL** command, followed by the letter assigned to your hard disk and a colon. For example, if your hard disk is drive C, enter the command **INSTALL C:**. Note that if you have not run the ID program discussed earlier, the installation process will stop, and you'll need to go back and run the ID program. If you have already run the ID program, just follow the prompts as they appear on the screen.

When prompted, remove System Disk #1 from drive A, and put in System Disk #2, then press any key to continue.

When System Disk #2 is copied, you'll be returned to the A> prompt. Log back onto drive C by typing **C:**, and remove System Disk #2 from drive A.

### STARTING dBASE

After the installation is complete, you can run dBASE directly from your hard disk by logging onto the appropriate directory (the one dBASE was installed on) and entering the command **DBASE** at the DOS prompt. You'll see a copyright notice and then the dBASE Assistant menu appear on the screen.

To leave dBASE III PLUS and return to the dot prompt, select the option **Quit dBASE III PLUS** from the menu, or press the Esc key and type **QUIT**.

### UNINSTALLING dBASE

If at some time in the future you wish to remove dBASE III PLUS from your hard disk, first log onto the directory where dBASE is stored using the usual DOS CD\ command. Then place the dBASE III PLUS System Disk #1 in drive A, and log onto drive A by entering the command **A:**.

When the A> prompt appears on the screen, enter the UNINSTAL command followed by the letter assigned to your hard disk and a colon. For example, if your hard disk is drive C, you would enter the command **UNINSTAL C:**.

Follow the prompts as they appear on the screen. When the UNINSTAL program is done, a message appears telling you that the uninstallation was successful, and the A> prompt reappears.

Log back onto the hard disk by typing **C:**, and then remove the floppy disk from drive A.

## Installing dBASE III PLUS on Floppy Disks

If your computer has only floppy disk drives and no hard disk, follow the steps in this section to install dBASE III PLUS on your computer. If your computer has only 256K memory, skip to the section entitled "Computers with 256K RAM" below.

### CREATING THE CONFIG.SYS FILE

The disk that you usually use to boot up your computer must have a file named Config.sys on it to tell DOS how many files and buffers to open. To check your boot-up disk, boot up your computer in the usual manner, and at the DOS A> prompt enter the command below:

**TYPE Config.sys**

If you get the error message **File not found**, you can use the DOS COPY command to copy the Config.sys file from the dBASE III PLUS System Disk #1 onto the disk that you normally boot up from. To do so, put the dBASE III PLUS System Disk #1 in drive B of your computer, and enter this command at the DOS A> prompt:

**COPY B:Config.sys**

If the Config.sys file already exists on your boot-up disk, you'll see its contents on the screen rather than the **File not found** error message. See whether the file contains the commands

**FILES = 20**
**BUFFERS = 15**

If it does, you need not make any changes. If it does not, change it so it looks exactly like the two lines above.

## STARTING dBASE

When you have successfully created the appropriate Config.sys file on your boot-up directory, you can run dBASE. To do so, place the dBASE System Disk #1 in drive A while the DOS A> prompt is still showing. Then enter the command **DBASE**.

If you have not run the ID program discussed at the beginning of this appendix, it will run now, and you will need to fill in the information requested. The serial number requested is the one typed on the label of the dBASE III PLUS System Disk #1.

You'll see a copyright notice and instructions to insert System Disk #2 into drive A. Remove System Disk #1 from drive A, put in System Disk #2, and press the Return key.

You should see the dBASE Assistant menu appear on the screen. To exit dBASE and get back to the A> prompt, select the **Quit dBASE III PLUS** option, or press the Esc key and type **QUIT**.

## MAKING COPIES

To prevent any accidents or excessive use from damaging your original dBASE III PLUS disks, you may want to make copies of the disks and use those instead. You'll need to copy the files from both the dBASE III PLUS System Disk #1 and System Disk #2 onto other floppy disks.

You can also make the disk on which you copy System Disk #1 bootable by using the /S parameter in the FORMAT command line. If you do wish to boot directly from the copied dBASE III PLUS System Disk #1, be sure to copy the appropriate Config.sys file to it, as well as the DOS Command.com program. See the FORMAT and COPY commands in your DOS manual if you need help with this.

Once you've made copies of the dBASE disks, use the copies in your work with dBASE, and store the originals in a safe place.

## Computers with 256K RAM

If your computer has only 256K RAM, you'll need to perform some extra steps to install dBASE on it. First, you need to copy the files named Config.sys and Config.db from the dBASE III PLUS System Disk #1 onto a separate, formatted disk. If you need help with this, see the FORMAT and COPY commands in your DOS manual.

Once the original Config.sys and Config.db files are copied to another disk, enter the command

**COPY Confi256.* CONFIG.***

These steps copy the contents of the Confi256.sys and Confi256.db files over the Config.sys and Config.db files on System Disk #1. Keep the original Config files that you copied from System Disk #1 in a safe place, in case you ever want to run dBASE III PLUS on a computer with more than 256K RAM.

You can use the DOS TYPE command to view the contents of the new Config files. The Config.sys file will contain the commands

```
FILES = 20
BUFFERS = 4
```

The Config.db file will contain

```
COMMAND = ASSIST
STATUS = ON
BUCKET = 1
GETS = 35
MVARSIZ = 3
HISTORY = 10
TYPEAHEAD = 10
```

These are the maximum settings allowed on computers with only 256K RAM. (The Config.db file is discussed in more detail in Appendix C, "Configuring dBASE III PLUS.")

The appropriate Config.sys file is now ready for your computer, so you can go back to the section that you left before skipping to this section. (Skip the discussion of the Config.sys file in that section, however. It is not relevant to 256K computers.)

## INSTALLING dBASE ON AN IBM PC NETWORK

This section discusses the steps required for installing dBASE ADMINISTRATOR, the multiuser version of dBASE III PLUS, on an IBM PC Network. It assumes that the network itself has already been set up, as per instructions in the IBM PC Network manuals. The sample commands in this section assume that the file server's hard disk is drive C. If this is not the case, substitute the appropriate file server drive name where appropriate.

### Running IDLAN

Before installing the dBASE ADMINISTRATOR on the file server, you need to run the IDLAN program to tag your copy of dBASE with your serial number and company name. Insert the ADMINISTRATOR Disk #1 into drive A of a computer. Enter the command **IDLAN** at the DOS prompt, and press Return. Enter the serial number, which is printed on the label of dBASE III PLUS System Disk #1, and your company or personal name. When you're done, the A> prompt will reappear.

### Making Working Copies

Next make a copy of each of the original dBASE disks. This is a safety precaution to prevent the original disks from accidental damage. Label the copies appropriately (e.g., System Disk #1, ADMINISTRATOR Disk #1), and use the copies instead of the originals when installing.

### Copying DOS Programs

To simplify the installation, copy the ATTRIB.exe file from the DOS disk onto a shared directory of the file server. You can use this program to assign file access privileges. Then include this directory's name in your DOS PATH command, so that all DOS programs will have access to the ATTRIB program.

## Creating the File Server Config.sys File

The root directory of the drive that the file server boots from must have a file named Config.sys. This file can be created or edited with any text editor or word processor with an ASCII text mode. The file should contain the statements below:

**FILES = 51**
**BUFFERS = 15**
**LASTDRIVE = <x>**

where <x> is a single letter, A through Z, indicating the highest logical drive used in the network. To allow each workstation to open as many files as possible, adjust the FILES setting accordingly, using the formula

**FILES = number of workstations × 17**

Hence, if there are four workstations on the network, you'll want to set the FILES setting to 68. (If other programs require still higher settings, use those higher settings instead.)

## Creating Workstation Config.sys Files

Each workstation should also have a Config.sys file on its boot-up directory, or on the floppy disk it boots from. The Config.sys settings on each workstation should be

**FILES = 20**
**BUFFERS = 15**
**LASTDRIVE = <x>**

where <x> is a single letter representing the highest-lettered logical drive on the network.

## Creating a dBASE Subdirectory

The IBM PC Network documentation suggests creating a directory named APPS on the file server for all application programs on the network. Individual programs, such as dBASE, should in turn be stored in subdirectories. You can use either the network NET command, or the DOS MD command, to create the subdirectory.

If you have not already created the APPS directory on the file server, you can enter the command **MD\APPS** on the file server to create the directory. Then, to create a subdirectory named DBASE for dBASE III PLUS, enter the command

**MD\APPS\DBASE**

Next, you can create any other shared or private directories that you want on the file server. For example, you might want to create a directory for all dBASE application programs and data files, and subdirectories beneath this directory for individual applications, such as Payroll, Ledger, and so forth.

## Installing the dBASE ADMINISTRATOR

To install dBASE ADMINISTRATOR on the file server, you'll need the dBASE ADMINISTRATOR Disk #1, ADMINISTRATOR Disk #2, and System Disk #1.

If you have any previous versions of dBASE on the file server that you do not want to overwrite, you should use the UNINSTAL program for that version to uninstall the old copy before installing the dBASE ADMINISTRATOR.

The following steps discuss how to install dBASE, using the example subdirectory named APPS\DBASE on drive C:

1. Log onto the directory with the command **CD\APPS\DBASE**.
2. Insert dBASE System Disk #1 in drive A.
3. Log onto drive A by entering the command **A:**.
4. Enter the command **INSTALL C: DBA**. The screen displays information about the hard disk system and presents several prompts for you to respond to.
5. When the program asks for it, insert the ADMINISTRATOR Disk #1 in drive A and press any key to continue. The files from the floppy disk will be copied onto the hard disk. (*Note:* If you haven't completed the IDLAN program discussed earlier in this section, the installation will abort. Go back to that section and run the IDLAN program.)
6. When the screen requests, place the ADMINISTRATOR Disk #2 in drive A and press any key to continue.

When the A> prompt reappears on the screen, the installation is complete. (If for some reason the installation fails, refer to Appendix A for a description of dBASE error messages, or your network manual for network-level errors.)

The installation process has created a directory named DBNETCTL.300 on the file server. This directory contains the necessary files for running both dBASE and the ADDUSER program (discussed below). You must not remove this directory or alter the contents of any of its files.

## Assigning Read-Only Status

Next, you'll need to assign read-only status to the dBASE files using the DOS ATTRIB command. First, log back onto the file server, by typing **C:**. Then enter the command

**ATTRIB +R *.***

This command will change the following files to read-only status:

DBA.COM
DBA.OVL
DBASE.MSG
HELP.DBS
ASSIST.HLP
PROTECT.EXE
ADDUSER.COM

Note that if you've previously logged onto dBASE on the network, you will have also changed your Login.db file to read-only. Check the directory using the usual DIR command to see whether Login.db exists. If it does, enter the command

**ATTRIB –R Login.db**

to remove the read-only status from that file.

## Assigning Shared Status

Before running dBASE, you need to make both the DBASE subdirectory and the DBNETCTL.300 shareable. The steps to follow are listed below:

1. From the file server, enter the command

   **NET SHARE DBASE = C:\APPS\DBASE /RWC**

   (assuming that dBASE is stored on drive C under the directory name APPS\DBASE). This command assigns the network name DBASE to these files, with the /RWC (Read Write Create) status.
2. To assign the network name DBUSERS to the DBNETCTL.300 directory, along with the appropriate status for these files, enter the command

   **NET SHARE DBUSERS = C:\DBNETCTL.300 /RWC**

3. Now you need to assign a logical drive name at each workstation where you want to access dBASE. The drive letters should be names of drives

that are not already in use. The examples below use the drive names D: and E:. From each workstation, enter the commands

**NET USE D: \\<name>\DBASE**
**NET USE E: \\<name>\DBUSERS**

where <name> is the network name of the file server.

To avoid retyping these commands in the future, you can store them in a DOS Autoexec.bat file on the root directory of each workstation. In addition, you can store the commands in steps 1 and 2 above to an Autoexec.bat file on the network file server root directory.

### Starting dBASE

Before you can run the dBASE ADMINISTRATOR, the DOS PATH command needs to be issued to use the two logical drives assigned in step 3 above. In this example, using drives D and E, you would enter the command **PATH = D:\;E:**. (You could store this command in the workstation Autoexec-.bat file as well.)

To run dBASE, enter the command **DBA #DF = E** where E:, once again, is the logical drive assigned earlier.

If the PROTECT program has been used to protect the files (see Chapter 20, "Networking and Security"), you will need to log in. If the system has not been protected, you will see the dBASE copyright message appear on the screen.

Until you use the ADDUSER program to add more users, only one person can use dBASE III PLUS. The following sections discuss how to use ADDUSER to add and subtract dBASE users.

## Adding Users

The ADDUSER program in the dBASE ADMINISTRATOR directory on the file server and the dBASE ACCESS disk that comes with the dBASE III PLUS LAN Pack let you add new users to dBASE. Each ACCESS disk allows you to add up to five users.

The steps for adding users are listed below:

1. Log onto the dBASE ADMINISTRATOR directory on the file server (which in the examples above is C:\APPS\DBASE).
2. Enter the command **ADDUSER**.
3. When prompted, enter the logical drive letter of the DBNETCTL.300 directory (which, in this example, was drive E:).

4. Select option 1 from the ADDUSER menu to add a new user. Follow the prompts that appear on the screen.
5. Repeat step 4 above for each user that you want to add. (Remember, you can add only one user with the dBASE System Disk #1, and five users with each ACCESS disk from the dBASE LAN Pack.)

To see the number of users added at any time, select option 3 from the ADDUSER main menu. When done adding users, select option 4 to exit ADDUSER. You may also want to jot down the file server name on each floppy disk that you used to add users, for future reference.

## Subtracting Users

To reduce the number of users who can have access to dBASE, run the ADDUSER program and select option 2 to subtract a user. You'll also need to have an ACCESS disk or System Disk #1 available so that the count of installed users on the disk can be reduced accordingly. The steps for subtracting users are listed below:

1. Log onto the dBASE ADMINISTRATOR directory on the file server (which in the examples above is C:\APPS\DBASE).
2. Enter the command **ADDUSER**.
3. When prompted, enter the logical drive letter of the DBNETCTL.300 directory (which in this example was drive E:).
4. Select option 2 from the ADDUSER menu to subtract a user. Follow the prompts that appear on the screen.
5. Repeat step 4 above for each user that you want to subtract.

To see the number of users added at any time, select option 3 from the ADDUSER main menu. When done subtracting users, select option 4 to exit ADDUSER.

If you want to subtract all the users, you must first uninstall the dBASE ADMINISTRATOR, as discussed below.

## Uninstalling the dBASE ADMINISTRATOR

If for some reason you wish to remove dBASE from the network system altogether, you need to use the UNINSTAL program. Before doing so, make sure that there are no users currently logged onto dBASE. (The **DISPLAY USERS** command, when entered at the dBASE dot prompt, will tell you whether any users are currently running dBASE.)

The steps below assume that you've installed the dBASE ADMINISTRATOR in drive C of the file server under the directory name \APPS\DBASE, as used in the installation examples above.

1. Log onto the dBASE ADMINISTRATOR directory by entering the commands

   **C:**
   **CD\APPS\DBASE**

2. Convert the dBASE files back to read/write status by entering the command

   **ATTRIB -R *.***

3. Insert dBASE System Disk #1 in drive A, and log onto that drive by typing **A:**.
4. From the DOS A> prompt, enter the command **UNINSTAL C: DBA** (where C: represents the drive letter assigned to the file server).

From this point on, you can just follow the prompts as they appear on the screen. You'll be informed when the uninstallation procedure is complete, and the DOS A> prompt will reappear. At that point, you can remove System Disk #1 from drive A and store it in a safe place.

Note that the UNINSTAL program leaves the DBNETCTL.300 directory intact on the file server. If you wish to remove this directory as well, use the usual **DOS ERASE** command to delete all the files in the directory, then the **RD** command to remove the directory.

## INSTALLING dBASE ON A NOVELL/86 NETWORK

This section discusses the steps required for installing dBASE ADMINISTRATOR, the multiuser version of dBASE III PLUS, on a Novell/86 Network. It assumes that the network itself has already been set up, as per instructions in the Novell manuals. The sample commands in this section assume that the default network drive is logical drive F, and the location of the dBASE ADMINISTRATOR directory is mapped to logical drive X. If your network uses different settings, substitute the appropriate drive letters where appropriate in the commands presented.

These instructions also assume that you are working in dedicated mode while installing dBASE, and that all the operations are performed from a workstation. (Dedicated mode is required, otherwise there will not be enough free memory to complete the installation.)

## Running IDLAN

Before installing the dBASE ADMINISTRATOR on the file server, you need to run the IDLAN program. Insert the ADMINISTRATOR Disk #1 into drive A of a computer. Enter the command **IDLAN** at the DOS prompt and press Return. Enter the serial number that is printed on the label of the dBASE System Disk #1 and your company or personal name. When you're done, the A> prompt will reappear.

## Making Working Copies

Make a copy of each of the original dBASE disks. This is a safety precaution to prevent the original disks from accidental damage. Label the copies appropriately (e.g., System Disk #1, ADMINISTRATOR Disk #1), and use the copies instead of the originals when installing.

## Copying DOS Programs

The DOS Command.com program needs to be stored on the root directory or boot-up disk of each workstation. Check each workstation on the network, and if necessary, copy the Command.com file from the DOS disk onto the root directory or boot-up disk of the workstation. Of course, you must remember not to violate any copyright laws while making these copies.

## Creating Workstation Config.sys Files

Each workstation must have a Config.sys file on its root directory or on the floppy disk it boots from. The Config.sys settings on each workstation should be

**FILES = 20**
**BUFFERS = 15**

Check each workstation, and add this file to the root directory or boot-up disk as necessary. You can use any text editor, word processor, or the DOS EDLIN program to create or modify the file.

## Creating a dBASE ADMINISTRATOR Directory

The steps below demonstrate how to create a directory named SYS:DBASE on the file server for installing the dBASE ADMINISTRATOR:

1. Log in as supervisor at any workstation, and create a directory named SYS:DBASE.

2. Enter the command below to make SYS:DBASE accessible through a search drive:

   **MAP SEARCH3: = SYS:DBASE**

   The MAP SEARCH command assigns a network drive and directory that specifies where to search for files that are not in the current directory. You can store the MAP commands in a log-in file at each workstation, so that individual users do not need to enter the MAP commands each time they want to access dBASE. Note that you need to map the dBASE directory on each workstation that will have access to dBASE.

3. At this point you can create any private or shared directories that will be used by dBASE, using the usual Novell commands. The example below uses a shared directory named SYS:DBFILES. To assign the directory to a logical drive letter, such as W: in the example below, enter the command

   **MAP W: = SYS:DBFILES**

   You must then store a mapping of the directory to a logical drive in each workstation's log-in file.

## Installing the dBASE ADMINISTRATOR

This section discusses the steps necessary to install the dBASE ADMINISTRATOR in a directory named SYS:DBASE on the network file server. To complete all of the steps, you'll need the dBASE ADMINISTRATOR Disk #1, ADMINISTRATOR Disk #2, and System Disk #1.

If you have any previous versions of dBASE on the file server that you do not want to overwrite, you should use the UNINSTAL program for that version to uninstall the old copy before installing the dBASE ADMINISTRATOR.

To install the dBASE ADMINISTRATOR, make sure you are logged in at a workstation as SUPERVISOR. Then follow the steps below:

1. Insert the dBASE System Disk #1 in drive A, and log onto that drive by typing **A:**.
2. Assuming that the dBASE ADMINISTRATOR directory is available as drive X (as discussed above), enter the command **INSTALL X: DBA**. The screen displays information about the hard disk system and presents several prompts for you to respond to.
3. When the program requests, enter the ADMINISTRATOR Disk #1 in drive A and press any key to continue. The files from the floppy disk will be copied onto the hard disk. (*Note:* If you haven't completed the IDLAN program discussed earlier in this section, the installation will abort. Go back to that section and run the IDLAN program.)

4. When prompted, place the ADMINISTRATOR Disk #2 in drive A and press any key to continue.

When the A> prompt reappears on the screen, the installation is complete. (If for some reason the installation fails, refer to Appendix A, "Error Messages," for a description of dBASE error messages, or your network manual for network-level errors.)

The installation process has created a directory named DBNETCTL.300 on the logical root of the file server. This directory contains the necessary files for running both dBASE and the ADDUSER program (discussed below). You must not remove this directory or alter the contents of any of its files.

## Assigning File Attributes

Now you must assign file attributes to the various installed files, using the steps below:

1. Log onto the network drive by entering the command **F:**.
2. Set the dBASE ADMINISTRATOR files to shareable read/write status by entering the command

   **FLAG X:*.* srw**

3. Assign a logical drive to the DBNETCTL.300 directory created during the installation by entering the command

   **MAP SEARCH4: = SYS:DBNETCTL.300**

4. Assuming that the search drive is logical drive Y on the network, enter the command below to set file attributes for the files in the DBNETCTL.300 directory (if you are not using drive Y, substitute the appropriate drive letter into the command):

   **FLAG Y:*.* srw**

5. Finally, use the Novell SYSCON command, as supervisor, to give each user trustee assignment to the DBASE and DBNETCTL.300 directories. (Refer to the Novell users manual for information on the SYSCON command.)

## Starting dBASE

The Novell MAP commands and the dBASE DBA command are used to start dBASE from any workstation. The commands below can be placed in the log-in script to specify the location of the dBASE ADMINISTRATOR and

DBNETCTL.300 directories:

**MAP SEARCH3: = SYS:DBASE**
**MAP SEARCH4: = SYS:DBNETCTL.300**

Next you need to map the locations of drives and directories containing applications programs, shared database files, and any private directories on the file server. For example, you could specify drive W as the SYS:DBFILES directory, containing database files and programs, by entering the command

**MAP W: = SYS:DBFILES**

When the network mapping is complete, you enter the command **DBA # DF = Y:** to start dBASE (where Y: is the logical drive of the DBNETCTL.300 directory).

If the PROTECT program has been used to protect the files (See Chapter 20, "Networking and Security"), you will need to log in. If the system has not been protected, you will see the dBASE copyright message appear on the screen.

Until you use the ADDUSER program to add more users, only one person can use dBASE III PLUS. The following sections discuss how to use ADDUSER to add and subtract dBASE users.

## Adding Users

The ADDUSER program in the dBASE ADMINISTRATOR directory on the file server and the dBASE ACCESS disk that comes with the dBASE III PLUS LAN Pack let you add new users to dBASE. Each ACCESS disk allows you to add up to five users.

The steps for adding users are listed below:

1. Log onto the dBASE ADMINISTRATOR directory on the file server (which in the examples above is SYS:DBASE).
2. Type **ADDUSER**.
3. When prompted, enter the logical drive letter of the DBNETCTL.300 directory (which in this example was drive Y:).
4. Select option 1 from the ADDUSER menu to add a new user. Follow the prompts that appear on the screen.
5. Repeat step 4 above for each user that you want to add. (Remember, you can add only one user with the dBASE System Disk #1, and five users with each ACCESS disk from the dBASE III PLUS LAN Pack.)

To see the number of users added at any time, select option 3 from the ADDUSER main menu. When done adding users, select option 4 to exit ADDUSER. You may also want to jot down the file server name on each floppy disk that you used to add users, for future reference.

## Subtracting Users

To reduce the number of users that can have access to dBASE, run the ADDUSER program and select option 2 to subtract a user. You need to have an ACCESS disk or System Disk #1 available so the count of installed users on the disk can be reduced accordingly. The steps for subtracting users are listed below:

1. Log onto the dBASE ADMINISTRATOR directory on the file server (which is SYS:DBASE in the examples above).
2. Enter the command **ADDUSER**.
3. When prompted, enter the logical drive letter of the DBNETCTL.300 directory (which in this example is drive Y:).
4. Select option 2 from the ADDUSER menu to subtract a user. Follow the prompts that appear on the screen.
5. Repeat step 4 above for each user that you want to subtract.

To see the number of users added at any time, select option 3 from the ADDUSER main menu. When done subtracting users, select option 4 to exit ADDUSER.

If you want to reduce the user count all the way to zero, you must first uninstall the dBASE ADMINISTRATOR, as discussed below.

## Uninstalling the dBASE ADMINISTRATOR

If for some reason you wish to remove dBASE from the network system altogether, you need to use the UNINSTAL program to remove dBASE. Before doing so, make sure that there are no users currently logged into dBASE. (The **DISPLAY USERS** command, when entered at the dBASE dot prompt, will tell you whether any users are currently running dBASE.)

The steps below assume that you've installed the dBASE ADMINISTRATOR in drive C of the file server under the directory name \APPS\DBASE, as used in the installation examples above.

1. Log onto the dBASE ADMINISTRATOR directory as supervisor.
2. Convert the dBASE files back to nonshared read/write status by entering the command

   **FLAG X:*.* nrw**

3. Insert the dBASE System Disk #1 in drive A, and log onto that drive by typing **A:**.
4. From the A> prompt, enter the command **UNINSTAL X: DBA**.

From this point on, you can just follow the prompts as they appear on the screen. You'll be informed when the uninstallation procedure is complete, and then the A> prompt will reappear. At that point, you can remove System Disk #1 from drive A and store it in a safe place.

Note that the UNINSTAL program leaves the DBNETCTL.300 directory intact on the file server. If you wish to remove this directory as well, delete all the files in the directory, and then delete the directory name.

## INSTALLING dBASE ON A 3COM 3+ NETWORK

This section explains how to install dBASE on the 3COM 3+ network. It assumes that you've already installed the network system, and that the network is running in a nonconcurrent mode so that the network administrator can work from a workstation. This section also assumes that you've made 3+ Share startup disks for each workstation, or that you have set up each workstation to start from its own hard disk.

Furthermore, it assumes that you've already created a shared directory named C:\APPS that users are linked to through drive D. If you've used other drive letters, substitute the appropriate drive letters into the example commands listed in this section. The \APPS directory should include the special share name APPSADMN with read\write\create privileges for the \APPS directory. Finally, the 3F.exe and Login.exe programs must be available in the \APPS directory.

### Running IDLAN

Before installing the dBASE ADMINISTRATOR on the file server, you need to run the IDLAN program. Insert the ADMINISTRATOR Disk #1 into drive A of a computer. Enter the command **IDLAN** at the DOS prompt and press Return. Enter the serial number that is printed on the label of the dBASE System Disk #1 and your company or personal name. When you're done, the A> prompt will reappear.

### Making Working Copies

Make a copy of each of the original dBASE disks. This is a safety precaution to prevent the original disks from accidental damage. Label the copies appropriately (e.g. System Disk #1, ADMINISTRATOR Disk #1) and use the copies instead of the originals when installing.

## Copying DOS Programs

For each workstation, you'll need to make a copy of the DOS disk that allows individual users to execute DOS commands. You'll also need a copy of the DOS disk to run the ATTRIB program when installing dBASE III PLUS. Of course, you must remember not to violate any copyright laws while making these copies.

## Creating Workstation Config.sys Files

Each workstation must have a Config.sys file on its root directory or on the floppy disk it boots from. The Config.sys settings on each workstation should be

**FILES = 20**
**BUFFERS = 15**
**LASTDRIVE = <x>**

where <x> is a single letter between G and Z, representing the highest-lettered logical drive on the network.

Check each workstation and add the Config.sys file to the root directory or boot-up disk as necessary. You can use any text editor, word processor, or the DOS EDLIN program to create or modify the file.

## Creating a dBASE ADMINISTRATOR Directory

The steps below demonstrate how to create a subdirectory called \APPS for the dBASE ADMINISTRATOR:

1. Log in as the server user at any workstation, and enter the command below to link the \APPS subdirectory, using the sharename APPSADMN, with full privileges:

   **3F LOGIN [server]; LINK D: APPS**

   where [server] is the name of the server on which you want to install dBASE.

2. Run the 3F program on drive D by entering the commands

   **D:**
   **3F**

3. Create a shared directory of \APPS for the dBASE ADMINISTRATOR by entering the command below, and responding to the prompts as shown:

   **SHARE ?**
   **Sharename? DBASE**

**Path? C:\APPS\DBASE**
**Password? [password1]**

where [password1] is the password that each user will have to enter to use the directory. (Just press Return instead of specifying a password if you don't want users to have to enter passwords.) The last prompt is

**Access (/RWC)?**

The message below will appear on the screen after you press Return:

**\\Server:Domain:Org\DBASE shared**

DBASE is now a subdirectory on the \APPS directory on drive C. This is the directory on which you will install the dBASE files.

4. Now you can create any other private or shared directories on the file server for storing dBASE data files or applications programs. For example, you can use the 3F SHARE command to create a root database file directory named C:\DBFILES, or a database file subdirectory of C:\APPS\DBASE, as shown in the steps below:

   **SHARE ?<↵>**
   **Sharename? DBFILES**
   **Path? C:\DBFILES**
   **Password [password2]**
   **Access (/RWC)?<↵>**

   The message below will appear on the screen:

   **\\Server:Domain:Org\DBFILES shared**

   Later, individual workstations can create subdirectories for storing files that are related to a particular dBASE application, for example, a directory named \DBFILES\LEDGER for a general-ledger application.

5. Next, assign the DBASE and DBFILES directories (and any other subdirectories you've created) to network logical drive letters, as in the examples below (which use drives F and G):

   **LINK F: DBFILES [/PASS = password2]**
   **LINK G: DBASE [/PASS = password1]**

   where the /PASS = options specify [password1] and [password2] assigned above.

6. Exit the 3F program by pressing Return, and log onto drive A by entering the command **A:**.

## Installing the dBASE ADMINISTRATOR

This section discusses the steps necessary to install the dBASE ADMINISTRATOR on the network file server. To complete all of the steps, you'll need the dBASE ADMINISTRATOR Disk #1, ADMINISTRATOR DISK #2, and System Disk #1.

If you have any previous versions of dBASE on the file server that you do not want to overwrite, you should use the UNINSTAL program for that version to uninstall the old copy before installing the dBASE Administrator.

1. Insert the dBASE System Disk #1 in drive A, and log onto that drive by typing **A:**.
2. Enter the command **INSTALL G: DBA**. The screen displays information about the hard disk system and presents several prompts for you to respond to.
3. When the program requests, enter the ADMINISTRATOR Disk #1 in drive A and press any key to continue. The files from the floppy disk will be copied onto the hard disk. (*Note:* If you haven't completed the IDLAN program discussed earlier in this section, the installation will abort. Go back to that section and run the IDLAN program.)
4. When the screen requests, place the ADMINISTRATOR Disk #2 in drive A, and press any key to continue.

When the A> prompt reappears on the screen, the installation is complete. (If for some reason the installation fails, refer to Appendix A, "Error Messages," for a description of dBASE error messages, or your network manual for network-level errors.)

The installation process has created a directory named DBNETCTL.300 on the logical root of the file server. This directory contains the necessary files for running both dBASE and the ADDUSER program (discussed below). You must not remove this directory or alter the contents of any of its files.

### Assigning File Attributes

Next, you must assign file attributes to the installed files. Put a copy of your DOS disk in drive A, and assign read-only status to the dBASE program files by entering the command below at the DOS A> prompt:

**ATTRIB +R G:*.***

This command will change the following files to read-only status:

DBA.COM
DBA.OVL

DBASE.MSG
HELP.DBS
ASSIST.HLP
PROTECT.EXE
ADDUSER.COM

Note that if you've previously logged onto dBASE on the network, you will have also changed your Login.db file to read-only. Check the directory using the usual DIR command to see whether Login.db exists. If it does, enter the command

**ATTRIB – R Login.db**

to remove the read-only status from that file.

## STARTING dBASE

To run dBASE, you must first set up logical drive assignments for the workstations' home directories and the dBASE ADMINISTRATOR directory. You can also specify a DOS PATH list for any logical drives that you'd like searched when executing programs. Examples of the appropriate steps are listed below:

1. To link drive D to the APPS directory and drive E to the user's home directory on the network, enter the command below:

   **3F LOGIN [user name]; LINK D: \\[server name]\APPS;**
   **LINK E:**

   where [user name] is a login name created by the network administrator, and [server name] is the name assigned to the file server.
2. To set up logical drive assignments, for example, linking drive F to the C:\DBFILES directory and drive G to the APPS\DBASE directory, you would enter the commands below:

   **3F LINK G: \\[server]\DBASE [/PASS = password1]**
   **3F LINK F: \\[server]\DBFILES [/PASS = password1]**

   where [server] is the file server name, and [password1] and [password2] are the optional passwords you created in previous steps.
3. To help organize dBASE applications programs and database files, you can create subdirectories on the DBFILES directory. For example, to create a subdirectory named LEDGER, use the commands

   **F:**
   **MD LEDGER**
4. To log onto and work from the \DBFILES\LEDGER directory, enter the command **CD LEDGER**.

5. To create a DOS PATH for locating the files on logical drive G, enter the command **PATH = G:**.
6. Finally, to start dBASE, enter the command **DBA #DF = G:** where #DF specifies the logical drive that the dBASE ADMINISTRATOR is stored on.

If the PROTECT program has been used to protect the files (see Chapter 20, "Networking and Security"), you will need to log in. If the system has not been protected, you will see the dBASE copyright message appear on the screen.

Until you use the ADDUSER program to add more users, only one person can use dBASE III PLUS. The following sections discuss how to use ADDUSER to add and subtract dBASE users.

## Adding Users

The ADDUSER program in the dBASE ADMINISTRATOR directory on the file server and the dBASE ACCESS disk that comes with the dBASE III PLUS LAN Pack let you add new users to dBASE. Each ACCESS disk allows you to add up to five users.

The general steps for adding users are listed below:

1. If, as shown in the examples above, you've linked drive G to the DBASE subdirectory, log onto drive G by entering the command G:
2. Type **ADDUSER**.
3. When prompted, enter the drive letter of the DBNETCTL.300 directory (which in this example is drive G).
4. Select option 1 from the ADDUSER menu to add a new user. Follow the prompts that appear on the screen.
5. Repeat step 4 above for each user that you want to add. (Remember, you can add only one user with the dBASE System Disk #1, and five users with each ACCESS disk from the dBASE LAN Pack.

To see the number of users added at any time, select option 3 from the ADDUSER main menu. When done adding users, select option 4 to exit ADDUSER. You may also want to jot down the file server name on each floppy disk that you used to add users, for future reference.

## Subtracting Users

To reduce the number of users who can have access to dBASE, run the ADDUSER program and select option 2 to subtract a user. You'll also need to have an ACCESS disk or System Disk #1 available, so that the count of installed users on the disk can be reduced accordingly. The general steps for subtracting users are listed below:

1. Log onto the drive containing the dBASE ADMINISTRATOR directory on the file server (which in the examples above is G).
2. Enter the command **ADDUSER**.
3. When prompted, enter the logical drive letter of the DBNETCTL.300 directory (which in this example is drive G).
4. Select option 2 from the ADDUSER menu to subtract a user. Follow the prompts that appear on the screen.
5. Repeat step 4 above for each user that you want to subtract.

To see the number of users added at any time, select option 3 from the ADDUSER main menu. When done subtracting users, select option 4 to exit ADDUSER.

If you want to reduce the user count all the way to zero, you must first uninstall the dBASE ADMINISTRATOR, as discussed below.

## Uninstalling the dBASE ADMINISTRATOR

If for some reason you wish to remove dBASE from the network system altogether, you need to use the UNINSTAL program to remove dBASE. Before doing so, make sure that there are no users currently logged into dBASE. The **DISPLAY USERS** command, when entered at the dBASE dot prompt, will tell you whether any users are currently running dBASE. You can also use the command below at the DOS prompt to see the list of users linked to the DBASE directory:

**3F DIR \\[server name]\DBASE /LINK**

When you are certain that there are no users logged onto dBASE, follow the steps below to uninstall dBASE ADMINISTRATOR:

1. Log in as the server user, link drive D to the APPSADMN share name with full privileges, and link drive G to the \APPS\DBASE directory by entering the commands below:

   **3F LOGIN SERVER;LINK D: APPSADMN**
   **3F LINK G: \\[server]\DBASE**

2. Using your DOS disk, convert the dbase files back to nonshared read/write status by entering the command

   **ATTRIB −R G:*.***

3. Put dBASE System Disk #1 in drive A, and enter the command

   **UNINSTAL G: DBA**

From this point on, you can just follow the prompts as they appear on the screen. You'll be informed when the uninstallation procedure is complete, and then the A> prompt will reappear. At that point, you can remove the System Disk #1 from drive A and store it in a safe place.

Note that the UNINSTAL program leaves the DBNETCTL.300 directory intact on the file server. If you wish to remove this directory as well, delete all the files in the directory, and then delete the directory name.

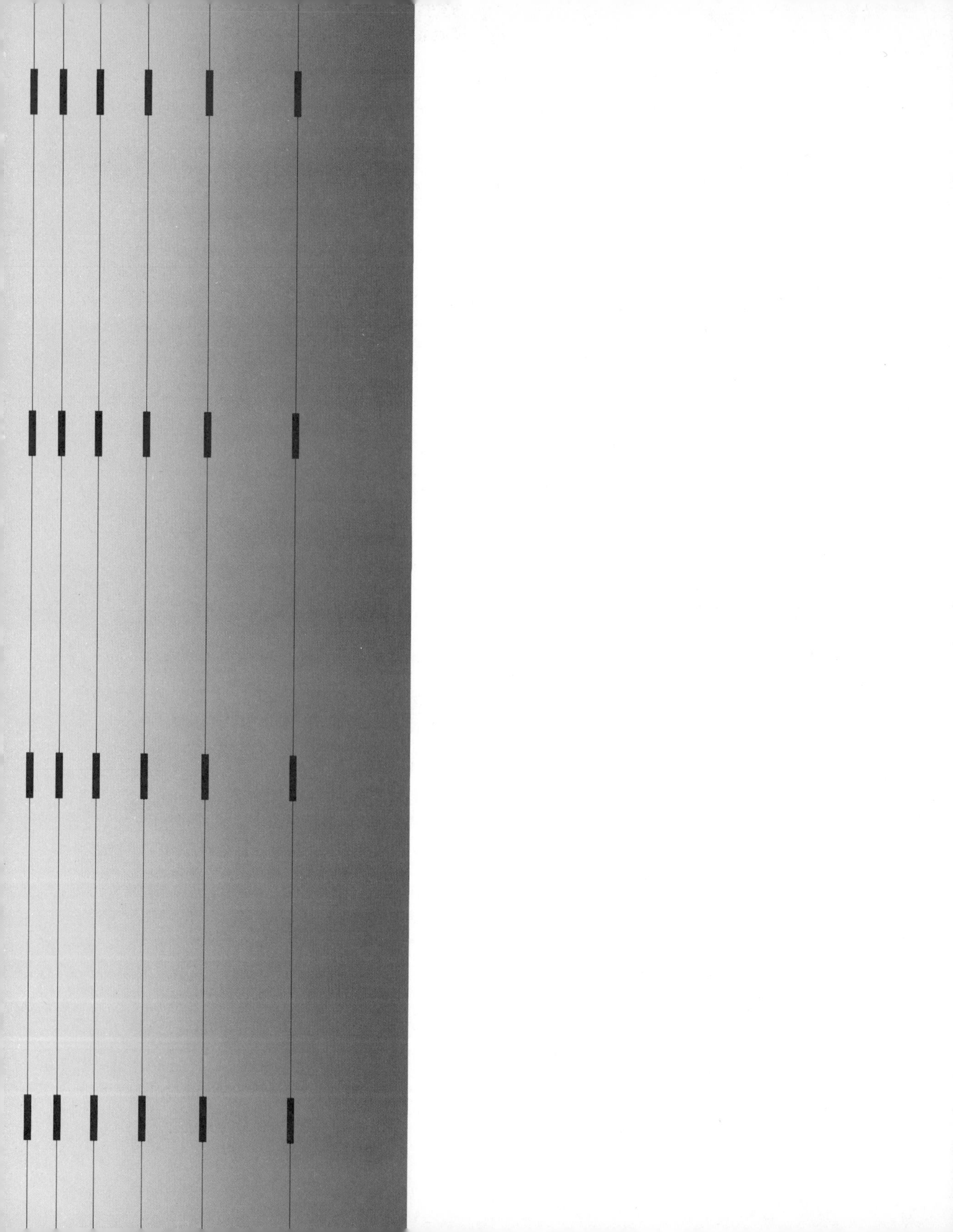

# CONFIGURING dBASE III PLUS

This appendix discusses the Config.db file, which dBASE reads automatically whenever you enter the command **dBASE** at the DOS prompt. dBASE executes all of the commands in the Config.db file before displaying the dot prompt, so you can use the Config.db file to customize the parameters dBASE starts with.

## INITIAL SETTINGS

The dBASE III PLUS System Disk #1 contains a file named Config.db, which you can modify to change the initial default settings in dBASE III PLUS. (When installed on a hard disk system, the Config.db file is on the same directory as dBASE itself.) Initially, the Config.db file contains only the commands

**STATUS = ON**
**COMMAND = ASSIST**

which ensure that dBASE begins with the status bar on and the Assistant menu showing. (If you were to remove these two commands, dBASE III PLUS would start with a dot prompt only, like earlier versions of dBASE.)

You can use any word processor in ASCII text mode or the dBASE MODIFY COMMAND editor to change the Config.db file to new settings.

## KEYWORDS USED IN THE CONFIG.DB FILE

Table C.1 lists the commands that Config.db recognizes (excluding the SET parameters, which are discussed later), along with a description of what each command does.

## SET PARAMETERS USED IN CONFIG.DB

You can set most of the dBASE SET parameters in the Config.db file, to establish their status before the dBASE dot prompt appears. The SET parameters recognized by Config.db, along with the values you can assign to them, are listed in Table C.2. (Chapter 18, "Setting Parameters," discusses each of these parameters in detail.) Note that the syntax used with SET parameters in the Config.db

| KEYWORD | EFFECTS |
|---|---|
| COMMAND | Any command listed with this option is executed the moment dBASE III PLUS begins. Therefore, the **COMMAND = ASSIST** line in Config.db causes the Assistant menu to appear the moment dBASE III PLUS is started. |
| BUCKET | Specifies the amount of memory allocated for PICTURE and RANGE commands. The default is 2, which stands for 2 × 1024 bytes. |
| GETS | Specifies the number of @...SAY...GET statements that can be active at any one time. The default setting is 128. |
| MAXMEM | Specifies the amount of memory preserved when dBASE III PLUS executes an external program. The default is 256K bytes. |
| MVARSIZ | Specifies the amount of space allocated for storing memory variables. The default is 6000 bytes (approximately 6K). |
| PROMPT | Specifies the dBASE III PLUS prompt, which appears as a dot (.) by default. |
| TEDIT | Specifies an external word processor to be used in place of MODIFY COMMAND. |
| WP | Specifies an external word processor to be used with memo fields. |

**TABLE C.1:** Commands Used in the Config.db File

file is different from that used in dBASE commands. Whereas dBASE commands use the syntax **SET <parameter> TO <setting>**, Config.db uses the syntax **<parameter>** = **<setting>**. Hence, when dBASE use the command **SET TALK OFF**, Config.db uses **TALK = OFF**.

## A Sample Config.db File

Figure C.1 shows a sample Config.db file, which demonstrates the proper syntax for the various commands.

The sample Config.db file has the following effects:

1. The **COLOR = GR+ /B,W+ /RB,BG+** command causes dBASE to start with yellow letters (GR+) on a blue background (B) for the standard screen, with white letters (W+) on a magenta background (RB) where reverse video is used. The screen border will be light blue (BG+).
2. **DEFAULT = C** specifies drive C as the default drive for storing and searching for files.

| SET KEYWORD | VALUES |
|---|---|
| ALTERNATE | <file name> |
| BELL | ON/OFF |
| CARRY | ON/OFF |
| CATALOG | <file name> |
| CENTURY | ON/OFF |
| COLOR | <color codes> |
| CONFIRM | ON/OFF |
| CONSOLE | ON/OFF |
| DEBUG | ON/OFF |
| DECIMALS | <0 to 14> |
| DEFAULT | <drive designator> |
| DELETED | ON/OFF |
| DELIMITER | ON/OFF |
| DELIMITER | <one or two characters> |
| DEVICE | SCREEN/PRINT |
| ECHO | ON/OFF |
| ESCAPE | ON/OFF |
| EXACT | ON/OFF |
| F<number> | <function key commands> |
| HEADING | ON/OFF |
| HELP | ON/OFF |
| HISTORY | <0 to 16000> |
| INTENSITY | ON/OFF |
| MARGIN | <1 to 254> |
| MEMOWIDTH | <0 to 80> |
| MENU | ON/OFF |
| PATH | <path name> |
| PRINT | ON/OFF |
| SAFETY | ON/OFF |
| SCOREBOARD | ON/OFF |
| STATUS | ON/OFF |
| STEP | ON/OFF |
| TALK | ON/OFF |
| TYPEAHEAD | <0 to 32000> |
| UNIQUE | ON/OFF |
| VIEW | <file name> |

**TABLE C.2:** SET Parameters Recognized by Config.db

```
COLOR = GR+/B,W+/RB,BG+
DEFAULT = C
PATH = C:\DBFILES\FW
TEDIT = WORD
WP = WS
F9 = "DISPLAY STRUCTURE;"
F10 = "DISPLAY STATUS;"
PROMPT = Command:>
HELP = OFF
TALK = OFF
COMMAND = DO MyProg
```

**FIGURE C.1:** This sample configuration file defines screen colors, a default disk drive, and a file search path. It sets up Microsoft Word to edit command files and WordStar as the editor for memo fields. The file assigns commands to function keys F9 and 10. The dot prompt is changed to **Command:>**, the SET HELP and SET TALK parameters are turned off, and the program MyProg is run automatically.

3. **PATH = C:\DBFILES\FW** tells dBASE to follow a route when looking for files. If a file cannot be found on the current directory, dBASE will search the DBFILES and FW directories for the file.
4. **TEDIT = WORD** causes dBASE to access Microsoft Word rather than the usual dBASE III PLUS MODIFY COMMAND editor. (This command requires more than 256K RAM.)
5. **WP = WS** causes dBASE to run WordStar when the user enters Ctrl-PgDn to enter or edit a memo field. (This command requires more than 256K RAM.)
6. **F9 = "DISPLAY STRUCTURE;"** and **F10 = "DISPLAY STATUS;"** assign the commands DISPLAY STRUCTURE and DISPLAY STATUS to function keys F9 and F10, respectively. The semicolon in the commands tells dBASE to perform a carriage return after the command (the equivalent of the user pressing the Return key).
7. **PROMPT = Command:>** causes dBASE to display the prompt **Command:>** instead of the usual dot prompt.
8. **HELP = OFF** turns the SET HELP parameter to the OFF setting.
9. **TALK = OFF** turns the SET TALK parameter to the OFF setting.
10. **COMMAND = DO MyProg** causes dBASE to run a program named MyProg.prg, which presumably already exists on the disk.

Neither the status bar nor the Assistant menu will appear when dBASE is first started, because the original STATUS = ON and COMMAND = ASSIST commands have been removed from the Config.db file.

Your Config.db file will not have any effect until dBASE is started from the DOS A> or C> prompt. Therefore, if you create a Config.db file using the MODIFY COMMAND editor, you'll have to QUIT dBASE and start it again from scratch to see the effects of the file.

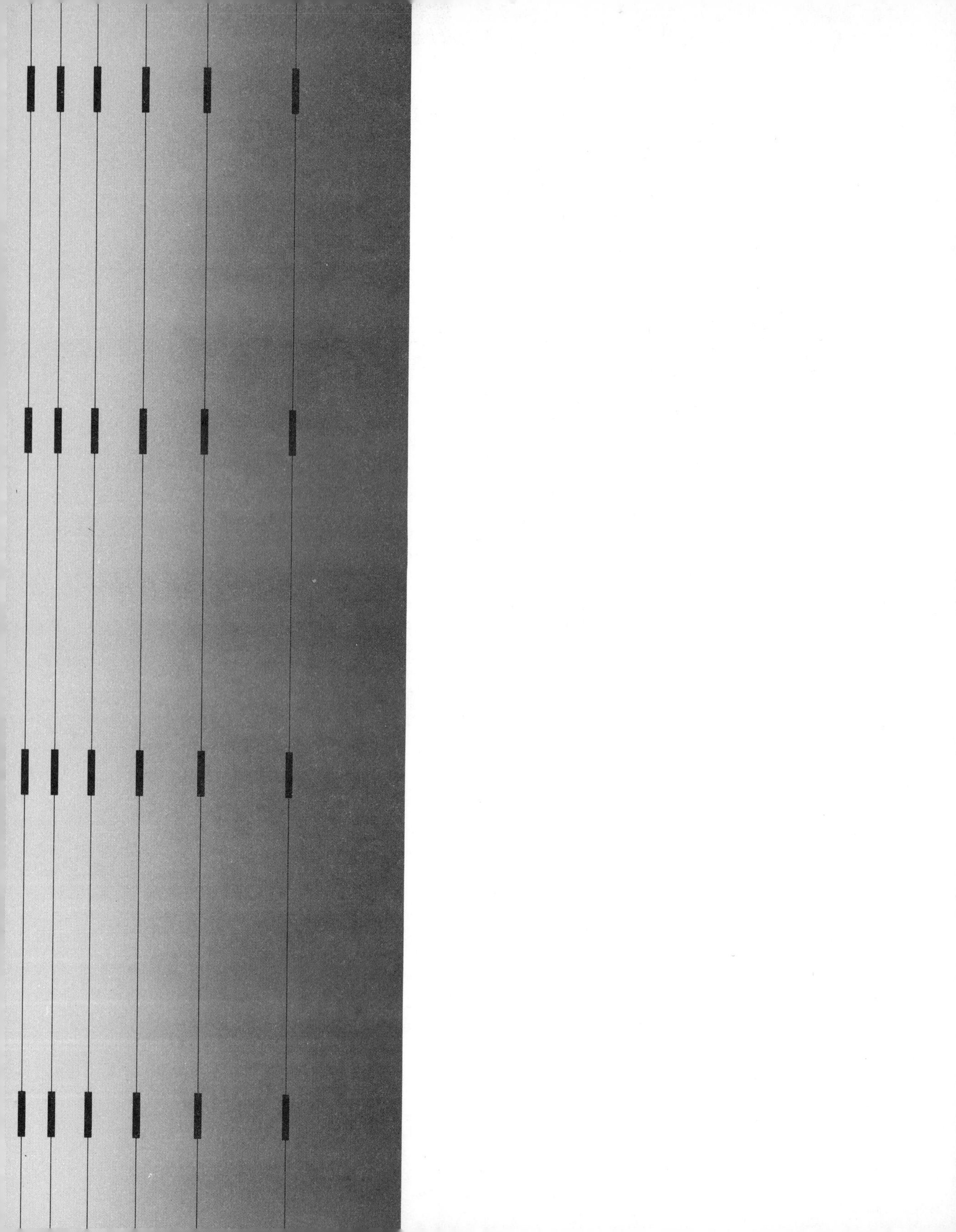

# ASCII CODES AND SYMBOLS

This appendix displays a chart of all the ASCII characters available on the IBM PC and compatible computers. The left column displays the decimal number for each character, the middle column displays the character, and the right column displays the hexadecimal value for each character.

To display any character on the screen, use the dBASE CHR( ) function with the appropriate decimal number. For example, the command **? CHR(3)** or **@ <row>,<col> SAY CHR(3)** will display a heart. The ASC( ) function displays the decimal number for a given character. For example, the command **? ASC("*")** displays **42**. The hexadecimal values are never used directly in dBASE, but are generally used in assembly language subroutines.

ASCII characters in the range of 32 to 127 are standard on all printers. ASCII values outside this range may vary on different printers, so the character on the screen may not be the same as the character displayed by the printer. On most printers, the command **? CHR(12)** produces a form feed, and **? CHR(10)** produces a line feed (assuming the **SET PRINT ON** command is in effect).

| ASCII | PRINTS | HEX | ASCII | PRINTS | HEX |
|---|---|---|---|---|---|
| 0* | | 0 | 16 | ► | 10 |
| 1 | ☺ | 1 | 17 | ◄ | 11 |
| 2 | ☻ | 2 | 18 | ↕ | 12 |
| 3 | ♥ | 3 | 19 | ‼ | 13 |
| 4 | ♦ | 4 | 20 | ¶ | 14 |
| 5 | ♣ | 5 | 21 | § | 15 |
| 6 | ♠ | 6 | 22 | ▬ | 16 |
| 7 | • | 7 | 23 | ↨ | 17 |
| 8 | ◘ | 8 | 24 | ↑ | 18 |
| 9 | ○ | 9 | 25 | ↓ | 19 |
| 10 | ◙ | A | 26 | → | 1A |
| 11 | ♂ | B | 27 | ← | 1B |
| 12 | ♀ | C | 28 | ∟ | 1C |
| 13 | ♪ | D | 29 | ↔ | 1D |
| 14 | ♫ | E | 30 | ▲ | 1E |
| 15 | ☼ | F | 31 | ▼ | 1F |

*Nonprintable character
**Space

| ASCII | PRINTS | HEX | ASCII | PRINTS | HEX |
|---|---|---|---|---|---|
| 32** | | 20 | 48 | 0 | 30 |
| 33 | ! | 21 | 49 | 1 | 31 |
| 34 | " | 22 | 50 | 2 | 32 |
| 35 | # | 23 | 51 | 3 | 33 |
| 36 | $ | 24 | 52 | 4 | 34 |
| 37 | % | 25 | 53 | 5 | 35 |
| 38 | & | 26 | 54 | 6 | 36 |
| 39 | ' | 27 | 55 | 7 | 37 |
| 40 | ( | 28 | 56 | 8 | 38 |
| 41 | ) | 29 | 57 | 9 | 39 |
| 42 | * | 2A | 58 | : | 3A |
| 43 | + | 2B | 59 | ; | 3B |
| 44 | , | 2C | 60 | < | 3C |
| 45 | - | 2D | 61 | = | 3D |
| 46 | . | 2E | 62 | > | 3E |
| 47 | / | 2F | 63 | ? | 3F |

*Nonprintable character
**Space

| ASCII | PRINTS | HEX | ASCII | PRINTS | HEX |
|---|---|---|---|---|---|
| 64 | @ | 40 | 80 | P | 50 |
| 65 | A | 41 | 81 | Q | 51 |
| 66 | B | 42 | 82 | R | 52 |
| 67 | C | 43 | 83 | S | 53 |
| 68 | D | 44 | 84 | T | 54 |
| 69 | E | 45 | 85 | U | 55 |
| 70 | F | 46 | 86 | V | 56 |
| 71 | G | 47 | 87 | W | 57 |
| 72 | H | 48 | 88 | X | 58 |
| 73 | I | 49 | 89 | Y | 59 |
| 74 | J | 4A | 90 | Z | 5A |
| 75 | K | 4B | 91 | [ | 5B |
| 76 | L | 4C | 92 | \ | 5C |
| 77 | M | 4D | 93 | ] | 5D |
| 78 | N | 4E | 94 | ^ | 5E |
| 79 | O | 4F | 95 | _ | 5F |

| ASCII | PRINTS | HEX | ASCII | PRINTS | HEX |
|---|---|---|---|---|---|
| 96 | ` | 60 | 112 | p | 70 |
| 97 | a | 61 | 113 | q | 71 |
| 98 | b | 62 | 114 | r | 72 |
| 99 | c | 63 | 115 | s | 73 |
| 100 | d | 64 | 116 | t | 74 |
| 101 | e | 65 | 117 | u | 75 |
| 102 | f | 66 | 118 | v | 76 |
| 103 | g | 67 | 119 | w | 77 |
| 104 | h | 68 | 120 | x | 78 |
| 105 | i | 69 | 121 | y | 79 |
| 106 | j | 6A | 122 | z | 7A |
| 107 | k | 6B | 123 | { | 7B |
| 108 | l | 6C | 124 | ¦ | 7C |
| 109 | m | 6D | 125 | } | 7D |
| 110 | n | 6E | 126 | ~ | 7E |
| 111 | o | 6F | 127 | ∆ | 7F |

| ASCII | PRINTS | HEX | ASCII | PRINTS | HEX |
|---|---|---|---|---|---|
| 128 | Ç | 80 | 144 | É | 90 |
| 129 | ü | 81 | 145 | æ | 91 |
| 130 | é | 82 | 146 | Æ | 92 |
| 131 | â | 83 | 147 | ô | 93 |
| 132 | ä | 84 | 148 | ö | 94 |
| 133 | à | 85 | 149 | ò | 95 |
| 134 | å | 86 | 150 | û | 96 |
| 135 | ç | 87 | 151 | ù | 97 |
| 136 | ê | 88 | 152 | ÿ | 98 |
| 137 | ë | 89 | 153 | Ö | 99 |
| 138 | è | 8A | 154 | Ü | 9A |
| 139 | ï | 8B | 155 | ¢ | 9B |
| 140 | î | 8C | 156 | £ | 9C |
| 141 | ì | 8D | 157 | ¥ | 9D |
| 142 | Ä | 8E | 158 | ₧ | 9E |
| 143 | Å | 8F | 159 | ƒ | 9F |

| ASCII | PRINTS | HEX | ASCII | PRINTS | HEX |
|---|---|---|---|---|---|
| 160 | á | A0 | 176 | ░ | B0 |
| 161 | í | A1 | 177 | ▒ | B1 |
| 162 | ó | A2 | 178 | ▓ | B2 |
| 163 | ú | A3 | 179 | │ | B3 |
| 164 | ñ | A4 | 180 | ┤ | B4 |
| 165 | Ñ | A5 | 181 | ╡ | B5 |
| 166 | ª | A6 | 182 | ╢ | B6 |
| 167 | º | A7 | 183 | ╖ | B7 |
| 168 | ¿ | A8 | 184 | ╕ | B8 |
| 169 | ⌐ | A9 | 185 | ╣ | B9 |
| 170 | ¬ | AA | 186 | ║ | BA |
| 171 | ½ | AB | 187 | ╗ | BB |
| 172 | ¼ | AC | 188 | ╝ | BC |
| 173 | ¡ | AD | 189 | ╜ | BD |
| 174 | « | AE | 190 | ╛ | BE |
| 175 | » | AF | 191 | ┐ | BF |

| ASCII | PRINTS | HEX | ASCII | PRINTS | HEX |
|---|---|---|---|---|---|
| 192 | └ | C0 | 208 | ╨ | D0 |
| 193 | ┴ | C1 | 209 | ╤ | D1 |
| 194 | ┬ | C2 | 210 | ╥ | D2 |
| 195 | ├ | C3 | 211 | ╙ | D3 |
| 196 | ─ | C4 | 212 | ╘ | D4 |
| 197 | ┼ | C5 | 213 | ╒ | D5 |
| 198 | ╞ | C6 | 214 | ╓ | D6 |
| 199 | ╟ | C7 | 215 | ╫ | D7 |
| 200 | ╚ | C8 | 216 | ╪ | D8 |
| 201 | ╔ | C9 | 217 | ┘ | D9 |
| 202 | ╩ | CA | 218 | ┌ | DA |
| 203 | ╦ | CB | 219 | █ | DB |
| 204 | ╠ | CC | 220 | ▄ | DC |
| 205 | ═ | CD | 221 | ▌ | DD |
| 206 | ╬ | CE | 222 | ▐ | DE |
| 207 | ╧ | CF | 223 | ▀ | DF |

| ASCII | PRINTS | HEX | ASCII | PRINTS | HEX |
|---|---|---|---|---|---|
| 224 | α | E0 | 240 | ≡ | F0 |
| 225 | β | E1 | 241 | ± | F1 |
| 226 | Γ | E2 | 242 | ≥ | F2 |
| 227 | π | E3 | 243 | ≤ | F3 |
| 228 | Σ | E4 | 244 | ⌠ | F4 |
| 229 | σ | E5 | 245 | ⌡ | F5 |
| 230 | μ | E6 | 246 | ÷ | F6 |
| 231 | τ | E7 | 247 | ≈ | F7 |
| 232 | Φ | E8 | 248 | ° | F8 |
| 233 | θ | E9 | 249 | • | F9 |
| 234 | Ω | EA | 250 | · | FA |
| 235 | δ | EB | 251 | √ | FB |
| 236 | ∞ | EC | 252 | ⁿ | FC |
| 237 | ø | ED | 253 | ² | FD |
| 238 | ∈ | EE | 254 | ■ | FE |
| 239 | ∩ | EF | 255* | | FF |

# INDEX

## E

# Selections from The SYBEX Library

## Software Specific

### *DATABASE MANAGEMENT SYSTEMS*

**UNDERSTANDING dBASE III PLUS**
**by Alan Simpson**
415 pp., illustr., Ref. 349-X
Emphasizing the new PLUS features, this extensive volume gives the database terminology, program management, techniques, and applications. There are hints on file-handling, debugging, avoiding syntax errors.

**ADVANCED TECHNIQUES IN dBASE III PLUS**
**by Alan Simpson**
500 pp., illustr., Ref. 369-4
The latest version of what ***Databased Advisor*** called "the best choice for experienced dBASE III programmers." Stressing design and structured programming for quality custom systems, it includes practical examples and full details on PLUS features.

**MASTERING dBASE III PLUS: A STRUCTURED APPROACH**
**by Carl Townsend**
350 pp., illustr., Ref. 372-4
This new edition adds the power of PLUS to Townsend's highly successful structured approach to dBASE III programming. Useful examples from business illustrate system design techniques for superior custom applications.

**ABC'S OF dBASE III PLUS**
**by Robert Cowart**
225 pp., illustr., Ref. 379-1
Complete introduction to dBASE III PLUS for first-time users who want to get up and running with dBASE fast. With step-by-step exercises covering the essential functions as well as many useful tips and business applications.

**UNDERSTANDING dBASE III**
**by Alan Simpson**
250 pp., illustr., Ref. 267-1
The basics and more, for beginners and intermediate users of dBASEIII. This presents mailing label systems, bookkeeping and data management at your fingertips.

**ADVANCED TECHNIQUES IN dBASE III**
**by Alan Simpson**
505 pp., illustr., Ref. 282-5
Intermediate to experienced users are given the best database design techniques, the primary focus being the development of user-friendly, customized programs.

**MASTERING dBASE III: A STRUCTURED APPROACH**
**by Carl Townsend**
338 pp., illustr., Ref. 301-5

**SIMPSON'S dBASE III LIBRARY**
**by Alan Simpson**
362 pp., illustr., Ref. 300-7
Our bestselling dBASE author shares his personal library of custom dBASE III routines for finance, graphics, statistics, expanded databases, housekeeping, screen management and more.

### UNDERSTANDING dBASE II

**by Alan Simpson**

260 pp., illustr., Ref. 147-0

Learn programming techniques for mailing label systems, bookkeeping, and data management, as well as ways to interface dBASE II with other software systems.

### ADVANCED TECHNIQUES IN dBASE II

**by Alan Simpson**

395 pp., illustr. Ref., 228-0

Learn to use dBASE II for accounts receivable, recording business income and expenses, keeping personal records and mailing lists, and much more.

### MASTERING Q&A

**by Greg Harvey**

350 pp., illustr., Ref. 356-2

An experienced consultant gives you straight answers on every aspect of Q&A, with easy-to-follow tutorials on the write, file, and report modules, using the Intelligent Assistant, and hundreds of expert tips.

### MASTERING REFLEX

**by Robert Ericson and Ann Moskol**

336 pp., illustr., Ref. 348-1

The complete resource for users of Borland's Reflex: The Analyst, with extensive examples and templates for practical applications.

### POWER USER'S GUIDE TO R:base 5000

**by Alan Simpson**

350 pp., illustr., Ref. 354-6

For R:base 5000 users who want to go beyond the basics, here is an in-depth look at design and structured programming techniques for R:base 5000—packed with expert tips and practical, usable examples.

### UNDERSTANDING R:base 5000

**by Alan Simpson**

413 pp., illustr., Ref. 302-3

This comprehensive tutorial is for database novices and experienced R:base newcomers alike. Topics range from elementary concepts to managing multiple databases and creating custom applications.

## Integrated Software

### MASTERING 1-2-3

**by Carolyn Jorgensen**

466 pp., illustr., Ref. 337-6

Here is a thorough, lucid treatment of 1-2-3, including Release 2, with emphasis on intermediate to advanced uses—complex functions, graphics and database power, macro writing, and the latest add-on products.

### SIMPSON'S 1-2-3 MACRO LIBRARY

**by Alan Simpson**

298 pp., illustr., Ref. 314-7

Share this goldmine of ready-made 1-2-3 macros for custom menus, complex plotting and graphics, consolidating worksheets, interfacing with mainframes and more. Plus explanations of Release 2 macro commands.

### ADVANCED BUSINESS MODELS WITH 1-2-3

**by Stanley R. Trost**

250 pp., illustr., Ref. 159-4

If you are a business professional using the 1-2-3 software package, you will find the spreadsheet and graphics models provided in this book easy to use "as is" in everyday business situations.

### THE ABC'S OF 1-2-3 (2nd Ed)

**by Chris Gilbert and Laurie Williams**

245 pp., illustr., Ref. 355-4

A complete introduction to 1-2-3, featuring Release 2—for first-time users who want to master the basics in a hurry. With comprehensive tutorials on spreadsheets, databases, and graphics.

" . . . an easy and comfortable way to get started on the program."

—*Online Today*

## MASTERING SYMPHONY (2nd Edition)

**by Douglas Cobb**

817 pp., illustr., Ref. 341-4

"*Mastering Symphony* is beautifully organized and presented . . . I recommend it," says *Online Today. IPCO Info* calls it "the bible for every Symphony user . . . If you can buy only one book, this is definitely the one to buy." This new edition includes the latest on Version 1.1

## ANDERSEN'S SYMPHONY TIPS AND TRICKS

**by Dick Andersen**

321 pp., illustr. Ref. 342-2

Hundreds of concise, self-contained entries cover everything from software pitfalls to time-saving macros—to make working with Symphony easy, efficient and productive. Includes version 1.1 and new Add-in programs.

## FOCUS ON SYMPHONY DATABASES

**by Alan Simpson**

350 pp., illustr., Ref. 336-8

An expert guide to creating and managing databases in Symphony—including version 1.1—with complete sample systems for mailing lists, inventory and accounts receivable. A wealth of advanced tips and techniques.

## FOCUS ON SYMPHONY MACROS

**by Alan Simpson**

350 pp., illustr., Ref. 351-1

Share Symphony expert Alan Simpson's approach to planning, creating, and using Symphony macros—including advanced techniques, a goldmine of ready-made macros, and complete menu-driven systems. For all versions through 1.1.

## BETTER SYMPHONY SPREADSHEETS

**by Carl Townsend**

287 pp., illustr., Ref. 339-2

For Symphony users who want to gain real expertise in the use of the spreadsheet features, this has hundreds of tips and techniques. There are also instructions on how to implement some of the special features of Excel on Symphony.

## MASTERING FRAMEWORK

**by Doug Hergert**

450 pp., illustr. Ref. 248-5

This tutorial guides the beginning user through all the functions and features of this integrated software package, geared to the business environment.

## ADVANCED TECHNIQUES IN FRAMEWORK

**by Alan Simpson**

250 pp., illustr. Ref. 257-4

In order to begin customizing your own models with Framework, you'll need a thorough knowledge of Fred programming language, and this book provides this information in a complete, well-organized form.

## MASTERING THE IBM ASSISTANT SERIES

**by Jeff Lea and Ted Leonsis**

249 pp., illustr., Ref. 284-1

Each section of this book takes the reader through the features, screens, and capabilities of each module of the series. Special emphasis is placed on how the programs work together.

## DATA SHARING WITH 1-2-3 AND SYMPHONY: INCLUDING MAINFRAME LINKS

**by Dick Andersen**

262 pp., illustr., Ref. 283-3

This book focuses on an area of increasing importance to business users: exchanging data between Lotus software and other micro and mainframe software. Special emphasis is given to dBASE II and III.

## MASTERING PARADOX (2nd Edition)

**by Alan Simpson**

463 pp., illustr., Ref. 375-9

Total training in Paradox from out bestselling database author: everything from basic functions to custom programming in PAL, organized for easy reference and illustrated with useful business-oriented examples.

### JAZZ ON THE MACINTOSH

**by Joseph Caggiano and Michael McCarthy**

431 pp., illustr., Ref. 265-5

Each chapter features as an example a business report which is built on throughout the book in the first section of each chapter. Chapters then go on to detail each application and special effects in depth.

### MASTERING EXCEL

**by Carl Townsend**

454 pp., illustr., Ref. 306-6

This hands-on tutorial covers all basic operations of Excel plus in-depth coverage of special features, including extensive coverage of macros.

### MASTERING APPLEWORKS

**by Elna Tymes**

201 pp., illustr., Ref. 240-X

This bestseller presents business solutions which are used to introduce AppleWorks and then develop mastery of the program. Includes examples of balance sheet, income statement, inventory control system, cash-flow projection, and accounts receivable summary.

### PRACTICAL APPLEWORKS USES

**by David K. Simerly**

313 pp., illustr., Ref. 274-4

This book covers a breadth of home and business uses, including combined-function applications, complicated tasks, and even a large section on interfacing AppleWorks with external hardware and software.

### APPLEWORKS: TIPS & TECHNIQUES

**by Robert Ericson**

373 pp., illustr., Ref. 303-1

Designed to improve AppleWorks skills, this is a great book that gives utility information illustrated with every-day management examples.

## *SPREADSHEETS*

### UNDERSTANDING JAVELIN

**by John R. Levine, Margaret H. Young, and Jordan M. Young**

350 pp., illustr., Ref. 358-9

A complete guide to Javelin, including an introduction to the theory of modeling. Business-minded examples show Javelin at work on budgets, graphs, forecasts, flow charts, and much more.

### MASTERING SUPERCALC 3

**by Greg Harvey**

300 pp., illustr., Ref. 312-0

Featuring Version 2.1, this title offers full coverage of all the sophisticated features of this third generation spreadsheet, including spreadsheet, graphics, database and advanced techniques.

### DOING BUSINESS WITH MULTIPLAN

**by Richard Allen King and Stanley R. Trost**

250 pp., illustr., Ref. 148-9

This book will show you how using Multiplan can be nearly as easy as learning to use a pocket calculator. It presents a collection of templates for business applications.

### MULTIPLAN ON THE COMMODORE 64

**by Richard Allen King**

250 pp., illustr. Ref. 231-0

This clear, straightforward guide will give you a firm grasp on Multiplan's function, as well as provide a collection of useful template programs.

## *WORD PROCESSING*

### MASTERING PAGEMAKER ON THE IBM PC

**by Antonia Stacy Jolles**

300 pp., illustr., Ref. 393-7

A guide to every aspect of desktop publishing with PageMaker: the vocabulary and basics of Page design, layout, graphics and typography, plus instructions for creating finished typeset publications of all kinds.

## dBASE III PLUS Programmer's Reference Guide

### Sample Programs

### Available on Disk

If you'd like to use the procedures and programs in this book but don't want to type them in yourself, you can send for a disk containing all the procedure files and command files in the book. To obtain this disk, complete the order form and return it along with a check or money order for $40.00. California residents add 6 percent sales tax.

**SMS Software**
**P.O. Box 2802**
**La Jolla, CA 92038-2802**
**(619) 943-7715**

**Name**________________________________________
**Company**______________________________________
**Address**_______________________________________
**City/State/ZIP**_________________________________

**Enclosed is my check or money order.**
**(Make check payable to SMS Software.)**
**dBASE III PLUS Programmer's Reference Guide**

## dBASE COMMAND INDEX (continued from inside front cover)



### LEGEND

| | | | |
|---|---|---|---|
| [...] | optional part of command or function | <l> | logical data |
| / | either option | <memvar> | memory variable name |
| <c> | character data | <n> | numeric data |
| <condition> | query condition | <skeleton> | ambiguous file name |
| <d> | date data | <path\> | directory path name |
| <exp> | expression | <procedure> | procedure name |
| <exp list> | list of expressions | <parameter list> | parameters passed |
| <file> | file name | <procedure file> | procedure file name |
| <field list> | list of field names | <scope> | quantity of records |